ACHI 2017

The Tenth International Conference on Advances in Computer-Human Interactions

March 19 – 23, 2017

Nice, France

ACHI 2017 Editors

Roy Oberhauser, Aalen University, Germany
Jaehyun Park, Incheon National University (INU), South Korea
Steffen Gerhard Schulz, Karlsruhe Institute of Technology, Germany
Paul Rosenthal, University of Rostock, Germany
Ljilja (Lilia) Ruzic Kascak, Georgia Institute of Technology, USA

Printed from e-media with permission by:

Curran Associates, Inc.
57 Morehouse Lane
Red Hook, NY 12571

Some format issues inherent in the e-media version may also appear in this print version.

Printed by Curran Associates, Inc. (2017)

International Academy, Research, and Industry Association (IARIA)
412 Derby Way
Wilmington, DE 19810

Phone: (408) 893-6407
Fax: (408) 527-6351

petre@iaria.org

Additional copies of this publication are available from:

Curran Associates, Inc.
57 Morehouse Lane
Red Hook, NY 12571 USA
Phone: 845-758-0400
Fax: 845-758-2633
Email: curran@proceedings.com
Web: www.proceedings.com

Table of Contents

ACHI 2017

Forward

The tenth edition of The International Conference on Advances in Computer-Human Interactions (ACHI 2017) conference was held in Nice, France, March 19 - 23, 2017.

The conference on Advances in Computer-Human Interaction, ACHI 2017, was a result of a paradigm shift in the most recent achievements and future trends in human interactions with increasingly complex systems. Adaptive and knowledge-based user interfaces, universal accessibility, human-robot interaction, agent-driven human computer interaction, and sharable mobile devices are a few of these trends. ACHI 2017 brought also a suite of specific domain applications, such as gaming, social, medicine, education and engineering.

The event was very competitive in its selection process and very well perceived by the international scientific and industrial communities. As such, it is attracting excellent contributions and active participation from all over the world. We were very pleased to receive a large amount of top quality contributions.

The accepted papers covered a wide range of human-computer interaction related topics such as graphical user interfaces, input methods, training, recognition, and applications.
We believe that the ACHI 2017 contributions offered a large panel of solutions to key problems in all areas of human-computer interaction.

We take here the opportunity to warmly thank all the members of the ACHI 2017 technical program committee as well as the numerous reviewers. The creation of such a broad and high quality conference program would not have been possible without their involvement. We also kindly thank all the authors that dedicated much of their time and efforts to contribute to the ACHI 2017. We truly believe that thanks to all these efforts, the final conference program consists of top quality contributions.

This event could also not have been a reality without the support of many individuals, organizations and sponsors. In addition, we also gratefully thank the members of the ACHI 2017 organizing committee for their help in handling the logistics and for their work that is making this professional meeting a success.

We hope the ACHI 2017 was a successful international forum for the exchange of ideas and results between academia and industry and to promote further progress in the human-computer interaction field.

We also hope that Nice provided a pleasant environment during the conference and everyone saved some time for exploring this beautiful city.

ACHI 2017 Chairs

ACHI Steering Committee
Leslie Miller, Iowa State University - Ames, USA
Alma Leora Culén , University of Oslo, Norway
Hermann Kaindl, Vienna University of Technology, Austria
Uttam Kokil, Kennesaw State University Marietta, USA
Flaminia Luccio, University Ca' Foscari of Venice, Italy
Jaehyun Park, Incheon National University (INU), South Korea

ACHI Industry/Research Advisory Committee
Jacki O'Neill, Microsoft Research, India
Weizhi Meng, Institute for Infocomm Research (I2R), Singapore
Harald Milchrahm, Institute for Softwaretechnology - Technical University Graz, Austria
Steffen Gerhard Schulz, Karlsruhe Institute of Technology, Germany
Ryo Ishii, NTT Corporation, Japan
Zahen Malla Osman, The National Center for Scientific Research (CNRS), France
Mohammed Korayem, Careerbuilder.com, USA

ACHI 2017

COMMITTEE

ACHI Steering Committee
Leslie Miller, Iowa State University - Ames, USA
Alma Leora Culén , University of Oslo, Norway
Hermann Kaindl, Vienna University of Technology, Austria
Uttam Kokil, Kennesaw State University Marietta, USA
Flaminia Luccio, University Ca' Foscari of Venice, Italy
Jaehyun Park, Incheon National University (INU), South Korea

ACHI Industry/Research Advisory Committee
Jacki O'Neill, Microsoft Research, India
Weizhi Meng, Institute for Infocomm Research (I2R), Singapore
Harald Milchrahm, Institute for Softwaretechnology - Technical University Graz, Austria
Steffen Gerhard Schulz, Karlsruhe Institute of Technology, Germany
Ryo Ishii, NTT Corporation, Japan
Zahen Malla Osman, The National Center for Scientific Research (CNRS), France
Mohammed Korayem, Careerbuilder.com, USA

ACHI 2017 Technical Program Committee

Andrea F. Abate, University of Salerno, Italy
Majed Alshamari, King Faisal University, Saudi Arabia
Tobias Blanke, King's College London, UK
Christos Bouras, University of Patras and Computer Technology Institute & Press «Diophantus», Greece
Christian Bourret, UPEM - Université Paris-Est Marne-la-Vallée, France
Jan Broer, ifib - Institut für Informationsmanagement Bremen GmbH, Germany
Marcin Butlewski, Poznan University of Technology, Poland
Nan Cao, NYU Shanghai, China
Jacek Chmielewski, Poznan University of Economics, Poland
Andre Constantino da Silva, Federal Institute of São Paulo – IFSP, Brazil
Daniel Costa, Universidade de Lisboa, Portugal
Rolf Drechsler, University of Bremen/DFKI, Germany
Carlos Duarte, Universidade de Lisboa, Portugal
Sophie Dupuy-Chessa, University Grenoble Alpes, France
Larbi Esmahi, Athabasca University, Canada
Sascha Fagel, KV Telematik GmbH, Germany
Peter Forbrig, University of Rostock, Germany
Somchart Fugkeaw, Mahidol University - Nakhonpathom, Thailand
Bernard Grabot, LGP-ENIT, France
Denis Gracanin, Virginia Tech, USA
Andrina Granić, University of Split, Croatia
Toni Granollers, University of Lleida, Spain
Celmar Guimarães da Silva, University of Campinas, Brazil
Maki Habib, The American University in Cairo, Egypt

Till Halbach, Norwegian Computing Center, Oslo, Norway
Ibrahim A. Hameed, Norwegian University of Science and Technology (NTNU), Ålesund, Norway
Sung H. Han, POSTECH, South Korea
José R. Hilera, University of Alcalá, Spain
Olivier Hugues, MINES ParisTech - PSL Research University, France
Francisco Iniesto, Institute of Educational Technology - The Open University, UK
Jamshed Iqbal, National University of Computer and Emerging Sciences (FAST-NU), Islamabad, Pakistan
Gökhan İnce, Istanbul Technical University, Turkey
Ryo Ishii, NTT Corporation, Japan
Suhas Govind Joshi, University of Oslo, Norway
Hanmin Jung, Korea Institute of Science & Technology Information, Korea
Katarzyna Kaczmarek, Systems Research Institute - Polish Academy of Sciences, Poland
Hermann Kaindl, Vienna University of Technology, Austria
Ahmed Kamel, Concordia College, Moorhead, USA
Ljilja (Lilia) Ruzic Kascak, Georgia Institute of Technology, USA
Jesuk Ko, Gwangju University, Korea
Uttam Kokil, Kennesaw State University Marietta, USA
Mohammed Korayem, Careerbuilder.com, USA
Jiyoung Kwahk, POSTECH, South Korea
Wen-Hsing Lai, National Kaohsiung First University of Science and Technology, Taiwan
Vidas Lauruska, Siauliai University, Lithuania
Dagmawi Lemma Gobena, Addis Ababa University, Ethiopia
Alma Leora Culén , University of Oslo, Norway
Tsai-Yen Li, National Chengchi University, Taiwan
Wenjuan Li, City University of Hong Kong, Hong Kong
Flaminia Luccio, University Ca' Foscari of Venice, Italy
Sergio Luján Mora, University of Alicante, Spain
Ameersing Luximon, Hong Kong Polytechnic University, Hong Kong
Yan Luximon, The Hong Kong Polytechnic University, Hong Kong
Zahen Malla Osman, The National Center for Scientific Research (CNRS), France
Weizhi Meng, Institute for Infocomm Research (I2R), Singapore
Daniel R. Mestre, CNRS Institute of Movement Sciences - Mediterranean Virtual Reality Center, Marseilles, France
Harald Milchrahm, Institute for Softwaretechnology - Technical University Graz, Austria
Les Miller, Iowa State University, USA
Yasser F. O. Mohammad, Assiut University, Egypt / KDDI Laboratories, Japan
Jaime Muñoz-Arteaga, Universidad Autónoma de Aguascalientes, Mexico
Roger Ng, Hong Kong Polytechnic University, Hong Kong
Jacki O'Neill, Microsoft Research, India
Jaehyun Park, Incheon National University (INU), South Korea
Marina Puyuelo, Universitat Politècnica de València, Spain
Didier Puzenat, LIRIS - University Lyon 2, France
Rafael Radkowski, Iowa State University, USA
Andreas Riener, University of Applied Sciences Ingolstadt, Germany
Antonio M. Rinaldi, Università degli Studi di Napoli Federico II - Napoli, Italy
Cuauhtémoc Rivera-Loaiza, Universidad Michoacana de San Nicolás de Hidalgo, Mexico
Covadonga Rodrigo San Juan, E.T.S.I. Informática - UNED, Spain
Paul Rosenthal, University of Rostock, Germany

Sandra Sanchez-Gordon, Escuela Politécnica Nacional, Ecuador
Antonio-Jose Sanchez-Salmeron, Universitat Politecnica de Valencia, Spain
Steffen Gerhard Schulz, Karlsruhe Institute of Technology, Germany
Trenton W. Schulz, University of Oslo / Norsk Regnesentral, Norway
Cristian Stanciu, University Politehnica of Bucharest, Romania
Tommaso Venturini, INRIA / Institut Rhônalpin des Systèmes Complexes, France
Guri B. Verne, University of Oslo, Norway
Connie Veugen, Vrije Universiteit Amsterdam, Netherlands
Michael L. Walters, University of Hertfordshire, UK
Alexander Wachtel, Karlsruhe Institute of Technology, Germany
Anja Zeising, ifib - Research Institute at the University of Bremen, Germany

Subjective Contribution of Vibrotactile Modality in Addition to or Instead of Auditory Modality for Takeover Notification in an Autonomous Vehicle

Valérie Duthoit[1,2], Eric Enrègle
[1]Direction de la Recherche
Renault, Guyancourt, France
e-mail: valerie.duthoit@renault.com

Jean-Marc Sieffermann, Camille Michon, and David Blumenthal
[2]UMR GENIAL, AgroParisTech,
INRA, Université Paris-Saclay
Massy, France

Abstract—**In future autonomous vehicles, drivers will be allowed to do anything else but driving. However, those autonomous cars may call the driver back to driving if all requirements for autonomous navigation are not met. Therefore, a call back sequence must be designed. The call back sequence must be efficient, as well as satisfying, in order not to annihilate the benefit of autonomous driving. Recent studies show the interest of using tactile channel for in-vehicle interfaces. In this study, we investigate the subjective contribution of vibrotactile signal instead or in addition to auditory modality for takeover sequences in an autonomous vehicle. We conducted a simulator survey on 41 subjects. The participants had to score their satisfaction and to evaluate the efficiency and some hedonic aspects of the sequence. According to the results, we recommend a multimodal signal for the takeover sequences in an autonomous vehicle. This must be confirmed with an evaluation of objective efficiency of the signal.**

Keywords- Interface design; Vibrotactile; Autonomous driving.

I. INTRODUCTION

During autonomous navigation phases, drivers can do anything they want but sleeping. Their attention may not be triggered by signals that may appear. According to NHTSA, level 3 of automation called "Limited Safe Driving Automation", implies that drivers must remain available to intervene with comfortable transition time if all conditions necessary to allow autonomous navigation are not met (e.g., the vehicle leaves highway, etc.) [1]. To ensure a safe and comfortable transition, a sequence of call back signals must be designed. To date, there are no standards about those call back signals.

Traditionally in an automobile environment, auditory and visual signals are used to convey information to the driver. However, many applications could benefit by using vibrations in the seat to transmit information [2], for instance lane departure warning [3][4], collision warning [4][5], hypovigilance alert [6], situation awareness [7], navigation [6][8], notifications [6][9] and even relaxing activities [10].

Several studies reported pros & cons of using tactile modality in vehicle (see [11] for a review). Even though no reason is given, this modality is rarely used in cars [10][12]. According to Wickens' multiple resource theories [13], tactile channel can convey information while auditory and visual channels are overloaded [14][15]. Firstly, a few studies reported that tactile modality has good alert properties. For instance, the reaction time decreases for a tactile or an auditory collision warning compared to a visual warning or no warning, or even an auditory warning when the driver is involved in an oral conversation [5][16]. Moreover, the tactile modality decreases the reaction time compared to the auditory modality for a navigation system and a Bluetooth hand-free system [6]. Secondly, depending on the context, the properties inherent to tactile modality can be relevant. For instance, tactile interactions are private, and subtle [17]. Furthermore, in most of the cases, it does not interrupt the current activity, which could let the subject choose the exact moment of interruption, and therefore reduce frustration.

There are also some practical limitations of using tactile modality. Tactile interfaces can convey limited information. Yet studies showed the possibility to recognize 7 haptic icons during a high visual load task [18]. The best compromise between number of possible in-vehicle tactile alerts, and efficiency and adequacy of reaction, could be with only 3 different tactile alerts [19]. Finally, there are some situations that may adversely affect perception of tactile warning. Some drivers are wearing thick clothes, which could affect their perception of vibrotactile stimuli in the seat [2] even though this effect may be relatively low [20]. Also, ambient vibration could mask the signal's vibrations [21][22]. Recent studies show the influence of attention, movement [23][24] and back pain [25] on tactile sensation.

Acceptability studies show mitigate results for vibrotactile interfaces. For a collision warning, it has better scored including on items like "trust", "overall benefit to driving" or "annoyance" [4]. Auditory warnings was clearly better accepted than tactile warning in the seat for a lane departure warning [3]. The subjective workload associated with a navigation system, and hand-free system were scored higher, and items like "quick to understand" or "easy to learn" were scored lower for tactile modality compared to auditory. This can adversely affect the acceptability of a tactile signal. The satisfaction evaluation may be influenced by the innovative nature of tactile feedback in the seat [6]. The meaning of the signal and the context may also have a great influence on acceptability.

Multimodality is proposed to find a good compromise between efficiency and acceptability [26]. However, it has been shown to increase perceived urgency [8][27].

In brief, tactile modality shows interesting performances for in-vehicle interfaces, but it must be tested for each given application. In this paper, we focus on takeover notifications in autonomous vehicles.

At least two types of evaluations are necessary to choose the most appropriate modality [28]: objective evaluation, on the measured performance, and subjective measure on acceptability. This study focused on the second one: we aimed to evaluate the subjective contribution of vibrotactile modality instead of, or in addition to auditory modality during a takeover phase in an autonomous vehicle. Moreover, we investigated on the relevance of a reminder: a second notification when half of the allocated time to take over has passed.

To answer our problematic, we conducted a customer study, described in Section II. The results are presented in Section III and discussed in Section IV. Lastly, we give our recommendations and perspectives in Section V.

II. Material and Method

To evaluate the signal in a realistic context, we conducted a customer survey in an autonomous driving simulated context.

A. Products

A takeover sequence, begins with a takeover notification one minute before the end of the autonomous driving mode. In our study, we used tactile modality, auditory modality or both.

1) Tactile signal

A haptic seat mock-up was created based on a commercialized seat (Renault, Espace 5). Several actuators were integrated in the seat backrest and cushion. The chosen actuators (voice-coil type, furnished by Lofelt) enable to independently set the frequency and the amplitude of the vibrotactile stimuli. Two preliminary studies were conducted before the present study: the first one aimed to define the right location of the actuators in the seat, and the second one aimed to define the pattern of the signal.

The locations of the actuators were chosen after a preliminary experiment for which eleven subjects participated. The participants of this first preliminary experiment were chosen to ensure a diversity of morphology in the panel. There were 6 men and 5 women. Height was from 147 to 200cm (mean: 176; sd: 13), and Body Mass Index (BMI) from 18.4 to 30 kg/m^2 (mean: 23.3; sd: 4). The actuators' locations allow an effective and acceptable perception of the vibration of each actuator, for all participants. Because we wanted to have a symmetric signal, and because it was not acceptable to place the actuators under the spine, they were set in two columns.

The tactile signal was designed after a second preliminary study measuring detection and acceptability of 16 signals. Those signals were designed based on a design of experiments, which enabled us to model detection rate and acceptability depending on signal characteristics. It was conducted on a large panel: 80 participants from 30 to 75 year old (mean: 49; sd: 11), BMI from 17.7 to 53.5 kg/m^2 (mean: 26.2; sd: 5.4). This signal is above detection threshold and supposed to be well accepted (estimated satisfaction score: 8.3/10).

2) Auditory signal

In this study, auditory signals previously designed for partially autonomous driving studies [29] were used. We only used the signal designed for a takeover notification, which is the equivalent of the vibrotactile signal. The signal was previously used in a few customer studies and was never reported as disturbing.

3) Takeover sequences

Five different takeover sequences were tested (see Table 1). Three are composed by a single notification occurring 1 minute before the end of autonomous mode. The other two were composed by two notifications: the first notification occurring 1 minute before the end of autonomous mode, followed by a second notification when half of the time to take over has passed (Fig. 1). We used either vibrotactile signal, auditory signal or a combination of those two signals.

TABLE I. MODALITIES OF THE NOTIFICATIONS FOR EACH SEQUENCES

Sequence	First notification	Reminder
V	Vibrotactile	-
A	Auditory	-
V+A	Mixed	-
V + reminder A	Vibrotactile	Auditory
V + reminder V+A	Vibrotactile	Mixed

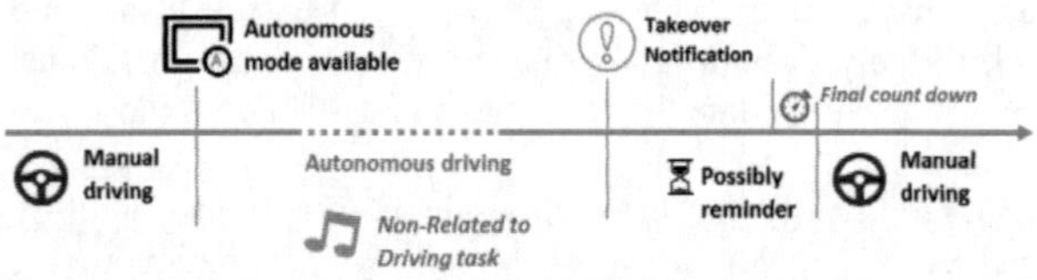

Figure 1. Driving trial with notification and possible reminder to takeover sequence.

B. Simulation

The study was conducted in a fixed-base simulator consisting of driver and passenger seats, steering wheel, and pedals (Fig. 2 a). The road was projected on a 60 inch screen (Samsung UE60D6500).Visual HMI (Human

Machine Interface) were disposed on two screens. The first one was a 15'' screen corresponding to the dashboard (Fig. 2 b, Litemax®, SSD 1515 ENB G01). The second was a 10,4'' touchscreen and corresponds to the central screen (Fig. 2 c, Litemax®, SLO1068 EGB I51). Visual interfaces related to autonomous system were developed to conduct autonomous driving studies at Renault. They remain the same for each takeover sequence. They continually display the state of the autonomous system (unavailable, available, activated, takeover notification, takeover required). The scenario was navigation on a highway road. The takeover notification was triggered by the experimenter without any scenario reason. The autonomous driving system used in this study was developed for an intern ergonomics study [30]. The simulation was generated using the simulation software SCANeR™ (v 1.4 ; Oktal), and the HMI were synchronized with the software RTMaps (v.4 ; Intempora).

Figure 2 : Picture of the simulator

C. Observers

41 volunteers were recruited after an internet screening survey. This screening survey had two objectives:

- Recruit people without motion sickness and without negative opinion on testing autonomous driving. This way we avoid eventual rejection effect due to this particular technology.
- Selecting observers by the activity they declared they want to do during autonomous phases: observers had to choose an activity among three before the test: reading on a hard copy, working or watching a movie. We tried to form three equivalent groups of people performing those three activities: 15 participants were reading, 15 were watching a movie and 11 were working.

The participants had to bring their own device or book with them for the test. We assumed that letting them choose and provide their own activity would give them more interest for the non-related to driving task (NRD) that they would perform during the autonomous driving phases, and therefore make the situation closer to the implication they would have in real situations.

The volunteers were all employees working at *the Technocentre Renault (Guyan*court, France). There were 39 males and only 2 females from 21 to 60 years old (mean: 40; sd: 12) and their body mass index varied from 14,5 to 32 kg/m² (mean: 21; sd:4). They were unaware of the nature of the research, except the fact that it deals with autonomous driving.

D. Procedure

First of all, the autonomous driving HMI were explained to participants. Moreover, the autonomous driving interfaces were presented. The experimenter explained that when the first takeover notification rings, there is 1 minute left to takeover. He also explained that driver safety is ensured by the system anyway, even if the driver does not take over on time.

After a familiarization phase with the autonomous driving HMI and with the simulator, the test procedure was explained to the participants.

The session consisted of five tests. For each test, the participant started to drive, engaged the autonomous mode, focused on a "non-related to driving" task, and then, resumed the driving after the takeover signal of the current test.

The current call back sequence was played before each test in order to make the subject identify the takeover notification.

After each sequence, the participants had to fill a survey with a global satisfaction score and to score 9 adjectives relative to hedonic evaluation ("pleasant", "soothing", "stressful", "frustrating", and "disturbing") and to perceived efficiency ("noticeable", "stimulating", "clear" and "efficient").

The test order was balanced among participants, using a Latin square design: each sequence was tested an equal number of times at a given rank.

The test took about 1 hour per participant. The experiment lasted one month during the summer of 2016.

III. Results

As the 41 subjects evaluated the 5 different sequences, there were 205 observations.

A. Satisfaction scores

We performed an analysis of variance (ANOVA) of the satisfaction score with sequence, NRD task and presentation rank as explicative variables. The sequence does have a significant influence on satisfaction but NRD task and presentation rank do not (Table 2).

There was no significant difference between the two unimodal sequences. The two unimodal sequences were worse scored than bimodal sequences. The reminder does not have any significant effect (Fig. 3).

TABLE II. RESULTS OF THE ANOVA ON THE SATISFACTION SCORES

Source	DoF	F	Pr > F
Rank	4, 194	0,805	0,523
Sequence	4, 194	6,685	< 0,0001
NRD task	2, 194	0,028	0,972

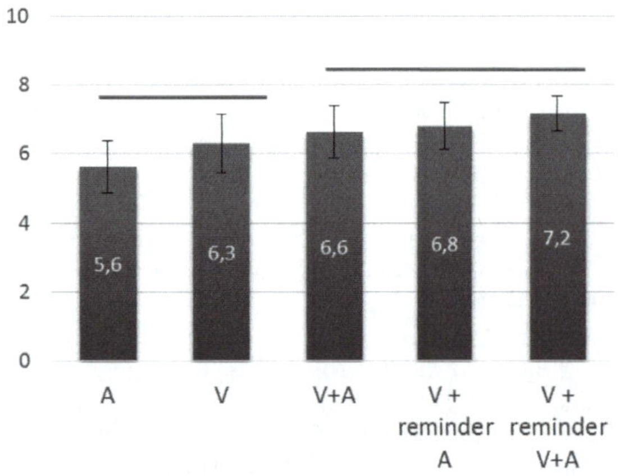

Figure 3. Mean satisfaction scores and Bonferroni pairwise comparison tests (α=0.05).

B. Adjectives

For each adjective, a one-way ANOVA was performed with sequence, NRD task, presentation rank and the interaction sequence*NRD task as explicative variables (Table 3), followed by a Bonferroni pairwise comparisons test (α=0.05).

TABLE III. RESULTS OF THE ANOVA ON THE ADJECTIVES

	Perceived efficiency				Hedonic evaluation				
	Noticeable	Stimulating	Clear	Efficient	Pleasant	Soothing	Stressful	Frustrating	Disturbing
$F_{(18, 186)}$	6,44	5,16	3,74	4,27	1,09	0,85	1,02	1,66	0,91
Pr > F	< 0,01	< 0,01	< 0,01	< 0,01	0,37	0,63	0,44	0,05	0,57
Sequence	23,31	17,93	10,70	13,81	1,67	1,62	1,43	0,34	2,44
	< 0,01	< 0,01	< 0,01	< 0,01	0,16	0,17	0,22	0,85	0,05
NRD-Task	2,36	4,01	4,74	4,08	1,25	1,05	1,57	11,29	1,61
	0,10	0,02	0,01	0,02	0,29	0,35	0,21	< 0,01	0,20
Rank	2,03	0,45	1,47	0,92	0,43	0,45	0,80	0,12	0,29
	0,09	0,77	0,21	0,45	0,79	0,78	0,53	0,97	0,89
Seq. * NRD-task	0,64	0,68	0,71	0,94	1,15	0,52	0,82	0,64	0,33
	0,74	0,71	0,68	0,49	0,33	0,84	0,58	0,74	0,95

The interaction type of sequence*NRD task and presentation rank had no effect on any adjective. In other words, the effect of the sequence was not dependent on the NRD task, and vice-versa.

1) *Influence of the sequence*

The sequence had a significant effect on the four adjectives about perceived efficiency (Fig. 4). For each, the score of the sequence with a single auditory signal was lower than the score of the other sequences. The reminder had no effect compared to single vibrotactile notification or a mixed single notification.

The adjectives "pleasant", "soothing", "stressful", "frustrating" and "disturbing" could not be explained with the chosen explicative variables.

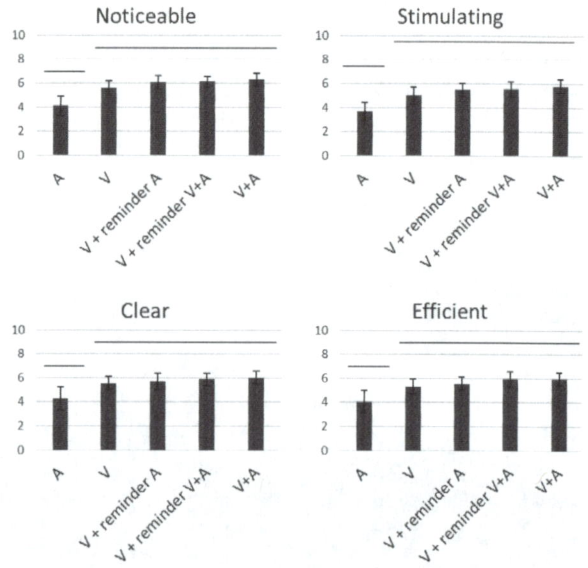

Figure 4 : Mean scores by sequences for the four adjectives related to perceived intensity. Bars correspond to a Bonferroni test (α=5%).

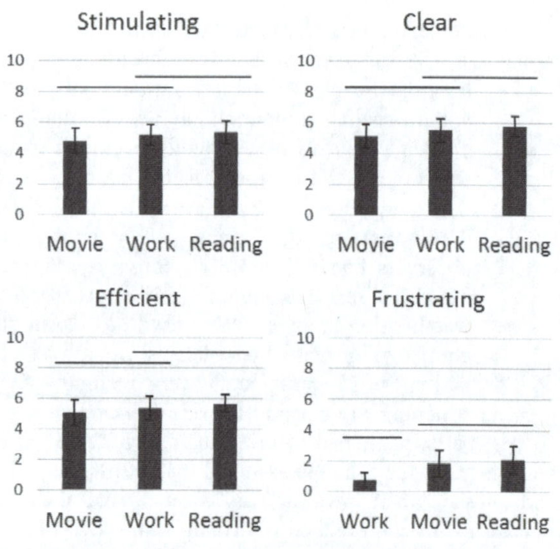

Figure 5: Mean scores by activity for 3 adjectives related to perceived efficiency and "frustrating". Bars correspond to a Bonferroni test (α=5%).

2) Influence of the NRD task

The NRD task had a significant influence on three adjectives about perceived efficiency: “stimulating”, “clear” and “efficient” (Fig. 5). For each adjective, the scores given by participants who were watching a movie were lower than the scores given by those reading.

Moreover, the NRD task had an influence on one adjective related with hedonic evaluation: “frustrating”. The participants who were working declared to be less frustrated than those who were reading a book or watching a movie.

IV. DISCUSSION AND LIMITATIONS

41 people participated to the study, who were divided in three group of activity. Those groups were composed by at least 11 participants. This was sufficient to find significant results. Increasing the number of participant could enhance the differences.

A. *Effect of the modalites used in the sequence*

Previous studies show that vibrotactile modality has mitigate results in terms of satisfaction. The hedonic properties of a signal seem to be dependent on the application. In our case, i.e., takeover phase in an autonomous vehicle, the vibrotactile modality in combination with the auditory modality increases the satisfaction score. The presence of a reminder has no effect compared to a mixed single notification. Our data show no differences for the satisfaction scores between the tactile signal and the auditory signal. Those results may not be generalized to other tactile and auditory signals because the two evaluated signals were previously optimized.

The vibrotactile modality in addition to, or instead of auditory modality increases the perceived efficiency. Most of the study show that tactile and auditory modality have comparable efficiency, unless in some cases including the driver involved in an oral conversation, where tactile alert has been shown to be more efficient [16]. We could assume that auditory background disturbs the efficiency of an auditory signal, but in our study, the interaction sequence*NRD task has no significant effect on the adjectives. Another explanation of the better perceived efficiency of tactile modality is the low familiarity of the participants with this kind of signal, whereas the automobile environment is full of auditory signals.

B. *Effect of the non related to driving task*

We found that watching a movie decreases the score on three adjectives related to efficiency. Two reasons could explain this. First, the auditory background of the movie disturbs the detection of the signals, regardless of their modality. Then the involvement of the subject in their task may be more important for those watching a movie than those working, which is consistent with the greater frustration of the first compared to the second.

C. *Limitations*

The 41 participants were mainly males with a low body mass index. The results should be validated with a more diversified panel, for instance, in terms of gender, age, body mass index.

As those results were obtained in a low fidelity simulator, a validation in real driving situation, taking into account vibro-acoustical background, as well as real risk perception for the driver is needed. To evaluate the takeover sequence, it is crucial, that the participant feels in the position of the driver. Because, we did not have an autonomous vehicle prototype for the experimentation, we conducted the study in a simulator.

It could also be interesting to reproduce the study with others tactile or auditory signals to evaluate the influence of the nature of the signal.

V. CONCLUSION

This paper focuses on the subjective evaluation of tactile modality in addition to, or instead of auditory modality during the takeover sequences in an autonomous vehicle. According to our results, we recommend the combination of vibro-tactile and auditory modality to improve the subject's satisfaction as well as the perceived efficiency of the takeover sequence.

Future studies must investigate on the objective efficiency of the five sequences, such as time to take over, situation awareness at takeover, in order to link the objective and the subjective evaluations.

ACKNOWLEDGMENT

The authors thank Pierre Hervé-Berdys for his work on set up and fields. They also thank Chunshi Guo for his kind help on setting up the simulator, Guillaume Willemotte for his technical support and Armenio Gomes for the help on recruiting.

REFERENCES

[1] SAE, 2014, Taxonomy and Definitions for Terms Related to On-Road Motor Vehicle Automated Driving Systems, SAE J3016.).

[2] C. Ho, and C. Spence, The Multisensory Driver: Implications for Ergonomic Car Interface Design, Ashgate Publishing, Ltd., 2008.

[3] J. Navarro, F. Mars, and J.-M. Hoc, "Lateral control assistance for car drivers: a comparison of motor priming and warning systems," Human Factors: The Journal of the Human Factors and Ergonomics Society, vol. 49, no. 5, pp. 950-960, 2007.

[4] J. D. Lee, J. D. Hoffman, and E. Hayes, "Collision warning design to mitigate driver distraction," Proc. SIGCHI conference on human factors in computing systems, ACM, 2004, pp. 65-62.

[5] J. Scott, and R. Gray, "A comparison of tactile, visual, and auditory warnings for rear-end collision prevention in simulated driving," Human Factors: The Journal of the Human Factors and Ergonomics Society, vol. 50, no. 2, pp. 264-275, 2008.

[6] W. Chang, W. Hwang, and Y. G. Ji, "Haptic seat interfaces for driver information and warning systems," International Journal of Human-Computer Interaction, vol. 27, no. 12, pp. 1119-1132, 2011.

[7] A. Telpaz, B. Rhindress, I. Zelman, and O. Tsimhoni, "Haptic seat for automated driving: preparing the driver to take control effectively," Proc. 7th International Conference on Automotive User Interfaces and Interactive Vehicular Applications, ACM, 2015, pp. 23-30.

[8] J. B. Van Erp, H. A. Van Veen, C. Jansen, and T. Dobbins, "Waypoint navigation with a vibrotactile waist belt," ACM Transactions on Applied Perception (TAP), vol. 2, no. 2, pp. 106-117, 2005.

[9] M. Schwalk, N. Kalogerakis, and T. Maier, "Driver Support by a Vibrotactile Seat Matrix--Recognition, Adequacy and Workload of Tactile Patterns in Take-over Scenarios During Automated Driving," Procedia Manufacturing, vol. 3, pp. 2466-2473, 2015.

[10] J. B. Van Erp, and H. Van Veen, "Vibro-tactile information presentation in automobiles," Proc. Eurohaptics, 2001, pp. 99-104.

[11] F. Meng, and C. Spence, "Tactile warning signals for in-vehicle systems," Accident Analysis & Prevention, vol. 75, pp. 333-346, 2015.

[12] G. H. Walker, N. A. Stanton, and M. S. Young, "What's happened to car design? An exploratory study into the effect of 15 years of progress on driver situation awareness," International journal of vehicle design, vol. 45, no. 1-2, pp. 266-282, 2007.

[13] C. D. Wickens, "Multiple resources and mental workload," Human Factors: The Journal of the Human Factors and Ergonomics Society, vol. 50, no. 3, pp. 449-455, 2008.

[14] A. Tang, P. McLachlan, K. Lowe, C. R. Saka, and K. MacLean, "Perceiving ordinal data haptically under workload," Proc. 7th international conference on Multimodal interfaces, (ICMI) ACM , 2005, pp. 317-324.

[15] I. Oakley, and J. Park, "Did you feel something? Distracter tasks and the recognition of vibrotactile cues," Interacting with Computers, vol. 20, no. 3, pp. 354-363, 2008.

[16] R. Mohebbi, R. Gray, and H. Z. Tan, "Driver reaction time to tactile and auditory rear-end collision warnings while talking on a cell phone," Human Factors: The Journal of the Human Factors and Ergonomics Society, vol. 51, no. 1, pp. 102-110, 2009.

[17] R. Hansson, P. Ljungstrand, and J. Redström, "Subtle and public notification cues for mobile devices," Proc. International Conference on Ubiquitous Computing, Springer, 2001, pp. 240-246.

[18] A. Chan, K. MacLean, and J. McGrenere, "Designing haptic icons to support collaborative turn-taking," International Journal of Human-Computer Studies, vol. 66, no. 5, pp. 333-355, 2008.

[19] G. M. Fitch, J. M. Hankey, B. M. Kleiner, and T. A. Dingus, "Driver comprehension of multiple haptic seat alerts intended for use in an integrated collision avoidance system," Transportation research part F: traffic psychology and behaviour, vol. 14, no. 4, pp. 278-290, 2011.

[20] V. Duthoit, J.-M. Sieffermann, E. Enrègle, and D. Blumenthal, "Perceived Intensity of Vibrotactile Stimuli: Do Your Clothes Really Matter?," in International Conference on Human Haptic Sensing and Touch Enabled Computer Applications, Springer International Publishing, 2016, pp. 412-418.

[21] J. C. Craig, "Difference threshold for intensity of tactile stimuli," Perception & Psychophysics, vol. 11, no. 2, pp. 150-152, 1972.

[22] J. Ryu, J. Chun, G. Park, S. Choi, and S. H. Han, "Vibrotactile feedback for information delivery in the vehicle," IEEE Transactions on Haptics, vol. 3, no. 2, pp. 138-149, 2010.

[23] A. Gallace, S. Zeeden, B. Röder and C. Spence, "Lost in the move? Secondary task performance impairs tactile change detection on the body," Consciousness and cognition, vol. 19, no. 1, pp. 215-229, 2010.

[24] S. Van Damme, L. Van Hulle, L. Danneels, C. Spence, and G. Crombez, "The effect of chronic low back pain on tactile suppression during back movements," Human movement science, vol. 37, pp. 87-100, 2014.

[25] L. Van Hulle, G. Juravle, C. Spence, G. Crombez, and S. Van Damme, "Attention modulates sensory suppression during back movements," Consciousness and cognition, vol. 22, no. 2, pp. 420-429, 2013.

[26] J.-M. Hoc, M. El Jaafari, J.-F. Forzy, J. Navarro, and F. Mars, "User acceptance and effectiveness of warning and motor priming assistance devices in car driving," Proc. European conference on human centred design for intelligent transport systems, 2008, pp. 311-320.

[27] I. Politis, S. Brewster, and F. Pollick, "Speech tactons improve speech warnings for drivers," The 6th International Conference on Automotive User Interfaces and Interactive Vehicular Applications, ACM, 2014, pp. 1-8.

[28] D. Warnock, "A subjective evaluation of multimodal notifications," Proc. 5th International Conference on Pervasive Computing Technologies for Healthcare (PervasiveHealth) and Workshops, IEEE, 2011, pp. 461-468.

[29] S. Langlois, and B. Soualmi, "Augmented reality versus classical HUD to take over from automated driving: an aid to smooth reactions and to anticipate maneuvers" The 19th International Conference on Intelligent Transportation Systems (ITSC 2016) IEEE, 2016, pp. 1571-1578.

[30] C. Guo, C. Sentouh, J.-C. Popieul, B. Soualmi, and J.-B. Haué, "Shared Control Framework Applied for Vehicle Longitudinal Control in Highway Merging Scenarios," Proc. IEEE International Conference on Systems, Man, and Cybernetics (SMC), IEEE, 2015, pp. 3098-3103.

Gesture-based User Interface Design for Static 3D Content Manipulation Using Leap Motion Controller

Naveed Ahmed

Department of Computer Science
University of Sharjah
Sharjah, United Arab Emirates
Email: nahmed@sharjah.ac.ae

***Abstract*—We present a new hand gesture-based user interface to efficiently manipulate static 3D content using the Leap Motion Controller. Our method uses intuitive gestures utilizing only the movement of the thumb and the index finger coupled with the hand rotation. These gestures not only allow the user to rotate the 3D content around the three axes but also scale the 3D content. We implement these gestures using the Leap Motion Controller and present the implementation details. We perform a comprehensive user study to demonstrate the effectiveness of our user interface in terms of both usability and user experience. The user study shows that a gesture-based user interface can be employed as a viable mechanism to manipulate 3D content and can be used in a number of applications.**

Keywords–Gestures; Leap Motion; Gesture-based User Interface; User Interface Design.

I. INTRODUCTION

The rapid change in technology has brought a number of ways to interact with software applications on a wide range of devices. Devices like Kinect, PS Move, Wii Remote brought motion controls to the gaming audience. Among these devices, Kinect [1] allows a complete passive motion capture solution without any direct physical interaction with the input hardware. Since, it can capture the motion of the person at real-time [2], Kinect has been widely employed to provide a gesture-based user interface to control a number of desktop applications [1]. It can detect high level arms and body motion, but it is not possible for it to capture fine grain hand movements up to the level of individual fingers.

With the advent of touch-based mobile devices, users are more comfortable with the use of hand gestures, especially finger-based multi touch interfaces, to control the applications. An interface that allows similar interactions on the desktop environment would be more efficient and user friendly. Any hand gesture control can also be easily employed in virtual and augmented reality applications. For a user, interacting with any application using a gesture controlled system is more natural, because it follows familiar user interface paradigm and unifies the user interaction across different platforms.

Incorporating gestures for user interaction first requires the detection of gestures. There has been a number of methods proposed to detect gestures using a number of devices. A number of methods have employed Hidden Markov Models to detect gestures [3] [4]. Other methods are proposed using AdaBoost [5], multi-layer perception [6], principal component analysis [7], Histogram of Oriented Gradients (HOG) features [8], and depth data [9]. A survey of 3D hand gesture recognition is presented by Cheng et al. [10].

Following the gesture recognition, there are a number of studies performed to evaluate the interfaces in terms of their usability and user experience. Farhadi-Niaki et al. [11] presented a usability study for arms and hand gestures to be used in common desktop tasks. Bragdon et al. [12] presented touch and air gestures for supporting developer meetings. A usability study of gestures in the virtual reality environment was presented by Cabral et al. [13]. Villaroman et al. [14] presented gesture-based user interface design using Kinect. Their work shows that even with the limitations of Kinect in terms of fine-grain gesture input, it works efficiently for common tasks. Bhuiyan et al. [15] presented gesture-based controls for common day-to-day tasks and studied their effectiveness in a number of real-world scenarios. Ebert et al. [16] show the limitations of a gesture-based interaction for manipulating CT scan data. Liao et al. [17] presented a gesture-based command system for interactive paper, and show that gesture-based interfaces are well suited for new technologies. Wachs et al. [18] presented a number of vision-based hand gesture applications.

Recently, Leap Motion [19] introduced a new way to interact with the desktop systems using hand and finger-based gestures. Leap Motion primarily targets hands recognition, and can track all 10 fingers with up to 1/100th millimeter accuracy [19]. The Leap Motion has a 150° wide, and 135° deep field of view (FOV). Within this FOV it can track within 8 cubic feet of 3D space. An example of the controller can be seen in Figure 1. In contrast to Kinect, which provides full body color, depth and pose data, the Leap Motion Controller provides specific set of parameters related to hands and fingers. Leap Motion SDK supports a limited number of gestures, e.g., Pinch, swipe, and tap [19]. Recognition of general purpose gestures from the Leap Motion data is an active research problem. Potter et al. [20] presented a study on viability of using Leap Motion for the sign language recognition. Guerrero-Rincon et al. [21] presented a gesture control system using Leap Motion to control a robot. Marin et al. [22] presented a generic framework to detect gestures using both Kinect and Leap Motion. In contrast, there are not many user studies that not only implement customize gestures but also perform a user study to demonstrate the effectiveness of usability and user experience of a hand gesture-based interface using the Leap Motion Controller.

In this work, we present a new user interface to manipulate

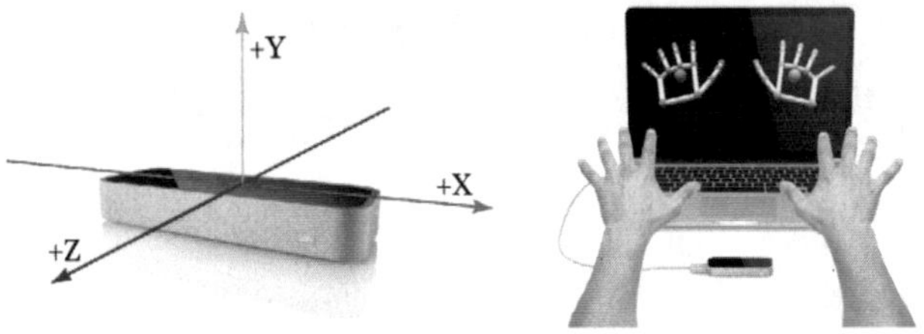

Figure 1. (left) Leap Motion Controller with the overlay of 3D right-handed coordinate system. (right) Tracking results are depicted on the computer screen if the hands are placed above the controller within the tracking distance.

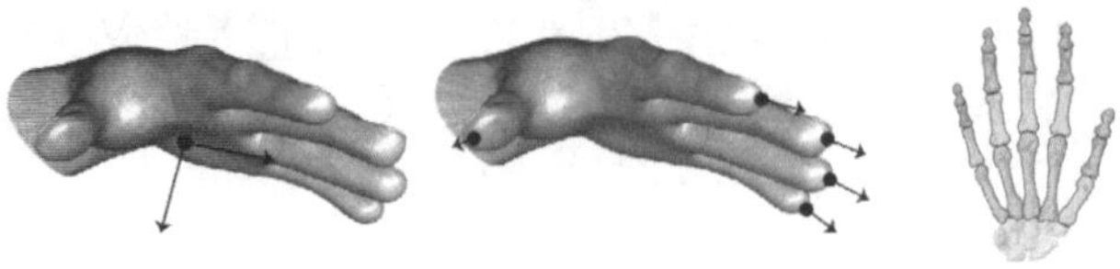

Figure 2. (left) Leap Motion Controller hand tracking. The palm normal and palm direction vectors are shown. (middle) Finger tracking with the direction vector of each finger is shown. (right) All the bones that are tracked by the Leap Motion Controller.

static 3D content using the Leap Motion Controller. Manipulation of 3D content is one of the widely performed user interaction in the computer graphics applications. A number of software, e.g., 3dstudio, Maya, CAD, Blender etc., employ the manipulation of 3D content. In general, a mouse-based interface is used for the user interaction. We implement four gestures, only using the thumb and the index finger to rotate and scale the 3D content. Three gestures are used to rotate the 3D content along the x, y and z axes, while the final gesture is used to uniformly scale the 3D content. We detail the implementation of the gestures, and then a comprehensive user study that evaluates the usability and user experience of the gesture-based user interface.

In the following section, we will first present the gesture-based user interface design and implementation (Sect. II), followed by the user study (Sect. III). Afterward, we will discuss the results (Sect. IV), followed by the conclusions (Sect. V).

II. User Interface Design & Implementation

Our gesture-based user interface is implemented using the Leap Motion Controller. As mentioned in the previous section, the Leap Motion Controller primarily focuses on the capturing of hands and fingers. The Leap Motion Controller uses optical sensors and infrared light, and the coordinate system is directed such that the y-axis is pointing upward when the device is placed horizontally on a surface. It employs a right-handed 3D coordinate system. It has a FOV of 150° wide, and 135° deep. The effective range of the Leap Motion Controller is from 25 to 600 millimeters or 1 inch to 2 feet above the device. The Leap Motion Controller coordinate system, along with the tracking result can be seen in Figure 1.

The Leap Motion Controller tracks hands and fingers in its field of view. The hand tracking provides the identity of the hand, along with its position, palm normal, direction, the arm to which the hand is attached and the list of fingers associated with the hand. A visualization of hand tracking can be seen in Figure 2(left). In addition, the Leap Motion Controller tracks individual fingers and tracks the position and direction of each finger. The visualization of the finger tracking can be see in Figure 2(middle). We make extensive use of these tracking parameters in our user interface design. If required, the Leap Motion Controller can return the position and orientation of each anatomical finger bone. Even though we do not use this data for our user interface, but it can be incorporated for more complex gestures. A visualization of the anatomical finger bones tracked by the Leap Motion Controller can be seen in Figure 2(right).

We implement four gestures to manipulate static 3D content using the Leap Motion Controller. The most general manipulation for the static 3D content is rotation and scaling. The rotation takes place along the x, y and z axes needing three gestures, and since we only implement the uniform scaling, it requires only one more gesture. Before describing the actual gesture recognition, we would like to formally define the hand and finger parameters that are used to implement the gestures:

- P_i is the 3 space position of each fingertip. The index i is from 0 to 4, identifying each finger starting from thumb (0) to the baby finger (4).
- D_i is the 3 space direction vector of each fingertip. The index i is from 0 to 4, identifying each finger starting from thumb (0) to the baby finger (4).
- N is the 3 space palm normal vector.

The first step before detecting any gesture is to define and identify a trigger. The trigger does not mean that a gesture will definitely occur but increases its likelihood. In our implementation, we define the trigger as the open hand with a spatial difference between the thumb and the index finger. We name the trigger as the "Neutral Pose", and all of gestures start form the Neutral Pose. An example of the Neutral Pose can be seen in top left image of the Figure 3, 4, 5, or 6. In principal, the Neutral Pose only depends on the thumb and the index finger, but for the gesture to work, it does not matter if other fingers are open or closed.

To detect the Neutral Pose, our system continuously monitors P_0, P_1, D_0, and D_1. If the distance between P_0 and P_1 is between 4 to 6 cm and D_0 and D_1 do not change over 30 frames, then it classifies the current pose as the Neutral Pose. Current values of P_0, P_1, D_0, D_1, and N are stored, and the system now actively searches for one of the four gestures, under the assumptions of each gesture. Henceforth the stored values for the Neutral Pose will be referred as P_0^{np}, P_1^{np}, D_0^{np}, D_1^{np}, and N^{np}. If there is a significant change in any of the four parameters then the Neutral Pose is classified as lost and the system again waits till the Neutral Pose is identified. Below we formally define the three rotation gestures and one scale gesture.

A. Rotation

3D rotation is characterized by the three rotations pitch, yaw and roll, which are the names given to rotations around x, y and z axes respectively. Once the Neutral Pose is detected, our implementation system actively searches for one of the three rotations or the scaling. Our rotation gesture is extremely

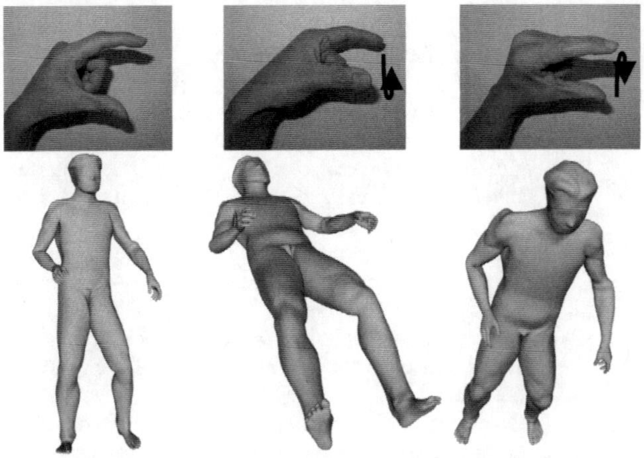

Figure 3. (left, top) The neutral pose is shown. (left, bottom) The 3D model in an arbitrary pose can be seen. Middle and right images show the rotation gestures with the corresponding rotated 3D model along the x axis.

intuitive as it is defined by the actual 3D rotation of the hand in the real world. Our system detects that if the values for P_0, P_1, D_0, and D_1 are similar to the Neutral Pose but the value of N is changing then one of the rotation gesture is being performed. Formally, the system actively monitors for $N.N^{np} > \sigma$. Where $N.N^{np}$ is the cosine of the angle between the two vectors. σ is the threshold that controls the sensitivity of the rotation gesture. In our case, it is equal to 0.349066, which implies that a rotation gesture is detected if the palm is rotated along one of the axes by more than $20°$ under the condition that the values of P_0, P_1, D_0, and D_1 are similar to P_1^{np}, D_0^{np}, and D_1^{np} respectively.

Once the rotation gesture is identified, we need to determine the axis of rotation. We determine the axis of rotation along one of the three axes using the following algorithm:

- Let N_{xy} and N_{xy}^{np} be the projection of N and N^{np} on the default xy plane at z=0.
- Let N_{xz} and N_{xz}^{np} be the projection of N and N^{np} on the default xz plane at y=0.
- Let N_{yz} and N_{yz}^{np} be the projection of N and N^{np} on the default yz plane at x=0.
- Compare $N_{xy}.N_{xy}^{np}$, $N_{xz}.N_{xz}^{np}$ and $N_{yz}.N_{yz}^{np}$, which is the dot product of the vectors projected on each plane respectively.
- If $N_{xy}.N_{xy}^{np}$ is maximum then the axis of rotation is along the z axis.
- If $N_{xz}.N_{xz}^{np}$ is maximum then the axis of rotation is along the y axis.
- If N_{yz} and N_{yz}^{np} is maximum then the axis of rotation is along the x axis.

Once the axis of rotation is determined, the corresponding dot product is used to work out the angle of rotation and the 3D model is rotated around that axis based on the angle of the rotation. An example of 3D rotations can be seen in Figure 3, 4, and 5.

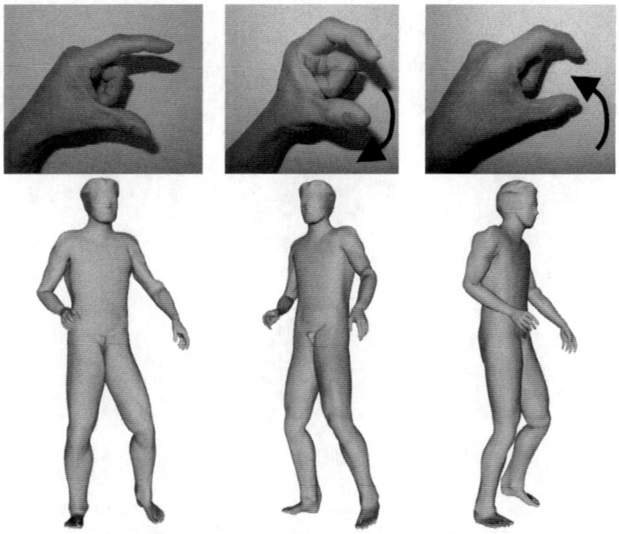

Figure 4. (left, top) The neutral pose is shown. (left, bottom) The 3D model in an arbitrary pose can be seen. Middle and right images show the rotation gestures with the corresponding rotated 3D model along the y axis.

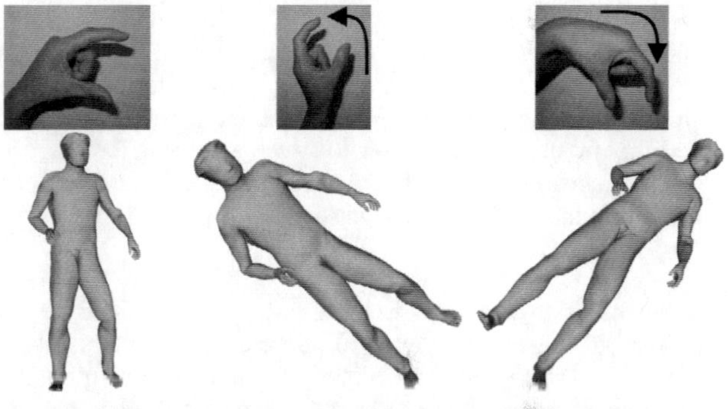

Figure 5. (left, top) The neutral pose is shown. (left, bottom) The 3D model in an arbitrary pose can be seen. Middle and right images show the rotation gestures with the corresponding rotated 3D model along the z axis.

B. Scaling

Since we only implement the uniform scaling, we need only one gesture to detect if the 3D content is being scaled up or down. The scaling gesture is defined by the fixed direction N with respect to N^{np}, but with the changing distance between P_0 and P_1 with respect to the distance between P_0^{np} and P_1^{np}. The following algorithm is used to detect the scaling gesture:

- Let $D^{np} = \sqrt{(P_0^{np} - P_1^{np})^2}$, which is the distance between the thumb and the index finger at the Neutral Pose.
- Let $D = \sqrt{(P_0 - P_1)^2}$, which is the distance between the thumb and the index finger after the detection of the Neutral Pose.
- if $D - D^{np} > \rho$ then the 3D content is being scaled up.
- if $D - D^{np} < -\rho$ then the 3D content is being scaled down.

The choice of parameter ρ controls the sensitivity of the scaling gesture. In our case, we set it to 1 cm, so that if the

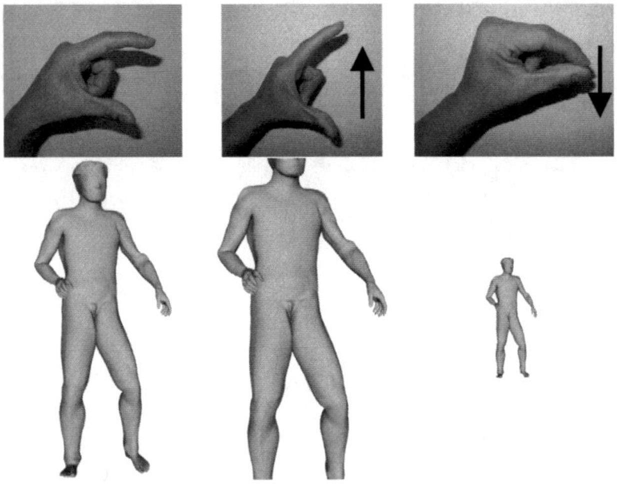

Figure 6. (left, top) The neutral pose is shown. (left, bottom) The 3D model in an arbitrary pose can be seen. Middle and right images show the scaling gestures with the corresponding uniformly scaled 3D model.

distance between the thumb and the index finger is increased by 1 cm then it is scaled up. Similarly, if it is decreased more than 1 cm then it is scaled down. An example of the scaling gesture can be seen in Figure 6. The above described gestures are used to manipulate the 3D content using both rotation and scaling. In the following section, we will describe the user study that validates the effectiveness of both the usability and the user experience of these gestures.

III. User Study

In order to evaluate the gesture-based user interface, we performed a user study over 20 participants (10 male, and 10 female). All the users were already familiar with manipulating 3D content using a mouse-based interface and their age was from 18 to 30. None of the users had any experience of manipulating 3D content using a gesture-based interface. At the beginning of the user study, they are asked to make note of the current scale of the 3D model. They performed the following steps in the user study:

- Rotate left along the x axis.
- Rotate down along the y axis.
- Scale up a little.
- Rotate right along the z axis.
- Scale down to half the size.
- Rotate right along the x axis.
- Rotate and scale the 3D model such that goes back to the original scale and facing towards the user.

After the completion of the user study, the users were asked the following questions:

1) Have you ever used a gesture-based interface before? (Yes/No).
2) Rate your satisfaction with the rotation interface on the scale of 1 to 9 with 1 being very simple, and 9 being very difficult.
3) Rate your satisfaction with the scaling interface on the scale of 1 to 9 with 1 being very simple, and 9 being very difficult.
4) Compared to a mouse-based interface how would you rate the effectiveness of the gesture-based interface in getting the tasks done? 1 very effective, 2 effective, 3 same, 4 worse, and 5 far worse.
5) Compared to a mouse-based interface how would you rate the learning curve of the gesture-based interface? 1 very easy, 2 easy, 3 same, 4 difficult, and 5 very difficult.
6) Compared to a mouse-based interface how would you rate the memorability of the gesture-based interface? 1 better, 2 good, 3 same, 4 bad, and 5 worse.
7) How would you define the experience of using the gesture-based interface in one word? e.g., exciting, fun, boring etc.
8) Given the choice of the mouse or gesture-based user interface, which one would you recommend?

On average, it took users less than a minute to perform the tasks, and they were immediately moved to the questionnaire after the completion of the tasks. On average it took 5 minutes for the users to complete the tasks and the user study. The results of the study are discussed in the next section.

IV. Results and Discussions

Our user study has seven closed questions (1 to 6, and 8), and one open question (7). Questions 1 to 6 focus on the usability, while the last two questions evaluate the user experience. Even though our usability questions have a scale of five or 9, we have consolidated the results into three classes for the ease of presentation. The results are presented as the percentages of the actual participants. The following table highlights the usability aspect of the gesture-based control:

TABLE I. USABILITY EVALUATION RESULTS BASED ON THE USER STUDY.

Question	Positive	Neutral	Negative
1	0%	0%	100%
2	70%	20%	10%
3	80%	20%	0%
4	70%	10%	20%
5	90%	10%	0%
6	95%	5%	0%

Similar to the usability analysis, to facilitate the presentation, we have classified the user experience analysis into two categories. For the question #7, we have classified the words e.g., fun, exciting, satisfactory etc., as positive, and the words e.g., boring, difficult etc., as negatives. Question #8 has only two possible answers, so there is no need for further classification. The following table shows the results of the user experience survey:

TABLE II. USER EXPERIENCE EVALUATION RESULTS BASED ON THE USER STUDY.

Question	Positive	Negative
7	95%	5%
8	90%	10%

As can be seen from the user study that the gesture-based interface is highly favored by the users both in terms of usability and the user experience. For the user experience, many of the users expressed that our interface is innovative and intuitive. It is evident from the results that the gesture-based interface is similarly effective to manipulate the 3D content compared to a mouse-based interface. Users not only managed to rotate and scale the 3D content easily using the gestures, but they are also able to complete the task efficiently without taking too much time. In addition, also in terms of learning the gesture-based interface proves to be easier to learn because users find it easy to pick up intuitively. Similarly, memorability of our interface is much better because once used they are easy to recall without any cues or prompts.

Our user study is subject to a couple of limitations. We do not specifically evaluate the ergonomics and fatigue factor associated with the gesture-based interface. Even though we did not receive any negative feedback in terms of user experience related to ergonomics or fatigue, these are important factors that must be evaluated using a long-term study. We will consider evaluating them in the future work. Similarly, we do not do a quantitative comparison of the time taken to complete various tasks using the mouse and the gesture-based interface. We plan to incorporate it in the future user study.

Despite the limitations, we show that it is possible to implement a single handed gesture-based interface to manipulate static 3D content using the Leap Motion Controller. Our user study demonstrates the effectiveness of the usability and user experience of such interface.

V. Conclusions

We presented a new hand gesture-based interface to effectively manipulate static 3D content using the Leap Motion Controller. We detailed the implementation of the four gestures. Our gesture recognition method first recognizes the Neutral Pose and then actively searches for either the rotation or the scaling gesture. The rotation gestures are recognized by using the rotation of the palm normal vector to find out the axis and angle of rotation. The scaling gesture is recognized by the changing distance between the thumb and the index finger. We performed a comprehensive user study to show the effectiveness of the usability and user experience of the gesture-based interface. The user study shows that gesture-based interface is easy to use, simple to learn and has a higher level of memorability. It resulted in a very positive user experience and most of the users recommended the interface over a mouse-based interface. The user study shows that our method is viable for manipulating static 3D content and can be employed in a number of applications. In future, we would like to add more gestures to add translation, in addition to rotation and scaling. We would also like to add gestures using both hands to control multiple 3D objects at the same time. In addition, we would also like to explore a gesture controlled system for controlling animated 3D content.

References

[1] MICROSOFT, "Kinect for microsoft windows. http://www.kinectforwindows.org/," November 2010, Last Access: Jan, 2017.

[2] R. Girshick, J. Shotton, P. Kohli, A. Criminisi, and A. Fitzgibbon, "Efficient regression of general-activity human poses from depth images," in ICCV, 2011, pp. 415–422.

[3] S. Marcel, O. Bernier, J. Viallet, and D. Collobert, "Hand gesture recognition using input-output hidden markov models," in 4th IEEE International Conference on Automatic Face and Gesture Recognition (FG 2000), 26-30 March 2000, Grenoble, France, 2000, pp. 456–461.

[4] F. Chen, C. Fu, and C. Huang, "Hand gesture recognition using a real-time tracking method and hidden markov models," Image Vision Comput., vol. 21, no. 8, 2003, pp. 745–758.

[5] Y. Liu and P. Zhang, "Vision-based human-computer system using hand gestures," in Computational Intelligence and Security, 2009. CIS '09. International Conference on, vol. 2, Dec 2009, pp. 529–532.

[6] C. Yu, X. Wang, H. Huang, J. Shen, and K. Wu, "Vision-based hand gesture recognition using combinational features," in Intelligent Information Hiding and Multimedia Signal Processing (IIH-MSP), 2010 Sixth International Conference on, Oct 2010, pp. 543–546.

[7] J. L. Raheja, R. Shyam, U. Kumar, and P. B. Prasad, "Real-time robotic hand control using hand gestures," in Proceedings of the 2010 Second International Conference on Machine Learning and Computing, ser. ICMLC '10, 2010, pp. 12–16.

[8] Y. Y. Pang, N. A. Ismail, and P. L. S. Gilbert, "A real time vision-based hand gesture interaction," in 2010 Fourth Asia International Conference on Mathematical/Analytical Modelling and Computer Simulation, May 2010, pp. 237–242.

[9] E. Ohn-Bar and M. M. Trivedi, "Hand gesture recognition in real time for automotive interfaces: A multimodal vision-based approach and evaluations," IEEE Transactions on Intelligent Transportation Systems, vol. 15, no. 6, Dec 2014, pp. 2368–2377.

[10] H. Cheng, L. Yang, and Z. Liu, "Survey on 3d hand gesture recognition," IEEE Transactions on Circuits and Systems for Video Technology, vol. 26, no. 9, Sept 2016, pp. 1659–1673.

[11] F. Farhadi-Niaki, S. A. Etemad, and A. Arya, "Design and usability analysis of gesture-based control for common desktop tasks," in Proceedings of the 15th International Conference on Human-Computer Interaction: Interaction Modalities and Techniques - Volume Part IV, ser. HCI'13, 2013, pp. 215–224.

[12] A. Bragdon, R. DeLine, K. Hinckley, and M. R. Morris, "Code space: Touch + air gesture hybrid interactions for supporting developer meetings," in Proceedings of the ACM International Conference on Interactive Tabletops and Surfaces, ser. ITS '11, 2011, pp. 212–221.

[13] M. C. Cabral, C. H. Morimoto, and M. K. Zuffo, "On the usability of gesture interfaces in virtual reality environments," in Proceedings of the 2005 Latin American Conference on Human-computer Interaction, ser. CLIHC '05, 2005, pp. 100–108.

[14] N. Villaroman, D. Rowe, and B. Swan, "Teaching natural user interaction using openni and the microsoft kinect sensor," in Proceedings of the 2011 Conference on Information Technology Education, ser. SIGITE '11, 2011, pp. 227–232.

[15] M. Bhuiyan and R. Picking, "A gesture controlled user interface for inclusive design and evaluative study of its usability." JSEA, vol. 4, no. 9, 2011, pp. 513–521.

[16] L. C. Ebert, G. Hatch, G. Ampanozi, M. J. Thali, and S. Ross, "You cant touch this: Touch-free navigation through radiological images," Surgical Innovation, vol. 19, no. 3, 2012, pp. 301–307.

[17] C. Liao, F. Guimbretière, and K. Hinckley, "Papiercraft: A command system for interactive paper," in Proceedings of the 18th Annual ACM Symposium on User Interface Software and Technology, ser. UIST '05. New York, NY, USA: ACM, 2005, pp. 241–244.

[18] J. P. Wachs, M. Kölsch, H. Stern, and Y. Edan, "Vision-based hand-gesture applications," Commun. ACM, vol. 54, no. 2, Feb. 2011, pp. 60–71.

[19] LeapMotion, "Leap motion controller, https://www.leapmotion.com/product/desktop," November 2012, Last Access: Jan, 2017.

[20] L. E. Potter, J. Araullo, and L. Carter, "The leap motion controller: A view on sign language," in Proceedings of the 25th Australian Computer-Human Interaction Conference: Augmentation, Application, Innovation, Collaboration, ser. OzCHI '13, 2013, pp. 175–178.

[21] C. Guerrero-Rincon, A. Uribe-Quevedo, H. Leon-Rodriguez, and J. O. Park, "Hand-based tracking animatronics interaction," in Robotics (ISR), 2013 44th International Symposium on, Oct 2013, pp. 1–3.

[22] G. Marin, F. Dominio, and P. Zanuttigh, "Hand gesture recognition with leap motion and kinect devices," in 2014 IEEE International Conference on Image Processing (ICIP), Oct 2014, pp. 1565–1569.

Toward a User Interface Adaptation Approach Driven by User Emotions

Julián Andrés Galindo, Sophie Dupuy-Chessa, Éric Céret

Université Grenoble Alpes, LIG, CNRS
Bâtiment IMAG, Domaine Universitaire, F-38000 Grenoble, France
e-mail: firstName.lastName@imag.fr

Abstract—**With the advent of ubiquitous computing, Human-Computer Interfaces must now be able to dynamically adapt to changes which may occur in their context of use while preserving usability. In this perspective, previous research evidences the need to adapt User interfaces (UIs) by taking into account dynamic user features like emotions at design time. To go one step further, this paper proposes an architecture to adapt the UI driven by user emotions at run-time. It is based on an existing adaptation approach which is extended to consider emotions. Hence, this proposition relies on three main components: the inferring engine, the adaptation engine and the Interactive System. We show an ongoing prototype to evaluate the feasibility of the approach for which we describe its implementation.**

Keywords-user interface adaptation; user modeling; emotion recognition; architecture.

I. INTRODUCTION

With the advent of ubiquitous computing, Human Computer Interfaces (HCI) must now be able to dynamically adapt to changes which may occur in their context of use (user, platform and environment) while preserving usability [1]. In this context, an important element for a suitable adaptation is to model users. A large variety of users' characteristics [2], profiles and preferences [3] need to be taken into account by designers to achieve users' satisfaction during interaction. In particular, authors state that the emotions felt by the user during interaction [4] should be taken into account by systems [5] and more specifically by user interfaces (UI) [6].

Indeed, during interaction with an UI, emotions are the user's response to aspects of objects, consequences of events and actions of agents [7]. Different user emotions were measured with respect to design factors: shapes, textures and color [8], visual features of web pages [9] and aesthetics aspects [10]. Emotions thus have the potential to highlight user's satisfaction [6]. However, adapting the UI regarding positive, negative or neutral emotions is a complex task because an effective adaptation needs mainly three elements: (1) emotion recognition [5], (2) adaptation to these emotions and (3) UI actions [6] to deal with dynamic changes in user's emotions. Indeed, humans seem to be inconsistent in their rational and emotional thinking evidenced by frequent cognitive dissonance [11] [12] and misleading emotions [13]. Therefore, this lack of user's harmony may lead the adaptation process to a fuzzy understanding of the user's emotions and to in effective adaptation changes.

Previous approaches consider a variety of users' elements, such as preferences [14], intentions [15], interactions [16] [17] [18], interests [19], physical states [20], controlled profiles [21] and clusters [22] ; however, they do not drive the UI adaptation by emotions as the main source of modeling and adaptation to the user [23]. Conversely, a spotlight was given by Nasoz providing an adaptive intelligent system with emotion recognition [6]. It mainly underlines the feasibility of adapting basic UI elements (dialogues) to affective states statically by analyzing stored user data. This work shows some highlights, such as emotion elicitation and recognition techniques, and a static user model with interface content actions from collected data. Nevertheless, it focuses on the understanding of physiological signals and does not provide a dynamic user model, nor UI adaptation rules and a consistent process to manage and execute these rules in the UI. Considering these limits, it cannot be considered as a complete solution for adapting UIs at runtime to user's emotions.

Our long term goal is to provide a tool that can adapt UIs to users' emotions. Here, the contribution focuses on a global architecture to adapt UIs regarding with user emotions at run-time. This proposal allows users to interact with the UI thanks to a cyclical process where (1) after recognizing the user's situation and in particular her emotions, (2) the best suitable UI structure is chosen and the set of UI parameters (audio, Font-size, Widgets, UI layout, etc.) is computed to (3) allow the UI to execute run-time changes aiming to find a better degree of user satisfaction. This architecture will be evaluated thanks to an empirical user experiment.

The reminder of the paper starts by explaining the state of the art about UI adaptation (Section 2), followed by a description of the approach (Section 3), and a presentation of the results of some observations of users' reacting to such adaptation (Section 4). It is based on the implementation of a preliminary prototype created for demonstrating the feasibility as well as the complexity of the approach. Finally, a conclusion summarizes the current findings, limitations and future work (Section 5).

II. Related work

Adapting the UI regarding emotions is at the intersection of two main areas: users' emotions modeling and UI adaptation.

First, several approaches have been proposed to model users' emotions in HCI[24] [25] [26] [27] [28] [29]. Although, these models study emotions when related to other users' features such as learnability, performance and communication. None of them deals with reusing these correlations to explore UI adaptation. For instance, the auto tutor project [25] shows a strong relation between emotions, learning and dialogues features during interaction with a vocal interface. Although, this finding is used to adapt the system content when user's uncertainty or frustration are detected, no UI change is considered.

Second, other proposals use emotion recognition to adapt the UI [6] [30] For instance, the Affect and Belief Adaptive Interface System (ABAIS) approach [29] applies changes in the GUI (Graphical User Interface) by following user's anxiety while interacting with a complex air force system. Despite these GUI adaptations can affect icons, displays, notifications and custom configuration, there is no significant evidence of considering other user's emotions, particularly positive ones. Moreover, this work does not allow adaptation of the structure of the UI depending on contextual elements such as the size of the screen.

Another adaptation proposal was made by Nasoz [6]. This approach consists in implementing an adaptive intelligent system relying on the recognition of affective states from physiological signals. It includes a user model with features such as personality traits, age, gender and recognized emotion (Sadness, Anger, Surprise, Fear, Frustration, and Amusement) attached to a set of automatic interface actions. This relation implies that UI adaptation can be driven by combining observable user's data with emotions at run-time. However, this inference is evidenced only in the design of the user model. Furthermore, while interacting with the UI, users may feel unconsidered emotions that may also be relevant in UI adaptation, such as dislike or contempt. In fact, dislikeness can be related to user's responses to the degree of appealing and familiarity with objects [7]. Consequently, we can suppose that users may often reflect dislike when they find that an UI adaptation is unfamiliar, unattractive, and therefore unsatisfactory. Overall, this contribution appears to be a partial solution in the field of UI adaptation.

To sum up, (1) there is a lack of UI adaptation by using user emotions models, (2) other relevant emotions (especially positive ones) need to be considered, (3) current changes mainly focus on content rather than UI itself. Considering the limits of related works, we investigate an approach that will permit UI adaptation to different kinds of emotions (positive, negative, and neutral) at runtime.

III. Global approach

This section provides an overview of our approach and introduces the global architecture of the tool supporting our approach.

A. *Overview*

Our approach proposes to adapt at run-time the UI to users' emotions. To prioritize the architecture's feasibility (emotion recognition), we choose mainly to consider 3 kinds of emotions: positive, negative and neutral. This categorization follows the valence model suggested by Russel in the circumflex model of affect [30]. In this model, emotional states are represented at any level of valence axis (positive or negative) or at a neutral level. For instance, happiness is located in the positive region of the axis while disgust in the negative one. The approach may thus recognize if one particular UI adaptation has been found as positive, negative or neutral (significant lack of expression) by the user as feedback for future adaptations.

The adaptation can be related to the widgets used, the font, the colors, etc., but also to the UI structure. Previously we proposed a patent [31] that considers the UI adaptation based on any contextual characteristics, such as the screen size or the brightness. We will reuse the principles of the patent to compute the appropriate adaptations and we will extend the tool for considering emotions. With this goal, we

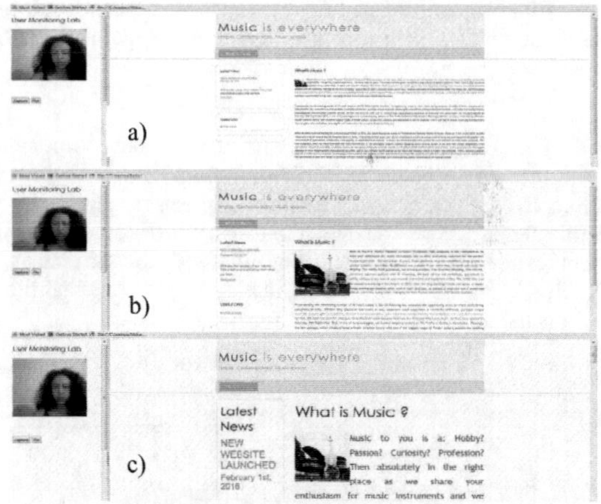

Figure 1. Prototype views during the UI adaptation

propose a new architecture which starts with the exposition of the main involved definitions.

B. *Definitions*

This section underlines the principal definitions in our architecture.

Context of Use*: a set of three models,* users, platforms and environment, representing the users who are intended to use the system, their hardware and software platform(s), and their physical and sociological environment while the interaction takes place in practice [1]. Consequently, the proposed architecture will deal with this context of use.

UI variant*: a variant is a variation of an UI* created for a specific context of Use (Figure 1, a, b, c). For instance, there can be two different structures for a laptop and a smartphone, leading to two variants of the same UI. A UI variant is modelled by the following elements: ui-name (the name of the UI it is a variation of), variant-id (its identifier), path (the path to the source code embodying this variant), and context-of-use (the subset of characteristics of the context of use this variant is dedicated to).

UI Parameters*: Defines a set of variables* which personalize UI elements (e.g., font-size, widgets, audio, display and dialogues) regarding with identified context values (e.g., user's emotions). For instance, if the user's emotion is happiness then the UI parameter named background-color could be set to light-yellow. Then, those variables sent to displayed UI for applying corresponding changes. To illustrate previous definitions, let's consider the UI variant shown in Figure 1(c). This variant of the Home page of a website is adapted to window-width is bigger than 900 (pixels). We consider here that, considering the user's emotions, the adaptation system has decided that the background of the UI should be yellow. It sets the UI parameter (background-color) to the chosen color (light-yellow) and sends it to the variant after it is displayed. This parameter will be applied by using a personalizing function which will be described in the architecture section.

Filtering emotions*:* Removes unneeded emotions during the interaction. Usefulness of emotions is defined by the designer.

C. *Architecture*

The architecture (Figure 2) articulates three components: the Inferring Engine ❶, the Adaptation Engine ❻ and the Interactive System ❾. An adaptation process might start from either (a) a need for a new UI to display or (b) a change in the context of use. (a) can be exemplified by the user entering a web site: the home page has to be displayed. An example of (b) is the ambient light: when it increases, the contrast on the UI might be increased as well. In (b), the overall process is the following: the Inferring Engine ❶ monitors sensors ❷ to detect changes in the context of use. From these values, it deduces the new context of use dynamically. It includes an Emotion Wrapper ❸ which makes it possible to include emotion values in the user model. The Inferring Engine ❶ sends ❺ the computed context of use to the Adaptation Engine ❻, which elicits accordingly a suitable UI variant and the UI parameters ❿. Finally, the Interactive System ❾ displays the variant ⓫ and executes the changes related to the parameters. The whole process runs cyclically by following a time period parameter defined by the designer.

The following sections describe the three main components of our global architecture with more details.

a) *Inferring Engine*

This component is in charge of dynamically deducing the value of the context of Use (users with their emotions, platform, environment) by executing inference rules (e.g., conversion, aggregation). The Emotion Wrapper ❸ takes sensor input data ❷ (e.g., user's face image) and sends it to an emotion detection tool ❹ such as FaceReader [32] or Affdex [33] that returns the set of detected emotions. The Wrapper ❸ filters and aggregates the acquired emotions values to find whether the current user emotion is positive, negative or neutral, and returns this value to the Inferring Engine, which includes it in the context of use (emotions, platform, environment) and in turn sends it ❺ to the Adaptation Engine ❻.

b) *Adaptation Engine*

The Adaptation Engine (AE) aims at (a) selecting the UI variant among all available variants for the UI and (b) computing the UI parameters for even better adapting the chosen variant to the context of use. First, the Adaptation Engines receives ❺ the current context of use from the Inferring Engine ❶ and the needed UI name from the Interactive System ❾. From the variants description ❽, it

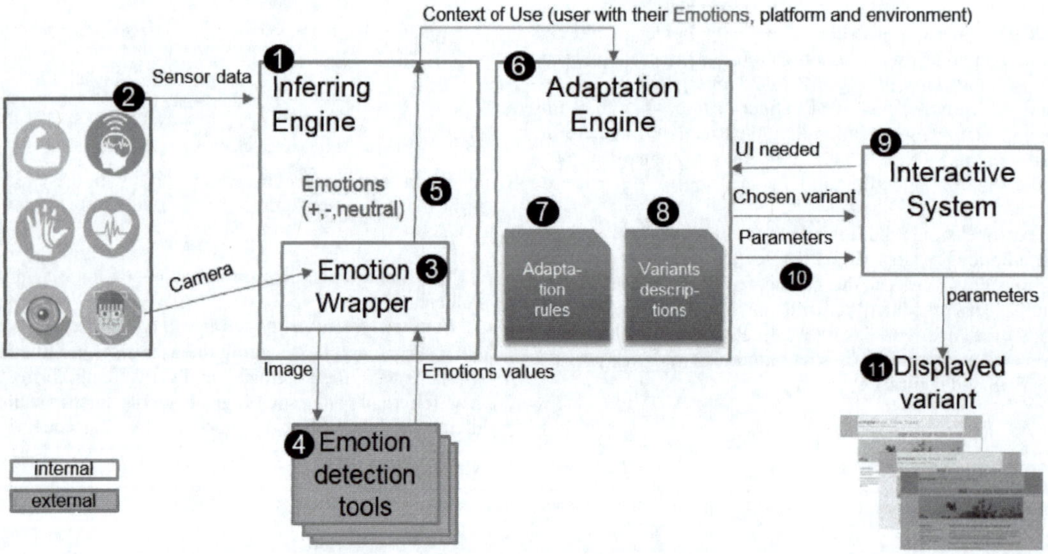

Figure 2. Global schema of the architecture.

computes which variant of the needed UI suits best the context of use, for instance a variant made for a screen width of 400px when the current screen is 450px width. Then it computes if some changes can be or have to be applied to the parameters of this variant for making it better, using rules that respect this format (F):

for every context-variable
do if <context-use-conditions> then
<define UI-parameters>.

For instance, *if <user-emotion=positive> then <background-color=light-yellow and font-size=normal>*

In this (fanciful) example, when the user is considered having a positive emotion, two parameters are defined for changing the variant: the background-color is set to light yellow and the font size is switched to normal. At the present time, adaptation rules are kept simple to show the feasibility of the architecture. If needed, we can choose another approach for specifying rules. This will require a continuous observation process to identity the suitable (1) context-use-conditions and (2) thresholds for the UI-parameters.

c) Interactive System

The last component is the Interactive System ❾. When needed, it sends the required UI name to the Adaptation Engine ❻, receives the chosen UI variant path and the UI parameters to apply, displays the UI variant and applies the UI parameters. This last action is made thanks to the following algorithm:

for every ui-parameter do
if <ui-parameter-condition> then <modify UI >.
For instance, if <background-color=light-yellow> then <addClass background-light-yellow to UI>.

As already mentioned, a change in the context of use may occur during interaction and induce the need of changing the displayed variant (e.g., the user has reduced the window size and a variant designed for a Smartphone would be more relevant) or applying new UI parameters (e.g., user's emotion has changed and the Adaptation Engine has decided that another color palette has to be used). The Interactive System is thus also in charge of watching for such updates and applying them dynamically by using the personalizing function.

This personalizing function executes a UI personalization thanks to the values of the UI parameters decided by the adaptation system. This function avoids selecting a UI variant that would have to suit all the characteristics of the context of use. Thus, variants can be reduced to only the variations that cannot be (or hardly be) modified at runtime. This makes it possible to deal with complexity, repetition and maintenance. First, if designers need to design as many UI variants as possible context of use, the combinations may lead to a complex design task to support <user emotions*platform*environment> combinations and ergonomic guidelines (e.g., 3700 in [34]). Second, even when designers deal with all designs diversity, there would be many UI repeated features across all variants (e.g., the same font-size across all different background colors). Lastly, designers would need to maintain all variants to have consistent UIs, which may be a tedious and ineffective task (e.g., change font-size=small for all UI variants).

D. *Current Prototype*

The architecture has been implemented for web pages. From the software perspective, all components rely on JavaScript and jQuery [35] to execute all steps in the adaptation process. Where the Interactive System uses also HTML and CSS. This first prototype (Figure 1) involves run-time adaptation in UI parameters (color, font-size, image-size) and variants regarding with positive (happiness and contempt), negative (anger, disgust, sadness, fear) and neutral emotions. Generic adaptation rules were implemented by following the format (F) shown in the architecture section to adapt the color, font-size and image-size according to user emotions (e.g., image-size=large when a negative emotion is evoked).

Moreover, the generic variable emotionFilter= {positive, negative, neutral} allows to filter the needed emotions to be considered by the Adaptation Engine. Two variants of a sample Home pages were used in our demonstrator. Variant home-1 is adapted to a PC platform as variant home-2 to a smartphone. The main structural change among them is the body-size:1024 and 480 pixels respectively. Those variants emphasize the adaptation engines selection of the variant depending on the current platform context. To illustrate the

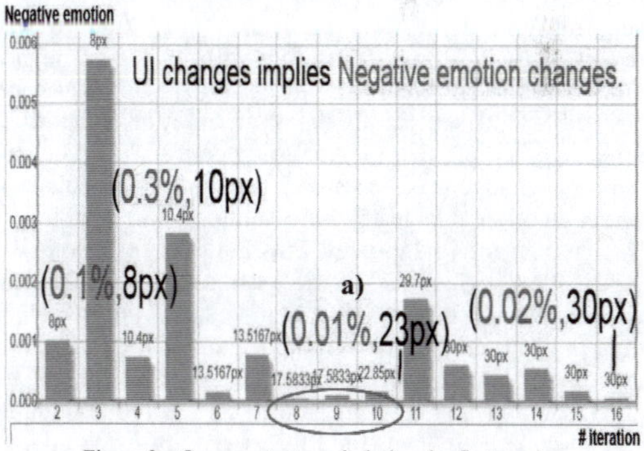

Figure 3. One user test result during the first session

current implementation, as the user is interacting with the website, the adaptation process may start with (a) a need for a new UI to display or (b) a change in the context of use. Emotions are detected every 10 seconds. In both cases, the Inferring Engine uses a camera for taking a picture of the user's face and sends it to the Emotion Wrapper. Then, it calls the Microsoft emotion detection tool [36] to get back the corresponding emotions. At this point, the Emotion Wrapper is configured to filter the neutral prediction. Basically, neutral emotions covered all positive and negative ones during the interaction with the current simple websites.

Then, with this set of emotion values, the inferring engine aggregates emotions to figure out whether the current user's emotion is positive or negative. Once the context of use is updated by the Inferring Engine, the Adaptation Engine finds the best UI variant (here an HTML path) and UI parameters thanks to a set of adaptation rules such as the following one which aims to show only the feasibility of the approach and does pretend to be relevant:

if <Context-Use-user-emotion=negative> then <Main-Background-Color=light-violet and Main-Font-Size=large>.

Consequently, the Interactive System displays the UI variant path (e.g., variants/home_pc.html) and adds CSS classes to the page.

IV. Feasibility User tests

As a first test of our architecture, we drove some observations with users. Their goal was to verify that the system is able to detect the correct emotion and to make changes. The test is designed to start with negative emotion then the changes in the user interfaces must make the emotions change to more positive ones. To test that the system runs correctly, we performed 10 tests with 5 users with a fixed emotion (negative). Tests involved two user sessions in a 2-minutes-period per session. The system run with a time period of 8 seconds leading to 16 iterations per session. Four men and one woman from a Computer Science profile between 25 and 33 years old. Users read a web page (Figure 1) by only looking at and scrolling up and down by interacting with the mouse in a PC (1920 x 1080 resolution) through a web browser (Firefox version 49.0.2). During every session, the system performed a gradual font-size growth (8px to 32px) regarding with the user negative emotion (emotionFilter=negative). As a result, the system was stable and reacted to the user emotion properly by increasing the font-size and image-size only when a negative emotional change was recognized. It means that it detects the correct emotion change and its evolution while adapting the UI (font-size and image-size). This initial observations were evidenced at asking users if the changes in the UI matched their emotions where 4 over 5 understood the correlation while the last one did not see the reason of the changes but agreed when an explanation was given. To illustrate, one user stated that the best font-size change was showed in middle of the experiment. In fact, for this user, Figure 3 shows the negative emotion across 16 iterations where a) evidences preliminarily that the lowest negative values were recognized just in between 8 and 10 iterations reaching almost 23 px. As a highlight, another user started with a close position to the screen when font-size was 8 px but then it was found relaxed at the end of the experiment (30 px). In such case, the user stated that he preferred the final UI change which may be also related with his low vision acuity.

Consequently, (1) the system was mainly able to detect changes in the emotion and (2) to induce UI variations which seems (3) to imply new and different user emotion values during the interaction. It leads to the need of driving a scientific experiment to consider more emotions and complex UI adaptations to validate the correlation between automatic detected emotions and user declared ones.

V. Conclussion and Future Work

This paper addresses UI adaptation by user emotions (positive, negative and neutral) at run-time. We proposed an architecture, which covered three components: The Inferring engine, the Adaptation engine and the Interactive System. The architecture was applied in a current prototype to test successfully how it reacts to emotions (negative). It was also evidenced that UI changes denotes negative emotion changes in run-time, which was particularly supported by most users. Even when empirical tests were relevant, it is necessary to go further to validate scientifically the architecture by considering more emotions, complex adaptation rules with larger case studies. To this, we envision to extend a current adaptation approach to include user emotions.

Filtering emotions seems to be not particularly useful at considering small interface changes. For instance, if font size changes from 10 to 11px then the user may often evoke a neutral emotion. As a perspective, we need to refine the emotion inferring engine so that it will not differentiate in which degree this minor change was positive or negative. A fact that might be beneficial to understand and define future and bigger adaptation changes. Hence, it is necessary to identify adaptations relevant to emotions and to validate them.

Acknowledgment

I wish to thank my family and supervisors for their priceless support.

References

[1] G. Calvary, J. Coutaz, D. Thevenin, Q. Limbourg, L. Bouillon, and J. Vanderdonckt, "A unifying reference framework for multi-target user interfaces," *Interact. Comput.*, vol. 15, no. 3, pp. 289–308, 2003.

[2] D. Browne, "Chapter 7 - Conclusions.," in *Adaptive User Interfaces*, London: Academic Press, 1990, pp. 195–222.

[3] P. Biswas, S. Bhattacharya, and D. Samanta, "User model to design adaptable interfaces for motor-impaired users," in *TENCON 2005 2005 IEEE Region 10*, pp. 1–6, 2005.

[4] B. Reeves and C. Nass, *How people treat computers, television, and new media like real people and places.* CSLI Publications and Cambridge university press Cambridge, UK, 1996.

[5] S. Carberry and F. de Rosis, "Introduction to special Issue on 'Affective modeling and adaptation,'" *User Model. User-Adapt. Interact.*, vol. 18, no. 1–2, pp. 1–9, Jan. 2008.

[6] F. Nasoz, "Adaptive intelligent user interfaces with emotion recognition," University of Central Florida Orlando, Florida, 2004.

[7] B. R. Steunebrink, "The Logical structure of emotions," Utrecht University, 2010.

[8] J. Kim, J. Lee, and D. Choi, "Designing emotionally evocative homepages: an empirical study of the quantitative

relations between design factors and emotional dimensions," *Int. J. Hum.-Comput. Stud.*, vol. 59, no. 6, pp. 899–940, 2003.
[9] G. Lindgaard, G. Fernandes, C. Dudek, and J. Brown, "Attention web designers: You have 50 milliseconds to make a good first impression!," *Behav. Inf. Technol.*, vol. 25, no. 2, pp. 115–126, 2006.
[10] E. Michailidou, S. Harper, and S. Bechhofer, "Visual complexity and aesthetic perception of web pages," in *Proceedings of the 26th annual ACM international conference on Design of communication*, pp. 215–224, 2008.
[11] *Cognitive dissonance: Progress on a pivotal theory in social psychology*, vol. xviii. Washington, DC, US: American Psychological Association, 1999.
[12] L. Festinger, *A Theory of Cognitive Dissonance*. Stanford University Press, 1962.
[13] P. Goldie, "Explaining expressions of emotion," *Mind*, vol. 109, no. 433, pp. 25–38, Jan. 2000.
[14] K. Gajos and D. S. Weld, "SUPPLE: automatically generating user interfaces," in *Proceedings of the 9th international conference on Intelligent user interfaces*, pp. 93–100, 2004.
[15] E. Horvitz, J. Breese, D. Heckerman, D. Hovel, and K. Rommelse, "The Lumiere project: Bayesian user modeling for inferring the goals and needs of software users," in *Proceedings of the Fourteenth conference on Uncertainty in artificial intelligence*, pp. 256–265, 1998.
[16] M. Hartmann, D. Schreiber, and M. Mühlhäuser, "AUGUR: providing context-aware interaction support," in *Proceedings of the 1st ACM SIGCHI symposium on Engineering interactive computing systems*, pp. 123–132, 2009.
[17] A. Krzywicki, W. Wobcke, and A. Wong, "An adaptive calendar assistant using pattern mining for user preference modelling," in *Proceedings of the 15th international conference on Intelligent user interfaces*, pp. 71–80, 2010.
[18] G. Weber and M. Specht, "User modeling and adaptive navigation support in WWW based tutoring systems," in *User Modeling*, pp. 289–300, 1997.
[19] J. Orwant, "Doppelgänger–a user modeling system," Massachusetts Institute of Technology, 1991.
[20] F. Nack *et al.*, "Pillows as adaptive interfaces in ambient environments," in *Proceedings of the international workshop on Human-centered multimedia*, pp. 3–12, 2007.
[21] C. G. Thomas and M. Krogs\a eter, "An adaptive environment for the user interface of Excel," in *Proceedings of the 1st international conference on Intelligent user interfaces*, pp. 123–130, 1993.
[22] B. Krulwich, "Lifestyle finder: Intelligent user profiling using large-scale demographic data," *AI Mag.*, vol. 18, no. 2, p. 37, 1997.
[23] M. Peissner, D. Häbe, D. Janssen, and T. Sellner, "MyUI: generating accessible user interfaces from multimodal design patterns," in *Proceedings of the 4th ACM SIGCHI symposium on Engineering interactive computing systems*, pp. 81–90, 2012.
[24] J. Rowe, B. Mott, S. McQuiggan, J. Robison, S. Lee, and J. Lester, "Crystal island: A narrative-centered learning environment for eighth grade microbiology," in *workshop on intelligent educational games at the 14th international conference on artificial intelligence in education, Brighton, UK*, pp. 11–20, 2009.
[25] K. Forbes-Riley and D. Litman, "Designing and evaluating a wizarded uncertainty-adaptive spoken dialogue tutoring system," *Comput. Speech Lang.*, vol. 25, no. 1, pp. 105–126, Jan. 2011.
[26] K. Porayska-Pomsta, M. Mavrikis, and H. Pain, "Diagnosing and acting on student affect: the tutor's perspective," *User Model. User-Adapt. Interact.*, vol. 18, no. 1–2, pp. 125–173, 2008.
[27] A. C. Graesser *et al.*, "The relationship between affective states and dialog patterns during interactions with AutoTutor," *J. Interact. Learn. Res.*, vol. 19, no. 2, p. 293, 2008.
[28] F. de Rosis, N. Novielli, V. Carofiglio, A. Cavalluzzi, and B. De Carolis, "User modeling and adaptation in health promotion dialogs with an animated character," *J. Biomed. Inform.*, vol. 39, no. 5, pp. 514–531, 2006.
[29] E. Hudlicka and M. D. McNeese, "Assessment of User Affective and Belief States for Interface Adaptation: Application to an Air Force Pilot Task," *User Model. User-Adapt. Interact.*, vol. 12, no. 1, pp. 1–47, Feb. 2002.
[30] J. A. Russell, "A circumplex model of affect.," *J. Pers. Soc. Psychol.*, vol. 39, no. 6, pp. 1161–1178, 1980.
[31] E. Céret, S. Dupuy-Chessa, G. Calvary, and M. Bittar, "System and method for magnetic adaptation of a user interface," TPI2015053 déposé via France INPI le 7 juillet 2015, 2ème dépôt le 7 juillet 2016.
[32] Noldus.com, "Facial expression recognition software." [Online]. Available: http://www.noldus.com/human-behavior-research/products/facereader. [Accessed: 01-Nov-2016].
[33] Affectiva.com, "Affdex - Affectiva." [Online]. Available: http://www.affectiva.com/solutions/affdex/. [Accessed: 02-Nov-2016].
[34] J. Vanderdonckt and F. Bodart, *The "Corpus Ergonomicus": A Comprehensive and Unique Source for Human-Machine Interface*. Namur (BE): Presses Universitaires de Namur, 1994.
[35] Jquery.com, "jQuery, write less, do more." [Online]. Available: https://jquery.com/. [Accessed: 02-Nov-2016].
[36] Microsoft.com, "Microsoft Emotion API." [Online]. Available: https://www.microsoft.com/cognitive-services/en-us/emotion-api. [Accessed: 05-Nov-2016].

Sonification of 3D Object Shape for Sensory Substitution: An Empirical Exploration

Torkan Gholamalizadeh, Hossein Pourghaemi, Ahmad Mhaish, Gökhan İnce and Damien Jade Duff
Faculty of Computer & Informatics Engineering
Istanbul Technical University
Email: djduff@itu.edu.tr, gokhan.ince@itu.edu.tr

***Abstract*—Different approaches to sonification of 3D objects as part of a sensory substitution system are experimentally investigated. The sensory substitution system takes 3D point clouds of objects obtained from a depth camera and presents them to a user as spatial audio. Two approaches to shape sonification are presented and their characteristics investigated. The first approach directly encodes the contours belonging to the object in the image as sound waveforms. The second approach categorizes the object according to its 3D surface properties as encapsulated in the rotation invariant Fast Point Feature Histogram (FPFH), and each category is represented by a different synthesized musical instrument. Object identification experiments are done with human users to evaluate the ability of each encoding to transmit object identity to a user. Each of these approaches has its disadvantages. Although the FPFH approach is more invariant to object pose and contains more information about the object, it lacks generality because of the intermediate recognition step. On the other hand, since contour-based approach has no information about depth and curvature of objects, it fails in identifying different objects with similar silhouettes. On the task of distinguishing between 10 different 3D shapes, the FPFH approach produced more accurate responses. However, the fact that it is a direct encoding means that the contour-based approach is more likely to scale up to a wider variety of shapes.**

Keywords–Sensory substitution; sensory augmentation; point clouds; depth cameras; sound synthesis.

I. Introduction

Sensory substitution is the use of technology to replace one sensory modality with another. In visual-to-audio sensory substitution, visual information captured by a camera is presented to users as sound. Such systems promise help for the sight-impaired: imagine users navigating using space/obstacle information, grasping novel objects, eating meals with utensils, and so forth. By not falling into the trap of many artificial intelligence-based assistive systems of aggressively abstracting the data provided to users, user agency is preserved and the user's own advanced cognitive data processing capabilities are leveraged. Sensory substitution systems also provide interesting platforms for exploring synaesthesia and cross-modal sensory processing [1].

Recent work in utilizing depth cameras for sensory substitution promises to increase the usefulness of such visual-to-audio sensory substitution systems [2][3]. Mhaish et al.'s system [2] uses a 3D depth camera to create point clouds characterizing the surfaces of objects in a scene and presents those surfaces to a user using spatial audio. See Figure 1 for a summary of the information flow in that approach. The present work extends that system, offering an investigation of different ways of encoding 3D spatial surfaces as audio, an area ripe for exploration in the context of sensory substitution systems.

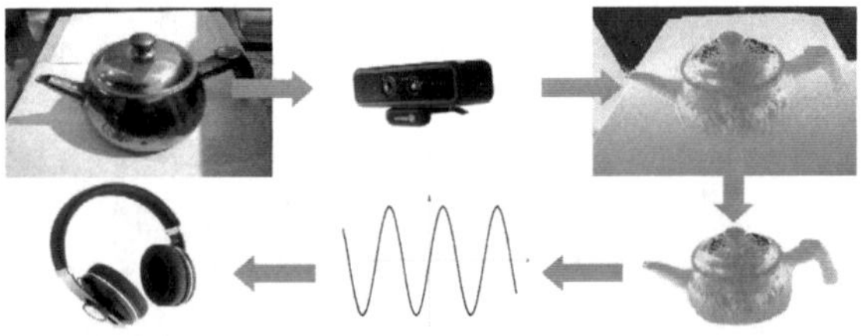

Figure 1. The flow of data in the full sensory substitution system, from real-world objects, via the depth camera, to a point cloud, and a segmented tracked object, and finally a sound waveform played to a user.

Figure 2. Left: the system being used "in the wild". Right: physical set-up of the experiments described in this paper.

Broadly speaking, the process of encoding information as (non-speech) sounds is called sonification. Sonification is used in applications such as medical imaging where it is used for example to differentiate a healthy brain from an unhealthy one, geological activity detection, and so forth. In the present paper, we present two approaches to sonification of object shape. Object shape is particularly important in providing functional information about objects, particularly for blind users who may wish to perceive objects in their environment in order to recognize them, avoid them, or manipulate them. The first approach to shape sonification described in the present paper is encoding based on 2D object contours and the second is based on a 3D object recognition descriptor called the Fast Point Feature Histogram.

The rest of this work will be presented in four sections. In the next section, a short summary of related work is presented. In Section 3, an overview of the sensory substitution system is given and two different sound generation approaches are explained in detail. Then in Section 4, details of experiments and results are shown. Finally, results are summarized and further work discussed in Section 5.

II. Related Work

Sensory substitution systems are systems that map visual information to audio in an attempt to create an effect like vision but channeled through a different sense. More broadly, systems that map any kind of information (including visual and graphical) to audio are called sonification systems. In general, there are two kinds of sonification systems, high-level and low-level sonification systems, where the high-level approaches are designed to convert information to speech. A significant subset of these systems are text-to-speech applications, widely used for visually impaired people. Examples include VoiceOver and JAWS [1]. In addition to text-to-speech applications there are some other high-level sonification systems which are more complex and can detect objects and identify them and return their names in real-time, like LookTel [4] and Microsoft Seeing AI project [5] that can read texts, describe people and identify their emotions. These high-level sonification systems are easy for users and do not require training, but they can fail in sonifying complex environment or shapes for which the system has not been adapted.

On the other hand, low-level sonification systems generate sound directly based on visual information. The main difference between these systems and high-level sonification systems is that users need to be trained before using these systems to be able to understand the relation between the generated sounds and properties of observed objects. Though these kinds of systems can seem difficult to use, they can be more flexible for new environments and undefined objects because they produce sounds based on characteristics directly calculated from input data [6]. One of the most well-known systems of this group is the sensory substitution system The vOICe [1], which uses the gray-level image of the scene and scans the image from left to right and generates and sums audible frequencies based on pixels' location with amplitude based on pixels' intensity. The disadvantages of the vOICe system are that it requires 1 second to scan the image. Further, the image-sound mapping is somewhat abstract if used with depth images without adaptation and does not explore physical or metaphorical synergies with shape in particular. However, our proposed system is conceived as a system for generating spatial audio generated based on surface and shape information for helping users to localize objects and identify them in real-time.

Systems closest to our own include the electro-tactile stereo-based navigation system ENVS of [7] with ten channels of depth information calculated from stereo transmitted to ten fingers, which focuses on navigation but not shape understanding and uses the tactile pathway, and the depth-camera visual-to-audio based sensory substitution system See ColOr of [3] which, though using depth-cameras, concentrates on bringing color (and not space or shape) to blind users by mapping different intervals of hue and value to instruments like violin, trumpet, piano etc. Conversely, finding a proper method for mapping shape information to audio is a vital step in many low-level sonification systems. In this area, the work of Shelley et el. [8] is close to the proposed system, focusing on sonification of shape and curvature of 3D objects in an augmented reality environment as part of the SATIN project, where the user of the system is able to touch and alter the 3D objects using the visual-haptic interface of the system. In that article, object cross sections (and associated curvature) are used to modulate the frequency of a carrier signal or the parameters of physical sound generation [8].

As discussed above choosing a good approach to sonification plays an important role in achieving good performance of low-level sonification systems. Therefore in the current work, two different sound generation methods are provided for Mhaish et al.'s [2] system and their accuracies are measured on the task of synthetic 3D object identification. The idea of using synthetic objects instead of real objects is to evaluate the performance of different sound generation methods isolated from the performance of other components and environmental noise. In future work, the best approach or mix of these approaches will be applied in the identification of real objects.

III. Technical Details

Output from a head-mounted depth camera (DepthSense 325 or ASUS Xtion) is converted to a head-centred point cloud, which is segmented by curvature and point-distance in real-time [9] into surface primitives. These surface primitives are tracked using simple data association, selected using size and closeness criteria, and presented to the user as spatially-located audio (played using a wrapper around the spatial audio library OpenAL [10], the wrapper taking care of time tracking and interpolation).

Heavy use of the Point Cloud Library [11] is made in the point-cloud processing steps and particular care is made to keep processing of point clouds at 15+ frames per second so as to provide responsive sensory feedback to user probing motions. An illustration of the system being tested can be found in the left picture of Figure 2.

Note that this system is designed to segment surface primitives rather than objects. Although for some applications, such as tabletop object manipulation, short-cuts can be taken to extract separate objects, general object segmentation is an unsolved problem. Since the current paper is focused on sonification (making sounds to represent data), the focus here is on the sonification of whole but mostly simple objects.

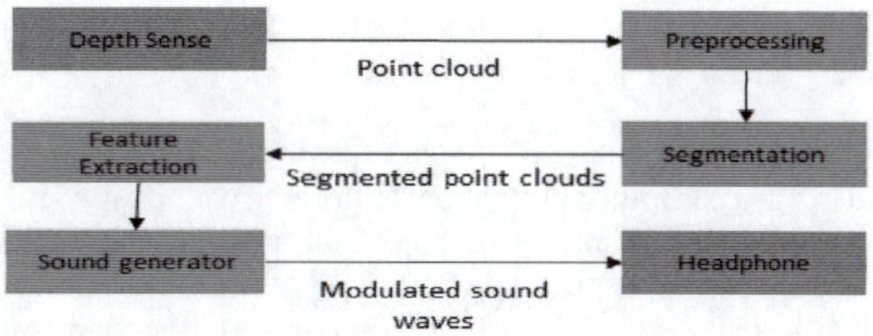

Figure 3. Software level of data flow diagram.

Before going into detail about the approaches used to sonify shape, the processing steps used by the system to extract visual information and process it to audio will be explained. Figure 3 shows the data flow architecture of the system. The steps in the architecture are further explained as follow:

1) Preprocessing: RGB and depth information produced by the time of flight or structured light camera is passed to a preprocessing step in the form of a point cloud and in this step normals are calculated from the point cloud "organized" in a 2D array of points, using a real time integral image algorithm supplied by Holzer et al [12].

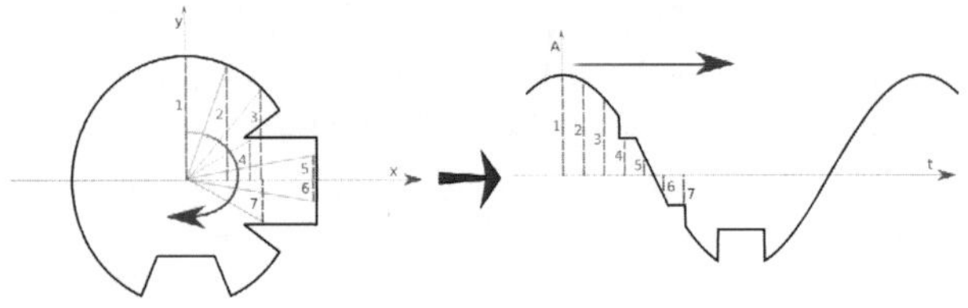

Figure 4. Rotary-contour-based encoding. **Left:** Original object contour in x-y image space. **Right:** Resulting waveform as a plot of amplitude(A) against time(t).

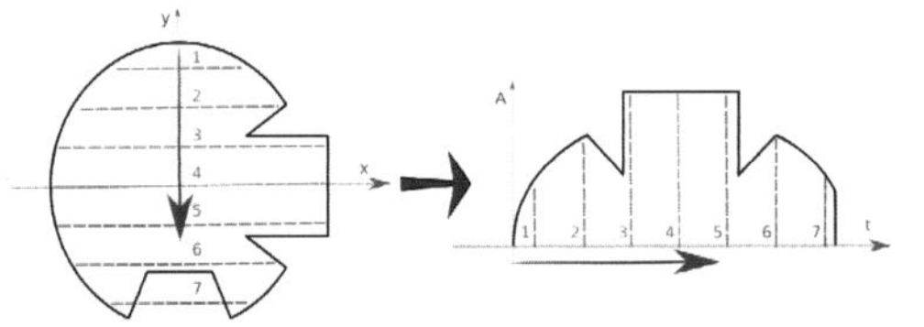

Figure 5. Vertical-contour-based encoding. **Left:** original object contour. **Right:** the resulting waveform as amplitude (A) against time (t).

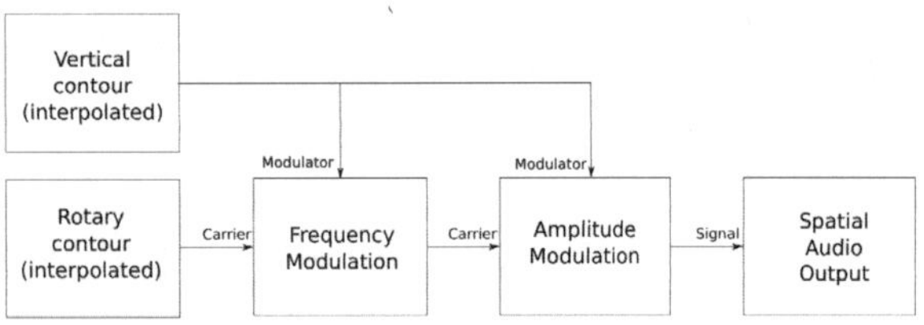

Figure 6. A simplified diagram of the direct encoding of an object contour as sound.

2) Segmentation: The 2D organized point cloud is then segmented by the method of Trevor et al [9] and segments are obtained characterized by slowly changing surface normal vectors and no intervening gaps. Further processing can be applied to find and remove tabletop surfaces for tabletop scenarios.

3) Feature Extraction: Information to characterize the acquired segments is extracted. In the current work, contour-based and FPFH-based approaches are explored.

4) Sound Generation: In the system presented by Mhaish et al. [2], a simple sonification approach was proposed based on a conversion of principle object dimensions to frequencies. A circular buffer is used to create, update and interpolate sound waves and their envelopes and the rate at which frames are arriving is estimated in order to send the appropriate number of samples to the OpenAL spatial sound system. In the current system, FPFH signatures are converted via a recognition step to different instruments from the STK simulation toolkit [13] and object contours are converted via interpolation and modulation data processing steps to sound waves.

The present paper focuses on the feature extraction and sound generation steps, proposing the contour- and FPFH-based approaches, explained in the next sections.

The sound is played using the OpenAl library which is provided as many samples as necessary from the filled circular buffer and generates spatial-audio based on binaural cues or, alternatively, Head Related Transform Functions (HRTFs).

A. *Contour-based sonification*

In the contour-based encoding, object contours are translated directly into auditory waveforms, and frequency and amplitude modulations of waveforms.

In the variation on this idea tested in this paper, the rotary-contour is extracted from the object and used to generate a carrier signal. In the rotary-contour-based encoding, a path is traced out around the contour of the object and the distance of each contour point from the object's horizontal axis (defined by the centroid of the points in the object) becomes an instantaneous amplitude in the sound waveform (normalized to fit within the range of acceptable sample amplitudes). Spherical or circular objects thus translate perfectly into sinusoidal waveforms. For instance, the object on the left side of Figure 4 becomes the waveform plot (amplitude vs time) on the right hand side, with radial distances converted into instantaneous amplitudes which are then potentially interpolated.

Because the signal waveform depends on the object contour, some timbre properties also depend on the object contour. The carrier signal is then modulated at a slower (consciously perceivable) time-scale using frequency and amplitude modulation by another time-varying function which we call here vertical-contour-based encoding. In this kind of encoding, which is illustrated in Figure 5, the top to bottom scanned width of the object silhouette is converted to the amplitude of a modulating signal which is then applied to the carrier signal as frequency and amplitude modulation. Thus, multiple perceptual channels are used to transfer information to the user. For a sketch of the signal processing flow used to generate the resulting waveform, see Figure 6.

The contour-based approach is motivated both by the conceptual clarity of the mapping, but also by the fact that sounds already arise as vibrations in objects and spaces, and travel through the objects, reflecting in the resulting waveforms the shape and size of these spaces; thus, the method, depending on the exact encoding used, has an analogue in the physics of real sound generation and consequently natural synergies with perception.

B. *FPFH-based sonification*

The FPFH is a feature extracted from point clouds or point cloud parts, designed for representing information about the shape of the cloud that is invariant to rotation. It is comparable to a histogram of curvatures measured in different ways across the object surface.

FPFH is a 33-bin histogram extracted from the points and normals in the point cloud. This histogram counts 3 different curvature measures with 11 bins for each measure. The relative position and surface-normal vector of each point is processed and the bin into which the point falls for each of the 3 dimensions incremented [14]. Note: the FPFH is not originally designed as a full object descriptor but it has proved sufficient for current purposes: other more or less viewpoint-invariant or object-global descriptors can also be easily adapted to this purpose. Examples of FPFH descriptors extracted from point clouds used in experiments in this paper can be found in Figure 7. As can be seen in the figure, different shapes generally correspond to different histograms and different sizes

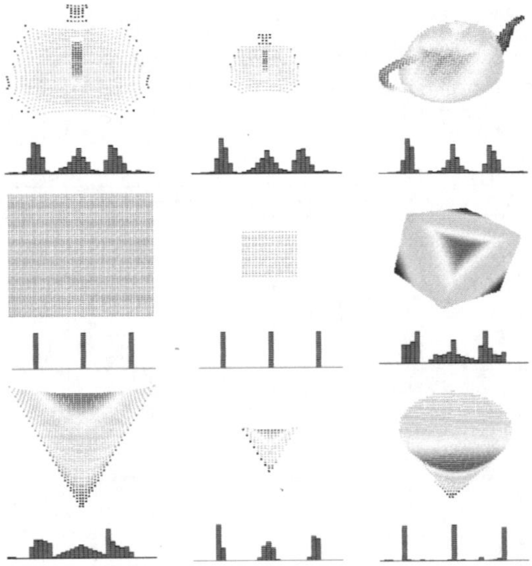

Figure 7. Sample point cloud views with normalized histogram shapes (FPFH). **Top row:** teapot. **Middle row:** cube. **Bottom row:** cone. **Left:** baseline view. **Middle:** a different object size. **Right:** a different view direction.

TABLE I. THE OBJECT-INSTRUMENT MAPPING IN THE FPFH-BASED APPROACH.

Object	Instruments
Teapot (Tp)	Shakers
Cube (Cb)	Struck Bow
Cuboid (Cd)	Drawn Bow
Cylinder (Cl)	High Flute
Cone (Cn)	Plucked String
Elipsoid (El)	Hammond-style Organ
Icosahedron (Ic)	Saxophone
Stretched Cylinder (SC)	Low Flute
Sphere (Sp)	Clarinet
Torus (Ts)	Sitar

and scales generally do not affect the histograms radically. However, the external contours do not always affect the result, as can be seen by comparing the bottom view of the cone and the side view of the cube.

After an object is encoded using FPFH, a database of existing FPFH descriptors is searched (using an indexing KD-tree) for the closest descriptor and the resulting object label retrieved. A mapping (Table I) is provided from object label to instrument type and the relevant instrument is synthesized using the Synthesis ToolKit (STK) [13].

3D object recognition techniques are attractive for the current application since the field of robotic vision has well-established approaches, and many descriptors are available for representing shape, having rotational invariance built in for example [14]. Moreover, synthetic instrument models provide highly discriminable sounds, which can support a sound-object mapping approach to the task under consideration.

IV. Training and Experiment

To evaluate the ability of the encodings discussed above to transmit shape as sound, the ability of users to identify objects under changing conditions was investigated. For a clear evaluation of the relationship between shape and sound, point clouds presented to the user were based on point-cloud samplings of views of the ten object meshes shown in Figure 8. Performance of the proposed encodings was measured by conducting two experiments. In the first experiment, the location from which objects are viewed was varied among five different equi-distant viewpoints, illustrated in Figure 9, and in the second experiment, five different scales of objects were presented, scale here stands for either size or viewing distance but only in the context of the encodings used in the present paper – not all point cloud encodings will confuse size and distance. The five sizes used are shown in Figure 10.

Figure 8. The set of objects used in experiments. Top: Teapot (Tp), Cube (Cb), Cuboid (Cd), Cylinder (Cl), Cone (Cn), Bottom: Elipsoid (El), Icosahedron (Ic), Stretched Cylinder (SC), Sphere (Sp), Torus (Ts).

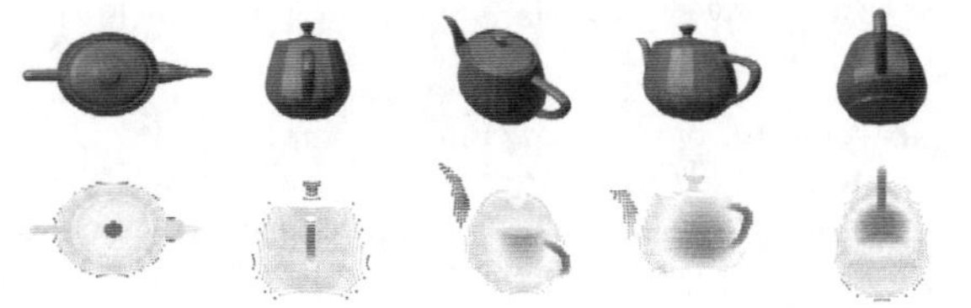

Figure 9. The set of poses used in the pose-varying experiment. **Top**: the object model as seen from different viewpoints. **Bottom**: the point cloud resulting from each viewpoint. Colour in the point cloud represents normalized distance from the camera of the points.

The main idea of choosing these two experiments is that these parameters are the most changing parameters in wild. Other possible parameters include lighting conditions, but our cameras use active lighting, or material properties, but these depend on the particular choice of depth-sensing device, to which our approach is designed to be mostly agnostic.

A. *Training session*

Each experiment comprises two conditions, the FPFH condition and the contour-based condition, presented to the individuals in a random order. For each condition, an independent training session was conducted. A single training session takes 15 minutes, including 2-3 minutes for describing the principles of the system followed by a free experimentation period. During the training sessions participants were given the ability to play sounds for all five different viewpoints of

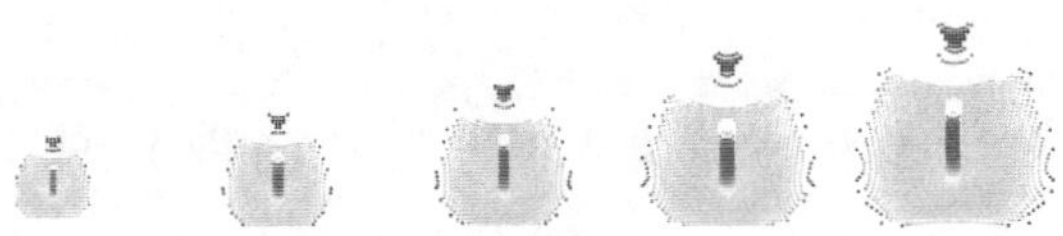

Figure 10. The set of object sizes used in the size-varying experiment.

TABLE II. THE VALUES OF RELEVANT PARAMETERS USED IN THESE EXPERIMENTS.

General parameters	
Input point cloud size (width × height)	320 × 240
Object distances to camera (metres)	3
Sound generation: Sample rate (Hz)	44100
Sound generation: Bits per sample	16
Contour-based approach	
Pixel-sample ratio: rotary-contour carrier	1:1
Pixel-sample ratio: vertical-contour modulator	600:1
Peak frequency deviation proportion: modulator	1.0
Peak amplitude deviation proportion: modulator	1.0
FPFH-based approach	
FPFH database size (num object views)	100
FPFH database size (num objects)	10

all ten objects for the viewpoint experiment and for all five scales for the scale/size experiment. Users were allowed to play with the system, choosing objects and viewpoints/sizes from the training set and playing the sounds as well as viewing a 3D visual representation from that viewpoint/size and they were asked to remember the sounds related to each object.

B. Experimental session

Experiments were conducted with 16 non-disabled participants with an average age of 24 years, divided into two groups with each group containing both male and female participants. Participants of each group performed only either the viewpoint or the scale experiment. Both sound generation approaches were tested with each participant. In experimental sessions, sounds of randomly selected objects with randomly selected viewpoints/sizes from the training set were presented and participants were asked to identify the objects. In these sessions, for each approach 30 trials were conducted with each participant and the participant was informed after each trial whether the answer was correct, and when the answer was wrong, the experimenter informed the participant the actual object identity. Answers were recorded in confusion matrices. In these experiments, users were not supposed to guess the viewpoints or scales; they were asked only to identify the objects based on the sound that they were hearing. The physical set-up of the experiment can be found on the right of Figure 2. Parameters of the system used in experiments are shown in Table II.

C. Results

The complementary properties of the two methods tested can be observed in the confusion matrices in Tables IV and III. In these matrices, numbers in cells represent the number of times the object in the row header was identified by participants as the object in the column header. Zero values are left blank. The inability of the contour-based approach to take account of the depth information in the interior of an object leading it to confuse objects with similar silhouettes, as it can be seen in the tables.

With an overall accuracy of 60% and 57% on the two experiments vs. 36% and 42% for the contour-based method, the FPFH approach performed better (verified with χ^2 tests, which are applicable when class sizes are balanced, 1 D.O.F., $p = 0.01$). However, the FPFH-based approach was still unable to account for the contour on the silhouette of an object, leading it to confuse objects with similar visible curvatures.

TABLE III. RESULTS OF SIZE-VARYING EXPERIMENT. (BOLD NUMBERS SHOWS THE MOST CHOSEN OBJECT(S) BY PARTICIPANTS, WHEN THE OBJECT IN THE ROW HEADER WAS PRESENTED).

Contour-based		Response									
		Tp	Cb	Cd	Cl	Cn	El	Ic	SC	Sp	Ts
Actual	TP	**33.3**				11.1	11.1	11.1	11.1		22.2
	Cb		**33.3**	25.0	8.3	8.3			8.3		16.6
	Cd		16.6	**50.0**							16.6
	Cl	6.6	13.3	13.3	**33.3**	6.6			13.3	13.3	
	Cn				10.0	**70.0**	10.0			10.0	
	El	11.1		11.1	11.1		11.1	**33.3**		11.1	11.1
	Ic	15.3			15.3	**23.0**		7.6	7.6	**23.0**	7.6
	SC					11.1	11.1	22.2	**55.5**		
	Sp	25.0							25.0	**50.0**	
	Ts						33.3				**66.6**

FPFH-based		Response									
		Tp	Cb	Cd	Cl	Cn	El	Ic	SC	Sp	Ts
Actual	TP	**100.0**									
	Cb		**76.9**		7.6					15.3	
	Cd		21.4	**64.2**	14.2						
	Cl		16.6		33.3			**50.0**			
	Cn		11.1	5.5	5.5	**55.5**		5.5	5.5	11.1	
	El	7.6			7.6		15.3	7.6	15.3	**46.1**	
	Ic	6.6			**33.3**	6.6		26.6	6.6	13.3	
	SC				37.5			6.2	**56.2**		6.6
	Sp		16.6		33.3					**50.0**	
	Ts							11.1			**88.8**

TABLE IV. RESULTS OF VIEWPOINT-VARYING EXPERIMENT. (BOLD NUMBERS SHOWS THE MOST CHOSEN OBJECT(S) BY PARTICIPANTS, WHEN THE OBJECT IN THE ROW HEADER WAS PRESENTED).

Contour-based		Response									
		Tp	Cb	Cd	Cl	Cn	El	Ic	SC	Sp	Ts
Actual	TP	**56.2**			6.2	25.0		6.2			6.2
	Cb		**29.4**	17.6	17.6			7.6			7.6
	Cd			**69.2**	7.6	7.6		7.6			7.6
	Cl	9.2	**28.5**	14.2	14.2	4.7	9.2		9.2	4.7	4.7
	Cn	9.0	9.0	4.5	4.5	**36.3**	9.0	4.5		18.1	4.5
	El		8.3		8.3	8.3	**41.6**		8.3		25.0
	Ic	6.6			**20.0**	**20.0**	**20.0**	**20.0**		13.3	
	SC			**50.0**	·		25.0		25.0		
	Sp	5.2	5.2		5.2	15.7	10.4	10.4		**36.8**	10.4
	Ts			11.1			22.2	11.1		22.2	**33.3**

FPFH-based		Response									
		Tp	Cb	Cd	Cl	Cn	El	Ic	SC	Sp	Ts
Actual	TP	**100.0**									
	Cb		**37.5**	**37.5**					25.0		
	Cd		23.5	**52.9**		11.7			11.7		
	Cl		13.3		**33.8**		7.0	13.3	7.0		
	Cn		**36.3**		9.0	**36.3**		9.0		8.0	
	El		12.5		12.5		**50.0**	12.5		12.5	
	Ic			28.5		14.2		**57.1**			
	SC		5.5	11.1	11.1				**66.6**		5.5
	Sp		9.0		9.0	9.0	18.1			**54.5**	
	Ts					7.1					**92.8**

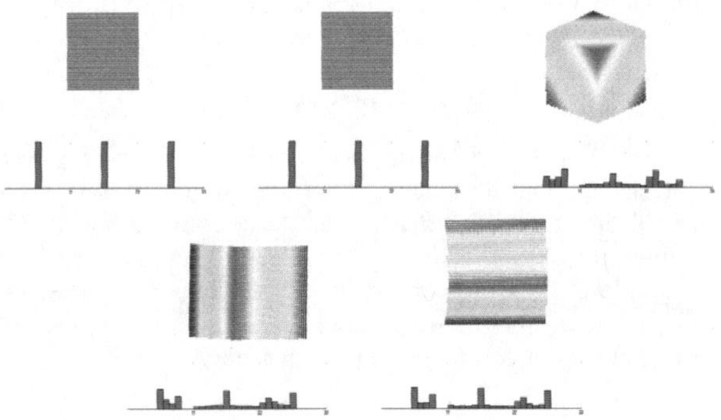

Figure 11. Five different view points of cube and their histograms.**Top:** Left: Top view. Middle: Frontal view. Right: Right front top corner view. **Bottom:** Left: Right Front edge view. Right: Front bottom edge view.

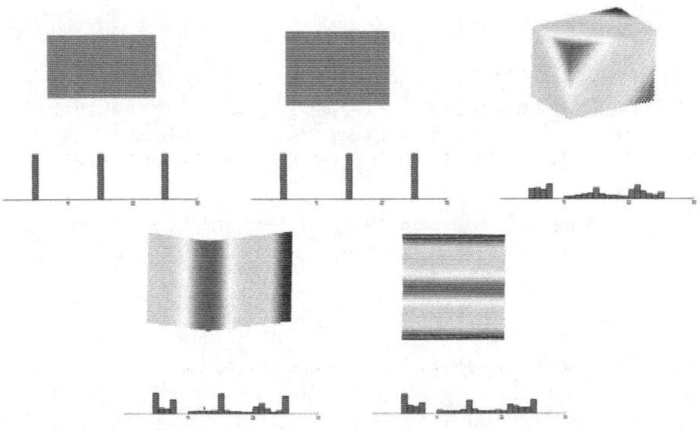

Figure 12. Five different view points of cuboid and their histograms.**Top:** Left: Top view. Middle: Frontal view. Right: Right front top corner view. **Bottom:** Left: Right Front edge view. Right: Front bottom edge view.

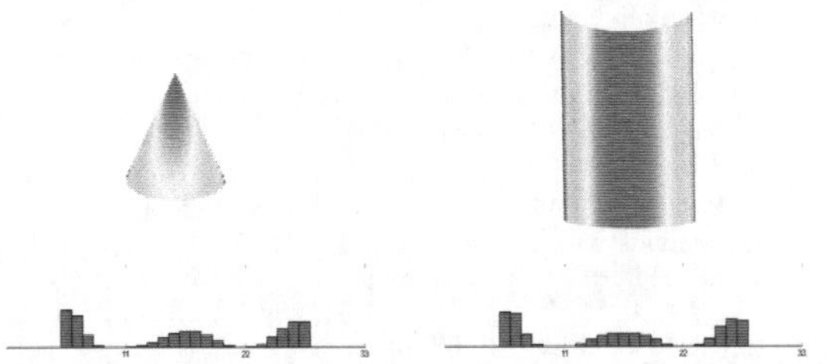

Figure 13. Similarity in histograms (FPFH) causes the system to mis-classify the objects. **Left:** FPFH for third view of cone. **Right:** FPFH of largest stretched cylinder(with second viewpoint)

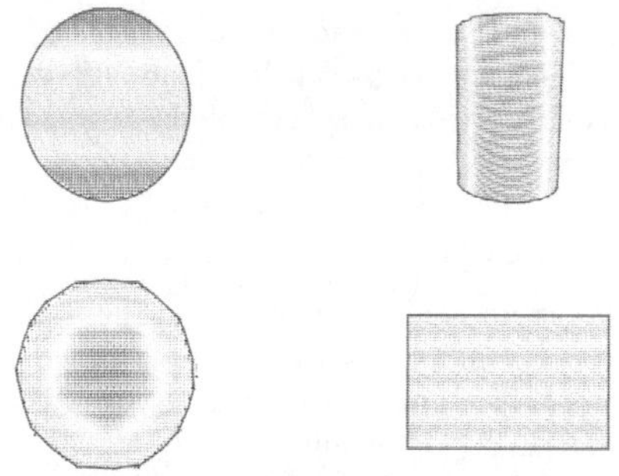

Figure 14. Example of objects contours for which the proposed contour based approach can not generate sufficiently distinguishable sounds(red lines around the objects represent objects contours). **Left column:** Top: sphere contour. Bottom: icosahedron contour. **Right column:** Top: cylinder(front view). Bottom: rectangle(front view)

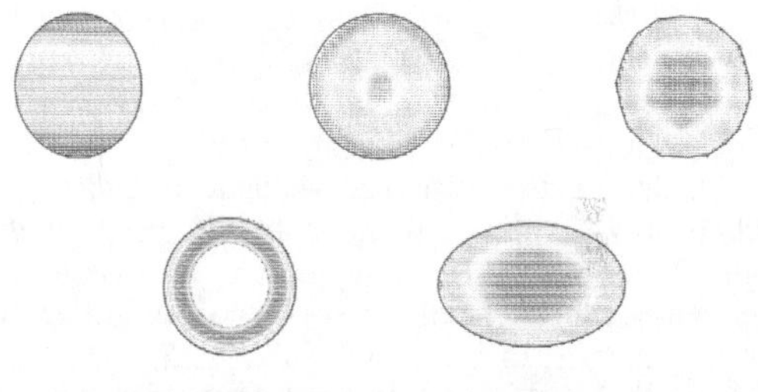

Figure 15. Similar contours of multiple objects used in experiment(red lines around the objects represent objects contours). **Top:** Left: sphere, Middle: cone, Right: icosahedron. **Bottom:** Left:torus Right: ellipsoid

For the FPFH-based approach, the natural user strategy to the identification problem is to learn a sound-object mapping. This worked as long as the system could find the correct mapping, but the system itself did not always use all available information. For instance, the flat bottom of a cone and cube or cuboid produce the same FPFH signature - see Figure 7. The same confusion occurred between cube and cuboid. Participants using the system frequently misclassified cube as cuboid in all the of 5 viewpoints of cube, as is shown in Figure 11 and Figure 12. The FPFH of the cube is so similar to cuboid as to cause the system to mis-classify the cube. This is sufficient to explain why in Table IV the cube is classified as a cuboid almost as much as it is a cube. The lack of distinguishability of FPFH signatures between the top view of the cylinder, the stretched cylinder and the cube is apparent because they all have a single flat surface visible. There are also some unexpected confusions such as the recognition system itself wrongly identifying third view of cone as largest scale of stretched-cylinder (see Figure 13). Since the frequency of occurrence of this confusion was low, participants were able to hear the related sound for the cone more frequently, so it did not affect their performance and they could treat the second sound as noise.

There were some objects that the system did not have any difficulty in identifying, such as the icosahedron, ellipsoid, sphere, teapot and torus. However, their classification accuracy varies from one-in-two to near-perfect. For example, ellipsoid, sphere and icosahedron are correctly identified in 50.0%, 54.5% and 57.1% of trials, while teapot and torus were identified perfectly (100% for teapot and 92.8% for torus-see Table IV). This high difference in confusion rates is due to the choice of instrument corresponding to each object, a fact that was mentioned by most of the participants during the experimental session. They believed that identifying the teapot and torus was easy because their sounds (shakers and sitar) are more distinct than the others. Hence, putting similar sound for shapes that are geometrically similar to each other may not be a good idea or work should be done to ensure that instruments are more distinguishable from each other. However, using dissimilar instruments for similar shapes can defeat any attempt to sonify subtle differences in shape.

In the contour-based approach, it was also observed that some participants preferred the abstract learning strategy of learning identity-sound associations rather than understanding the sound-shape mapping representation as well. For this approach, participants reported that some important object properties were not available to them, leading them to confuse objects like the sphere with the icosahedron or the front view of the cuboid with the same view of the cylinder (see Figure 14). For these two pairs of objects, the output of the system does not produce exactly the same result but similar results which makes it hard for users to distinguish them from each other and they need to put in more effort to understand the differences. However, it should be noted at this point that visually similar objects should be expected in any successful system to pose a larger challenge. Moreover, as discussed before, this approach is viewpoint-variant and for some viewpoints of different objects which have similar contours, it generates identical or too-similar sounds which causes the user to choose the wrong object. For instance, as shown in Figure 15, the top view of cylinder, cone, torus and sphere all have a circular contour which makes their sounds exactly the same.

V. Conclusion and Future Work

Two different encodings of 3D shape into sound were presented, i.e., *contour*-based and *FPFH*-based. The contour-based approach presented maps directly from shape to sound. This is an advantage in that any new object can be represented in sound, and that similarly shaped objects produce similar sounds. However, the encoding attempted here only transmits the image-contour of the object and is not robust to viewpoint. Some participants also preferred to learn the abstract object mapping, suggesting that work is needed on making this approach more intuitive when it comes to the relationship between shape and sound.

The FPFH-based approach solves these problems by using data about the full 3D object shape and by representing features that are somewhat invariant to viewpoint (though only to the extent that surfaces are visible). The FPFH-based approach also has the advantage when creating distinguishable sounds of using a mature sound-synthesis system with highly recognizable objects. However, again, the use of discrete instruments reduces flexibility in encoding different shape properties. In order to make the system work, object exemplars must be paired with sounds, restricting the generalizability of the system to new objects and abstracting some of the user's agency, not fully utilizing their cognitive capacity.

The next step in this work is to extend these approaches to reduce the above-mentioned limitations. In the case of the contour-based approach, a more sophisticated encoding is needed, that takes into account 3D aspects of the object. Adding some viewpoint invariance may be desirable, but it would be a subject of empirical investigation as to whether this viewpoint invariance would actually be helpful when considering other tasks that users might want to do with objects, such as manipulation, in which users need to perceive also the orientation of the object. In the case of the FPFH-based approach, a way is needed of generalizing from the exemplars in an appropriate way, for example by using machine learning techniques in conjunction with user input. Other point cloud features with different properties also should be systematically investigated.

Further work also involves testing these sonifications "in the wild" and with multiple objects, which will require work on more aggressive noise elimination and object (or surface primitive) tracking. In both approaches, it is important to exploit and extend the intuitive mappings from shape to sound whose exploration was begun here, for quick learning and application of the system, as well as for recruiting the advanced cognitive capabilities of users.

Acknowledgments

This work was supported by the Scientific and Technological Research Council of Turkey (TÜBITAK), Project No 114E443.

References

[1] M. Auvray, S. Hanneton, and J. K. O'Regan, "Learning to perceive with a visuo-auditory substitution system: Localisation and object recognition with 'The vOICe'," Perception, vol. 36, no. 3, 2007, pp. 416 – 430, URL:http://www.perceptionweb.com/abstract.cgi?id=p5631 [retrieved: 2017-02-04].

[2] A. Mhaish, T. Gholamalizadeh, G. İnce, and D. Duff, "Assessment of a visual-to-spatial audio sensory substitution system," in Signal Processing and Communications Applications(SIU). Zonguldak, Turkey: IEEE, May 2016 24th, pp. 245–248, URL:http://ieeexplore.ieee.org/stamp/stamp.jsp?arnumber=7495723 [retrieved:2017-02-04].

[3] J. D. Gomez Valencia, "A computer-vision based sensory substitution device for the visually impaired (See ColOr)," Ph.D. dissertation, University of Geneva, 2014, URL:http://archive-ouverte.unige.ch/unige:34568 [retrieved:2017-02-04].

[4] J. Sudol, O. Dialameh, C. Blanchard, and T. Dorcey, "Looktel—A comprehensive platform for computer-aided visual assistance," in IEEE Computer Society Conference on Computer Vision and Pattern Recognition Workshops (CVPRW). IEEE, 2010, pp. 73–80, URL:http://ieeexplore.ieee.org/abstract/document/5543725/ [retrieved:2017-02-01].

[5] "Microsoft," 2016, URL: https://news.microsoft.com/videos/microsoft-cognitive-services-introducing-the-seeing-ai-app/#sm.00001gckhn7usbfpbyeceij35wz8i#570rbWhUTwooz7X5.97 [accessed: 2017-02-02].

[6] T. Yoshida, K. M. Kitani, H. Koike, S. Belongie, and K. Schlei, "EdgeSonic: image feature sonification for the visually impaired," in Proceedings of the 2nd Augmented Human International Conference. ACM, 2011, p. 11, URL:http://dl.acm.org/citation.cfm?id=1959837 [retrieved:2017-02-01].

[7] S. Meers and K. Ward, "A vision system for providing 3d perception of the environment via transcutaneous electro-neural stimulation," in International Conference on Information Visualisation. London, UK: IEEE, Jul. 2004, pp. 546–552, URL:http://ieeexplore.ieee.org/abstract/document/1320198/ [retrieved:2017-02-02].

[8] S. Shelley, M. Alonso, J. Hollowood, M. Pettitt, S. Sharples, D. Hermes, and A. Kohlrausch, "Interactive Sonification of Curve Shape and Curvature Data," in Haptic and Audio Interaction Design. Springer, Berlin, Heidelberg, Sep. 2009, pp. 51–60, DOI: 10.1007/978-3-642-04076-4_6, URL:http://link.springer.com/chapter/10.1007/978-3-642-04076-4_6 [retrieved:2017-02-01].

[9] A. J. Trevor, S. Gedikli, R. B. Rusu, and H. I. Christensen, "Efficient organized point cloud segmentation with connected components," Semantic Perception Mapping and Exploration (SPME), 2013, URL:https://pdfs.semanticscholar.org/c96b/ad70db489701ade007b365fe215478303003.pdf [retrieved: 2017-02-04].

[10] G. Hiebert, "Openal 1.1 specification and reference," 2005, URL:http://www.citeulike.org/group/12573/article/6483595 [retrieved: 2017-02-04].

[11] R. B. Rusu and S. Cousins, "3d is here: Point cloud library (PCL)," in IEEE Intl. Conf. on Robotics & Automation. Shanghai, China: IEEE, 2011, pp. 1–4, URL:http://ieeexplore.ieee.org/xpls/abs_all.jsp?arnumber=5980567 [retrieved:2017-02-04].

[12] S. Holzer, R. B. Rusu, M. Dixon, S. Gedikli, and N. Navab, "Adaptive neighborhood selection for real-time surface normal estimation from organized point cloud data using integral images," in Intelligent Robots and Systems (IROS), 2012 IEEE/RSJ International Conference on. IEEE, 2012, pp. 2684–2689, URL:http://ieeexplore.ieee.org/xpls/abs_all.jsp?arnumber=6385999 [retrieved:2017-01-20].

[13] G. P. Scavone and P. R. Cook, "RtMidi, RtAudio, and a synthesis toolkit (STK) update," Synthesis, 2004, URL:http://citeseerx.ist.psu.edu/viewdoc/download?doi=10.1.1.143.997&rep=rep1&type=pdf [retrieved: 2017-02-04].

[14] R. B. Rusu, N. Blodow, and M. Beetz, "Fast point feature histograms (FPFH) for 3d registration," in IEEE Intl. Conf. on Robotics & Automation. Kobe, Japan: IEEE, 2009, URL:http://ieeexplore.ieee.org/xpls/abs_all.jsp?arnumber=5152473 [retrieved: 2017-02-04].

Multi-Operator Gesture Control of Robotic Swarms Using Wearable Devices

Sasanka Nagavalli, Meghan Chandarana, Katia Sycara
Robotics Institute, School of Computer Science
Carnegie Mellon University
Pittsburgh, Pennsylvania 15213
email: snagaval@andrew.cmu.edu, mchandar@cmu.edu
katia@cs.cmu.edu

Michael Lewis
School of Information Sciences
University of Pittsburgh
Pittsburgh, Pennsylvania 15260
email: ml@sis.pitt.edu

***Abstract*—The theory and design of effective interfaces for human interaction with multi-robot systems has recently gained significant interest. Robotic swarms are multi-robot systems where local interactions between robots and neighbors within their spatial neighborhood generate emergent collective behaviors. Most prior work has studied interfaces for human interaction with remote swarms, but swarms also have great potential in applications working alongside humans, motivating the need for interfaces for local interaction. Given the collective nature of swarms, human interaction may occur at many levels of abstraction ranging from swarm behavior selection to teleoperation. Wearable gesture control is an intuitive interaction modality that can meet this requirement while keeping operator hands usually unencumbered. In this paper, we present an interaction method using a gesture-based wearable device with a limited number of gestures for robust control of a complex system: a robotic swarm. Experiments conducted with a real robot swarm compare performance in single and two-operator conditions illustrating the effectiveness of the method. Results show human operators using our interaction method are able to successfully complete the task in all trials, illustrating the effectiveness of the method, with better performance in the two-operator condition, indicating separation of function is beneficial for our method. The primary contribution of our work is the development and demonstration of interaction methods that allow robust control of a difficult to understand multi-robot system using only the noisy inputs typical of smartphones and other on-body sensor driven devices.**

Keywords–Robotic Swarms; Gesture Control; Wearable Devices.

I. INTRODUCTION

There has been significant interest in effective operator interaction methods for human-robot teams consisting of multiple humans and robots. Work in this area has been classified along multiple dimensions including the degree of coordination between individual humans or robots on the team (e.g., independent robots or coordinating robots) [1] [2], the association between robots and humans (i.e., shared pool of robots or robots assigned to individual humans) [3] [4] [5] and the physical distance between the humans and the robots (e.g., remote operators or humans working alongside the robots) [6] [7]. For a multitude of application scenarios ranging from urban search and rescue (USAR) [8] to supply support activities, a variety of operator interfaces for teleoperation [9] have been considered including those based on conventional keyboard, mouse and joystick, voice commands [6], haptic feedback [10] [11] and many more.

In recent years, there has also been significant interest in a particular class of multi-robot system known as a *robotic swarm*. Each individual in the swarm obeys a simple control law that allows interactions only with the robot neighbors. Local interactions between individual robots and their communication and sensing neighbours within a robotic swarm lead to *emergent collective behaviors*. Swarms exhibit various behaviors, such as flocking, rendezvous, dispersion. The swarm control law aims to keep the swarm coherent, meaning that the robots execute the commanded behavior and do not disconnect from the swarm and avoid collisions with one another. One way to control a swarm is via the selection of a *leader* robot. The leader robot is given a command by the human operator to perform a particular motion (e.g., move forward). The other robots align their headings to the leader heading (or an average heading that is dominated by the leader heading) so the flocking behavior is realized. Robot swarms are inherently robust and scalable because robots can fail or be added and removed with minimal system reconfiguration required to keep the swarm operational. Robotic swarms have enormous potential in applications including search and rescue, environmental monitoring and exploration, environmental cleanup. Prior work has considered supervisory control of *remote* swarms and associated issues such as bandwidth constraints and latency [12], control input propagation [13], input timing [14] and intelligibility of swarm motion to humans [15].

This paper considers an interaction method based on a wearable gesture control interface for use in scenarios involving humans working alongside or in close proximity to swarms of coordinating ground robots. Such interaction is very suitable for soldiers in an area of operations where voice or long-range radio communications may not be appropriate due to the presence of adversaries. Gesture control [16] [17] is of specific interest because it enables operators to interact with robots within their spatial vicinity in an intuitive fashion without the use of an additional device (e.g., laptop, joystick) that may prevent the operator from using hands for other tasks. In contrast to prior work that considered collaborative recognition of gestures [18] [19], communication via gestures drawn on tablets [17] or vision-based gesture recognition [16] for control of swarms, we use a wearable gesture recognition device combined with our gesture translation interface, which translates gestures to a variety of swarm commands. Wearable gesture recognition devices, such as the Myo we use in our work, recognize muscle signals of the operator and map them to particular gestures. The advantage of this technique is that it obviates the need to instrument the environment (which is necessary for vision-based recognition), thus making it useful in any environment, such as indoor or outdoor, despite varying visibility (e.g., occlusions) and lighting. The disadvantage and challenge is that wearable gesture recognition must rely on sensors (e.g., accelerometer, electromyography) without direct human interpretation for input. Consequently, discriminability of gestures by both the system and the human, rather than intuitiveness of the gestures, must be the primary criterion for gesture selection. Current wearable gesture devices have only a limited number of gestures that provide good discriminability. Increasing the number of gestures, thus providing a richer command vocabulary, would decrease the discriminability. In this research, we investigate whether wearable gesture control with a limited number of gestures can be made suitable for the complex interactions needed to command a robotic swarm.

The main contributions of this work are (a) the design of an interaction method using a gesture-based wearable device with a limited number of gestures for robust control of a complex system, a robotic swarm, and (b) an experiment on a real robot swarm comparing system performance in a one- vs two-operator scenario. In Section II, we examine the related work. In Section III, we describe the robotic swarm system. In Section IV, we describe our gesture-based interaction method. We outline the experimental design in Section V, followed by the experimental results in Section VI and a discussion in Section VII. Finally, in Section VIII, we state our conclusions and ideas for future work.

II. RELATED WORK

Over the years, researchers have focused on developing multi-operator control of multi-robot teams. These methods typically either assign a subset of the robots to each operator [4] or assign operators jointly to control of the whole team [20]. Results have been equivocal with some researchers reporting advantages for joint control [1] [20] and others [4] [21] finding better performance from operators assigned responsibility for subsets of robots. Separability of function appears to be a key to this difference with studies in which operators performed clearly distinguished tasks [1] [20] benefiting from joint control while those with less well differentiated tasks [2] [4] [21] suffered from diffusion of responsibility.

In naturalistic settings, where tasks are clearly separable, responsibility is often allocated by function. Flocks of sheep and other domesticated animals are commonly controlled by a shepherd through use of collaborating agents, such as sheep dogs, who maintain coherence within the herd while the shepherd determines the overall direction of the flock [22]. Whether this division of labor is inherent to the task and extends to control of robotic swarms as well or is simply an artifact of the shepherd's inability to control the periphery of the swarm is an empirical question. The selection of a leader and choice of swarm behaviors are less clearly separable tasks and might either benefit from division of labor or impose coordination and communication overheads outweighing the advantages of a second operator. In this study, we investigated this issue by comparing two experimental conditions: (1) where swarms were controlled in both heading and coherence (coherently performing the commanded behavior) by a single operator with (2) swarms controlled in heading by a "shepherd" and for coherence by a second operator playing the role of the sheep dog.

III. ROBOTIC SWARM SYSTEM

Our robot swarm consists of five TurtleBots running the Robot Operating System (ROS Indigo) under Ubuntu 14.04 LTS. Each TurtleBot is outfitted with a USB-controlled LED (BlinkStick) and with an AprilTag in a known location on its body so that the TurtleBot can be identified and visually tracked via a set of overhead cameras. AprilTags [23] are a visual fiducial system that encode data into a pattern of white and black squares on a grid. In our case, we encode the unique identifier (UID) for the robot into the tag. The use of this fiducial system enables us to identify and track each TurtleBot in the swarm using a set of overhead monocular cameras. Note that the AprilTags and overhead localization for the TurtleBots were used to collect experimental data. In a real world deployment, such instrumentation of the environment would not be present.

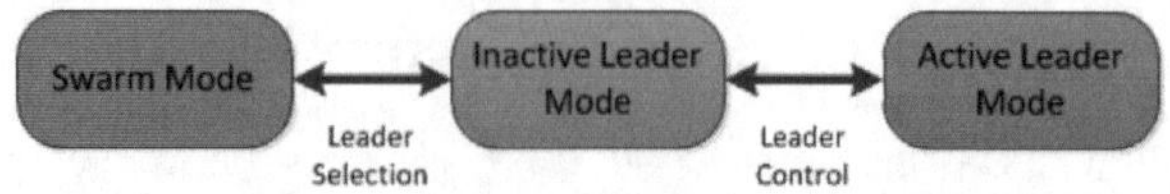

Figure 1. Each robot may be in one of three modes of operation: Swarm Mode, Inactive Leader Mode or Active Leader Mode. Only one robot may be leader (inactive or active) at any time.

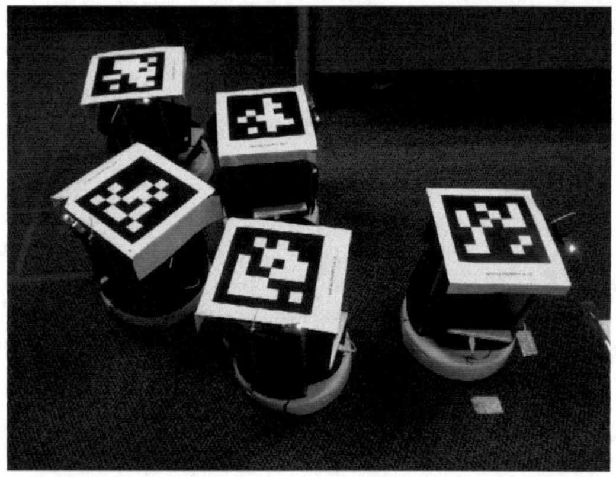

Figure 2. The TurtleBot swarm always has one leader. The leader may be an Active Leader (green LED, shown) or an Inactive Leader (blue LED).

The USB-controlled LED enables the human operator(s) working alongside the robot to identify its current mode of operation (Figure 1). Each individual robot in the swarm may be in one of three modes of operation. When the LED is red, the robot is in Swarm Mode, obeying local control laws based on the selected swarm behavior (discussed later) and the poses of other robots within its spatial neighborhood. When the LED is green (Figure 2), the robot is in Active Leader Mode and can only be directly controlled by a human operator (i.e., it ignores the behavior of other swarm robots). When the LED is blue, the robot is in Inactive Leader Mode and behaves similarly to a robot in Swarm Mode, but may be switched to an Active Leader when desired by the operator.

For our swarm, only one robot may be a leader (whether inactive or active) at any given time, but the operator may select a different leader robot during operation. The distinction between Inactive Leader Mode and Active Leader Mode is one that is practically useful to the operator. For example, consider the situation where the operator would like to select a different leader before making the decision to directly influence the leader. In our system, the operator would (1) switch the current Active Leader to Inactive Leader Mode, (2) select a new Inactive Leader and (3) only switch the new Inactive Leader to

Active Leader when desired. Until then, the operator has visual confirmation (blue LED) that the desired Inactive Leader has been selected without actually influencing that robot.

A. Robot Dynamic Model

Each robot in the swarm has the following dynamic model, where x^i, y^i and θ^i represent the position and orientation of robot i. The control inputs to the robot are given by u_v^i and u_ω^i, which represent the commanded linear velocity and commanded angular velocity respectively.

$$\dot{x}^i = u_v^i \cos\left(\theta^i\right), \quad \dot{y}^i = u_v^i \sin\left(\theta^i\right), \quad \dot{\theta}^i = u_\omega^i \tag{1}$$

For convenience, we define the position vector $\mathbf{p}^i \in \mathbb{R}^2$, which is the xy-coordinates of the robot as given above, and bearing vector $\mathbf{b}^i \in \mathbb{R}^2 : \|\mathbf{b}^i\| = 1$, which is a unit vector in the heading direction θ^i. The function $\phi(\mathbf{v}_1, \mathbf{v}_2)$ finds the smallest angle required to rotate from $\mathbf{v}_1$ to $\mathbf{v}_2$. It is assumed that the sign is adjusted accordingly (deliberately omitted from equation below for simplicity of exposition).

$$\begin{aligned} \mathbf{b}^{ij} &= \frac{\mathbf{p}^j - \mathbf{p}^i}{\|(\mathbf{p}^j - \mathbf{p}^i)\|_2} \\ \phi(\mathbf{v}_1, \mathbf{v}_2) &= \cos^{-1}\left(\frac{\mathbf{v}_1^T \mathbf{v}_2}{\|\mathbf{v}_1\|_2 \|\mathbf{v}_2\|_2}\right) \end{aligned} \tag{2}$$

B. Swarm Behaviors

Our swarm obeys a variety of behaviors chosen by the operator. These behaviors are outlined below. Note that the control law given in [14] was used for the formation behaviors.

1) Stop Moving (Default): Robots stop moving.

$$\forall i : u_v^i = 0, \quad \forall i : u_\omega^i = 0 \tag{3}$$

2) Move Forward: Robots move forward (in their local coordinate frame) with a constant linear velocity V.

$$\forall i : u_v^i = V, \quad \forall i : u_\omega^i = 0 \tag{4}$$

3) Move Backward: Robots move backward (in their local coordinate frame) with a constant linear velocity V.

$$\forall i : u_v^i = -V, \quad \forall i : u_\omega^i = 0 \tag{5}$$

4) Turn Clockwise: Robots rotate clockwise with a constant angular velocity Ω.

$$\forall i : u_v^i = 0, \quad \forall i : u_\omega^i = -\Omega \tag{6}$$

5) Turn Anti-Clockwise: Robots rotate anti-clockwise with a constant angular velocity Ω.

$$\forall i : u_v^i = 0, \quad \forall i : u_\omega^i = \Omega \tag{7}$$

6) Flocking: Regions around each robot are divided into three zones for flocking as shown in Figure 3. Each robot experiences a virtual attractive force toward robots in its "attraction" zone, a virtual torque to align heading with neighbour robots in the "alignment" zone and a virtual repulsive force away from robots in the "repulsion" zone. Strictly speaking, we use a first-order model, so the virtual forces and torques are actually virtual biases in the linear and angular velocity control inputs u_v and u_ω. Note that all three zones were

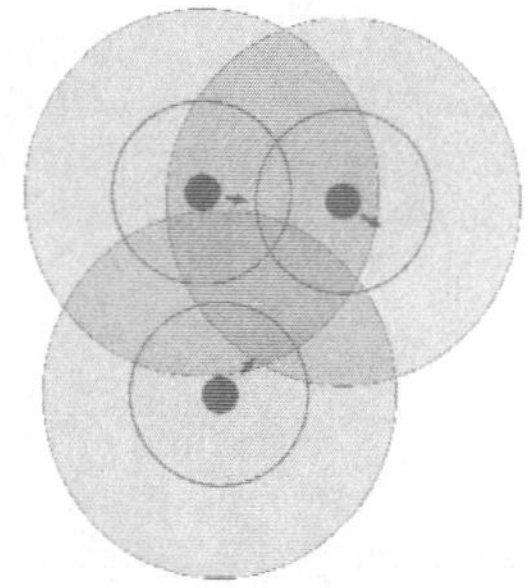

Figure 3. Zones of attraction (all white), heading alignment (green) and repulsion (red) for each robot (blue).

(a) Double Tap (b) Fist (c) Spread Fingers (d) Wave In (e) Wave Out

Figure 4. The five gestures recognized by the Myo as shown on the Thalmic Labs website [24].

implemented on the robots, but for simplicity of exposition, only the attraction portion of the control law is given below.

$$\begin{aligned} \forall i : u_v^i &= \frac{K_v}{|\mathcal{N}(i)|} \sum_{j \in \mathcal{N}(i)} \|(\mathbf{p}^j - \mathbf{p}^i)\|_2 \\ \forall i : u_\omega^i &= K_\omega \phi\left(\frac{\sum_{j\in\mathcal{N}(i)} \mathbf{b}^{ij}}{\|\sum_{j\in\mathcal{N}(i)} \mathbf{b}^{ij}\|_2}, \mathbf{b}^i\right) \end{aligned} \tag{8}$$

7) Align Heading: Robots align heading with other robots within their spatial neighborhood

$$\forall i : u_v^i = 0, \quad \forall i : u_\omega^i = \frac{K_\omega}{|\mathcal{N}(i)|} \sum_{j \in \mathcal{N}(i)} \phi(\mathbf{b}^i, \mathbf{b}^j) \tag{9}$$

8) Line Formation - X Direction: Robots move into a line formation along the world frame's X direction.

9) Line Formation - Y Direction: Robots move into a line formation along the world frame's Y direction.

10) Circle Formation: Robots move into a circle formation.

IV. Gestures for Robot Swarm Control

In this section, we describe the wearable gesture recognition devices we used and our gesture-based interaction method.

A. Wearable Gesture Recognition Devices

In our system, each of the human operators for the robot swarm wears one or more gesture recognition devices and receives feedback about swarm state via LEDs on the robots. For the gesture recognition device, we chose to use an off-the-shelf device called the Myo developed by Thalmic Labs [24]. The Myo is an armband that combines eight EMG sensors for measuring myoelectric muscle signals with a nine-axis IMU (three-axis gyroscope, three-axis accelerometer and three-axis magnetometer) to detect hand gestures. There are five standard hand gestures shown in Figure 4 that were used to develop the gesture-based interaction for our experiment: *Double Tap*, *Fist*, *Spread Fingers*, *Wave In* and *Wave Out*. The device can also provide simple haptic feedback via vibration, but that feature was not used in this work. Data is received from the device via Bluetooth.

B. Gesture-Based Interface

Our design for robust interaction of robotic swarms, given a limited number of gestures whose recognition is error prone, relies on three key ideas: (a) constructing a rich vocabulary of commands, a command grammar, out of a small number of gestures, (b) providing safeguards against errors in gesture recognition and (c) a gesture-based "virtual menu" that allows selection of robots as leaders. These ideas were operationalized. The first idea was implemented by giving different semantic mappings to the same gesture (semantic overloading) depending on context (role). The second idea was operationalized by a multi-step process, rather than letting the operator switch from one behavior to another on the fly, thus running the risk of poor signal recognition. For example, in the two-operator case, where the heading is given, the process is stop, select robot (and mode), give heading command. The third idea is implemented by mapping the "wave in" and "wave out" operations to a selection action for selecting the next behavior or the next robot depending on the role and whether there was a single or multiple operators (see swarm behavior selection section for examples). Albeit complicated in the single operator case, this design allowed for robust operation as shown by our experimental results. Note that in this work, we deliberately made the control task challenging (small crowded room, box obstacles) so the operator would be continuously occupied with guiding the robots through the environment. In a real outdoor environment, the operator would spend less time engaged in controlling the swarm with gestures.

Our gesture-based interface for operating the swarm is divided into two distinct roles: (1) Swarm Behavior Selection and (2) Swarm Leader Selection. Each role is allocated to a different Myo armband and all gestures recognized by that armband are interpreted in the context of the associated role. In this way, one operator can wear both armbands and try to fulfill both roles or two operators can each wear an armband and only fulfill their own role.

As already discussed, there is a trade-off between the intuitiveness of the interface and the discriminability of the gestures. Although work can be done to develop an interface that includes more intuitive gestures for the various robot leader and behavior mappings, there are many cases where these gestures are more difficult for the sensor to characterize. Our gesture-based interaction was designed to be as intuitive as possible while still keeping the limited number of five standard gestures, leveraging the higher discriminability of these gestures.

1) Swarm Behavior Selection: In this role, the operator selects a swarm behavior that will be followed by all robots in Swarm Mode. The operator is given a circular list (the virtual menu) of the swarm behaviors described in Section III-B. The *Wave In* and *Wave Out* gestures allowed the operator to select the previous or next behavior in the list respectively. This mapping leverages most operators' prior experience with swiping left or right on a touch screen device to switch between screens. Once the operator moves to the desired

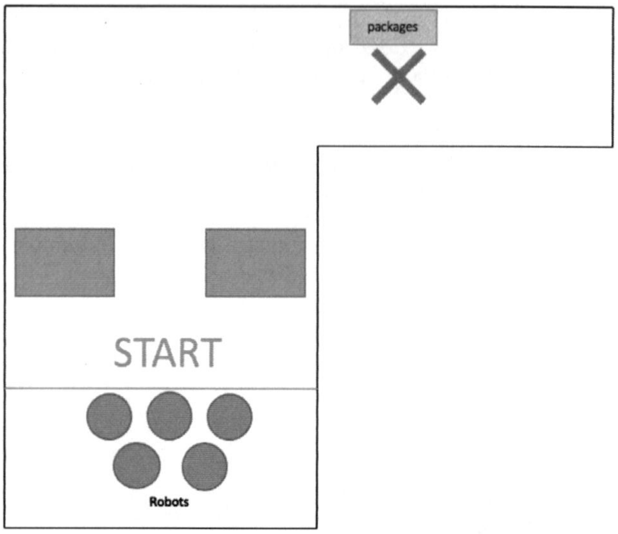

Figure 5. Diagram of environment used for trials. Robots begin in the region indicated by Start and packages are located in the region indicated by red X.

swarm behavior in the menu they can activate it by performing the *Spread Fingers* gesture. Unless the behavior is activated, the swarm will not follow the selected behavior. The *Spread Fingers* gesture is intended to correlate the fingers moving away from the palm to the robots moving away from their starting position via the activated swarm behavior. The *Fist* gesture is commonly used for signifying someone or something to hold or wait. Therefore, it is mapped to the default behavior ('Stop Moving'). For this role the operator ignores the *Double Tap* gesture.

2) Swarm Leader Selection: In this role, the operator selects an Inactive Leader (indicated by blue LED) or controls an Active Leader (indicated by green LED) within the swarm. Assume there is an implicit circular list of robot UIDs ordered numerically. When the selected robot is in Inactive Leader Mode, the *Wave In* gesture selects the previous robot on the list and the *Wave Out* gesture selects the next robot on the list. The *Wave In* and *Wave Out* gestures were chosen for moving through the list of UIDs for the same reason they were chosen to select a swarm behavior. The *Double Tap* gesture switches the selected robot from Inactive Leader Mode to Active Leader Mode or vice versa. A *Double Tap* gesture was used instead of a *Spread Fingers* gesture so as to distinguish between choosing a robot and choosing a movement. Once a new leader robot is chosen with the *Double Tap* gesture and is placed in Active Leader Mode, the *Wave In* gesture causes the chosen leader robot to rotate counterclockwise, the *Wave Out* gesture causes the robot to rotate clockwise. These mappings are chosen such that the direction of the operator's hand when they perform the gesture corresponds to the direction of rotation of the leader robot. The *Spread Fingers* gesture once again signifies a robot movement away from its current location – in this case a forward movement. A *Fist* gesture causes the robot to stop moving for the same reason as in the swarm behavior selection.

V. Experimental Design

Our experiment investigates the resulting performance in two conditions: one-operator condition where the operator

Figure 6. Actual environment used for trials with robots in their initial locations. The large boxes are obstacles.

Figure 7. Leader selection participant (left) and the behavior selection participant (right) during a double operator trial. Each participant is wearing a Myo on their right arm.

performs both roles versus two-operator condition where each operator has a single role, but the two must coordinate. In other words, we want to compare the difficulty and workload resulting from these two conditions. This investigation is conducted in a package retrieval scenario that requires operators to guide the swarm to a target location, retrieve packages and return to the start location. Two conditions were tested: two operator and one operator. In the two operator condition, the subject would wear one armband and fulfill the Swarm Behavior Selection role and an experienced human operator (same person for all two operator experiments) would wear another armband and fulfill the Swarm Leader Selection role. Both operators wore their respective armbands on their right arm. For the second condition (one operator condition), the subject would wear both armbands and fulfill both the Behavior Selection and Leader Selection roles simultaneously. The armband associated with the Leader Selection role was always worn on the right arm of the subject and the armband associated with the Swarm Behavior Selection was worn on the left arm during the one operator trials.

Each subject participated in both the two operator and one operator trials. All subjects participated in the two operator trial first (with the experienced operator partner) before participating in the one operator condition trial. This experimental design was used to mitigate any bias due to possible learning effects. In this setup, if the subjects did get better over time, it would only help their performance in the one operator trial. The order was also chosen to reduce any bias the two operator condition trial had because of the experienced operator's performance.

Before each trial the subject was instructed to wear the Myo armband(s) and allow the sensors to warm up. When the armband(s) was/were warm enough (5-10 minutes) the subject would then sync the armband(s) with the system using the *Wave Out* gesture. Once the armband(s) was/were properly synced the subjects were allowed to practice the 5 standard gestures. As soon as the subject was comfortable performing all gestures with each armband they were wearing, the researchers explained the complete mapping of the gestures to the robot behavior and leader selection. No additional training was done. The subjects did not try the behavior and/or leader selection before the trial began.

A. *Experimental Task*

The experimental task was a package retrieval task and the same experimental task was used across all trials in both the one operator and two operator conditions. There were three distinct parts to each trial. First, the operator(s) was/were required to use the gestures to guide the swarm of TurtleBots from the start region to the region indicated by the red X in Figure 5. Second, the operator(s) was/were required to load packages (small boxes) onto each swarm robot. Finally, the operator(s) was/were required to guide the swarm back to the start region. The trials began when the operators began using the gestures to move the TurtleBots and ended when the TurtleBots made it back to the start area. Large boxes were setup in the environment as obstacles through which the operators guided the robots in order to reach the package pickup location. For a sense of scale, the actual environment used for trials is shown in Figure 6. The traversable area of the main portion of the environment containing obstacles was approximately 20 feet long and 14 feet wide. The traversable area of the narrow corridor was approximately 4 feet wide and 10 feet long. The obstacles were placed 4.25 feet apart. For comparison, an individual TurtleBot is 1 foot in diameter. Both operators were located within visual range of the robots and audible range of each other such that they could coordinate commands sent to the robots (Figure 7).

The human operators faced several challenges navigating through the environment including boxes which narrow the passage, as well as turning into the narrow corridor. In addition, there were several "blind spots" on the map where overhead cameras could not detect AprilTags, so TurtleBots in Swarm Mode would behave erratically due to incorrect localization. TurtleBot wheel odometry and gyroscope were intentionally not used to correct for this effect, so that operator(s) would be forced to intervene to correct for the effect.

B. *Participants and Data Collection*

There were a total of 8 participants in the experiment (excluding the experienced operator). Participants were all graduate students (five male, three female). Only one of the subjects had previous experience using the Myo armband and none of the participants had previously used the armband to control our robotic swarm. Data was recorded using the 'rosbag' program included with ROS. Recorded data included AprilTag poses detected by overhead cameras, gestures detected by the armbands and the active behavior and leader for the swarm. Videos of each trial were also recorded.

VI. RESULTS

The data collected are presented in terms of performance measures and operator measures below. Performance measures include (1) the distance traveled by the robots – maximum of any robot and total of all robots – and (2) the average dispersion from the calculated centroid of the robots' location. Operator measures are presented for both the behavior selection armband and the leader control armband. The measures included are (1) the total number of gestures recognized by the armband, (2) the number of extraneous gestures performed, (3) the count of activated behaviors and leader robots, (4) the total time spent on each behavior and leader robot, and (5) the average time spent each time a behavior or leader robot is chosen. Data were analyzed using the number of roles simultaneously fulfilled by the subject as a factor.

A. Performance Measures

1) Completion Time: Figure 8 shows a plot of trial completion times for each subject under the two operator and one operator conditions. Most subjects were able to complete trials in the two operator condition significantly more quickly than in the one operator condition. The sample means for the two operator and one operator condition trial completion times were 12.115 minutes and 23.806 minutes, respectively. The difference in means was significant at the $p < 0.05$ level ($F_{(1,17)} = 8.082$, $p = 0.011$).

2) Distance Traveled: The sample means for the total distance traveled by all TurtleBots was 127.21 meters and 190.12 meters for the two operator and one operator trials respectively. Figure 9a shows the total distance traveled by all robots in each trial. The sample means for the maximum distance traveled by any TurtleBots was 27.75 meters for the two operator trials and 49.44 meters for the one operator trials. Figure 9b shows the maximum distance traveled by a TurtleBot in all trials. Both differences were significant at the $p < 0.05$ level ($F_{(1,17)} = 6.652$, $p = 0.02$; $F_{(1,17)} = 4.525$, $p = 0.048$ respectively). The average dispersion of the TurtleBots throughout the trials was calculated by summing the average squared euclidean distance between each TurtleBot and the centroid at each time point. The two operator trials had an average dispersion of 66.4 centimeters while the one operator trials had an average of 73.4 centimeters.

B. Operator Measures

Figures 9c and 9d show the total number of recognized gestures performed using the behavior selection armband and leader selection armband respectively. The two operator trial results are shown in blue and the one operator trial results are shown in red. The number of gestures performed with the leader armband was significant at the $p < 0.01$ level ($F_{(1,17)} = 8.599$, $p = 0.009$).

The number of extraneous gestures made by subjects using the Behavior and Leader Selection armbands were calculated. In Behavior Selection, an extraneous gesture was characterized as one of the following two cases: (1) the gesture repeated a gesture immediately before it, or (2) the operator performed an unmapped gesture, which in this case was the *Double Tap* gesture. A gesture was characterized as extraneous when using the Leader Selection armband if one of the following two cases

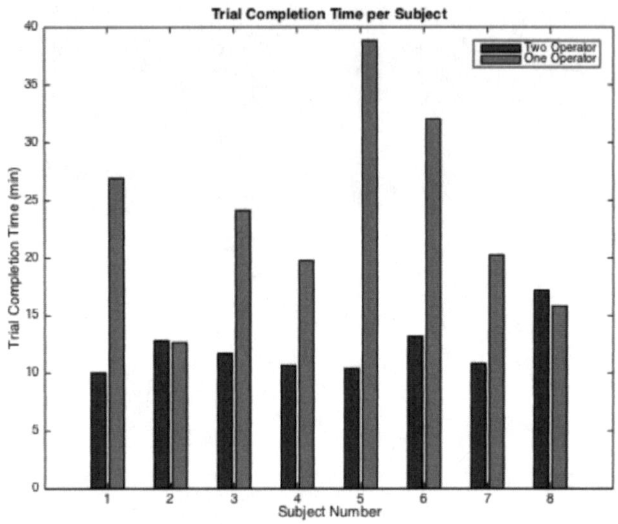

Figure 8. Trial completion times for each subject under both the two operator and one operator conditions.

was true: (1) the gesture repeats a gesture immediately before it or (2) the gesture is an unmapped gesture in the Inactive Leader mode. In the Inactive Leader mode (while an operator is switching to a new leader robot), the *Fist* and *Spread Fingers* gestures are unmapped. The two operator results are from the expert user while the one operator's are from the subject. Subjects using the behavior armband performed an average of 48.67 and 55.40 extraneous gestures for the two operator and one operator conditions respectively. An average of 126.89 extraneous gestures were performed using the leader armband in the two operator condition and 251.70 for the one operator condition. The number of extraneous gestures performed with the leader armband was significant at the $p < 0.05$ level ($F_{(1,17)} = 6.157$, $p = 0.024$).

On average subjects selected the 'Stop Moving' behavior the most followed by 'Flocking' (Figure 11). Subjects spent an average total time of 7.49 minutes and 15.01 minutes on the 'Stop Moving' behavior in the two operator and one operator condition respectively (Figure 12). The average time spent on the 'Stop Moving' behavior each time it was selected was 21.54 seconds in the two operator condition and 38.75 seconds in the one operator condition. Both the total time and average time spent on the 'Stop Moving' behavior were significant at the $p < 0.05$ level ($F_{(1,17)} = 7.292$, $p = 0.015$; $F_{(1,17)} = 4.971$, $p = 0.04$ respectively).

C. Correlations

High correlations were found between operator behavior and performance measures at the $p < 0.01$ significance level. Figure 10 shows that completion time was found to correlate to the 'Stop Moving' behavior, the number of gestures performed using the Behavior Selection armband, the total distance traveled by all TurtleBots, and the maximum distance traveled by a single TurtleBot ($r = 0.987$, $r = 0.709$, $r = 0.949$, and $r = 0.886$ respectively). The number of gestures performed with the Behavior Selection armband and number of errors occurring with the Leader Selection armbands were highly correlated with the time spent in the 'Stop Moving' behavior ($r = 0.703$ and $r = 0.935$ respectively). The total time spent

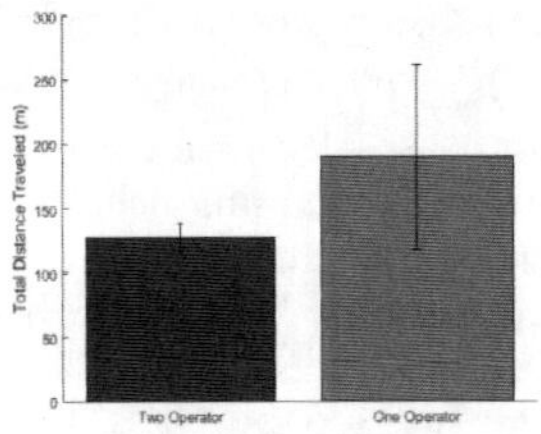

(a) Average total distance traveled by all TurtleBots per trial.

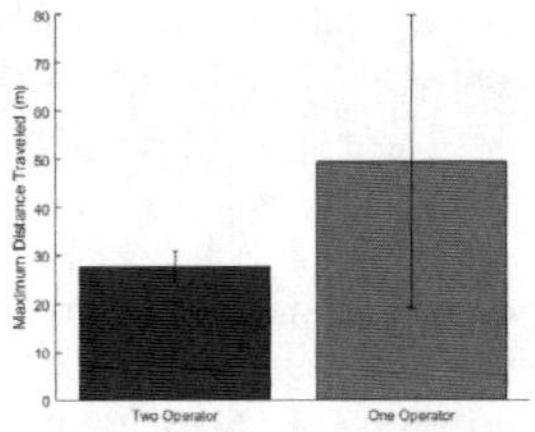

(b) Average maximum distance traveled by any TurtleBot per trial.

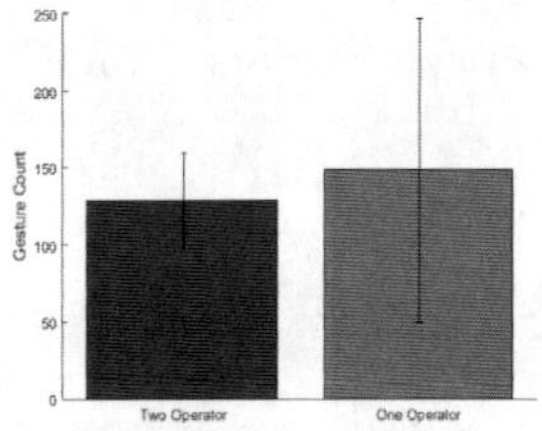

(c) Average total number of recognized gestures performed with behavior armband per trial.

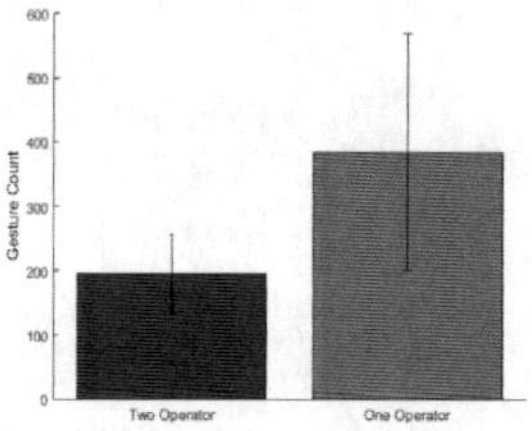

(d) Average total number of recognized gestures performed with the leader armband per trial.

Figure 9. Average measures for single and double operator conditions per trial.

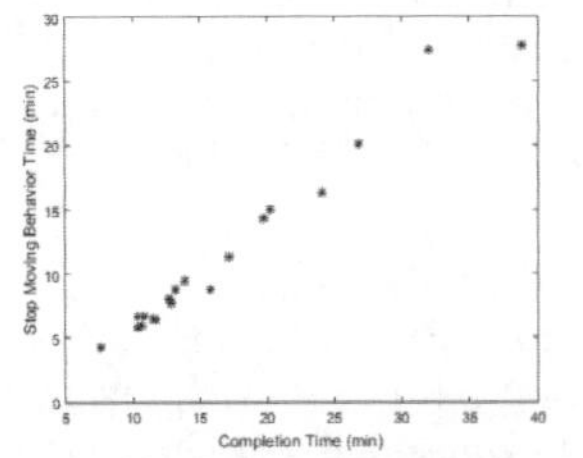

(a) Correlation between time spent on the 'Stop Moving' behavior vs. trial completion time.

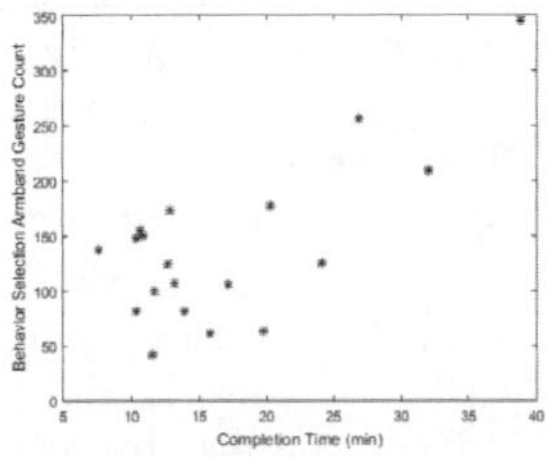

(b) Correlation between total number of gestures performed using Behavior Selection armband vs. trial completion time.

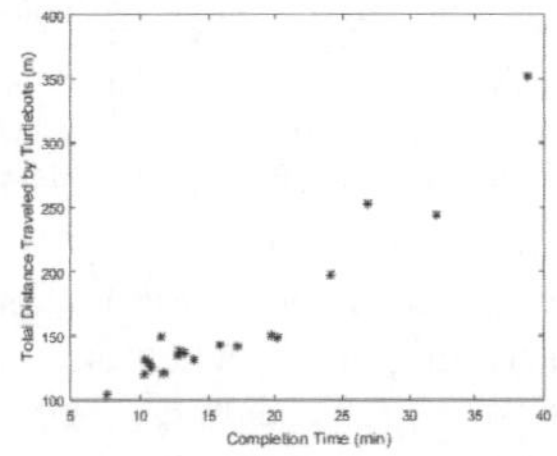

(c) Correlation between total distance traveled by the TurtleBots vs. trial completion time.

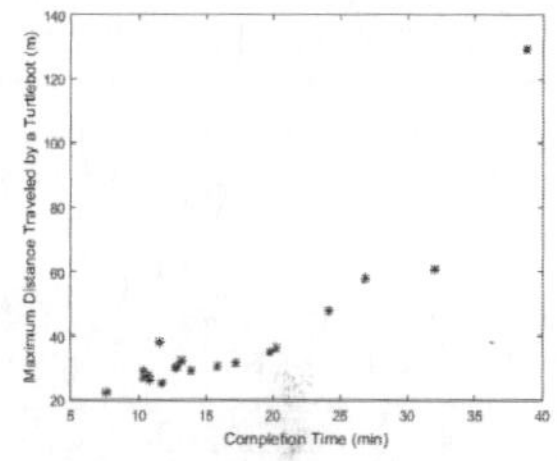

(d) Correlation between the maximum distance traveled by a single TurtleBot vs. trial completion time.

Figure 10. Correlations

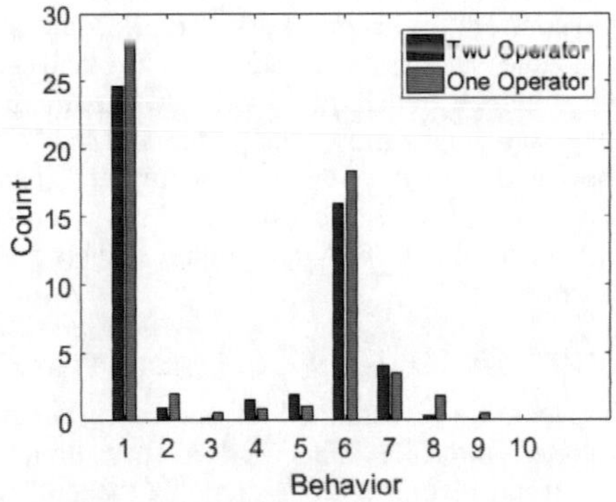

Figure 11. The average number of behavior selections. They are numbered according to Section III-B

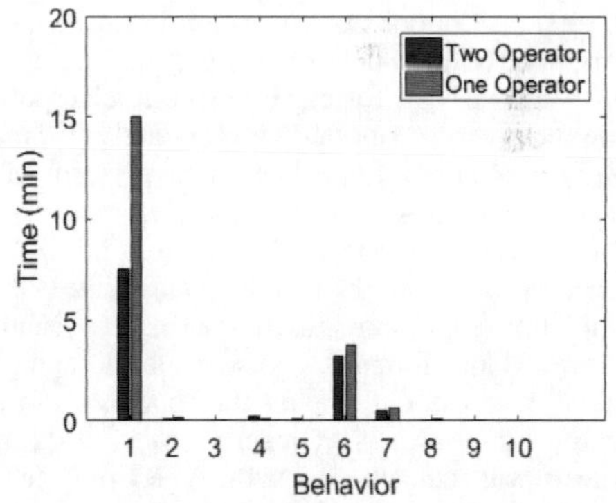

Figure 12. The average total time spent on each behavior. They are numbered according to Section III-B.

on the 'Stop Moving' behavior was also highly correlated with the total distance traveled by all TurtleBot and the maximum distance traveled by a single TurtleBot ($r = 0.737$ and $r = 0.728$ respectively).

Among measures of command usage only the average times spent stopped and flocking were significantly correlated ($r = 0.68, p = 0.001$). As shown in Figure 13, counts of commands and errors were intercorrelated with errors in behavior selection closely paralleling the number of behavior selections while leader selection errors followed the number of leader selections. Behavior and Leader Selection errors were uncorrelated, however, each was correlated with the number of commands of the other type. This pattern shows strong interaction between the behavior selection and leader control task suggesting that they may not be fully separable.

The time spent stopped was the only aspect of a command showing strong correlations with performance. It was correlated with Total Distance ($r = 0.916, p < 0.001$), Maximum Distance ($r = 0.836, p < 0.001$), Completion Time ($r = 0.987, p < 0.001$) and marginally correlated with Average Dispersion ($r = 0.43, p = 0.066$). The Average Time Stopped was correlated only with the Average Dispersion

		Behavior		Leader	
		Errors	**Total**	**Errors**	**Total**
Behavior	**Errors**				
	Total	0.853			
Leader	**Errors**	-	0.622		
	Total	0.464	0.610	0.984	
$R = 0.456, p = 0.05, r = 0.693, p = 0.001$					

Figure 13. Correlations between errors and total commands for behavior selection and leader selection.

	Behavior		Leader	
	Errors	**Total**	**Errors**	**Total**
Total Distance	0.687	0.788	0.866	0.870
Max Distance	0.602	0.779	0.817	0.786
Completion Time	0.598	0.709	0.906	0.930
$R = 0.575, p = 0.01, r = 0.693, p = 0.001$				

Figure 14. Correlations between commands issued for behavior selection or leader selection and subject performance according to total distance traveled by all robots, maximum distance traveled by any robot, trial completion time.

($r = 0.602, p < 0.01$). These relations suggest that longer times spent stopped either in selecting new behaviors or deciding on a course of action was strongly predictive of poor performance on other aspects of the task. Figure 14 shows a pattern of strong correlations between aggregate measures of command usage and performance. As with use of the Stop command, larger numbers of commands and errors led to poorer performance on each of the measures.

VII. Discussion

Subjects performed significantly better in the two operator condition, where they were only required to fulfill the Behavior Selection role, than in one operator condition, where they were required to fulfill both Behavior Selection and Leader Selection roles. This suggests that for our interface, the responsibilities for a role have been selected appropriately to match the level of effort required for a human to perform effectively in that role. Attempting to perform multiple roles seems to have a significantly detrimental effect on human operator performance. In addition, the results demonstrate the viability of the implemented gesture-based interface in controlling a robotic swarm since all operator(s) successfully completed the experimental task without driving the robotic swarm into an unrecoverable state, as was frequently observed during initial informal tests with only the Behavior Selection role.

Although the subjects participated in the two operator trial before the one operator trial, they performed better in the two operator trial. This could be attributed to the experience of the expert outweighing learning effects seen in the subjects' performance, although it cannot be said for certain that this is the sole cause. The operators in the two operator trials seemed to effectively communicate throughout the trial which was apparent in the lower total and maximum distances traveled, and the number of extraneous gestures performed with the behavior armband. For most subjects, the total number of gestures performed with the behavior armband in the one operator trial was close to or lower than the number performed in the two operator trials. This can be attributed to the learned effects seen from the subjects first participating in the two operator trial. However, the number of gestures was less in the two operator condition when the subjects were not required to split their attention between the behavior and leader selection.

The 'Stop Moving' behavior was selected most by subjects. Observations saw that subjects made this behavior the prerequisite for selecting all other movement behaviors. In many instances subjects selected the 'Stop Moving' behavior while they walked around and inspected the TurtleBots' current positions so as to determine the next command(s) required to accomplish their goal. This in between behavior planning stages were almost double in the one operator trials than in the two operator trials as seen by the average time spent on the 'Stop Moving' behavior each time it was selected. The second most used behavior was the 'Flocking' behavior. Subjects seemed to prefer the efficiency of coordinated movement seen when the TurtleBots followed the direction and movements of the leader robot controlled by the leader armband. This significantly reduced the commands that would be necessary to send to the TurtleBots with more primitive commands like 'Move Forward', 'Move Backward', 'Turn Clockwise', and 'Turn Anti-Clockwise.'

The high correlations between the completion time and (1) the 'Stop Moving' behavior, (2) the number of gesture performed using the Behavior Selection armband, (3) the total distance traveled by all TurtleBots, and (4) the maximum distance traveled by any TurtleBot suggests that excessive time spent in the stopped state generating erroneous gestures coincided with poor control and excessive travel for the TurtleBots. The one operator trials sent commands less efficiently to the TurtleBots and stopped more often to make decisions. The lower control resulted in larger total distances and maximum distances traveled in the one operator condition than the two operator condition.

Although the current interface seems to effectively allow operators to control the current swarm size, as additional robots are added to the swarm the interface as it stands now may cause the operators to reach their workload maximum. A more intuitive interface would allow the operators to send commands to the robots with added efficiency. By further expanding the interface to provide a way to control a subset group of robots, the system will be able to provide a more scalable solution for robot swarm control.

VIII. Conclusion and Future Work

In this paper, we investigated an interaction method using a gesture-based interface that used a very limited set of gestures for robust control of a complex system, namely a robotic swarm. The approach was based on 3 key ideas: (a) constructing a rich vocabulary of commands, a command grammar, out of a small number of gestures, (b) providing safeguards against errors in gesture recognition and (c) a gesture-based "virtual menu" that allows selection of robots as leaders. The gesture-based interface incorporated multiple roles (i.e., Behavior Selection, Leader Selection) and each gesture recognition device was associated with a different role. Our experiments indicated that human operators performed significantly better when each operator was fulfilling one role than with one operator fulfilling both roles. Single operators performing both the Behavior and Leader Selection roles tended to be less efficient with their control of the TurtleBots, which resulted in larger total distances traveled by all TurtleBots and maximum distance traveled by any TurtleBot.

The results also demonstrated the viability of the gesture-based interface in enabling human operators to robustly control robotic swarms in proximal interactions.

In future work, we plan to run a larger number of subjects in multiple trials for each subject to study performance improvement with experience. We also plan to perform sensitivity analysis, varying system parameters (e.g., number of robots, course layout). Additionally, we will explore methods for gesture-based control of subsets of swarms to provide a more scalable solution.

ACKNOWLEDGEMENTS

This research has been sponsored in part by AFOSR Grant FA9550-15-1-0442 and an NSERC PGS D scholarship.

REFERENCES

[1] J. M. Whetten, M. A. Goodrich, and Y. Guo, "Beyond robot fan-out: Towards multi-operator supervisory control," in *Systems Man and Cybernetics (SMC), 2010 IEEE International Conference on*. IEEE, 2010, pp. 2008–2015.

[2] F. Gao, M. L. Cummings, and L. F. Bertuccelli, "Teamwork in controlling multiple robots," in *Proceedings of the seventh annual ACM/IEEE international conference on Human-Robot Interaction*. ACM, 2012, pp. 81–88.

[3] M. Lewis, H. Wang, S. Y. Chien, P. Velagapudi, P. Scerri, and K. Sycara, "Process and performance in human-robot teams," *Journal of Cognitive Engineering and Decision Making*, vol. 5, no. 2, pp. 186–208, 2011.

[4] M. Lewis *et al.*, "Teams organization and performance in multi-human/multi-robot teams," in *Systems Man and Cybernetics (SMC), 2010 IEEE International Conference on*. IEEE, 2010, pp. 1617–1623.

[5] F. Gao, M. L. Cummings, and E. T. Solovey, "Modeling teamwork in supervisory control of multiple robots," *Human-Machine Systems, IEEE Transactions on*, vol. 44, no. 4, pp. 441–453, 2014.

[6] S. Teller *et al.*, "A voice-commandable robotic forklift working alongside humans in minimally-prepared outdoor environments," in *2010 IEEE International Conference on Robotics and Automation*, May 2010, pp. 526–533.

[7] M. Lewis, "Human interaction with multiple remote robots," *Reviews of Human Factors and Ergonomics*, vol. 9, no. 1, pp. 131–174, 2013.

[8] E. Olson *et al.*, "Progress toward multi-robot reconnaissance and the magic 2010 competition," *Journal of Field Robotics*, vol. 29, no. 5, pp. 762–792, 2012.

[9] J. Y. Chen, E. C. Haas, and M. J. Barnes, "Human performance issues and user interface design for teleoperated robots," *Systems, Man, and Cybernetics, Part C: Applications and Reviews, IEEE Transactions on*, vol. 37, no. 6, pp. 1231–1245, 2007.

[10] S. Nunnally, P. Walker, M. Lewis, N. Chakraborty, and K. Sycara, "Using haptic feedback in human robotic swarms interaction," in *Proceedings of the Human Factors and Ergonomics Society Annual Meeting*, vol. 57, no. 1. SAGE Publications, 2013, pp. 1047–1051.

[11] T. Setter, A. Fouraker, H. Kawashima, and M. Egerstedt, "Haptic interactions with multi-robot swarms using manipulability," *Journal of Human-Robot Interaction*, vol. 4, no. 1, pp. 60–74, 2015.

[12] P. Walker, S. Nunnally, M. Lewis, A. Kolling, N. Chakraborty, and K. Sycara, "Neglect benevolence in human control of swarms in the presence of latency," in *Systems, Man, and Cybernetics (SMC), 2012 IEEE International Conference on*. IEEE, 2012, pp. 3009–3014.

[13] S. A. Amraii, P. Walker, M. Lewis, N. Chakraborty, and K. Sycara, "Explicit vs. tacit leadership in influencing the behavior of swarms," in *Robotics and Automation (ICRA), 2014 IEEE International Conference on*. IEEE, 2014, pp. 2209–2214.

[14] S. Nagavalli, L. Luo, N. Chakraborty, and K. Sycara, "Neglect benevolence in human control of robotic swarms," in *Robotics and Automation (ICRA), 2014 IEEE International Conference on*. IEEE, 2014, pp. 6047–6053.

[15] S. Nagavalli, S.-Y. Chien, M. Lewis, N. Chakraborty, and K. Sycara, "Bounds of neglect benevolence in input timing for human interaction with robotic swarms," in *Proceedings of the Tenth Annual ACM/IEEE International Conference on Human-Robot Interaction*. ACM, 2015, pp. 197–204.

[16] G. Podevijn, R. O'Grady, Y. S. Nashed, and M. Dorigo, "Gesturing at subswarms: Towards direct human control of robot swarms," in *Towards Autonomous Robotic Systems*. Springer, 2014, pp. 390–403.

[17] D. Perzanowski *et al.*, *Communicating with teams of cooperative robots*. Springer, 2002.

[18] A. Giusti, J. Nagi, L. Gambardella, and G. A. Di Caro, "Cooperative sensing and recognition by a swarm of mobile robots," in *Intelligent Robots and Systems (IROS), 2012 IEEE/RSJ International Conference on*. IEEE, 2012, pp. 551–558.

[19] J. Nagi, A. Giusti, L. M. Gambardella, and G. A. Di Caro, "Human-swarm interaction using spatial gestures," in *Intelligent Robots and Systems (IROS 2014), 2014 IEEE/RSJ International Conference on*. IEEE, 2014, pp. 3834–3841.

[20] B. Mekdeci and M. Cummings, "Modeling multiple human operators in the supervisory control of heterogeneous unmanned vehicles," in *Proceedings of the 9th Workshop on Performance Metrics for Intelligent Systems*. ACM, 2009, pp. 1–8.

[21] T. D. Fincannon, A. W. Evans, F. Jentsch, E. Phillips, and J. Keebler, "Effects of sharing control of unmanned vehicles on backup behavior and workload in distributed operator teams," in *Proceedings of the Human Factors and Ergonomics Society Annual Meeting*, vol. 53, no. 18. Sage Publications, 2009, pp. 1300–1303.

[22] B. Bennett and M. Trafankowski, "A comparative investigation of herding algorithms," in *Proc. Symp. on Understanding and Modelling Collective Phenomena (UMoCoP)*, 2012, pp. 33–38.

[23] E. Olson, "AprilTag: A robust and flexible visual fiducial system," in *Proceedings of the IEEE International Conference on Robotics and Automation (ICRA)*. IEEE, May 2011, pp. 3400–3407.

[24] T. Labs, "Myo gesture control armband - wearable technology by thalmic labs," 2017, [Retrieved: February, 2017]. [Online]. Available: https://www.myo.com/techspecs

Natural Language User Interface For Software Engineering Tasks

Alexander Wachtel, Jonas Klamroth, Walter F. Tichy

Karlsruhe Institute of Technology
Chair for Programming Systems Prof. Walter F. Tichy
Am Fasanengarten 5, 76131 Karlsruhe, Germany
Email: alexander.wachtel@kit.edu, jonas.klamroth@student.kit.edu, walter.tichy@kit.edu

***Abstract*—In this paper, we present the idea to use natural language as the user interface for programming tasks. Programming languages assist with repetitive tasks that involve the use of conditionals, loops and statements. This is what is often challenging users. However, users can easily describe tasks in their natural language. We aim to develop a *Natural Language User Interface* that enables users to describe algorithms, including statements, loops, and conditionals. For this, we extend our current spreadsheet system to support control flows. An evaluation shows that users solved more than 60% of tasks. Although far from perfect, this research might lead to fundamental changes in computer use. With natural language, programming would become available to everyone. We believe that it is a reasonable approach for end user software engineering and will therefore overcome the present bottleneck of IT proficients.**

***Keywords*–Natural Language Processing; End User Development; Natural Language Interfaces; Human Computer Interaction; Programming In Natural Language; Dialog Systems.**

I. Introduction

Since their invention, digital computers have been programmed using specialized, artificial notations, called programming languages. Programming requires years of training. However, only a tiny fraction of human computer users can actually work with those notations. With natural language and end user development methods, programming would become available to everyone and enable end users to program their systems or extend their functionality without any knowledge of programming languages. Myers [1] and Scaffidi [2] compared the number of end users and professional programmers in the United States. Nearly 90 million people use computers at work and 50 million of them use spreadsheets. In a self-assessment, 12 million considered themselves as programmers, but only 3 million people are professional programmers. According to Liberman [3], the main question in the End User Development (EUD) area of research is, how to allow non-programming users who have no access to source code, to program a computer system or extend the functionality of an existing system. In general, spreadsheets have been used for at least 7000 years [4]. The created spreadsheets are not only the traditional tabular representation of relational data that convey information space efficiently, but also allow a continuous revision and formula-based data manipulation. It is estimated that each year hundreds of millions of spreadsheets are created [5].

Our Vision

Programming languages assist with repetitive tasks that involve use of loops and conditionals. This is what is often challenging for spreadsheet users. We work on *Natural Language User Interface (NLUI)* that enables users to describe algorithms in their natural language and provides a valid output by the dialog system for given user description:

- *Find the maximum element of a set:*
  Use an auxiliary variable. Initialize the variable with an arbitrary element of the set. Then visit all the remaining elements. Whenever an element is larger than the auxiliary variable, store it in the auxiliary variable. In the end, the maximum is in the auxiliary variable.
- *Selection sort of a set:*
  The result is a vector. Initially it is empty. Find the minimal element of the set and append it to the vector. Remove the element form the set. Then, repeatedly find the minimum of the remaining elements and move them to the result in order, until there are no more elements in the set.
- *Switching sort of an array:*
  If there are two elements out of order, switch them. Continue doing this until there are no more elements out of order. Out of order means that an element is larger than its right neighbor. The right neighbor of an element x[i] in a vector x is x[i+1].

Ordinary, natural language would enable almost anyone to program and would thus cause a fundamental shift in the way computers are used. Rather than being a mere consumer of programs written by others, each user could write his or her own programs [6]. However, programming in natural language remains an open challenge [7].

Our paper is structured as following: section II describes our previous work on NLUI. Followed by the Section II-D that presents our current work on control flows, discussing conditional and loop statements. Section III evaluates prototype in an user study. Section IV presents related work in the research areas of programming in natural language, End User Programming and natural language dialog systems. Finally, section V presents a conclusion of our topic and future work.

II. Natural Language User Interface

In 1979, Ballard et al. [8][9][10] introduced the Natural Language Computer (NLC) that enables end users to program simple arithmetic calculations using natural language.

A. Dialog System

In 2015, first prototype of an assistant has been presented that uses natural language understanding and a dialog management system to allow inexperienced users to manipulate spreadsheets with natural language [11]. Motivated by a pilot study based on the selected problems from Frey's book *Microsoft Excel 2013* [12] the system requests missing information and is able to resolve ambiguities by providing alternatives to choose from. Furthermore, the dialog system must resolve references to previous results, allowing the construction of complex expressions step-by-step. The system architecture consists of a user interface responsible for human interaction, as well as a natural language understanding and a dialog management unit (See Figure 1).

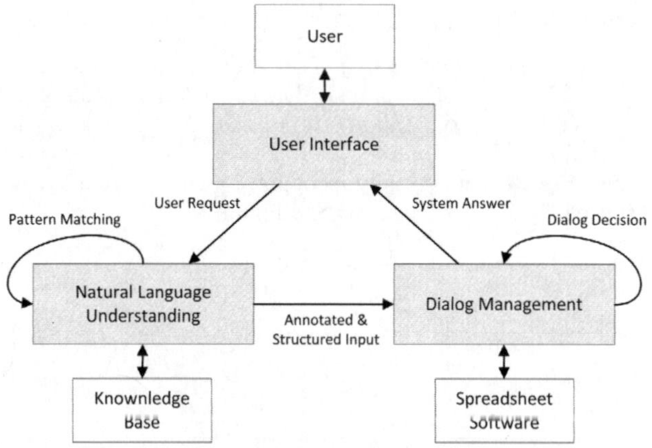

Figure 1. Architecture Overview

In a first step, the natural language understanding unit (NLU) performs essential language analysis relying on a basic vocabulary specifically built to cover the system's domain. Synonyms are substituted using a handcrafted synonym database. Mathematical terms and numerical values as well as references to regions within the spreadsheet are tagged. In the following step, the system groups elements representing a sentence or clause to enable subsequent analysis.

The purpose of the dialog management unit (DMU) is to deal with the tree structure that has been created by the NLU unit, resolve references, create a valid spreadsheet formula and generate a human-like response to the user input.

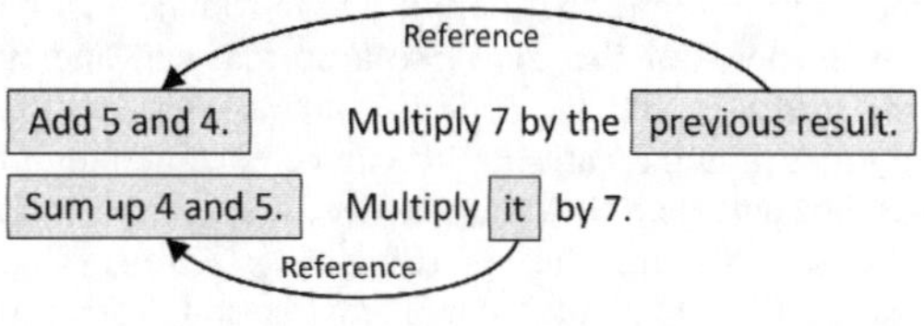

Figure 2. Resolution of references

The evaluation of the prototype exceeded expectations. 80% of 170 tasks have been solved successfully. The system helped users to solve tasks and received positive feedback from nearly two thirds of the users. Inspired by the Turing Test, the authors asked 17 independent spreadsheet users to formulate requests for particular calculation tasks. Each task was answered by both, the prototype and a human, independently. Afterwards the participants were encouraged to identify the computer generated response. This however turned out to be surprisingly hard to decide. With 34 decisions made in total, 47.1% falsely identified the dialog system answer as human. This result indicates that the prototype is capable of generating suitable responses for sufficiently specific requests within the language domain.

B. Active Ontologies

In early 2016, the natural language dialog system has been extended with a natural language dialog system based on active ontologies which enables the user to create and manipulate excel sheets without having to know the complex formula language of excel [13]. Our system is able to resolve references, detect and help resolve ambiguous statements and ask for missing information if necessary. While already quite powerful this system was not able to handle conditions properly or understand statements involving loops or instructions affecting multiple cells. In this paper, we will present an approach on how to attack these weaknesses.

By adding additional information to an ontology, such as a rule evaluation system and a fact store, it becomes an execution environment instead of just being a representation of knowledge. Sensor nodes register certain events and store them in the fact store. An evaluation mechanism tests the new facts against the existing rules and performs the associated action if one or more rules apply to the stored facts. The old system consists mainly of two active ontologies. One in charge of interpreting the user input and one generating answers according to the interpretation.

In our system each rule is represented by a separate node in the active ontology. By connecting nodes the developer decides which type of facts are relevant to which node. In [13], we presented four different types of nodes:

1) Gather-Nodes: These nodes gather the information of all children nodes and only create a new fact if all necessary children facts exist.
2) Selection-Nodes: These nodes gather all information of their children and pass on the most fitting according to some score.
3) Pass-Nodes: These nodes bundle all obtained information of their children into 1 new fact.
4) Sensor-Nodes: These nodes are the "leaves" of the ontology and react directly to the user input.

Each node-type can be seen as one possible evaluation mechanism. While with these types a developer is able to cover most parts of standard domains of dialog systems one can think of far more complex ones. This is where our new system comes into play. By allowing the developer to use his own evaluation mechanisms we created an infinite amount of new possibilities what our system is capable of.

C. Interactive Spreadsheet Processing Module

Interactive Spreadsheet Processing Module (ISPM) [14] is an active dialog management system that uses machine learning techniques for context interpretation within spreadsheets and connects natural language to the data in the spreadsheets. First, the rows of a spreadsheet are divided into different classes and the table's schema is made searchable for the dialog system (See Figure 3).

	A	B	C	
1	**Table 1: persons**			CAPTION
2	**name**			SUPER HEADER
3	**first name**	**last name**	**age**	HEADER
4	**group A**			GROUP HEADER
5	Sloane	Morgan	37	DATA
6	Dustin	Brewer	33	DATA
7	Valentine	Yates	38	DATA
8	Michael	Gregori	50	DATA
9	**group B**			GROUP HEADER
10	Ina	Hoffman	40	DATA
11	Oliver	Hopkins	27	DATA
12	Damon	Vasquez	22	DATA
13	Mark	Richards	25	DATA

Figure 3. A spreadsheet table annotated with row labels

In the case of a user input, it searches for headers, data values from the table and key phrases for operations. Implicit cell references like "people of age 18" are then resolved to explicit references using the schema. Using the ISPM, end users are able to search for values in the schema of the table and to address the data in spreadsheets implicitly, e.g., *What is the average age of people in group A?* (See Figure 4).

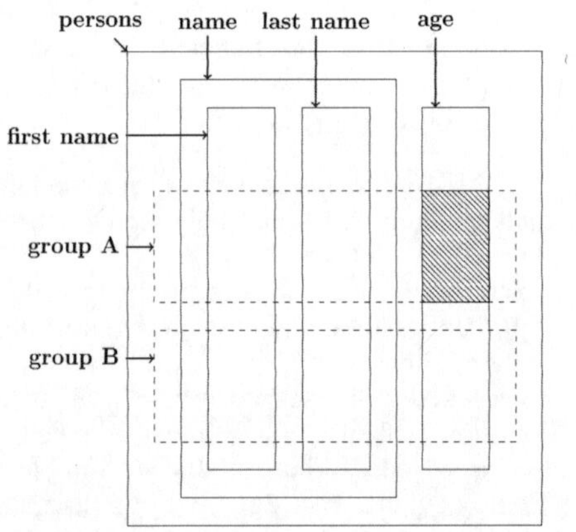

Figure 4. Context detection of user input

Furthermore, the system enables users to select (88% successfully solved), sort (88%), group (75%) and aggregate (63%) the spreadsheet data by using natural language for end user software engineering.

D. Control flows

Two new modules have been developed to extend the current system for support of control flows. The first module is capable of handling conditional instructions and the second is able to understand statements that contain loops.

1) Conditional Statements: Conditional instructions are often hard to understand due to their complex grammatical and contextual structure. Also references are complicated to resolve in this kind of sentences. The advantage of conditions is that they have a small set of key-words (such as if, in case of, etc.) that indicate that the user uses a conditional statement. In domain of spreadsheet manipulation to be able to understand, the condition has to result in a boolean operation. These two facts enable us to develop a specialized service dealing with conditional statements. We react to the keywords and try to find a boolean value in the user input. If we can not find any boolean operation, dialog system asks the user directly for it. After user answers, it is just recognizing which action the user wants to perform. Unconditional statements were already supported in our older system, so we can rely on it to find the proper action.

As already annotated *if* gets recognized as a condition keyword. The system already knows that it is dealing with a conditional statement. *A1 is greater than 3* is a boolean operation and may be used as condition. The trivial statement *save 5 in B1* can be easily recognized as unconditional action and handled by our system (See Figure 5).

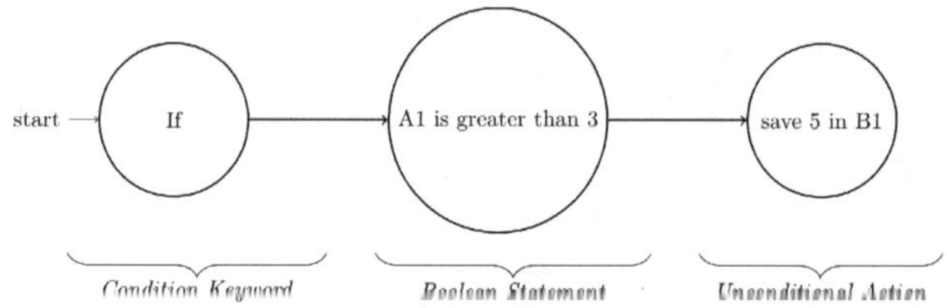

Figure 5. Example for a conditional statement

2) Loop Statements: Dealing with statements that affect more than one cell can be seen as a looped instruction. In that case, the target of the instruction is the loop variable. Knowing this, we can handle it in a similar way we used for conditional statements. In contrast to conditions, loop do not necessarily have to contain clear keywords. Often times these keywords are hidden within the sentence like *for all, for each, as long as*. However, there may also be explicit instruction like *do something three times.*

Once any of these keywords are recognized, the system has to find the corresponding action and execute it for the given range of cells. In order for our active ontology to be able for recognition the proper action, we introduced a Looptarget. This is an operator that acts like a normal cell and is able to be recognized by normal actions (such as save, multiply), but at the same time indicates that it can be executed on a range of cells. Once activated by a loop keyword, the loop service reacts to actions containing the regarding targets. In this case, next step is to split input into several instructions for each cell of the given range. This may also be combined with conditional instructions. User input *add 2 to B2 for each cell of column A which is greater than B2* is correctly handled by our system (See Figure 6).

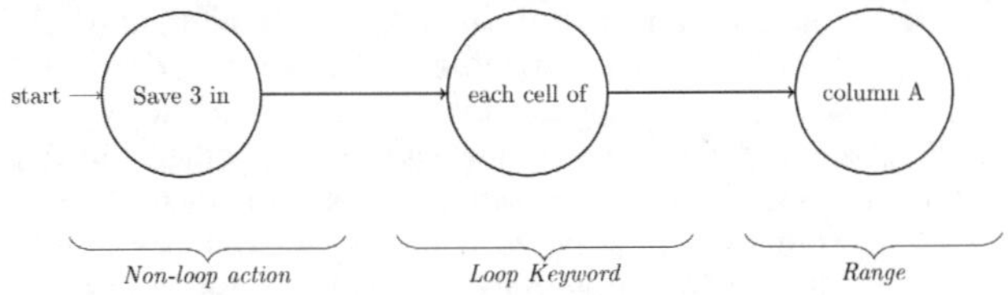

Figure 6. Example for a loop statement

3) Sample Dialog: To demonstrate the extended features, we present a short dialog between the NLUI and user. For each iteration of the dialog we listed the user input (User), the operation the system executed as consequence of this input (NLU) and the response generated by the system (DMU):

User: Write 30 in all cells of column A

NLU: save(30, A:A)

DMU: Already done. Is there anything else i can do?

User: Subtract 10 from each cell between A1 and A10

NLU: save(A1:A10 - 10, A1:A10)

DMU: Ok, I did that for you.

Can I do something else for you?

User: No

DMU: Alright

...After a break, user turns back to the NLUI

User: For each cell of column A which is greater than 25

add 2 to B2

NLU: conditionalAction(A:A>25, save(B2 + 2, B2))

User: If A3 is greater than A2 write 2 in A3 else in B3

NLU: conditionalAction(A3>A2, save(2, A3), save(2, B3))

DMU: Ok, I did that for you.

User: If A5 is greater than B5

NLU: NoAction

DMU: I see you used a condition.

What do you want to do if the condition is true?

User: Save 4 in B3

NLU: conditionalAction(A5 > B5, save(4, B3))

DMU: Everything done as you wished.

III. Evaluation

To evaluate the quality of our system we conducted an user study. We asked 12 participants to solve given tasks by using our system and recorded their experience with it. In detail we asked for each task

- whether they were able to solve the task,
- if the system was helping them to solve the task,
- if the system output was natural,
- and if the system was able to understand their input.

The participants were Non-native English speakers and the majority of them have never used our system before. Most of them stated that they knew and already used excel before, but not on a regular basis.

Since we already evaluated our system for standard arithmetic tasks, response time as well as scalability in our last paper [13], we specifically designed the tasks to test the discussed control flow features. e.g.:

- Insert the specified value 10 into all cells of a column.
- Multiply all cells in a range (between A1 and A10) that are greater than 2 by 3.
- If the value in cell A3 is greater than A2, they should add 2 to B1, else to B2.

The results show that the users where able to solve more than 60% of the tasks at least partially and found our system as useful in over 60% of the cases (see Figure 7). Additionally nearly 70% of the system outputs were considered as natural by the participants. The participants stated in over 50% of the cases that the system didn't understand their input. The improvement of the systems output has to be worked on. Overall, the system's quality was rated at 3.33 out of 5 stars, and except for one participant all participants said that they would use our system.

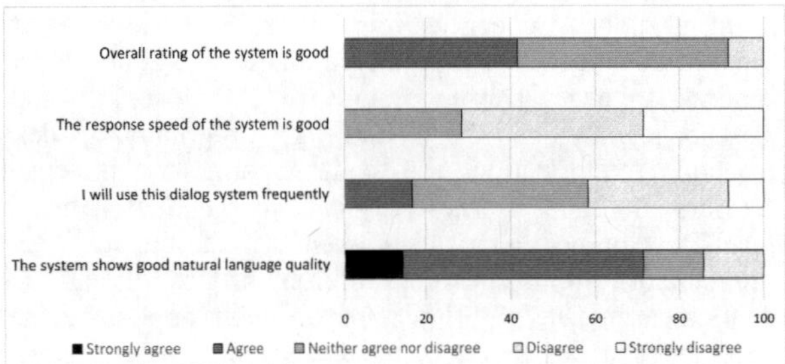

Figure 7. Overall results in %

While this result demonstrates that our system is far from perfect it also shows that there is added value when using the system especially for inexperienced users. Knowing that nearly half of the unsolved tasks stemmed from the same question and the most common problem were synonym problems which are easy to fix the results we achieved are auspicious. Since our system will most likely only improve in coming versions due to the growing number of services and the size of our word databases we consider this a promising approach.

IV. Related Work

The idea of programming in natural language was first proposed by Sammet in 1966 [15], but enormous difficulties have resulted in disappointingly slow progress. One of the difficulties is that natural language programming requires a domain-aware counterpart that asks for clarification, thereby overcoming the chief disadvantages of natural language, namely ambiguity and imprecision. In recent years, significant advances in natural language techniques have been made, leading, for instance, to IBM's Watson [16] computer winning against the two Jeopardy! world champions, Apple's Siri routinely answering wide-ranging, spoken queries, and automated translation services such as Google's becoming usable [17][7]. In 1979, Ballard et al. [8][9][10] introduced their Natural Language Computer (NLC) that enables users to program simple arithmetic calculations using natural language. Although NLC resolves references as well, there is no dialog system. Metafor introduced by Liu et al. [18] has a different orientation. Based on user stories the system tries to derive program structures to support software design. A different approach regarding software design via natural language is taken by RECAA [19]. RECAA can automatically derive UML models from the text and also keep model and specification consistent through an automatic feedback component. A limited domain end-to-end programming is introduced by Le. SmartSynth [20] allows synthesizing smartphone automation scripts from natural language description. However, there is no dialog interaction besides the results output and error messages.

Paternò [21] introduces the motivations behind end user programming defined by Liberman [3] and discusses its basic concepts, and reviews the current state of art. Various approaches are discussed and classified in terms of their main features and the technologies and platforms for which they have been developed. In 2006, Myers [1] provides an overview of the research in the area of End-User Programming. As he summarized, many different systems for End User Development have already been realized [22][23][24]. However, there is no system such as our prototype that can be controlled with natural language. During a study in 2006, Ko [22] identifies six learning barriers in End User Programming: design, selection, coordination, use, understanding and information barriers. In 2008, Dorner [25] describes and classifies End User Development approaches taken from the literature, which are suitable approaches for different groups of end users. Implementing the right mixture of these approaches leads to embedded design environments, having a gentle slope of complexity. Such environments enable differently skilled end users to perform system adaptations on their own. Sestoft [26] increases expressiveness and emphasizing execution speed of the functions thus defined by supporting recursive and higher-order functions, and fast execution by a careful choice of data representation and compiler technology. Cunha [27] realizes techniques for model-driven spreadsheet engineering that employs bidirectional transformations to maintain spreadsheet models and synchronized instances. Begel [28] introduces voice recognition to the software development process. His approach uses program analysis to dictate code in natural language, thereby enabling the creation of a program editor that supports voice-based programming.

NLyze [29], an Add-In for Microsoft Excel that has been developed by Gulwani, Microsoft Research, at the same time as our system. It enables end users to manipulate spreadsheet data by using natural language. It uses a separate domain-specific language for logical interpretation of the user input. Instead of recognizing the tables automatically, it uses canonical tables which should be marked by the end user. Another Gulwani's tool QuickCode [30] deals with the production of the program code in spreadsheets through input-output examples provided by the end user [24]. It automates string processing in spreadsheets using input-output examples and splits the manipulations in spreadsheet by entering examples. The focus of his work is on the synthesizing of programs that consist of text operations. Furthermore, many dialog systems have already been developed. Commercially successful systems, such as Apple's Siri, actually based on active ontology [31], and Google's Voice Search [32][33] cover many domains. Reference resolution makes the systems act natural. However, there is no dialog interaction. The Mercury system [34] designed by the MIT research group is a telephone hotline for automated booking of airline tickets. Mercury guides the user through a mixed initiative dialog towards the selection of a suitable flight based on date, time and preferred airline. Furthermore, Allen [35] describes a system called PLOW developed at Stanford University. As a collaborative task agent PLOW can learn to perform certain tasks, such as extracting specific information from the internet, by demonstration, explanation, and dialog.

V. Conclusion and Future Work

In this paper, we presented the new idea to use of natural language as the user interface. Nowadays, users can easily describe a tasks including conditionals, loops and statements (See Section I). To enable the system for end user development, these parts should be recognized correctly by the system. In the current version of our prototype, the system supports control flows, such as conditionals and loops, but the challenge is to understand the user input at run time and put the different statements in the right order. There is a lot of work on our system still needs to be done. The goal is to implement valid scripts from natural language input that describes some sorting algorithm. We are also exploring ways to extend the system functionality with the help of the dialog. The system needs to be extended for handling graphs, and charts. Furthermore, there are some properties of tables, which are not considered in the current system and can potentially lead to problems.

References

[1] B. A. Myers, A. J. Ko, and M. M. Burnett, "Invited Research: Overview End-User Programming," CHI, 2006.

[2] C. Scaffidi, M. Shaw, and B. Myers, "Estimating the numbers of end users and end user programmers," in Visual Languages and Human-Centric Computing, 2005.

[3] H. Liberman, F. Paternò, M. Klann, and V. Wulf, "End-user development: An emerging paradigm, human-computer interaction series, volume 9," 2006.

[4] M. Hurst, "The interpretation of tables in texts," University of Ediburgh, Ph.D., 2000.

[5] R. Abraham, "Header and Unit Inference for Spreadsheets Through Spatial Analyses," in IEEE Symposium on Visual Languages - Human Centric Computing, 2004.

[6] W. F. Tichy, M. Landhäußer, and S. J. Körner, "Universal Programmability - How AI Can Help. Artificial Intelligence Synergies in Software Engineering," May 2013.

[7] C. L. Ortiz, "The Road to Natural Conversational Speech Interfaces," IEEE Internet Computing, March 2014.

[8] B. W. Ballard and A. W. Biermann, "Programming in natural language: NLC as a prototype," Association for Computing Machinery (ACM), Volume 10, 1979.

[9] A. W. Biermann and B. W. Ballard, "Toward Natural Language Computation," American Journal of Computational Linguistics, Volume 6, Number 2, 1980.

[10] A. W. Biermann, B. W. Ballard, and A. H. Sigmon, "An experimental study of natural language programming," International Journal of Man-Machine Studies, 1983.

[11] A. Wachtel, S. Weigelt, and W. F. Tichy, "Initial implementation of natural language turn-based dialog system," International Conference on Intelligent Human Computer Interaction (IHCI), December 2015.

[12] C. D. Frye, "Microsoft Excel 2013, Step by Step," O'Reilly Media, 2013.

[13] A. Wachtel, J. Klamroth, and W. F. Tichy, "A Natural Language Dialog System Based on Active Ontologies," The Ninth International Conference on Advances in Computer-Human Interactions, April 2016.

[14] A. Wachtel, M. T. Franzen, and W. F. Tichy, "Context Detection In Spreadsheets Based On Automatically Inferred Table Schema," 18th International Conference on Human- Computer Interaction, rated with Best Paper Award, October 2016.

[15] J. E. Sammet, "The Use of English as a Programming Language," Communication of the ACM, March 1966.

[16] D. Ferrucci, "Building Watson: An Overview of the DeepQA Project," Association for the Advancement of Artificial Intelligence, 2010.

[17] H. Liu and H. Liebermann, "Toward a programmatic semantics of natural language," Visual Languages and Human Centric Computing, 2004.

[18] H. Liu and H. Lieberman, "Metafor: Visualizing stories as code," 10th international conference on Intelligent user interfaces, 2005.

[19] S. J. . Körner, M. Landhäußer, and W. F. Tichy, "Transferring Research Into the Real World - How to Improve RE with AI in the Automotive Industry," 2014.

[20] V. Le, S. Gulwani, and Z. Su, "SmartSynth: Synthesizing Smartphone Automation Scripts from Natural Language," Proceeding of the 11th annual international conference on Mobile systems, applications, and services (MobiSys), 2013.

[21] F. Paternò, "End user development: Survey of an emerging field for empowering people," in ISRN Software Engineering, vol. 2013, 2013.

[22] A. J. Ko and B. A. Myers, "Designing the whyline: a debugging interface for asking questions about program behavior," in Proceedings of the SIGCHI conference on Human factors in computing systems. ACM, 2004.

[23] S. Gulwani, W. R. Harris, and R. Singh, "Spreadsheet data manipulation using examples," in ACM, 2012.

[24] A. Cypher, "Watch what I do: programming by demonstration," in MIT Press, 1993.

[25] C. Dorner, M. Spahn, and V. Wulf, "End user development: Approaches towards a flexible software design," in European Conference on Information Systems, 2008.

[26] P. Sestoft and J. Z. Sorensen, "Sheet-defined functions: Implementation and initial evaluation," 2013.

[27] J. Cunha, J. P. Fernandes, and J. Mendes, "Bidirectional Transformation of Model-Driven Spreadsheets," Springer Lecture Notes in Computer Science, 2012.

[28] A. Begel, "Spoken Language Support for Software Development," Ph.D. Thesis, Berkeley, 2005.

[29] S. Gulwani and M. Marron, "NLyze: Interactive programming by natural language for spreadsheet data analysis and manipulation," SIGMOD, 2014.

[30] S. Gulwani, "Automating string processing in spreadsheets using input-output examples," in ACM SIGPLAN, 2011.

[31] D. Guzzoni, "Active: A unified platform for building intelligent web interaction assistants," in IEEE, Web Intelligence and Intelligent Agent Technology Workshops, 2006.

[32] J. R. Bellegarda, "Spoken Language Understanding for Natural Interaction: The Siri Experience," Springer New York, 2014.

[33] J. D. Williams, "Spoken dialogue systems: challenges and opportunities for research," 2009.

[34] S. Seneff, "Response planning and generation in the MERCURY flight reservation system," 2002.

[35] J. Allen, N. Chambers, and G. Ferguson, "PLOW: A Collaborative Task Learning Agent," Association for the Advancement of Artificial Intelligence, 2007.

"Fly Like This": Natural Language Interfaces for UAV Mission Planning

Meghan Chandarana
Dept. of Mech. Eng.
Carnegie Mellon University
Pittsburgh, PA, USA
mchandar@cmu.edu

Erica L. Meszaros
Dept. of Linguistics
Eastern Michigan Unversity
Ypsilanti, MI, USA
ewicks@emich.edu

Anna Trujillo and Bonnie Danette Allen
Crew Systems & Aviation Operations
NASA Langley Research Center
Hampton, VA, USA
{a.c.trujillo,danette.allen}@nasa.gov

***Abstract*—With the increasing presence of unmanned aerial vehicles (UAVs) in everyday environments, the user base of these powerful and potentially intelligent machines is expanding beyond exclusively highly trained vehicle operators to include non-expert system users. Scientists seeking to augment costly and often inflexible methods of data collection historically used are turning towards lower cost and reconfigurable UAVs. These new users require more intuitive and natural methods for UAV mission planning. This paper explores two natural language interfaces – gesture and speech – for UAV flight path generation through individual user studies. Subjects who participated in the user studies also used a mouse-based interface for a baseline comparison. Each interface allowed the user to build flight paths from a library of twelve individual trajectory segments. Individual user studies evaluated performance, efficacy, and ease-of-use of each interface using background surveys, subjective questionnaires, and observations on time and correctness. Analysis indicates that natural language interfaces are promising alternatives to traditional interfaces. The user study data collected on the efficacy and potential of each interface will be used to inform future intuitive UAV interface design for non-expert users.**

Keywords–natural language; gesture; speech; flight path

I. Introduction

Many current unmanned aerial vehicle (UAV) enriched applications such as disaster relief [1] and intelligence, surveillance and reconnaissance (ISR) [2], are executed by highly trained operators equipped with a comprehensive knowledge of the vehicle(s) and its control behaviors [3]. Similar to ISR, search and rescue (SAR) missions [4][5] typically employ an intelligent search strategy based on human-defined areas of interest (AOI), and only rely on onboard machine intelligence to locate and identify a target(s) and track to it. This same approach is also employed in suborbital earth and atmospheric science missions that may be collecting data for trend analysis over time across a set of predefined AOIs. In addition to manned flight campaigns, air balloons and satellites are traditionally used to collect data. As new applications emerge, such as atmospheric data collection, the user base shifts from one of experienced operators to one of non-expert users. Therefore, human-robot interaction methods must distance themselves from traditional controllers [5] – whose complexity often makes it arduous for untrained users to navigate – to a more natural and intuitive interface. Systems that work to simulate human-human interaction are found to be more accessible to non-expert users [6].

If available and easily programmable, earth and atmospheric scientists would utilize UAV platforms to collect their data in-situ. UAVs provide a viable method for conducting more comprehensive studies, which may require correlative data to be taken using multiple, coordinated vehicles [3]. Of particular interest is their ability to take in-situ sensor measurements in historically hostile or congested environments. Further, data-driven collection based on real-time sampling to point sensors towards, for example, transitions in ozone data or to identify the flow of biomass burning is enabled via real-time replanning for updates of UAV missions and flight paths. Figure 1 illustrates an exemplar science mission AOI and initial search pattern where three UAVs search for the source of a pollutant and then perform a sweeping pattern once within range (Fig. 2) [7]. The UAVs share and fuse maps along with sensor information across platforms during the mission to increase efficiency in locating and tracking the target.

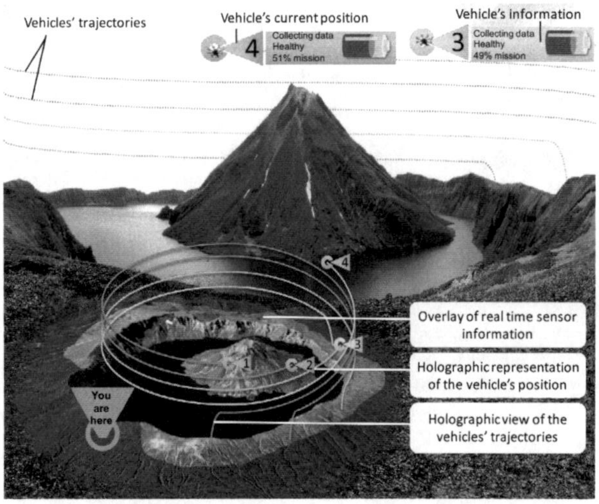

Figure 1: Example science mission area of interest (AOI) [7].

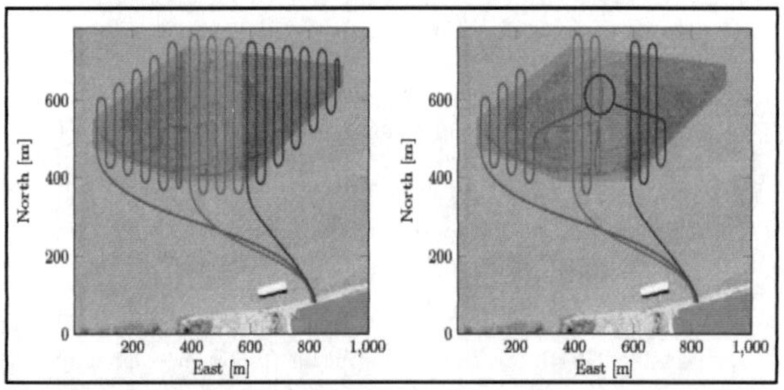

Figure 2: UAV search pattern for locating a pollutant [7].

Given current interface and control methods, skilled roboticists and pilots can easily define and program instructions for UAVs. This is made possible by their background knowledge

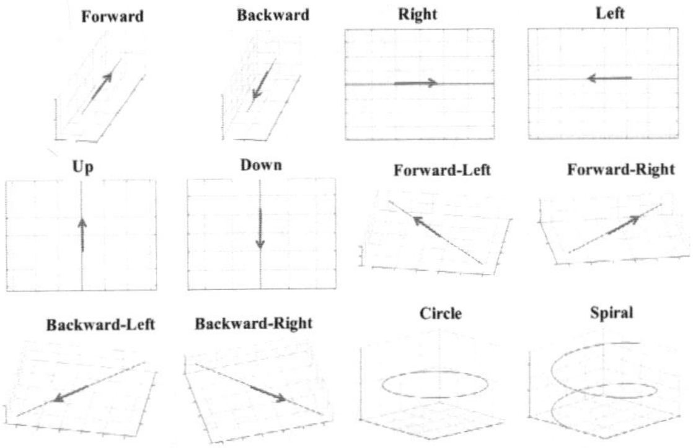

Figure 3: Gesture library of 12 trajectory segments developed by Chandarana et al. [3].

in the controls architectures required to command complex flight systems. Further, researchers in the area of autonomous aerial missions possess knowledge and insight typical of roboticists and pilots. An understanding of path planning approaches and air vehicle performance is typically required. Airborne (manned) earth science missions are supported by large teams of scientists, engineers, and pilots. Scientists, much like mission commanders, communicate their intent to the engineers and pilots who create a flight profile. This process involves trajectory/route planning of complex, flyable patterns given vehicle and environment. The trajectory/route is generated via negotiation between scientists and engineers such that the desired mission is completed while maintaining safe, executable flight paths. The complex trajectories are often generated/modified in hostile environments (e.g., cargo area of an airplane) where precise, point-and-click interfaces are challenged by factors, such as vibration and dexterity limits (e.g., gloves). The ubiquity and promise of small unmanned aerial systems (sUAS) bring the possibility of reducing dependence on vehicle-specific support, but the gap between science and engineering must be bridged.

Previous researchers looked at several methods for facilitating natural human-UAV interaction. Frequently, these interfaces adopt only a single natural language input. Ng and Sharlin [8] developed a gesture-based library and interface built on a falconry metaphor. Other gesture-based interfaces explore the concept of human-robot teaming where commands like "come here," "stop," or "follow me" communicate intent to the robot or UAV [9] without explicitly defining a flight path [10]. Alternatively, interfaces such as a speech-based interface [11] and a 3D spatial interface [12] have been explored to directly define the flight path of UAV. The work we present here explores the adequacy of common human-human interactions – gesture and speech [13][10] – in the context of an earth science data collection application.

Typically, humans use a combination of gesture and speech for communication. As an initial iteration we explore two distinct natural language interfaces – gesture and speech – for UAV flight path generation. This paper assumes the use of a single autonomous UAV. We compare the performance, efficacy, and ease-of-use of the three interfaces through user studies. Participants use a library of trajectory segments to build several flight paths. The library was developed by gathering information from atmospheric scientists about typical desired UAV flight paths to obtain measurements and further breaking them into easily defined primitives [14][15]. Although the given flight paths seen in the remainder of this paper are designed to reflect those of interest to an atmospheric scientist, the same requirement for flight path generation can be seen in variety of other applications such as search and rescue, reconnaissance, etc. This paper evaluates the current instantiation of both natural language interfaces as compared to the mouse baseline. The results will aid in the future development of a multimodal interface that makes use of the strengths from both the gesture and speech interfaces.

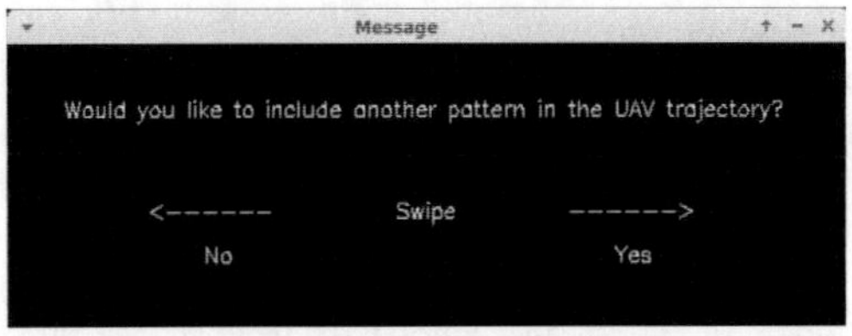

Figure 4: Yes/No message window for the gesture interface.

The paper is organized as follows. Section 2 describes the three interface frameworks. Section 3 gives an overview of the experimental setup. The results and discussion are given in Sections 4 and 5 respectively. Finally Section 6 provides some concluding remarks and identified future work.

II. Interface Frameworks

The remainder of this paper will focus on the gesture and speech interfaces, as well as a mouse baseline. The interfaces allow the user to build complex flight paths by defining individual trajectory segments. The subjects are able to use the library of 12 trajectory segments developed by Chandarana et al. [3] to build their desired final flight path (Fig. 3). Using the framework developed by Chandarana et al., each of the natural language interfaces are built with a user flow as follows: (1) define a desired trajectory segment, (2) image of the chosen segment is displayed as confirmation, (3) message asks the user if they would like to define another trajectory segment, if **Yes** (4) repeat step 1, if **No** (5) the user defined flight path is displayed. The framework then combines the segments into one flight path by automatically defining additional parameters [3]. The segments are then automatically combined into a flyable path. All systems make two assumptions about the trajectory library: (1) the *Circle* segment is defined as parallel to the ground and clockwise and (2) the *Spiral* segment is defined as a spiral upward in the clockwise direction.

A. Mouse Interface

The mouse interface consists of a drop-down menu, which includes the 12 trajectory segments in the library (Fig. 3). It assumes that the user will not choose the same trajectory segment two times in a row. A drop-down menu was chosen for this study because it is a selection method familiar to users of a mouse interface and can therefore serve well as a baseline. The user can select a desired trajectory segment by clicking on it in the drop-down menu. As mentioned previously, once a segment is chosen an image of the segment is displayed on the screen to the user as visual confirmation of their choice. For the case of the mouse interface, the user can click on the yes/no window in order to include another segment or finish the flight path.

B. Gesture Interface

For these user studies the gesture interface developed by Chandarana et al., was used [3]. In the gesture interface, a user's gestures are tracked using a commerical-off-the-shelf sensor – a Leap Motion Controller (Leap) SDK v2.2.6 – which has sub-millimeter accuracy. The three infrared cameras provide 8 ft^3 of interactive space [16]. The Leap is placed on the table in front of the user while they sit/stand based on their comfort. The current system assumes that the user is performing the gestures with their right hand.

In contrast to the mouse interface, the gesture interface users perform gesture movements to represent each trajectory segment. The Leap sensor provides more of a natural language interface for the user. This allows them to represent trajectory segments by imitating their shape rather than systems such as the Myo armband, which selects gestures based on discriminability alone [17]. The gesture input is characterized using the linear support vector machine (SVM) model trained by Chandarana et al. For each gesture movement the Leap tracks the palm of the user's hand for three seconds. The eigenvalues and movement direction throughout the gesture are then extracted from the raw data and classified using the trained model [3]. For the yes/no message window, the user must swipe *Right* for **Yes** and *Left* for **No** (Fig. 4).

C. Speech Interface

The speech interface uses a commercial-off-the-shelf headset microphone from Audio-Technica PRO 8HEmW [18] in conjunction with the speech-to-text software CMUSphinx4-5prealpha ("CMU Sphinx"). The CMU Sphinx software was used with the built-in US-English acoustic and language models. This software is a product of Carnegie Mellon University and benefits from more than 20 years of research on speech-recognition. It is ideally suited to this project because it allows for easy customization. The standard version of CMU Sphinx was modified for this application through the creation of a dictionary of allowable words. Four of the formation segments specified in Figure 3 are compound words, e.g., "Forward-left," which consists of both the word "Forward" and the word "left." Therefore, this dictionary contains only eight formation words ("Forward", "Backward", "Right", "Left", "Up", "Down", "Circle", and "Spiral") plus "yes" and "no" for the **Yes** and **No** choices in the message window. In addition, a rule-based grammar was created in order to allow the system to hear the compound formation names.

Similar to the mouse interface, the speech interface presents users with a drop-down selection of the 12 trajectory segments. Rather than selecting the desired segment using the mouse, however, users specify a segment by speaking its name into the microphone. The speech input is then broken down into *phonemes*, or small and distinct units of sound that usually correspond to consonants and vowels, which are in turn compared to the application-specific dictionary of phones and mapped to one of the twelve formations. For the yes/no message window, the system only listens for the words "yes" or "no".

III. Experimental Setup

Two single input user studies were conducted. Each subject who participated was asked to use two different natural language interfaces: (1) either a gesture or speech natural language interface (Sections 2B and 2C respectively) and (2) a baseline mouse interface (Section 2A). All subjects were allowed to sit or stand in front of the computer screen.

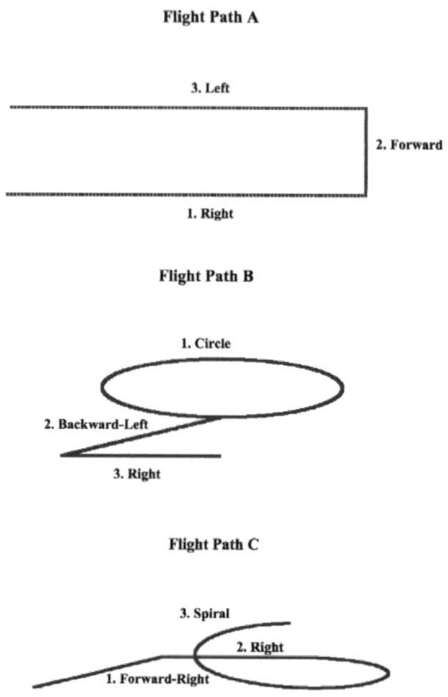

Figure 5: The three flight paths subjects were asked to build in the single input user studies.

The user studies were designed to test the ease-of-use and efficacy of each natural language interface for the purpose of UAV flight path generation. For each trial the subject was asked to define three complete flight paths. Each flight path included three segments. The flight paths ranged in difficulty level and included one common segment — a *Right* — for comparison (Fig. 5). The *Right* segment appeared at different positions in the three flight paths to avoid any bias in segment order. The order of the flight paths was randomized and counterbalanced among the subjects. Each user study was carried out in the following order: (1) subject reads and signs Privacy Act Notice and Informed Consent Form, (2) researcher(s) explains purpose of experiment, (3) subject fills out background questionnaire, (4) researcher trains subject, (5) subject builds given flight paths one at a time (for each interface), and (6) subject fills out subjective questionnaire and NASA TLX (for each interface type) [19][20]. As part of step 2 subjects were told they would be asked to build three flight paths with three segments each.

The subjects were given a printout of the trajectory segment library (Fig. 3) during training and were allowed to keep the printout during testing. Before each trial, the subject was given a printout – with labels – depicting the desired flight path to be built (one of the three shown in Fig. 5). They were allowed to study the flight path for only five seconds before the trail began, but were allowed to keep the printout for reference throughout the entire duration of the run.

In order to correctly define each flight path subjects needed to define the first segment, select *Yes* to add another segment, define the second segment, select *Yes* to add another segment, define the third segment, select *No* to complete the flight path. All errors seen from defining a segment can be attributed to one of six: (1) misinterpreted by system, (2) extra segment, (3) human error – misinterpreted flight path or ended trial too early, (4) combination error – segment misinterpreted

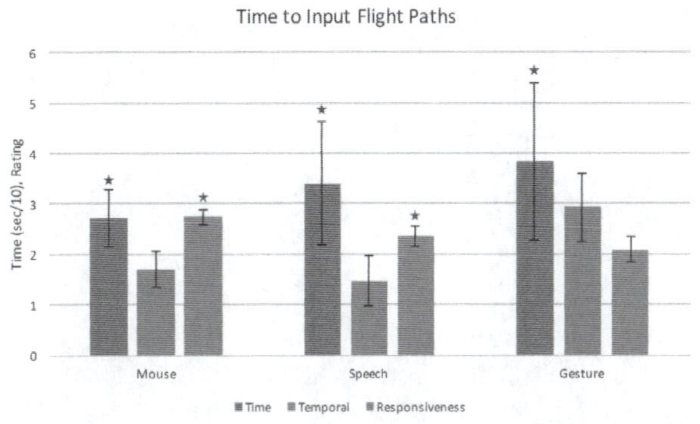

Figure 6: The normalized average time to input flight paths and subject's rating of temporal load and responsiveness of the interfaces.

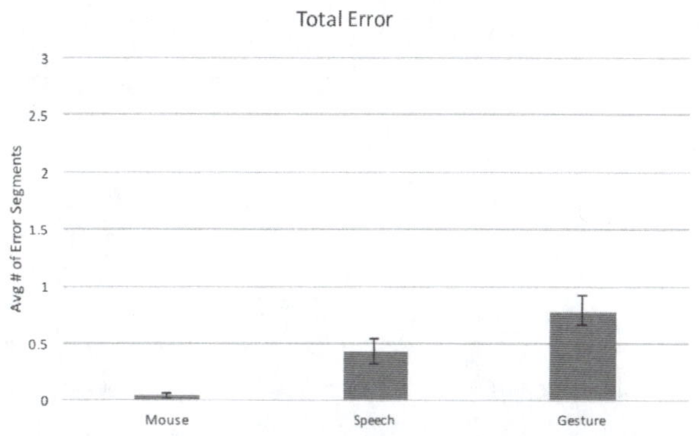

Figure 7: The average number of errors segments for each input method on a scale from 0 to 3 segments.

by system + human error, (5) combination error – segment misinterpreted by system + extra segment, and (6) combination error – extra segment + human error.

There were 13 subjects who participated in the gesture user study and 14 who participated in the speech user study. All subjects were full time employees at a research center. Subjects who participated in the gesture user study did not participate in the speech user study and vice versa. All participants also used the mouse interface for a baseline comparison. The order of interface use was counterbalanced throughout the subject pool. For both gesture and speech user studies, the same three flight paths were used (Fig. 5). The order in which each subject was asked to build the flight paths was counterbalanced throughout the subject pool, but was kept the same for the mouse interface and the natural language interface runs within the same subject. The subject was asked to fill out a subjective questionnaire and NASA TLX workload assessment survey after using each interface. Researchers also collected time to complete each given flight path and correctness of each flight path defined. The correctness data was collected through observations made by the researcher(s).

IV. RESULTS

The following results were derived from the background questionnaire, NASA TLX(s), and subjective questionnaire. The results will show the time taken to input the given flight paths, the subject's impression of the temporal workload and responsiveness of all 3 interfaces. Input errors will be given for each interface. Mouse interface results are combined as the same interface was used for both sets of user studies. Lastly, we will present the subjective measures of overall impression of how likely subjects are to use the interface method again in the future.

All data was analyzed using an analysis of variance (ANOVA) with IBM SPSS version 24. Tests of Between-Subject effects were run on the independent variables: (1) subject, (2) run, (3) input method, (4) flight path, (5) input x flight path, (6) subject x flight path, and (7) subject x input. A Tukey HSD Post-Hoc test was then run on any non-interaction significant independent variables. The significance values reported assume a $p \leq 0.05$. Error bars are shown for the standard error of the mean in each figure.

The NASA TLX asked each subject to rate their temporal workload on a scale from 0 to 10 – 0 being low temporal load and 10 being high. A separate NASA TLX was used for each interface used by the subject. In the subjective questionnaire, each subject rated their overall impression (difficulty) of the interface, the responsiveness (speed) of the interface and how likely they were to use the interface again in the future. All subjective questions used a likert scale between 1 and 5. The 1 for the impression rating represented the interface was easy to use and 5 meant it was difficult. In responsiveness, 1 indicated that the interface was too slow, 3 meant it responded at the right speed, and 5 meant the system was too fast. A 1 for likelihood represented that the subject was not likely to use the interface again and 5 that the subject was very likely to use the interface again.

23.08% of Mouse-Gesture user study subjects had previous experience with flying UAVs for an average of 170.67 hours of flight time. 76.92% of subjects said they were right-handed, but all were comfortable using their right hand. Only 7.69% of the subjects had previous experience with a gesture-based interface (other than a cell phone or tablet).

Only 7.12% of Mouse-Speech subjects had previous experience with flying UAVs for an average of 30 hours of flight time. 71.43% of the subjects had previous experience with using a speech-based interface before. This included interfaces such as Siri and Amazon Echo.

A. Time to Input Flight Paths

Figure 6 displays the average time to build a flight path (blue), the average rating of temporal load (orange), and the average rating of responsiveness (gray) for each interface. The average time values given in blue were normalized (divided by 10) to fit on the same graph as the responsiveness and temporal load ratings. The colored stars indicate the input methods that were significantly different from each other.

The time it took for subjects to build a flight path and the subject's temporal load were statistically significant for the input interface method ($F_{(2,58)} = 43.601$, $p \leq 0.01$; $F_{(3,32)} = 3.867$, $p \leq 0.02$ respectively). Responsiveness ratings given by each subject were not significant ($F_{(3,31)} = 2.284$, $p = 0.098$). The time taken to implement flight paths was statistically different as indicated with the blue stars. The mouse method was the fastest input method, however, the responsiveness and temporal load indicated that the different between the mouse, speech and gesture input methods was small. The responsiveness of the mouse interface was statistically different from the speech, but not the gesture (gray stars). Although the time taken to define flight paths with the speech interface was

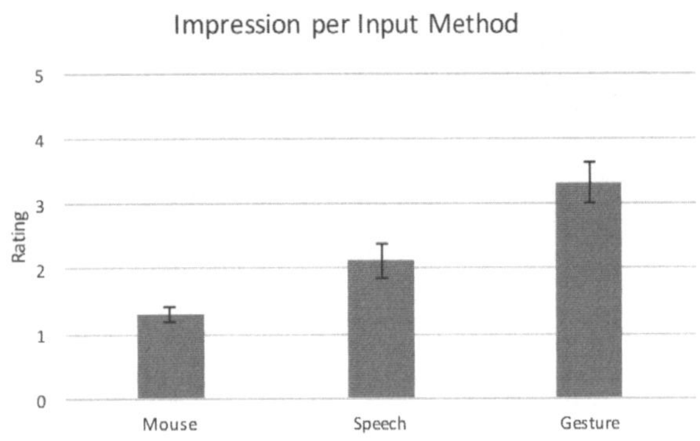

Figure 8: The average impression subjects had about the difficulty of each input method.

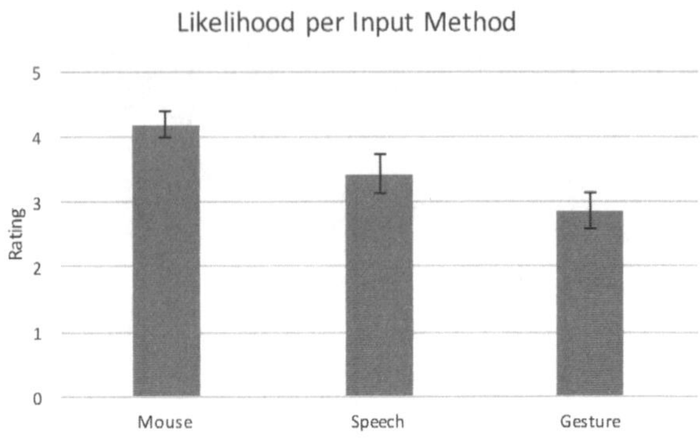

Figure 9: The average likelihood that the subjects would use each interface again.

TABLE I: AVG. % OF FLIGHT SEGMENTS CORRECT

	Flt A % Cor	Flt B % Cor	Flt C % Cor
Mouse	97.62%	100%	98.81%
Speech	95.24%	69.05%	92.86%
Gesture	87.18%	71.79%	64.10%

more than the time taken with the mouse interface, subjects rated their temporal workload lower for the speech interface.

B. Input Errors

The average percentages of correct segments for each flight path are given in Table I. The mouse interface values shown are the average of the values calculated in the all trials combined. For each flight path built, the number of incorrectly defined trajectory segments was counted. The average number of incorrect segments per input method is given in Figure 7. The average number of errors per flight path is statistically significant for the input interface ($F_{(2,58)} = 27.903$, $p \leq 0.01$). All input methods are statistically different from each other.

C. Subjective Preferences

The average impression of each input method given by the subjects was statistically significant ($F_{(3,32)} = 25.458$, $p \leq 0.01$). Similar to the results in the total error per input method, Figure 8 shows that all input methods are statistically different from each other. Figure 9 shows the average likelihood that subjects would use each input method again. Although the ratings are statistically significant ($F_{(3,32)} = 8.618$, $p \leq 0.01$), none of the interfaces are statically different from each other.

V. DISCUSSION

Initial analysis indicates that differences among the input modalities does not seem to drive the total number of errors. The total number of wrong segments was fairly low, with almost no errors using the mouse input method and a low number of errors using the speech interface. This is likely due to familiarity with these types of interface; most subjects use mouse-based interfaces on a daily basis, with 71.43% reporting that they have used speech-to-text systems such as Siri or Amazon Echo previously. The error rate for the speech interface is just above the error rate for the mouse input, except for Flight Path B, potentially indicating an area of focus for improvements to the speech interface system.

Similar to results seen from Trujillo et al. [21], users tended to perform relatively well on each individual flight path segment, though observations indicated that they frequently performed better than they thought they did. With limited contemporaneous feedback and no ability to compare performance to other users or other sessions, users were frequently unaware of their level of success. This often surfaced in their own assessment of their performance on the NASA TLX, as well as, in comments made during experimentation.

Unsurprisingly, the mouse input method proved the fastest method to input flight paths. However, the difference between the mouse, speech, and gesture modalities, as indicated by the temporal and responsiveness responses, was small. The mouse and speech interface temporal results are comparable, while the gestural interface temporal results are only slightly elevated. The responsiveness of all three interfaces is remarkably similar, with mouse and speech both being statistically different.

Users indicated a lower overall impression of difficulty for the mouse interface than for the natural language interfaces. Despite this, users still expressed a likelihood for choosing to use a speech interface again in the future. Users were almost neutral about using the gesture interface again. For both categories, the mouse interface received better scores, which is unsurprising as it is the most familiar. However, the differences were not substantial. Instead, these two subjective categories provide valuable data on user acceptance and willingness to use the natural language interfaces in the future.

Based on observations made throughout training and the user studies, most subjects who participated in the gesture user study seemed to think that using gestures to indicate the shape of a trajectory segment was natural. Most of the errors arose due to a simplification of the interface that required users to perform the gestures at a specific time in relation to feedback shown on the screen. For the most part, using speech to define the trajectory segment shapes did not seem extensible for more complex shapes, which could be more easily defined with gestures. Instead, speech would be better suited to providing information that could augment the gesture input, such as specifying length, radius and height. Such numerical data would otherwise be difficult to intuitively convey with gestures.

While both the speech recognition software and hardware suggest that they work in noisy environments, this initial user study was run with limited background noise conflicting with the speech commands. Because real-life situations will often include at least some degree of background noise, continued research should endeavor to include the effect of noisy environments on the accuracy of the speech recognition system. Similarly, while this study used flight paths consisting of three segments, actual science missions may require more complex or lengthy flight paths. Further research should examine whether such changes to flight path length effect the usability of natural language interfaces by leading to fatigue.

Overall, however, analysis of these interfaces has indicated that the natural language interfaces show some promise. Users still successfully used speech and gesture interfaces to define flight paths in only slightly slower times. Continued advancement of their design will enable intuitive, natural language communication between UAVs and human operators, as well as, offer a compelling alternative to traditional interface designs.

Additionally, despite performing faster than other input methods, mouse-based interfaces become a less viable or desirable option outside of the sterile office environment. In the field or on an emergency call, a mouse-based system becomes ill-suited for a trajectory definition application. The results of this study show that alternate natural language interfaces are well-received by users. These alternative interfaces allow for novel ways of defining missions and generating trajectories that lend themselves better to fast-paced field work. Based on these results we can therefore work to improve the next iteration of natural language interfaces so that they are comparable to the results seen by using the mouse-based interface.

VI. Conclusion and Future Work

This paper presented two natural language interfaces for UAV mission planning. User studies were conducted to test the ease-of-use, efficacy and overall acceptance of each interface as compared to a mouse baseline. Overall, the experimental setup proved adequate for gathering data on the efficacy and the potential of individual mouse, speech, and gesture interfaces. This analysis shows that the experimental setup allow for comparison not only of the gesture interface to the mouse interface and the speech interface to the mouse interface, but due to the purposefully similar setup it allows for comparison between gesture and speech interfaces. The analysis indicates that even if users performed better using a mouse interface, they were still able to use the natural language interfaces successfully and were interested in using them in the future. This indicates that natural language interfaces offer an appealing alternative to conventional interfaces, and may provide a more intuitive method of communication between humans and UAVs. Moreover, the data produced in this analysis have indicated areas of each interface that were well-accepted by users, and areas that need to be supported. This is critical information for the design of next generation natural language interfaces.

The focus of this work has been on individual mouse, gesture, and speech interfaces. The data have indicated that while each interface was successfully used to develop UAV flight paths, complementary aspects of each interface were more intuitive and met with greater success. Having identified these strengths, a multimodal interface that combines aspects of the speech and gestural interfaces can be developed to further increase usability and accuracy. Such a combination of both verbal and gestural languages is critical to a truly natural interface [10]. Humans naturally and instinctively use both gestural and verbal modes of communication, indicating that a truly natural language interface should also leverage both [22]. Such a multimodal interface would work to limit any barriers to communication, establishing trust between non-expert users and the system and facilitating improved interaction [13]. More importantly, it would draw on the strengths of the individual interfaces – gesture and speech – and compensate for any limitations in one interface through the use of the other. Future work will examine a next generation multimodal natural language interface used to interact with UAVs.

Acknowledgment

The authors would like to thank Kyle McQuarry (Analytical Mechanics Associates, Inc.) for helping to create the mouse interface.

References

[1] G. Saggiani and B. Teodorani, "Rotary wing uav potential applications: an analytical study through a matrix method," *Aircraft Engineering and Aerospace Technology*, vol. 76, no. 1, pp. 6–14, 2004.

[2] D. Weatherington and U. Deputy, "Unmanned aircraft systems roadmap, 2005-2030," *Deputy, UAV Planning Task Force, OUSD (AT&L)*, 2005.

[3] M. Chandarana, A. Trujillo, K. Shimada, and B. D. Allen, "A natural interaction interface for UAVs using intuitive gesture recognition," in *Advances in Human Factors in Robots and Unmanned Systems*. Springer, 2017, pp. 387–398.

[4] M. L. Wald, "Domestic drones stir imaginations, and concerns," *New York Times*, 2013.

[5] H. Chen, X.-m. Wang, and Y. Li, "A survey of autonomous control for uav," in *Artificial Intelligence and Computational Intelligence, 2009 International Conference on*, vol. 2. IEEE, 2009, pp. 267–271.

[6] D. Perzanowski, A. C. Schultz, W. Adams, E. Marsh, and M. Bugajska, "Building a multimodal human-robot interface," *IEEE intelligent systems*, vol. 16, no. 1, pp. 16–21, 2001.

[7] B. D. Allen and N. Alexandrov, "Serious gaming for test & evaluation of clean-slate (ab initio) national airspace system (nas) designs," 2016.

[8] W. S. Ng and E. Sharlin, "Collocated interaction with flying robots," in *2011 RO-MAN*. IEEE, 2011, pp. 143–149.

[9] T. Naseer, J. Sturm, and D. Cremers, "Followme: Person following and gesture recognition with a quadrocopter," in *2013 IEEE/RSJ International Conference on Intelligent Robots and Systems*. IEEE, 2013, pp. 624–630.

[10] T. Ende *et al.*, "A human-centered approach to robot gesture based communication within collaborative working processes," in *2011 IEEE/RSJ International Conference on Intelligent Robots and Systems*. IEEE, 2011, pp. 3367–3374.

[11] M. Quigley, M. A. Goodrich, and R. W. Beard, "Semi-autonomous human-uav interfaces for fixed-wing mini-uavs," in *Intelligent Robots and Systems (IROS). Proceedings. 2004 IEEE/RSJ International Conference on*, vol. 3. IEEE, 2004, pp. 2457–2462.

[12] N. Li, S. Cartwright, A. Shekhar Nittala, E. Sharlin, and M. Costa Sousa, "Flying frustum: A spatial interface for enhancing human-uav awareness," in *Proceedings of the 3rd International Conference on Human-Agent Interaction*. ACM, 2015, pp. 27–31.

[13] J. R. Cauchard, J. L. E, K. Y. Zhai, and J. A. Landay, "Drone & me: an exploration into natural human-drone interaction," in *Proceedings of the 2015 ACM International Joint Conference on Pervasive and Ubiquitous Computing*. ACM, 2015, pp. 361–365.

[14] A. C. Trujillo *et al.*, "Operator informational needs for multiple autonomous small vehicles," *Procedia Manufacturing*, vol. 3, pp. 936–943, 2015.

[15] A. C. Trujillo *et al.*, "Collaborating with autonomous agents," *15th AIAA Aviation Technology, Integration, and Operations Conference, AIAA AVIATION Forum*, 2015.

[16] D. Bassily, C. Georgoulas, J. Guettler, T. Linner, and T. Bock, "Intuitive and adaptive robotic arm manipulation using the leap motion controller," in *ISR/Robotik 2014; 41st International Symposium on Robotics; Proceedings of*. VDE, 2014, pp. 1–7.

[17] T. Labs, "Myo gesture control armband - wearable technology by thalmic labs," 2015, retrieved: Nov. 2016. [Online]. Available: https://www.myo.com/

[18] Audio-Technica, "Pro 8hemw hypercardioid dynamic headworn microphone," 2016, retrieved: Nov. 2016. [Online]. Available: http://www.audio-technica.com/cms/accessories/b119dcfe66995ac5/index.html

[19] S. G. Hart and L. E. Staveland, "Development of nasa-tlx (task load index): Results of empirical and theoretical research," *Advances in psychology*, vol. 52, pp. 139–183, 1988.

[20] J. Byers, A. Bittner, and S. Hill, "Traditional and raw task load index (tlx) correlations: Are paired comparisons necessary?" *Advances in Industrial Engineering and Safety*, pp. 481–485, 1989.

[21] A. C. Trujillo, J. Puig-Navarro, S. B. Mehdi, and A. K. McQuarry, "Using natural language to enable mission managers to control multiple heterogeneous uavs," in *Advances in Human Factors in Robots and Unmanned Systems*. Springer, 2017, pp. 267–280.

[22] "Put-that-there: Voice and gesture at the graphics interface," vol. 14, no. 3. New York, NY, USA: ACM SIGGRAPH Computer Graphics, 1980, pp. 262–270.

Building Mobile Health Applications Using Archetypes

André Magno Costa de Araújo, Valéria Cesário Times, and Marcus Urbano da Silva
Center for Informatics, Federal University of Pernambuco, Recife, Brazil
e-mail:{amca,vct,mus}@cin.ufpe.br

Carlos Andrew Costa Bezerra
CESAR – Recife Center for Advanced Studies and Systems
Recife, Brazil
e-mail: andrew@r2asistemas.com.br

Abstract — **The use of archetypes in the development of health applications standardizes the data attributes, terminologies, and constraints of the electronic health record, as well as improves the flexibility of health information systems. However, we have noticed in the literature that little attention has been given to researching tools that dynamically build mobile health applications using archetypes, which is what we present in this work - a cloud service for automatic generation of applications from archetypes. The approach hereby proposed specifies a mechanism that generates graphical user interfaces for mobile devices and creates relational data schemes for storing data in the cloud. In addition to that, we present a mobile application named Mobile4EHR that dynamically synchronizes the cloud-generated application with the mobile device, and creates the data schema that allows for local data storage. Finally, aiming to validate the service introduced in this paper, we selected available archetypes in the Open Electronic Health Record Foundation repository to build an application that registers patients' vital signs. The main contributions of our research are i) making the patients' clinical data registration more agile, and ii) reducing the dependence on programmers when creating mobile applications for the health sector.**

Keywords-Graphical user interfaces; Interface generators; Mobile devices and services; Medical informatics; Archetypes.

I. Introduction

Health Information Systems (HIS) currently play an important role in society. They assist organizations in automating patient care activities, improve the productivity of healthcare professionals, and popularize access to Electronic Health Record (EHR) information. In recent years, the software industry has debated how to develop flexible HIS by harnessing the benefits of cloud computing and the agility provided by mobile devices [1][2]. Cloud computing provides convenient and on-demand access to process and store applications made available in the Internet.

Similar to any other software category, HIS faces problems caused by high maintenance costs, lack of uniformity in EHR modeling, and difficulty in managing the large volume of processed data in the health sector [3].

It is a natural characteristic of software to change over time, and in addition, it must adapt to the new demands of its context, even while it is in execution. HIS deal with a large number of concepts that continually change or are specialized after a short period of time. Consequently, HIS which follow these standards are expensive to maintain. Generally, necessary changes in an application require effort and provoke a high dependence on programming teams. On the other hand, one may notice that HIS are not designed to support dynamic changes, i.e., they are not flexible systems adaptable to the context of the problem domain, and do not allow end users to create new instances of an application or develop new functionalities.

Among the Health standards that promote interoperability, extensibility, and minimize high maintenance costs in the development of the HIS, the dual modeling model proposed by the Open Electronic Health Record (OpenEHR) Foundation stands out [6]. The openEHR architecture separates the generic characteristics that model the EHR structure, also known as the reference model, of the constraints and patterns associated with clinical data, known as the knowledge model.

The concept of dual modeling consists in the separation between the information contained in the EHR from the knowledge associated with the terminologies of the Health area. The first level of dual modeling involves components related to software development (e.g., data schemes, class diagrams, etc.), while the second level is represented by archetypes and templates. An archetype can be defined as a computational expression represented by Health domain constraints, while templates represent user interaction interfaces created at runtime to validate and ensure that data entered conforms to constraints defined in the archetypes [7].

Recent research studies based on openEHR specifications include the construction of the EHR using and specializing archetypes [8], the development of Computer-Aided Software Engineering (CASE) tools for data schema creation [9], and a study on development patterns for Health computing [10]. Moreover, openEHR archetypes have been used to create Graphical user interfaces (GUI) for web applications [11], to store EHR data in heterogeneous databases [12], and to model the EHR in proprietary database systems [13]. However, one may notice that little attention has been given to researching how to dynamically build applications for mobile devices from archetypes.

This work presents a cloud service that dynamically builds Health apps from archetypes. The approach hereby proposed allows Health professionals to construct and distribute applications according to the following pipeline: a representational state transfer (REST) application program interface (API) extracts the EHR specifications from the archetypes (i.e., data attributes, terminologies, and constraints) and dynamically generates relational data schemes and GUI. After that, the application generated is synchronized with the application named Mobile4EHR, and all the functionality generated through the service is ready to use. It is worth mentioning that, at the moment the synchronization between Mobile4EHR and the application created occurs, the cloud-generated data schema is replicated on the mobile device. Therefore, when there is no network or Internet connection, the application will store the data locally. When the connection is reestablished, the EHR data is automatically synchronized with the cloud data scheme.

There are three main advantages in using the service proposed here. Firstly, Health applications are built dynamically following a standard, which makes EHR requirements uniform. Secondly, through mobile devices, Health professionals can expedite the registration of the patient's clinical data. Finally, the service presented here minimizes dependence on programmers in order to develop Health applications.

The rest of this paper is organized as follows: Section II describes the basic concepts used in this work and provides an analysis of the main related works. Section III presents and describes the service proposed in this article, while Section IV demonstrates the creation of a Health application for Mobile4EHR. Finally, Section V presents the final considerations and suggestions for future work.

II. Background and Related Work

In this section, we describe the main concepts that are essential to understand our service proposal. In Section II-A, the definition of archetypes is given, while Section II-B outlines the main issues related to cloud computing. Finally, Section II-C describes the related works.

A. Archetypes

Several research projects and many applications have been developed from the specifications of the openEHR system architecture and the concept of archetypes [8]-[11]. The openEHR software architecture for HIS is aimed at developing an open, interoperable and computational platform for the Health domain [6]. This architecture separates generic information that represents the structures of the EHR and demographic characteristics of the patients of a reference model, from the constraints and standards associated with the clinical data of a given specific domain, which composes the knowledge model. An archetype consists of a computational expression that is based on the reference model and is represented by domain constraints and terminologies [3] (e.g., data attributes of a blood test), while templates are structures used to group archetypes for allowing their use in a particular context of application, and are often associated with a graphical user interface.

Dual modeling is the separation between information and knowledge of health care system architectures. In this approach, the components responsible for modeling the clinical and demographic data of EHR are specified through generic data structures, which are composed of data types, constraints and terminologies.

In an archetype, the specification of attributes is achieved through data entry builders named generic data structures. Such structures allow the representation of EHR data heterogeneity through the following types: ITEM_SINGLE, ITEM_LIST, ITEM_TREE and ITEM_TABLE.

ITEM_SINGLE models a single data attribute such as a patient's weight, height and age. ITEM_LIST groups a set of attributes in a list. A patient's address containing number, street and zip code for example. ITEM_TREE specifies a hierarchical data structure that is logically represented as a tree. It can be used, for instance, to model a patient's physical or neurological evaluations. Finally, ITEM_TABLE models data elements by using columns for field definition and rows for field value respectively. Each attribute of a data structure is characterized by a type of data and can have a related set of associated domain restrictions and terminologies. The terminologies give semantic meaning to clinical data and can be represented as a set of health terms defined by a professional.

B. Cloud Computing

Cloud computing defines every computational environment, which consists of numerous servers, be they physical or virtual, which have the ability to process and store applications, platforms and services made available in the Internet [14]. As its main feature, it provides convenient and on-demand access to a set of configurable computing resources that can be acquired quickly and released with minimal effort regarding configuration or interaction with the service provider [15]. The term *cloud* is a metaphor for the Internet or communication infrastructure among the architectural components, emphasizing an abstraction that conceals from the user all the complexity of the infrastructure and technologies used to offer such services [14].

Another important feature is that the necessary infrastructure for processing, connectivity, and data storage, is hosted by providers (e.g., *Microsoft Azure e Amazon*) specialized in this type of service. Contrariwise, in a traditional Health domain environment, in order to build or manage a HIS, IT professionals must consider the development, installation, configuration, and software update, aside from other expenses such as software licenses.

The architectural outline of cloud computing consists of three layers: Software as a Service (SaaS), Platform as a Service (PaaS) and Infrastructure as a Service (IaaS). The definition of each layer is given below:

- **Software as a Service:** In this layer, software is offered as a service or on-demand. The software runs on a remote server and there is no need to install the application on the client's computer, just access it over the Internet.
- **Plataform as a Service:** A feature provided by the cloud that enables IT professionals to port, within

the cloud, applications built using the programming languages and tools available in the cloud.

- **Infrastructure as a Service:** It consists in the provision of infrastructure for processing, storage, networks, among others. This service, like the others, has its resources shared with several users simultaneously.

The development of a service which generates data schemes and GUI using archetypes is one of the topics encompassed in this study on cloud computing. The service aims at creating relational data schemes and storing EHR in a cloud platform.

C. Related Works and Motivation

Based on the main works investigated in the state of the art, this section presents an analysis of the main characteristics of each study, and discusses the main contributions of the work hereby proposed. In order to facilitate the understanding, Table 1 presents a comparative table with four significant criteria that guide the comparison of existing works in the state of the art. The criteria evaluated were: C1) generation of graphical interfaces using archetypes; C2) generation of data schemes; C3) EHR storage in the cloud; and C4) support for mobile applications.

TABLE 1. COMPARATIVE ANALYSIS OF RELATED WORKS

Tool	C1	C2	C3	C4
Template Design	✔	✖	✖	✖
EhRScape Framework	✔	✔	✖	✖
EhRGen Framework	✔	✔	✖	✖
Mobile4EHR	✔	✔	✔	✔

Considering the solutions available in the market, we identified three tools that generate GUIs for the Health sector using archetypes. The Template Design tool, and the EhrScape and EhRGen frameworks support the development of Health applications based on the specifications by openEHR. As shown in Table 1, Template Design, EhrScape, EhRGen, and Mobile4EHR generate their GUIs from archetypes; nevertheless, only EhRScape, EhRGen, and Mobile4EHR generate data schemes and offer the ability to manipulate data in the generated GUI. Lastly, features of EHR storage in the cloud and generation of GUIs for mobile applications is only available on Mobile4EHR. Indeed, the creation of relational data schemes for EHR storage and GUI generation using archetypes is one of the main contributions of the present work. Mobile4EHR is an extension of the GUI generation and customization approach proposed in [33], i.e., it extends GUI generation to mobile applications and proposes to store EHRs in relational data schemes in the cloud.

The main motivation of the proposed work is to develop a cloud service that dynamically builds Health apps from archetypes. For this, we specify a REST API that extracts the EHR specifications from the archetypes (i.e., data attributes, terminologies, and constraints) and dynamically generates relational data schemes and GUI. After that, the application generated is synchronized with the mobile device, and all the functionality generated through the service is ready to use.

III. THE PROPOSAL

This section introduces the Health tool generation service from archetypes and is organized as follows: subsection III-A describes the architecture and main features developed, while subsection III-B details the generation of relational data schemes for EHR storage.

A. Architecture and Overview

The cloud service proposed in this work consists in a computational environment focused on the dynamic development of applications using archetypes. As mentioned previously, we extend the approach proposed in [11] in the following aspects: Firstly, we modify the GUI generation algorithm to support mobile device usage. Secondly, we have developed a cloud service (i.e., REST API) from the extended algorithm, in order to generate the GUIs. Finally, we developed a mechanism for generating cloud data schemes to persist the EHR data from the generated GUIs.

As shown in Figure 1, by taking advantage of the cloud service, Healthcare professionals can import archetypes and build apps to be used in the Healthcare industry.

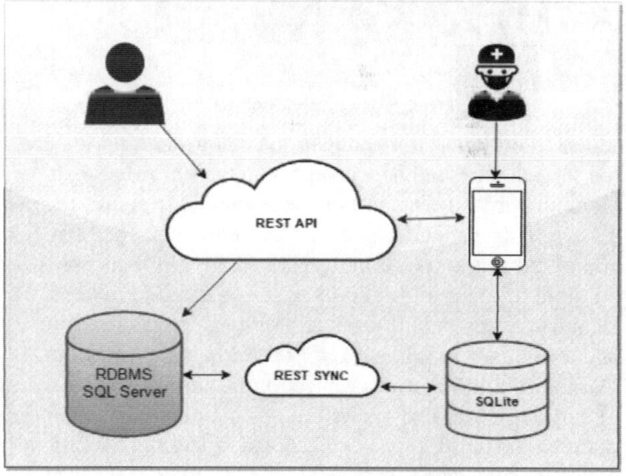

Figure 1. Cloud service architecture for generating apps

To achieve this, a REST API generates relational data schemes and GUI from the extraction of data attributes, terminologies, and constraints from archetypes. As shown in Figure 2, while running Mobile4EHR, the application created is synchronized in the mobile device, and all the features generated in the cloud are available for use. At the time of synchronization, the relational data schema created is replicated in the mobile device. Mobile4EHR stores data locally when there is no network or Internet connection. Once the application identifies a connection, the data is automatically synchronized and the data is uploaded to the cloud.

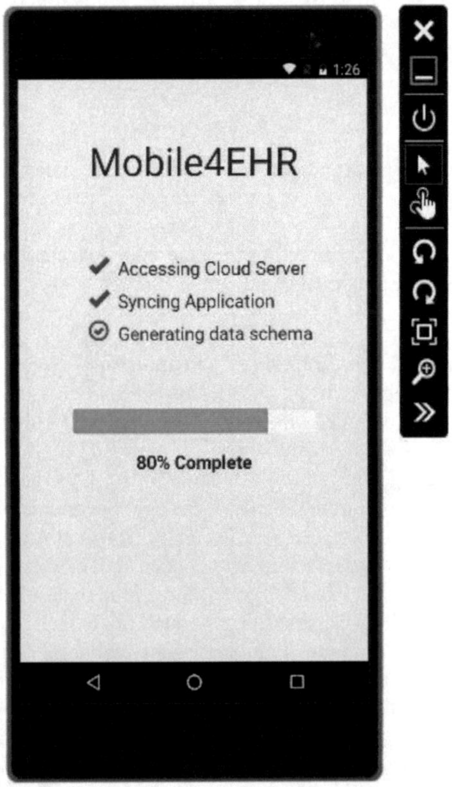

Figure 2. Interface of Mobile4EHR

In addition to GUI and data schema generation features, the service proposed here counts with the following features: **Demographic Information Management**: This feature allows for managing the actors who will be directly connected to the use of the generated app. In this case, it is possible to manage and link the organization providing the Health services and the professionals (e.g., physicians, nurses and technicians) responsible for the caring for the patient. **Domain Creation:** An organization may offer various types of health services to society. For example, a hospital can perform laboratory tests, diagnostic imaging, emergency care, hospitalization, among others. Having that in mind, Mobile4EHR allows the user to create and configure domains and subdomains that represent the services offered by each organization. This enables to link and access generated GUIs through domains and subdomains.

B. Relational Data Schema Generation

The relational data schema created contains 6 tables, 5 integrity constraints and a set of fields, which store the extracted elements from archetypes. The *Archetype* table stores the informed XML configuration file metadata, e.g., the type of archetype, its author, the file version, among other information. The *Archetype_Details* table stores the type of the data structure and constraints found in the archetype, while the *Terminology* table stores reference data attributes alongside their respective terminologies.

An archetype data specification may be done via a single attribute, a vertical list of attributes, a hierarchical data structure or a table with rows and columns. Aiming to store the data attributes into an archetype while respecting all possible layouts, we use the *ITEM_TREE* and *ITEM_TABLE* tables. Since the organization of a hierarchical structure already includes the definition of one or multiple attributes, we have mapped the attributes of the SINGLE, LIST and TREE types to the ITEM_TREE table. As the name suggests, the ITEM_TABLE table maps the attributes of the archetypes that are arranged in rows and columns. Once all data attributes are mapped to their respective tables, the user can choose which data attributes will generate the GUI, and therefore store the data manipulated by end-users. In this case, the selected attributes are added at runtime as columns in the Data_Item table.

Each element of an archetype is referenced by an identifier. All identifiers begin with the letters *at* followed by a sequential value. For example, the *at000* identifier stores the name given to an archetype. We have applied the naming standard defined by this identifier to name the fields in our data schema. Whenever a new field is inserted in the *Data_Item* table, the service verifies whether it already exists, avoiding repetitions.

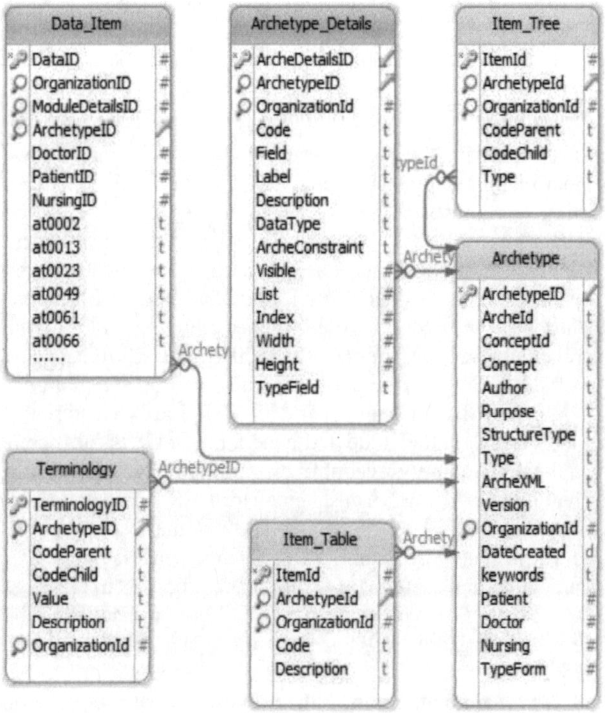

Figure 3. Relational data schema created from archetypes

Figure 3 shows a data schema instance built from Blood Pressure and Apgar archetypes, both available at the openEHR repository.

IV. Results

In this section, we demonstrate the generation of an app for the Healthcare industry using the service described in this article. Our goal is to exemplify the activities carried out by a Health professional, such as collecting and registering patients' vital signs. We chose three archetypes related to such activities, all available in the openEHR repository: Blood Pressure, Body Temperature and Respiration.

First of all, a Health unit named Hospital was registered. Subsequently, we registered a domain called Vital Signs and three subdomains named Blood Pressure, Body Temperature and Respirations, which will later be linked to the GUI generated from the archetypes. Afterwards, the archetypes were imported, linked to their respective subdomains and the application was released and available to be used. At that moment, opening Mobile4EHR triggers the synchronization and installs the cloud-generated service. Figure 4 shows the domain (i.e., Vital Signs) and subdomains (i.e., Blood Pressure, Body Temperature and Respirations) created to access the GUIs created in this demonstration, while Figure 5 depicts the GUI created from the Body Temperature archetype.

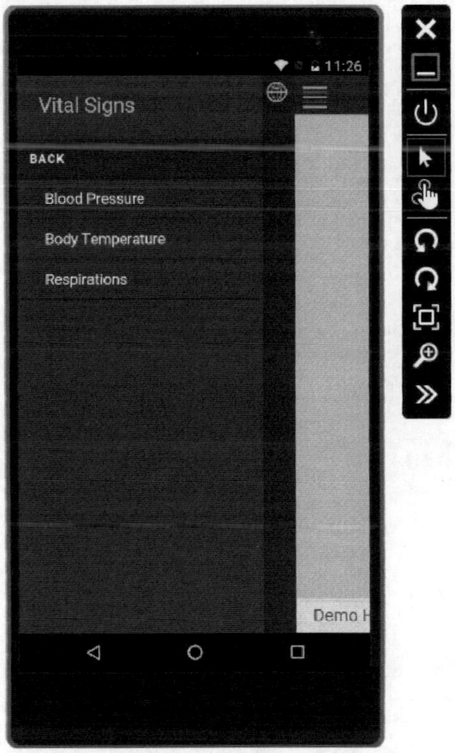

Figure 4. Menu of the app created

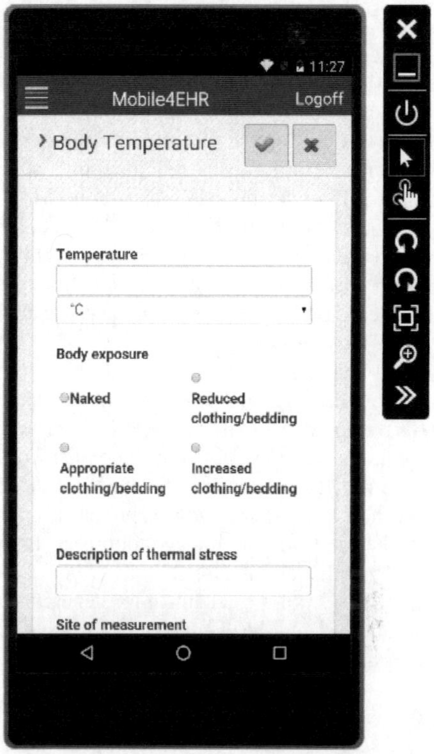

Figure 5. GUI created from the archetype Body Temperature

Each generated GUI has data persistence features. (i.e., insert, update, delete, and select). The data manipulated from the GUI is stored in the local relational data schema or in the cloud.


```
[
  {
    "Temperature": "33°C",
    "BodyExposure": "Reduced clothing/bedding",
    "DescriptionThermalStress": "",
    "Measurement": "Axilla"
  },
  {
    "Temperature": "39°C",
    "BodyExposure": "Appropriate clothing/bedding",
    "DescriptionThermalStress": "",
    "Measurement": "Urinary bladder"
  }
]
```


Figure 6. Data synchronization

Figure 6 portrays the records of the local data schema in JSON format, extracted through the REST API responsible for synchronizing data with the cloud database. In this task, only records that are in the local database and not in the cloud are synchronized. This validation aims to minimize application performance problems.

V. Final Considerations

This article presented a cloud service that enables users to build mobile Health applications using archetypes. As the main contributions, we highlight: i) we created a GUI generation service for mobile devices; ii) we have specified a mechanism for generating cloud relational data schemes for EHR storage; iii) we developed an app called Mobile4EHR that synchronizes the application created in the cloud, and generates the data schema locally on the mobile device. Furthermore, we have demonstrated the creation of a Health app from openEHR archetypes to register patients' vital signs.

Four main characteristics stand out in our work. Firstly, Health applications are built dynamically from a standard that makes EHR requirements uniform. Secondly, through mobile devices, Health professionals can speed up the recording of a patient's clinical data. Thirdly, the EHR is stored on a platform in the cloud. Finally, the approach proposed here minimizes the dependence on programmers in order to develop Health applications.

The development of a mechanism for generating NoSQL cloud data schemes and the evaluation of usability tests with health professionals are the next aims of our future works. In this paper, we limited the scope of research to data schemes and GUIs generation. A forthcoming work will address privacy and security issues by presenting an algorithm to encrypt EHR data on a cloud service or local storage.

Acknowledgment

This work was partially supported by Fundação de Amparo à Ciência e Tecnologia do Estado de Pernambuco (FACEPE), under the grants APQ-0173-1.03/15 and IBPG-0809-1.03/13.

References

[1] C. C. Martínez, T. M. Menárguez, B. J. T. Fernández, and J. A. Maldonado, "A model-driven approach for representing clinical archetypes for Semantic Web environments," Journal of Biomedical Informatics, pp.150–164, 2009.

[2] V. Dinu and P. Nadkarni, "Guidelines for the Effective Use of Entity-Attribute-Value Modeling for Biomedical Databases," International Journal of Medical Informatics, pp. 769-779, 2007.

[3] S. Garde, E. Hovenga, J. Buck, and P. Knaup, "Expressing clinical data sets with openEHR archetypes: A solid basis for ubiquitous computing," International Journal of Medical Informatics, pp. 334–341, 2007.

[4] B. Bernd, "Advances and Secure Architectural EHR Approaches," International Journal of Medical informatics, pp. 185-190, 2006.

[5] K. Bernstein , R. M. Bruun, S. Vingtoft, S. K. Andersen, and C. Nøhr, " Modelling and implementing electronic health records in Denmark," International Journal of Medical Informatic, pp. 213-220, 2005.

[6] J. Buck, S. Garde, C. D. Kohl, and G. P. Knaup, "Towards a comprehensive electronic patient record to support an innovative individual care concept for premature infants using the openEHR approach," International Journal of Medical Informatics, pp. 521-531, 2009.

[7] L. Lezcano, A. S. Miguel, and S. C. Rodríguez, " Integrating reasoning and clinical archetypes using OWL ontologies and SWRL rules," Journal of Biomedical Informatics, pp.343-353, 2010.

[8] R. Chen, G. O. Klein, E. Sundvall, D. Karlsson, and H. Åhlfeldt. "Archetype-based conversion of EHR content models: pilot experience with a regional EHR system," BMC Medical Informatics and Decision Making, pp. 9-33, 2009.

[9] A. M. C. Araujo, V. C. Times, and M. U. Silva, "A CASE Tool for Modeling Healthcare Applications with Archetypes and Analysis Patterns," The Eleventh International Conference on Software Engineering Advances, pp. 206-211, 2016.

[10] M. B. Späth and J. Grimson, "Applying the archetype approach to the database of a biobank information management system," International Journal of Medical Informatics, pp. 205-226, 2010.

[11] A. M. C. Araujo, V. C. Times, and M. U. Silva, "Template4EHR: Building Dynamically GUIs for the Electronic Health Records Using Archetypes," 16th IEEE International Conference on Computer and Information Technology, pp. 26-33, 2016.

[12] A.M.C Araujo, V.C Times, and M.U Silva, "PolyEHR: A Framework for Polyglot Persistence of the Electronic Health Record", Int'l Conf. Internet Computing and Internet of Things, pp. 71-77, 2016.

[13] L. Wang, L. Min, X. Lu, and H. Duan, "Archetype relational mapping - a practical openEHR persistence solution," BMC Medical Informatics and Decision Making, pp. 1-18, 2015.

[14] R. S. Seelam, P. Dettori, P. Westerink, and B. B. Yang, "Polyglot Application Auto Scaling Service for Platform As A Service Cloud," IEEE International Conference on Cloud Engineering, pp. 84-91, 2015.

[15] M. Ellison, R. Calinescu, and R. Paige, "Re-engineering the Database Layer of Legacy Applications for Scalable Cloud Deployment," IEEE/ACM 7th International Conference on Utility and Cloud Computing, pp. 976-979, 2014.

A Comparative Assessment of User Interfaces for Choreography Design

Tafadzwa Joseph Dube, Gökhan Kurt, Gökhan İnce

Computer Engineering Department
Istanbul Technical University
Istanbul, Turkey
Email: dube@itu.edu.tr, kurt@itu.edu.tr, gokhan.ince@itu.edu.tr

Abstract—**Choreography design is a vital creative art that benefits vastly from digital applications. In this study, we investigate the effects of different interaction techniques on user experience for a choreography generator interface. We develop an augmented reality choreography generator and compare it with 1) a personal computer based choreography generator and 2) a mobile application for choreography generation. We evaluate user performance and user experience on the interfaces in terms of task completion times, as well as subjective criteria, such as mental stress, physical stress, and pleasure experienced. Our research contributes to the study of how different interaction methods of the same application affect user experience. The paper also contributes to human-computer interaction in education and training. The results verify the effectiveness of augmented reality in developing training and design applications.**

Keywords–choreography; augmented reality; user experience; natural user interfaces.

I. INTRODUCTION

Choreography is a creative process that has evolved over years. With the advent of technology, different ways that embraced digital tools for choreographing emerged. Thus, allowing choreographers to benefit a lot from this evolution. It is imperative to develop interfaces that are robust and suite well for hand-held devices and computers. Furthermore, to enhance user experience in choreographing tools it is important to design human friendly user interfaces.

One emerging field of Natural User Interfaces (NUI) shows much promise shows much promise in the Human Computer Interaction(HCI)field. The approach put more emphasis on developing interfaces that allow users to perform tasks in a natural way, including touch based techniques, gestures and voice; it runs away from the traditional approach of using keyboard and mouse [1]. In this study we develop interfaces that utilize the traditional interactive approach and also interfaces that seek aspects of NUI. NUIs have a pivotal role to play in HCI in education and training.

Augmented Reality (AR) presents an interesting approach to interface development. AR coupled with touch screen presents aspects of NUI, which potentially improves user experience. AR combines the real world and the virtual worlds, it provides interaction with 3 dimensional objects superimposed onto a real world [2]. AR provides a simultaneous way for users to interact with the virtual and real world. With the surge in mobile devices, mobile AR is quickly gaining momentum [3]. This growth in mobile AR applications has been facilitated by the increasing processing power of modern day mobile devices [4]. The ability to process intensive applications has seen a swift shift from the bulky hardware that has symbolized AR since the 20th century. AR promises to be a major player in interface design in the 21st century. Whenever 3D objects appear superimposed onto the real world, a novel experience is created that adds pleasure and creates amazement and curiosity to the user [5]. This has seen AR being embraced by the mobile gaming industry. The year 2016 saw a major shift for AR in the gaming industry with the launch of "Pokemon Go" that has revolutionized how people viewed AR. New York Times suggests that Pokemon go represents the moment AR breaks through the current position to something bigger [6]. As the trend continues, it is imperative to embrace AR in interface development. Technological advances have allowed cheaper ways to develop AR applications.

Over the years different digital platforms have been developed for choreography generation. 3D animation is a preferred choice for dance learning [5]. Furthermore, choreographers have been fascinated by the use of digital tools when perfoming their tasks. The use of these digital tools encourages choreographers to observe the creative compositional process as new through confines alongside new possibilities [7]. In this study, we complement existing choreographing tools by adding AR. Several researchers have suggested that AR can aid reinforce motivation of students and trainees through improving their educational realism [8]. AR applications in mobile platforms provide a lot of promise with respect to training and planning [9].

In this study, we design, implement and compare the mobile AR interface with 1) the Personal Computer (PC) based choreography generator and 2) the mobile application for choreography generation. Our aim is to investigate the effects of different interactive techniques of the same application on user experience. We also investigate how AR affects user experience on training tools. The results of the experiments are important in understanding the impacts of different interaction techniques on user experience, as well as understanding the effects of AR on training applications. In this study, we provide an important contribution presenting a choreography application bridging the gap in the creative technological field. This study also contributes in evaluating aspects of NUI with respect to user experience.

The rest of the paper is structured in this way; Section 2 discusses related work. Section 3, 4 and 5 discuss the PC based, the mobile application and the AR based interfaces respectively. In Section 6, we discuss the experiments that we carried out and share the results obtained. Finally, in Section 7 we discuss the results, challenges and future work.

II. Related work

As the digitization of choreographing continues, different approaches have been explored to fully embrace technology for this creative process. However, the lack of standards with regards to development of choreograph applications slows down the advances of the development process of these applications. Therefore, as attempts to digitize choreography appear many open questions in relation to the support tools and consensus on the standards exist [7]. Standardizing choreography applications remains a major challenge. This has seen different choreographing tools being developed. Lack of standards allows creativity thereby encouraging more developers to come up with different idea. However, at the same time this leads to development of applications that lack a proper structure.

As early as the 1960s digital tools were introduced for choreography generation. The first choreographing computer system was developed in 1967. It was influenced by the need to create dance annotations without the need of a physical space or the physical dancers [10]. The system developed made use of a two dimensional interface, which utilized stick figure representation of dancers displayed on the computer screen. The choreographers crafted dance annotations using different buttons and controls to control the stick figure representations. The system played an important role in crafting a way for choreographing in the digital space. It was initially developed for ballet dancing, although with time it included other choreographs. However, the major weakness of such a system is dependence on 2D which hinders the natural feel of the interface. Furthermore, early systems suffered from limited input techniques and low processing power of computers. However, the modern century has seen an increase in processing power and the availability of different input techniques.

As digital tools evolved augmented reality has been incoperated in different applications. AR has gained a lot of use in teaching, training and visualization for many different institutions over the last decade [9]. Choreography has also embraced AR and virtual reality in recent years. An interactive mixed reality system for stage management and choreography is mentioned in [11]. The system developed is a hybrid choreography system that uses both virtual reality and augmented reality to achieve the desired goals. The system facilitates planning for stage shows and events. It makes use of head mounted devices to allow the choreographer to design choreographs for 3D generated characters. Furthermore, 3D pops can be used in stage set up to visualize how the real stage will look like. These 3D props include different stage set up items like drums and guitars. Choreographers can define different choreographs and play them on the miniature stage. Interior designers can also use this mixed reality stage. However, the major downside of this approach is the dependence on bulky and expensive hardware. Furthermore, it requires a lot of space for setting up the miniature stage, making it difficult for mobile users. However, this cumbersome approach to AR has been improved by recent advances in mobile hand-held devices like smart phones [12].

Another digital approach to dance learning that is based on a Web3D environment is described in [13]. This interactive system realizes dance animations for training and education. Using the application a choreographer can compose various dance annotations. The Web3D environment is effective for interactive dance steps observation, slow movement of fast steps and different angles of view. The choreographer is presented with a rich interface that enables the creation of choreographs with a good zooming level. The system enables the dancer to learn the annotations defined by the choreographer from different angles and speed. This 3D animation environment provides an easy way for dancers and choreographers to perform their work without the need of a physical platform. However, the interface is effective on desktop browsers. In this approach portability is a challenge.

Much work has been conducted to compare different interactive techniques. A study mentioned in [1] investigates the usability of the mouse-based and touch based interactive approaches in manipulating objects in a 3D virtual environment. In the study, they measure subjective aspects such as fatigue, workload, and preference. The researchers used docking tasks on participants to accomplish the investigation. The experiments were conducted in a well controlled environment, which allowed the users to continuously give feedback. The results were important in showing that the two approaches provide relatively similar levels of precision, however time of interaction differs. The subjective results also showed which of the interactive techniques users preferred. The study conducted contributed to the study of interactive techniques and usability of applications. However, as per our knowledge there is no work comparing the different interactive techniques on user experience for choreographing applications which also takes AR into consideration. Therefore, our study focuses mainly on user experience on a choreographing tool. Furthermore, we focus on AR for training and education. We seek to develop a clear understanding on the effects of mobile AR on user experience.

III. PC based interface

We first developed a desktop application for choreography generation. We engaged various stakeholders in the arts field to obtain the necessary functionality of a choreography application. This interactive process played a big role in crafting the control for the characters in the choreographing scene. In the application, we limit choreography animation to movement only, for the sake of simplicity.

The interface is a 3D choreographing environment that a choreographer uses to define different annotations. The presented stage is rich in props and presents a well modeled stage that resembles real stages for theaters. The choreographer is presented with controls to add dancers and props into the stage. The props that can be added include trees and boxes. Figure 1 shows the PC based interface with dancers and props added. The choreography generator interface can be customized to suit well for different set ups ,this enables flexibility to choreographers. In this way users can define their stages in different ways depending on the type of choreographing they are working on. Furthermore, individual character profile for the dancer can be created when adding a character, the profile contains attributes such as name, age, gender and height. This functionality allows the choreographer to define 3D virtual characters with attributes that makes it easier for the real performing artists to follow in order to understand their roles in the choreography.

The stage can be viewed from different angles, allowing the choreographer and the dancer to view the defined annotations from various views. The user can zoom into and out of the

Figure 1. A screen shot from the PC based interface showing props added.

scene using a mouse, and also rotate the scene to view it from different angles. The interface provides high levels of zooming that permits both the choreographer and the dancers to view the defined annotations clearly.

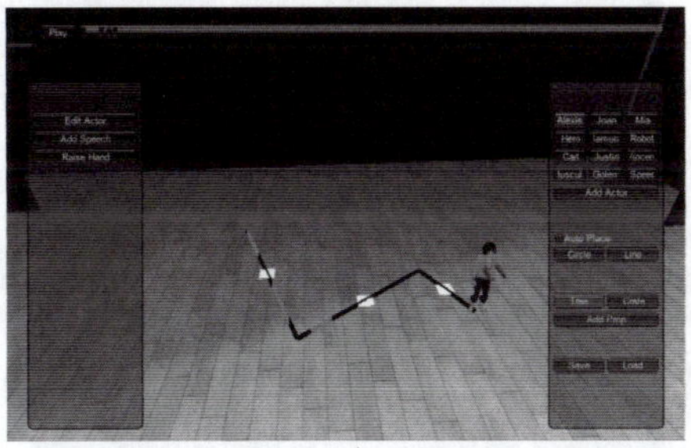

Figure 2. PC based interface: draw path.

To add a dancer into the scene the user utilizes the "add dancer" button, then selects the character from the presented grid. Once the dancer is added into the scene the choreographer can then define the path that the dancer must follow. The "draw path" button is used to set the scene into a mode for defining the path. The user uses the mouse to drag the character along the path to follow. A line trail is used to show the user the path they are defining as shown in Figure 2. After defining the choreography the "play" button is used to play the defined choreography. While the scene is playing the choreographer can use a slider to control the speed of the characters.

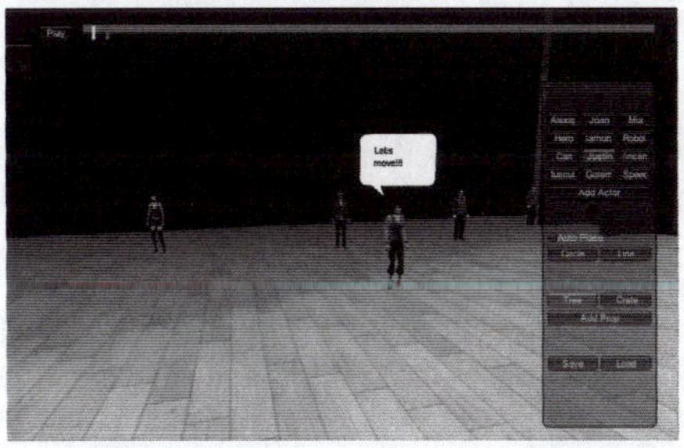

Figure 3. PC based interface: text bubble.

Other animations include a bubble to keep track of any text that a performing artist utters in the scene, and also the ability to raise hands as a sign for different signals. The choreographer can set different signals that dancers use in the scene, including voice signals which come in the form of note bubbles on the interface. The bubble carries a message that a character must utter as shown in Figure 3. This is analogous to a lead dancer hailing out instructions during the dance or an actor telling his lines.

IV. Mobile Application Interface

The PC based choreography generator functions as the foundation for the mobile application for choreography generation and the AR application. Mobile touch screens such as those of phones and tablets remove reliance on the keyboard and mouse for interaction, and present the touch based interaction technique. The touch based approach present a new dimension of controlling the characters and interacting with the interface. This interface is designed to function on hand-held devices of different screen sizes.

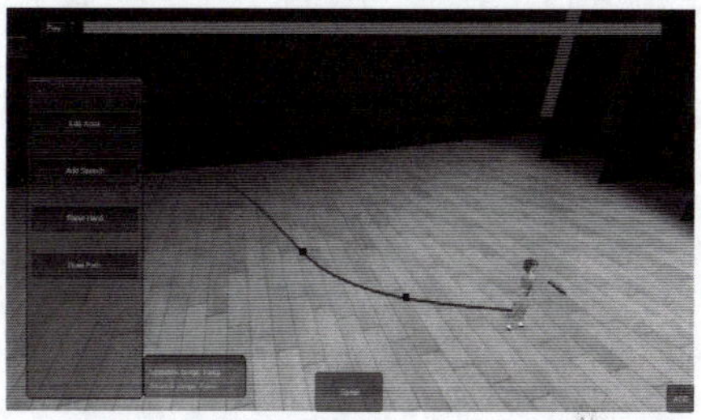

Figure 4. Mobile application interface: draw path.

The application retains the same functionality and graphics as the PC based application, but relies on the finger to define different controls. The user can select the actors to add into the scene by touching a specific button from the character grid presented in the interface. Once the character has been added the finger is used to draw the path the character follows. The user uses his/her finger to drag the character towards a path to follow. A line trailer utility is developed to set the trail behind the path to show the user the path being defined as shown in Figure 4. Drawing the path using the finger allows a natural way of performing this task. This enables an easy way for the user to achieve the required result, in addition it facilitates defining paths that are difficult to achieve using the mouse.

To play the scene the "play" button is used. Whilst playing the choreography the choreographer can view the scene from different angles and zooming levels, by utilizing the touch screen. To zoom in or out the interface allows the simultaneous use of two fingers to open up or close down the interface. Rotating the scene is achieved by dragging the view towards the required viewing angle using just one finger. The mobile application also allows the user to add different props to decorate the scene. The underlying visual graphics for the PC based interface and the mobile application interface are generally the same with a little difference owing to the nature of mobile devices' screens.

V. AR Based Interface

Mobile AR presents an interesting approach to interface development. AR changes the users' real view by superimposing computer generated graphics using a smart-phone screen or a headset. AR is important in choreographing as it takes away the need for physical resources to set up a choreographing environment. Using AR a virtual stage can be created anywhere and virtual 3D characters can be added.

The AR based interface presents the same functionality as the two previous interfaces. However, the graphical interface of the AR based application differs significantly due to the nature of AR. The AR application is a mobile based AR tool that utilizes marker based detection. The application uses marker-based augmented reality approach. The marker is used as the stage set up required to initiate the interface. Marker based AR uses a camera and a visual marker to determine the center, orientation and range of its spherical coordinate system [3]. The marker used for this application is shown in Figure 5.

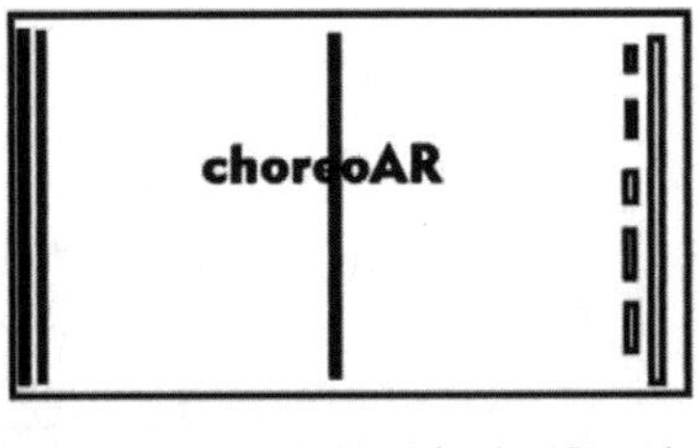

Figure 5. Template designed for the AR marker.

Using AR, different real world tangible objects can be added on top of the marker apart from the computer generated imagery. This aspect gives the choreographer ability to use different real world tangible objects. Therefore, using AR the stage is not a fixed environment but rather it allows the choreographer to creatively define different environments for choreographing. AR's inherent nature provides a unique opportunity to create authentic extraordinary environments that make use of both digital and physical material [14]. In Figure 6 two physical objects are utilized as props and an image as a background scenery. In mobile or PC based interfaces only computer generated imagery can be used in the background for stage setup.

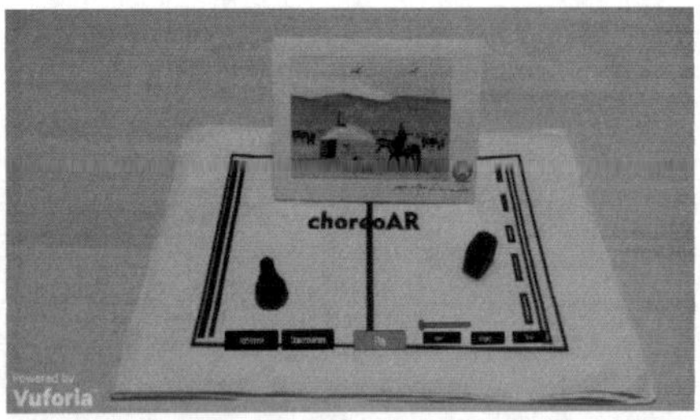

Figure 6. A screen shot from the AR interface, which shows interactive buttons, physical objects as props and an image as background scenery.

The user utilizes his/her mobile device's camera to view the marker and initiate the interface. To interact with the interface the user also utilizes the touch screen of the mobile device. Once the marker is detected the user is presented with the application's interface on the mobile device's screen. The interface presented has controls for adding a dancer, drawing the path, adding props to decorate scene, controlling speed of the characters and resetting the scene. To add the characters into the scene the "add button" is utilized. The user can then position the dancers anywhere on top of the marker. To define the choreography the user drags the 3D character along the path to follow; this is achieved using the finger. The line trailer utility of unity is also utilized to draw a trailer behind the path being defined, so that the choreographer has a visual aspect of the path being defined. Figure 7 shows a simple path defined for a single character.

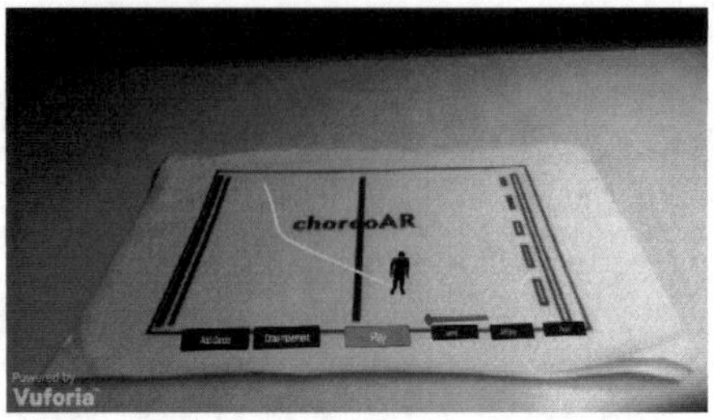

Figure 7. AR based interface: draw path.

Figure 8. A screen shot from the AR interface, which shows characters and a prop added.

A play button to play the defined choreography is presented to the user as shown in Figure 7. Whilst playing the defined choreography, the user can control the speed of the characters, view the choreography from different angles and zoom in or out. To achieve different zooming levels the user moves the mobile device closer or further from the marker, whilst keeping the marker at a fixed position in the screen. This same functionality can also be achieved by moving the marker closer to the device's camera, whilst keeping mobile device on a fixed position. In order to view the scene from different angles the user can move the camera around the marker. The scene can also be reset to correct any errors that arise. This functionality enables the choreographer to explore the interface further without fear of making errors. Figure 8 shows the implementation of the AR interface with a tree and four dancer characters added into the scene.

VI. EXPERIMENTS

Experiments were conducted to evaluate the performance of users on the three developed interfaces, the PC based version, the mobile application for choreography generation and the AR based version. We investigated four of Nielsen's factors of usability: satisfaction, effectiveness, ease of learning and efficiency [15]. We obtained satisfaction levels from the post user questionnaire form. The effectiveness is shown by how the test subjects completed the given tasks. The user's feedback on how easy it is to learn the system gives an indication of the time needed to learn the different interfaces. The time scores determines the efficiency of the interface.

A. *Software and Hardware*

To develop the three interfaces we used Unity3D software, a cross-platform game engine used to develop video games for computers, consoles, mobile devices and websites [16]. Unity is a powerful platform for developing 3D based graphical applications with rich interfaces. The PC based interface is available as a standalone desktop application or as a web based application, but works only on browsers that support Unity3D plugin. The user interacts with the interface using a keyboard and a mouse.

The mobile application for choreography generation is designed for hand-held devices. For the experiments we published the application for Android devices. The users use the touch screen to interact with the interface. The AR application makes use of an additional plugin for Unity3D named Vuforia. Vuforia facilitates for the creation of robust AR applications on the Unity3D platform. It uses computer vision technology to recognize and track planar images and simple 3D objects in real-time [17]. Vuforia and Unity3D have a seamless combination that enables the development of rich interfaces.

To test the PC application the participants accessed it as a web application from the Mozilla Firefox web browser, and also as a standalone desktop application. To test the mobile AR application and the mobile application we used an LG G4 stylus and a Samsung S5. These devices have good cameras that are very effective for AR applications.

B. Participants

We used a total of 15 unpaid test subjects for the experiments. From the 15, 9 were males and 6 were females. Their ages ranged between 19 and 28, with a mean age of 24. We selected the participants based on their ability to use computers. The experiments were carried out primarily to evaluate the usability of the applications therefore the use of non-professional test subjects, this is a preliminary study. With respect to expertise in AR, four participants had experience with AR applications whilst the others stated that they had no significant previous experience.

C. Tasks

For this comparative study, we chose these simple tasks that are easier to handle for users since all of them are first time users of a choreographing application. The participants were expected to complete these tasks on the three interfaces. The participants had to add a dancer to the left and to the right of scene. After adding the dancer, the user then adds a prop into the scene, the prop being the tree or the box for decoration. After adding the prop the user then draws a simple path for the dancer to follow. Finally, the user is expected to play the defined choreography. In addition to this task, users were required to zoom in and out, and also increase speed of characters in the scene. This was to allow users to explore the interfaces further.

The four tasks that the users were expected to perform:

- Task 1) Add dancer to the left and right of the scene
- Task 2) Add prop to the left and right of the scene
- Task 3) Draw a simple path from the back to the front
- Task 4) Play the choreography (free play time)

D. Procedure

The participants performed the four tasks in sequence on each of the three interfaces. The participants were each given a brief description of the task to be performed. During the experiments, our participants used the interfaces in a random order to avoid task adaptation and to obtain fair scores for the three interfaces. We encouraged the users to think aloud during the process and we recorded their feedback at each stage.

We recorded the time the users took to complete each tasks to obtain the objective test results. We only recorded completion time for the first three tasks, whilst the last task of playing the scene had a free time so as to allow the users to explore the system more.

At the end of the experiment the users were presented with post test questionnaire that assisted in obtaining subjective analysis of the experiments. The users gave feedback on satisfaction, the pleasure they experienced, time to learn the interface, their frustration levels and they also gave feedback on their preferred interface. Difficult measures of using the interfaces in the type of mental stress and physical stress scores were also attained. Furthermore, we required our participants to express their preferred interface from the three given interfaces. These results gave us a fair comparison of the interfaces to have a conclusive analysis.

The user experience test conducted on the interfaces investigated the following issues:

- Users' awareness and experience with AR technology
- Users' preference on touch based or pointer based interactive technique
- Users' reaction to the different zooming approaches
- How the users interact with the two interfaces.
- Time taken to complete tasks

To measure the different aspects of user experience we used a scale 1 to 10. Satisfaction, pleasure, physical stress and mental stress level were attained from this scale. We also expected users to give a feedback on the effects of the different interactive approaches on viewing the choreography from different angles, and also the effects of the different zooming interactive techniques.

E. Results

The results of the experiments are shown the Tables 1-6. Table 1 gives mean time scores, Table 2 gives mean mental stress scores, Table 3 gives mean physical stress scores, Table 4 gives mean satisfactions scores, Table 5 gives mean pleasure scores and Table 6 gives mean frustration scores. Best scores are highlighted in bold.

TABLE I. TIME RESULTS[IN SECONDS]

	PC based	Mobile application	AR interface
Task 1	9.3±1.2	8.3±1.0	**7.5±1.2**
Task 2	**8.9±1.2**	9.0±2.5	9.1±1.3
Task 3	12.4±2.10	7.2±1.2	**6.5±0.8**
Task 4	free time	free time	free time
Average	7.7±1.1	6.1±1.2	**5.4±0.8**

The results in Table 1 indicate that completing the tasks was generally faster on the touch based interactive approaches of the AR and the mobile application interface as compared to the mouse approach of the PC based interface. The total average time for completing the first three tasks in sequence is 30.6 seconds for the PC based interface, 24.5 seconds for the mobile application interface and 23.1 seconds for the AR based interface. The total average scores show that AR

TABLE II. MENTAL STRESS RESULTS [IN LIKERT SCALE 1-10]

	PC based	Mobile application	AR interface
Task 1	3.1±0.9	3.0±0.7	**2.9±0.9**
Task 2	1.5±0.8	**1.4±1.0**	1.7±1.1
Task 3	6.7±1.00	2.9±1.2	**1.3±0.7**
Task 4	1.5±1.1	2.0±1.0	**1.3±1.2**
Average	3.2±0.9	2.3±1.0	**1.8±0.9**

TABLE III. PHYSICAL STRESS RESULTS [IN LIKERT SCALE]

	PC based	Mobile application	AR interface
Task 1	**1.5±1.3**	2.0±0.7	4.3±1.0
Task 2	**1.6±1.2**	2.8±0.4	4.2±1.3
Task 3	2.9±0.9	1.7±3.6	**1.35±0.7**
Task 4	**1.6±1.6**	4.8±0.7	6.6±1.7
Average	**1.9±1.2**	2.8±1.4	4.1±1.1

TABLE IV. SATISFACTION RESULTS [IN LIKERT SCALE 1-10]

	PC based	Mobile application	AR interface
Task 1	**7.0±1.1**	6.5±1.2	6.8±0.8
Task 2	7.9±0.9	7.3±1.3	**8.0±0.5**
Task 3	6.7±2.1	7.64±0.2	**8.2±0.8**
Task 4	7.2±0.5	7.0±0.9	**8.6±1.0**
Average	7.2±1.2	7.1±0.8	**7.8±0.8**

TABLE V. PLEASURE RESULTS [IN LIKERT SCALE 1-10]

	PC based	Mobile application	AR interface
Task 1	7.0±1.1	6.7±1.6	**7.4±1.0**
Task 2	7.6±1.0	7.6±1.2	**8.0±1.1**
Task 3	6.7±1.2	8.2±1.3	**8.6±0.9**
Task 4	6.6±0.7	7.0±1.1	**8.9±0.6**
Average	6.9±0.9	7.4±1.5	**8.2±0.9**

TABLE VI. FRUSTRATION RESULTS [IN LIKERT SCALE]

	PC based	Mobile application	AR interface
Task 1	1.90±0.8	**1.4±0.9**	2.3±0.9
Task 2	**1.4±1.30**	1.8±1.1	1.8±0.9
Task 3	3.1±0.8	2.8±0.9	**1.0±0.8**
Task 4	3.0±0.9	4.10±0.8	**1.8±0.9**
Average	2.4±0.9	2.5±0.8	**1.7±0.9**

produces faster task completion rates compared to PC based interface and the mobile application interface. Especially *Task 3* drawing path shows significant difference on the mean time values. Drawing path on the mobile based application and the AR interface is performed drastically faster than on the PC based. The AR has 6.5 seconds , 7.2 seconds for the mobile application and 12.4 seconds for the PC based interface. Furthermore, we note from the standard deviation scores that the divergence of AR results is rather small, showing that the task was performed almost similar by all users. Drawing the path on the touch based interfaces using the finger was simpler and faster as compared to using the mouse to define the path. The time scores generally show that the touch based approach is more efficient than the mouse based approach as they produce faster task completion rates. Furthermore, although time was not measured for *Task 4* it was observed that zooming in and out or changing the viewing angles was faster in the AR based interface. This further highlighted the efficiency of AR as it gives users a quicker way of achieving different viewing positions.

The levels of mental stress on all the three interfaces are generally low owed to the simplicity of the tasks and the interfaces, as shown in Table 2. However, we note a significant difference on the result for the PC based interface when drawing the path. This was a result of the approach that required more time to grasp. The mental stress scores for the PC based is 6.7, whilst it is 2.9 for the mobile application interface and 1.3 for the AR interface. This shows that the users experienced a lot of stress mentally in this task. Furthermore, the standard deviation score of 1.0 shows that almost all the users agree on the high mental effort needed to perform *Task 3* on the PC based interface. On the AR interface users experienced the least mental stress on three of the four tasks.

Physical stress is significantly high on the AR interface. The AR interface has an average physical stress of 5.6 as compared to 3.1 and 1.8 of the mobile application and PC based interface respectively. *Task 4* "playing the scene" shows the highest level of physical stress experienced by the users on the AR interface. Having a physical stress score of 6.60 as compared to 1.60 and 2.75 of the PC based interface and mobile application interface respectively. This highlights one big disadvantage of mobile AR on user experience as it requires more physical effort over time. However, for *Task 3* we observe that AR has the lowest physical stress. This result highlights that users needed less physical effort when drawing the path using the finger as compared to using the mouse. The high levels of physical stress on the AR interface are due to the movement of hands, as the user moves the device closer and further from the marker to achieve different angles and zooming levels. This effect is also the cause for the physical stress scores on the mobile application as the fingers need to constantly interact with the interface for any activity. Thus, the touch based interfaces require users to use more physical effort to perform the tasks. From Table 3, best scores are achieved most on the PC based interface highlighting that the mouse as an interaction device requires low physical effort. The main source of physical stress on the PC based interface is the movement of the mouse through small movements of the hand while the arm lies in rest-up position. This explains the low levels obtained in this regard.

Users expressed high levels of satisfaction from completing their tasks on all the interfaces. These results are attributed to the simplicity of the interfaces themselves. The standard deviation scores that are generally less than 1.0 also indicate that users experienced almost similar effects. As shown in Table 4 users expressed more satisfaction on the AR interface as compared to the two other interfaces. For *Task* 4 the satisfaction scores are 7.2 for the PC based interface, 7.0 for the mobile application interface and 8.6 for the AR based interface. These high scores are attributed to the fact that users managed to complete all their tasks to a satisfactory level. Users expressed satisfaction in the quicker and easier way they managed to move around the scene using the AR interface.

Table 5 shows the scores recorded for the pleasure experienced by users when performing the tasks. The results show significant excitement when using the AR interface. The main excitement is brought by the curiosity that the interface introduces as stated by [8]. On all the tasks the highest pleasure is recorded on the AR interfaces with scores of 7.4, 8.0, 8.6 and

8.9, for *Task 1* up to *Task 4* respectively. Of particular interest are the results for *Task 4* where the users were allowed a free time to explore the interfaces. The pleasure results for the PC based interface, the mobile application interface and the AR interface are 6.6, 7.0 and 8.9 respectively. These results show a significant difference; on the AR interface users experienced the greatest pleasure. The ability to zoom in and out of the scene by only moving the mobile device closer or further from the marker, brought about such a compelling effect to the users when using the AR interface. This approach of changing viewing position gave users an easier way to move around the scene. This ability also reduces the time to achieve the required zooming position or angle as compared to using the touch screen to zoom in or using the mouse to zoom into the scene. Therefore on the overall the AR interface is more effective than the other two interfaces. The results also indicate that users experienced more excitement on the mobile application than on the PC based interface.

The mobile based interface produced high level of errors when the user was zooming in and out of the scene, thus more frustration as shown in Table 6. This was largely due to the user rotating the scene instead of zooming. A number of errors were also experienced on the PC based interface, but this was less than the ones on the mobile based. This result is attributed to the level of control a pointer device has on the scene largely due to the small point of contact with interface as compared to the finger's surface. However, we note that with the AR based interface this error does not exist as the AR interface allows a more natural way of zooming which is analogous to moving closer to an object to view it clearly. The frustration scores for *Task 4* demonstrate the effects of the errors on the interface as the users were frustrated on interfaces with many errors. The score for *Task 4* for the PC based interface, the mobile application and the AR interface is 3.00, 4.10 and 1.81 respectively. This shows that users were less frustrated on the AR interface whilst playing the scene. This is largely due to the easiness of changing viewing angles and zooming levels. However, we note that when adding the characters the AR presents the highest frustration scores (2.3 compared to 2.1 and 1.43 of the PC based interface and mobile application interface respectively). This result is caused by the tilting effect of the mobile device whilst the user is positioning the characters. Therefore, this makes it difficult for the user to correctly position the characters in the scene in the way they wanted. On the contrary, in the PC based interface and the mobile application this difficulty does not exist. Table 6 also highlights that frustration levels differed on the tasks the users were performing on the different interfaces. The AR interface gave the least frustration levels on the last two tasks whilst the PC based interface gave the least on *Task 2* and for *Task 1* the mobile application interface gave best result. The main source of frustration for the AR interface is the tilting of the device whilst performing tasks that are more effectively done with a static device, such as adding the character on the scene.

The simplicity of the interfaces is further shown by the "easy to learn" results we obtained from the users, which have scores of 8.4 for the AR based application, 8.01 for the mobile application interface and 8.10 for the PC based interface. The AR interface has fewer visual buttons than the other two interfaces this makes it easier to learn as shown by the results. Generally, the interfaces provided the same basic functions and controls that explains why the scores for the easiness to learn are very close to each other. It is of high importance to develop interfaces that are easy to grasp for the users, especially for applications that are used in training and education. This was also demonstrated by the willingness of the participants to explore the interfaces further. This also helps the users retain over time.

After completing the experiments, we also asked which interface for choreography generation the users prefer best after having performed tasks on all the three interfaces. Seven preferred the AR interface, four preferred mobile application and four preferred the PC based interface. These results show that the AR based interface was the preferred option by the users. From the users that already had prior experience with AR only one of the users did not choose the AR based application as a preferred interface for choreography generation.

VII. Discussion

The experiments were carried out to complete the same task on three different interfaces using different interactive techniques: 1) the PC based application that uses pointer based interaction approach utilizing a mouse and keyboard, 2) the mobile application interface and 3) the AR application that used touch based interaction approach. The results obtained from the experiments contributes to the study of how different interaction techniques affect user experience and also the effects of augmented reality on user experience.

The touch based approaches produced faster task completion times compared to the mouse based approach. The touch based interactive approach of the AR interface and the mobile application showed faster times using the finger to draw path demonstrating the power of interfaces that provide a natural way of interaction to the users [1]. Using the finger to define choreographs presented a natural approach to define movement as compared to using the mouse, this explains the significant time differences. The AR interface gives the best overall task completion rate compared to that of the PC based and mobile application interfaces. However, the mobile application and the AR interface show a small difference of 1.4 seconds since both approaches use the touch based interactive approach. Furthermore, the ability to zoom in and out of the scene by only moving the hand-held device closer to the scene gave users a quicker way to complete the task. This further demonstrates the effectiveness of having interfaces that facilitates a natural way to complete the tasks. Thus, interfaces which facilitate a natural way to complete tasks possess a great advantage in as far as user experience is concerned.

The results showed that when adding the dancer and the props into the scene the rate of errors was high in the AR interface as compared to the other two interfaces. This result is influenced by the changing position of the interface as the phone tilts or is held in an unstable manner and also the underlying design of the interfaces. Maintaining a mobile device in a stable position during interaction is a big challenge for all mobile AR applications. This is attributed to the natural hand tremor [18]. This effectively undermines AR's effectiveness for mobile devices in applications that require accurate positioning. Nonetheless, depending on the application these errors can be tolerated. However, AR interface had no errors associated with zooming or rotating the scene since this was achieved by only moving closer or around the scene. The mobile application had more errors in this regard compared to the PC based application owing to the larger surface area of the finger as compared to the mouse pointer. The mouse facilitates an easier zooming approach compared to using the finger. The mouse utilizes the scroll wheel to change the levels by scrolling it towards the required direction. In addition, changing the viewing angles by dragging the scene using the mouse pointer produces faster and more accurate results, compared to using the finger on the touch screen of the mobile device. This effect is influenced by the small contact area of the mouse pointer which gives the user more control to perform the required task. The touch based approach is efficient, however care has to be given when dealing with interfaces that have many controls in the same line. This gave many errors on the mobile based application where a user was zooming but instead found himself/herself rotating the scene. This is a drawback for the touch approach. However, rarely experienced on the PC based approach due to the small area of contact on the mouse pointer as compared to the larger surface area of the finger.

It very important to develop interfaces that are easy to learn. The simplicity of the graphical user interface goes a long way in achieving faster "time to learn" scores as demonstrated by the results from the experiments. Time to learn eventually affects the usability of the interface, especially with regards to training tools. Interfaces that are simple to understand also help boost the users' retention rate. In our experiments, the interfaces were easy to learn, this made users more interested in exploring different functionality of the interfaces. We also noted that AR interface produced the best "time to learn" score. This also led to the interface being the preferred choice of the users, as they felt more relaxed while using the interface.

The results of the experiments also show that AR has an important part to play in crafting training tools as stated in [9]. It gives a compelling effect to the users and excitement through the curiosity it creates. Furthermore, AR allows the addition of physical objects into the scene in addition to the computer generated objects. For training applications this helps explore many objects to illustrate concepts without the need of completely changing the graphical interface. Therefore, AR allows flexibility in interface design. The user preference results demonstrate that AR has a great promise, this reenforces the findings in [14]. This demonstrates that AR is effective in teaching and training.

The AR interface affords users the ability to interact with the characters by only moving the phone around the marker. The ability to move closer to the dancers on the scene and easily shift the viewing angle provided pleasure and excitement to the users. This is similar to moving closer to an object or further from the object, which is a natural approach to changing positions. This approach gave users an easier and quicker way to move around the scene. However, mobile AR for hand-held devices presents high levels of physical stress on the hands of the user and also a high error rate when interacting with the touch screen as the mobile device tilts and shifts positions on the hand of the user. The interface requires a lot of physical effort from the user's hand to achieve the desired results, this in turn leads to the high levels of physical stress. Another contributing factor to physical stress in mobile AR is the screen size of the device as limited screen size tend to restrict the covered field of view as stated in [19], thereby forcing the user to continuous adjust viewing positions.

Therefore, wearable glasses or goggles can prove more effective for AR in training applications. For example, using wearable glasses like Google's cardboard the user does not need to continuously use the hand to position the mobile device correctly, but rather by positioning the eyes in the required position. This is an approach we leave as future work, it will give an understanding on the effects of wearable devices on AR and training tools. Furthermore, we intend to extend the interactive approach for the AR interface by allowing the choreographer to use virtual buttons on the marker and draw on the marker. In this approach the mobile phone screen becomes a merely viewing screen but no longer the means of interaction. To achieve more of the natural interface approach voice commands will be important in the future work. For the time being, voice is used as a means to enter text into speech bubbles using the Google speech API. Therefore, future work will complement the current interfaces by having voice commands to add and control characters especially on the AR interface. This future work study focuses more on the natural user interface aspect by having an application that combines virtual buttons and voice commands to control characters in a real environment superimposed with 3D graphics. It is also imperative to extend the interfaces to include a virtual reality interface and compare user experience too.

VIII. Conclusion and Future Work

In the study, we designed and implemented three interfaces for choreography generation a PC based interface, a mobile application interface and an AR based interface from which we compared the performance of users in terms of user experience. The interfaces allow a choreographer to define choreographs and makes the choreographer in charge of the actors just like in the real world. The results indicated that using touch based approaches the users obtained faster task completion rates as compared to using a mouse on the PC based interface. Users were more comfortable completing tasks using natural approaches, for example defining choreographs using their finger on the touch based interface. The result demonstrates the need to develop natural user interfaces to improve user experience. Excitement and pleasure obtained was highest on the AR interface, followed by the mobile application interface and lowest on the PC based interface.

The results of the experiment showed that AR has a big role to play in the development of training and educational applications. Researchers can build upon this to further investigate AR coupled with natural user interface aspects like voice and gestures. Another aspect to be implemented in the future includes virtual buttons and virtual drawing of paths where the user only interacts with the marker and not the mobile device screen. In this approach the mobile device screen becomes just a screen to view the real world but the user only interacts with the marker. We plan to add more forms of movement and special animation for choreography generation and test the interfaces on experts working in the arts domain.

Acknowledgment

The authors would like to thank Güneş Karababa, Çağatay Koç and Ege Sarıoğlu for the fruitful discussion sessions and their invaluable ideas.

REFERENCES

[1] L. Besançon, P. Issartel, M. Ammi, and P. Isenberg, "Usability comparison of mouse, touch and tangible inputs for 3d data manipulation," CoRR, vol. abs/1603.08735, 2016, pp. 1–10, URL: http://arxiv.org/abs/1603.08735/[accessed: 2017-02-01].

[2] R. M. Yilmaz, "Educational magic toys developed with augmented reality technology for early childhood education," Computer Humam Behaviour Journal, vol. 54, 2016, pp. 240–248, ISBN: 0747-5632, URL: http://dx.doi.org/10.1016/j.chb.2015.07.040 [accessed: 2017-02-02].

[3] A. B. Craig, Understanding augmented reality: concepts and applications. Morgan Kaufmann, 2013, ISBN: 978-0-240-82408-6.

[4] G. A. Lee, U. Yang, Y. Kim, D. Jo, K. Kim, J. Kim, and J. Choi, "Freeze-set-go interaction method for handheld mobile augmented reality environments," in Proceedings of the 16th ACM Symposium on Virtual Reality Software and Technology November 18–22, 2009, Kyoto, Japan. ACM, Nov. 2009, pp. 143–146, ISBN: 978-1-60558-869-8, URL: http://doi.acm.org/10.1145/1643928.1643961/ [accessed: 2017-02-01].

[5] K. R. Bujak, I. Radu, R. Catrambone, B. Macintyre, R. Zheng, and G. Golubski, "A Psychological Perspective on Augmented Reality in the Mathematics Classroom," Computer Education Journal, vol. 68, Oct. 2013, pp. 536–544, ISSN: 0360-1315.

[6] "Pokémon Go Brings Augmented Reality to a Mass Audience," Jun. 2016, URL: http://www.nytimes.com/2016/07/12/technology/pokemon-go-brings-augmented-reality-to-a-mass-audience.html?_r=1 [accessed: 2017-02-02].

[7] S. F. Alaoui, K. Carlson, and T. Schiphorst, "Choreography As Mediated Through Compositional Tools for Movement: Constructing A Historical Perspective," in Proceedings of the 2014 International Workshop on Movement and Computing June 16–17, 2014, Paris, France. ACM, Jun. 2014, pp. 1–6, ISBN: 978-1-4503-2814-2, URL: http://doi.acm.org/10.1145/2617995.2617996/ [accessed: 2017-02-01].

[8] G. Chang, P. Morreale, and P. Medicherla, "Applications of augmented reality systems in education," in Proceedings of Society for Information Technology Teacher Education International Conference March 29, 2010, San Diego, USA. Association for the Advancement of Computing in Education (AACE), March 2010, pp. 1380–1385, URL: https://www.learntechlib.org/p/33549 [accessed: 2017-02-01].

[9] L. K., "Augmented reality in education and training," TechTrends: Linking Research and Practice to Improve Learning, vol. 56, no. 2, 2012, pp. 13–21, ISSN: 8756-3894,URL: https://www.learntechlib.org/p/65711/ [accessed: 2017-02-01].

[10] A. M. Noll and A. Hutchinson, "Choreography and computers," Dance Magazine, vol. 41, 1967, pp. 43–45.

[11] W. Broll, S. Grünvogel, I. Herbst, I. Lindt, M. M. J. Ohlenburg, and M. Wittkämper, "Interactive Props and Choreography Planning with the Mixed Reality Stage," in Proceedings of the 3rd International Conference Entertainment Computing (ICEC) , September 1–3, 2004, Eindhoven, The Netherlands,. Springer Berlin Heidelberg, Sep. 2004, pp. 185–192, ISBN: 978-3-540-28643-1, URL: http://dx.doi.org/10.1007/978-3-540-28643-1_25/ [accessed: 2017-02-01].

[12] D. W. F. Van Krevelen and R. Poelman, "A survey of augmented reality technologies, applications and limitations," International Journal of Virtual Reality, vol. 9, 2010, pp. 1–20, URL: http://citeseerx.ist.psu.edu/viewdoc/download?doi=10.1.1.454.8190&rep=rep1&type=pdf/ [accessed: 2017-02-01].

[13] D. Davcev, V. Trajkovic, S. Kalajdziski, and S. Celakoski, "Augmented reality environment for dance learning," in Proceedings of the Information Technology Research and Education International Conference (ITRE) August 11–13, 2003, New Jersey, USA, Aug. 2003, pp. 189–193, URL: http://ieeexplore.ieee.org/stamp/stamp.jsp?tp=&arnumber=1270600&isnumber=28360/ [accessed: 2017-02-01].

[14] M. Dunleavy, C. Dede, and R. Mitchell, "Affordances and limitations of immersive participatory augmented reality simulations for teaching and learning," Journal of Science Education and Technology, vol. 18, 2009, pp. 7–22, ISSN: 1573-1839, URL: http://dx.doi.org/10.1007/s10956-008-9119-1/ [accessed: 2017-02-01].

[15] J. Nielsen, Usability Engineering. Morgan Kaufmann Publishers Inc., 1993, ISBN: 0125184050.

[16] "Unity3D," URL: http://www.unity3d.com [accessed: 2017-02-02].

[17] "Vuforia," URL: http://www.vuforia.com [accessed: 2017-02-02].

[18] T. Vincent, L. Nigay, and T. Kurata, "Handheld Augmented Reality: Effect of registration jitter on cursor-based pointing techniques," in Proceedings of the 25th Conference on l'Interaction Homme-Machine (IHM) November 12–15, 2013, Bordeaux, France. ACM, Nov. 2013, pp. 1–6, URL: https://hal.inria.fr/hal-00875440/file/1-1.pdf/ [accessed: 2017-02-01].

[19] O. Bimber and R. Raskar, "Modern approaches to augmented reality," in ACM SIGGRAPH 2006 Courses July 30–August 03, 2006, Boston, USA. ACM, Jul. 2006, pp. 1–88, ISBN: 1-59593-364-6, URL: http://doi.acm.org/10.1145/1185657.1185796/ [accessed: 2017-02-01].

Product Design in the Smart City

Investigation of priority needs in terms of human interaction in the Smart City

Marina Puyuelo Cazorla, Lola Merino Sanjuán, Mónica Val Fiel
Escuela Técnica Superior de Ingeniería del Diseño ETSID
Universitat Politècnica de València, UPV
Valencia, Spain
e-mail: mapuca@ega.upv.es, mamesan@ega.upv.es, movalfie@ega.upv.es

***Abstract*—The concept of Smart City refers to a developed city, which incorporates the required infrastructures and available technology to increase its economic and environmental sustainability, as well as the quality of life for its inhabitants. It involves a city equipped with the latest communication technologies in order to "function" by providing "intelligent" solutions to multiple issues. This control of technology in the management of resources, services and information in the city can increase the risk of threatening the interaction between people and the environment. In order to get feedback about people's concerns and priorities as future users of this Smart City, a preliminary research has been developed. This paper presents the study carried out at the School of Design Engineering, whose objective is to look for design concepts for the city, which increase the relationship of citizens with products and services intended for public use, and the "potential benefits" of the "smart city". The first results reveal that it is a priority to work on the urban elements which show citizens the contributions of technology to the care and welfare of the environment in which they operate.**

Keywords-Smart City; Shared Artefacts; Product Design; Smart products; Technology Design

I. INTRODUCTION

The Smart City is an emerging concept with a broad and diffuse scope, whose limits have yet to be defined, and where many initiatives are in the project phase. We highlight, as an essential feature, the implementation of Information and Communications Technologies (ICTs) in multiple existing products and services, and the connectivity of objects [1]. This development will make it possible to manage and control energy resources with greater efficiency, and provide a faster response to the constant maintenance requirements. It is understood that a digital platform will be constructed, which will make it possible to improve the society, environment and welfare of cities in a sustainable manner, and in accordance with the degree of "CONTROL" which technology allows. Everything offers controllable information in real time and, which will foreseeably result in a better response to citizens' needs. Public spaces have been transformed into more interesting and entertaining sites where many topics are shared and where everything is recorded [2].

The public space, which historically has been a meeting place open to all citizens, is now undergoing smart, as result of the implementation of the new communication technologies and their application in personal use devices. These devices have transferred part of the interaction that took place in the physical space, to a new public domain, which is partly physical and virtual, and is modifying many social habits and individual behaviours.

According to the European Smart Cities initiative, the six main elements, which constitute a Smart city [3] are: *Smart Mobility,* which gives priority to public transportation and "soft" transportation services. *Smart people,* which includes services that have an impact on comfort, health and safety, permanent learning and training, care for senior citizens, meeting points and leisure, etc. *Smart economy,* which relies on decentralized work areas, mobile offices and teleworking, entrepreneurship, development of co-working, etc.
Smart living, which focuses on the use of intelligent sensors that control confort and safety in buildings, sustainability, pollution and their remote management. *Smart Environment,* which focuses on optimising the smart grids through sustainable electricity production and management systems, controlling public and household lighting, integrating home automation systems, and through the coexistence of clean energy cogeneration processes. Finally *Smart Governance,* which involves communication and participation in the city's management, managing its employment, relations with the public administration, etc.

Furthermore, the European Commission has set a challenge and priority for these smart cities, to make it viable to reduce pollution by 40% in the short term, and thus improve the economy and the quality of citizens' lives. This approach prioritises investing in buildings, energy and transportation [4]. The role of ICTs is also essential for the development of these concepts, since they require the implementation of powerful infrastructures and communication systems, which permit data exchange and storage, as well as its analysis, in order to improve the processes, which have a repercussion on the citizens. Major investments are required to carry out this technological upgrade of our cities that, in 2020, will have billions of devices connected to Internet [5].

Faced with this highly technified, automated and virtual environment, we must address the need for tangible interaction with these concepts proposed and developed in the Smart City. We strongly believe in the pertinence of designing products for the environment, which have a physical presence, and with which, citizens directly become users.

This paper presents in Section II the Smart City as context for product design, and the need for interaction with users. In Section III, we point out the relevance of the *augmented city* concept and some projects that influence people's demands and expectations. The Research Methods and materials used in this local research are presented in Section IV, followed, in Section V, by some of the results from the research made. These results have allowed us to define in Section VI the scope of a design project, and to draw some specific proposals for the Smart City.Finally, some general conclusions are given.

II. Product Designs For The "Use" Of The Smart City

As claimed in the report *Smart City Trends* [6], there is no doubt that Smart Cities are a fertile sector for innovation, an open space where proposals and categories of services and products arise. This field opens up opportunities and new market challenges for industrial design and for companies, and it constitutes an enormous space for innovation. Based on the elements of the Smart City listed above, this prospective study features some areas of urban innovation. We are interested on some of them, such as products on a human scale, bicycles first, predictive systems, flexible furniture, outdoor offices, sustainable lighting and access to energy.

Coming from the Design Engineering sector, and having had experience in the development of projects for the public space [7] since 2001, the concept of Smart City has made it necessary, to devote a specific line of work to enhance the role of design in the development of elements for the users of this technological and sustainable city. The exhibition *Smart City, Design, Technologies and Services for the Citizens*, was the first outcome regarding the state of art of this sort of product design. Pioneer applications at present time, which merit attention to interrelate connectivity, energy efficiency with products for public use, power charge and generation systems for the citizens and pollution reduction by means of innovative devices [8].

In the framework of Smart Cities multiple developments can be integrated responding the new needs and the integration of communication technologies, which provide new services and knowledge for citizens. In particular, from the design sector dedicated to urban elements, five action areas were outline, at the Smart City Expo World Congress. These action areas are related to each other, and priority has been given to those, which have the greatest potential as innovative objects for the public space [9].

These five areas are planned to be thoroughly permeable with each other, and they focus on:

- Data processing systems for society, communication and information services and participation. Education, welfare, commitments, ideas, entrepreneurship, etc.
- Launching technologies and access to platforms and urban media.
- Sustainability and clean energies, fair water consumption, increase of green areas, etc.
- Products for welfare and leisure.
- Clean mobility, bicycles, car sharing and participation in energy generation.

The goal of our research is planning a practical design project for the city of Valencia. Since previous works have been realized analysing the urban elements and services, technologies to be implemented, materials, and systems of energy, we have made a prospective research of the potential target of users, attempting to know their needs and expectations. The outcome of this ethnographic research is to find out new possibilities and values for designing and innovation at the contemporary city.

III. The Augmented City

Closely linked to communication technologies in the urban scope and, consequently, to the Smart City, we highlight the "augmented city", which involves the new physical space, expanded by the supply of graphic formats and information generally derived from Internet.

Augmented Reality (AR) applications in the public space are creating a new dimension within the city, an overlapping layer consisting of information, which augments the experiences in real time of the individuals who interact simultaneously in their urban environment [10]. To cite several examples of these technologies in dynamic situations, we highlight the application for cell phones GeoTravel, the project proposed by architect Keiichi Matsuda, in which the virtual and the real form a continuum offering amazing possibilities, while also controlling the way we understand the world (Figure 3). In the same way the famous Google Glass proposes a dynamic and constant individual visual connection with the on-line information and the environment It will be the glue between every interaction and experience everywhere [11] -[13].

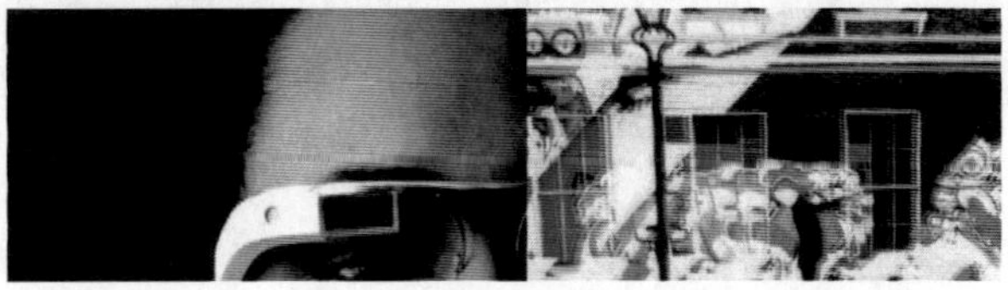

Figure 1. Some technologies provide individual experiences of Augmented Reality outdoors. Google Glass and Domesti/City The Dislocated Home in Augmented Space.

In augmented city, the physical space and the virtual space are not separate, but two spaces, which constitute a whole. Real is combined with the digital environment, so that concepts such as public space, identity, knowledge, citizenship, and public participation are inevitably affected by technology, by mobile communication, which modifies the enjoyment of the public space and the way in which the users relate to the environment and with the activities that take place in these environments. With the implementation of this technology, surprising and immediate results have been obtained within the scope of wayfinding. Orientation and location of spaces and places make the urban environment more attractive for users because it allows them to expand and express their own identity and experiences [14].

IV. Research Methods

With the aim of getting information of products and citizen's expectations, this research focused four areas:

A. *Urban scenario and field research*

Ethnographic methods were used; walking and visiting the city to get information about what already exists, the potential lack of aspects or things which could be improved, and observe where most people spend their time outside. This part leads us to a favourite place in the city of Valencia: the Turia Park, a riverbed transformed into an urban park in the nineties.

Nowadays, as it passes through the city of Valencia, the old Turia riverbed is a big urban park that allows for different leisure activities, consistent with the contemporary concept of sustainable city that is active, healthy and participative. In this longitudinal space that runs through the city, natural elements play a key role in connecting leisure, mobility (walking or cycling) and a variety of uses (recreational, sportive, cultural, touristic).

B. *Desk research*

This involved information about Valencia's plan to become a Smart City. We made an inventory of street furniture elements and classified it in categories pertaining to their contribution to this aim.

C. *Interviews*

The survey had the aim of verifying which existing facilities were highly valued, and what the interviewees found to be lacking in an urban environment very frequented by multiple users. These interviews performed 3 times per week at different times of the day, in September 2015 and, again in May 2016. We choose people randomly, trying to cover different user profiles.

We interviewed a range of 25-30 people from each of the four different groups, who are relevant users of this site: citizens, young athletes, elderly people and tourists/visitors.

D. *On-line Survey*

Simultaneously, a short public-opinion poll was conducted online to complement the previous one, about preferences regarding services and design. This online survey targeted to people who live in Valencia or have been living in the city, such as exchange students or foreign workers (short-term residents).

V. Results of the Local Research

The city of Valencia has an action plan to become a Smart City and it has a major potential as an urban environment, due to its socio-demographic and environmental features. However, the first field research realized shows only ten public facilities, currently identified as Smart products in the city:

1) Information panels, with real-time traffic information throughout the city.

2) App-Valencia, car park information, also in real time

3) QR codes for disabled people, so they can reach things, such as a parking meter

4) E-card, an electronic public transport card (4,000 passengers per day)

5) Municipal bicycle rental service (*Valenbisi*): 2,750 bikes, 5,500 access points, 75,114 daily bike journeys.

6) Monitoring Valencia through cameras

7) Intelligent lights throughout the city

8) EMT bus service, 100% ecological

9) Online City Council administration services (100% paperless)

10) VLCi Platform for urban information

This list summarizes the answers to the open question: "Give an example of the Smart City concept in Valencia" in On-line interviews conducted and the inventory made on the desk research.

What we observe overall in terms of participation is that both, the interviews and the surveys show, from a sample of 100 individuals distributed equally as users, that young people have been more interested in this research.

The two graphs (the Figure 2) illustrate the age of the participants in the study, and the main areas of changes that they perceive as part of the Smart City. The first graph shows clearly the prevalence of young people (18-29) over the different groups of the answers, while the second one describes the value given to the changes perceived at the city as context of public life. So the graphs clearly illustrate the relation between people age and the tendencies on what they expect from the city places nowadays.

In terms of participation, both the interviews and the surveys show, from a sample of 100 individuals distributed equally as users, that young people have been more interested in the research presented. This result is not surprising, as, compared to other groups, young people tend to go out more often and furthermore, they find easier to participate in on-line applications such as this interview and what is more, they prefer this way. Young people like to share places outside even when they are using their own personal devices. They usually mentioned the quality of the environment as place to rest and stay. They ask for urban elements and services, which involve spending time (charge a mobile phone, to use a computer, information in real time, social areas…).

It's worth observing that de second group of participants more relevant (45-64), represents people situated as professionals, workers who have more time in front of the computer and who practice sports and healthy habits. On the contrary, the group (30-44) years corresponds to a group affected by the economic crisis that shows a more sceptical and slightly participative attitude.

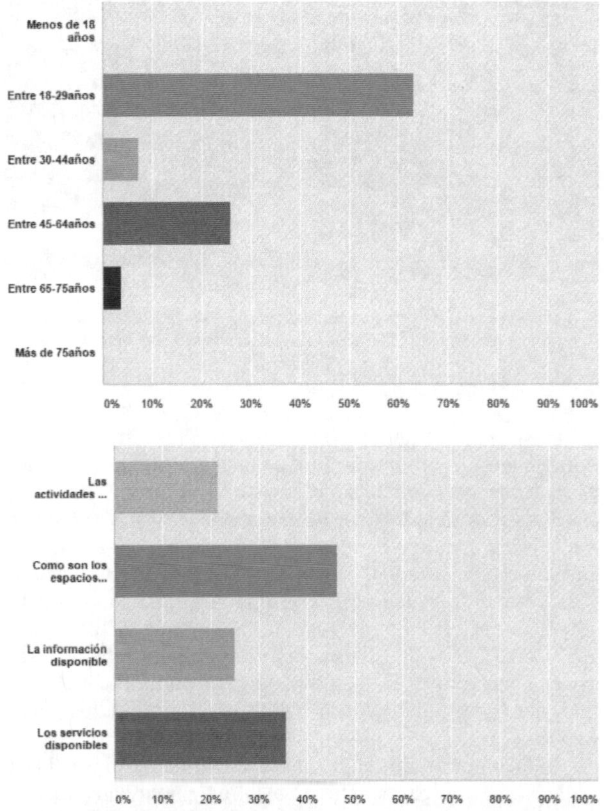

Figure 2. Participation by ages. Activities and changes in the city

What is perhaps more significant for design is that on the second graph, how are the places and the facilities provided, got more percentage than the access to information and other activities that people do outdoors. It is relevant to point out that image appreciation raise almost a 50% getting the double than the others.

Research also suggests that people much concentrate attention on the place they are. Through the outdoor interviews, we found what was missing, and what people would like to improve in Valencia, both from the local and from the tourist perspective. One complaint was about dim lighting at night when using urban elements (which makes people feel unsafe and scared).

Tourists pointed out that there are not enough signs, they are often poorly located and only in Spanish. They also ask for more areas in the shade with rest elements. Young people would like to have Wi-Fi zones in order to recharge or use devices comfortably. Elderly citizens would like screens to display events or beautiful sites to visit in the city.

The analysis of these ethnographic data shaped ideas and requirements for some new smart products. These elements have to include in their features those needs: simplicity, interaction, light, be sustainable, provide energy, easy information displayed, etc. Design has to provide the city with elements with a clean image adapted to the current needs.

Following these considerations, we define the scope of this project as the conceptual design of an urban services booth, which combines sustainability and communication. This urban element has to integrate the principles of the Smart City, linking technology with a pleasant interface, inviting the citizens to use it and participate in social public life.

The service booths are more or less enclosed structures, located in the public space, whose aim is to permit the use of different types of installations; electricity, voice and data are the most common. These cabins have a direct antecedent in phone booths and share with them some characteristics. These sort of elements need to have sufficient space for an individual to carry out the required actions; lighting that facilitates both, their location and use at night; an enclosure system, or a partial or total roof to protect the technological elements; and specific insulation to create the suitable conditions for its possible function as an oral/audio communication terminal.

VI. Design Proposals For The Smart City and Further Work

The methodology followed corresponds to the general design process, which starts with the definition and conceptual design phases. Using creativity, design and the principles of the green engineering in an innovative way can be a force for positive change, in the cities of the future. From the social view of the product, that involves with the community and the public space, sustainable design gains added interest: The street furniture can be an active support in public and political life of the community enabling new forms of participation and civic engagement.

The objectives of this proposal are two:

- Suggest an ecological solution for an innovative public use product, owing to the offered services, which will be determining the optimum implementation of materials and sustainable processes.
- Design a product of public use evidencing this ecological efforts contributing to ecological social awareness.

Assuming the range of available technologies allow to create truly "ecofriendly" products that actively contribute in a responsible and respectful use of the community environment. This raises interest in technology, renewable energy and design, as key aspects for generating futuristic, attractive and fully viable street furniture.

In this direction this proposal also focus on looking for new solutions to be incorporated in elements of collective use, making use of current and low cost communication technologies, which are materialized in a self-sufficient infrastructure that also clearly demonstrate this vocation. Following these ideas, ten projects were developed in detail in the workshop Designing Products for Collective Use at the Technical School of Design Engineering UPV.

They propose different ways of using the contemporary public space in a sustainable, aware, useful and attractive way. It is important to note that, the element/topic proposed, involves complex urban elements, which have a direct contact with the user and require a specific interactivity to be efficient. Consequently, they require immediate comprehension by the user, and the dimensions of their components must ensure the accessibility.

The two projects presented in this paper, show different design solutions based in the *10 principles of Green Engineering* [14]. In the case of *Algui* focuses on the awareness and communication of its energy system: the biomass, and its visual-natural qualities. While in *Eco cabin*, the main values reference to the experience of nature and domestic comfort.

Algy (Figure 3) is an urban booth for services and information with a lively and fresh appearance. A self-sufficient design that employs the developed technology for the BIQ house, located in Hamburg. The project inquires into the combination of new technologies, like augmented reality (AR) and biomass energy, in a product for public use designed as an ecological, attractive and functional element. This piece of street furniture reduces environmental impact and has as further goal: the communication of these values. With this aim, the central element in the design is the bio-reactor itself. In this way the booth is a vertical element of simple geometric shapes that works independently or accompanied by other strategically located, generating a comfortable micro-climate that provides certain soundproofing and insulation, suitable for some of its functions. As a street furniture, at dimensional level this universal and ergonomic design incorporates a floating screen that adjusts to the height of each individual by means of a sensor, without the need for direct tactile contact. Also, one can interact with the booth by voice. All of this with all the necessary accessories to fulfil the offered services satisfactorily, highlighting among them AR applications, and supported by intuitive and very accessible interface

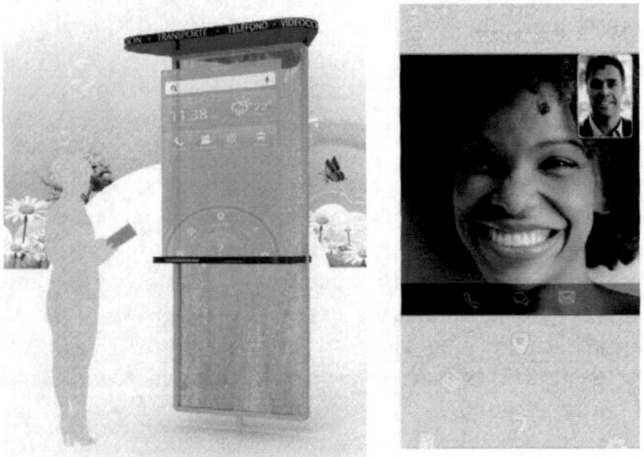

Figure 3. Algy is a service booth inspired in the management of energy with biomass processes. Projected by Marta Jiménez.

Figure 4. Eco Cabin Project allows users to work outdoor in a pleasant environment. Provides energy and plants are watered. Projected by Greta Gulienetti

EcoCabin (Figure 4), provide the city with a comprehensive urban design element that offers a pleasant place for busy people to stop for a while.

Two walls and a cover form a stay zone. One of the two walls is a vertical garden that takes the water needed for drip irrigation from a small container lodged at the top, which stores water from the rain. This allows the irrigation of the plants in perfect autonomy. As far as lighting is concerned, the use of LEDs and its photovoltaic cells installed on the cover, reduce by 50% the power consumption. Plants, water and sun energy also reduce pollution all around this urban element.

In the interior, this cabin has different facilities, such as a table with electrical outlets fed by a few photovoltaic panels installed in the cover. The height of both the work surface and the seats, are adjustable to adapt to different users, in particular to people using wheelchairs. There is a tactile LCD screen on the opposite wall, which presents information of interest (itineraries, transport, etc.), surveillance camera and SOS button.

VII. CONCLUSIONS

It is unquestionable that the development of the Smart City will result in the improvement of the quality of city life. However, it is a true challenge to make people aware of the real changes and participate in their benefits. In this sense, the contribution of this particular research paper is bridging the gap between new concepts and design methods, ideas and smart products.

Coinciding with other authors, the study carried out in the city of Valencia also states clearly that the "Smart" concept seems rhetorical and overvalued, especially when specific products already implemented are observed in operation [15]. It can be state, that it is a priority to gather more information about the needs and expectations of citizens and how they enjoy collective facilities. The parking meters, public transportation, ticket machines or the bicycle rental system, are examples of this product concept, regardless of how intelligent they are.

A strong point of public use elements is their availability and acceptance by the users. This is a great advantage for social communication of new habits at the public space. These products are suitable for communicating contents, which can reinforce information and training strategies linked to the opportunities and improvements of the Smart concept itself. The new materials and lighting applications based on the design make it possible to offer low consumption solutions and greater energy efficiency to face the new urban requirements and the growing environmental sensitivity. Several urban applications such as digital lighting and signage, adds multiple attributes and utilities to the urban experience by combining technologies, architectural integration and design of more interactive contents." [16]

The design projects described show the suitability of the service booths as first-class elements of interactive urban furniture for the Smart City, since they allow integrating conventional analogical uses (rest, protection, safety, etc.) and connectivity and augmented reality systems. Furthermore, these products promote user interest and participation. In addition to communicating the technologies applied to the city, they encourage their use by all types of audiences who are already familiar with these types of interfaces, thanks to the multiple applications in other mobile devices. Thanks to the great versatility of technology and its progress, creativity and multidisciplinarity, viable projects can be developed.

These projects allow monitoring how well paired is the implementation of new technologies and sustainability, which may lead to very interesting products with applications that today are still unimaginable. Society is becoming increasingly receptive to ecological policies; therefore, it is of great interest to take the utmost advantage of the opportunities that technology can bring to really competitive design.

Future work may include usability analysis and the evaluation of these design projects, when used by different people and circumstances.

ACKNOWLEDGMENTS

Thanks to ETSID for the support given to the *Exposition Smartcity: Design, Technology, and Services for Public Use*. This exhibition has shown the interest of the public in these proposals, and has encouraged the development in detail of some of these projects, as well as their submission to different forums.

REFERENCES

[1] N. Vidal, "The smart city: smart cities of the future", Barcelona: Editorial UOC, D.L. 2015, ISBN 9788490649053.

[2] L. Verweij, "Public Spaces More Public or Private than Ever?", Experimenta, vol. 55, pp. 67-73, April 2006, ISSN: 1133-9675.

[3] C. Manville, et al. "Mapping Smart Cities in the EU", Policy Department A Economic and Scientific Policy, pp.21, January 2014. http://www.europarl.europa.eu/RegData/etudes/etudes/join/2014/507480/IPOL-ITRE_ET(2014)507480_EN.pdf , Accessed: November, 2016.

[4] European Initiative on Smart Cities, https://setis.ec.europa.eu/set-plan-process. Accessed: November, 2016.

[5] N. Vidal, "The smart city: smart cities of the future", Barcelona: Editorial UOC, pp.29–30, October 2015, D.L. ISBN 9788490649053.

[6] M.G. Casado, C. Revert, V. Sales, and S. Veral, "Smart Cities Trends: Trends in smart cities and opportunities for sectors habitat", ITC y ADIMA, pp.3–4, March 2015, ISBN: 978-84-941029-3-6.

[7] M. Puyuelo, et al. "Street furniture. Design and Accessibility", Valencia: Editorial Universitat Politècnica de València, 2010.

[8] F. Domínguez and U. Fogué, "Technifying Public Space and Publicizing Infrastructures: Exploring New Urban Political Ecologies through the Square of General Vara del Rey" International Journal of Urban and Regional Research, vol. 37, Urban Research Publications Limited, pp.1035-1052, April 2013.

[9] M. Jiménez, M. Puyuelo, and L. Merino "Urban furniture for Smartcity. Augmented Reality and sustainability for public use" Information Systems and Technologies (CISTI), 2014 9th Iberian Conference on, IEEE, pp. 100-105, June 2014, doi:10.1109/CISTI.2014.6876969

[10] http://www.todoiphone.net/geotravel-un-guia-turistico-en-tu-iphone-con-realidad-aumentada Accessed: November, 2016.

[11] K. Matsuda, "DOMESTI/CITY The Dislocated Home in Augmented Space", Keiichi Matsuda / Unit 15 / Year 5 Diploma/March Thesis. http://km.cx/projects/domesticity-the-dislocated-home-in-augmented-space/. Accessed: November, 2016.

[12] Project Glass of Google develops an augmented reality device that allows individual use Internet to interact with information via voice. Wikipedia: the free encyclopedia [Wiki a Internet]. St. Petersburg (FL): Wikimedia Foundation, Inc. 2001. Available from: https://es.wikipedia.org/wiki/Google_Glass. Accessed: November, 2016.

[13] Smart City Expo World Congress, Fira Barcelona, Noviembre 2015, http://www.smartcityexpo.com/en/program. Accessed: November, 2015.

[14] P. T. Anastas and J. B. Zimmerman, "Design through the 12 principles of Green Engineering", Environmental Science & Technology pp. 94A, 2003

[15] T. Paris, "Desirable intelligence", diid disegno industriale/industrial design, vol.58, Rdesignpress, pp.124, 2014.

[16] G. Flore and A. Pozzoni, "Smart cities, smart lights. Digital signage and urban experience", Elisava Temes de Disseny, vol. 28, pp.39, 2012, eISSN: 2385-7951.

Investigating Self-disclosure and the Amount of Speaking in an Online Meeting Under the Rule of Casual Talking and Casual Listening

Yoshihiro Ichikawa*, Satsuki Ayaya†, Shinichiro Kumagaya†, Fumihide Tanaka*

*Faculty of Engineering, Information and Systems,
University of Tsukuba,
1-1-1 Tennodai, Tsukuba, Ibaraki 305-8577 Japan
Email: {ichikawa@ftl., tanaka@}iit.tsukuba.ac.jp
†Research Center for Advanced Science and Technology,
The University of Tokyo,
3-8-1 Komaba, Meguro, Tokyo 153-8902 Japan
Email: {ayayamoon@live.jp, kumashin@bfp.rcast.u-tokyo.ac.jp}

Abstract—**This paper investigates an online meeting under the rule of casual talking and casual listening (CTCL). Four different meeting styles with respect to spatial and temporal viewpoints were compared by recruiting a total of 60 university students using questionnaires. The results revealed the followings: (1) the degree of participant' self-disclosure in the online meetings was not significantly different from the baseline; (2) it was preferred to use a more familiar interface like a timeline; (3) an online meeting under the CTCL rule was more effective for people with a lower disclosure than the case with a higher disclosure; (4) it is important to provide an appropriate discussion subject to improve the self-disclosure of participants; and (5) a Delay function was suitable to talk with participants who had various degrees of social anxiety.**

Keywords–Tojisha-kenkyu; Social networking system; Text chat system; Casual talking casual listening; Communication Interface; Self-disclosure; Social anxierty.

I. INTRODUCTION

A. Background

The Japanese word, *tojisha-kenyu* means a research by interested persons for themselves. It is a practical activity in which people with a difficulty or a mental disorder engage in to recover from their problems. The activity consists of sharing ways to deal with various difficulties and finding words to explain what is happening to yourself [1][2]. The most basic activity is to gather and share information with persons who have the same difficulties. There is a fundamental rule of casual talking and casual listening (CTCL) that is a facilitating technique used by self-help groups, such as Alcoholics Anonymous. These activities are expected to uncover new finding.

However, it is not easy to increase the number of participants in *tojisha-kenkyu* because of the following reasons: (1) when the number of participants increases, the recording effort also increases; (2) it is often difficult for many people to gather at one site because of the constraints of location, time, and the physical problems of participants; and (3) there is a limit to the number of participants in a meeting because time and space are limited. A web-based system for conducting a meeting online will solve these problems. However, to the authors' knowledge, there is no research on online meetings with the CTCL rule.

B. Objective

The aim of this study is to investigate an online meeting under the CTCL rule. From the study, we also expect to draw out implications about designing a suitable online meeting interface for each user.

C. Method

In this study, we conducted an experiment in which university students participated in online meetings with the CTCL rule using a web-based interface. Since it is important for participants to be able to speak and hear more easily and this is strongly affected by the interface, examining the effectiveness of the interface was important. Then, we constructed four interfaces that were different from each other on two aspects: spatial and temporal. The spatial difference in the interfaces was whether spoken texts were displayed on one line, which is called a timeline, or at random positions. The temporal difference was whether there was a delay in displaying a text inputted by a user. The intention was to weaken the relationship between multiple text messages. It was expected that if the context became weaker, the conversation would become difficult to maintain. In addition, participants' name and ID were not visible to others (the meetings were held anonymously). In the experiments, we first evaluate whether an online meeting using the standard interface led to a good outcome for participants by measuring self-disclosure. Second, to investigate the effect of different interfaces, we measured the relationship between an index called self-disclosure and social anxiety and the number of words inputted from the participants.

D. Structure of this paper

This paper is organized as follws: In Section II, we introduce to practice *tojisha-kenkyu* and CTCL rule. In Section III, we show the experiment which is conducted in this paper, and we also show the results of the experiment in Section IV. After that, Section V discusses about the results. And, in Section VI and VII, we mention about an implication and limitation, respectively. In Section VIII, we conclude this paper.

II. How to Practice Tojisha-Kenkyu

In *tojisha-kenkyu*, the most basic activity is to gather and share information with persons with similar difficulties. This section shows an example of a *tojisha-kenkyu* meeting with the CTCL rule.

A. Proceess

An organizer announces information, date, place, meeting theme, and basic precautions through a mailing list several weeks in advance. If a receiver is interested in attending the meeting, he or she can apply for participation. Cancelling the participation is also allowed.

On the meeting day, participants gather at the venue and conduct a face-to-face meeting with the CTCL rule. Participants seat in a circle along with the facilitator, who takes the initiative. First, the participants are informed about the meeting and the rules. Next, starting from the facilitator, the participants speak one by one in turn to warm up. After that, they speak about some topics in the same way. For convergence of the meeting, a time limit (from 1 to 3 minutes) is imposed on each speaker.

B. Keep talking and keep listening (CTCL) rule

It is recommended that the participants follow the CTCL rule. The rule has two components: speaking and hearing. According to the speaking component, the participants need to speak based on their experiences and feelings. The participants are recommended to try to speak even if it is difficult for them to express themselves. But the participants should not be forced to speak. Participants are also allowed to pass their turn. According to the hearing component, a participant needs to hear the others' stories without talking, nodding, or eye contact.

C. Self-disclosure and CTCL rule

In a CTCL meeting, participants need to speak only about the meeting theme. It is important that the speaking is based on self-experiences and feelings. Such a speaking from a subjective viewpoint, which is not based on an objective opinion or knowledge, is closely related to a self-disclosure [3]. The word *self-disclosure* is defined as *"act of revealing personal information to others in phycology."* Autobiographies that include an element of self-disclosure contribute to the development of *tojisha-kenkyu*. However, it is not easy for everyone to publish an autobiography. There is a function in *tojisha-kenkyu* that gets the story out of many persons.

D. Social anxiety and CTCL rule

Audiences and being judged by them create anxiety in people, called social anxiety [4]. The word *social anxiety* is defined as *"anxiety resulting from the prospect or presence of personal evaluation in real or imagined social situations."* In a CTCL meeting, to reduce such a psychological anxiety, talking, nodding, and eye contact is not allowed. An online meeting system can also help reduce the anxiety. In particular, almost all persons with developmental disabilities have such anxiety because they have little experience sharing their difficulties.

III. Experiment

This section describes the experiment to evaluate the effectiveness of a CTCL meeting using an online system and to examine the effects of interfaces implementing our spatial and temporal concepts.

A. Method

1) Analyzing data: We analyzed the questionnaire responses and contents spoken by participants in meetings. The meeting participants used one of four interfaces. The analysis employed a between-subjects comparison. The participants answered questions about self-disclosure and social anxiety in their regular life in prior questionnaires. After the meeting, the participants answered another questions about self-disclosure for the online system using in the experiment.

2) Measuring self-disclosure: In order to measure the self-disclosure of participants, we employed the questionnaire ESDQ-45, which was developed by Enomoto [5] and translated and inspired from JSDQ-60 [6]. It is a questionnaire in Japanese on a 5-point Likert scale and consists of 45 items belonging to 15 categories (c01, c02, . . ., c15). Points 1 to 5 mean respectively *"do not disclose at all the contents,"* *"not disclose much,"* *"neutral,"* *"disclose,"* and *"disclose enough about the contents."* For example, one of the content is *"own current goal,"* and it is categorized as c03 (*"intentional aspect of spiritual self"*). In the experiments, to measure the degree of disclosure in the usual living environment, we asked the participants whether they have someone to talk about each item. The revised meanings of points 1 to 5 are respectively *"have no one to talk about the contents,"* *"have few person to talk"* *"neutral,"* *"have someone to talk,"* and *"have someone to talk enough about the contents."* The aim was to evaluate how much the online system can support a participant compared to the existing environment. Therefore, in the questionnaire after the meeting, we measured the degree of disclosure of participants using the online system. Then, points 1 to 5 in this case mean respectively *"do not disclose at all the contents,"* *"do not disclose much,"* *"neutral,"* *"disclose,"* and *"disclose enough about the contents."* In both the cases, the value of self-disclosure is expressed as the total score of the answers to 45 questions. Thus, the value ranges from 45 to 225.

3) Measuring social anxiety: In order to measure the social anxiety of participants, we used a questionnaire of Interaction-Audience Anxiety (I-AA) scale translated and modified by Okabayashi et al. [7] from Leary's social anxiety scale [8]. It is questionnaire in Japanese on a 5-point Likert scale and consists of 14 items about two aspects, audience anxiety and interaction anxiety. Points 1 to 5 mean respectively *"strongly disagree,"* *"disagree,"* *"neutral"* *"agree,"* and *"strongly agree."* The value of social anxiety is expressed as an average of the answer to the 14 questions. For exsample, one of the questions in audience anxierty aspect is *"I usually get nervous when I speak in front of a group."*

B. Using interfaces

In this study, we employed a text-chat system as a way to conduct an online meeting. Text-based systems have higher anonymity compared with sound- or video-based systems. If an unspecified number of people participate through the system, it is better to have high anonymity from the viewpoint of privacy. We also employed a real-time chat system. It is close to the concept of *tojisha-kenkyu* that participants share the same place and time while discussing.

In a text-based communication system, the contexts of conversations are constructed and arranged by time, space, and user IDs such that texts are spatially arranged with time stamps or user information. Computer-mediated communication (CMC) contributes to increasing the anonymity of people; however, it also brings a behavior based on a lack of social morality [9]. To suppress the problem and to let the participants focus on the meeting obeying the CTCL rule, we think that it is effective to blur the relationship between each text spoken by participants. Such blurring can be implemented using two kinds of ways that are spatial and temporal rearrangement.

Spatial rearrangement is to display texts spoken by participants without spatially organizing. A CTCL meeting is similar to the brainstorming process because the participants do not need to consider evaluation by others and they can speak freely about the current topic [10]. In this method, it is important that everyone just expresses their ideas without organizing them. For this reason, displaying text without spatially arranging may also promote speaking in a CTCL meeting. In order to implement the concepts into a real-time chat system, we propose the method of spatial rearrangement.

Temporal rearrangement is to intentionally delay for displaying text spoken by participants. Conversation is constructed by turn-taking [11]. Such conversation causes unnecessary evaluation and advice from others. For this reason, to complicate to do turn-taking between participants may promote concentration on thinking and speaking of each person. In order to implement the concepts into a real-time chat system, we propose the method of temporal rearrangement.

These spatial and temporal concepts make it difficult for users to recognize contexts, and establish conversations. For this reason, participants will not try to talk each other. There is an etiquette of not replying to a malicious person in an online system with higher anonymity. Our proposal is expected to contribute to compliance with such etiquettes.

In our spatial rearrangement, the interface displays texts at random positions as staggered rows without aligning in a line, which is called "*timeline*" (Figure 1). In our temporal rearrangement, the interface delays displaying of texts sent from participants. Our proposal is to weaken relationship between spoken texts. Then, we implemented four interfaces that differ from two viewpoints, spatial and temporal, as shown in Table I. In the case of Timeline (TL), new text is displayed at the top of other texts. In the case of Random (RND), new text is displayed randomly in blank spaces, which are tiled constantly. In the case of No delay (Nodelay), new text is displayed as soon as it is sent. In the case of Delay, new text is displayed after a delay of few seconds after it is sent. In all cases, the oldest text is archived when the display area becomes full. Thus, there are four different combinations possible: TL-Nodelay, TL-Delay, RND-Nodelay, and RND-Delay. These can also be treated as experimental conditions.

C. Experimental settings and conditions

The participants (33 males and 27 females, having the age between 19 and 24) were undergraduate and graduate students in the university of the first author. They were enrolled in this experiment as part-time employees. The theme of

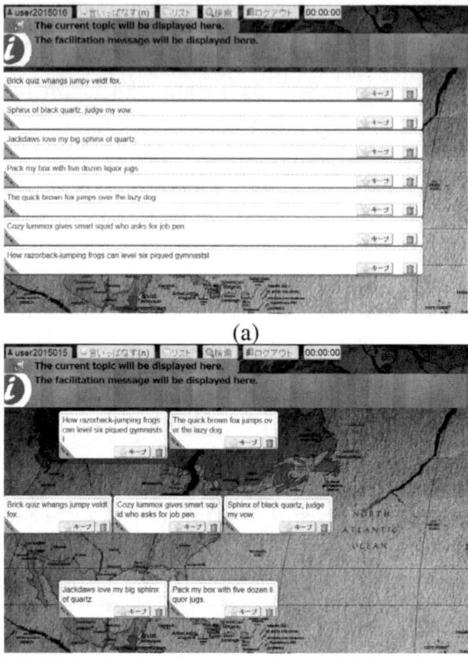

Figure 1. Using interfaces: (a) shows an exsample of the timeline interface, and (b) shows an exsample of the random interface.

TABLE I. INTERFACES COMBINING SPATIAL AND TEMPORAL REARRANGEMENT. THE INTERFACES ARE ALSO EXPERIMENTAL CONDITIONS.

Interfaces (Conditions)		Spatial	
		Timeline (TL)	Random (RND)
Temporal	No delay	TL-Nodelay	RND-Nodelay
	Delay	TL-Delay	RND-Delay

the meetings was "*worries about interpersonal relationships,*" which has high commonality between the subjects. The setting was close to the premise of *tojisha-kenkyu* that all participants have the same worries or difficulties. Each interface was an experimental condition, and each participant took part in experiments in only one condition. Concretely, three meetings with five participants each were hold for each condition, and thus, the total number of participants was 60 (4 conditions $\times$ 3 meetings $\times$ 5 participants/meeting). Each mechanism of the interface was explained to the participants on ahead. In the case of Delay, the delay time was set from 15 to 60 seconds during the experiments. Each meeting was held about 36 minutes (the first half of 18 minutes and the second half of 18 minutes). A topic of the first half was about above theme, and a topic of the second half was "*what are you dealing with about worry about interpersonal relationships and what do you want to do?*"

IV. RESULTS

A. Major relations

In order to outline the major relations between variables, we show Pearson's correlation coefficient between each data point (N = 60) in Table II. "*IAA*" indicates the degree of social anxiety, "*ESDQpre*" indicates the degree of self-disclosure

TABLE II. PEARSON'S CORRELATION COEFFICIENT BETWEEN EACH DATA POINT (N = 60).

	IAA	ESDQpre	ESDQsys	dESDQsys	#words
IAA	1.00				
ESDQpre	−.28*	1.00			
ESDQsys	−.02	.11	1.00		
dESDQsys	.22	−.74***	.59***	1.00	
#words	−.19	.24	.18	−.07	1.00

TABLE IV. PEASON'S CORRELATION COEFFICIENT BETWEEN IAA AND OTHER DATA FOR EACH CONDITION (N = 15).

	IAA			
	TL-Nodelay	TL-Delay	RND-Nodelay	RND-Delay
dESDQsys	.61	−.08	.16	−.03
#words	−.31	−.14	−.36	−.03

in the usual living environment, "*ESDQsys*" indicates the degree of self-disclosure of participants in the online system, "*dESDQsys*" indicates the difference between ESDQpre and ESDQsys, and "*#words*" indicates the number of words in texts posted by a participant. Note that the same base word was counted only once and symbols were not counted, and the morphological analysis was conducted using MeCab [12]. The test statistic of IAA and ESDQpre was $p = .033$; thus, it met the significance level of 5%. There is a weak negative correlation between the two parameters. No correlation was observed between IAA and ESDQsys, IAA and #words, ESDQpre and ESDQsys, and ESDQsys and #words. However, there is a strong negative correlation between ESDQpre and dESDQsys.

B. Interface effects

In order to investigate the interface effects, we show the values of mean and standard deviation of each data for each condition (N = 15) in Table III. The IAA of the persons in TL-Nodelay and RND-Nodelay was high, but that of persons in TL-Delay and RND-Delay was not high. The ESDQpre was also different accordingly. This result confirms that there is a correlation between IAA and ESDQpre. Despite this result, dESDQsys was positive in TL-Delay and negative in RND-Nodelay. By the two-way factorial ANOVA for spatial and temporal factors, it was found that there was no effect of interaction between the factors and there was a significant difference between the spatial factors whether timeline or random ($p = .049 < .05$).

C. Relevance between personality and interface

In order to investigate the relevance of the effects between participants' personality and interfaces, we show Pearson's correlation coefficient between IAA or ESDQpre and other data for each condition (N = 15) in Table IV and Table V. A correlation was observed between IAA and dESDQsys in TL-Nodelay. In TL-Nodelay and RND-Delay, there was a weak negative correlation between IAA and #words. On the other hand, there was no correlation between IAA and #words in TL-Delay and RND-Delay. In TL-Nodelay and RND-Nodelay, there was a very strong negative correlation between ESDQpre and dESDQsys. The correlations in TL-Delay and RND-Delay were lower than those in the other conditions. In TL-Delay, there was a positive correlation between ESDQpre and #words.

TABLE V. PEARSON'S CORRELATION COEFFICIENT BETWEEN ESDQPRE AND OTHER DATA FOR EACH CONDITION (N = 15).

	ESDQpre			
	TL-Nodelay	TL-Delay	RND-Nodelay	RND-Delay
dESDQsys	−.88	−.68	−.91	−.67
#words	−.04	.64	.16	.14

V. DISCUSSION

The interface of TL-Nodelay is baseline of online meeting with CTCL rule, because it was made based on a conventional interface. The results revealed that the degree of self-disclosure for unfamiliar (anonymous) people on the system is almost the same from the disclosure for the usual living environment. The degree of self-disclosure was not only maintained but also increased by using a system. We think there are two reasons that are application of the CTCL rule and using the CMC system. But, it is not only necessary to use an online system but also preferred to use a more familiar interface like timeline. On the other hand, the degree of self-disclosure in the usual living environment is the major factor contributing to changing of the disclosure in an online system. The online system and the CTCL rule are more effective for a person with a lower disclosure than a person with higher disclosure. It can be said that the online system and the CTCL rule are useful for the person who has many worries relatively.

Table VI shows the results about the fifteen categories of the self-disclosure assessment. The value of p indicates the test statistic with student's t-test of ESDQpre and ESDQsys. The scores of categories c03 and c07 were especially increased by using the conventional interface system. The student's t-test statistics of ESDQpre and ESDQsys are $p = 0.059$ and 0.063; thus, they met the significance level of 10% ($p < 0.1$). The categories c03 and c07 are "*intentional aspect of spiritual self*" and an "*informal interpersonal aspect of social self (same sex),*" respectively. We think that the results occurred because several categories have high relevance to the meeting theme. For this reason, to improve the self-disclosure of participants, it is important to provide an appropriate theme. In contrast, the category c15, which is about "*rumors,*" was not easy to be disclosed in the online system. That is a reasonable result because in the meeting, the participants spoke based on their own experiences and feelings. Further investigation is necessary to discuss the effect of self-disclosure for each category.

The result that there was no correlation between IAA and #words suggests that the participants with higher social anxiety did not speak much in the meeting despite having difficulties related to the meeting theme. However, there was a weak negative correlation in TL-Nodelay and RND-Nodelay, and there was no correlation in TL-Delay and RND-Delay (Table IV). From the results, when the participants with higher social anxiety use the Nodelay interfaces, they find it difficult to speak. In contrast, since the Delay interfaces have no such effect, they are suitable for all participants who have various degrees of social anxiety.

VI. IMPLICATION

The contents of the I-AA questionnaire administered before the experiment were included the meeting theme, which was about worries of interpersonal anxiety. As a result, it may have

TABLE III. MEAN AND STANDARD DEVIATION OF EACH DATA POINT FOR EACH CONDITION (N = 15).

	TL-Nodelay		TL-Delay		RND-Nodelay		RND-Delay	
	M	*SD*	*M*	*SD*	*M*	*SD*	*M*	*SD*
IAA	2.97	0.96	3.21	0.74	2.99	1.00	3.32	0.79
ESDQpre	176.80	30.15	170.60	34.98	186.67	29.06	162.80	29.81
ESDQsys	189.13	21.93	183.53	30.39	173.73	25.01	158.20	22.63
dESDQsys	12.33	43.03	12.93	39.94	−12.93	48.39	−4.60	23.97
#words	97.73	35.63	123.47	59.34	121.80	44.00	103.80	41.65

TABLE VI. MEAN AND STANDARD DEVIATION OF THE FIFTEEN CATEGORIES OF THE SELF-DISCLOSURE IN TL-NODELAY (N = 15).

	TL-Nodelay				
	ESDQpre		ESDQsys		*p*
	M	*SD*	*M*	*SD*	
c01	12.93	1.87	13.40	1.88	.509
c02	11.20	3.26	12.47	2.83	.360
c03	11.73	2.69	13.33	2.23	.059+
c04	11.13	3.18	12.33	2.41	.294
c05	12.53	2.23	13.07	2.22	.502
c06	8.07	3.49	7.53	3.23	.636
c07	11.80	2.68	13.53	1.81	.063+
c08	10.53	4.02	11.80	2.51	.350
c09	12.73	2.60	13.27	2.02	.508
c10	12.93	2.22	13.67	1.29	.326
c11	11.87	2.50	12.40	2.82	.569
c12	11.47	3.09	13.20	2.04	.159
c13	13.67	1.72	14.53	0.92	.155
c14	12.60	2.41	13.60	1.68	.221
c15	11.60	2.23	11.00	2.45	.591
total	176.80	30.15	189.13	21.93	.302

promoted speaking or improved self-disclosure of participants. It may have also biased the contents of speaking. However, conducting a questionnaire before a meeting for the participants to have a deeper consciousness about meeting themes may be useful. In the field of *tojisha-kenkyu*, there is room for consideration also in preparation for a meeting stage.

From the result, there is not necessarily a relationship between the degree of self-disclosure and the number of spoken words (Table II). The fact suggests that there is a gap between feeling and actually action. From the subjective viewpoint of a participant, it is a better environment where self-disclosure tends to be higher. On the other hand, from the objective viewpoint, it is better to have an active environment where many things are spoken by others. Both factors are important for constructing a better meeting environment for *tojisha-kenkyu*.

The result that the TL interfaces improve self-disclosure may be interpreted as RND deteriorates self-disclosure. In RND, there is a risk of participants lacking concentration in the meeting because the display position of the spoken text is not fixed. In contrast, it can be inferred that application of the CTCL rule or the CMC environment greatly contributed to improve self-disclosure. It is important to verify which factor is more important in some way, e.g., by conducting a meeting without the CTCL rule.

By comparing #words in TL-Nodelay, TL-Delay, and RND-Nodelay, both spatial and temporal rearrangements seem to have promoted speaking (Table III). However, #words are the same in RND-Delay and TL-Nodelay. Since there is no statistical difference anyway, the contribution of the interface to promote speaking in a meeting may be small.

If we want to just increase the number of spoken text in a meeting environment, introducing a bot agent using logs of another meeting may be a solution. We are conducting research on the construction of such agents [13].

According to previous research, gender affects self-disclosure [14][15]. Specifically, females have higher self-disclosure than males. In fact, the degree of self-disclosure in the preliminary questionnaire tended to be higher in experimental groups with more women. Considering the result that the degree of self-disclosure in the usual living environment is the major factor contributing to the disclosure change in an online system, the system may be more effective for males.

VII. LIMITATION

This experiment was conducted as a part-time job for university students. It may be implicitly bringing confidence that the other participants are also in the same part-time job. The implicit assumption that the participants belong to a close community can also create security. It is undeniable that the sense of security and responsibility as an employee may have established the meetings online. It is necessary to investigate the influence of these two factors by application to the groups of tojisha-kenkyu or general population who are not part-time employees.

For the same reason, few spoken texts ignoring the meeting rule were observed. Therefore, similar verification is required for the relationship between interface and rule compliance.

Although we did not control the sex, such a control is necessary for more precise evaluation.

In order to make university students a *tojisha*, we adopted very general worries as a meeting theme. Since the difficulties of tojisha-kenkyu are not general, their meetings are more serious and useful.

The evaluation is based on the experimental result of only one meeting by the participants who used the rule and the system for the first time. As tojisha-kenkyu is continual in practice, the evaluation of the system by observations of a number of meetings is necessary.

This paper does not discuss the content of the meeting. It is interesting to study whether using the system essentially has an influence on tojisha-kenkyu.

We assumed that participants access the web-system from thier desktop or laptop PC in this experiment. It is desirable that the system can also be used in other devices such as smartphones so that a large number of people can participate. However, it is difficult to operate the RND interface when using it on a device with a small screen.

VIII. CONCLUSION AND FUTURE WORK

Tojisha-kenkyu is used to share difficulties that many participants cannot express well. In this research, to construct a system to conduct CTCL meetings online, we investigated the effect of an online meeting with the CTCL rule. Concretely, we constructed four interfaces that are different from two viewpoints, spatial and temporal, and we examined the effect on the conventional interface and the relationship between the effects of the proposed interfaces. From the experimental results on undergraduate and graduate students, following findings were obtained:

- The degree of self-disclosure for unfamiliar people on the system is almost the same from the disclosure for the usual living environment. However, it is not only necessary to use an online system but also preferred to use a more familiar interface like TL.
- The degree of self-disclosure in the usual living environment is the major factor contributing to change the disclosure in the online system. The online system and the CTCL rule are more effective for a person with a lower disclosure than one with a higher disclosure.
- It is important to provide the appropriate theme to improve the self-disclosure of participants.
- The Delay interfaces are suitable for all participants who have various degrees of social anxiety.

As future work, it is necessary to investigate the influence of the sense of security and responsibility by application to the groups of *tojisha-kenkyu* or general population who are not part-time employees.

ACKNOWLEDGEMENT

This work was supported by JSPS KAKENHI Grant Number 24119003.

REFERENCES

[1] K. Ishihara, "Learning from tojisha kenkyu," in Disability Research Today: Interactional Perspectives. London: Routledge, 2015, pp. 27–42.

[2] S. Ayaya and S. Kumagaya, Hattatsu Shougai Tojisha Kenkyu (A Tojisha-Kenkyu of Developmental Disorders). Tokyo: Igaku-shoin, 2008.

[3] S. M. Jourard, Self-disclosure : An experimental analysis of the transparent self. New York: Wiley-Interscience, 1971.

[4] B. R. Schlenker and M. R. Leary, "Social anxiety and self-presentation: A conceptualization model," Psychological Bulletin, vol. 92, 1982, pp. 641–669.

[5] H. Enomoto, Psychological study of self-disclosure. Kyoto: Kitaohji-syobo, 1997.

[6] S. M. Jourard and P. Lasakow, "Some factors in self-disclosure," Journal of Abnormal & Social Psychology, vol. 56, 1958, pp. 91–98.

[7] N. Okabayashi and H. Seiwa, "A study on the reliability and validity of Learys social anxiety scale," Studies in Information and the Behavioral Sciences, vol. 15, 1991, pp. 1–9.

[8] M. R. Leary, "Social anxiousness: The construct and its measurement," Journal of Personality Assessment, vol. 47, 1983, pp. 66–75.

[9] L. Sproull and S. Kiesler, "Computers, Networks and Work," Scientific American, vol. 265, 1991, pp. 116–123.

[10] A. F. Osborn, Applied Imagination. Charles Scribners Sons, Inc., 1953.

[11] H. Sacks, E. A. Schegloff, and G. Jefferson, "A Simplest Systematics for the Organization of Turn-Taking for Conversation," Language, vol. 50, 1974, pp. 696–735.

[12] T. Kudo, K. Yamamoto, and Y. Matsumoto, "Applying Conditional Random Fields to Japanese Morphological Analysis," in Proc. of the 2004 Conference on Empirical Methods in Natural Language Processing (EMNLP-2004), 2004, pp. 230–237.

[13] Y. Ichikawa and F. Tanaka, "Displaying Speeches Method for Non-Crosstalk Online Agent," in Proc. of the 2016 AAAI Spring Symposium Series, 2015, pp. 354–355.

[14] S. M. Jourard, The Transeparent Self. New York: D. Van Nostrand, 1964.

[15] D. M. Pedersen and V. J. Breglio, "Personality correlates of actual self-disclosure," Psycological Reports, vol. 22, 1968, pp. 495–501.

WeaveStudio: An Object-Oriented Toolkit for Textile Pattern Colouring and Visualization

Ahmed Mohamed Fahmy Yousef
Fayoum University
Fayoum, Egypt
amf00@fayoum.edu.eg

Mahmoud Kamel Mahmoud Abdalaziz
Digitex Software Corporation
Cairo, Egypt
m-kamel@digitexit.com

Abstract— **Textile industry includes a large number of practices and complex technical issues that operate in a competitive global industry. Recently, researchers have shown an increased interest in textile design software solution for all designing and coloring needs. However, for massive production textile designers are facing several problems related to Color Matching, Design Export, and Customize pantone coloring. Thus, textile designers need to take into account not only the design but also manufacture and technological development and the application of the final product. In order to enhance textile designers' with an optimization tools, this paper presents the design, implementation, and evaluation details of WeaveStudio Toolkit for textile pattern coloring and visualization. A combination of quantitative and qualitative approaches was used in the data analysis. Therefore, this study makes a major contribution to research on textile pattern coloring and visualization by demonstrating a valuable toolkit on the textile design suiTable for design professionals in the textile and fashion industries, as well as in academia.**

Keywords- Textile; usability; Customize pantone coloring; fashion; textile manufacture.

I. TEXTILE DESIGN

Textile designing is a creative field that is important for a wide range of scientific and industrial processes. Textile designing is a major area of interest within the field of fashion design, carpet manufacturing and any other cloth-related field [1]. This industry includes a variety of purposes, e.g., clothing, carpets, drapes, towels, and rugs are all a products of textile design [2]. It is now well established from a variety of studies, that, textile industry is now one of the most influential sectors, in the global economy, garment industrialization has become the world's third biggest industrial industry [3][4].

Textile designers should have the ability to inspire collections, trends, and styles of fashion [5]. In this regard, different textile design software's have been developed in order to making the garment industrialization more productive. Most of these textile applications share some combinations of functions such as, setup any number of style templates. The design output can be linked to specific style components, such as fabrics or size specs as well as designers specified number of solutions to be saved [6].

Despite its long experiments success, the textile software has a number of problems in use. Customize pantone coloring is one of the most frequently stated problems with the current versions of textile applications, that limits the amount of designs and hinders designers creativity growth. Moreover, there is increasing concern that some textiles applications are being disadvantaged with color matching. Therefore, these major issues have been shown to be related to adverse effects the massive design export [7]. In addition, that lack of textile software usability has been highlighted in several studies [8].

There is an urgent need to address these issues in order to make the garment industrialization more productive. This paper addresses these issues and presents design, implementation, and evaluation details of WeaveStudio toolkit for textile pattern coloring and visualization. The specific objective of WeaveStudio is to shift away from traditional textiles software where designers are limited to customize pantone coloring towards a more dynamic and productive one. In fact, WeaveStudio is built on a vision to rethink of textile production and make it more accessible and enabled designers to create their own unique brand line.

The remainder of the paper is organized as follows. In Section 2 begins by laying out the theoretical dimensions of the research, and looks at how field of textiles computer-aided design software is still relatively new and extending due to technology miniaturization. The third Section is concerned with the methodology used for this study including the WeaveStudio design and requirements. Section 4 analyses the results of interviews and focus group discussions undertaken during the implementations of WeaveStudio toolkit. Finally, we summarize our findings and outline perspectives for future work.

II. RELATED WORK

The textile design process often begins with different art mediums to match concepts for the finished product design. Nowadays, most professional textile designers are using some kinds of design software created expressly for this purpose [9]. The field of textiles computer-aided design software is still relatively new and extending due to technology miniaturization [10]. We selected the following ten textile design application for our analysis due to their particular focus on the textile pattern design and color matching.

- Pointcarre Textile Software [11].
- Vetigraph [12]
- Apparel Innovator [13]
- Color Matters International Software [14]
- Coyote [15]

- Design Suite by Bontex [16]
- DesignSew Diva [17]
- Evolution Textile Design by DigiFab Systems [18]
- Modaris 3D [19]
- SmartDesigner [20]

we analyze each system for low-level features (e.g., CAD Tools, Color Matching, Design Export , Fabric Matching , Fashion Illustrations , Pattern Grading, Pattern Layout/ Print/ Cut, Pattern, Color & Art Storage, Presentation Tools, Textile Pattern Design and) as well as high-level features (e.g., Customize pantone coloring, flexible and user friendly). A summary of the analysis results and a comparison with the WeaveStudio software are presented in Table 1.

TABLE I. SUMMARY OF THE TEXTILE SYSTEMS ANALYSIS

Functionality	System	Pointcarre	Vetigraph	Apparel Innovator	Color Matters	Coyote	Bontex	DesignSew Diva	Evolution Textile	Modaris 3D	SmartDesigner	WeaveStudio
Low-Level Features	CAD Tools	√	(√)	(√)	(√)	√	(√)	√	(√)	(√)	√	√
	Color Matching	√	(√)	√	√	√	√	√	√	√	√	√
	Design Export	√	√	√	√	√	√	√	√	-	√	√
	Fabric Matching	√	√	√	√	-	√	√	√	√	√	√
	Fashion Illustrations	√	√	√	-	√	-	√	√	√	√	√
	Pattern Grading	√	√	-	-	-	√	√	-	√	-	√
	Pattern Layout / Print / Cut	√	√	√	-	-	√	√	√	√	-	√
	Pattern, Color & Art Storage	√	√	√	-	√	√	√	√	-	√	√
	Presentation Tools	√	√	√	√	√	√	√	√	√	√	√
	Textile Pattern Design	√	√	√	(√)	√	√	√	√	√	√	√
High-Level Features	Customize pantone coloring	-	-	-	-	-	-	-	-	-	-	√
	Flexible and user friendly	(√)	(√)	-	-	-	-	(√)	(√)	-	-	√
legend		✓ Completely supported			(✓) Partly			- Not supported				

It can be seen from the data in Table 1 that, these textile applications are support the basic features of textile design, namely CAD Tools , Color Matching , Presentation Tools, Textile Pattern Design. However, only Pointcarre, Vetigraph, DesignSew Diva, and Evolution Textile Design by DigiFab Systems are providing more advanced features, such as user friendly and usable interface. This analysis has been demonstrated that the lack of Customize pantone coloring is a major cahalenge of texttile applications that, makes their usage unpractical and out of context.

III. WEAVESTUDIO DESIGN

Driven by the wish to enhance textile software with a complete package solution for all designing and coloring needs, we follow spiral model as a combination of both, iterative model, which mixed some key aspect of the waterfall model and rapid prototyping models, in an attempt to combine wide range advantages of top-down and bottom-up concepts. [23]. We analyzed the existing textile software to identifying which functionalities they have in common, which functionalities were most frequently used, and what are the additional functionalities that are still required as presented in the related work Section 2.

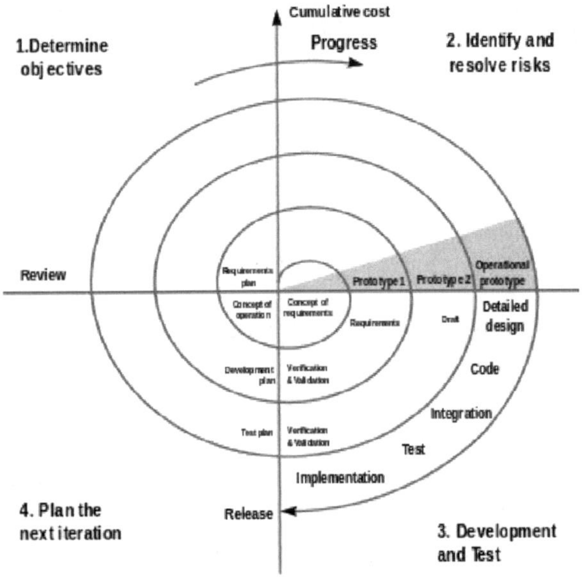

Figure 1. Spiral model [23]

A. Survey Results

Based on the literature review and the analysis of the existing systems, we collected design requirements regarding the main textile grading and electronic prototyping to the product design, ensuring better finish, fit and accuracy. Then, we designed a survey to collect feedback from different textile stakeholders concerning the importance of the collected requirements. The demographic profile of this survey was distinguished into academic professors and textile industrial designers as follows:

- **Academic Professors**: 23 professors who had experiences in the field of textile completed this survey. 37% from Europe, 42% from the US and 21% from Asia.
- **Textile Industrial Designers**: 42 textile industrial designers who had worked in the field of textile completed this survey. 55% from Europe, 34% from the US and 11% from Asia.

A summary of the survey analysis results are presented in Table 2. It strengthens the collected requirement to support WeaveStudio Design in order to enhance designers with an object-oriented toolkit that enable them to spend as little time as possible for entering data. From styles and trims to design sizing, sewing operations and style prototype, moreover, designers can create templates or groups of objects that can be instantly retrieved and editable if appropriate.

TABLE II. WEAVESTUDIO DESIGN REQUIREMENTS

	Design Requirements	M	SD
1	Provide CAD tools where appropriate.	3.7	0.88
2	Support color matching.	4.66	0.68
3	Provide a design export box for prototypes design.	4.23	0.56
4	Enable easier fabric matching.	4.33	0.69
5	Provide a fashion Illustrations solution.	4.68	0.89
6	Provide opportunities for pattern grading.	4.78	0.45
7	Use editing features e.g. pattern Layout / Print / Cut.	4.10	0.97
8	Framing: arrange objects Pattern, Color & Art Storage.	4.12	0.89
9	Offer a usable presentation tool.	4.41	0.82
10	Offer a textile pattern design.	4.90	0.45
11	Provide a customize pantone coloring	4.91	0.34

1. Strongly disagree … 5. Strongly agree

B. WeaveStudio Implementation

WeaveStudio implementation that includes dynamic interface of linked design data, supported by an integrated object-oriented technology. In the next Sections, we will discuss the main components of the WeaveStudio user interface in some detail.

IV. WEAVESTUDIO COMPONENTS

There are several different types of layouts for repeated patterns. WeaveStudio provides a flexible workflow of product specifications modeled after the actual design.

A. WeaveStudio Workflow

WeaveStudio uses a common color palette to relate every aspect of style specification including graphics and textual information as shown in Figure 2. Some of the most common repeats are straight and half drop. Often, the same design is produced in many different colored versions, which are called live models as illustrated in Figure 3.

Figure 2. WeaveStudio Workflow.

Figure 3. WeaveStudio live models.

B. *Customize pantone coloring*

Customize pantone coloring is the other method to make your textile unique. In WeaveStudio Customize pantone coloring as an expression of textile design power provide designers with a usable tool of color in constructing identity, the creation of color via contemporary technical advances,

From the icons in Figure 4, designers can create new textile designs in a matter of hours rather than days or weeks. alongside the classification and codification of color as presented in Figure 4.

Therefore, customize pantone coloring a powerful design studio at fingertips that allows textile designers to:

- Modifying designs with advanced color management
- Using a variety of color modes.
- Including knits and weaves, as you create a choice of textiles and colorways.
- Printing digital textile design.
- Creating multiple colorways and palettes.
- Designing, creating and manipulating the textile prototypes.
- Repeats, drops, engraving sizes
- Work with different file formats.
- Allows the view of one repeat, many repeats, and real image size.
- Efficiently and quickly design custom fabrics and results appear immediately.
- Export multiple designs at once.
- Its user friendly workflow enables to make the textile design faster and error free.

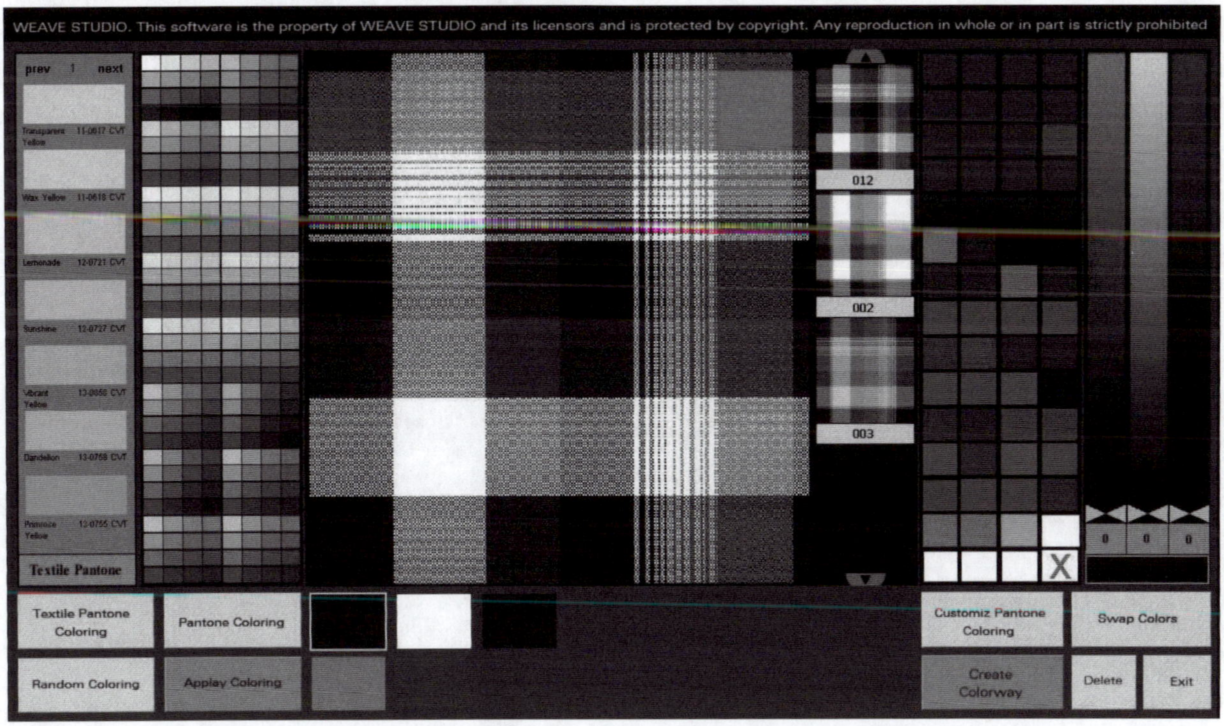

Figure 4. WeaveStudio customize pantone coloring.

V. WeaveStudio Evaluation

In this Section, we are going to present the empirical evaluation of usability and effectiveness of WeaveStudio. Each evaluation method is described with its methodology and the used metrics. After that, we continue with detailed discussion of the findings.

A. *Usability Evaluation (ISONORM 9241/110-S)*

The ISONORM 9241/110-S questionnaire was designed based upon the International Standard ISO 9241, Part 110 [21]. Recently, researchers have shown an increased interest in using this questioner for testing the user-friendly and usability [22]. Thus, we used this questionnaire as a general usability evaluation for the WeaveStudio toolkit. ISONORM questionnaire consists of 21 questions distributed into seven main Sections. Participants were asked to respond to each question scaling from (7) a positive exclamation and its mirroring negative counterpart (1) and it's used. The questionnaire comes with an evaluation framework that computes several aspects of usability to a single score between 21 and 147. A total of 34 questionnaires were completed. Table 3 illustrates the summary of the ISONORM 9241/110-S usability evaluation.

The majority of respondents were in the 23-42 age range. Male respondents formed the majority (90%). Participants have a high level of educational attainment: 66% of participants are studying bachelor's degree in Textile Technology and Design and 34% are worked in textile production.

TABLE III. ISONORM 9241/110-S EVALUATION MATRIX (N= 34)

Factor	Aspect	M	Sum
Suitability for design tasks	Integrity	4.6	
	Streamlining	4.9	15.2
	Fitting	5.7	
WeaveStudio Self-descriptiveness	Information content	4.9	
	Potential support	5.2	15.4
	Automatic support	5.3	
Conformity with user expectations	Layout conformity	4.9	
	Transparency	5.8	16.6
	Operation conformity	5.9	
Suitability for learning	Learnability	5.8	
	Visibility	4.9	15.5
	Deducibility	4.8	
Controllability	Flexibility	5.4	
	Changeability	4.9	15
	Continuity	4.7	
WeaveStudio Error tolerance	Comprehensibility	3.9	
	Correct ability	3.2	10.6
	Correction support	3.5	
Suitability for individualization	Extensibility	4.8	
	Personalization	4.7	14.7
	Flexibility	5.2	
ISONORM score		103	

The collect feedback from ISONORM 9241/110-S questioner reflect higher level of satisfaction; the total score was 103, which translates to "Everything is all right. Currently, there is no reason to make changes to the software in regards to usability"[21]. In particular, the handling of the WeaveStudio interface was considered by most of the designers to be easy and the majority reported that they did not have difficulties when going through the required textile design tasks (i.e. design coloring). The general design of the interface was perceived to be pleasant and interactive (i.e. every thing in one screen). Most designers also agreed that the used terminology and icons (e.g., Customize pantone coloring; create color way) were clear and self-describing. In general, the ISONORM 9241/110-S evaluation results reflect a user satisfaction with the usability of the WeaveStudio toolkit.

B. *Effectivness Evaluation*

In this Section, we will focus on the perceived quality and usefulness on the best practices of WeaveStudio. We will analyze the results per question basis for all textile design tasks. A summary of the average scores per question are given in Figures 5-10. Likert items are used to measure respondents' attitudes to a particular question.

The first question investigates if the proposed objective of WeaveStudio to make any suggestions for the client designs ideas. As shown in Figure 5, 64% of responders are strongly agree with that WeaveStudio helps them accurately interpreting and representing clients' designs ideas.

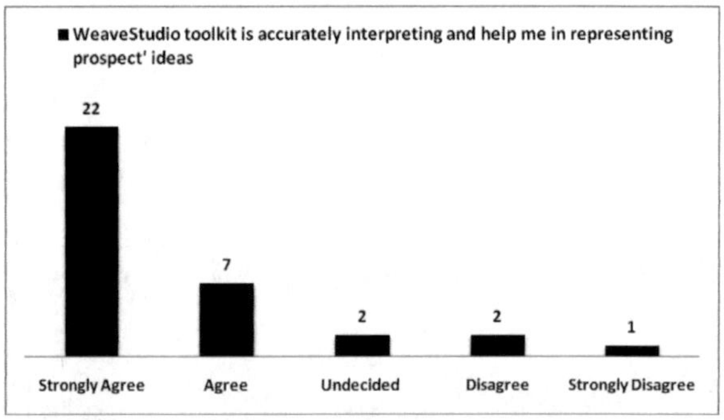

Figure 5. Representing clients' designs ideas

Further, we have observed that, applying color management on textile printing substrates. As can be seen from Figure 6, the overall response to the evaluation item is over 70% strongly agree with that WeaveStudio helps designers in understanding of color matching and color management issues for digital textile printing. This indicates that WeaveStudio toolkit is a powerful method for color management software in the field of digital printing onto a textile substrate.

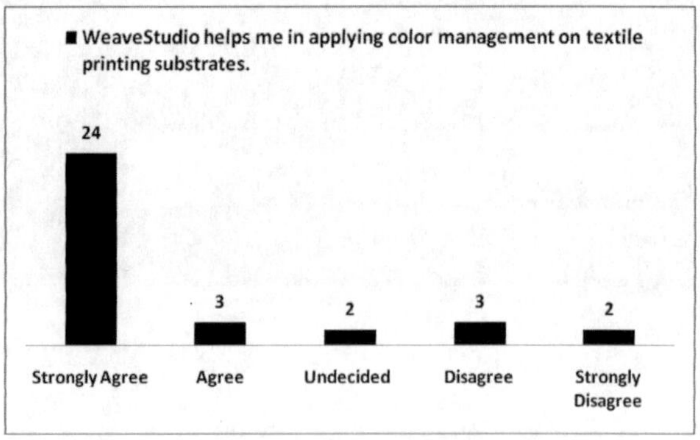

Figure 6. Applying color mangment in WeaveStudio

Moreover, participants in this survey are noted that, aggregate all the design elements in one screen (See Figure 4) is the best feature in WeaveStudio. Furthermore, following, we elaborate the ability of the WeaveStudio to produce novel and attractive in designing the structure and properties of nonwoven fabrics for different purposes.

It can be seen from the data in Figure 7, the majority are agreed that WeaveStudio enable them to create *beautiful* repeating patterns using different color patterns and make it possible to create a novel *textile design* for different perspectives.

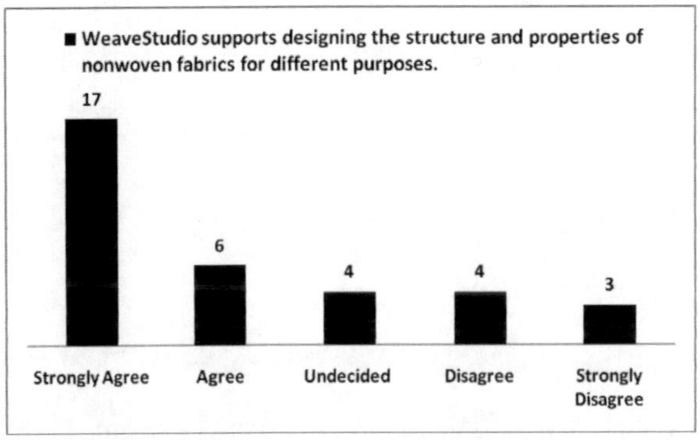

Figure 7. Novel and ttractive textile design

WeaveStudio further fosters customize panton coloring in order to improving the design of men's, women's and children's clothing for different purposes.

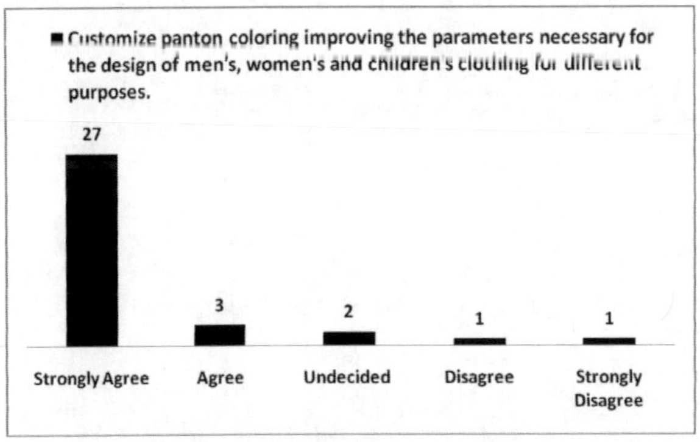

Figure 8. Customize panton coloring

In WeaveStudio designers can with the color picker in place, you can now integrate it with their design (Re-Coloring), the most used icons are presented in Figure 9.

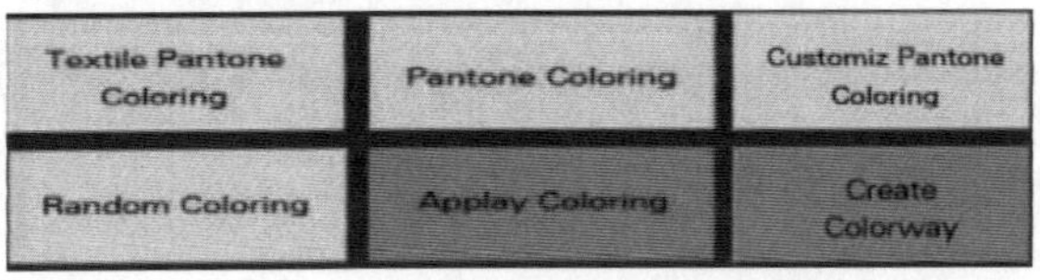

Figure 9. Most used icons in WeaveStudio

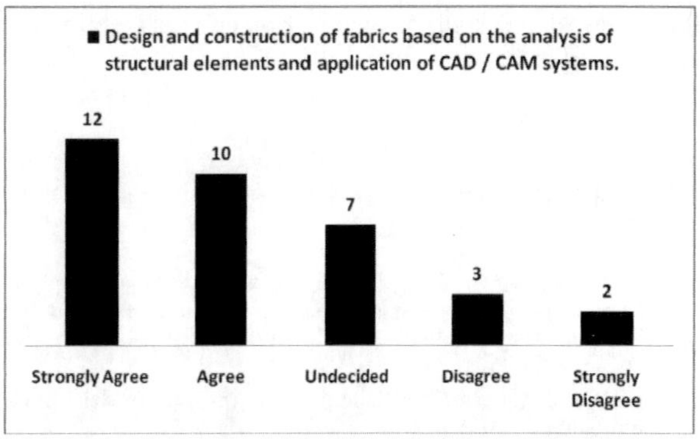

Figure 10. Supporting CAD / CAM systems

Computer-aided design (CAD) has brought a new revolution in the textile industry. In our context WeaveStudio helps textile designers to visualize and see their imaginative design in final layout without producing any cloths sample. The themes identified in these responses are summarized in Figure 10.

Finally, we asked designers whether WeaveStudio helps them to export and share design production-ready assets with textile developers. In Figure 11 there is a clear trend of agreeing that, WeaveStudio supports textile design artboards and helps them to export them individually to files.

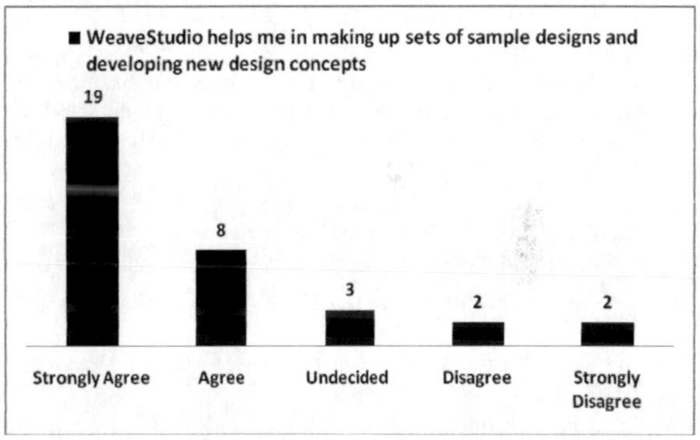

Figure 11. Export final textile designs

VI. CONCLUSION

Textile designing is a creative field that is important for a wide range of scientific and industrial processes. This study was undertaken to design, implement and evaluate the WeaveStudio toolkit as a textile designing solution for pattern coloring and visualization. WeaveStudio includes a dynamic interface of linked design data, supported by an integrated object-oriented technology. A combination of quantitative and qualitative approaches was used in the data analysis. The preliminary evaluation results revealed a user acceptance of WeaveStudio toolkit as a helpful, easy to use, and useful textile design tool that has the potential to foster customize panton coloring in order to improving the design of men's, women's and children's clothing for different purposes.

REFERENCES

[1] L. D. Burns, and N. O. Bryant. "The business of fashion: Designing, manufacturing, and marketing" Fairchild Books, 2002.

[2] J. M. Hawley "Digging for diamonds: A conceptual framework for understanding reclaimed textile products" Clothing and Textiles Research Journal, vol. 24, no. 3, pp. 262-275, 2006.

[3] L. Welters, and A. Lillethun "The fashion reader. Berg Publishers", 2011.

[4] D. Francis. " Mending the Capitalist Model", Financial Post., 2014, Retrieved: http://www.financialpost.com

[5] S. J. Jones. "Fashion design". Laurence King Publishing, 2005.

[6] I. Verpoest and S. V. Lomov. "Virtual textile composites software WiseTex: Integration with micro-mechanical, permeability and structural analysis" Composites Science and Technology, vol. 65 no. 15, pp. 2563-2574, 2005.

[7] R. Kamiya, B. A. Cheeseman, P. Popper, and T. W. Chou, "Some recent advances in the fabrication and design of threedimensional textile preforms: a review," Composites science and technology, vol. 60, no. 1, pp. 33-47, 2000.

[8] N. Lintu, J. Holopainen, and O. Hänninen. "Usability of textile-integrated electrodes for EMG measurements" University of Kuopio, Department of Physiology, Laboratory of Clothing Physiology, Kuopio, Finland, 2005.

[9] C. Gale, and J. Kaur. "The textile book". Berg Publishers, 2005.

[10] S. Kursun-Bahadir, V. Koncar, F. Kalaoğlu, I. Cristian, and S. Thomassey. "Assessing the signal quality of an ultrasonic sensor on different conductive yarns used as transmission lines" Fibres & Textiles in Eastern Europe, 2011.

[11] www.pointcarre.com/Textile Design Software. last accessed on 1st December 2016

[12] www.vetigraph.com last accessed on 1st December 2016

[13] www.pluraltechnology.com last accessed on 1st December 2016

[14] www.colormattersintl.com last accessed on 1st December 2016

[15] www.generation-digital.net last accessed on 1st December 2016

[16] www.bontex.it last accessed on 1st December 2016

[17] www.designsew.com last accessed on 1st December 2016

[18] www.digifab.net/systems/ last accessed on 1st December 2016

[19] www.lectra.com last accessed on 1st December 2016

[20] okmodern.wix.com/smartdesigner

[21] J. Prümper. "Der Benutzungsfragebogen ISONORM 9241/10: Ergebnisse zur Reliabilität und Validität" In Software-Ergonomie'97, pp. 253-262, Vieweg+ Teubner Verlag, 1997.

[22] A. M. F. Yousef, M. A. Chatti, U. Schroeder, and M. Wosnitza. "A usability evaluation of a blended MOOC environment: An experimental case study" The International Review of Research in Open and Distributed Learning, vol. 16 no 2, 2015.

[23] B. Boehm. "Spiral Development: Experience, Principles,and Refinements", Special Report CMU/SEI-2000-SR-008, July 2000

Visualizing Workload and Emotion Data in Air Traffic Control - An Approach Informed by the Supervisors Decision Making Process

Linda Pfeiffer, Tabea Sims

Institute for Media Studies
Chemnitz University of Technology
Email: <firstName>.<familyName>@phil.tu-chemnitz.de

Paul Rosenthal

Institute of Computer Science
University of Rostock
Email: research@paul-rosenthal.de

***Abstract*—The work of a supervisor, working in an area control center in air traffic control, seems to be rarely addressed by research. Within this paper, we present a preliminary study that deals with the supervisors decision making process, current practices and interfaces. Based on this study, we derived design guidelines to the development of a visualization, displaying the air traffic controllers' workload and emotional state, thus supporting the supervisors decision making.**

Keywords–air traffic control supervisor; visualization, workload data, emotional data, decision making

I. Introduction

Usually known for having one of the most stressful jobs or causing huge delays when being on a strike, air traffic controllers provide a safe, orderly and fluent handling of the air traffic. Not only do tower controllers coordinate departing and landing aircraft on airports, but also while being airborne, air traffic is constantly monitored, managed, and sustained by area center controllers. In order to overview the whole air space, it is divided into sectors, where each one is overseen by two controllers. In fact this job can be very demanding, so someone is needed to keep an overview of what is going on across sectors and prevent them and the assigned controllers from getting overwhelmed.

This task goes to the air traffic controllers' supervisors, who administer air traffic on a bigger scale, mostly by supporting and directing controllers. Especially since the controller's job is taxing and emotions can have a big impact on ones condition, it might help supervisors to know about their controllers' mental states, in order to balance out their workload and to offer better support to them.

Within this paper, we present preliminary studies, that analyze the supervisor's work and point out the usefulness of an emotion data display. We end up with the design requirements for such a visualization.

We start in Section II by introducing the StayCentered project that frames this piece of work. In Section III, a brief description of air traffic control supervisors' work is presented, followed by some related work in Section IV. The methodology and the results are presented in Sections V and VI. Finally, we give our interpretation regarding the emotion display in Section VII and finish with the conclusion and aims for future work in Section VIII.

II. The StayCentered Project

The main goal in air traffic control is to assure safe, orderly and fluent handling of the air traffic. This is a highly demanding task. Thus, the project "'StayCentered - Methodenbasis eines Assistenzsystems für Fluglotsen (MACeLot)"' at the university of technology Chemnitz aims for giving support to air traffic controllers in stressful situations. The resulting system should be capable of identifying the emotional and cognitive state of the air traffic controllers and simulating their state with regard to upcoming air traffic some hours in advance. Galvanic skin response, facial action coding, body posture, vocal properties, eye movements and pupil dilation are recorded and used to infer an emotion valence, arousal level, and cognitive load. The assistance of the air traffic controllers will be realized by self-adapting interfaces [1] and by providing this information to their supervisors. Such a visualization of the controller's emotional and cognitive state may support the supervisors decision upon the opening of a sector, in order to reduce the controller's workload. This paper presents preliminary studies of the supervisors work and the resulting design requirements.

III. The Air Traffic Control Supervisor

Before going into detail of our studies, we want to give a short description of what an air traffic control supervisor does and what tools and general environment he is provided with.

As a superior and shift leader of air traffic controllers, the main work of a supervisor is to manage assignments and shift-structures of controllers, while regulating their workload by handling air traffic flow across sectors.

The regulation of traffic flow is done by splitting or merging sectors, permitting or forbidding special maneuvers (like, e.g., skydiving or air force trainings) and in extreme cases even regulating sectors by setting a maximum number of allowed planes and rejecting any exceeding traffic, which usually leads to delay. However, the amount of traffic that can be handled is limited by the number of present controllers and the Supervisor's job is to assign them in such a way that simultaneously no employee is overexerted and air traffic can flow undisturbed.

We experienced that supervisors do not work alone but divide their work by region, where each one can operate independently but still help each other if necessary.

The actual work place is located within the area air traffic control center, often in the middle of the operations room or a little elevated, providing a good overview. Other non-controller positions can be found alongside. These include technical surveillance, data assistants, flight data agents/operators, flow management position, and the technical supervisor.

Each supervisor's workplace comes with a computer, equipped with two monitors, serving as their main working tool. Among other work specific software, the most important one is a shift management program, where active sectors are scheduled, air traffic controller's shifts are organized and controllers can be notified by publishing the current plan on a separate screen.

In addition supervisors have several information systems, specific to each center, as well as communication devices, such as an email program, a land-line telephone and a direct-dial telephone.

IV. RELATED WORK

This section presents literature related to various aspects of the topics tackled in this paper.

A. Supervisors

In order to assess the supervisor's work, research in this field should be taken into consideration. Broach et al. [2] showed the importance of the supervisor's position. They found a correlation between the supervisor-controller-ratio and the number of errors made by air traffic controllers. Unfortunately we did not find any further literature on air traffic control supervisors, suggesting we might be first to focus on this group.

However, research shows that the general supervisor-employee relationship has a direct impact on the employees work motivation, organizational identification, and perceived career relevance [3]. Furthermore, emotional intelligence on both, a personal and a group level, has been proven to improve collaboration and communication, while emotional contagion can increase efficiency and decrease conflict potential [4][5].

B. Decision Support System Design

As the emotion visualization should support the supervisors decision making, some general work about decision support systems and design implications is introduced here.

The design process of decision support systems should always go from the "inside" to the "outside", meaning desired functions should get identified first and then restrictions of the outside world should be taken into account. Ariav et al. [6] propose to start with analyzing task characteristics and making a decision on the intended level of support.

Different implications for a visualization can be derived from the task. Well-structured problems, are best supported by showing possible outcomes and eventually the underlying model. Whereas a lot of visualization techniques can help to explore and evaluate available data, when a person is required to base a decision on this data. Sometimes conclusions are based on previous experience, domain knowledge, and situation awareness, where the last two could get enhanced visually [7].

Researchers keep stressing the importance of adequately including users during the whole process. As Miah et al. [8] report many projects fail because of different goals of users and designers as well as insufficient involvement of stakeholders. And when the systems do not get used in the intended way, the reason often is a mismatch of requirements between users and designers or unfamiliarity with the provided functions [9].

Benbasat also recommends to consider cognitive styles of users. As for example analytic decision makers might trust mathematically or quantitatively supported reports easily, while heuristic decision makers usually like to explore and analyze,

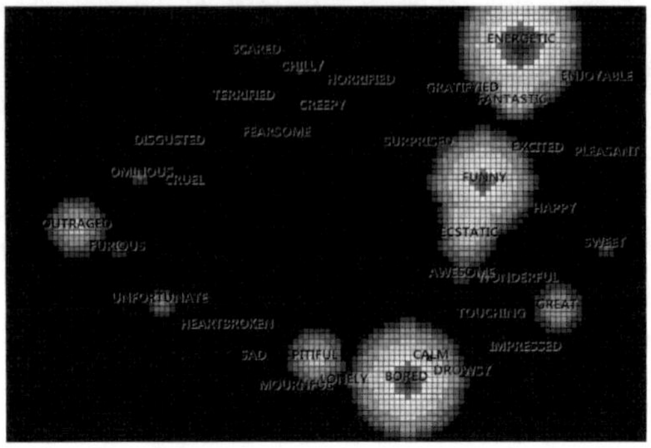

Figure 1. A visualization of the value and amount of emotional connections to a movie as a heat map on a valence-arousal-coordinate system [10].

suggesting the implementation of the possibility to switch between different levels of detail.

C. Emotion Visualizations

A lot of work has already be done in the field of visualizing emotions, especially in the context of social media.

For example Ha et al. [10] visualize sentiments connected to movies with their focus on easy recognition of clusters and intricate network structure. The visualization in Figure 1 is a detail view for one node within that structure, showing emotions connected to a single movie as a heat map on the valence-arousal-coordinate system. Additionally some points in the coordinate system are labeled with the common name of that emotion.

Steed et al. [11] constructed a similar view, shown in Figure 2a, within their visual application to dynamically analyze twitter sentiment. Their coordinate system uses arousal and dominance as axes while showing valence in color (orange for negative and blue for positive). However, this again is just an additional display, next to a geographical depiction of tweets, while the main view is a visualization of the amount of tweets (divided in binary valence) over time, shown in Figure 2b. This view is designed interactive to select time intervals for further inspection in the other images.

Working on the same problem, of analyzing twitter sentiments over time, Wang et al. [12] came up with a solution integrating valence, arousal and time into a single visualization, as shown in Figure 3. Each ring in the circle represents a different step in time (designed to resemble the view in a tunnel) while the amplitude within the ring is defined by the valence-arousal-coordinate-system. Since the curve is additionally color coded by valence and arousal, the rings could also be displayed as straight lines, which might be a little less disorienting for some users. Thus, the amount of tweets, currently shown by the bar on the left, could also be aligned.

A completely different application is that of Cernea et al [13], who designed an emotion visualization on touch displays, giving users direct feedback in the color and shape of the selection highlighting. However, they also created a separate view, showing the different emotions of the touch events over time, in order to let users reflect and compare themselves with other users (Figure 4). They displayed time on the horizontal axis while valence is shown in direction and size of the bars and arousal is color coded (blue is little and red is much).

The program in Figure 5 [14] was developed to directly track user emotions while they are watching or listening to

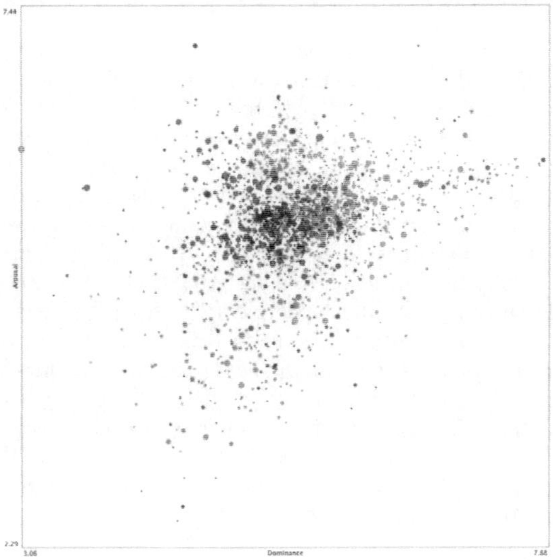

(a)

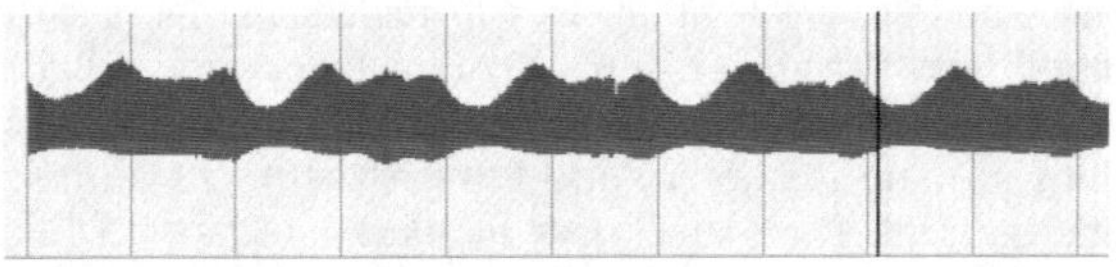

(b)

Figure 2. A sentiment visualization concerning a specific topic on twitter [11]. (a) The emotion is shown as arousal and dominance on the axes, the valence is color coded and its amount is shown as the size of each dot. (b) The number of positive and negative posts is shown over time.

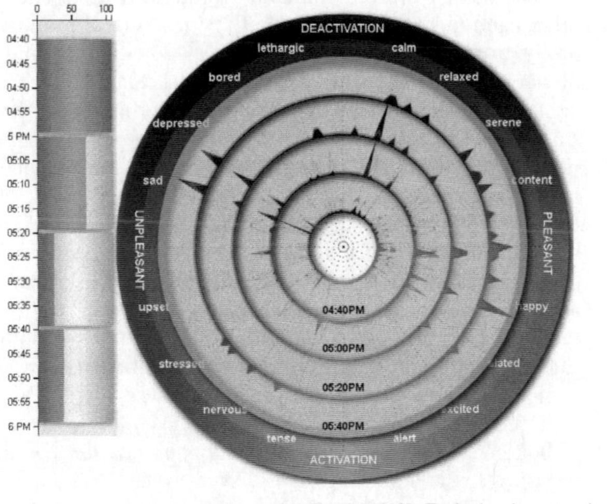

Figure 3. Another twitter-sentiment visualization [12]. Each ring is a step in time, while the curve depicts the valence and arousal.

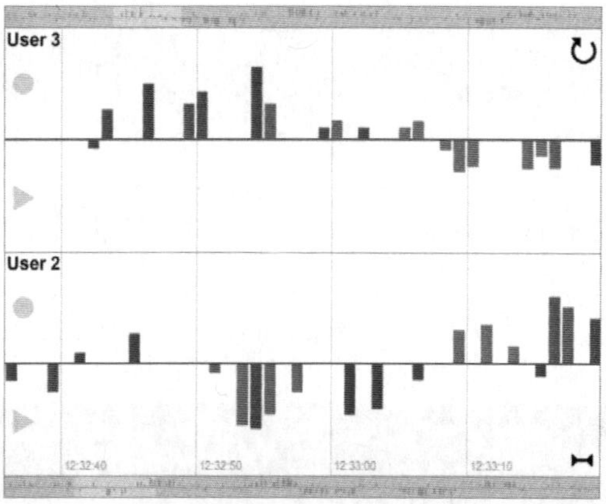

Figure 4. An emotion visualization over time for individual users by Cernea et al. [13].

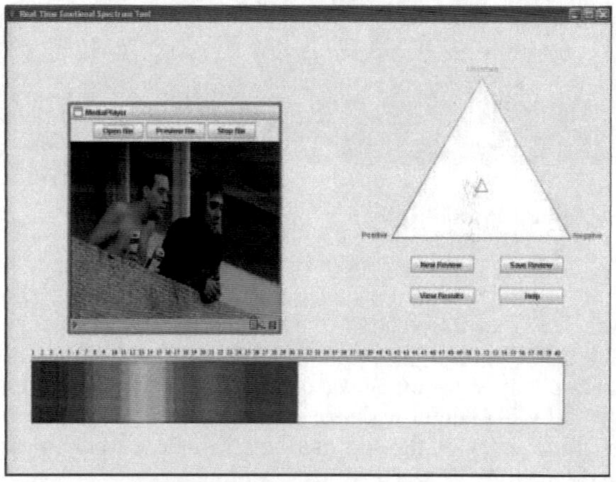

Figure 5. An emotion input interface concerning a video [14]. The bottom bar shows collected emotions on a time line, while the color shows the value of each step.

some kind of media playing. Thus the media player box on the left. On the triangle to the right the recipient is supposed to report current emotions by accordingly placing his mouse within that triangle. Thus, valence and uncertainty are measured. The input gets tracked and displayed in the bottom bar as visual feedback of the opinion development. Time is the horizontal axis in the bar while the color gets computed as the distance to each corner of the triangle mapped on the opacity of one of the base colors in RGB. It is also possible to render the results of multiple users on top of each other, showing the mean opinion of all of them.

Yet another approach is to use some kind of emoticon, like the manikins in Figure 6, designed for visual feedback, e.g., in questionnaires. Sonderegger et al. [15] even found in a user study, comparing different pictographs, that the ones shown in Figure 6 could be further enhanced by using an animated heart as arousal indicator instead of the rather abstract shape depicted here. This might be the most intuitive way for emotion visualization. However, research shows that the bigger the set size and complexity of the icons, the harder they are to identify, even more so when they are rather similar [16][17].

Finally, there is also the work of McDuff et al. [18], who created a very detailed visualization of emotions connected to work. Their goal was to use the device for personal reflection over longer periods of time. The result is shown in Figure 7.

Figure 6. An emotion visualization in manikins [15]. The facial expression shows valence while the shape on his chest depicts arousal.

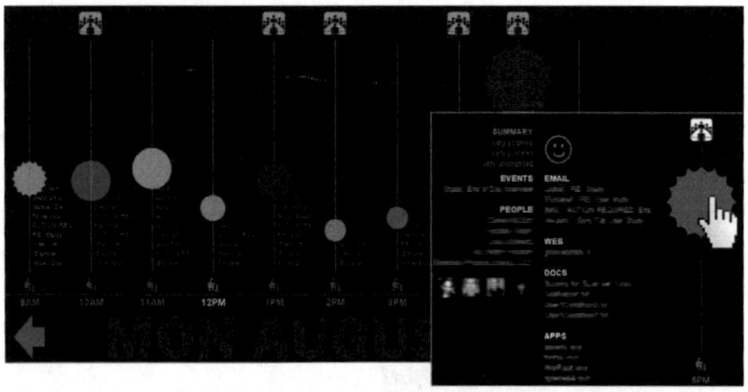

Figure 7. A visualization of emotion during a work day for personal reflection [18].

They encoded emotions in the bubbles with color showing valence (pink is positive, purple neutral and blue negative), shape showing arousal (calm is round and aroused is pointy) and opacity showing engagement. Work related information is given by the height and size of the bubbles (desktop activity), by little icons at the top and bottom of each bar (meetings) and text (further work related information).

The summary in Table I gives an overview of the just described visualizations and how different variables are presented.

V. METHODOLOGY

Main goal of the preliminary studies was the identification of design requirements such that the intended visualization serves the supervisors needs best. This implies first establishing an understanding about the supervisors tasks and their way of decision making. Furthermore, we wanted to find about the qualities of stress and emotion data needed by the supervisors and we wanted to learn from the use of the current interfaces and from its positive and problematic impact on the supervisors work.

We did two full-day observations at the end of September 2016 of the supervisors working place in the Munich area control center. The researchers had the chance to ask clarifying questions during the observation and collected the data by handwritten notes. Furthermore, we interviewed seven supervisors, each interview lasting 18 - 51 minutes on their decision-making process, their information needs, as well as on the role of the air traffic controller's workload and emotional situation in their decision-making process and the data's level of detail favored by the supervisors. During the interview, we invited the supervisors, to sketch their decision process and the considered information, this was done to make them reflect their decisions structured and not forgetting anything. The data was audio recorded during the interviews and transliterated. For analysis, the data was coded and categorized. We did not use a standardized coding scheme, because of the exploratory nature of the research questions.

TABLE I. OVERVIEW OF ENCODINGS OF DIFFERENT VARIABLES IN THE GIVEN EMOTION VISUALIZATIONS.

Vis.	Valence	Arousal	Time	No of Persons
1	horizontal axis	vertical axis	-	multiple
2a	color	vertical axis	-	multiple
2b	direction + color	-	horizontal axis	multiple
3	horizontal amplitude + color	vertical amplitude + color	rings (tunnel view)	multiple
4	size + direction	color	horizontal axis	single
5 Triangle	horizontal axis	-	-	single
5 Bar	color	-	h. axis	single
6	facial expression	shape	-	single
7	color	shape	horizontal axis	single

VI. RESULTS AND DISCUSSION

Our first step in preparation of designing a well suited stress and emotion visualization, was to understand the supervisors tasks. The supervisors task area includes tasks concerning ongoing operations and tasks beyond. Beyond ongoing operations, the supervisors have to fulfill tasks in human resources management. Each supervisor is responsible for 15 to 20 air traffic controllers. Additionally they may have optional special tasks like the participation in research projects or committees. As our visualization is most beneficial in ongoing operations we concentrated on this part of the supervisors work.

The principal task of a supervisor is to keep ongoing operations fluently going. This means, doing everything, so that the circumstances allow the air traffic controllers safe, orderly and fluent handling of the air traffic. The supervisors called themselves well-paid secretaries, in order to express that they are responsible for every concern in the operation room. The principal task can be divided into sub tasks. At the one hand there are somehow formalized tasks and at the other hand more informal tasks. Even the formalized tasks are rarely provided with clear instructions, allowing for a multitude of alternatives. The only task with clear instructions is the documentation of events, that happened during the supervisors shift. This task is not very favored by the supervisors, according to them they are spending too much time documenting insignificant events. This may be a task that is very suitable for automation. Each day, there are two briefings scheduled, wherein the supervisor updates the controllers. Most of their time the supervisors spend on planning the day's shift schedule and solving occurring bottlenecks and problems. We observed two ways of planning: some supervisors prefer planning of the whole shift and changing the schedule if necessary. Others avoid this strategy, because of the numerous changes and prefer a piecewise planning. On the other hand, there is the solving of bottlenecks and problems, that may put the safety of aircraft in risk. This is a very creative task, because of the numerous possible solutions. Sometimes supervisors even consult their colleagues and the air traffic controllers on this behalf.

The informal tasks are rather some kind of good practice and skills. Their implementation depends on the individual supervisor. Over the entire shift, even if the supervisor seems to relax a while, he is observing the current situation at the operation control room and looking for abnormal situations. Each abnormality may induce safety problems. A controller speaking to the technician holding his interaction device in his hand, may be an indicator for a malfunction of equipment. Especially if a controller switches his status on the status display to a warning level, the supervisor will go to the controllers working position to asses the situation. In order to assure the controller's ability to work under pressure, the supervisor is trying to determine their daily emotional state and basic stress level, thus he can consider this in the shift schedule or, in extreme cases, advising a controller to rest. Generally, the supervisor tries to prevent controllers from stress by using formal means, like splitting up a sector or by regulating the number of aircraft that are allowed to enter the sector, or by using more informal means like warning the controllers of a short high traffic peak. Usually the supervisor complies with flat hierarchies. This has practical effects, like asking the controllers for their opinion about suggested solutions or by considering the controllers wishes in the shift schedule. They are also trying to support the air traffic controllers on their issues, even if they are not in their field of responsibility, e.g., they check for the location of a meeting. Altogether, a supervisor needs interpersonal skills, he should be sensible to individual communication patterns. It is a well known issue in leadership studies, that the political skills of a supervisor, including social asturence, may have a positive impact on the team performance [19][20]. The ability to identify the others needs by observation and to attune to divers social situations allows for better communication and improvements in supporting the controllers.

However, the supervisor is not just concerned about the controllers issues, but he also tries to support his colleague. He stands in for his colleague during breaks and he reminds him of important tasks. This is appreciated by the other supervisor.

There are some typical decisions a supervisor has to face in his daily work. Besides the decision of the briefing topics, the most critical decisions are made in the tasks of planning the day's shift schedule and preventing and solving bottlenecks and problems. The planning task includes the decision which controller has to work at which position. This decision is guided by several constraints. The solution should be safe as well as cost effective. That means that safety rules need to be met, e.g., considering breaks, two controllers should be responsible for one sector, assuring that no controller is overstrained. Simultaneously every controller should be busy, taking special tasks, trainings and so on into consideration. Potential bottlenecks and problems may be caused by external demands or extraordinary circumstances. The supervisor has to decide whether to allow for external demands, like photo flights, gliding flight areas, or planned detonations. Other external demands are obligatory (e.g., activation of special air spaces or military trainings) and the supervisor has to decide on a suitable reaction to this. The decision on the reaction to extraordinary circumstances includes malfunction of the technical equipment, potential overloads in traffic quantity, which may result in splitting up a sector or a regulation of the number of aircraft. In addition there may occur staff concerns, like illness or spontaneous meetings, that force the supervisor to alternative solutions or looking for someone replacing the missing controller, and there other troubles may occur, e.g., fire alarms. None of these decisions can be seen separated. each decision on one variable of the system has impact on another and may result in new decisions to be made. For instance, the decision on splitting up a sector entails a change in the shift schedule or regulating the number of aircraft in one sector increases the number of aircraft in other sectors.

Based on their experience, the supervisors identified variables, that are affecting the capacity of a sector or constraining their scope of action. Information upon these variables should be available to the supervisors. They should know about the standard sector plan, that tells which sectors should be open. It is based on statistics of the past years and is the basis for the shift schedule. The available staff is a framing variable for the scope of action, this includes the air traffic controllers on duty as well as controllers, who are around but fulfilling other tasks (paperwork, trainings, meetings, and so on). The latter may be consulted in the case of staffing shortage, but usual the information is hardly available. Also, the staffs condition is a factor to the capacity of a sector: their daily performance, fatigue, their satisfaction. To keep satisfaction high the supervisors, try to assure that the controllers are facing variable demands, that they are sharing a position with someone with whom they accord, and that some of their preferences will be met. The information about alternative tasks a controller has to do is necessary in order to assure cost efficiency, but it is often incomplete. The main factors on a sectors capacity are the expected traffic load and the weather conditions. The weather forecast is needed 2 hours in advance, but up to this day, weather predictions are not always reliable. The quantity of the expected traffic is also automatically predicted, by considering the aircraft's flight plans. A 2 hours forecast is highly unreliable, but with each minute this estimation is getting more precise. In contrast, to the quantity predicting the traffic quality is even challenging for an expert. 15 aircraft flying straight in a line may be less demanding than 7 aircraft climbing and descending with a different headings. Extraordinary circumstances as safety issues in the area control center (e.g., fire alarms) and technical concerns (malfunction of equipment or the use of backup systems) may reduce the capacity of a sector extremely. Also, visual clutter on the radar screen, coming from a lot of aircraft below or above the sector, is limiting the sectors capacity. A variable that is consulted rather unconscious, is the own constitution, it has some effect on the consideration of external demands or controllers wishes. When a supervisor has not the full overview on the current situation he is not willing to generate any additional workload to his controllers or himself. This listing of variables is an attempt to get a structured view on the variables needed by the supervisors and is not complete, as every situation is unique and may require other information.

Altogether the supervisors are facing complex problems [21][22]. They have to address many variables that are interrelated, the time for decision making is limited, and some events occur unexpected (illness, external demands, emergencies, etc.). They have to outweigh different goals (safety, cost efficiency, controllers satisfaction) and the information needed is incomplete and sometimes not reliable. They make decisions for the future based on current data, personal heuristics and unreliable predictions. The heuristics they use for problem solving are based on their experience. They are able to anticipate the effect of the variables on the sectors capacity and they know how to weigh the influence of a variable to a specific type of problems.

As we are interested in designing a stress and emotion visualization, we wanted to have a further look on the role of stress, workload and emotion data. As stated above, the supervisors already take the controllers basic stress level and severe emotional states into consideration. By now they have to look for this information during conversations with the controllers. The information on the controllers workload, stress and boredom is considered as useful in two terms: A prediction of the workload in a specific sector, is seen as alternative approach to current traffic quantity predictions and may thus help with the planning of the shift schedule. Moreover, an information upon the controllers former and current stress level may help in assigning suitable tasks to the controller. The relevance of detecting stress seems to be much more important than boredom. During periods of boredom, controllers lean back and start chatting. Thus, the supervisors stated, that they can easily observe boredom. In contrast, stress is sometimes not even recognized by the controllers themselves. The use of emotion data is seen much more diverging than the workload data. On the one hand the emotion data may be useful when the controllers emotional state in extremely emotional situations hinders him from doing his job. On the other hand they refuse using this data. This arises from the expected professionalism, from the fear of treating other controllers unfair, when someone is pretending to be in a bad mood, and from concerns about privacy. Both, showing the data linked to an individual controller and showing it linked to a sector, may be useful. Sector related data is similar to current traffic quantity predictions, whereas individual data may help by assigning each controller a suitable task. There are ethical concerns about showing the data person related.

As already mentioned in Section III, the supervisors working place offers a multitude of tools and information systems to support their decision making. The three main tools are the shift management program, an overview of the planned controllers and a notepad. This physical notepad, is an important tool since it allows for quick note taking and thus remembering important tasks and lines of thought. This is necessary because the supervisors thoughts are often interrupted by incoming demands and information. These main tools are complemented by a multitude of information and communication systems, where information can be retrieved and is pushed through. Conspicuous about the interfaces was the importance of clear arrangement. Consistency of representations and data between systems and tools are as important as unambiguous interaction strategies [23][24][25]. Using different time zones and coding same meanings differently led to misunderstandings and cognitive resources were occupied. The supervisors had to transfer data from one tool to another manually, this took time and cognitive resources. Further more several similar interaction devices, each of them belonging to another system, were confounded, thus slowing the progress down.

VII. Implications to a Workload and Emotion Visualization

As workload and emotion data turned out to be relevant to the supervisors task, an automation of the detection of the controllers workload and emotional state seems to be promising. However, this data is useless without an effective visualization of the data.

Based on the findings of this preliminary study and completed by general visualization guidelines, we developed a set of design requirements to a workload and emotion visualization for supervisors working at an area control center:

- R1 In order to consider the controllers state during scheduling, the workload data needs to be accessible in an overview over a period of time ranging from 2 hours in the past to 2 hours in the future.
- R2 Emotion data will be restricted to extreme situations, in order to address ethical issues.
- R3 Extreme situations should be visible at a glance. Extreme stress, extreme boredom, as well as extreme negative emotions may hinder the air traffic controllers work, so that intervention of the supervisor may be appropriate.
- R4 The visualization should support the supervisors notional categories. Thus, the data should be available related to the individual controller as well as to the working positions.
- R5 The visualization must concentrate on a minimal set of primitives to produce an expressive and effective visualization [26] with minimal disturbance of the work flow. All important features should be easily identifiable and all visual elements should have an important meaning. Color should only be used when really needed to highlight very important features and taking into account human visual perception [27].

VIII. Conclusion and Future Work

We presented a preliminary study on the work process of air traffic control supervisors. We investigated the supervisors tasks and decision making process as well as their current interfaces and ended up with design requirements for the development of a workload and emotion visualization.

Next steps in our project will be the design of the intended visualization within a human centered iterative process. It will be integrated into the StayCentered system and evaluated. Beyond that, further investigation of the application area and the design of a complete decision support system seem to be promising, as the application area is rarely addressed by research so far.

Acknowledgments

This work was supported by the German Federal Ministry of Education and Research in the project StayCentered - Methodenbasis eines Assistenzsystems für Centerlotsen (MACeLot). Furthermore, we thank the German air navigation service provider DFS Deutsche Flugsicherung GmbH and the participating supervisors for their support.

References

[1] L. Pfeiffer, G. Valtin, N. H. Müller, and P. Rosenthal, "The mental organization of air traffic and its implications to an emotion sensitive assistance system," International Journal on Advances in Life Sciences, vol. 8, 2016, pp. 164–174.

[2] D. Broach and C. S. Dollar, "Relationship of employee attitudes and supervisor-controller ratio to en route operational error rates," US Department of Transportation, Federal Aviation Administration, Office of Aerospace Medicine, Tech. Rep., 2002.

[3] M. Sollitto, M. M. Martin, S. Dusic, K. E. Gibbons, and A. Wagenhouser, "Assessing the supervisor-subordinate relationship involving part-time employees," International Journal of Business Communication, vol. 53, no. 1, 2016, pp. 74–96.

[4] V. U. Druskat and S. B. Wolff, "Building the emotional intelligence of groups," Harvard business review, vol. 79, no. 3, 2001, pp. 80–91.

[5] S. G. Barsade and A. P. Knight, "Group Affect," Annual Review of Organizational Psychology and Organizational Behavior, vol. 2, no. 1, Apr. 2015, pp. 21–46.

[6] G. Ariav and M. J. Ginzberg, "DSS design: a systemic view of decision support," Communications of the ACM, vol. 28, no. 10, 1985, pp. 1045–1052.

[7] B. Zhu and H. Chen, "Information visualization for decision support," in Handbook on Decision Support Systems 2: Variations. Berlin, Heidelberg: Springer Berlin Heidelberg, 2008, pp. 699–722.

[8] S. J. Miah and J. McKay, "A New Conceptualisation of Design Science Research for DSS Development Research," in Proceedings of the Pacific Asia Conference on Information Systems (PACIS) 2016, 2016. [Online]. Available: http://aisel.aisnet.org/pacis2016/384

[9] I. Benbasat, "Cognitive style considerations in DSS design," ACM SIGMIS Database, vol. 8, no. 3, 1977, pp. 37–38.

[10] H. Ha, G.-n. Kim, W. Hwang, H. Choi, and K. Lee, "CosMovis: Analyzing semantic network of sentiment words in movie reviews," in Large Data Analysis and Visualization (LDAV), 2014 IEEE 4th Symposium on. IEEE, 2014, pp. 113–114.

[11] C. A. Steed, M. Drouhard, J. Beaver, J. Pyle, and P. L. Bogen, "Matisse: A visual analytics system for exploring emotion trends in social media text streams," in Big Data (Big Data), 2015 IEEE International Conference on. IEEE, 2015, pp. 807–814.

[12] F. Y. Wang, A. Sallaberry, K. Klein, M. Takatsuka, and M. Roche, "SentiCompass: Interactive visualization for exploring and comparing the sentiments of time-varying twitter data," in Visualization Symposium (PacificVis), 2015 IEEE Pacific. IEEE, 2015, pp. 129–133.

[13] D. Cernea, C. Weber, A. Ebert, and A. Kerren, "Emotion-prints: interaction-driven emotion visualization on multi-touch interfaces," in Proc. SPIE 9397, Visualization and Data Analysis 2015, D. L. Kao, M. C. Hao, M. A. Livingston, and T. Wischgoll, Eds., Feb. 2015, pp. 93 970A–93 970A–15.

[14] J. Ohene-Djan, A. Sammon, and R. Shipsey, "Colour Spectrum's of Opinion: An Information Visualisation Interface for Representing Degrees of Emotion in Real Time," in Tenth International Conference on Information Visualization. IEEE, July 2006, pp. 80–88.

[15] A. Sonderegger, K. Heyden, A. Chavaillaz, and J. Sauer, "Anisam & aniavatar: Animated visualizations of affective states," in Proceedings of the 2016 CHI Conference on Human Factors in Computing Systems, ser. CHI '16. New York, NY, USA: ACM, 2016, pp. 4828–4837.

[16] M. D. Byrne, "Using icons to find documents: simplicity is critical," in Proceedings of the INTERACT'93 and CHI'93 conference on Human factors in computing systems. ACM, 1993, pp. 446–453.

[17] L. Nowell, R. Schulman, and D. Hix, "Graphical encoding for information visualization: an empirical study," in Information Visualization, 2002. INFOVIS 2002. IEEE Symposium on. IEEE, 2002, pp. 43–50.

[18] D. McDuff, A. Karlson, A. Kapoor, A. Roseway, and M. Czerwinski, "AffectAura: an intelligent system for emotional memory," in Proceedings of the SIGCHI Conference on Human Factors in Computing Systems. ACM, 2012, pp. 849–858.

[19] J. Liu, W. Wang, and K. Cao, "Leader political skill and team performance: a moderated mediation model," Nankai Business Review International, vol. 2, no. 1, 2011, pp. 5–22.

[20] R. L. Brouer, C.-Y. C. Chiu, and L. Wang, "Political skill dimensions and transformational leadership in china," Journal of Managerial Psychology, vol. 31, no. 6, 2016, pp. 1040–1056.

[21] J. Funke, "Complex problem solving: a case for complex cognition?" Cognitive Processing, vol. 11, no. 2, 2010, pp. 133–142.

[22] J. Quesada, W. Kintsch, and E. Gomez, "Complex problem-solving: a field in search of a definition?" Theoretical Issues in Ergonomics Science, vol. 6, no. 1, 2005, pp. 5–33.

[23] J. Nielsen, Coordinating User Interfaces for Consistency. Morgan Kaufmann, 1989.

[24] C. Ware, Information visualization: perception for design. Morgan Kaufmann, 2013.

[25] W. Lidwell, K. Holden, and J. Butler, Universal Principles of Design, Revised and Updated: 125 Ways to Enhance Usability, Influence Perception, Increase Appeal, Make Better Design Decisions, and Teach Through Design. Rockport Publishers, 2010.

[26] A. Sears and J. A. Jacko, Eds., The Human-Computer Interaction Handbook: Fundamentals, Evolving Technologies, and Emerging Applications. Lawrence Erlbaum Assoc Inc, 2007.

[27] E. Tufte, Envisioning Information. Graphics Press, 1990.

Changes in Small Eye Movements in Response to Impressions of Emotion-Evoking Pictures

Tetsuya Furuta
Control and System Engineering
Tokyo Institute of Technology
Ookayama, Meguro-ku, Tokyo, Japan

Minoru Nakayama
Information and Communications Engineering
Tokyo Institute of Technology
Ookayama, Meguro-ku, Tokyo, Japan
email: nakayama@ict.e.titech.ac.jp

Abstract—**The possibility of evaluating the emotional impressions of pictures was examined using the cross power spectrum density (CPSD) of small eye movements. Pictures were employed as a set of normative emotional stimuli and were presented to 7 male subjects in order to evoke emotional impressions. The eye movements resulting from each stimulus were measured using a video based eye tracker while the viewer's subjective impression for each picture was rated. The stimuli were then grouped as "Pleasant" or "Unpleasant". In comparing the CPSDs of eye movements between two groups, the powers of the CPSDs for the "Unpleasant" group were significantly higher, at 3.75-7.5Hz during the 400-1033.3ms after stimulus onset. This result confirms that eye movements reflect viewer's emotional impression.**

***Keywords*–eye movements; emotional assessment; subjective assessment; cross power spectrum**

I. INTRODUCTION

Emotional impressions require the highest level of information processing, and emotions are an essential facet of human behavior. Therefore, this activity has been studied psychologically and clinically, and has often been referred to in the study of applied sciences, such as marketing. The emotional state which is created in some patients is often measured using eye oscillations such as small eye movements [1]–[3]. As the eye oscillations also reflect the mental workload in a specific task [4], a more detailed analysis is required.

However, as the definition of an emotional state remains ambiguous, facial expressions were used to evoke viewer's responses. During the experiment, the frequency power of small eye movements can indicate the degree of "Unpleasant" impressions of facial expressions [5]. Whether the phenomenon is maintained when various images are used should be confirmed. In addition to this, the observation procedure has not yet been established.

This paper confirmed the possibility of using a set of normative emotional stimuli of photos and a typical video based eye tracker to detect viewer's emotional responses using the responses of their eye movements. Also, a procedure for evaluating eye movement was established. This paper is organized as follows. Section II gives a brief description of previous works, and Section III presents the experimental method. In Section IV, the results of the experiment are shown, and the discussion is summarized in Section V. Section VI concludes the overall results.

II. PREVIOUS WORK

The relationships between facial expressions and the observer's eye movements has been studied previously [6]. An observer's emotional impressions are stimulated by the viewing of facial expressions, due to a kind of emotional synchronization [7]. The responses of both eye movements and event related potentials (ERPs), such as the observation of brain activity, were analyzed after pictures of facial emotions that had been prepared as the Japanese and Caucasian Facial Expression of Emotion (JACFEE) collection [8] were shown to participants. The individual impressions of the facial expressions in the pictures were evaluated using a scale called the "Affect Grid" [9]. The results of viewer's rating patterns were extracted using cluster analysis, and assigned to two clusters labeled "Pleasant" and "Unpleasant" [10]. Also, there were some significant differences in the waveforms of ERPs between the two clusters [10]. All of the differences suggest that the degree of two dimensional eye oscillation for "Unpleasant" facial images is significantly higher than for "Pleasant" images.

To extract perceptual differences between the two groups of emotional face images, ERP potentials were compared at three typical positions on the scalp, such as the Frontal (Fz), Central (Cz) and Occipital areas, according to the international 10-20 system. Significant differences in frontal electrode Fz from 142.5ms to 192.5 ms and central electrode Cz from 132.5ms to 195.0 ms were observed [10]. The difference was not detected in waveforms at the Oz (Occipital) electrode. Emotional recognition is a thought process at the highest level, and the differences appear on potentials at an early stage, from between 130 to 195 milliseconds after the introduction of the stimulus at the mid and frontal areas [10].

In regard to these results, as ERP responses to facial expressions occur earlier than the reactions to eye movements [11] [12], some specific area of brain activation may trigger these eye movements. As there are some latencies in eye movement after stimulus onset [13], eye movement may follow a rapid physiological response such as an ERP. In order to examine the phenomenon, the relationships between the two indices were analyzed for every 160msec. time interval. The results provide evidence that the activity of an electrode at the central area of the scalp affects eye movement between 220 and 540ms when "Unpleasant" images of facial expressions are displayed. This phenomenon is more highly emphasized during the viewing of "Unpleasant" facial expression images than it is during the viewing of "Pleasant" images [5].

During the experiment, eye movement was measured using electro-oculograms (EOGs) at a sampling rate of 400Hz. Eye oscillation activity was calculated as a cross power spectrum density (CPSD) using the two dimensional positions of eye movement. The EOG observation requires four electrodes which are placed directly around the eyes of the subjects, so that viewing activities are restricted. In addition to this, the measuring technique did not focus on the frequency powers of lower frequency ranges where eye oscillations during fixation increase the power of CPSDs. While most eye trackers are designed for use during unrestricted viewing, observations were measured at a sampling rate of 60Hz. Therefore, the sampling rate and the period of observation used to detect eye oscillation should be considered carefully.

In order to determine the feasibility of observing eye oscillations at a lower sampling rate, the EOG data was re-sampled at 60Hz and analyzed using CPSD measurements and an observation interval set at 640 ms (256 data points). Frequency power can be calculated every 1.5625Hz. The frequency powers of the CPSDs of the two groups of emotions were compared across several periods of time. As a result, significant difference ($p < 0.05$) in two of the groups was detected at a frequency range between 3.125 and 6.25Hz in 650–1440ms. The result is a reasonable range of frequency and duration for eye oscillation.

The possibility of evaluating eye oscillations at lower frequency which would be comparable to the 60Hz rate was examined, and a procedure was developed [14].

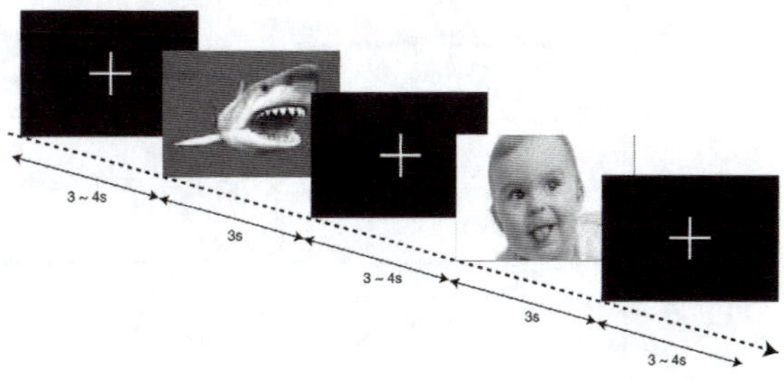

Figure 1. Diagram of stimuli shown.

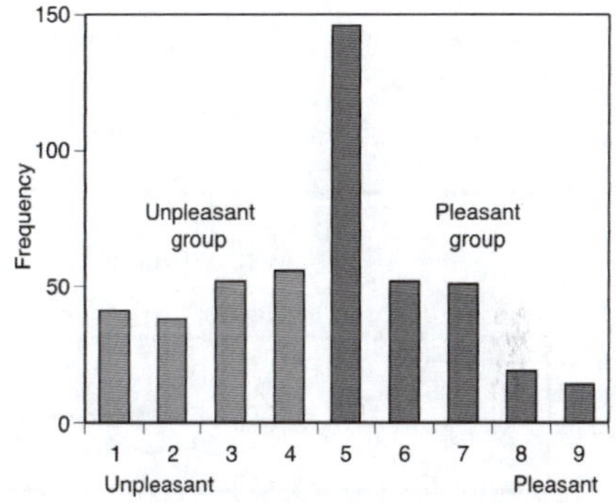

Figure 2. Results of viewer's ratings of photos using an "Unpleasant" – "Pleasant" scale.

III. Experimental Method

The stimulus and experimental design are organized as follows.

A. Stimulus

To evoke viewer's emotions, a set of pictures from the International Affective Picture System (IAPS) was employed [15]. According to the license, the images are not allowed to be presented in any format. This data set consists of scene images which produce specific impressions and is well known as a set of normative emotional stimuli for use in the experimental investigation of emotions. The contents of the photographs are completely different from the photographs of facial emotions mentioned above in Section II. Sixty seven pictures were selected that would produce the anticipated responses within a range of emotional impressions. Since the photos consisted of natural expressions, the level of brightness varied widely. The color range also varied widely. This is known as saliency, when the features of images presented affect a viewer's eye movement [16]. To reduce the effects of color, all pictures were converted into grayscale images. However, the brightness levels were not adjusted for presentation in this experiment.

B. Experimental design

The photos were displayed on a 19 inch LCD which was 60cm away from subjects. The eye tracker unit (nac:EMR-ACTUS) was set under the LCD monitor, and the observer did not wear any equipment. A presentation diagram is shown in Figure 1. Each photo was displayed for 3 seconds, followed by a blank image used to produce eye fixation. The stimulus presentation was controlled using the software of the eye tracker. Subjects were not asked to produce any responses before an image had been viewed. The eye movements of both eyes in response to every photo were recorded at 60Hz, and the data of the left eye was used in the analysis which follows.

Three trials were conducted during which the same set of images was shown to each subject, followed by a short break. All photos were evaluated by each participant following each of the sessions, using a 9 point scale which ranged between "Pleasant" and "Unpleasant". The numerical rating was used as one of the two dimensions of an Affect grid [9].

The subjects, who possessed sufficient visual acuity, were 7 male university students aged between 21 and 24 years old. The contents of the experiment were explained to all participants in advance, and informed consent was then obtained.

IV. Results

The rating responses for stimuli and the analyses of eye movements are summarized as follows.

A. Subjective evaluation

All photographs were rated by each subject using a 9-point scale. The overall frequencies of the scale are summarized in Figure 2. The frequency is the cumulative value of the responses of all participants to each photograph, since individual ratings are different and independent. The responses

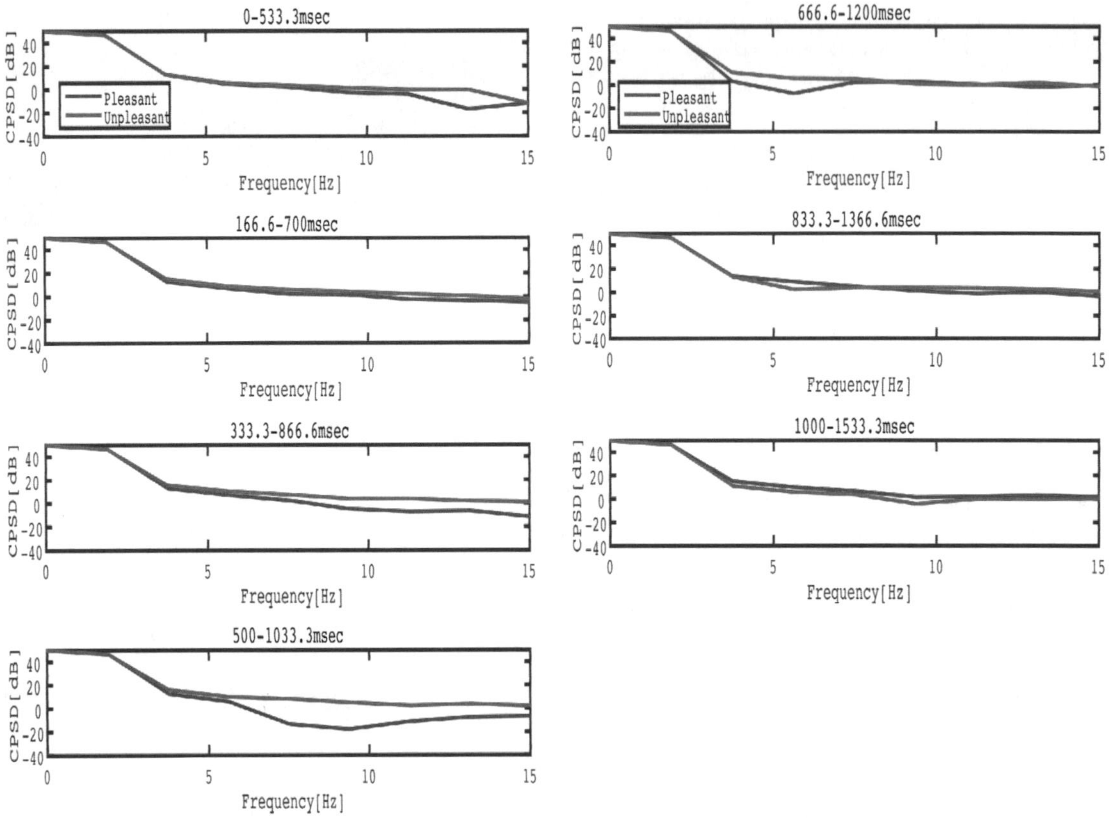

Figure 3. Comparison of cross power spectrum densities for every 533.3ms between 0 and 1533.3ms.

were widely distributed as was intended by the experimental design. The result suggests that some pictures are rated as the most "Pleasant" ones while others were rated as the most "Unpleasant". The most common responses to pictures were in the neutral category "5". Therefore, the photographs have been divided into two groups using the rating scale. The responses between two groups were compared, in order to rate them according to the factor of their emotional impressions. In the following analysis, ratings less than 5 are classified as "Unpleasant" (N_u = 187) and the remainder of the ratings are classified as "Pleasant" (N_p =282). As the responses consist of individual impressions of each photo, the grouping patterns between individuals are different.

B. Cross power spectra of eye movements

To detect evoked eye movements during picture observation, frequency analysis was conducted using the two dimensions of eye movement. Cross power spectrum densities (CPSDs) were calculated for every 533.3ms (32 data points at a 60Hz sampling rate). As the frequency power of the CPSD is generated every 1.875Hz, it is comparable to the calculations used for the condition mentioned above in Section II. When eye blinks occurred during observations, the trials were omitted. Since the eye tracker measures pupil diameters simultaneously, eye blinks can be used to detect the sudden drop in the diameter of the eye.

To examine the emotional difference factor of the pictures, frequency powers of CPSDs of eye movements were calculated for 7 periods: 0–533.3ms, 166.6-700ms, 333.3-866.6ms, 500-1033.3ms, 666.6-1200ms, 833.3-1366.6ms, and 1000-1533.3ms. The duration was shifted every 166.6ms. The power spectra of CPSDs of eye movements are summarized in Figure 3. In the figures, the blue line indicates the powers of the "Pleasant" group, and the red line indicates the powers of the "Unpleasant" group. The powers are at almost the same levels at 0–533.3ms and 166.6–700ms. For the periods 333.3-866.6ms, 500-1033.3ms and 666.6-1200ms, the powers of the "Unpleasant" group gradually become greater than the ones for the "Pleasant" group, and the frequency range of the difference becomes lower.

In examining the significant differences in frequency powers between the two emotional groups, some significant differences exist. The results are summarized as a 3D graph in Figure 4. The horizontal axes represents the frequencies and duration analyzed, and the vertical axis represents the levels of significance. A cuboid indicates that there is a significant difference between the two groups. As the figure shows, significant differences appear, depending on frequency and duration. At an early stage, a significant difference between 333.3 and 866.6ms at 5.625Hz was observed. Some additional differences which were significant followed at an early stage. In addition, the possibility of detecting the differences occurred between 400 and 1033.3ms at 3.75–7.5Hz. The duration of

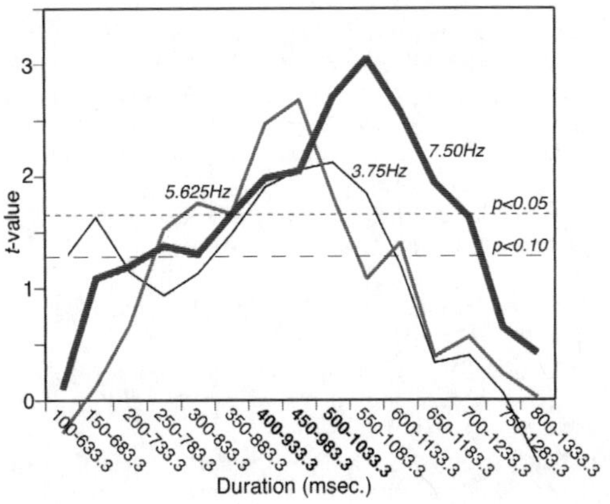

Figure 4. Results of t-tests which confirm significant differences in cross power spectrum densities of eye movements between two emotional groups.

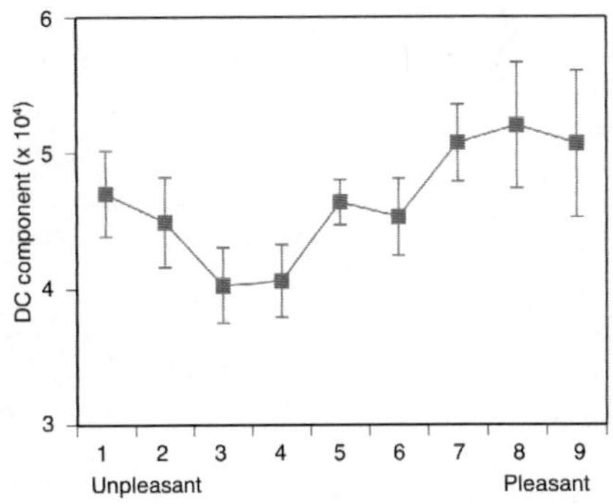

Figure 5. Relationship between viewer's rates and the brightness of photographs presented (Error bars indicate STD Errors)

observation time is shown as red cuboids in Figure 4. When this condition was analyzed, it was confirmed that the difference in the frequency power of eye movement CPSDs for the "Unpleasant" group is significantly higher than the CPSDs for the "Pleasant" group across all periods of time.

V. DISCUSSION

The activation of eye oscillation in response to "Unpleasant" images was confirmed when photographs of emotional expressions were introduced in addition to the facial images which were presented. The frequency ranges and duration were also confirmed during this experiment.

The brightness level of the pictures was not considered during the design of this experiment, though several features and especially brightness affect the saliency of the visual attention of the viewers. In a previous study, the influence of the level of brightness was ignored, as all visual stimuli were similar photos of facial expressions. To confirm the factor of brightness in the experiment, the relationships between picture brightness and viewer's subjective evaluations are summarized in Figure 5. The horizontal axis indicates the rating values, and the vertical axis indicates the values for DC components of photographic data, using DCT analysis. The error bars show the standard errors of DC components as a level of brightness. In regards to the relationships between picture brightness and viewer's subjective evaluations, a small correlation was observed. The effectiveness of viewer's ratings of the deviation of DC components is not significant however, according to the results of one-way ANOVA ($F(8,460) = 1.69, p = 0.10$). Therefore, the degree of contribution of picture brightness should be considered carefully in the feature studies.

Another question is the mechanism which causes eye oscillation when "Unpleasant" images are displayed. The phenomenon was observed when both facial images and normal pictures were viewed. The latencies in appearance of the differences in CPSD powers and chronological analysis suggest that the oscillations may be caused by image recognition and the activation of some area of the brain. The details of the information processing process are unclear. In regards to our daily experience, as we may be reluctant to view unpleasant images, the detailed of this phenomenon should be examined in greater detail.

As the phenomenon may be a stable one, responses can be used to evaluate the viewer's emotional impressions of images such as those used in HCI design or psychological analysis. To examine the validity of using this technique, the influence of various factors such as brightness or the color of stimuli should be confirmed. The study of these factors will be the subject of our further study.

VI. CONCLUSION

The possibility to evaluating viewer's emotional condition when evoked by their viewing photographs was examined using frequency analysis of eye movements. As the previous studies suggested, at lower frequencies some cross power spectrum densities of eye movements were generated by the invoked emotional conditions created using the facial images which were shown to subjects. To create the stimulus using images, a set of normative emotional stimuli photographs was introduced, and a typical video based eye tracker was employed to measure eye movement.

In regard to the chronological analysis of the cross power spectrum densities (CPSDs) of eye movement, a significant difference was confirmed at 400–1033.3ms after stimulus onset in the frequency range of 3.75-7.5Hz. From the differences that were extracted from the durations and frequency ranges, the powers of CPSDs for "Unpleasant" images were significantly higher than were the ones for "Pleasant" images. Also, as the differences began between 333.3 and 866.6ms, it suggests that an early response has occurred.

ACKNOWLEDGMENT

This research was partially supported by the Japan Society for the Promotion of Science (JSPS), Grant-in-Aid for Scientific Research (KAKEN, B-26282046: 2014-2016).

REFERENCES

[1] P. Tseng et al., "High-throughput classification of clinical populations from natural viewing eye movements," Journal of Neurology, vol. 260, Jan 2013, pp. 275–284.

[2] M. Watanabe, Y. Matso, L. Zha, D. P. Munoz, and Y. Kobayashi, "Fixational saccades reflect volitional action preparation," Journal of Neurophisiology, vol. 110, 2013, pp. 522–535.

[3] Y. Matsuo et al., "Gap effect abnormalities during a visually guided pro-saccade task in children with attention deficit hyperactivity disorder," PLoS ONE, vol. 10, no. 5, 2015, p. e0125573.

[4] M. Nakayama and M. Katsukura, "Development of a system usability assessment procedure using oculo-motors for input operation," Universal Access in Information Society, vol. 10, no. 1, 2011, pp. 51–68.

[5] M. Nakayama and M. Yasuda, "Relationships between eegs and eye movements in response to facial expressions," in Proceedings of ACM Symposium on Eye Tracking Research & Applications 2016 (ETRA2016), 2016, pp. 291–294.

[6] G. J. Walker-Smith, A. G. Gale, and J. M. Findlay, "Eye movement strategies involved in face perception," Perception, vol. 6, 1977, pp. 313–326.

[7] A. Suzuki, "Facial expression recognition and embodied simulation," Japanese Psychological Review, vol. 57, no. 1, 2014, pp. 5–23.

[8] D. Matsumoto and P. Ekman, "Japanese and Caucasian facial expression of emotion (JACFEE) and neutral faces (JACNeuF)," 1988, san Fransisco State University, San Francisco, CA, USA.

[9] J. A. Russell, A. Weiss, and G. A. Mendelsohn, "Affect grid: A single-item scale of pleasure and arousal," Journal of Personality and Social Psychology, vol. 57, no. 3, 1989, pp. 493–502.

[10] M. Yasuda, Z. Dou, and M. Nakayama, "Features of event-related potentials used to recognize clusters of facial expressions," in Proceedings of International Conference on Bio-inspired Systems and Signal Processing (BIOSIGNAL 2015), 2015, pp. 165–171.

[11] M. G. Calvo and L. Nummenamaa, "Eye-movement assessment of the time course in facial expression recognition: Neurophysiological implications," Cognitive, Affective, & Behavioral Neuroscience, vol. 9, no. 4, 2009, pp. 398–411.

[12] M. Eimer and A. Holmes, "Event-related brain potential correlates of emotional face processing," Neuropsychologia, vol. 45, 2008, pp. 15–31.

[13] S. Palmer, Vision Science –Photons to Phenomenology. Cambridge, MA, USA: The MIT Press, 2000.

[14] T. Furuta and M. Nakayama, "The relation between eye movements and subjective evaluation of emotional pictures," IEICE Technical report, Tech. Rep. HCS2016-05, 2016.

[15] P. Lang, M. Bradley, and B. Cuthbert, "International affective picuture system (IAPS): Affective ratings of pictures and instruction manual," University of Florida, Tech. Rep. Technical Report A-8, 2008, http://csea.phhp.ufl.edu/media.html, Last accessed at 22nd Feb. 2017.

[16] L. Itti, "Quantifying the contribution of low-level saliency to human eye movements in dynamic scenes," Visual Cognition, vol. 12, no. 6, 2005, pp. 1093–1123.

Hierarchy Visualization Designs and their Impact on Perception and Problem Solving Strategies

Nicholas H. Müller, Benny Liebold, Daniel Pietschmann, and Peter Ohler
Institute for Media Research
Chemnitz University of Technology
Chemnitz, Germany
Email: {nicholas.mueller, benny.liebold, daniel.pietschmann, peter.ohler}@phil.tu-chemnitz.de

Paul Rosenthal
Institute of Computer Science
University of Rostock
Rostock, Germany
Email: research@paul-rosenthal.de

***Abstract*—Visualizing hierarchical structures is of great importance in many economic and scientific applications. Many different approaches have been developed and enhanced in the last decades. Each of them claims specific advantages over competing methods, usually referring to visual or structural properties. Although several user studies investigated the usefulness of specific approaches, for practitioners it often remains unclear what the practical advantages of the approaches are and in which contexts they are useful. In our user study, we systematically investigated the value of three frequently used visualization types for the intuitive understanding of hierarchical data: treemap, icicle plot, and nodelink. We measured user performance in terms of correctness and time and tracked eye movements for each participant. The results regarding the user performance revealed that nodelink and icicle plot yield expected and comparable results, whereas treemap is only exceeding chance level for one easy task. Still, the analysis of eye-tracking measures suggests that treemaps draw visual attention better to relevant elements. Finally, implications for facilitating human intuition and problem solving strategies are discussed.**

***Keywords*–User Study; Hierarchy Visualization; Perception; Eye-tracking.**

I. Introduction

Visualizing hierarchical data has a long tradition going back to the drawings of medieval family trees. A wide research field with very different visualization approaches developed over the last three decades, investigating a multitude of different visualization properties and aiming at all kinds of different applications. However, despite this long tradition there are still new developments in the field through new applications and demands [1].

A comprehensive overview over most of the proposed hierarchy visualization techniques is maintained by treevis.net [2]. Every approach was published with several advantages in mind and was at the time of publication an advancement to the state of the art. However, for most practitioners the value of new (and sometimes even older) visualization techniques for their data remains unclear with the result that they are unsure, which visualization would fit their needs best. This issue becomes even more eminent considering the importance of hierarchical data structures in science [3] and especially economy [4], where visualizations can significantly influence large-scale decisions [5].

In this paper, we make a step towards studying which visualizations are intuitively understandable by non-expert users. Additionally, we investigate why different visualization techniques impact the users' understanding of the data differently. Since we are treating the visualizations as objectively as possible, our goal is not to show which visualization is superior, but to try to understand what problems and pitfalls arise when typical users try to use different visualizations to solve typical tasks. Preliminary results of the reported study were presented at EuroRV^3 [6]. In this paper, we report an extended analysis.

In this first step, we restricted our study to static and non-interactive visualizations, which are, apart from being much easier to interpret especially when analyzing problem solving patterns, still highly practice relevant, since many practitioners mainly rely on static visualizations on paper or digital presentations. Since Burch et al. [7] showed that radial techniques for the visualization of hierarchies are understood less intuitively, we further restricted our study to linear visualization techniques. After a thorough analysis of several well-established reporting and analysis software packages, we decided to compare nodelinks, treemaps, and icicle plots, because they represent the most common visualization techniques.

In addition, we restrict our considerations to the area of visualizing hierarchical data with additional scalar dimension, which are highly relevant especially in the business environment. More precisely, the data consists of a rooted tree $T = (V, E, v_{\text{root}})$, where V is the set of n data elements (nodes), E is a subset of $V \times V$ representing the hierarchy relations (edges), and $v_{\text{root}} \in V$ is the root node of the hierarchy. Additionally, a function $f : V \to \mathbb{R}^+$ is given, which assigns each node a specific positive value and respects the hierarchy, i. e., the sum of values of all children of a node is always smaller or equal than the value of the node. One example for such data is a company structure with annual expenses.

In Sections III and IV, we present background about the tackled visualizations and the relations to cognitive science. We give a precise description of our study setup in Section V. In Section VI, we present a detailed analysis of the results of the user study with respect to participants' performance and eye-gaze data.

II. Related Work

General design rules for good visualizations have been discussed in the last decades intensively and are often based on the investigation of visual attention [8] and the understanding of the human cognitive system. In this regard, the effects of colors in visualizations received much research attention, because they represent a particular powerful visual cue [9], [10]. A comprehensive overview about those design rules and general strategies was presented by Ware [11].

One of the most-used practical examples when visualizing hierarchies with an additional scalar component is the file system of computers. Stasko et al. [12] evaluated the two visualization techniques treemap [13] and sunburst [14] with respect to their capabilities for standard file-management tasks, like locating files or comparing file sizes. They measured user performance by logging their number of correct answers and their reaction times. They found that sunburst significantly outperforms the treemap representation, presumably because of the more explicit representation of hierarchy relations in sunburst.

In a very similar study, Bladh et al. [15] evaluated the usefulness of encoding the depth of nodes in a treemap using the third dimension in comparison to a traditional treemap visualization. Again, users had to complete typical file-management tasks. It turned out that both visualizations were not significantly different in most tasks, i. e., the third dimension did not result in a performance loss due to the additional navigational and cognitive efforts. However, users' performance was significantly better with the 3D visualization when having to identify the node with the highest depth in the hierarchy.

Wang et al. [16] had a very similar experimental setting by comparing a standard file browser to rings [17] and treemap [13]. They evaluated the effectiveness of the methods based on complex questions, such as finding two similar directories or the most homogeneous directory. The users' performance was measured by assessing their answering time. Additionally, they were asked to rate the difficulty of each question with the respective visualization. In summary, the file explorer performed significantly worse than both other methods with no significant difference between rings and treemap.

In a quite different user study, Ziemkiewicz and Kosara [18] showed that the methaphoric presentation of tasks influences users' performance during the work with hierarchy visualizations. In our study, we follow the findings and only formulate the tasks abstractly with respect to the hierarchy.

Borkin et al. [19] presented a new method for visualizing filesystem provenance data, which relies on a combination of a radial-based tree layout and a time-based node grouping. The system was evaluated with domain experts and compared to a state-of-the-art nodelink tool [20] by measuring accuracy and efficiency. Results show that the new tool outperforms the state of the art. A very interesting additional finding was, that there was a significant gender effect in the state-of-the-art method, which was not the case for the proposed method.

Teets et al. [21] stressed the need for evaluation of the effectiveness of visualizations especially in the business environment. They analyzed a very specific application in the field of process monitoring, which was based on production data of a can factory. Their evaluation relied on cognitive fit theory, i. e., they investigated how good the visualizations and induced mental models fit to the problem solving strategies. They found no information loss when not displaying accurate values in a tabular fashion as well as a significantly faster solution time when using visual representations.

While most studies rely on user performance data in terms of the number of correct answers and reaction times, eye-tracking studies have been the exception. However, Burch et al. [7] investigated the impact of different layouts of nodelinks using eye-tracking. They used one question type and an explanatory task. The users were confronted with two different linear layouts with four different placements of the root node and a radial layout of the nodelink. Burch et al. assessed both eye-movements and performance data, allowing to systematically compare the results from different measurement approaches. The users performed much better with the axis-aligned layouts than with the circular one, which might be a result of the typically linear fashion of information display, the users are familiar with. In line with this argument, the traditional layout with the root node at the top performed best, which further emphasizes the role of individual experience with visualizations in understanding them intuitively and using them for problem solving.

A recent variation of the treemap design is the angular treemap [22] with the goal to enhance comprehension of hierarchy levels by rotating parts of the treemap. Liang et al. [23] conducted an experiment comparing traditional and angular treemaps. The study mainly investigated search tasks and measured completion time. While it turned out that the new design was significantly better, the flexible method needs several well-tuned parameters and, thus, should be set up by visualization experts to achieve comparable results.

The need for visualization expertise is true for many new and sophisticated visualization techniques. However, there is an ever growing demand for easily usable and reliable visualization techniques for hierarchical data in practice that can be used without much prior knowledge. Therefore, we investigated the properties of three of the most-used and practice-relevant visualization techniques with respect to fast and accurate data comprehension for users with low visualization knowledge and only a short time of familiarization with the type of visualization.

III. Visualizations for Hierarchical Data

For our user study, we wanted to choose the most-used and most practice-relevant visualization techniques for hierarchies with additional scalar dimension. After elaborate inspection of the treevis repository and several software packages for productive use, we decided to compare nodelinks, treemaps, and icicle plots.

The use of nodelinks for drawing trees is very intuitive since it replicates the structure of botanical trees. Consequently, nodelinks have already been used for ages to represent hierarchies and the research on optimal drawing of nodelinks has a long tradition [24]. The strengths of the nodelink representation is typically its intuitiveness and clear representation [25]. However, many competing techniques produce less empty space and allow a more integrated visualization of the additional scalar dimension.

The concept of treemaps has been introduced by Johnson and Shneiderman [13]. Since then a lot of different modifications, additions, and enhancements were proposed [26], [27], still respecting the initial idea of maximizing screen space usage and implicit encoding of the hierarchy. These aspects are often referred to as the main advantages of the concept. Problematic properties, which are nowadays still constant topic of further research [28], are the inherent overplotting, problems with hierarchy perception, and complications with node distribution.

The icicle plot is a concept with a long tradition and was originally proposed by Kruskal and Landwehr [29] for the display of cluster hierarchies and based on the trees and castles of Kleiner and Hartigan [30]. Although it has been shown that users perform worse, when using radial layouts [7], icicle plots are used less often in practical applications [31] than their radial counterpart, the sunburst diagram [14], [32], [33]. The icicle plot combines two strengths of nodelink and treemap, namely the intuitive top-down design and the implicit hierarchy encoding. In addition, it inherently features a one-dimensional encoding of the additional scalar dimension. On the other hand, the screen-space usage is less efficient than the one of treemaps.

IV. Cognitive Processing of Visualizations

When we want to assess the effectiveness of visualizations, we first need to distinguish between the visual search phase and the stage of central information processing. In the visual search phase, the user has to identify relevant elements of a visualization. During this process the user constantly reallocates the attention to different elements of a visualization. Following Schneider and Shiffrin [34], this process can be characterized as an interplay of bottom-up (automatic) and top-down (controlled) attention allocation.

Our visual field can be considered as an assembly of elements competing for our attention [35]. Bottom-up processes are triggered by elements, which stand out from their environment. A node of a visualization could for example be colored differently or have a different shape compared to other elements. Top-down attention, on the other hand, is moderated by the user's intention and previous knowledge. For example, when the user's goal is to compare two elements of a visualization, the user employs a strategy of visual search, during which the positions of all relevant entities are identified. The search process itself can be carried out both by chaotically searching for relevant elements (bottom-up) or deducting the relative position of an element from other elements through previous knowledge about the type of visualization (top-down) [36].

The first strategy is suited for users without any previous knowledge and its efficiency depends on the visualization's complexity. The latter strategy, however, can be employed by users, who understood the basic principles of a visualization, and should result in a more efficient use. Regardless of the user's prior experience, both modes are constantly directing our attention to elements that are relevant to the organism with one or the other mode being predominant in a certain situation. Bottom-up attention allocation can be overridden by top-down processes, which allows users to focus their attention at specific elements of a visualization. If, however, a stimulus exceeds a certain threshold it automatically triggers bottom-up attention towards this stimulus, thereby interrupting top-down attention allocation. These so-called "orienting responses" are usually triggered by sudden changes in the environment [37], such as movement in the peripheral visual area, flashing lights, or loud sounds.

As we can only observe eye movements by users, we are usually not able to distinguish between bottom-up and top-down attention allocation. Both mechanisms directly impact which elements our eyes fixate. Additionally, the mere fact that users fixate an element of a visualization does not imply that this element is being processed centrally. Moreover, it does not even imply that the user is looking at the element, because attention can also be allocated towards elements outside of central vision [38]. Although we are not able to see elements as clearly when using peripheral vision, humans are still able to estimate object shape and size rather accurately.

When the relevant elements of a visualization are identified, the user enters the stage of central information processing. The success and the efficiency of a visualization depend both on user and visualization properties. User properties affecting visualization processing are previous knowledge about the type of visualization, general intelligence components, especially those related to visuo-spatial information processing, and possible impairments (e.g., color or stereo blindness). In terms of information processing, nearly all properties of a visualization, like color usage, descriptiveness, intuitiveness, alignment, or visual data preparation affect success and efficiency. In this paper, we assess indicators for both phases of visualization processing.

V. Method

We conducted a laboratory experiment, during which participants had to solve problems using different visualization techniques. For each participant, the performance in terms of accuracy and completion times as well as eye movements were recorded.

A. Stimulus Materials

We employed a $3 \times 4 \times 2$ within-subjects factor design with visualization type, task, and hierarchy complexity as independent variables.

1) Visualization Types: All hierarchies with additional positive scalar values per node were visualized using three different visualization types, illustrated in Figure 1. The nodelinks were generated using Reingold and Tilford's algorithm [24]. The additional scalar value per node was indicated by the area of each node's circle. As for all three different visualization types, each non-root node was annotated with an alphanumeric code to allow for unique identification by the users. The treemaps were generated using the squarified approach [39], again encoding each node's scalar value by area. To enhance the perception of different hierarchy levels, nodes were color coded in different grey scales and, following Bladh et al. [15], stacked in a 2.5D fashion. The icicle plots were generated in the top-down fashion that is used most often. Screen space was divided in rows of equal height, depending on the height of the hierarchy. The root node's width was set to the full width. For each node, all children were drawn below the node with a width proportional to the scalar values, respectively.

2) Tasks: We interviewed several researchers from different fields of economics and social sciences, who regularly deal with hierarchical data. We identified four tasks, which are commonly performed when confronted with the given visualizations. From these tasks, three are hypothesized to favor one of the visualization types, respectively. For the fourth tasks, we could not find any strong indications on what visualization might be favored and added it as an exploratory task. In detail, the tasks were:

- T1: Count all leaf nodes of the hierarchy.
- T2: Count all nodes of the hierarchy.
- T3: Compare the combined area of two pairs of nodes within one level of the hierarchy.
- T4: Compare the combined area of two pairs of nodes across different levels of the hierarchy.

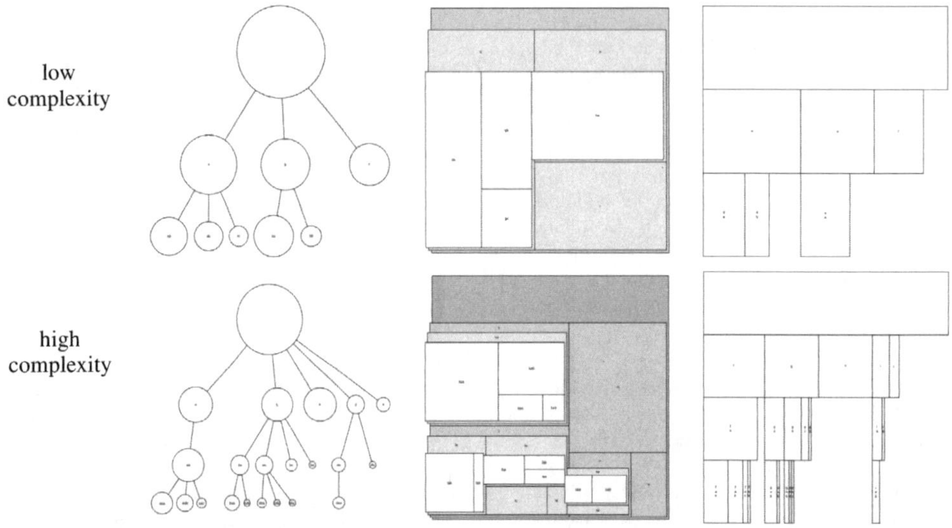

Figure 1. Example stimuli that where used for the user study. For each of the four questions, we presented three different visualization types (nodelink, treemap, icicle plot) of equivalent hierarchies with additional scalar values per node. In addition, we varied the complexity of the hierarchies, resulting in visualizations with low (height two, maximum three children per node) and high complexity (height three, maximum five children per node).

It is obvious that tasks differ in difficulty: Counting leaves and nodes is less cognitive exertive than comparing the sizes of nodes. However, this does not affect our main goal, the analysis of differences between the visualization methods.

3) Hierarchy Complexities: As base data set we used two artificial hierarchies with different levels of complexity. The hierarchy with low complexity had height two and had a maximum of three children per node. In contrast, the height of the hierarchy with high complexity was three with a maximum number of five children per node. An illustration of the different complexities can be seen in Figure 1.

Since the hierarchy for all visualizations was initially equal per complexity level and question, it could have happened that participants remembered their choice from a different visualization and just replicated it. To overcome this problem, we slightly changed hierarchies (changed size of one node or added/removed one node/leaf) for each visualization of one complexity-task combination. Consequently, tasks and answers were not equal per visualization but still comparable in terms of difficulty. Participants were informed that similar hierarchies might not always result in the same answers.

B. Hypotheses

From a review of relevant literature and recommendations in software packages, we extracted several claims of what benefits the used visualizations should have. Together with the tailored questions, this resulted in the following hypotheses, that we wanted to check with our experiment.

H1: Task **T1** favors the treemap over both other visualization types.
Counting leaves reduces to the simple task of counting all non-occluded rectangles when using a treemap. Users have to traverse the whole hierarchy to count the leaves in both other visualizations.

H2: Task **T2** favors the nodelink over both other visualizations.
Counting nodes is reduced to simply counting all circles in the nodelink visualization, which are, even in contrast to the icicle plot, clearly distinguishable from background and auxiliary lines.

H3: Task **T3** favors the icicle plot over both other visualizations.
Comparing sizes of nodes within one level of hierarchy reduces to the much easier one-dimensional task of comparing lengths on one straight line when using the icicle-plot visualization. In contrast, users have to sum up and compare areas of different proportions when using a treemap and, even more difficult, sum up differently-sized circular areas in the case of the nodelink.

H4: Treemap performs worst in the tasks **T1**, **T3**, and **T4** due to overplotting.

H5: When only varying hierarchy complexity, users perform better with the low complex hierarchy compared to high complexity.

C. Sample

We recruited $N = 69$ second year university students of the local communication studies program (age: $M = 21.09$, $SD = 2.40$, female = 53). The students were well-skilled in reading academic publications and working with statistical analyses and charts. Apart from their general experience, they had no specific knowledge in either of the presented visualization methods nor in visualization of hierarchies in general. They received study credit for their participation.

D. Procedure

To control for sequence effects, we generated two different pre-randomized sequences respecting a non-repetition restriction. Each participant was assigned to one of the sequences in which the combinations were presented, respectively. Both sequences did not differ in their performance ($t(67) = -0.238$, n.s.). The hierarchies were presented on a 19" computer screen with a resolution of 1280×1024 pixels via E-Prime 2.0. An SMI RED eye-tracker from SensoMotoric Instruments was installed below the screen and recorded eye movements at 50 Hz. The stimuli were presented at a head distance of about 700 mm. However, due to the contact-free setup, slight variations of the distance during the experiment were possible, which should not affect the results due to the within-subjects factor design. All participants were calibrated using a five point matrix according to the standard SMI RED setup procedure. Each event in E-Prime was logged within the eye-tracking data file, which allowed to synchronize stimulus presentation and eye-tracking data. In the first part of the instructions, the definition of a hierarchy, the difference between leaves and nodes, and the different types of visualizations were explained to the participants by showing examples. They also received a speed-accuracy instruction (i. e., "Please answer as quickly and accurately as you can!").

During the experiment, participants were first shown a textual description of the task (e. g., "How many leaves does the hierarchy have?") as well as the possible answers and then had to press a key to proceed. This allowed each participant to read and understand the task and the answers at its own pace. Next, the hierarchy visualization was presented in addition to the task and the answers. Participants then had to respond by pressing one of three answer keys, with one correct answer and two distractors, resulting in a chance level of $p = 0.33$. E-Prime automatically logged the participant's answer and completion time, i. e., the time of stimulus onset until the participant's response. In average, the response time for an item was M = 19.6 sec (SD = 5.9). This procedure allowed us to be able to judge users reaction times without the delay of having them typing in the correct number. All participants were shown a training sequence of the visualizations. Afterwards, all three visualizations in both the high and low complexity were presented. Nodes to be compared were named in the question before the visualization was shown and remained visible during the task until an answer was given. The whole procedure took less than 25 minutes per participant. After the computer test, participants filled out an electronic questionnaire with items concerning manipulation checks and demographic data.

VI. Results

We recruited undergraduate students from Chemnitz University of Technology and therefore conducted the study with a very homogeneous set of participants. Thus, demographic assessments did not show any correlations or other interesting variables regarding age, gender, or occupation. Since part of our analysis was already reported before [6], we focus on the findings that are relevant to our hypotheses. A plot of the participants' performance with respect to the independent variables is shown in Figure 2.

To test our hypotheses we used a $3 \times 4 \times 2$ repeated measures ANOVA (analysis of variance) with participants' performance as dependent variable. Alpha levels for all calculations were set to $p < 0.05$. Due to the violation of the sphericity assumption, Greenhouse-Geisser-corrected dfs are reported, if necessary. We found a significant main effect for the type of visualization ($F(2, 136) = 53.77$, $p < 0.001$, $\eta^2_{\text{part}} = 0.442$). More specifically, performance was significantly lower when using treemap compared to nodelink and

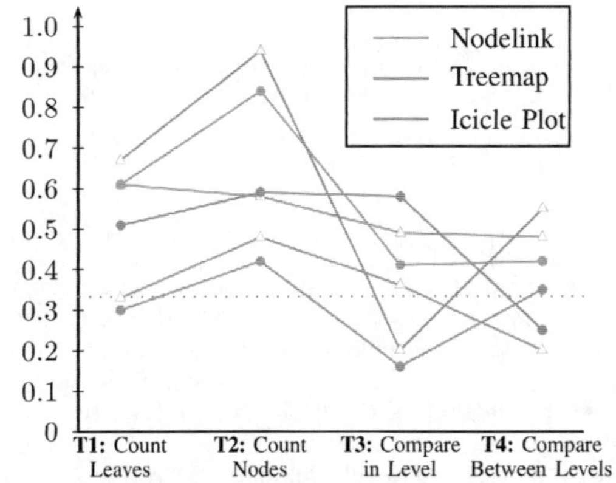

Figure 2. Plot of the average correctness of participants' answers to the four questions with respect to visualization type (encoded by color) and hierarchy complexity (Δ = low complexity, • = high complexity). Chance level is indicated by the dotted horizontal line at 0.33.

icicle plot, whereas the latter two did not differ significantly. Participants performed well above chance level with both nodelink ($M = 0.55$, $t(68) = 8.73$, $p < 0.001$) and icicle-plot visualizations ($M = 0.54$, $t(68) = 9.03$, $p < 0.001$). However, participants did not perform above chance when presented the treemap ($M = 0.33$, $t(68) = -0.332$, n.s.). These first results validate hypothesis **H4**. Furthermore, we found that participants were able to perform above chance level only in task **T2** when using a treemap, i. e., counting nodes at low complexity ($M = 0.48$, $t(68) = 2.40$, $p < 0.05$). This discovery directly opposes hypothesis **H1** and lets the treemap stand out as the worst choice for all tasks. Even at its best performing task **T2**, nodelink and icicle plot performed significantly better ($F(1, 74) = 50.02$, $p < 0.001$, $\eta^2_{\text{part}} = 0.403$).

Results did not show a significant main effect for complexity of hierarchies, ($F(1, 68) = 2.607$, n.s.). Consequently it seems that, in the current setting, hypothesis **H5** can not be confirmed. However, revisiting the stimuli and analyzing the after-test feedback resulted in at least two possible factors influencing the results with respect to this hypothesis. One surprising fact is, that participants performed significantly better with the complex nodelink compared to the less complex nodelink for task **T2**, counting nodes ($t(74) = -4.32$, $p < 0.001$, $\eta^2_{\text{part}} = 0.20$). It is apparent, that some participants were uncertain if the root node is also counted as a node and, consequently, counted one node less. In the high complex stimulus, this was compensated, because, as all answering options were above their count, the participants simply chose the lowest possible answer, which was the right one. In the low complex stimulus, this strategy did not work, as indicated in Table I. Due to this occurrence, it is not possible to validate hypothesis **H2** although the performance of the nodelink is still significantly better than both other visualizations when only using the complex hierarchy ($F(1, 74) = 32.85$, $p < 0.001$, $\eta^2_{\text{part}} = 0.307$).

We encountered another surprising result when we compared icicle plots of high and low complexity for task **T3**. Again, the less complex hierarchy is performing significantly worse than the complex hierarchy ($t(74) = -5.11$, $p < 0.001$). The performance is even significantly below chance level ($t(74) = -2.52$, $p < 0.05$), leading to the conclusion

TABLE I. OBSERVED RELATIVE FREQUENCIES FOR TASK **T2** USING NODELINK REPRESENTATION. FOR LOW AND HIGH COMPLEX HIERARCHIES, THE CORRECT ANSWER IS RESPECTIVELY HIGHLIGHTED WITH GREY.

Answer	Low Compl.	Answer	High Compl.
7	6.8%	22	84.7%
8	34,7%	23	13.6%
9	58.5%	24	1.7%

that the participants were confident in their (wrong) answers. After carefully inspecting the stimulus for the low complex hierarchy, illustrated in Figure 3, we assume that participants' confidence was based on a wrong assumption about the pictorial information. The Gestalt-laws [40] suggest certain cognitive grouping tendencies when confronted with images. Based on the Gestalt-laws of proximity, closure, and common region, the nodes da, db, and dc are perceived as belonging together. The task, however, asks to judge the combined size of the first two ($da + db$) against the other node and an "external one" (dc+ea). Due to this, we assume a misleading perception, which lets the participants underestimate the size of $da + db$. The cognitive process of "moving" area dc over to ea (or reverse) might be influenced by the distance between the two because of the impression that both nodes together (a gestalt) require more space due to the empty space between them. This overestimation could be the reason, why hypothesis **H3** cannot be supported, although in the high complex setting icicle plot performed, as predicted, significantly better than nodelink and treemap at **T3** ($F(1, 74) = 22.57$, $p < 0.001$, $\eta^2_{\text{part}} = 0.234$).

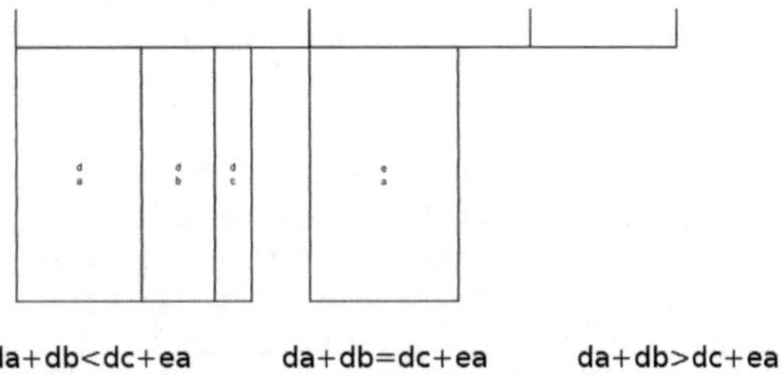

Figure 3. Close-up view of the stimulus for task **T3** using the low complex hierarchy and the icicle-plot visualization. The area $da + db$ is actually larger than $dc + ea$ but the latter is overestimated due to the empty space between both areas.

A. Heatmaps

Beyond looking into the participants' performance, we also recorded the eye-movement of all participants during the tasks. For the analysis, the areas of interest were defined with respect to each task and fixations were detected, based on 80 ms duration. After careful inspection of the heatmaps for each task, we decided to enlarge each area of interest by 20 pixels beyond the actual node to account for measurement error and peripheral vision when looking at rather small nodes (see for example Figure 6). As a first approach we analyzed the heatmaps of different tasks and visualizations and their evolution over time. The heatmaps were generated by accumulating fixations over a specified period of time and the calculation of the smoothed average density of fixations for each pixel. The resulting density function was color-coded in the range between minimum and maximum using the built-in color scheme of the eye-tracking software, depicted below:

In Figure 4, we illustrate the heatmaps for different subsequent periods of time for nodelink and icicle plot of the high complex hierarchy and task **T2**. The heatmaps suggest a top-down and left-right movement of participants' fixations which is consistent with the top-down screen-space structure of the visualizations. This coincides with the expected gaze direction that is deeply rooted into cultural education. Eye-tracking research regarding reading and comprehension in Saudi-Arabia revealed fixation patterns from right to left [41], in contrast to the typical findings in western countries. Li and Briley [42] therefore differentiate between a habitual eye movement and a situational one, which, on occasions, might be in conflict.

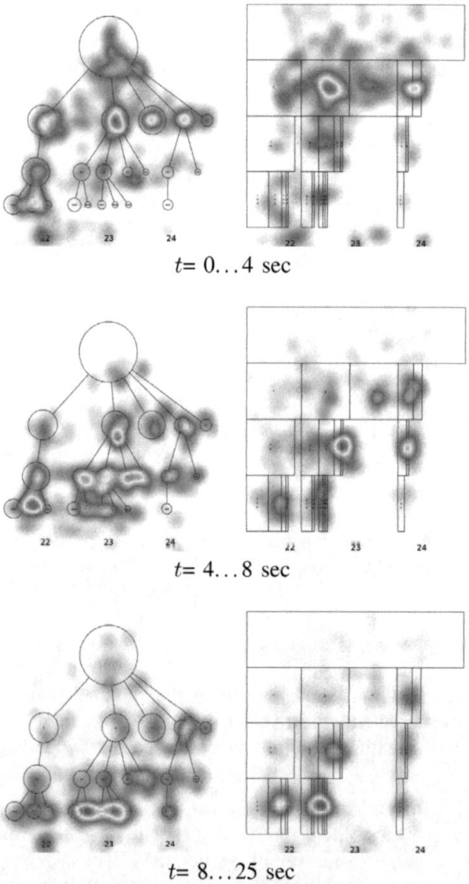

Figure 4. Accumulated heatmaps for the task **T2** and the complex hierarchy for three subsequent periods of time. Note the apparent top-down and left-right pattern of participants' gazes when counting the nodes of the hierarchy.

Since the participants for the presented study were all originating from Germany, we assume homogeneous habituated reading patterns: Since most of their reading materials in everyday life are dextrograde, a gaze movement pattern from left to right and top to bottom was to be expected. One of the most prominent indications for this habituated behavior is visible in the fixations on the answer options at the bottom of the screen moving from left to right on every visualization within this study.

A very similar habitual top-down pattern in the heatmaps

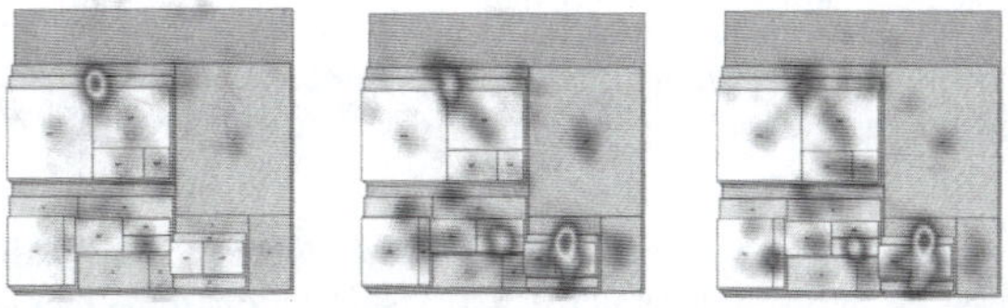

t= 0…7 sec t= 7…21 sec t= 21…30 sec

Figure 5. Accumulated heatmaps for the task **T2**, counting all nodes of the hierarchy, and the complex hierarchy. For three subsequent periods of time, we indicate the heatmaps of the treemap visualization. Although treemaps feature only limited top-down characteristics in screen space, the typical European pattern of top-down processing is apparent.

is encountered when visualizing the same hierarchy with a treemap (Figure 5), although this visualization does not imply an inherent top-down screen-space structure. Because treemaps do not explicitly follow this structural order with several clearly distinct hierarchy levels, participants constantly have to reorient and remember which elements were already processed. We suspect that this discrepancy is partially responsible for the participants' bad performance with treemaps. The same applies to task **T1** where participants again followed a top-down strategy, as illustrated in Figure 6.

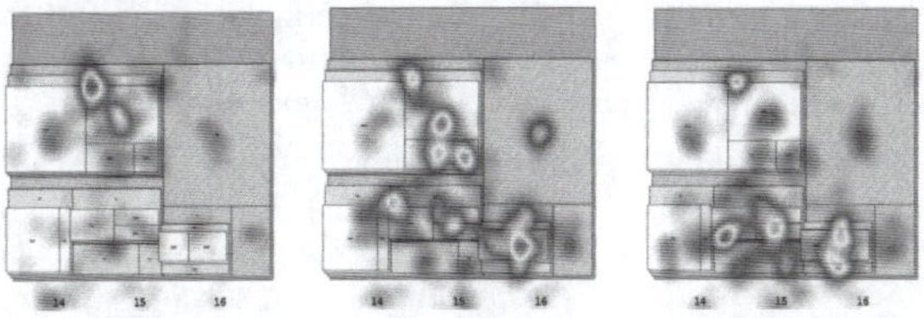

t= 0…5 sec t= 5…10 sec t= 10…40 sec

Figure 6. Accumulated heatmaps for the task **T1**, counting all leaves of the hierarchy, and the complex hierarchy. The heatmaps of the treemap visualization are depicted for three subsequent periods of time. Again, the top-down tendency of processing, although the screen space design of the treemap has no such component, is apparent.

One further interesting, but unexpected finding with respect to the treemap visualization was that participants' performance at **T3** with the complex hierarchy performing significantly worse than chance level ($t(74) = -4.54$, $p < 0.001$). This again indicates that participants were confident in giving a wrong answer. When inspecting the respective heatmap for the whole task processing time (Figure 7), it becomes apparent that fixations concentrate mainly in the upper parts of the relevant regions. Due to the self-occluding design of treemaps, these are the only parts of occluded regions that are directly observable. When only concentrating on the non-occluded parts the areas of nodes l and k are quite equal, although the area of node k is in fact much larger than the area of l. This might have, in combination with the very small area of node o and the relatively large, but mostly occluded area of n, led to the impression that the area of $l+n$ is smaller than the area of $k+o$. Thus, the participants might have followed a misconception of the treemap visualization. The same explanation can account for the significantly lower-than-chance performance of the less complex treemap at **T4** ($t = -2.52$; $p < 0.05$).

B. Odds Ratios

In addition to inspecting the heatmaps, we used a measure for the chance that fixations in task-relevant areas of interest are succeeded by task-relevant fixations, i. e., the participants

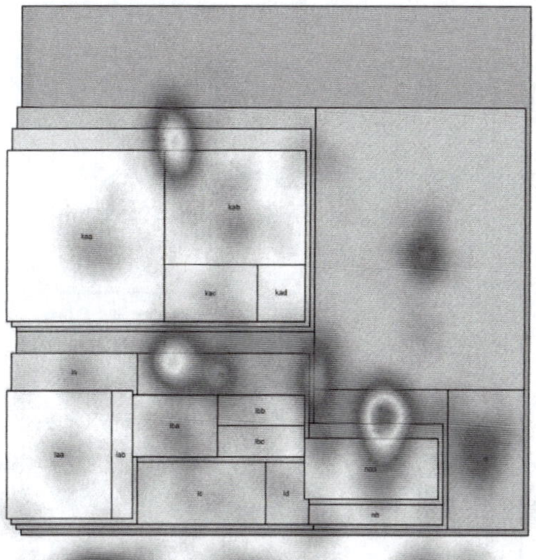

Figure 7. Accumulated heatmap for the whole time of **T3** using the treemap visualization for the complex hierarchy. Participants' fixations concentrated mainly on the upper, non-occluded, parts of the relevant regions, making it hard to correctly estimate the areas.

visual attention remains at task-relevant nodes. For this, we computed odds ratios, which compare the odds of remaining at task-relevant nodes of two visualizations for each task. We first divided the chance of task-relevant fixations by the chance of irrelevant fixations after looking at relevant areas of interest. This gives us an odd of relevant follow-up fixations for each visualization. We then divided the odds of one visualization by the odds of another visualizations to get the respective odds ratio. We used the nodelink visualization as a baseline for the other two visualizations, because it is the most established one. Respective confidence intervals (95%) for the odds ratios allow comparisons of the suitability of a given visualization to promote fixations that remain within task-relevant areas. Odds ratios of around 1.0 indicate that the chance of hitting an important area of interest is not significantly different in both visualizations. Non-overlapping confidence intervals of different visualization combinations indicate a significant difference between them. An illustration of the different odds ratios and confidence intervals with respect to task and visualization type combinations is given in Figure 8.

T1 produced significant differences between all visualizations in their ability to draw user attention to task-relevant areas of interest. Within this particular task, the treemap visualization outperforms the other visualizations, regarding its chance to draw attention to task-relevant areas. The odds of looking at important areas of a treemap during the task are four times higher compared to a nodelink ($\Delta\text{odds}_{T/N} = 4.22$; CI: $[3.36, 5.30]$). Comparing icicle plots and treemaps also indicates a one-to-two advantage for the treemap ($\Delta\text{odds}_{I/T} = 0.51$; CI: $[0.42, 0.63]$). Furthermore, the odds for the icicle-plot visualization are twice as high compared to the nodelink ($\Delta\text{odds}_{I/N} = 2.17$; CI: $[1.71, 2.75]$). These results can be explained by the ratio of relevant to irrelevant screen space, which is highest for the treemap and lowest for nodelink. However, the significant advantage of the icicle plot over the nodelink cannot be explained by the small difference in relevant screen space, but might be a result of the eye-trackers

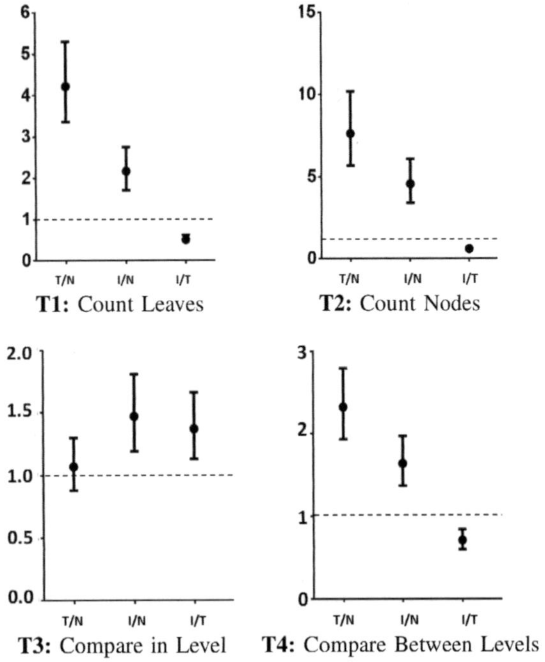

Figure 8. Plots of odds ratios and confidence intervals. For each task and combination of visualizations (N = nodelink, T = treemap, I = icicle plot), the respective odds ratio is indicated together with its 95% confidence interval.

resolution.

T2 presents a similar pattern, but with overall higher odds ratios. The improvement in odds for treemap compared to icicle plot relative to nodelink, however, is only marginally significant. Still, both perform again better than the nodelink in keeping the participants' attention within task-relevant areas. However, when counting nodes, the ratio of relevant screen space to overall screen space is nearly one for the treemap and close to one for the icicle plot. Consequently, participants have only few chances to actually look at non task-relevant positions, directly explaining the very high odds.

The tasks of comparing the volume of two groups of areas **T3** and **T4** reveal rather different odds ratios. Within one level of the hierarchy there is almost no difference between the treemap and the nodelink visualization ($\Delta\text{odds}_{T/N} = 1.07$; CI: $[0.88, 1.3]$), but a slightly higher odds ratio for the icicle plot compared to nodelink ($\Delta\text{odds}_{I/N} = 1.47$; CI: $[1.19, 1.81]$) and treemap ($\Delta\text{odds}_{I/T} = 1.37$; CI: $[1.13, 1.66]$). When looking at comparisons between different levels of hierarchy, however, both treemap ($\Delta\text{odds}_{T/N} = 2.32$; CI: $[1.93, 2.79]$) and icicle plot ($\Delta\text{odds}_{I/N} = 1.64$; CI: $[1.37, 1.97]$) again outperform the nodelink visualization. Additionally, the treemap is again significantly better than the icicle plot ($\Delta\text{odds}_{I/T} = 0.71$; CI: $[0.6, 0.84]$).

These results suggest that the treemap visualization is indeed effective in promoting task-relevant fixations due to its maximization of screen space. Additionally, the icicle plot performs better in guiding user gaze compared to nodelinks. However, these benefits in visual perception are not reflected in the user performance measure, because nodelinks still perform rather good compared to the visually more efficient visualization techniques. This could be seen as an indicator of the high relevance of previous experience with visualization techniques compared to their visual arrangement.

VII. Conclusions

We presented a user study which allowed us to analyze three of the most commonly used visualizations for hierarchical data with additional scalar dimension, namely nodelink, treemap, and icicle plot. These three visualization techniques of two hierarchy complexities (high, low) were tested at four tasks that are common for these types of visualizations. In addition to measuring completion time and correctness of responses, we analyzed the participants eye movements during problem solving. The statistical analysis of the participants' performance revealed that the treemap visualization performed worst. It barely exalted chance level and never performed better than fifty percent. For nodelink and icicle plot, our hypotheses were mostly supported due to well-known properties of both visualizations. However, we also found some puzzling effects: The analysis of gaze heatmaps revealed that the 2.5D representation format of treemaps was possibly misleading participants during area judgments of occluded nodes. Additionally, we found that the use of icicle plots, with a better screen-space usage compared to nodelinks, comes along with the problem that areas might be judged differently simply because of their mutual distance, i. e., the sum of closely spaced nodes is perceived smaller than nodes with a higher distance.

A deeper analysis of the eye-tracking data enabled us to calculate the odds of continued visual attention at relevant nodes. Here, treemaps performed superior in most tasks, which can be seen as proof of its optimized screen-space usage. However, the user performance contradicts this finding: Optimized screen-space usage is no guarantee for good user performance. Interestingly, icicle plots outperformed nodelinks in both comparison tasks with respect to odds ratios, suggesting that icicle plots concentrate participants' attention to the relevant areas by omitting unimportant structures.

In sum, we were able to replicate several findings from earlier studies, especially about the problematic properties of treemaps. Our analyses also revealed several pitfalls for visualization design as well as for visual user-study planning and execution, particularly dealing with the powerful Gestalt-laws. Those findings facilitate different directions for future analyses, for example if the choice of nodes' positions plays a crucial role for area perception or if area shape, circular or squared, is a significant factor for good counting, finding, or comparing performance.

References

[1] E. Bakke, D. Karger, and R. Miller, "Automatic layout of structured hierarchical reports," IEEE Trans. Vis. Comput. Graphics, vol. 19, no. 12, 2013, pp. 2586–2595.

[2] H.-J. Schulz, S. Hadlak, and H. Schumann, "The design space of implicit hierarchy visualization: A survey," IEEE Trans. Vis. Comput. Graphics, vol. 17, no. 4, 2011, pp. 393–411.

[3] D. M. Kidd, "Geophylogenies and the map of life," Systematic Biology, vol. 59, no. 6, 2010, pp. 741–752.

[4] W. N. Dilla, D. J. Janvrin, and C. Jeffrey, "The impact of graphical displays of pro forma earnings information on professional and non-professional investors' earnings judgments," Behavioral Research in Accounting, vol. 25, no. 1, 2012, pp. 37–60.

[5] E. Tufte, The visual display of quantitative information, 2nd ed. Cheshire, Conn: Graphics Press, 2001.

[6] N. H. Müller, B. Liebold, D. Pietschmann, P. Ohler, and P. Rosenthal, "Gaze into hierarchy: A practice-oriented eye tracking study," in Proceedings of the EuroVis Workshop on Reproducibility, Verification, and Validation in Visualization, 2013, pp. 9–10.

[7] M. Burch, N. Konevtsova, J. Heinrich, M. Hoeferlin, and D. Weiskopf, "Evaluation of traditional, orthogonal, and radial tree diagrams by an eye tracking study," IEEE Trans. Vis. Comput. Graphics, vol. 17, no. 12, 2011, pp. 2440–2448.

[8] C. G. Healey and J. Enns, "Attention and visual memory in visualization and computer graphics," IEEE Trans. Vis. Comput. Graphics, vol. 18, no. 7, 2012, pp. 1170–1188.

[9] C. Healey, "Choosing effective colours for data visualization," in Proceedings of IEEE Visualization, 1996, pp. 263–270.

[10] S. Lin, J. Fortuna, C. Kulkarni, M. Stone, and J. Heer, "Selecting semantically-resonant colors for data visualization," Computer Graphics Forum, vol. 32, no. 3pt4, 2013, pp. 401–410.

[11] C. Ware, Information Visualization: Perception for Design. Morgan Kaufmann Publishers Inc., 2004.

[12] J. Stasko, R. Catrambone, M. Guzdial, and K. McDonald, "An evaluation of space-filling information visualizations for depicting hierarchical structures," International Journal of Human-Computer Studies, vol. 53, no. 5, 2000, pp. 663–694.

[13] B. Johnson and B. Shneiderman, "Tree-maps: a space-filling approach to the visualization of hierarchical information structures," in Proceedings of IEEE Visualization, 1991, pp. 284–291.

[14] K. Andrews and H. Heidegger, "Information slices: Visualising and exploring large hierarchies using cascading, semi-circular discs," in Proceedings of the IEEE Information Visualization Symposium, 1998, pp. 9–12.

[15] T. Bladh, D. Carr, and J. Scholl, "Extending tree-maps to three dimensions: A comparative study," in Computer Human Interaction, ser. Lecture Notes in Computer Science, M. Masoodian, S. Jones, and B. Rogers, Eds. Springer Berlin Heidelberg, 2004, vol. 3101, pp. 50–59.

[16] Y. Wang, S. T. Teoh, and K.-L. Ma, "Evaluating the effectiveness of tree visualization systems for knowledge discovery," in Proceedings of EuroVis, 2006, pp. 67–74.

[17] S. Teoh and M. Kwan-Liu, "Rings: A technique for visualizing large hierarchies," in Graph Drawing, ser. Lecture Notes in Computer Science, M. T. Goodrich and S. G. Kobourov, Eds. Springer Berlin Heidelberg, 2002, vol. 2528, pp. 268–275.

[18] C. Ziemkiewicz and R. Kosara, "The shaping of information by visual metaphors," IEEE Trans. Vis. Comput. Graphics, vol. 14, no. 6, 2008, pp. 1269–1276.

[19] M. Borkin, C. Yeh, M. Boyd, P. Macko, K. Gajos, M. Seltzer, and H. Pfister, "Evaluation of filesystem provenance visualization tools," IEEE Trans. Vis. Comput. Graphics, vol. 19, no. 12, 2013, pp. 2476–2485.

[20] P. Macko and M. I. Seltzer, "Provenance map orbiter: Interactive exploration of large provenance graphs," in Proceedings of the 3rd USENIX Workshop on the Theory and Practice of Provenance, 2011.

[21] J. Teets, D. Tegarden, and R. Russell, "Using cognitive fit theory to evaluate the effectiveness of information visualizations: An example using quality assurance data," IEEE Trans. Vis. Comput. Graphics, vol. 16, no. 5, 2010, pp. 841–853.

[22] J. Liang, Q. V. Nguyen, S. Simoff, and M. L. Huang, "Angular treemaps - a new technique for visualizing and emphasizing hierarchical structures," in Proceedings of the International Conference on Information Visualisation, 2012, pp. 74–80.

[23] J. Liang, M. L. Huang, and Q. V. Nguyen, "Perceptual user study for combined treemap," in Proceedings of the International Conference on Machine Learning and Applications, vol. 1, 2012, pp. 300–305.

[24] E. M. Reingold and J. Tilford, "Tidier drawings of trees," IEEE Trans. Software Eng., vol. SE-7, no. 2, 1981, pp. 223–228.

[25] C. Plaisant, J. Grosjean, and B. B. Bederson, "Spacetree: Supporting exploration in large node link tree, design evolution and empirical evaluation," in Proceedings of IEEE Information Visualization, 2002, pp. 57–64.

[26] M. Balzer and O. Deussen, "Voronoi treemaps," in Proceedings of the IEEE Symposium on Information Visualization, 2005, pp. 49–56.

[27] R. Blanch and E. Lecolinet, "Browsing zoomable treemaps: Structure-aware multi-scale navigation techniques," IEEE Trans. Vis. Comput. Graphics, vol. 13, no. 6, 2007, pp. 1248–1253.

[28] S. Tak and A. Cockburn, "Enhanced spatial stability with hilbert and moore treemaps," IEEE Trans. Vis. Comput. Graphics, vol. 19, no. 1, 2013, pp. 141–148.

[29] J. B. Kruskal and J. M. Landwehr, "Icicle plots: Better displays for hierarchical clustering," The American Statistician, vol. 37, no. 2, 1983, pp. 162–168.

[30] B. Kleiner and J. A. Hartigan, "Representing points in many dimensions by trees and castles," Journal Am. Stat. Assoc., vol. 76, no. 374, 1981, pp. 260–269.

[31] J. Zhao, F. Chevalier, C. Collins, and R. Balakrishnan, "Facilitating discourse analysis with interactive visualization," IEEE Trans. Vis. Comput. Graphics, vol. 18, no. 12, 2012, pp. 2639–2648.

[32] C. Rohrdantz, M. Hund, T. Mayer, B. Wälchli, and D. A. Keim, "The world's languages explorer: Visual analysis of language features in genealogical and areal contexts," Computer Graphics Forum, vol. 31, no. 3pt1, 2012, pp. 935–944.

[33] J. Stasko and E. Zhang, "Focus+context display and navigation techniques for enhancing radial, space-filling hierarchy visualizations," in Proceedings of IEEE Information Visualization, 2000, pp. 57–65.

[34] W. Schneider and R. M. Shiffrin, "Controlled and automatic human information processing: Detection, search, and attention," Psychological Review, vol. 84, no. 1, 1977, pp. 1–66.

[35] R. Desimone and J. Duncan, "Neural mechanisms of selective visual attention," Annual Review of Neuroscience, vol. 18, no. 1, 1995, pp. 193–222.

[36] A. Torralba, A. Oliva, M. S. Castelhano, and J. M. Henderson, "Contextual guidance of eye movements and attention in real-world scenes: The role of global features in object search," Psychological Review, vol. 113, no. 4, 2006, pp. 766–786.

[37] A. Lang, "The limited capacity model of mediated message processing," Journal of Communication, vol. 50, no. 1, 2000, pp. 46–70.

[38] J. Intriligator and P. Cavanagh, "The spatial resolution of visual attention," Cognitive Psychology, vol. 43, no. 3, 2001, pp. 171–216.

[39] M. Bruls, K. Huizing, and J. van Wijk, "Squarified treemaps," in Proceedings of the Joint Eurographics and IEEE TCVG Symposium on Visualization, 1999, pp. 33–42.

[40] J. Wagemans, J. H. Elder, M. Kubovy, S. E. Palmer, M. A. Peterson, M. Singh, and R. von der Heydt, "A century of gestalt psychology in visual perception: I. Perceptual grouping and figure-ground organization," Psychol Bull., vol. 138, no. 6, 2012, pp. 1172–1217.

[41] A. Al-Edaily, A. Al-Wabil, and Y. Al-Ohali, "Interactive screening for learning difficulties: Analyzing visual patterns of reading arabic scripts with eye tracking," in HCI International 2013 - Posters Extended Abstracts, ser. Communications in Computer and Information Science, C. Stephanidis, Ed. Springer Berlin Heidelberg, 2013, vol. 374, pp. 3–7.

[42] E. Li and D. Briley, "Attitudes shaped by eye movements: The reading direction effect," Advances in Consumer Research, vol. 39, 2011, pp. 666–667.

Topic-based Revision Tool to Support Academic Writing Skill for Research Students

Harriet Nyanchama Ocharo
School of Information Science
Japan Advanced Institute of Science and Technology
Nomi City, Japan
Email:harriet.ocharo@jaist.ac.jp

Shinobu Hasegawa
Research Center for Advanced Computing Infrastructure
Japan Advanced Institute of Science and Technology
Nomi City, Japan
Email:hasegawa@jaist.ac.jp

Kiyoaki Shirai
School of Information Science
Japan Advanced Institute of Science and Technology
Nomi City, Japan
Email:kshirai@jaist.ac.jp

Abstract— **When students write academic articles, they undergo a revision process where they receive feedback in the form of comments from their supervisors to improve the quality of the articles. The comments can be broadly classified into three categories: grammatical comments, format-related comments and topic-related comments. Comments related to the topic of the research are the hardest to resolve because students may lack discipline-specific writing skills needed to resolve such comments. This research developed an interactive tool to enable students search an archive of previous students' articles showing the revision history and comments. A machine learning approach was used to automatically classify the comments in the database into the three categories so that only topic-related comments were brought up in the search result. The result of the search was presented to the student in a way that clearly showed the process previous students used to resolve related comments, thereby showing them a similar way they could use to resolve any difficult topic-related comments. As the student's writing skill level increases, the amount of detail presented to the student reduces so as to avoid over reliance on the tool. In this way, students could improve their academic writing skills.**

Keywords- research support system; academic writing; writing tools; writing skill.

I. Introduction

Students in higher education and other researchers measure their achievements through the number of quality research articles they publish. Quality writing is therefore important in research in order to convey ideas clearly. It is the final stage of research and a culmination of effort that deserves to be done properly. However, students sometimes face difficulties revising their articles due to various reasons, such as lack of understanding, focusing too much on the formatting rather than the content and an inability to estimate the time it takes to revise an article because of lack of experience in academic writing [1]. In other words, they may not have sufficient academic writing skill.

Academic writing skill is the ability to write logically organized research papers, essays or reports in a well-structured, concise format. It is the ability to present complex ideas objectively while following the academic writing style, such as writing in third-person style, passive writing, proper citations etc. General academic writing skill may be taught in formal language lectures. However, there are variations in the structure and style of research papers in different research fields. Young researchers therefore feel the need to acquire discipline-specific writing style or skill from previous articles by researchers in the same field [2]. The challenge is that usually, the articles they read and learn from are in the final version. If they face a problem during revision of their own articles, they have no way of knowing how the previous students went through the revision process.

This research therefore proposes a support system for revision of articles based on a revision history database. When students write articles, they have to go through a revision process to improve the drafts based on comments from their supervisors. However, students may lack discipline-specific writing and revision skills needed to resolve such comments. We built an archive of previous students' articles and the corresponding comments they received when they were revising their articles. With a revision history database, students can learn revision skills by looking up similar or related comments and see how the other students resolved their comments.

The comments can be broadly classified into three categories: grammatical comments, format-related comments and topic-related comments. There are many tools, commercial or otherwise, to check the grammatical structure of documents. Format-related comments are also easy to resolve by following some standard guidelines set out for academic papers. However, there is not much research into tools or interfaces to help students resolve topic-related comments and that is why our focus is on comments related to content and meaning – where students take the longest time during revision. A machine learning approach was used to automatically classify the comments in the database into the three categories, so that only topic-related comments appeared when students looked up the comments database. The student would then be able to easily focus on resolving the topic-related comments. The result of the archives database search was presented to the student in a way that clearly showed the changes in subsequent drafts, thereby showing them a similar process they could use to resolve any difficult topic-related comments. If students resolve topic-related comments quickly, then the duration of the revision process is shortened.

As the student's writing skill level increases, the amount of detail presented to the student reduces so as to avoid over-reliance on the tool. To improve academic writing skill, there is a need to reduce the cognitive support for the students as their level of skill increases. This approach is called fading, where the functions of the supporting tool can be *fadable* according to the student's meta-cognitive skill [3]. This raises the issue of measuring the student's skill level, which we can estimate by the number of comments raised in each article the student is revising.

The rest of this paper is constructed as follows: section II is a review of related work with a view of identifying the research gap in academic writing and the potential impact of this research. In section III, our approach is discussed in detail covering the writing and revision process, the data collection procedure used to gather previous students' articles and the technical details related to the process of automatic classification of the comments. Section IV includes the results and discussion of the comment classification, and section V is the conclusion and future work.

II. RELATED WORK

With the advent of the use of computers in learning, there has been an increase in research on writing tools to aid academic writing. Earlier research into important linguistic aspects of a good writing style such as readability, sentence and word length, sentence type, word usage and sentence openers [4] enhanced the capability of word processors beyond mere spellchecking. In addition to word processors, grammar checking tools are available that can automatically recognize and clean up grammatical errors in writing [5].While these grammatical tools are beneficial in helping researchers clean up errors in their writing, the quality of writing cannot be evaluated by grammatical accuracy alone [6].

This therefore raises the question of whether these tools can also be useful in improving students' competency in academic writing. Students can of course learn directly from language teachers, but research students are often pressed for time and are likely to end up copying from bibliography, or working in a relationship of informal apprenticeship with more experienced members of their team [2].

Online interactive tools offer a promising way for students to improve their grammar skills. A corpus is one way for novice students to learn from experienced researchers. Narita [6] states that a corpus-based tool of previous students' work can be vital for improving second language learners' grammatical knowledge. Aluisio [7] proposed a design for a tool that made explicit the writing skills performed by language expert authors so that novice researchers could develop their academic drafting and revision skills in a foreign language. Alusio [8] further developed a tool to assist non-native novice researchers in achieving a cohesive schematic structure for their articles.

In their research, Hasegawa and Yemane [1] created an article revising support system that facilitates article revision by managing all the comments as tickets, such as in an issue-tracking system. However, the comments are not classified by categories, as is the case in this research where the focus is on topic-related comments and how to solve them.

Once a research student has written an initial draft, he/she will receive feedback from their supervisor to improve the draft. These comments may not only be related to their grammatical errors, but also to the format or structure of the paper. A third type of comments are those related to the topic of research. As described previously, there are a lot of tools to help students improve their grammatical knowledge as well as the structure of their scientific articles. However, there has not been much research into helping students improve their revision skills.

This paper expands the scope of previous research by presenting a way for researchers to improve their topic-related revision skills and hence resolve comments relating to the content of their research articles.

III. OUR APPROACH

In this section, the process a student goes through when writing and revising an academic article is discussed in detail. We also discuss how our revision tool can help the student to shorten the revision process by automatically filtering out non topic-related comments. In addition, we discuss the process of collecting the necessary data and developing the tool.

A. The Writing and Revision Process

After a student writes the first draft of a research article, he/she sends it to the supervisor for feedback. The supervisor inserts comments to help the student improve the draft and sends it back to the student. The student then revises the draft based on the comments and sends it back to the supervisor for feedback and so on, until the final draft is approved. This is illustrated in Figure1.

The main objective of this tool is to increase the efficiency of the revision process resulting from a reduction in the number of comments and number of drafts, and a shorter duration of the revision process. Increased efficiency implies that the writing skill level of the student has improved as they are able to revise their articles much faster. When the student uploads the draft with comments into the tool, the comments are automatically labelled as grammatical, format or topic-related. If the student were to do this manually, it would take too much time. The student can then quickly revise the format and grammatical comments before focusing on the topic-related comments. He/she can look up in the archive for similar comments and see how previous students resolved their comments.

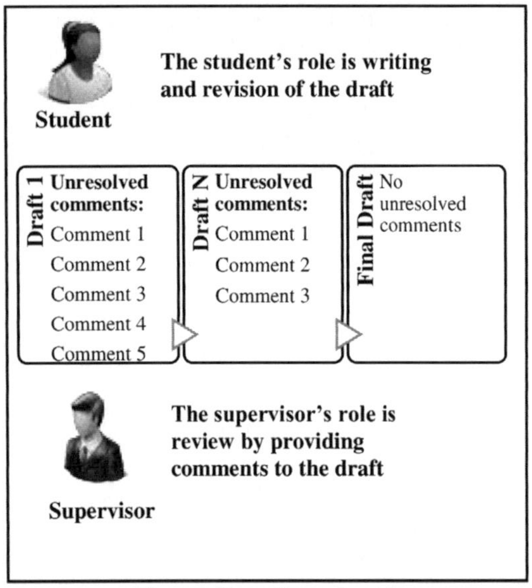

Figure 1. The writing and revision process

B. Data Collection Procedure

The revision history of articles from previous students in the same laboratory was collected. 19 articles were obtained with an average of 6.6 drafts (126 drafts in total). Each draft had an average of 20 comments. The total number of comments was 1,338.

The comments and corresponding comment ranges were extracted from the original Microsoft Word documents and uploaded to a MySQL database. This formed the backend for the web-interface that was developed using Django, a Python framework. The web interface was used to search for matching comments and for viewing a history of the revision process for the documents containing similar comments.

C. Comments Classification Process

The comments were classified into 3 types – format, grammatical, and topic-related. The comments were classified as per the below definition:

- **Format**: comments about font type and size, positioning of figures and tables, page limitations etc. *Example: Change font style for section title*
- **Grammatical**: comments about correction of grammatical or spelling mistakes etc. *Example: Is paragraph structure OK? (Main topic). However, the contrary situation?- On the other hand?*
- **Topic-related**: comments about actual content or topic of the article *Example: I cannot catch the goal of community based learning from this document. What types of knowledge and skill do the community members have through the CBL?*

If a comment belonged to both topic-related and any other category, then that comment was labeled as being topic-related in the training model because it was considered useful to the revision process.

Natural language processing and machine learning techniques were used to automatically classify comments into the three categories. Each comment was analyzed and annotated using the Stanford CoreNLP [9]. The annotation included tokenization, sentence splitting, POS tagging and lemmatization. The machine learning algorithm LIBSVM [10] was used for training because of its simplicity in rapidly obtaining acceptable results, even with texts short in length (the average length of the comments was 90 words). For simplicity reasons, this classification test used only the lemmas of the comment words as features. The comment words included were nouns, verbs, adjectives and adverbs. Pronouns, articles and other parts of speech were not considered relevant features for the classification algorithm.

IV. Results and Discussion

This section details the results of using machine learning to automatically classify comments into the three categories discussed earlier, and a discussion of the implications of the results as well as the practical application of the revision tool in a laboratory setting.

A. Classification Results

After obtaining the features, the number of unique comments was down to 612. The number of features considered was 902. Each comment was manually assigned a label as SVM is a supervised learning method. There was an imbalance in the distribution of the target classes with topic-based comments accounting for 56% of the total number of comments. Grammatical and format comments accounted for 25% and 19% respectively. Stratified k-fold validation was applied, with k=10. Data was split into 10 groups, with each group containing 552 (137 grammar, 105 format, 310 topic-related) training data items and 60 (15 grammar, 11 format, 34 topic-related) testing data items. The ratio of relative class frequencies was approximately preserved in each training and testing fold. An average prediction accuracy rate of 56.21 was obtained using the LIBSVM tool (default parameters).

B. Case Study:

In order to observe the usability of the tool, we obtained a student's article with reviewer comments. There are two stages:

Stage 1: The student uploads the article and the comments are automatically extracted and classified. There were 15 comments, which were automatically extracted and classified as grammatical, format or topic-related. In this case, all the 612 unique comments were used as training data and the resulting model was used to predict the category of the 15 comments. 13 of the 15 comments were accurately predicted as being topic related, having an accuracy rate of 86.67%. In Figure 2, the topic-related comments are presented to the student.

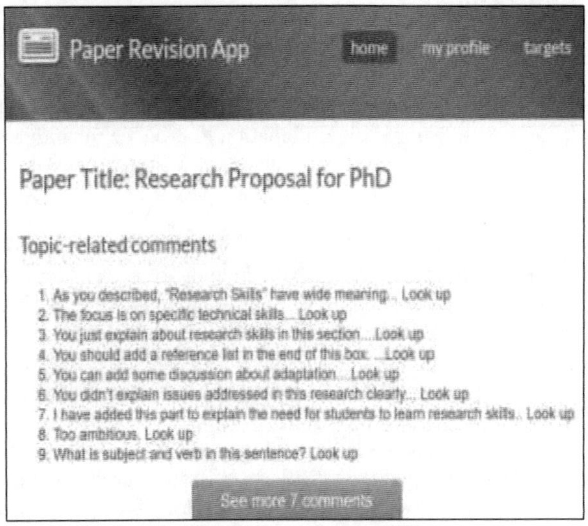

Figure 2. Results of the classification of the case study article presented in the web interface

Stage 2 is looking up the comment in the database of previous work to see how other students resolved similar comments. In this case, clicking "look up" on the first comment presents a list articles whose results closely match the key word "skills". The first step in the search is to look for specific content-related keywords in the comment. The reason keyword searches are used is because the comments are stored in a relational database as string fields. Therefore, the search is a simple database lookup. Only the papers containing comments in the database marked as topic-related by the SVM algorithm were brought up in the lookup results. The search results are shown in Table I.

Selecting one of paper titles presented "HCII2016_Ocharo", the revision history of the article i.e. the changes the phrase in question had gone through various draft versions, was presented as in Table II. From this result, they may notice how to define technical terms in research and also how to focus and narrow down the focus of their research.

In summary, there were positive search results for other comments containing key topic-related words such as "testing, analysis, abstract, methodology". The results of the matching comments and revision history of corresponding articles were displayed as expected. In future, the system will be tested by the target students to evaluate its actual effectiveness in reducing the average number of drafts and comments, thus reducing the time it takes to revise academic articles.

TABLE I. THE SEARCH RESULTS IN TABLE FORM

Paper Title	Version no	Matching Comment
GLS2014_Didin	2	These sentences are similar to the ones in Abstract?. Basically, it is OK. But you can add some examples. ?such as, decision-making, team-working, and communication skills?
SIG-ALST2012_Didin	2	Why should the volunteers improve their skills independently?
HCII2016_Ocharo	3	Can you describe a couple of examples of the research skills?
HCII2016_Ocharo	3	What is the research skills in this context? Maybe you define it at section 2 or later. But it would be better if you explain a simple example of the skill in this section so that the audience can easily understand the concept.
ICCE2013_Didin	4	Magnitude which enables the novice volunteers to develop their ethical decision-making skills at all times during official disaster management training inside and outside of class, and expect them to improve their performance in disaster response activities.?

C. Discussion

Considering the prediction accuracy of the classification algorithm, more comment data is needed. In machine learning, a large amount of data is needed in order to improve the accuracy of the prediction algorithm but in this case, there was only an initial number of 1,338 comments. A lot of the grammatical and format related comments were misclassified as being topic-related. Even with the limited data set, the factors below could have affected the accuracy.

- Even after using stratified k-fold cross validation, that more than half of the comments were topic-related could have introduced bias in the training model. In addition, the large number of features (902) relative to the data set (612) may have also had an impact on the performance of the prediction model.
- In addition, a single model with three outputs (grammar, format, topic-related) was trained and used for prediction. Instead, three different models each predicting whether a comment belonged to the group or not, may improve accuracy.

TABLE II. COMMENT REVISION HISTORY

Paper Title: HCII2016_Ocharo	**Version 1**	**Version 2**	**Version 3**
Matching comment	But it would be better if you explain a simple example of the skill in this section so that the audience can easily understand the concept	Can you describe a couple of examples of the research skills?	Describe specific examples of the research skills?
Comment range	Research skills	Research skills can be widely categorized into two: discipline specific and general research skills.	Research skills include such generic skills as planning and scheduling, communication and presentation; and specific skills such as trend analysis, problem definition and data analysis

- Thirdly, the classification algorithm only used the content words (nouns, adjectives, verbs and adverbs) of the comments without considering their meaning or context. For example, topic-related comments contain keywords such as 'abstract', 'originality', 'design', 'develop', 'usability' etc. Topic-related comments also apply to certain sections of the article, such as the title, section headers etc. Grammatical comments contained keywords or phrases such as 'redundant', 'sentences', 'misspell' etc. while format comments typically contained keywords such as 'font', 'Calibri', 'style', 'move figure', 'change order' etc. Including other information like the document version, author, and comment metadata such as comment author, comment replies etc. may improve the prediction accuracy.
- Fourthly, the comment range – the words in the document that are covered by the comment – was not considered either and this combined with the comment text could also improve the accuracy of classification.
- Fifthly, the comment length was not considered for convenience purposes as it would require scaling between a range of (0,1). However, it is an important feature to consider as topic-related comments were typically longer than any other, while grammatical comments' length could be as short as a single word.
- Lastly, the kernel and parameter selection of the SVM algorithm also affect the accuracy of the results. In this research, the default parameters were applied. It would require several trials to discover the best kernel-parameter combination to produce the highest accuracy. However, in this research, we focused on rapidly obtaining acceptable results.

D. Practical Application in Laboratory Setting

The revision tool can be applied in a laboratory setting so that the student can look up similar comments in the archive of previous students, since the results are more likely to be relevant if all the students belong to the same laboratory. For the search results to be more useful, the database of revision histories also needs to be large enough to allow more informative searches. The current database is limited to only 19 articles. However, it is difficult to build a large database as even with an average of 10 students publishing 3 times each year, that would only amount to 30 articles in a year. Therefore, finding ways of improving accuracy even with a limited data set is the most important element of future research. Students could help with the annotation, by manually correcting misclassified comments and this feedback would in turn be used to improve future prediction.

When it comes to research involving comments, other factors to be considered include whether or not the system will manage comments or leave it to an external application such as text processors. In our case, the tool only provides look up but not comment management. Furthermore, metadata contained in the comments such as author, date, comment replies, comment status (open or closed) could be useful data for students carrying out revision of their academic articles. Some comments are also persistent throughout the revision process, which could mean they are harder to solve, while others occur more frequently. Such an analysis could be combined with search results to push the most relevant comments to the top of the search result.

The student's skill level should be taken into account when presenting the student with the search results. In other words, the system should *adapt* to the student's skill level by presenting a more detailed version of the results to students with low skills, while presenting a less detailed version to students with higher skills. As the student's writing skill level increases throughout the revision process, the amount of detail presented to the student reduces so as to avoid over-reliance on the tool. This would avoid automated writing, which impends student learning.

The student's skill level can be estimated by the number of comments raised in their drafts by their supervisor. More comments show that the student has a lot of revision points to consider, which could mean that the student is lowly skilled. Fewer comments imply the student is highly skilled. This estimate of skill is calculated with each draft to ensure adaptation to the skill level of the student.

V. CONCLUSION AND FUTURE WORK

This paper described an article revision tool that helps students resolve difficult topic-related comments they encounter during the writing process by looking up the revision process of previous students in an archived database. In this way, the students can improve on their knowledge of academic writing. In future, the efficiency of this tool in improving the writing skills of students will be evaluated by the target students in the same laboratory. In this research, the comments were simply classified into grammar, format and content-related. In future, other types of comments such as comments related to the logical structure of the documents will be considered. In addition, if there are many similar corrections in grammatical errors, it should be shared as pre-requisites for paper writing. Such a summarization function would be useful for novices.

Academic writing is an integral part of research in universities and other institutions of higher education, and as such, any computer tools to aid this process can have a significant impact on the quality of output from such institutions. Future work will focus on evaluating the impact of the revision tool discussed in this paper.

REFERENCES

[1] S. Hasegawa and K. Yamane, "An Article/Presentation Revising Support System for Transferring Laboratory Knowledge," 19th International Conference on Computers in Education, Chiang Mai, Thailand, pp.247-254, 2011.

[2] K. Hyland, Disciplinary Discourses: Social Interactions in Academic Writing, Harlow: Person Education, 2000.

[3] S. Hasegawa, K. Mannari, S. Ooiwa, and A. Kashihara, "A Portal Site for Supporting Research Activities," 15th International Conference on Computers in Education, Hiroshima, Japan, pp. 59-60, 2007.

[4] L. Cherry, "Writing Tools," IEEE Transactions on Communications, vol. Volume: 30, no. Issue: 1, pp. 100-105, 1982 .

[5] R. Blake, "Current trends in online language learning," Annual Review of Applied Linguistics, *31*, pp. 19-35, 2011.

[6] M. Narita, "Developing a corpus-based online grammar tutorial prototype," The Language Teacher, pp. 23-29, 2012.

[7] S. M. Aluisio, I. Barcelos, J. Sampaio and N. O. Oliviera Jr., "How to learn the many unwritten 'rules of the game' of the academic discourse: a hybrid approach based on critiques and cases to support scientific writing," Proceedings IEEE International Conference on Advanced Learning Technologies, Madison, WI, USA, pp.257-260, 2001.

[8] S. M. Aluisio and R. E. Gantenbein, "Towards the Application of Systematic Functional Linguistics in Writing Tools," Computers and their applications: Proceedings of the ISCA 12th international conference, Tempe, Arizona, US, pp. 181-185, 1997.

[9] C. D. Manning, et al., "The Stanford CoreNLP Natural Language Processing Toolkit," Proceedings of the 52nd Annual Meeting of the Association for Computational Linguistics: System Demonstrations, pp. 55-60, 2014. http://stanfordnlp.github.io/CoreNLP/index.html [Retrieved: Aug, 2016]

[10] C. Chih-Chung and L. Chih-Jen, "LIBSVM : a library for support vector machines," ACM Transactions on Intelligent Systems and Technology, p. 27, 2011. Software available at http://www.csie.ntu.edu.tw/~cjlin/libsvm [Retrieved: Aug, 2016]

Annotation and View Synchronization of Shared 3D Models

Hiroshi Shimada, Kengo Imae
Graduate School of Frontier Informatics
Kyoto Sangyo University,
Kyoto, Japan
Email: {i1658083,i1558048}@cc.kyoto-su.ac.jp

Naohiro Hayashibara
Faculty of Computer Science and Engineering
Kyoto Sangyo University,
Kyoto, Japan
Email: naohaya@cc.kyoto-su.ac.jp

***Abstract*—Many pictures and videos have been shared on the Web. Thus, it is easy to find what one needs by using a Web search engine. Given the popularity of 3D printers, it is expected that 3D models will also be shared in the same manner. We focus here on 3D models with camera viewpoint and propose a prototype implementation of the annotation sharing system of 3D models. We also implement the synchronization mechanism for 3D models based on Publish/Subscribe model. Then, we evaluate the resource overhead of a server and the response time of clients in our prototype.**

Keywords–3D model; annotation; viewpoint synchronization; publish/subscribe systems

I. Introduction

Pictures and videos are major contents on the Web. We can find favorite ones using a search engine and share them with social network services. Sharing annotations on such contents is particularly interesting in terms of promoting communication.

On the other hand, 3D models are getting popular in the area of virtual reality and 3D printing in recent years. So, they are expected to be shared on the Web like pictures and videos, and will be used in teleconference and distance education for an intuitive awareness (e.g., [1]). However 3D models have a problem that the appearance changes by rotation and zoom operations. For this reason, we have to consider a new way of annotation on 3D models and their sharing.

Now, we take a look at the difference between 2D contents (e.g., pictures and movies) and 3D contents in terms of annotation.

2-Dimensional Contents: One of the features of 2-dimensional (2D) contents is to be able to display all information in the same plane. In the case of pictures, annotations can be added simply on pictures. Video contents include much more information than pictures. A video can be considered to be a sequence of pictures, and changes the view over time. However, it is still the same as a picture at the moment. Thus, annotations for videos is also realized by adding it directly on the contents.

3-Dimensional Contents: For shared 3-dimensional (3D) contents, it is important to consider a view through a camera. When a user operates a shared 3D model, the camera position is changed by the operation. Thus, the view changes according to the position. To represent the intention of an annotation precisely, it should be associated with the camera position. It is also appeared with the same view as when it was added.

In this paper, we focus on the problem on the visual appearance of a 3D model caused by operations, such as rotation and zoom. When a user adds some annotation on a 3D model, it should be stored together with the current camera position. To display annotations, it is important to select some of them according to the camera to emphasize their intention. Despite the problem, most of the existing approaches display all annotations of a 3D model in the same plane.

Some of the recent research work take into account of the visual appearance of a 3D model and annotations are associated with a part of the model by using explicit links. However, such approaches become more complicated when many annotations are added by users.

Contribution: We propose (i) the approach of the perspective-oriented display of annotations and (ii) the viewpoint synchronization mechanism for 3D models. The former one is realized by annotations with position information of a camera. Each annotation is associated with an implicit link from the camera position, which realizes the user's perspective, to the corresponding 3D model going through the annotation. The latter one is the viewpoint sharing mechanism based on the Publish/Subscribe (Pub/Sub) model. It realizes the synchronization on the visual appearance for 3D models among multiple users. Moreover, we have evaluated the proposed system regarding resource consumption and the response time. Our contribution is expected to be useful for distance education and teleconferencing using 3D models.

II. Related work

In this section, we introduce several existing work related to mechanisms to annotate 3D models and applications using 3D models.

A. Annotation on shared 3D models

Although there are a lot of work on the annotation of 3D models such as ones in the context of CAD drawing [2], [3], we now explain some of them which have motivation similar to ours.

Kahan et al. developed a Web-based shared annotation system for Web documents, called Annotea [4]. It is based on an open Resource Document Framework (RDF) infrastructure standardized by W3C. Annotations, which are attached by users, are managed by Annotation servers separated from the corresponding document. The protocol between clients and the server has been defined as Annotea Protocols [5].

Kadobayashi et al. proposed notions of Physical viewpoint for annotations of 3D models [6]. It is the way to put annotations based on the camera position at which a user is looking. Hunter and Yu proposed the 3D semantic annotation system for digital 3D artifacts [7] and crystallography models [8] including annotations. The problem of those systems is to be complicated if many annotations (i.e., windows and links) have been put into a 3D model.

1) Teleconference and e-Learning using 3D models: There are so many applications using 3D models for realizing the virtual environment in teleconferencing, e-Learning, and training in the medical, educational and business fields. In particular, they are sophisticated in terms of devices because lots of VR devices such as head-mount display (HMD) have been developed in recent years.

Goeser et al. developed the web-based 3D virtual framework for e-Learning, called VIEW [9]. It consists of two modules for tensile testing and mechanical assembling. In the result of their experiments, the proposed system and modules using 3D models give students the learning experience equivalent to the physical one.

Kleven et al. developed a virtual operating room of surgery for medical training of surgical nurses [10]. The proposed system integrates the use of a head-mount display, Oculus Rift. The experiment through the role-play with the system shows that the sense of presence and immersion has been enhanced in the majority of the participants. It is a good alternative for medical training. It is also used for anatomy lectures with 3D anatomical models.

III. Annotation of Sharing for 3D Models

In this work, we propose an annotation sharing and a viewpoint sharing mechanisms for 3D models. The former one is a mechanism for displaying annotations in consideration of the camera position. It means that an annotation to be displayed with a 3D model is stored with the position information of the camera, which decides the visual appearance of the 3D model. The system selects annotations of the 3D model properly based on the camera viewpoint changed by operations (i.e., rotation and zoom). An annotation does not use a link to express its context because the implicit line from the camera position to the 3D model going through the annotation takes the same role of the link. Thus, we realize the way of seamless display for 3D models with annotations.

The second one is a viewpoint sharing mechanism based on the Pub/Sub model. The mechanism provides viewpoint synchronization among multiple users who look at the same 3D model without mutual exclusion. Thus, it is capable of offering a scalable service.

A. Operations on 3D Models

Shared 3D models can be operated by users. This system suppose rotation and zoom as operations on 3D

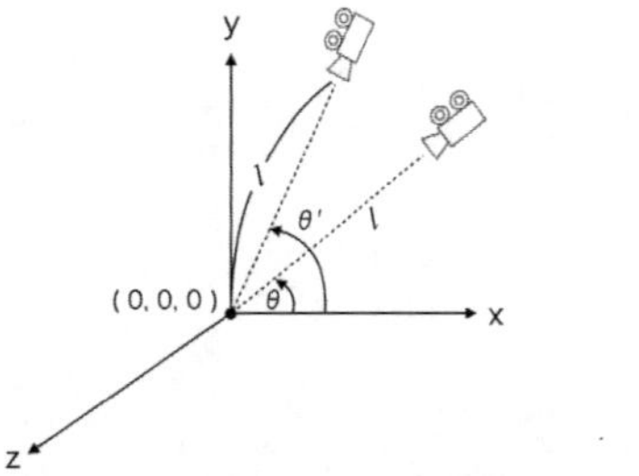

Figure 1: Rotation of a 3D model

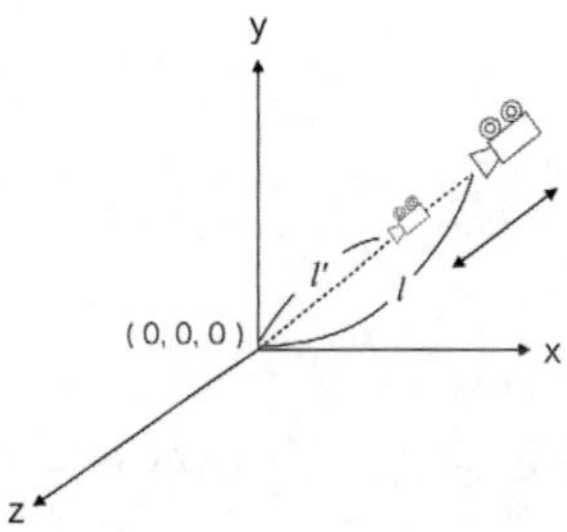

Figure 2: Zoom of a 3D model

models. Rotation is defined as an operation of changing the angle θ without changing the distance l from the origin (see Figure 1). It is represented by $rotate(\theta, d)$, where d is the value of the angle to be changed from the current position. Rotation is primarily an operation for vertical and horizontal movement of the camera angle to change the face of the 3D model.

Contrary to the rotation, zoom is defined as an operation for changing the distance l from the origin (see Figure 2). It is represented by $zoom(l, d)$. Zoom is to change the depth of the camera viewpoint to the model.

B. Annotation with Position Information

As mentioned above, the appearance of 3D models is different depending on the camera angle. Existing approaches introduced in Section II associated annotations with its context and semantics by using links explicitly. However, it makes the display complicated when there are lots of annotations on a 3D model in those methods.

We attempt to solve the problem using annotation with the camera position. Our approach selects annotations to be displayed properly according to the current camera angle. It also realizes implicit links between annotations and the 3D model to express their context.

1) Definition of annotations: When we consider the implementation, it is necessary to define the notion of the annotation with position information. First of all, we describe the definition of a set of annotations as follows.

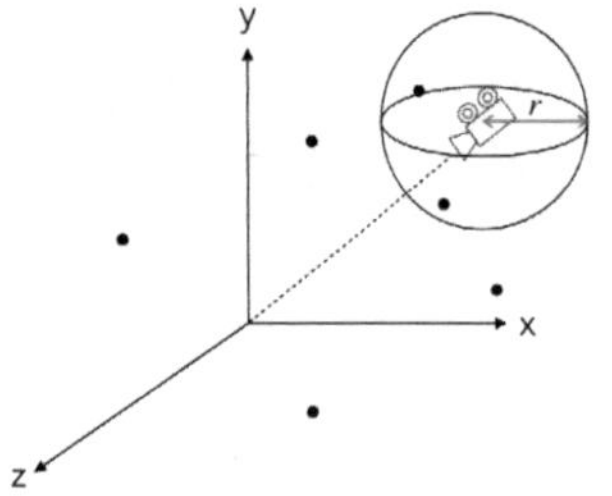

Figure 3: Selection of annotations

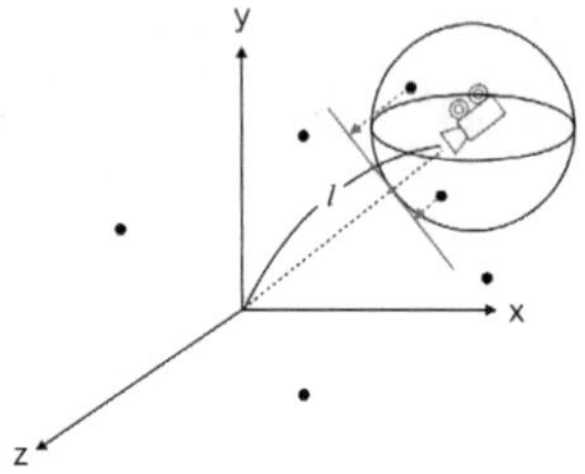

Figure 4: Converting 3D position information into 2D one by the Map function.

$$X = \{C_1, C_2, C_3, C_4, ..., C_n\} \tag{1}$$

In Equation (1), annotations are represented by the elements of X. Each annotation C_i is an ordered pair which consists of two elements $C_i \overset{\text{def}}{=} (s, c_i)$; s is an annotation content (e.g., a character string) and a three-dimensional coordinates of the position $c_i = (x_i, y_i, z_i)$.

2) Selection of annotations: We describe a method for selecting annotations on a 3D model. To display annotations, they are selected from the set of annotations X based on the current camera position a. Let $f_x(a, c_i)$, $f_y(a, c_i)$ and $f_z(a, c_i)$ be functions which return the distance between the camera position a and a position of a certain annotation c_i in x, y and z axis, respectively. So, we define $d(a, c_i)$ as the function to calculate the relative distance between a and c_i in a three-dimensional space, as follows.

$$d(a, c_i) = \sqrt{f_x(a, c_i)^2 + f_y(a, c_i)^2 + f_z(a, c_i)^2} \tag{2}$$

The set of annotations $D \subseteq X$ displayed on a screen is defined as follows.

$$D = \{C_d \in X | d(a, c_d) \leq r\} \tag{3}$$

Each annotation $C_d \in D$ is selected based on the sphere with the radius r from the camera position as the central point of it (see Fig. 3).

3) Display of annotations: Each annotation $C_d \in D$ should be converted its position c_d into two-dimensional one for showing on a flat display. So, we introduce a function $Map(c_d)$ for converting a position information. Figure 4 shows how it works. The advantage of this function is to preserve the relative position between annotations in a 2D plane. When a user rotates the 3D model (i.e., changes the camera position), positions of annotations in a display should be updated. The Map function updates those positions for following such operations as shown in Figure 5. As a result, annotations move to the same direction of the rotation.

4) Solving the scale problem: In the case that there exists a gap between the size of the 3D space and the display size as shown in Figure 6, we have to adjust the difference between them properly. The $Comp$ function

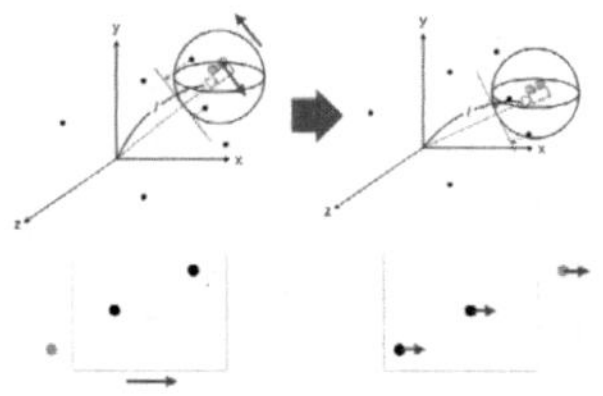

Figure 5: Updating positions of annotations in a display.

defined below adjusts the positions of annotations for the display to solve the scale gap (see Figure 7).

$$Comp(c_i) = (W + k_w x_i, H + k_h y_i) \tag{4}$$

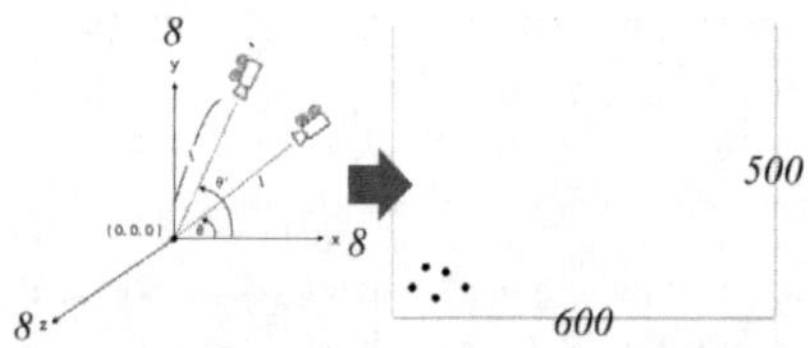

Figure 6: The scale problem caused by the gap between the size of the 3D space and the display.

W is the half of the width and H is the half of the height in the display. k_w and k_h are correction factors for x-axis and y-axis, respectively. They are calculated by the following equation:

$$k = \frac{L + \frac{L}{2}}{|l_{min}| + |l_{max}|} \tag{5}$$

Let L be the width or the height of the display area. l_{min} and l_{max} indicate the minimum and the maximum of

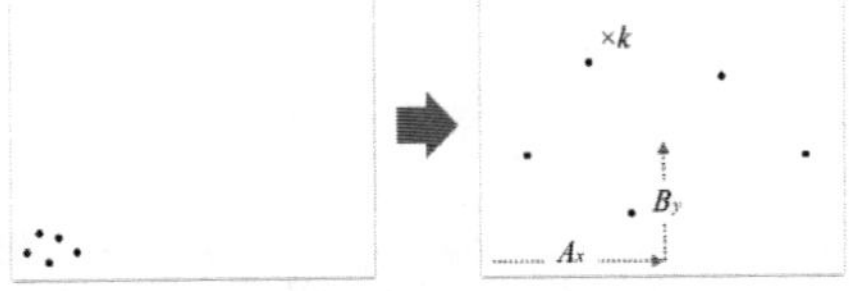

Figure 7: Position adjustment for annotations by the *Comp* function.

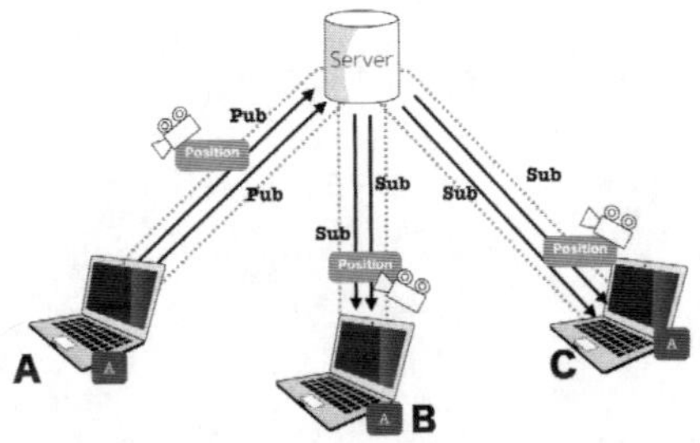

Figure 8: Sharing viewpoint based on the Pub/Sub model

the 3D space (i.e., $\forall x, y, z \in [l_{min}, l_{max}]$). To obtain k_h, you set the height of the display as L. While, you can set the width of the display as L to obtain k_w.

IV. Viewpoint Sharing for 3D Models

We propose a mechanism of viewpoint synchronization among multiple users for shared 3D models. We apply the Pub/Sub communication model, which is mostly used in distributed system community [11], [12], to the mechanism to solve the performance degradation.

Suppose that all users in Figure 8 have registered to the server to subscribe the same 3D model. In the viewpoint sharing mechanism, the current viewpoint information (i.e., camera position) of a user is published to the server when the user makes some operation to a shared 3D model (i.e., the user A in Figure 8). While, other users behave subscribers in the Pub/Sub model. It means that such users receive the camera viewpoint on the shared one.

Advantage: The advantage of this approach is that it provides viewpoint sharing for 3D models in a scalable manner. Thus, we expect that it is capable of offering real-time service to multiple users. Moreover, a camera viewpoint on a 3D model will be delivered to appropriate users based on the registration information which associates users (or clients) and 3D models.

Applications: Our proposed system including viewpoint and annotation sharing mechanisms can be useful, for instance, for teleconference systems in medical practice. 3D models of internal organs which are obtained by fMRI are used for preparing or practice for surgical operations. In this case, annotation and viewpoint sharing can be building blocks of teleconference systems for a meeting using 3D models among multiple sites (hospitals). Practically speaking, we can build a teleconference system using 3D models with our mechanism of annotation and viewpoint sharing together with some communication service. It is also possible to implement a system for distance learning with molecular structure models using the proposed system. 3D models can be helpful to understand chemical structures, molecular dynamics, universal gravitation among planets.

V. Details of Implementation

In this section, we explain the implementation details of our prototype for sharing annotation and viewpoint on 3D models.

The architecture of our prototype is shown in Figure 9. The prototype consists of the server and clients. Clients have been implemented on the browser Google Chrome version 54. We describe the details of them below.

1) Implementation of the server: The server is implemented using the Web application framework Express of Node.js and Socket.io that is a module related to WebSocket. Socket.io provides the push-style communication interface between the server and clients. If a user changes the camera position by rotating the 3D model, this information is sent to the server immediately. It is like *publish* in a Pub/Sub system. The server manages the subscription information and 3D models in Redis which is an in-memory Key-Value-Store (KVS) supporting pub/sub-style messaging.

2) implementation of client side: Clients register a certain 3D model and *subscribe* the change of the viewpoint from the server. In this architecture, a client that executes a certain operation (e.g., rotation or zoom) becomes a *publisher* and any other clients are *subscribers*. We adopt WebGL for displaying 3D models on a browser. In the implementation of clients, we mainly use Three.js which is a wrapper library of WebGL. A Client implemented on a browser is provided as an extension of the browser (i.e., add-on). This is because, we suppose that the proposed system is used with some messaging service such as Google Hangouts, Skype and so on.

3) Advantage of the prototype: The advantage of this messaging style is that a publisher does not care about the destination. It sends the viewpoint information to the server as a message after executing an operation, and the server delivers it to subscribers properly. Moreover, Redis takes place the pattern matching between published messages and subscribers. Thus, our prototype can execute the view synchronization with low overhead.

VI. Evaluation

We have measured our proposed mechanism of the viewpoint sharing mechanism from two points of view; the resource consumption in the server and the response time in clients. The former one would be useful for system administrators, or service providers that provide some

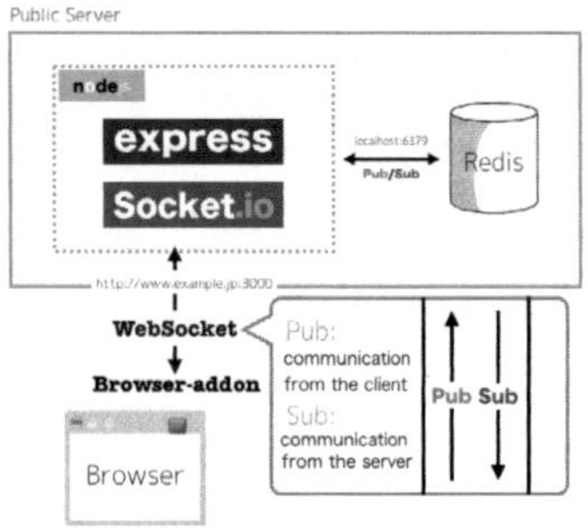

Figure 9: Architecture of the system

service using our proposed mechanism and the latter one might be interesting in terms of user experience.

A. Environment and Experimental Setup

Our experiments have been done in a LAN including a single server and 20 clients where they are interconnected with a wired 1000Base-T Ethernet connection. The average RTT (round trip time) is 0.71 msec. in the LAN. Clients run on Mac OSX version 10.9.5.

The number of clients is set from 2 to 20 in the experiments. We used the regression testing tool Selenium Web Driver running on web browsers to realize a heavy load to the server during the experiments.

Both the average of CPU load and Network load were measured using the System Admin Reporter (sar). We have measured the number of received packets and number of sent packets and the CPU utilization of the server process for 200 sec. for each configuration. We have also measured the response time between the server and clients as observing the time difference between a pair of sent and received packets in clients.

B. On Resource Consumption

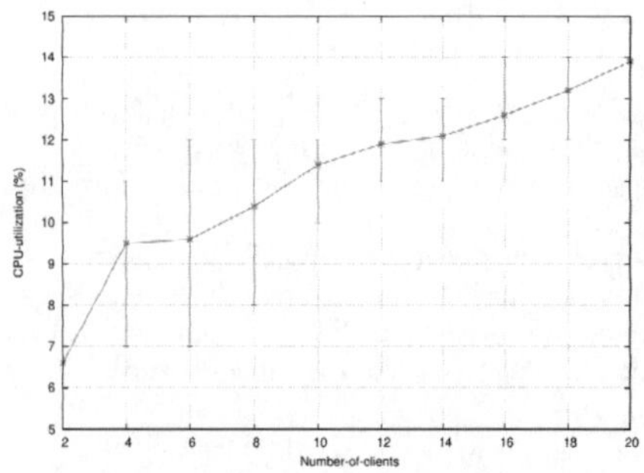

Figure 10: The CPU load of the server

1) CPU Load: Figure 10 shows the result of the number of clients v.s. the average value of CPU load (%) at the server. The average CPU load of the server process is shown in the y-axis, and the number of clients is shown in the x-axis.

The average CPU load of the server is 13.9% with 20 clients. It is increased by about 2.1 times from the one with 2 clients. If we suppose an increase of the CPU load is same as our experimental result, the average CPU load is expected to be about 43% with 100 clients.

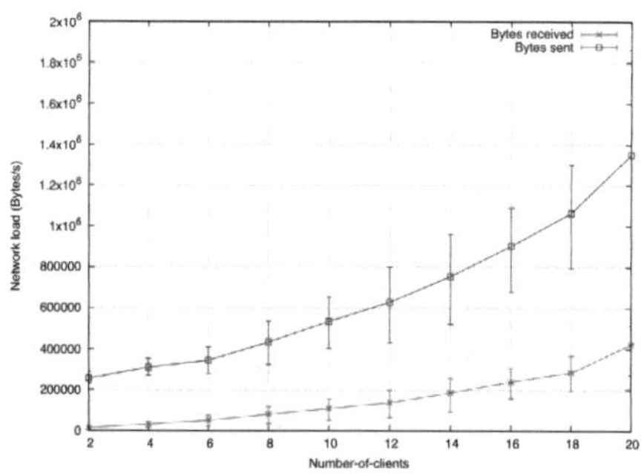

Figure 11: Network load on the server

2) Network Load: Figure 11 shows the result of the number of clients v.s. the average network load (Bytes/s) at the server. The number of sent and receive packets is shown in the y-axis, the number of clients is shown in the x-axis.

Packets received in the server increases 150 Kbytes/s to 323 Kbytes/s as the number of clients increases from 2 to 20. On the other hand, packets sent from the server becomes 1,067 Kbytes/s from 256 Kbytes/s by the number of clients increases. As a result, the architecture of the experiment can be practical with 1,000 clients because the number of packets is expected to be 40 Mbytes/s.

C. On Response Time

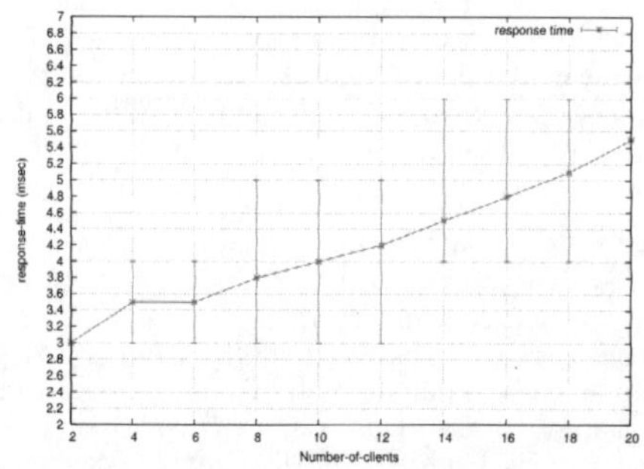

Figure 12: Response time on the number of clients

Figure 12 shows the time for processing a request of updating a viewpoint at the server. We call it the response time.

According to the result, the response time is expected to be about 100 msec if we suppose 700 clients. 100 msec. is considered to be the limit of response time for having users feel that the system is reacting instantaneously [13]. Thus, our prototype is capable of having the real-time property with about 700 users.

VII. Conclusion

We showed our prototype for sharing annotation and the viewpoint synchronization mechanism based on the Pub/Sub model for 3D models in this paper. It realizes the scalable collaboration using 3D models for multiple users.

We also measured resource consumption of the server and response time in clients on the viewpoint synchronization mechanism. As a result, the system showed the capability of providing the real-time service to at least 100 users. It means that the prototype can provide the high-level user experience with low overhead.

The proposed system, for example, can be used for teleconferencing in the medical field. It is useful for an online meeting using a 3D model of an internal organ, which is the target for a surgical operation. It can also be used for e-Learning in physics and chemistry. The simulation of planetary motion and chemical synthesis using the prototype provides an additional learning experience for students.

In our project, we are developing the collaborative editing system for 3D models using a conflict-free data type, called ChainVoxel [14]. The next goal of the work is to combine the annotation and the view synchronization mechanism with the collaborative editing system and develop the integrated framework of 3D models for e-Learning, teleconferencing, digital archiving, city design, and training in the medical field.

Acknowledgement

This work was supported by JSPS KAKENHI Grant Number JP16K00449.

References

[1] J. Jang-Jaccard, S. Nepal, B. Celler, and B. Yan, "WebRTC-based video conferencing service for telehealth," *Computing*, vol. 98, no. 1, pp. 169–193, 2016.

[2] T. Jung, E. Y.-L. Do, and M. D. Gross, "Immersive redlining and annotation of 3d design models on the web," in *the 8th International Conference on Computer Aided Architectural Design Futures*, pp. 81–98, 1999.

[3] T. Jung, M. D. Gross, and E. Y.-L. Do, "Annotating and sketching on 3d web models," in *Proceedings of the 7th International Conference on Intelligent User Interfaces*, ser. IUI '02. New York, NY, USA: ACM, pp. 95–102, 2002.

[4] J. Kahan, M.-R. Koivunen, E. Prud'Hommeaux, and R. R. Swick, "Annotea: An open rdf infrastructure for shared web annotations," in *Proc. of the 10th International World Wide Web Conference*, pp. 623–632, 2001.

[5] R. Swick, E. Prud'Hommeaux, M.-R. Koivunen, and J. Kahan, "Annotea protocols," W3C, 2002, http://www.w3.org/2002/12/AnnoteaProtocol-20021219#AnnotProtocol retrieved: March 2017.

[6] R. Kadobayashi, J. Lombardi, M. P. McCahill, H. Stearns, K. Tanaka, and A. Kay, "3d model annotation from multiple viewpoints for croquet," in *Proc. of The Fourth International Conference on Creating*, ser. Connecting and Collaborating through Computing, pp. 10–15, 2006.

[7] J. Hunter and C. hao Yu, "Supporting multiple perspectives on 3d museum artefacts through interoperable annotations," in *Cultural Computing*, R. Nakatsu, N. Tosa, K. W. Wong, and P. Codognet, Eds. Springer Berlin Heidelberg, pp. 149–159, 2010.

[8] J. Hunter, M. Henderson, and I. Khan, "Collaborative annotation of 3d crystallographic models," *Journal of Chemical Information and Modeling*, vol. 47, no. 6, pp. 2475–2484, 2007.

[9] P. T. Goeser, W. M. Johnson, F. G. Hamza-Lup, and D. Schaefer, "View: A virtual interactive web-based learning environment for engineering," *Advances in Engineering Education*, vol. 2, no. 3, pp. 1–24, 2011.

[10] N. F. Kleven, E. Prasolova-Førland, M. Fominykh, A. Hansen, G. Rasmussen, L. M. Sagberg, and F. Lindseth, "Training nurses and educating the public using a virtual operating room with oculus rift," in *Proc. of the 2014 International Conference on Virtual Systems and Multimedia (VSMM)*, pp. 206–213, 2014.

[11] P. T. Eugster, P. A. Felber, R. Guerraoui, and A.-M. Kermarrec, "The many faces of publish/subscribe," *ACM Comput. Surv.*, vol. 35, no. 2, pp. 114–131, Jun. 2003. [Online]. Available: http://doi.acm.org/10.1145/857076.857078

[12] Y. Liu and B. Plale, "Survey of publish subscribe event systems," Indiana University, Tech. Rep. TR574, May 2003.

[13] J. Nielsen, *Usability Engineering*, 1st ed. Morgan Kaufmann, 1993.

[14] K. Imae and N. Hayashibara, "ChainVoxel: A data structure for scalable distributed collaborative editing for 3d models," in *Proc. of The 14th IEEE International Conference on Dependable, Autonomic and Secure Computing (DASC-2016)*, 2016.

A System to Depict the Cognitive Process of Trainees Based on Multiple Skill Parameters

System validation involving normal individuals with an electrician's license

Norikatsu Fujita, Hiroshi Takeshita, Hirotada Fukae, Sho Aoki, Kazushige Matsumoto, Tomohiro Murakami, Minoru Hoshino
Ability Development Dept. Polytechnic University of Japan
e-mail:fujita@uitec.ac.jp

Abstract— **Instructors of vocational training are increasingly encountering trainees, such as individuals with developmental disorders, who need special accommodations. Flexible teaching of diverse trainees requires the characteristics of trainees to be comprehensively ascertained from an educational perspective. This paper describes a system to depict the cognitive process of trainees based on multiple skill parameters to comprehensively ascertain the characteristics of trainees from an educational perspective. The system to depict the cognitive process while feeding back to the trainee skills essential for vocational training. Instructors of vocational training will give optimum instruction to each trainees based on the cognitive process generated by the system. From the simulation using the theoretical value and the verification by the field, we confirmed that the cognitive process visualization of the trainee can be performed with 32 multi-dimensional skill parameters.**

Keywords-Vocational Training; Theory of Multiple Intelligences; Action Research; M-GTA; Developmental Disabilities; Cognitive Information Processing Model.

I. Introduction

In vocational training, trainees in every age group have various vocational and educational backgrounds. Over the past few years, there have been an increasing number of situations where trainees, such as individuals with developmental disorders, need special accommodations. Instructors of vocational training have to teach them in accordance with their abilities.

In general schools for vocational training, a method to learn from causality analysis of successes and failures is used to deal with people with developmental disabilities[1] [2] [3]. However, the information obtained from this method is only the causal relationship between factors that affect a specific situation. Therefore, dealing with various situations encountered in reality is difficult. In other fields, there have been attempts to explore parameters with which to comprehensively ascertain the characteristics of subjects, and these parameters have been used in national policies and education[4]. However, parameters with which to comprehensively ascertain developmental disorders are mainly those used for diagnosis[5], and there are no parameters from an educational perspective.

Until now, there are training practices that use evaluation scales such as interpersonal skills and social skills[6] [7]. In addition, a system to measure skill gap by measuring physical exercise skill using a haptic device has been reported[8] [9]. However, these efforts target specific skills necessary for vocational training.

This paper describes a system to depict the cognitive process of trainees based on multiple skill parameters to comprehensively ascertain the characteristics of trainees from an educational perspective. The system to depict the cognitive process while feeding back to the trainees skills essential for vocational training. Instructors of vocational training will give optimum instruction to each trainee while judging whether the deficient multiple skill parameters are due to under-experience or ability based on the cognitive process generated by the system.

II. A Theoretical Model of Teaching Competencies Formation Process of Vocational Training Instructors

In vocational training, conventional teaching methods do not work, and struggling to respond to trainees who need consideration to cause unexpected reactions and behaviors. From such a problem, the purpose of this study is to realize evidence-based training from the cognitive process of trainees generated by the system. In a previous study, the current authors analyzed the development of teaching competencies in experienced instructors of people with developmental disabilities using a modified grounded theory approach [10].

Figure 1 shows a theoretical model of teaching competencies formation process of experienced instructors(hereinafter referred to as the theoretical model). This theoretical model was constructed by M-GTA. The M-GTA makes unique modifications to technique, improving GTA [11] for greater practicability, developed by Kinoshita. Unlike GTA, M-GTA does not use technique of slicing data, but uses the concepts of the Analytical Theme and Analytically-Focused Person[12]. M-GTA is an inductive method for creation of a theoretical model, requiring skill and experience in analysis and involving a high degree of

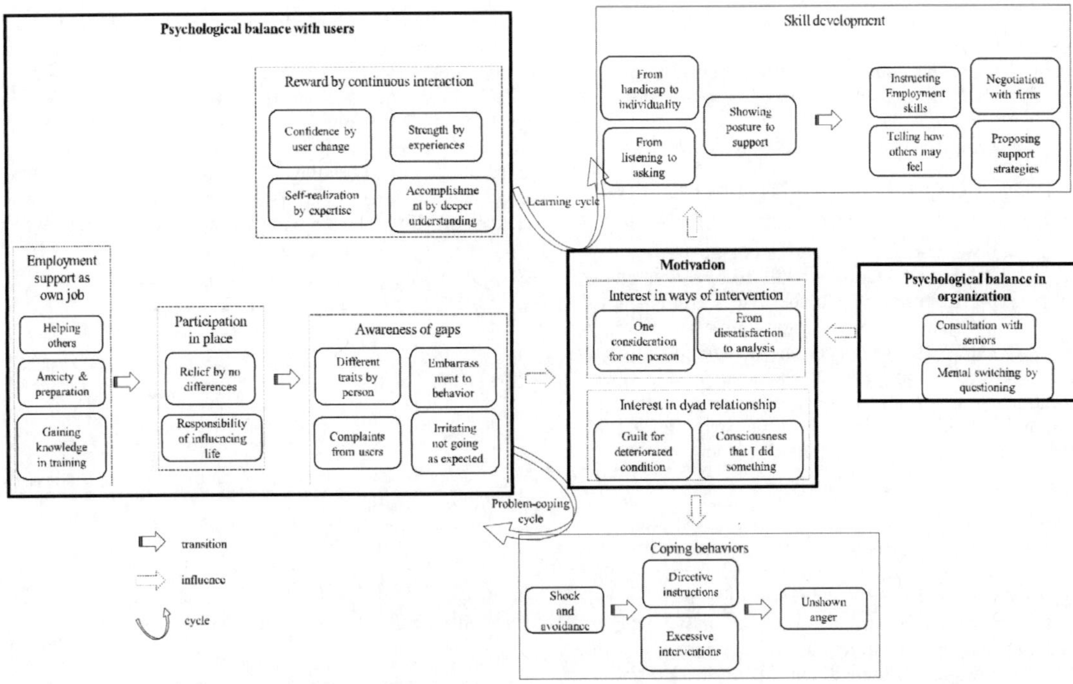

Figure 1. A theoretical model of teaching competencies formation process of experienced instructors (Details of the concept are shown in Figure 6.)

TABLE I. INTERVIEW GUIDE

No	Questions
1	Please tell me about your current job. (A) responsible work, (b) teaching skills, (c) stakeholders
2	Please tell me about your experience of employment assistance. (A) year, (b) content, (c) number of students
3	Compared to the past, is the concept of trainees different from now? (What triggered the event)
4	Compared to the past, is the way of teaching trainees different from now? (What triggered the event)
5	Compared to the past, is the relationship with the trainee different now?
6	What kind of troubles or problems you have ever had?
7	What kind of idea did you do?
8	When do you feel joy, pleasure, rewarding?
9	In the beginning, what did you most want?
10	What is the biggest problem at work?

difficulty. Dr. Takeshita, one of the authors, is a supervisor of the M - GTA Study Group and has sufficient experience.

This theoretical model was constructed by semi-structured interview with 15 senior instructors who specialize in teaching people with developmental disabilities. The semi-structured interview was conducted by the interview guide shown in Table 1.

In this theoretical model, Instructors first are interested in investigating the causes of problems dealing with persons with developmental disabilities by recognizing their lack of experience. Then, instructors will "skill formation" against "user" and "organization". The instructors will grow to become an experienced instructor through such "learning cycle". If a problem-coping cycle occurs, instructors become frustrated that trainees fail to meet their expectations and instructors see no way out. The plight of people with developmental disabilities worsens, and instructors who are "Interested in ways of intervention" fall into a Problem-coping cycle as they become "Coping behavior". To escape from such a Problem-coping cycle, it is necessary to make a "Psychological balance in organization" by consultation with seniors and mental switching by questioning. In other words, the theoretical model shows the need to improve the environment of "Psychological balance in organization" and the smooth circulation of "learning cycle ".

The basic approach to this study is to adopt an action research methodology involving mutual feedback of "theories" and "practice." This system realizes "skill development" by circulating "learning cycle" in the theoretical model. The multiple skill parameters are a common measure for "skill development". By storing best practices with multiple skill parameters as key, we can construct a training environment based on evidence.

III. DEPICTION OF THE COGNITIVE PROCESS OF TRAINEES

In Section3, we describe depiction of cognitive processes of trainees. The system measures skill factors that cause trainee's unexpected reactions and behaviors from actions selected in a part-time job interview and training at a family restaurant. The trainees will deepen the recognition of his / her skills while receiving feedback on the selected actions. The vocational training instructors decide the overall class guidance and individual guidance from the state of the skill output by the system, and aims to train all participants.

A. *Definition of theoretical construct*

Depiction of the cognitive process of trainees are realized by three processes: definition of theoretical constructs, design of questions by stories, and implementation in the system. This section describes definition of the theoretical construct. A theoretical construct abstracts cognitive patterns from human behavior and predict human behavior.

Figure 2 shows the theoretical construction based on the cognitive information processing model of Card[13]. The theoretical construct is based on a simple Card cognitive information processing model which is easy for the instructors to understand. The cognitive information processing model of Card is widely known in the cognitive science field trying to understand the intellectual system and the nature of intelligence from the viewpoint of information processing. Card's cognitive information processing model consists of three systems, "perception system", "cognitive system", and "motor system", and each system includes a memory and a processor. However, since human perception is known to have a deep relationship with psychology, we define a theoretical construct that consists of four systems that add "emotional system". The multiple skill parameters of "cognitive system" and "motor system" are measured by computer. Meanwhile, "perception system" and "emotion system" are measured by instructors by trainee observation.

The multiple skill parameters are the root of problem behavior in vocational training and are the minimum elements for instructor to develop teaching skills. Many problem behaviors in vocational training are thought to have resulted from a combination of 32 multiple skill parameters. Instructors learn basic countermeasure strategies for each multiple skill parameters, and as a next step, respond to the combined case.

Extraction of multiple skill parameters is extracted from 192 cases occurred in the vocational training written in "Support and correspondence guide for trainees who need special consideration" published by Japan Organization for Employment of the Elderly[14]. Dr. Fukae is one of the authors of this book. Multiple skill parameters are extracted based on a theoretical construct by inductive reasoning which considers the cause from the problem behaviors in vocational training. The extracted multiple skill parameters are classified into six categories in the MI theory shown in Table 2. In the MI theory[15], " Naturalistic " " Musical-rhythmic and harmonic " exists in addition to these six categories, but excluded because they are intelligences not related to vocational training. The MI theory advocates that the human frame of mind is 8 intelligences. Educational practices of MI theory are widely practiced in the world[16] [17].

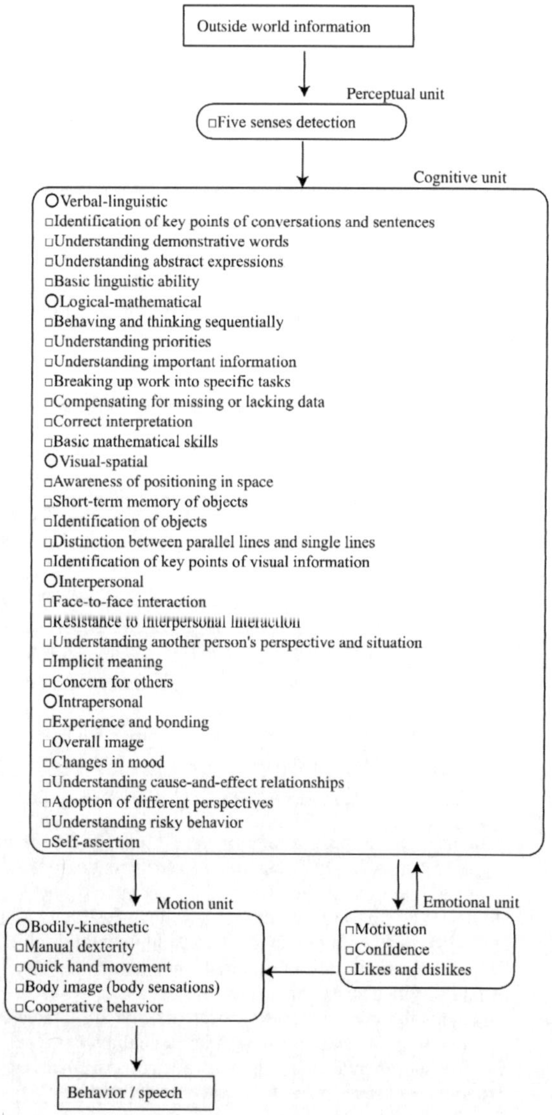

Figure 2. Cognitive information processing model using Card

TABLE II. MULTIPLE SKILL PARAMETERS CATEGORIES

Multiple intelligences	Characteristic	Typical example
○Verbal-linguistic (Vl)	Word smart	I like the teaching materials explained in detail.
○Logical-mathematical (Lm)	Number reasoning smart	I like to be reasonably explained.
○Visual-spatial (Vs)	Picture smart	I like to think about while drawing.
○Bodily-kinesthetic (Bk)	Body smart	I like to memorize with the body.
○Interpersonal (Ie)	People smart	I like to learn in groups.
○Intrapersonal (Ir)	Self smart	I like to learn while looking at examples.

TABLE III. MULTIPLE SKILL PARAMETERS

Multiple skill parameters	Typical example
○Verbal-Linguistic	
Vl1: Identification of key points of conversations and sentences	Copying unnecessary information from a blackboard into a notebook.
Vl2: Understanding demonstrative words	Only understands words superficially.
Vl3: Understanding abstract expressions	Unable to understand sarcasm or indirect references.
Vl4: Basic linguistic ability	Has difficulty reading.
○Logical-mathematical	
Lm1: Behaving and thinking sequentially	Confused by a complicated description of steps involved in wiring.
Lm2: Understanding priorities	Unable to understand what to do when instructed to perform several tasks.
Lm3: Understanding important information	Confused when several friends talk at the same time.
Lm4: Breaking up work into specific tasks	Unable to appropriately allocate time when taking a test.
Lm5:Compensating for missing or lacking data	Fails to understand when a conversation is not logical.
Lm6: Correct interpretation	Becomes upset after mistaking instruction directed at another student as intended for oneself.
Lm7:Basic mathematical skills	Has difficulty performing simple calculations.
○Visual-spatial	
Vs1: Awareness of positioning in space	Collides with objects and desks more often than other students do.
Vs2: Short-term memory of objects	Confused when an instructor returns to a previous slide to explain a point.
Vs3: Identification of objects	Cannot draw a straight line (either by freehand or with drafting equipment).
Vs4: Distinction between parallel lines and single lines	Cannot clearly draw a double line.
Vs5: Identification of key points of visual information	Cannot adeptly hit a ball or shuttlecock with a bat or racket.
○Bodily-kinesthetic	
Bk1: Manual dexterity	Beautifully written script and notes.
Bk2: Quick hand movement	Unable to copy information from the blackboard during class.
Bk3: Body image (body sensations)	Often hits his hand when using a hammer.
Bk4: Cooperative behavior	Has difficulty choosing clothing appropriate to the season due to hypersensitivity.
○Interpersonal	
Ie1: Face-to-face interaction	Always alone in class.
Ie2: Resistance to interpersonal interaction	Agonizes when working in a group or in a lab.
Ie3: Understanding another person's perspective and situation	Unable to converse if a friend suddenly strikes up a conversation.
Ie4: Tacit understanding	Fails to understand when called on rule violations during a game.
Ie5: Concern for others	Coolly points out things people may be self-conscious about.
○Intrapersonal	
Ir1: Experience and bonding	Is always exploring something.
Ir2: Overall image	Unable to envision the positioning of parts when drawing a schematic.
Ir3: Changes in mood	Strikes things when he dislikes something.
Ir4: Understanding cause-and-effect relationships	Unable to envision his position or role as part of a team.
Ir5: Adoption of different perspectives	Starts work without knowing or even thinking about procedures.
Ir6: Understanding risky behavior	Preoccupied with comics or games during class.
Ir7: Self-assertion	Immediately asks a question if he is curious about something.

Table 3 shows the details of the multiple skill parameters. The multiple skill parameters consists of 32 in six categories in MI theory. The minimum factor for the instructors to develop teaching skills are the correspondence to the case shown in the typical case in Table 3. After that, instructors will be able to teach closer to experienced instructors by learning correspondence to typical cases combined cases.

B. *Design and implementation of questions with story by cartoon*

Next, design and implementation of questions with story by cartoon. Questionnaires using psychometric measures are commonly used for grasping behavior with psychological phenomena. However, question papers written in language have problems such as dependency on language

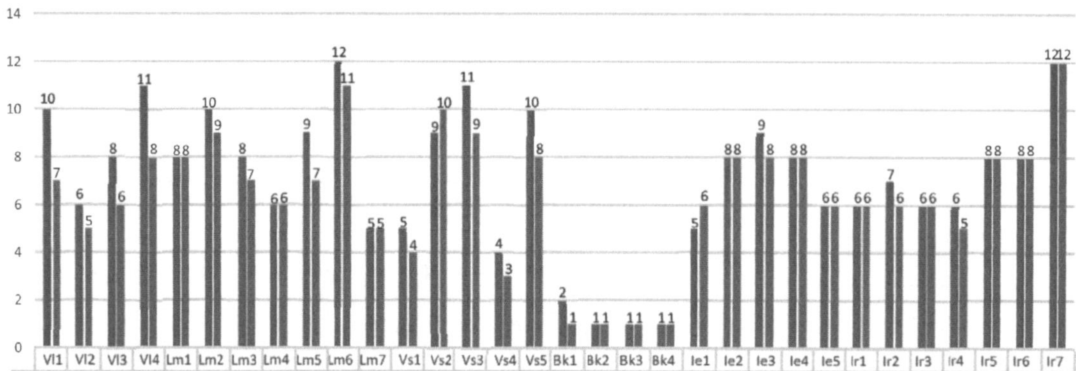

	Vl1	Vl2	Vl3	Vl4	Lm1	Lm2	Lm3	Lm4	Lm5	Lm6	Lm7	Vs1	Vs2	Vs3	Vs4	Vs5
■ Number of questions	10	6	8	11	8	10	8	6	9	12	5	5	9	11	4	10
■ Maximum score	7	5	6	8	8	9	7	6	7	11	5	4	10	9	3	8

	Bk1	Bk2	Bk3	Bk4	Ie1	Ie2	Ie3	Ie4	Ie5	Ir1	Ir2	Ir3	Ir4	Ir5	Ir6	Ir7
■ Number of questions	2	1	1	1	5	8	9	8	6	6	7	6	6	8	8	12
■ Maximum score	1	1	1	1	6	8	8	8	6	6	6	6	5	8	8	12

■ Number of questions ■ Maximum score

Figure 3. Number of questions and scores of the system

comprehension degree, difficulty in deeply grasping inner side in linguistic expression, existence of false and socially desirable answers[18]. Therefore, it is difficult to guarantee "reliability" and "validity" in vocational training conducted in various "age", "occupation history", "learning history". Therefore, this system develops a system with a story by cartoon, not questionnaire by language. To set up questions, make the case shown in Table 4 on an episode basis. After that, we implemented questions with a comic story on the system, implemented on the group of subjects to be measured, and repeated individual interviews to ensure practical "reliability" and "validity".This system converts typical cases of multiple skill parameters into context to work part-time at family restaurant. Trainees have visualized cognitive processes by choosing actions in the context of performing work at family restaurants. The standard implementation time is 30 minutes. The total number of questions are depending on the answer and is 24 to 34 subjects. The question format has problems involving work on the computer and questions asking actions in 5 alternatives. In the question of asking actions by choosing one of the five questions, we always have the option of "I do not know". In addition, although it does not count to the number of questions, as a reference information, it is a free description formal, and prepares a question "hobby" and " requests from my teacher". Development of the system is made with ArticulateStoryline[19] authoring tool for e-learning which is widely prevalent globally.

Figure 3 shows the number of questions and scores of the system. Depending on the multiple skill parameters, the number of questions and points involved are different. There are not only plus points but also minus points as options. For example, Vl1 has a maximum score of 7 for 10 problems. The number of related questions and the score are determined normatively between members. Also consider the independence of the six categories in the MI from the score. In the trial production of the system, one question was associated with one multiple skill parameter. However,

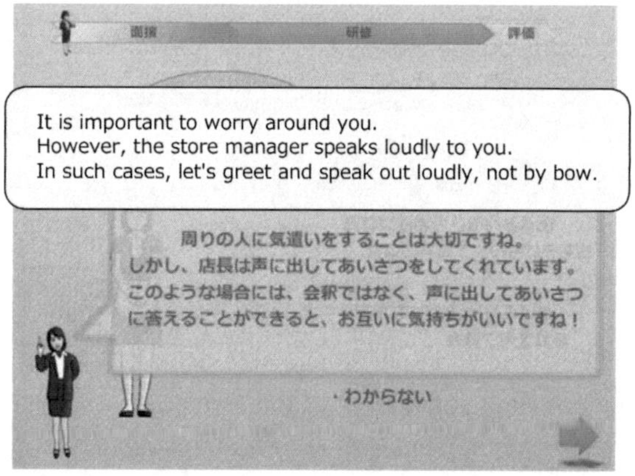

Figure 4. An example of feedback to the trainees

without increasing the number of questions, accurate viewpoints of this study demonstrated that the cognitive process of the trainees can depict thirty-two multiple skill parameters from 34 questions(Total number of questions 274 in Figure 3).

Figure 4 shows an example of feedback to the trainee. This example is the scene of the first greeting to the manager with part-time job interview. People differ in behavior depending on skill characteristics. For example, some people greet themselves with a small voice, paying attention to people around outside, others always say a loud voice regardless of the surrounding circumstances. That is, the skill characteristics are related to the actions to be selected. The system depicts the cognitive process of the trainees based on which skills are emphasized. After the trainees respond, the system will feed back to the socially desirable direction that respects the individuality of the trainees. The role of many feedbacks is to inform trainees of the characteristics of their cognitive processes and to realize training in which both trainee and instructor cooperate.

Figure 5 shows a question example with a branching structure. This is a scene where the store manager instructs to take an order machine. If you can not take the order machine correctly, it will become a scene where customers waiting for accounting will get angry for slowly working clerks. The multiple skill parameter common to these two scenes is "tacit understanding" in the conceptual model of Figure2. If there is only one trainee who does not have the skill of "tacit consent", the overall guidance of the class will teach using the language, gesture, model, body using the sequential proximity method based on behaviorism[20]. Until now, the usefulness of overall guidance design that matches the skill characteristics of individual classes has been confirmed in practical cases of active learning[21] using Just-In-Time[22] Teaching. In this way, this system is useful for both guidance design and individual guidance design of the whole class.

Figure 5. A question example with a branching structure

IV. EVALUATION

As system evaluation, from the simulation using the theoretical value and the verification by the field, confirm depiction of the cognitive process of the trainee through 32 multi-dimensional skill parameters. This study was approved by the Ethical Committee of the Polytechnic University of Japan(No.607).

Table 4 shows simulation results of abnormal values using theoretical values. The system outputs the evaluation value in five stages. For abnormal value detection, output with evaluation value of 2 or less. The theoretical value A 'is a simulation of a trainee who detected an abnormality in a specific skill such as tacit consent. The theoretical value B 'is a simulation of a trainee who detects an abnormality in the language category and also has another category. The theoretical value C 'is a simulation of a trainee who detects abnormality by skill of physical movement category and other category has high skill. From these simulation results, the system is able to output outliers with categories and skills.

Table 5 shows the assessment results of 10 Trainees. Subjects are the top trainees in the class who acquired the electrician's license. It is understood that the skill level

TABLE IV. SIMULATION RESULTS OF ABNORMAL VALUES USING THEORETICAL VALUES

	Vl1	Vl2	Vl3	Vl4	Lm1	Lm2	Lm3	Lm4	Lm5	Lm6	Lm7	Vs1	Vs2	Vs3	Vs4	Vs5	Bk1	Bk2	Bk3	Bk4	Ie1	Ie2	Ie3	Ie4	Ie5	Ir1	Ir2	Ir3	Ir4	Ir5	Ir6	Ir7
A′	5	3	①	5	4	4	4	3	5	5	3	4	5	5	3	5	5	5	5	5	②	5	①	①	5	4	4	①	②	②	①	5
B′	②	②	②	②	②	②	3	3	3	3	3	3	4	3	②	5	5	5	5	5	4	4	3	4	3	4	②	4	3	3	②	4
C′	4	4	4	4	5	4	5	4	5	4	4	4	4	4	4	5	①	①	①	①	4	4	5	5	4	4	4	4	4	4	4	4

TABLE V. TRAIAL RESULTS

	Vl1	Vl2	Vl3	Vl4	Lm1	Lm2	Lm3	Lm4	Lm5	Lm6	Lm7	Vs1	Vs2	Vs3	Vs4	Vs5	Bk1	Bk2	Bk3	Bk4	Ie1	Ie2	Ie3	Ie4	Ie5	Ir1	Ir2	Ir3	Ir4	Ir5	Ir6	Ir7
A	4	4	4	4	4	5	3	4	4	3	4	5	3	3	3	4	5	5	5	5	5	5	5	4	4	4	4	4	3	3	3	4
B	4	5	4	4	3	4	3	3	4	4	4	5	3	4	4	4	5	5	5	5	4	3	4	3	4	4	4	4	3	4	3	5
C	4	3	3	4	4	4	3	4	4	3	4	3	4	5	5	5	5	5	5	5	5	4	5	4	4	4	5	4	3	4	4	5
D	4	5	4	4	4	4	5	4	5	5	4	5	4	4	4	5	5	5	5	5	5	3	4	4	4	4	5	5	5	5	4	5
E	4	5	5	4	4	4	4	4	5	4	4	5	3	4	4	5	5	5	5	5	5	5	5	5	4	4	5	4	3	4	4	5
F	4	4	4	4	4	4	5	4	5	4	3	4	5	3	4	4	5	5	5	5	4	3	5	4	4	4	5	4	5	4	4	5
G	4	5	②	4	4	4	5	4	5	4	4	4	5	4	4	4	5	5	5	5	4	3	4	4	5	5	5	4	5	3	4	5
H	3	②	①	5	5	5	②	5	①	3	5	①	3	4	4	②	5	5	5	5	4	4	3	3	4	4	4	②	3	②	3	3
I	5	5	4	4	4	4	4	4	5	5	3	4	4	3	4	4	5	5	5	5	4	4	4	4	4	4	5	4	3	4	5	5
J	5	5	5	4	4	5	5	4	4	4	4	4	5	4	4	4	5	5	5	5	4	4	4	4	4	4	4	4	5	4	4	5

related to qualification acquisition is uniformly high and there are variations in skills. However, Trainee H has many items with low skill level. Trainee H has a low skill level overall. In a later interview, he said that he had worked in a hurry without time. In this system, we emphasized familiarity by embedding context, but it is not perfect.

From the simulation using the theoretical values and the verification by the field, we confirmed that the cognitive process of the trainees can be depicted by the multiple skill parameters defined in this paper.

V. CONCLUSION

In this paper, we described a cognitive process depiction system of trainees based on multiple skill parameters which comprehensively grasp the skills necessary for vocational training from the viewpoint of education. From the simulation using the theoretical values and the verification by the field as described above, we confirmed that the cognitive process of the trainees can be depicted by the multiple skill parameters defined in this paper.

The originality of this work has been to comprehensively ascertain developmental disorders from an educational perspective. This originality is achieved through the followings:

1) We defined a theoretical construct based on a simple Card cognitive information processing model, which the instructor can easily understand.

2) We extracted and weighted the pluralistic skill parameters from the theoretical construct.

3) We classified the pluralistic skill parameters in the intellectual category of MI theory from the viewpoint of education in vocational training.

Future tasks are verification for people with developmental disabilities and construction of a database of teaching methods carried out by skilled instructors.

ACKNOWLEDGMENT

This work was supported by JSPS KAKENHI Grant Number JP26350303.

REFERENCES

[1] Japan Organization for Employment of the Elderly, Persons with Disabilities and Job Seekers, " Research on promoting employment of people with developmental disabilities using technology and support for continuing work, " Research ReportNo.149, 2010, Japanese.

[2] Japan Organization for Employment of the Elderly, Persons with Disabilities and Job Seekers, " Effective vocational training examples for people with developmental disabilities, "Research ReportNo.119, 2007.Japanese.

[3] Japan Organization for Employment of the Elderly, Persons with Disabilities and Job Seekers, "Vocational training handbook of people with developmental disabilities, " 2008.Japanese.

[4] Alfred B, Jacqueline C, "Characterizing Criminal Careers, "Science, Vol.237, No.4818, pp.985-991, 1987.

[5] Kaufman, Alan S. , "Lichtenberger, Elizabeth (2006). Assessing Adolescent and Adult Intelligence (3rd ed.)," Hoboken (NJ): Wiley. pp. 3, 2010.

[6] Japan Organization for Employment of the Elderly, Persons with Disabilities and Job Seekers, " Research on characterization of communication skills of people with developmental disabilities, " Research ReportNo.119, 2014.Japanese.

[7] Japan Organization for Employment of the Elderly, Persons with Disabilities and Job Seekers, " Research on human resource development program using SST, " Research ReportNo.124, 2014.Japanese.

[8] Fujita, N., Hayashi, T., Yamasaki, T., "Torch Operation Learning System Based on Welding Skill Parameters, "The IEICE transactions on information and systems (Japanese edetion), J90-D, Vol.9, pp.2522-2529, 2007. Japanese.

[9] Aswathi P., Amritha Natarajan, Namitha K., "Bridging the skill gap using vocational training simulators:Validating skill assessment metrics, " IEEE Conference Proceedings, Vol.2016, No.ICACCI, pp.645-651, 2016.

[10] Takeshita, H. and Fujita, N, "Psychological intervention in an Employment transition support center: Support staff psychological balance", Poster session presented at the 22nd World Congress of Social Psychiatry-WASP2016, New Delhi, 2016.

[11] Glaser B, Strauss AL., " The discovery of grounded theory. Chicago (IL)", Aldine, 1967.

[12] Nishigaki, K., "Changes in Mothers' Psychosocial Perceptions of Technologydependent Children and Adolescents at Home in Japan:Acknowledgement of Children's Autonomy, "Asian Nursing Research, pp100-105, 2016.

[13] S.K.Card and T.P.Moran, "The Psychology of Human – Computer Interaction, " Lawrence Erlbaum Associates, 1983.

[14] Japan Organization for Employment of the Elderly, Persons with Disabilities and Job Seekers, "Support/ correspondence guide for students who need special consideration in the progress of training / learning (practical edition), "2015 .Japanese.

[15] Gardner, H. , "Multiple Intelligences: The Theory in Practice, Basic Books; Reprint Edition edition, " 1993.

[16] Gardner, H., "Assessment in context:The alternative to standardized testing.In B.R. Gifford , & M.C.O'Connor(Eds.) , Changing assrssment:Alternative views of aptitude, achievement, and instruction., "Boston: Kluwer., 1991.

[17] Gardner, H., Krechevsky, M., Sternberg, R. J., & Okagaki, L., " Intelligence in context: Enhancing students' practical intelligence for school. In K. McGilly(Ed.), " Cambrige: Bradford Books/MIT Pree, 1994.

[18] Yokouchi, H, " Basic understanding of psychometric scale,"J Jpn Soc Intensive Carw Med, Vol.14, No.4, pp.555-560, 2007.Japanese.

[19] Articlute Storyline
http://www.articulate.com

[20] Dennis H. Reid, Carolyn W. Green, "Preference-Based Teaching: Helping People with Developmental Disabilities Enjoy Learning without Problem Behavior, "Habilitative Management Consultants, Inc., 2005

[21] Novak, G. M. and Patterson, E. T. , "Just-in-Time Teaching:Blending Active Learning with Web Technology, " Addison-Wesley,pp1-188,1999

[22] Deslauriers, L., Schelew, E., Wieman, C., "Improved Learning in a Large-Enrollment Physics Class", SCIENCE, Vol.332, No.862, pp862-864,2011

No.	Concept	Definition (This phenomenon is that ...)
1	From dissatisfaction to analysis	A staff considers the causes of communication failure, without accusing the user.
2	Guilt for deteriorated condition	A staff feels responsibility because his/her intervention led user condition deterioration.
3	Anxiety & preparation	A staff thinks facing with users' disability traits as a part of own job.
4	Self-realization through expertise	A staff utilizes their experiences on their welfare and business practice through supporting users.
5	Helping others	A staff finds value in supporting other's life.
6	Shock and avoidance	A staff is shocked by user's background and trying to leave the user to his colleagues.
7	From handicap to individuality	A staff accepts the user's disability traits as individuality.
8	From listening to asking	A staff receives the user's reaction and asks the cause and background.
10	Unshown anger	A staff does not take attitude even if feels anger in the user's behavior, and dissatisfaction is accumulated.
11	Consciousness that I did something	A staff feels sad by thinking that he/she did something for the user but the user did not responded.
12	Accomplishment by deeper understanding	A staff feels accomplishment by understanding the background of a user's behavior.
14	Awareness of gaps	A staff notices the gap between the goals and the reality.
15	Consultation with seniors	A staff can ask a senior whenever he / she can not understand the user's behavior.
16	Relief by no differences	A staff pleasantly surprises because the users' behaviors do not differ from his / hers.
17	One consideration for one person	A staff notices that each user needs one consideration.
18	Embarrassment to behavior	A staff is surprised by the sudden behavior of user and feel uncomfortable.
19	Irritating not going as expected	A staff is irritated and exhausted, as having no sign of improvement of user's condition.
20	Telling how others may feel	A staff tell a user how the user's behavior is seen from the third party.
22	Mental switching by questioning	By being asked by seniors about the cause of user's behavior, frustration will switch to questioning.
25	Gaining knowledge in training	A business-experienced staff learns basic knowledge of supporting persons with disabilities in training.
26	Proposing support strategies	A mid-level staff creates and proposes support plans each other in various viewpoints.
29	Confidence by user change	A staff gains self-confidence by the progress of users.
30	Responsibility of influencing life	A staff feels responsible because his / her intervention influences the employment (life) of users.
35	Showing posture to support	A staff lets the user disclose thoughts and circumstances by showing posture to support.
36	Instructing Employment skills	A business-experienced staff trains necessary skills for employment to users.
37	Strength by experiences	By having experienced, a staff will not be upset by the disastrous background of individual users.
38	Different traits by person	Since the situation of users is different for each person, basic knowledge is not applicable.
42	Negotiation with firms	A staff can negotiate with the company about employment of users.
43	Directive instructions	A staff instructs and requests at the ordinary workplace level to a user.
59	Excessive interventions	A staff has excessive interest and intervention to a user.
60	Complaints from users	A staff receives complaints concerning oneself and facility from a user.

Figure 6. Details of the concept

Interactions with Projected Augmented Relief Models (PARM)

Nachnoer Arss
School of Geography
University of Nottingham
Nottingham, United Kingdom
e-mail:
lgxnna@nottingham.ac.uk

Alastair D. Smith
School of Psychology
University of Nottingham
Nottingham, United Kingdom
e-mail:
alastair.smith@nottingham.ac.uk

Gary Priestnall
School of Geography
University of Nottingham
Nottingham, United Kingdom
e-mail:
gary.priestnall@nottingham.ac.uk

Abstract—**Techniques for enhancing physical landscape models with dynamic maps and imagery, termed Projected Augmented Relief Models (PARM), are part of a revival of interest in the power of relief models as tools for geographic visualization. This method enables the creation of dynamic and engaging public displays, which appear attractive but also promote discussion and interaction as revealed through direct observation and video. This paper explores the capabilities of physical relief models as tangible displays for geographic information, and considers the role of interaction using the Kinect sensor for finger detection. The focus of interaction is on making solid landscape models of real geographic areas reactive to touch.**

Keywords: Physical 3D model; augmented reality; landscape visualisation.

I. INTRODUCTION

From ancient times, geographic visualization has played a significant role in human life and it has become even more popular during the digital age. The evidence of ancient people using geographic visualization includes cave paintings and carvings that look like maps. The techniques of map creation have continually developed to make human life easier by supporting many daily activities, as well as being of fundamental importance to diplomacy and defence from the early modern period.

In the past, people drew maps using cartographic methods in 2-dimensional (2D) form to represent the terrain of the earth. They developed these methods further and visualized the landscape in 3-dimensional (3D) models, some of the earliest examples being for military purposes [1]. This kind of model was considered the most representative 'map' before the digital era.

The starting point of digital technology was between the late 1950s and the early 1970s, during which time technology developed rapidly in every field, including geography. The development of mapping technology started with field data acquisition, data processing and data representation. Drawing maps using digital technology helps users produce maps faster and more precisely, and the development of geographical information systems combined spatial analysis with map making. However, such complex maps remained the preserve of specialists until the late 1990s, when the increasing popularity and use of the internet popularized digital maps and made them increasingly desirable and useful. In contrast, developments in geographic physical models were not as rapid as with digital maps, being considered less practical for many applications despite their inherent value as representations of terrain.

Since the turn of the 21st Century, the nature of 3D physical geographic models has become more dynamic and there has been a revival in their use, in part due to technologies to increase their interactivity. The Illuminating Clay project [2] illustrated how landscape models made from clay could be manipulated by hand and the resulting changes in the surface model detected, triggering new contour and water flow maps that could be projected back on to the model. TanGeoMS [3] used a malleable surface model connected to the GRASS Geographical Information System (GIS). The Illuminating Clay approach was further extended to use sand as a more modifiable surface in the Augmented Realty Sandbox (Fig. 1) which has been used in an educational context to engage students with topographic mapping and earth science [4].

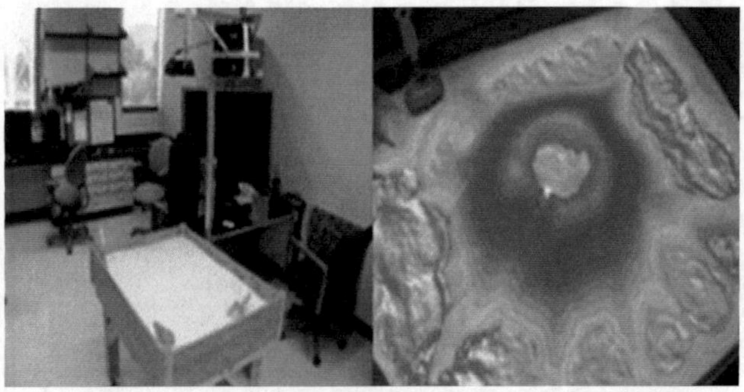

Figure 1: The Augmented Reality Sandbox. Sandbox unit when not in operation (left). In operation with projected contours and water flow (right) [4].

Whilst the ability to manipulate surface models offers a powerful environment for education and outreach in relation to generic landform and process relationships [5] there are contexts where more geographically specific models are required. Solid relief models are able to replicate details of real geographic environments, with digital elevation data being used to manufacture faithful representations of the terrain. It is easier than ever before to produce physical models either through subtractive techniques like milling or additive techniques like 3D printing, where layers of material build up a surface. Today accurate physical relief models are produced commercially, including examples by manufacturers such as Solid Terrain Modelling [6] and Howard Models [7]. At certain scales it is possible to represent surface features like buildings to allow urban environments to be visualised. Conventional relief models are static in terms of surface texture, typically painted to reflect the land cover. When augmented with projection, solid models can allow alternative forms of information to be displayed, but are generally limited in terms of interaction except where buttons around the model illuminate certain points of interest within the model.

In terms of interactivity the sandbox approach used the Kinect sensor, initially introduced by Microsoft to support the Xbox games console, to detect deformations of the surface, as well as to detect certain gestures for example to instigate rainfall over the model. For solid models the interaction could involve making the static surface responsive to touch. This could trigger certain algorithmic responses for example to route water from that point or to display a visibility map (or view-shed) but could also simply act as a query operation to display information about that place on the model.

This paper describes work in progress towards exploring the potential of making solid relief models more dynamic in terms of surface representation and interactivity. It describes an experimental approach building upon previous work to develop the Projection Augmented Relief Model (PARM) technique for public display, as described by Priestnall et al [8]. The investigation aims to examine whether they offer measurable benefits for the presentation of geographic information to people, and whether people's expectations of interactivity can be addressed, so that interaction delivers geographic information that is best suited to the needs of the viewer. In particular the potential for adding a degree of interaction so the solid model responds to touch, exploiting the ability of the Kinect sensor to detect the position of the finger [9] is being explored.

II. PROJECTION ONTO SOLID RELIEF MODELS

Projection onto solid objects [10] effectively allows dynamic texture maps to be applied to physical models in the real world as might be applied to virtual models. These textures could be a series of static images of video. An example of a landscape model being textured by video is the Dresden Elbe Valley model exhibited in Dresden Museum [11]. A solid terrain model measuring 2m x 1.5m was augmented by a film showing the development of the area since the year 8000 BC.

The development of design and evaluation protocols for projecting detailed spatially referenced information onto equally detailed static physical landscape models has been the focus of the PARM project (Fig. 2). The typical PARM configuration comprises a physical landscape model, a projector, a monitor to display related information and a computer to synchronise digital map and image content across model and monitor. The combination of model and projected content creates a holographic effect that has been seen to be both engaging and informative for viewers, enabling them to explore the model by inspecting it closely from different angles or taking in the broader overview.

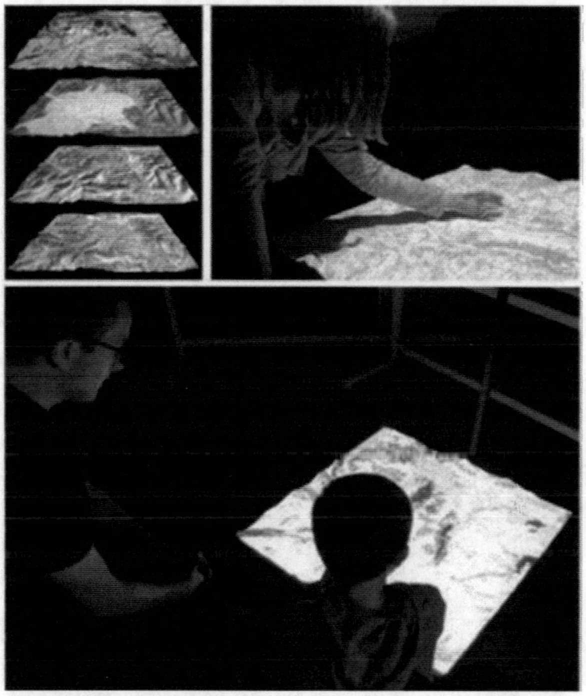

Figure 2: Projection Augmented Relief Model (PARM): Tangible Displays for Geographic Information. A selection of data layers used for projection (upper left); demonstrating at a community event at the University of Nottingham, 2011 (upper right and bottom) [8].

An opportunity to study PARM in a public context over a long period of time came with the *Spots of Time* display at the Wordsworth Trust gallery in Grasmere, Cumbria, UK. The model was used to represent key events in the childhood of the poet William Wordsworth (1770 – 1850), connecting them with particular parts of the landscape. Furthermore, those key events also related to poetry that Wordsworth created in adulthood, notably *The Prelude*. The purpose of the model was not only to raise the awareness of the importance of place and memory in Wordsworth's work, but also to encourage the visitor to study the original manuscripts on display elsewhere in the gallery. The PARM configuration used for this display also features a touch screen to trigger three separate projected sequences and an audio shower above the display to allow passages from the poems to be played aloud.

The *Spots of Time* display was in the gallery for over nine months and for around four weeks video observation was undertaken at the display, in addition to direct observation in the gallery. The observation data showed the display was effective in holding visitor attention but also for promoting discussion, often accompanied by pointing or tracing gestures. Even though the model surface itself was not interactive there seemed to be an expectation from some visitors of some kind of touch sensitivity, especially when certain landscape features were highlighted through projection (Fig. 3).

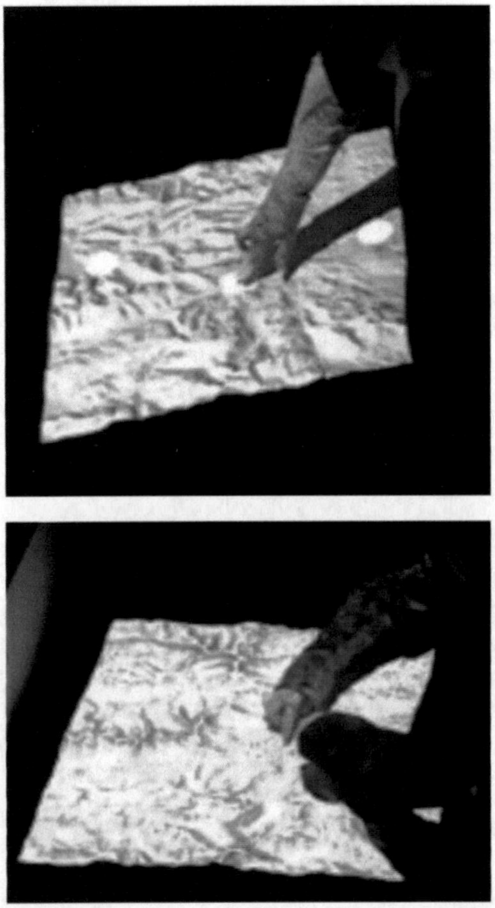

Figure 3: Finger-based interactions observed from video analysis of the Spots of Time display

The *Spots of Time* display went some way towards demonstrating that physical relief models offer viewers a rapid overview of a landscape with the added attraction of physical touch. There is clearly potential for some form of touch-based interaction to extend the capabilities of techniques such as PARM. To underpin this it would be valuable to understand more about the particular aspects of physical models that proved effective, for example in increasing people's ability to orient themselves, to measure distances or relative elevations, and to achieve a quick understanding of a location or recognizing landmarks. A set of experiments is being undertaken to establish whether such subtle measurable differences can be observed.

III. EXPLORING THE CAPABILITIES OF PARM

A first experiment was designed to explore PARM's capabilities in the portrayal of relief features using the model of the Lake District used in the *Spots of Time* display. The experiment posed questions of participants about topographic characteristics on both the relief model and a flat surface. A number of different measures were designed to gauge people's understanding of the landscape form in an attempt to unpick the elements that could be seen as contributing to the viewer's spatial frame of reference, these were:

- Deciding which of two points was the highest
- Deciding which of two lines was the steepest
- Deciding which of two target points would receive water flow from a single origin point
- Deciding which of two target points was visible from one observer point
- Deciding which cone of vision symbol corresponded to a first person perspective image shown on screen

These measures therefore ranged from a simple comparison of two local topographic characteristics to more complex measures which required a degree of landscape interpretation, and in the case of the cone of vision the ability to take the perspective of viewers 'on the landscape'. As well as the projected shapes to implement the above tests the backdrop images on the model were also a variable. Earlier observation had indicated a number of projected backdrop textures were effective but it was of interest here to establish if they helped viewers make judgements about various characteristics of the landscape. These backdrop images were a satellite image, a hillshade effect image, a map including contours and a subdued version of the hillshade image.

In order to assess whether there were benefits to adding a third dimension a core manipulation was to present half of the questions about landscape characteristics over the relief model, then the other half over a flat surface. The order of presentation was counterbalanced across all participants and questions were fully randomized. From observation of a pilot study the viewing position of each participant was not the same, so it was decided that the participants' head and body movement should be restricted to control against some participants gaining additional information from changing their perspective (Fig. 4) even though in practice this would be common, and is one of the virtues of having free movement around a relief model.

Figure 4: The environment for PARM experimentation.

Outcomes from ongoing analysis suggest that for all measures the relief model generated more accurate performance across participants particularly when the satellite image was the backdrop. The model proved particularly effective in terms of accuracy of response when asking participants to interpret the landscape scene, particularly the judgement of water-flow, the cone of vision test and intervisibility. Overall response times were slower for these tests than simple height comparisons, though were quicker for the model than the map. This may suggest that the extra information provided by the physicality of the model allows viewers to construct more complex cognitive models more effectively to support their decisions.

Figure 5. The Nottingham University Park Campus Model.

Since the model in this first experiment was an unfamiliar environment to most participants, an ongoing follow-up study uses a model that represents a familiar area, so that we can observe whether existing knowledge affects the utility of PARM. Here we modelled the University Park Campus at the University of Nottingham (Fig. 5). As well as being a familiar environment for participants, the scale and the nature of the data (airborne laser-scanning) also meant that the model was able to represent major buildings and landmarks. Questions were based on the measures from the first experiment but adapted for the current environment. Early results suggest that the model is most effective in supporting cone of vision judgements along with assessments of intervisibility. We are also interested in the ability of participants to judge the location of newer buildings that are not represented on the model, and there is evidence to suggest that PARM facilitates accuracy for this task, compared to the flat equivalent.

IV. Interacting with PARM

A third experiment is focussing on direct interaction with the model surface, in particular to establish whether finger point detection algorithms can be used to identify the coordinate where a finger touches the model. This kind of interaction had been observed at the *Spots of Time* display when there was no prompt to interact and no mechanism to offer a response. The aim is to explore whether the Kinect sensor could be exploited to identify the last position of the finger when it touches the model and whether this offers an accuracy which is fit-for-purpose for general geographical query or even analytical activities.

The PARM rig for this experiment has the addition of the Kinect sensor mounted 47cm above the relief model. From experimentation (Fig. 6) this proved to be the most effective distance to discriminate the finger location. The projector is an Optoma HD131Xe mounted 2m above the model which measured 60cm x 60cm. The specification of the computer is an AMD FX-6100 of processor, 16 Gb of memory DDR3 and 4 Gb NVidia GeForce GTX 970 graphic card.

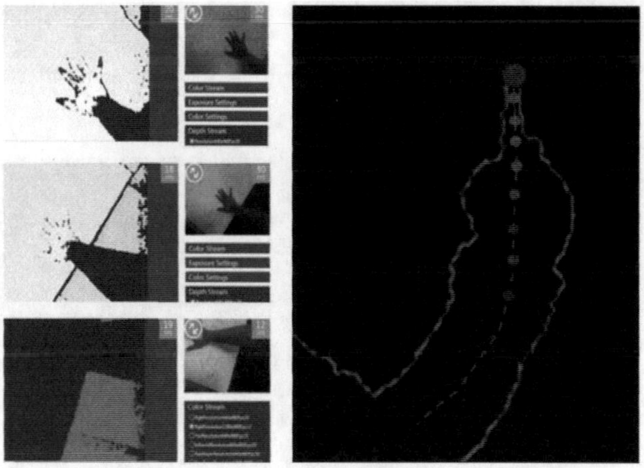

Figure 6: Distance between Kinect sensor and PARM, from top to bottom, 47 cm, 51 cm, 37 cm, shown variations in ability to detect fingertips. The coordinates of the finger as it approaches the model can be tracked and the last coordinate recorded before the finger merges with the model object is indicated in blue (right).

Sequences of finger point coordinates are detected as the finger approaches the model and the last coordinate in theory represents the position of the model just before it merges with the model. Early experimentation suggests the accuracy of this finger point touch detection is in the range of 1.5 – 2.5cm. A full and rigorous test will be conducted to explore the repeatability and robustness of this process by projecting randomized points of interest over the models and recording finger touch coordinates against the known target coordinates. These points should include a wide range of conditions over the model that represent typical points of interest which for rural models may include mountain peaks and valleys and for urban models may include buildings and flat areas between buildings. The aim is to assess how the accuracy of touch relates to the scale of geographical features represented on the model. This would inform both the design of future interactive PARM models and also the nature of any interaction design built in to the system. The proposed query interface (Fig. 7) includes a projected information panel beside the model so touch actions can trigger responses in terms of information about the object queried so as to confirm this response matched the user's expectations.

V. Further Possibilities

The discussion of previous research presented above indicates a niche between geospatial visualization, spatial cognition and tangible interface that requires further research to improve human perception about topographical surfaces in relation to certain potential application domains. Interactions could relate to simple query operations but could also be task-driven. There are many possible application to explore including: Storytelling in a cultural heritage setting; Military training; Disaster management simulation and awareness (for example flooding); Route planning and tourist orientation, showing visitors the shape of the landscape and relative positions of features of interest around them.

Figure 7. Proposed query interface

Tablet-based Augmented Reality (for example AR Toolkit) could also be explored in order to add dynamic 3D content to augment the projected surface. This could be used to explore elements with a vertical dimension that cannot easily be portrayed using projected images over the model, for example volcanic eruptions, tornadoes, or glaciation. One could also simulate past structures on the surface, such as reconstructing building structures over their landscape footprint.

VI. Conclusion

This work has begun to demonstrate that solid relief models of real geographic environments can be usefully augmented with projection, and that there is some potential for detecting finger point touch on the model surface. Experiments that attempt to isolate the most useful aspects of physical relief models in judging landscape characteristics have suggested that models may support more complex understandings of topographic form. Observations of displays have also indicated some expectation of touch-based interaction and early experiments with the Kinect sensor show some promise. The accuracy of such touch interactions need to be fully investigated and assessed against the scale of object in the model that would be the focus of such actions.

Acknowledgment

This research is funded by Indonesia Ministry of Research, Technology and Higher Education (Kementrian Riset, Teknologi dan Pendidikan Tinggi) and supported by Indonesia Geospatial Information Agency (Badan Informasi Geospasial)

References

[1] A.W Pearson, "Allied military model making during world war II", Cartography and Geographic Information Science, vol. 29, No. 3, pp. 227-241, 2002.

[2] B. Piper, C. Ratti, and H. Ishii, "Illuminating clay: a 3-d tangible interface for landscape analysis". In *Proceedings of the SIGCHI Conference on Human Factors in Computing Systems*, 355-362, 2002.

[3] L. G. Tateosian, H. Mitasova, B.A. Harmon, B. Fogleman, K. Weaver, and R.S. Harmon, "Tangible geospatial modeling system". *IEEE Transactions on Visualization & Computer Graphics* 16, 6: 1605-1612, 2010.

[4] K. Oliver, "Augmented reality sandbox". Institute Data Analysis and Visualization (IDAV). Retrieved February 19, 2017, available from http://idav.ucdavis.edu/~okreylos/ResDev/SARndbox/, 2012

[5] T. L. Woods, S. Reed, S. Hsi, J.A. Woods, and M.R. Woods, "Pilot study using the augmented reality sandbox to teach topographic maps and surficial processes in introductory geology labs", Journal of Geoscience Education, vol. 64, pp. 199–214, 2016.

[6] Solid Terrain Models, *Solid Terrain Models*, Retrieved February 19, 2017, available from: http://www.solidterrainmodeling. com

[7] E. Howard, "Architectural models, renderings, terrain models - howard models". Retrieved February 19, 2017, available from http://www.howardmodels.com/index.html, 2014

[8] G. Priestnall, J. Gardiner, J. Durrant, and J. Goulding, "Projection augmented relief models (PARM): Tangible Displays for Geographic Information". *Electronic Visualisation and the Arts,* 180-187, 2012

[9] A. Kulshreshth, C. Zorn, and J. J. LaViola Jr., "Real-time markerless kinect based finger tracking and hand gesture recognition for HCI". In *IEEE Symposium on 3D User Interfaces 2013*, 187-188, 2013

[10] P. Dalsgaard and K. Halskov, "3D projection on physical objects: design insights from five real life cases", In Proc CHI. ACM Press, pp. 1041-1050, 2011.

[11] T. Hahmann, C. Eisfeldwer, and M. F. Buchroithner, "Cartographic representation of dresden's historical development by projecting a movie onto a solid terrain model". *In True-3D in Cartography: Auto stereoscopic and solid visualization of geodata* (revised ed.), Manfred Buchroithner (Ed.). Springer, Heidelberg, Germany, 281-296, 2012.

A Comparative Study between Younger and Older Users on Mobile Interface Navigation

Qingchuan Li and Yan Luximon
School of Design
The Hong Kong Polytechnic University
Hung Hom, Hong Kong
e-mails: qingchuan.li@connect.polyu.hk, yan.luximon@polyu.edu.hk

Abstract— **Mobile interface navigation is an important aspect when directly manipulating the mobile technologies, yet the navigation behavior is not well understood at the level of visual presentation of navigation elements and task complexity for users among different age groups. This comparative study utilized an experiment to compare the mobile interface navigation between younger and older user groups, by examining three types of visual presentations and three levels of task complexity. The results showed that there were significant differences between age groups in navigation efficiency, effectiveness and subjective evaluation. In addition, the navigation performance was significantly lower when the task required more information sources to be remembered and integrated, especially for older users. However, no significant effect of visual presentation was reported on the navigation performance and subjective evaluation. Understanding the mobile interface navigation behavior among different age groups will assist in designing appropriate visual presentation of navigation elements and keeping task complexity to an accepted level for targeted user groups.**

Keywords- age; mobile interface; navigation; task complexity; visual presentation.

I. Introduction

With the prevalence of mobile technologies, navigation through mobile interfaces is becoming an important aspect to search for the contents and utilize relevant functions provided by the mobile websites or applications [1]. Instead of interacting with the mouse and keyboard, mobile technologies generate their specific mobile navigation patterns due to the different interactive mode, limited interface space, and complex information architectures. Thus, it poses a considerable challenge of how to improve the user experience of mobile interface navigation for diversified user groups.

In particular, the direct user interface allows users to navigate through the applications by directly pointing or clicking the navigation elements on the interfaces, such as touch-screens [2]. The well-designed navigation elements can help users accomplishing tasks efficiently and effectively [3]. For instance, the menu navigation is a typical and popular way of representing the mobile application structures and functions [4]. Users can navigate their way to the desired target by selecting navigation elements (i.e., icons, hyperlinks, and buttons). In this way, the visual presentation of navigation elements is recognized as an important design consideration that helps users to better use navigation elements to find relevant information and complete tasks [5].

To fulfill the functional goals of the application or website, the designers may start from collecting specific navigation elements, to further grouping or arranging them into different hierarchies or categories. Also, designers could use these visual presentations to guide users' navigation patterns [6]. In fact, there is a long history examining the visual presentation in terms of icon characteristics on computer tasks [7][8]. They mainly emphasized the importance of icon characteristics on visual searching, such as concreteness, semantic distance, color quality, size, shape and location arrangement. However, most of the previous studies were mainly considered within the context of visual recognition and function matching tasks. It is still unknown how the visual presentation of navigation elements matters in the mobile navigation tasks.

Currently, an increasing number of older users are using mobile technologies for health management and social interactions, which involves information searching, decision-making, and problem-solving tasks [9]. Thus, the mobile interface navigation should also be concerned with the task complexity [10]. Task complexity, as defined by Campbell [11], lies in the nature of multiplicity, and deals with the collections of paths needed to reach the directions and even conflicts between the paths and expected results. Specifically, navigation task is concerned with how to organize the sequences of actions to search for desired information in order to achieve the task goals [12].

Previous studies normally defined the task complexity based on the page complexity and path complexity [13] [14], which concerned the number of navigation elements on the pages, the difficulty of judging the relevance of these elements and task goals, as well as the total steps and depth to gain the target information. Yet, we think it is also important to consider the task complexity based on the cognitive load and mental work needed. If the more complex a task is, the more information resources users need to remember and integrate, thus acquiring for more working memory and information processing. Therefore, this study examined the task complexity with the number of information sources needed to be remembered or integrated during the whole task.

Although strides have been made in studying web navigation, little investigation existed about the user experience of mobile interface navigation. This study was conducted as the first phase of a larger study to investigate the possible effects of visual presentation of navigation elements and task complexity on the mobile interface navigation. In order to include a diverse group of users, this study examined the differences of mobile interface navigation between age groups. The user experience of navigation was highlighted by aspects of task performance and subjective evaluation [15].

Overall, this study aims to contribute to a better comprehension of the user experience with mobile interface navigation among different age groups. It will assist designers in choosing the appropriate visual presentation of navigation elements and keeping the number of information sources to an accepted level of task complexity for targeted user groups. The organization of this article is as follows. Section II describes the details of participants recruitment and experiment design. Section III outlines the results of participants' navigation performance and subjective evaluation, with relevant correlations analyzed. Then, the section IV detailed discusses and interprets the results with some previous literatures. Finally, the section V presents the main conclusions, discusses the major limitations, and points out the possible directions to be explored in the future.

II. METHODS

The method of experiment was employed in present study to investigate participants' navigation performance and subjective evaluation.

A. Participants

A total of 15 participants were involved in this study. The majority of the participants were recruited from local universities and elderly centers. All the participants were in good physical and cognitive conditions, and had the ability to read Chinese characters. The participants were divided into two age groups: the younger group with an average age of 28.63 years old (SD= 4.60; age range: 24-38); and the older group with an average age of 69.57 years old (SD=11.62; age range: 52-81).

Figure 1. Interface design for menu navigation page (left) and sub-page: medication (right).

B. Experimental Design

In order to test the effects of visual presentation of navigation elements and task complexity on navigation performance and subjective evaluation, 9 tasks were planned with a 3 (visual presentation of icon-text, icon-only, and text-only) × 3 (level 1, level 2 and level 3) factorial design.

As shown in Figure 1, a simulated iOS mobile application that used to remind users to take medicine was implemented by Unity: users could browse the four sub-pages through a menu navigation page. A total of 8 real size navigation elements were presented in the menu navigation page, in which, 4 of them can be clicked to direct users to the 4 sub-pages: patient, medication, dose and time. In each of the four sub-pages, participants needed to choose the answers according to different task instructions. There was also some relevant information provided in the sub-pages.

1) Visual presentation manipulation: Three kinds of visual presentations were used for the menu navigation page: icon-text, icon-only, and text-only. The visual presentation followed the principles of applying concrete, semantic-closed, simple colored, and uncomplicated shapes for icons and text with dynamic hit provided [8]. The sizes of icon and text were controlled to be exactly the same. The positions of navigation elements were randomly presented for each task.

2) Task complexity manipulation: Three levels of task complexity were manipulated in this study.' At the complexity of level 1, participants were asked to choose the answers directly following the task instructions, which didn't require any memory load or information integrating (e.g., please remind Awen to take one piece of aspen after lunch). At the level 2, the task instruction was as similar as level 1, whereas, the task instruction disappeared after the task began. Thereby, it required a memory load to remember the task instructions. At the level 3, participants were asked to choose the answers based on both of task instruction and the relevant information provided by each sub-page. The process required users to remember task instructions and integrate relevant information across all the sub-pages (e.g., please help Awen who got cold to make the medication plan).

C. Measurement

Navigation performance was measured using data that automatically recorded by the background system. It was assessed based on the efficiency, effectiveness, and the number of return steps and incorrect clicks. Specifically, efficiency was measured by the completion time, which was the seconds the participants required to finish each task. Effectiveness was measured by the correctness of answers, which was the percentage of correct answers chosen for each task. The number of returns was defined as the number of returning to previous sub-pages. The number of click was defined as the number of incorrect click of the navigation elements on the main menu page.

Subjective evaluation was measured by the 5-point Likert scales based on five aspects of ease-of-use, disorientation, effort needed, helpfulness, and satisfaction [16] [17]. For the first three questions of ease-of-use, disorientation and effort needed, it scored 1-5 from a rating of very agreed to very disagreed. Specifically, the ease-of-use was evaluated by whether the application is hard to learn; the disorientation was asked by whether it is easy to get lost and disorientated; the effort needed was assessed by whether a lot of efforts were needed to fulfill these tasks. In addition, the last two questions of helpfulness and satisfaction were used to examine users' overall feelings from the rating of very dissatisfied to very satisfied (1-5).

D. Procedure

The experiment was conducted in a separated and quiet room, with one participant and two experimenters there at one time. Before the experiment, the experimental instruction and consent form were given to the participants. Each participant was allowed to free explore the experimental application for 5 minutes. At the same time, the experimenters provided the task description document with the participants and instructed them how to use this application. Following that, participants completed three trials to familiarize himself or herself with the experiment without the task description document. After a 2-min rest, the experiment began. Each participant was given 9 tasks to complete. Following each task, the subjective evaluation was collected respectively. The whole interactions between users and application will be recorded by the background system and the whole process for each participant was controlled in one hour.

E. Data analysis

Normality test was first performed to assess the normality of the data. Since the data were collected from only 15 participants, it is unsurprised that they were not normally distributed. The non-parametric testing was then utilized to analyze the results in SPSS. Specifically, the Mann-Whitney test was employed to compare the differences of navigation performance and subjective evaluation between the younger and older user groups. The Friedman test was utilized to test for differences in navigation performance and subjective evaluation when participants were measured at different visual presentations and task complexities. Based on the results from the Friedman test, the Wilcoxon signed-rank test was further used to compare the differences between each of the two measurements from the same participants.

III. RESULTS

The experiment compared the navigation performance and subjective evaluation between age groups. The possible effects of visual presentation and task complexity were also investigated.

A. Navigation performance

The descriptive data of navigation performance between younger and older user are shown in graphical forms in Figure 2 and Figure 3, including the completion time, correctness of answers, and the number of return steps and incorrect clicks.

1) Comparison between age groups: Analysis of Mann-Whitney test was used to compare the difference of navigation performance between age groups. In terms of the completion time, the results revealed that younger users completed the tasks significantly faster than older users with all the visual presentations of icon-text, icon-only and text-only when the task complexity was level 1 (U = 4.00, p =

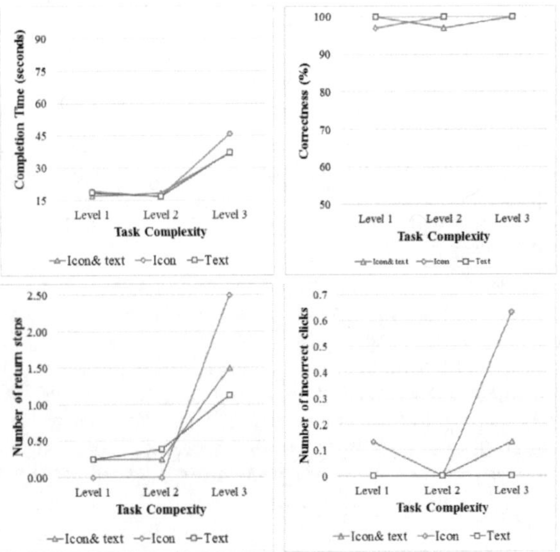

Figure 2. Navigation performance of younger users with different visual presentation and task complexity.

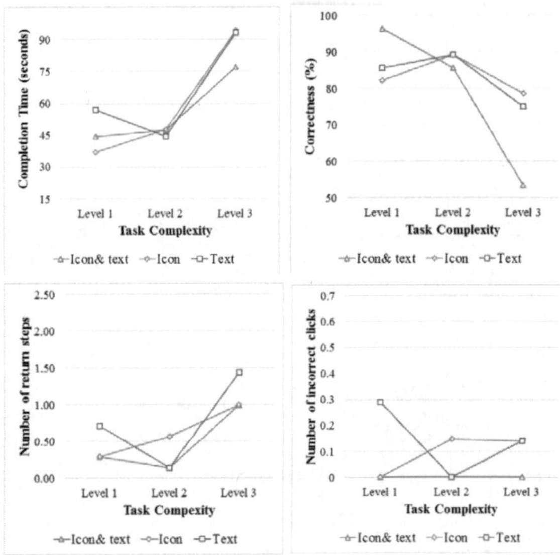

Figure 3. Navigation performance of older users with different visual presentation and task complexity.

0.004; $U = 1.50$, $p = 0.001$; $U = 1.00$, $p = 0.001$), and level 2 ($U = 0.00$, $p = 0.000$; $U = 0.00$, $p = 0.000$; $U = 0.00$, $p = 0.000$). The same results were found for the visual presentations of icon-text and text-only when the task complexity was level 3 ($U = 6.00$, $p = 0.009$; $U = 0.00$, $p = 0.000$).

The correctness was found no significant difference between age groups, except for the visual presentation of icon-text at the task complexity of level 3 ($U = 4.00$, $p = 0.004$), in which younger users had a significant higher correctness of answers. Similarly, no significant difference was found for the number of return steps and incorrect clicks between age groups.

2) Effects of visual presentation on navigation performance:

a) The younger group of users: Analysis of Friedman test was firstly employed to examine the statistical differences between navigation performances of 9 tasks. The results reported significant differences in completion time (χ^2 (2) = 44.228, $p = 0.000$) and the number of return steps (χ^2 (2) = 27.591, $p = 0.001$). Then, the Wilcoxon signed-rank test was used to test where the differences actually occurred. However, the results did not reveal significant differences of completion time and the number of return steps between different visual presentations for all of three levels of task complexity.

b) The older group of users: Friedman test also reported significant differences in older users' completion time (χ^2 (2) = 20.086, $p = 0.010$), the correctness of answers (χ^2 (2) = 16.597, $p = 0.035$), and the number of return steps (χ^2 (2) = 15.504, $p = 0.050$). Nevertheless, in the further analysis of Wilcoxon signed-rank test, no significant difference was found in terms of navigation performance between different visual presentations across all the levels of task complexity.

3) Effects of task complexity on navigation performance:

a) The younger group of users: Followed the previous Friedman test, a Wilcoxon signed-rank test was also used to examine the effects of task complexity on navigation performance among younger users. The results reported statistically significant differences in navigation performance between different levels of task complexity. Specifically, it indicated there were significant differences of completion time between the task complexity of level 1 and 3 (icon-text: Z = -2.524, $p = 0.012$; icon-only: Z = -2.524, $p = 0.012$; text-only: Z = -2.521, $p = 0.012$), as well as level 2 and 3 (icon-text: Z = -2.533, $p = 0.011$; icon-only: Z = -2.521, $p = 0.012$; text-only: Z = -2.521, $p = 0.012$), in which the task complexity of level 3 induced longer completion time. The same results were also found in the number of return steps between the task complexity of level 1 and 3 (Z = -2.207, $p = 0.027$), level 2 and level 3 (Z = -2.207, $p = 0.027$), in which the task complexity of level 3 elicited more return steps, but only for the visual presentation of icon-only.

b) The older group of users: Based on the previous Friedman test's results of older users, the Wilcoxon signed-rank test was conducted. Significant longer completion time was reported at the task complexity of level 3 when comparing with level 1 (Z = -2.371, $p = 0.018$; Z = -2.028, $p = 0.043$) for the visual presentation of icon-text and icon-only, and level 2 for the visual presentation of text-only (Z = -2.028, $p = 0.043$). The same results were found in the correctness of answers between the task complexity of level 1 and 3 (Z = -2.220, $p = 0.026$), level 2 and 3 (Z = -2.041, $p = 0.041$) for the visual presentation of icon-text.

B. Subjective evaluation

1) Subjective evaluation between age groups: Analysis using Mann-Whitney test revealed that older users evaluated significantly higher in the aspect of helpfulness compared with younger users when the task complexity was level 1 (icon-text: $U = 10.00$, $p = 0.040$; text-ony: $U = 6.00$, $p = 0.009$), level 2 (icon-only: $U = 10.50$, $p = 0.040$), and level 3 (icon-text: $U = 6.50$, $p = 0.009$; icon-only: $U = 4.00$, $p = 0.004$; text-only: $U = 10.00$, $p = 0.040$). The same result was also found in the evaluation for the satisfaction when the task complexity was level 1 (icon-text: $U = 10.00$, $p = 0.040$; icon-only: $U = 10.00$, $p = 0.040$; text-ony: $U = 5.00$, $p = 0.006$), level 2 (icon-only: $U = 9.50$, $p = 0.029$), and level 3 (icon-text: $U = 10.00$, $p = 0.040$; icon-only: $U = 5.00$, $p =$

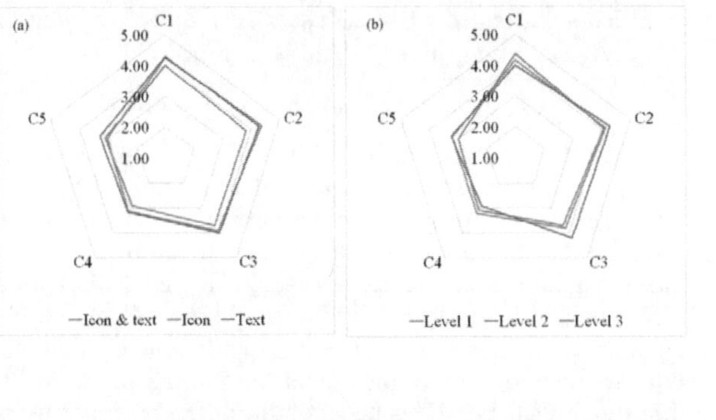

Figure 4. Subjective evaluation of younger users with different (a) visual presentation and (b) task complexity (C1: ease-of-use; C2: disorientation; C3: efforts; C4: helpfulness; C5: satisfaction).

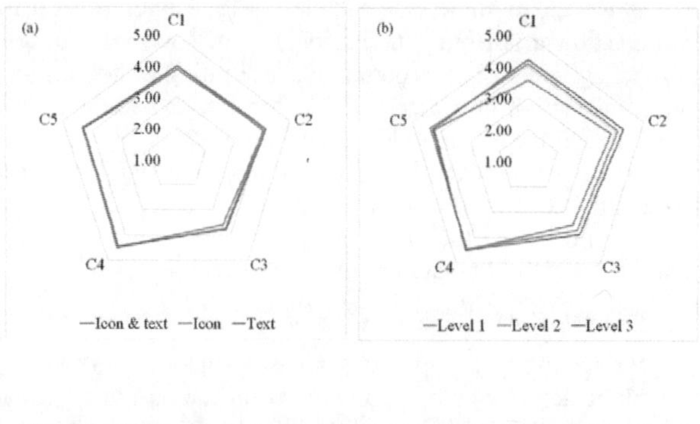

Figure 5. Subjective evaluation of older users with different (a) visual presentation and (b) task complexity (C1: ease-of-use; C2: disorientation; C3: efforts; C4: helpfulness; C5: satisfaction).

0.006).

2) Subjective evaluation on visual presentation and task complexity: To further analyze the differences between subjective evaluations of 9 tasks, Friedman test was used. Nevertheless, there were no significant differences in subjective evaluation between different visual presentations and task complexities. The descriptive data of subjective evaluation from younger and older users were shown in Figure 4 and Figure 5. Generally, for younger users, the visual presentation of text-only and icon-only resulted in the feelings of less disorientation and efforts needed. Nevertheless, the other aspects of subjective evaluation between different visual presentations and task complexities followed quite a similar pattern.

IV. DISCUSSION

Mobile interface navigation is an important aspect when interacting with mobile technologies to complete different tasks. In contrast to previous studies focusing on menu item searching [18] [19], or specific digital tasks [20] [21], this study obtained a unique perspective of simulating different levels of task complexity for mobile navigation tasks. One question of interest for the present study was whether the age matters for navigation performance as well as subjective evaluation. Also, the effects of visual presentation and task complexity were concerned.

A. Comparison of mobile interface navigation between age groups

Consistent with the previous findings within the context of information finding [19] and menu navigation tasks [22], older users indicated poorer navigation efficiency in our studies. They averagely spent twice the length of younger users' completion time. There are also some differences between their navigation strategies. The younger users tended to make more return steps and incorrect clicks when the task complexity is high. On the other hand, the older users tended to be consistent with their navigation paths. The fatigue issue should also be considered for older users in this experiment. Older users were not consistent with their performance between tasks because they were easier to feel tired.

However, to some extent, older users showed a positive attitude towards digital tasks. Despite of lower navigation efficiency, older users reported a higher rating of helpfulness and satisfaction towards their navigation experience. The reason could be that older adults normally show positive feelings of experience [23]. In this way, we suggest rather than only relying on analyzing user's subjective feelings, tasks and experiments could help to enhance the comprehension of what happened in the real world.

B. Effects of visual presentation of navigation elements

Navigation tasks involve a lot of visual exploration and searching actions; thereby, it emphasizes the design of visual presentation for navigation elements. However, the present study found no statistical and significant differences between three kinds of visual presentations, i.e., icon-text, icon-only and text only. On the one hand, the possible reason is that the duration of searching for specific navigation element in the menu navigation page only accounts for a quite small portion of the whole task completion time. On the other hand, the navigation element used in this study was quite different with each other, which didn't cause many efforts in searching and recognizing processes.

Little evidence in previous studies exists in examining the effects of visual presentation of navigation elements on mobile interface navigation. Although there was no significant result reported in this study, the pattern of different visual presentations could be preliminarily deduced from this study. For younger users, in agreement with the previous study [24], the visual presentation of text-only seemed to have better navigation performance when the task complexity was high; whereas the icon-only design induced a lot of return steps and incorrect clicks.

C. Effects of task complexity

Task complexity is a broad-defined concept in navigation tasks. This study took a specific perspective from the task requirements for remembering and integrating different numbers of information sources. As expected, the higher level of task complexity led to the lowest navigation efficiency both for the younger and older groups. Nevertheless, the younger users still kept high navigation effectiveness when the task complexity was high compared with the older users.

Previous studies stated that user's visual ability of scanning and searching largely influence the number of navigation elements that should be displayed [25]. Nevertheless, to fulfill the specific functional goals, users also need to remember a lot of information that generated from the task itself, as well as integrating information from some other sources. Consistent with the previous study examining mobiles' complexity levels [26], the present study also found that older users performed worse than younger users when the task complexity was higher, however their performance was similar to younger users when the task complexity was lower. Specifically, this study shows that the navigation performance could not be affected when the memory load is low, such as remembering one-sentence task description. However, the navigation performance could be significantly affected when the users are required to integrate a lot of information sources at the same time.

V. CONCLUSION AND FUTURE WORK

This study compared the differences of mobile interface navigation between younger and older groups with three types of visual presentations of navigation elements and three levels of task complexity. Firstly, it can be concluded that navigation performance and subjective evaluation were significantly different between age groups. Secondly, the navigation performance was significantly lower when the task requires users to remember and integrate a lot of information sources. This occurs more often for older users. However, no significant effect of the visual presentation of navigation elements was found in present study. Thus, in extending the finding in improving the user experience of mobile interface navigation, we suggest that the task complexity could be important design considerations especially for older users.

This study should also be considered in the light of limitations. For instance, the age of older users varied a lot in present study. Thereby, their navigation performances were quite different with each other. For future research, more participants will be recruited to cover more age groups, and the demographics factors and technology experience will also be investigated. Furthermore, it is better to employ a better evaluation method (e.g., task analysis) to investigate participants' mobile navigation behavior in details. For example, it is interesting to examine how long the user spends on each section of tasks including information searching, decision-making and checking.

ACKNOWLEDGMENT

The authors would like to thank the Research Grants Council for the UGC Funding Scheme from the Hong Kong Polytechnic University.

REFERENCES

[1] J. J. Garrett, Elements of user experience: user-centered design for the web and beyond. Berkeley, CA: Pearson Education, 2010.

[2] R. Michalski, J. Grobelny, and W. Karwowski, "The effects of graphical interface design characteristics on human–computer interaction task efficiency," International Journal of Industrial Ergonomics, vol. 36(11), pp. 959-977, 2006.

[3] N. Yu and J. Kong, "User experience with web browsing on small screens: Experimental investigations of mobile-page interface design and homepage design for news websites," Information Sciences, vol. 330, pp. 427-443, 2016.

[4] E. P. dos Santos, S. de Lara, and W. M. Watanabe, R. P. Fortes, "Usability evaluation of horizontal navigation bar with drop-down menus by middle aged adults," Proc. the 29th ACM international conference on Design of communication, ACM, pp. 145-150, 2011.

[5] M. C. Puerta Melguizo, U. Vidya, and H. van Oostendorp, "Seeking information online: the influence of menu type, navigation path complexity and spatial ability on information gathering tasks," Behaviour & Information Technology, vol31(1), pp. 59-70, 2012.

[6] M. S. Chen, M. C. Lin, C. C. Wang, and C. A. Chang, "Using HCA and TOPSIS approaches in personal digital assistant menu–icon interface design," International Journal of Industrial Ergonomics, vol. 39(5), pp. 689-702, 2009.

[7] C. J. Kacmar and J. M. Carey, "Assessing the usability of icons in user interfaces," Behaviour & Information Technology, vol. 10(6), pp. 443-457, 1991.

[8] R. Leung, J. McGrenere, and P. Graf, "Age-related differences in the initial usability of mobile device icons," Behaviour & Information Technology, vol. 30(5), pp. 629-642, 2011.

[9] Q. Li and Y. Luximon, "Older Adults and Digital Technology: A Study of User Perception and Usage Behavior," in Advances in Physical Ergonomics and Human Factors, R. Goonetilleke and Q. Karwowski, Eds. AG Switzerland: Springer International Publishing, pp. 155-163, 2016.

[10] J. Gwizdka and I. Spence, "Implicit measures of lostness and success in web navigation," Interacting with Computers, vol. 19, pp. 357–369, 2007.

[11] D. J. Campbell, "Task complexity: A review and analysis," Academy of management review, vol. 13(1), pp. 40-52, 1988.

[12] J. Gwizdka and I, Spence, "What can searching behavior tell us about the difficulty of information tasks? A study of web navigation" The 69th annual meeting of the American Society for Information Science and Technology (ASIS&T 2006) American Society for Information Science and Technology, vol. 43(1), pp. 1-22, 2006.

[13] M. C. Puerta Melguizo, U. Vidya, and H. van Oostendorp, "Seeking information online: the influence of menu type, navigation path complexity and spatial ability on information gathering tasks," Behaviour & Information Technology, vol. 31(1), pp. 59-70, 2012.

[14] P. Van Schaik and J. Ling, "A cognitive-experiential approach to modelling web navigation," International Journal of Human-Computer Studies, vol. 70(9), pp. 630-651, 2012.

[15] H. Petrie and N. Bevan, "The evaluation of accessibility, usability and user experience," in The universal access handbook, C. Stepanidis Eds, Florida, USA: CRC Press, PP. 10-20, 2009.

[16] J. S. Ahuja and J. Webster, "Perceived disorientation: an examination of a new measure to assess web design effectiveness," Interacting with computers, vol. 14(1), pp. 15-29, 2001.

[17] S. Leuthold, P. Schmutz, J. A. Bargas-Avila, A. N. Tuch, and K. Opwis, "Vertical versus dynamic menus on the world wide web: Eye tracking study measuring the influence of menu design and task complexity on user performance and subjective preference," Computers in human behavior, vol 27(1), pp. 459-472, 2011.

[18] I. Etcheverry, T. Baccino, P. Terrier, J. C. Marquié, and M. Mojahid, "Age differences in information finding tasks: Performance and visual exploration strategy with different web page layouts," Computers in Human Behavior, vol. 28(5), pp. 1670-1680, 2012.

[19] A. C. de Barros, R. Leitão, and J. Ribeiro, "Design and evaluation of a mobile user interface for older adults: navigation, interaction and visual design recommendations," Procedia Computer Science, vol. 27, pp. 369-378, 2014.

[20] S. Sayago and J. Blat, "Telling the story of older people e-mailing: An ethnographical study," International Journal of Human-Computer Studies, vol. 68(1), pp. 105-120, 2010.

[21] D. Castilla, A. Garcia-Palacios, I. Miralles, J. Breton-Lopez, E. Parra, S. Rodriguez-Berges, and C. Botella, "Effect of Web navigation style in elderly users," Computers in Human Behavior, vol. 55, pp. 909-920, 2016.

[22] C. Gatsou, A. Politis, and D. Zevgolis, "Text vs visual metaphor in mobile interfaces for novice user interaction," Information Services and Use, vol. 31(3-4), pp. 271-279, 2011.

[23] H. Sayers, "Desktop virtual environments: a study of navigation and age," Interacting with Computers, vol. 16(5), pp. 939-956, 2004.

[24] S. Schröder and M. Ziefle, "Making a completely icon-based menu in mobile devices to become true: a user-centered design approach for its development," Proc. the 10th international conference on Human computer interaction with mobile devices and services, ACM, pp. 137-146, 2008.

[25] L. Rosenfeld and P. Morville, Information architecture for the world wide web. Sebastopol, CA: O'Reilly & Associates, Inc, 2002.

[26] M. Ziefle and S. Bay, "How older adults meet complexity: aging effects on the usability of different mobile phones," Behaviour & Information Technology, vol. 24(5), pp. 375-389, 2005.

Two-button Mobile Interface: Touchscreen Based Text-Entry for Visually-Impaired Users

Hanseul Cho and Jae-joon Kim
Department of Creative IT Engineering
POSTECH
Pohang, Korea, Republic of
e-mail: {johanseul, jaejoon}@postech.ac.kr

***Abstract*—As the usage of mobile devices grows explosively, texting on a touchscreen becomes everyday routines for communication. For visually-impaired people, however, text-entry on the touchscreen is largely cumbersome and time-consuming due to the difficulty of locating keyboard buttons without any physical signifiers. We present new text-entry methods based on the Braille system to address this issue. The proposed Left Touch and Double Touch schemes are based on the two-button interface for Braille input, so that visually-impaired users can type textual characters without moving their fingers to find target buttons. We conducted experiments to evaluate the usability of the proposed methods and compared them with the One Finger Method and VoiceOver. The results show that the speed of the Double Touch is 3.94 second per letter (SPL) while that of the Left Touch is 2.60 SPL. The Left Touch was twice as slow as the VoiceOver but 39% faster than the One Finger Method. Although the typing speeds of the proposed schemes were slower than the VoiceOver, we found that the subjects felt the proposed schemes more comfortable to use than the VoiceOver. The convenience of using only two buttons in the mobile interface also enabled visually-impaired users to be less dependent on auditory feedback while typing texts.**

Keywords-visullay-impaired; touchscreen; text-entry; Input; Braiile.

I. Introduction

Despite the technological advances, there are still groups of people that cannot benefit from the recent innovation because such advances usually aim to address the demand of the general public. One example is the touchscreen technology that fails to serve visually-impaired people. They acquire information mainly through auditory and tactile senses, whereas touchscreens require high dependency on vision. Touchscreens lack physical components to support auditory and tactile senses of visually-impaired people. Because visually-impaired cannot find a target to touch on the screen [3][8][16], regardless of the inventors' intention, visually-impaired people are naturally excluded from using touchscreens. As mobile devices and interfaces for smartphones become an essential element of modern life and communication, visually-impaired people have been facing unprecedented frustration.

Among a number of issues associated with touchscreens, we focused on text-entry methods on touchscreens for visually-impaired people. Although there are numerous assistive typing devices for visually-impaired people, such as the Braille Hansone [6], these devices are typically not light and portable, thus less desirable for smartphones. There are also existing text-entry tools for visually-impaired users. For example, iPhone, the most popular smartphone among visually-impaired users, has its own eye-free interface called VoiceOver [1]. It supports text-entry based on the standard QWERTY keyboard, using a split-tapping method [7] to find and touch each character. Although VoiceOver is a dominant text-entry interface among visually-impaired users, it still has a problem. The number of target buttons is too large, while the size of each target is too small for visually-impaired users to locate and touch easily. In addition, because VoiceOver requires high dependency on auditory sense, it is difficult to use in noisy places. Most of other existing text-entry methods have similar audio-related problems. Therefore, there is a pressing need to develop an appropriate text-entry method for touchscreens that is specifically targeted to visually-impaired people

In this research, we first review the previous approaches of alternative text-entry methods for visually-impaired users, and evaluate the advantages and disadvantages of each approach. Based on the review and evaluation, we developed new Braille based text-entry methods, called Left Touch and Double Touch. These two text-entry methods use only two buttons in the mobile interface, so visually-impaired users can input letters without changing finger positions. That is, visually-impaired users do not need to scan and search the touchscreen to find a target. At the same time, the level of dependency on auditory sense is relatively low in the proposed method.

We begin this paper with the analysis of background (Section 2), followed by the detailed presentation of our text-entry methods, Left Touch and Double Touch (Section 3). Then we report the methodology and results of our experiment (Section 4, 5). As a conclusion, we discuss the analysis of the experiment result and its implications for future research directions (Section 6).

II. Background

In this section, we discuss basic Braille system and researches related to text-entry for visually-impaired users to provide background knowledge of our research.

A. Text-entry Methods Based on Braille

Since developed in 1825, the Braille system has been used for reading and writing characters by visually-impaired people. One Braille character consists of six dots with three rows and two columns as shown in Figure 1, so 64 different letters can be represented in principle.

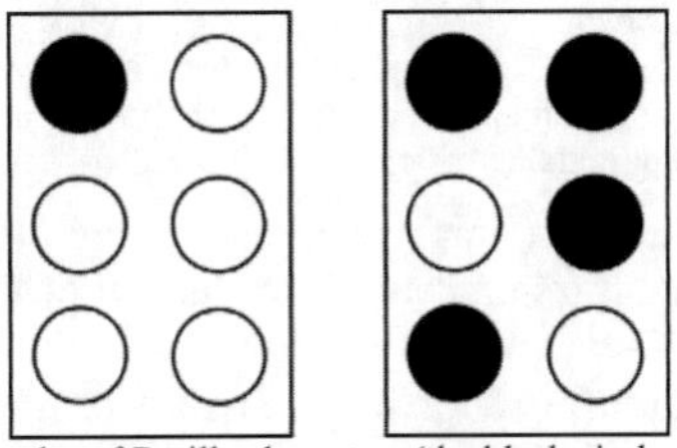

Figure 1. Examples of Braille characters (the black circle means a raised dot, and the white means a flat): Lower-case 'a' (left); Lower-case 'n' (right).

Each dot could be raised or remain flat so that people can figure out characters with tactile sense. Since most of visually-impaired people learn Braille, the advantage of text-entry based on the Braille system is the relatively low barrier for learning compared to non-Braille based entry methods.

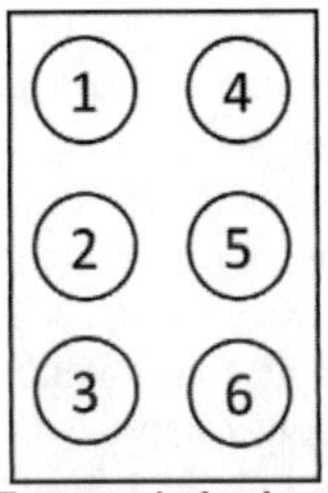

Figure 2. The numerical order of each dot

There is a numerical order for the dots in a Braille character. As shown in Fig. 2, the three dots in the left column have an order of 1 to 3, whereas three dots in the other column have an order of 4 to 6. Since this order is widely known to visually-impaired people, recognizing Braille in different orders would be challenging for them [11]. Therefore, it is important to keep the same order when designing new text-entry methods.

Naturally, many previous Braille based text-entry methods place six buttons on a touchscreen to map the Braille cell directly. An example is *BrailleType* presented by Olivia et al [12]. In *BrailleType*, the user inputs one dot at a time by touching a corresponding button on the touchscreen. The speed was 1.45 wpm, which was relatively slower than the speed observed in other similar studies [10][14]. Paisios et al. presented four text-entry methods based on the Braille system [11]. The most preferred one was the *One Finger Method*, which is similar to *BrailleType*. In *BrailleTouch* presented by Southern et al., users input six dots in the Braille cell simultaneously using six fingers [14]. To use *BrailleTouch*, users hold a device with two hands and the screen faces away from them. This method, however, may cause difficulties since the general holding posture is opposite from the typing posture. Usually, users hold smartphones to face them for general use. In *BrailleTouch,* the average speed of experts group was 23.2wpm, while that of non-experts group was 9.4 wpm.

Mascetti et al. presented *TypeInBraille*, where users input one row at a time [10]. The speed was 6.3 wpm. Although there are no quantitative data available to be compared with other Braille-based input methods, it is possible that visually-impaired users may experience some confusion by the different order of the dots from the conventional Braille character and the need for additional training and practices [11].

Based on the review of the previous methods, we view that there are three advantages in the Braille-based text-entry method. First, visually-impaired users are already familiar with the Braille layout and the function of buttons. Second, users do not have to newly learn how to input in the Braille-based system different from VoiceOver since the input methods use Braille characters. Third, the number of target button decreases. For example, the maximum number of target in text-entry methods based on Braille is six. That is a relatively small number of target button compared to other text-entry methods, such as QWERTY. To leverage these advantages, we propose a simple text-entry layout with a smaller number of targets, for easy input way and small cognitive load. In this research, we use the *One Finger Method* as a baseline for our experiment, because it is the simplest way of input based on the standard six buttons format of Braille characters.

B. Other Text-entry Methods

Kane et al. presented *Slide Rule*, an eye-free interface for touchscreens with audio-based multi-touch techniques [7]. Later, *Slide Rule* was incorporated into the *Apple*'s *VoiceOver,* which supports QWERTY-based eye-free text-entry. In *VoiceOver*, since there are too many tiny targets, visually impaired users have to explore the keyboard with the finger to find targets [10]. Due to the small size and the lack of tactile feedback [13], even skilled users can rarely find a key without initial scanning. Due to the difficulty of recognizing the visual layout, QWERTY may not be a viable solution of text-entry design for visually-impaired users. Bonner et al. presented *No-Look Notes,* which uses the multi-touch interface and audio feedback [2]. In *No-Look Notes*, 26 letters of the English alphabet are arranged around the screen in an 8-segment pie menu reminiscent. In one segment, there are three to four letters. When a user touches a target segment, the letters in the targeted segment appear in the alphabetical order from top to bottom on the screen. The speed was 1.32 wpm. Niazi et al. applied similar mobile 3*4 keyboard concept to touch screen text-entry, and compared the results with QWERTY keyboard [18].

Oliveira et al. also presented *NavTouch,* which is a gesture-based interface [5]. The average speed was around 1.7 wpm. Heni et al. also proposed gesture based text-entry and the speed was about 12 WPM [19]. On the whole, it appears that text-entry methods not based on Braille have fundamental problems that visually-impaired users need additional training and prolonged experience to skillfully use such methods.

III. THE PROPOSED TEXT-ENTRY METHODS

Based on the review of the existing text-entry methods, in the initial stage of our research, we set the following three design principles to propose a new mobile text-entry interface for visually-impaired users:

- Principle 1: Design a text-entry method based on the Braille system for the simplicity of the interface layout, and the fewer burdens for additional training and practices.
- Principle 2: Design a text-entry method with a minimal number of targets, thereby users do not have to move their position of fingers extensively.
- Principle 3: Design a text-entry method less dependent on auditory sense, so that visually-impaired people can use it in noisy places without solely depending on auditory feedback.

A. *Two-Button Interface*

Based on the first and second design principles, we designed text-entry methods that have only two vertical buttons for Braille character input as shown in Fig. 3. In the rest of the paper, we use the term LEFT button for the button on the left side and RIGHT button for the other one.

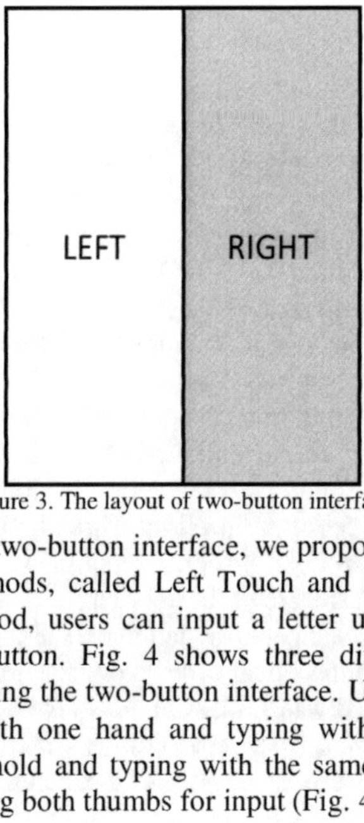

Figure 3. The layout of two-button interface.

Using this two-button interface, we propose two types of text-entry methods, called Left Touch and Double Touch. For each method, users can input a letter using the LEFT and RIGHT button. Fig. 4 shows three different holding postures for using the two-button interface. Users can hold a smartphone with one hand and typing with another hand (Fig. 4, left), hold and typing with the same hand (Fig. 4, middle) or using both thumbs for input (Fig. 4, right).

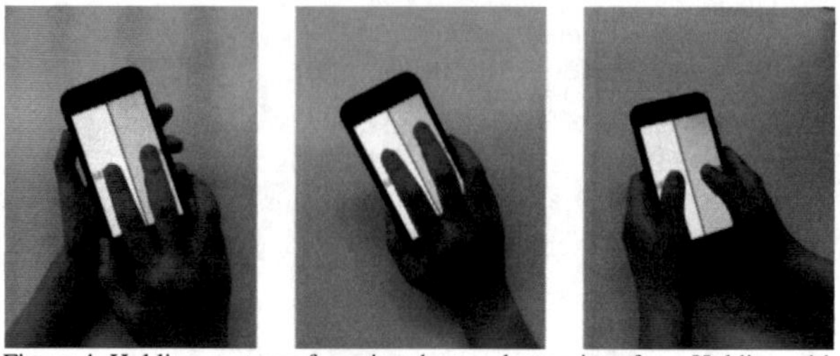

Figure 4. Holding postures for using the two-button interface: Holding with one hand, and typing with the other (left); holding and typing with the same hand (middle); typing with both thumbs (right).

One of the most important features of the two-button interface is that it minimizes the movement of fingers on the touchscreen. Users only need to lift fingers up and down at the same position. By applying the two-button interface, it is expected that Braille input on touchscreens can be convenient and easy for visually-impaired users. In the following section, we provide more detailed descriptions about each text-entry method in the two-button mobile interface.

B. *Left Touch*

Visually-impaired people recognize the numerical order of dots when understanding Braille characters. To leverage on this learned behavior, in the Left Touch method, users input dots in a regular order. The operating mechanism is simple. If a user wants to mark a dot, touch the LEFT button; otherwise, touch the RIGHT button. Users always touch buttons six times to complete one letter since one Braille character is composed of six dots. After typing one letter, the system presents audio feedback that informs users of the typed letter for confirmation.

For example, the sequence of touching the alphabet 'n' is 'LEFT→RIGHT→LEFT→LEFT→LEFT→RIGHT' as shown in Fig. 5 (top).

Users can delete letters by swiping upward on the LEFT button, and input a 'space' by swiping downward on the RIGHT button. When users want to restart inputting a letter, they can cancel an inputted pattern and restart input by swiping down on the LEFT button.

Visually-impaired people that are familiar with Braille can easily adopt the Left Touch method because the touching sequence is same as the natural order for the original Braille system. The layout is highly simple to reduce the need for memorizing locations and functions of buttons. Finally, the dependency on auditory sense is relatively low because users can easily recognize the completion of a letter input through the fixed number (6) of touches for each letter.

C. *Double Touch*

In the Double Touch method, a user touches a button twice to mark a dot and touches a button once to mark an empty dot. Different from the Left Touch method, users input dots in the order of row, not in numerical order of

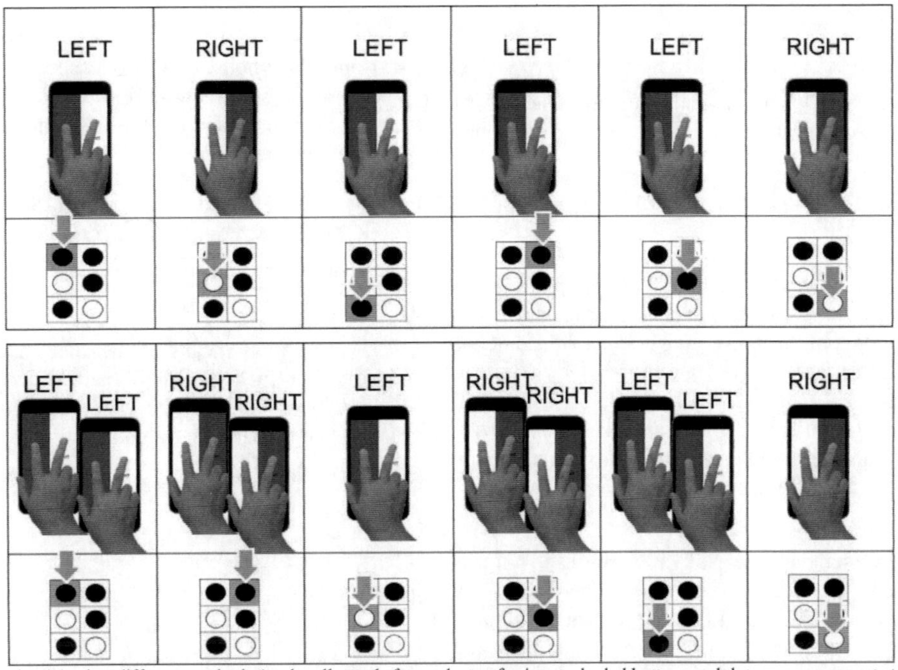

Figure 5. Way of inputting 'n' using different methods (each cell stands for each step for input, shaded buttons and dots mean a current step): Left Touch (top); Double Touch (bottom).

Braille. For example, users input dots for the first row, then for the second row, and finally for the third row. In the same row, left dots are inputted first. Therefore, the order should be 'left dot (1st row) - right dot (1st row) - left dot (2nd row) - right dot (2nd row) - left dot (3rd row) - right dot (3rd row)'. In this scheme, we use the LEFT button for entering Braille characters in the left column and the RIGHT button for entering Braille characters in the right column. If users want to input left dots in a row as marked, they need to touch the LEFT button twice. Otherwise, if users want to input right dots in a row as empty, they need to touch the RIGHT button once. Following this rule, the sequence of entering the alphabet 'n' is '(LEFT-LEFT)→ (RIGHT-RIGHT)→LEFT→(RIGHT-RIGHT)→(LEFT-LEFT)→RIGHT' as shown in Fig. 5 (bottom).

The same audio feedback as in the Left Touch method is presented to inform users of the completion of letter input. Deleting, spacing and restarting mechanisms are also same as the ones for Left Touch. Since the order of entering each dot (1-4-2-5-3-6 in Fig. 2) is different from the conventional one (1-2-3-4-5-6), users may feel some confusion in the beginning. However, in Double Touch, dots and corresponding buttons mapped spatially to reduce cognitive load to remember the layout. Also, the way the buttons are pressed is rhythmical because a user touches the LEFT and RIGHT button alternately. The downside of this method, however, is that the number of touching may vary depending on the letters. In the worst case, the buttons have to be pressed 12 times (all dots are marked).

IV. EXPERIMENTS

We conducted an experiment with four visually-impaired participants. In the experiment, we compared the efficacy of our proposed methods, Left Touch and Double Touch with the existing methods including the One Finger Method, and VoiceOver.

A. Participants

We recruited four visually-impaired users for the experiment. All participants are university students from the same university located in a mid-sized city in Korea. As shown in Table 1, the average age was 24 (standard deviation=1.63, range: 22-26). Three participants were visually-impaired from birth. All of them were iPhone users, and used VoiceOver for more than two years. Also, all of them used Braille Hansone at least once. We asked the participants about their experiences with using the English Braille, since the tasks in the experiment were to type English letters. The average period of the English Braille experience was 10.75 years (standard deviation=4.03, range: 5-14).

TABLE I. PARTICIPANTS' CHARACTERIAZATION

	Age	Gender	C/A (age)	P/E(year)	P/V(year)
1	26	male	acquired(18)	5	3
2	22	female	congenital	11	2
3	24	female	congenital	13	3
4	24	female	congenital	14	3

*C/A(age)[Congenital or Acquired(age)];P/E[Period of Using English Braille];P/V[Period of Using VoieOver].

B. Apparatus

We used Galaxy S3 from Samsung for the One Finger Method, Double Touch, and Left Touch, and used iPhone4 for VoiceOver.

C. Tasks

1) Dictation

We used dictation as the main task. First, participants listened to specific sentences, and then entered the sentences with the given input method. We delivered sentence uniformly by using the Google translator [4] for Text-to-Speech method as suggested in [14]. Because all participants were not native English speakers, they were allowed to ask questions before starting text input when having troubles in identifying spellings.

2) Phrase Set

We used the 'standard set of 500 English phrases commonly used in text entry studies' developed by MacKenzie and Soukoreff [9]. Participants inputted alphabets in lower-case only. There were no numbers and punctuation marks. We recorded inputted logs and times to calculate second per letter (SPL) and to evaluate the accuracy of each entry method.

3) Procedure

Participants had four sessions of twenty-minute typing tasks. Before starting main tasks, they had a training session to learn and practice each text-entry method. Since all participants were familiar with VoiceOver, they did not have the training time for VoiceOver.

Each method was tested for one day, not to overburden participants and to reduce confusion and learning effects across the different methods compared. We did not conduct experiments for Left Touch and Double Touch continuously to avoid the ordering effect because two methods commonly use the two-button interface style. Half of the participants were given the Left Touch test first, whereas the others tried the Double Touch method first.

For data collection, we recorded both audio and video data. After finishing all experiments, the participants were asked to complete a survey concerning usability issues such as ease of use, willingness to use, and satisfaction. All survey questions were given in a five-point Likert scale (1=strongly disagree, 5=strongly agree), and open questions about the personal opinion on the method. The experiments were followed by semi-structured interviews for further details about participants' qualitative opinions.

4) Experimental Design and Data Analysis

For quantitative data, the dependent variables are speed and accuracy, with a 4 x 4 within-subjects analysis of variance: the four text-entry methods (Left Touch, Double Touch, One Finger Method, & VoiceOver) X four sessions (from the 1st to the 4th). To test the significance of the main effect, a Student Newman-Keuls (SNK) test was conducted as a post-hoc analysis. For the analysis, we assumed that for text-entry methods, the input speed would increase as sessions progress. Furthermore, we assumed that there would be significant differences among the four different input methods in terms of input speed.

V. RESULTS

In this section, we report results of the experiments; speed, accuracy and survey results.

A. Speed

Fig. 6 shows means of the speed measured in the four sessions for each text-entry method. The unit for speed is SPL, which indicates the time taken to input one letter. Hence, the higher SPL value means that it takes longer time to input.

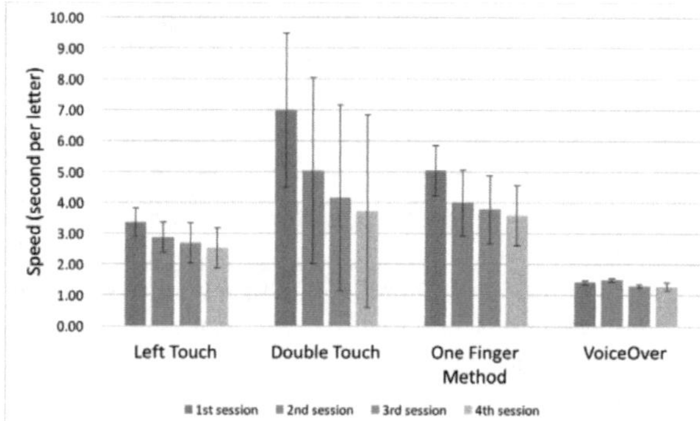

Figure 6. Speed results for the four text-entry methods across sessions (error bars± standard error).

Fig. 6 shows that VoiceOver (Mean SPL=1.38, SD=0.11) is the fastest among the four different text-entry methods compared ($F_{3,9}=14.69$, $p<0.001$). It was then followed by Left Touch (Mean SPL=2.86, SD=0.55), One Finger Method (Mean SPL=4.10, SD=0.91), and Double Touch (Mean SPL=4.98, SD=2.06). There was no significant difference between Double Touch and One Finger Method. The speeds among Left Touch, Double Touch and VoiceOver were significantly different from each other.

In terms of sessions, there was a significant effect ($F_{3,9}=23.98$, $p<0.001$). The first session was much slower than the others, with means of 4.20 SPL, 3.35 SPL (2nd), 2.99 SPL (3rd), and 2.78 SPL (4th), respectively. The SNK analysis indicates that the 1st session was significantly different from the 3rd, the 4th sessions. There was no significant difference in terms of speed for sessions of the 2nd, the 3rd and the 4th sessions.

There was a significant text-entry × session interaction ($F_{9,27}=3.84$, $p<0.01$).

To find the learnability effect of each text-entry, an ANOVA test was performed with the speed of sessions for each text-entry method as the dependent variables.

1) Left Touch

For Left Touch, the ANOVA test results show that there is a significant effect of session ($F_{3,9}=28.82$, $p<0.0001$). Although there was no significant difference between the 2nd and 3rd sessions, the 1st, 2nd, and 4th sessions were significantly different from each other. Since the speed became faster in the later sessions, the analysis result confirms that there is the learnability effect in Left Touch.

2) Double Touch

There were significant effects of session for Double Touch ($F_{3,9}=7.08$, $p<0.01$). Similar to the Left Touch, the speed became faster as sessions are repeated. However, the learnability effect was less than the effect observed in Left Touch. There was no significant difference in the 2nd, 3rd, and 4th sessions. Only the 1st session was significantly different from other sessions.

3) One Finger Method

Similar to the Double Touch method, significant effects in session were found for One Finger Method ($F_{3,9}=9.22$, $p<0.01$). While the speed became faster as sessions were repeated, there was no significant difference in the 2nd, 3rd, and 4th sessions. Only the 1st session was significantly different from other sessions. From that, it was found that the learnability effect of the One Finger Method was less than that of the Left Touch method.

4) VoiceOver

As expected, VoiceOver had little effect on learnability because the participants were already familiar with this method. Although the test results show that there was a significant effect of session ($F_{3,9}=5.85$), it was mainly due to the fastest speed of the 2nd session, which is significantly different from others. There was no significant difference in the 1st, 3rd, and 4th sessions. Note that Voiceover did not have any significant improvement in speed, whereas other text-entry methods showed about 20% improvements in speed from the first session and onward.

B. Accuracy

Regarding accuracy, there was no significant difference among the four text-entry methods, as measured in the number of errors in text input, because all participants corrected errors whenever they found them. Therefore, we analyzed the number of deleting action during the experiments instead. We set the number of deleting per letter, NPL, as a unit of analysis.

There were no significant main effects in both text-entry method ($F_{3,9}=2.26$, $p>0.05$) and session ($F_{3,9}=2.99$, $p>0.05$).

The mean number of deleting for Left Touch, Double Touch, One Finger Method, and VoiceOver were 0.0201 NPL, 0.0398 NPL, 0.0882 NPL, and 0.0507 NPL respectively. In other words, when the user types 100 letters, he/she only deleted letters 2 to 8 times only.

C. Survey Results

After completing all the experiments, we asked for participants' opinion through the survey and semi-structured interview. As shown in Table 2, in terms of ease of use, Left Touch and One Finger Method received the highest scores. VoiceOver received the highest score in willingness to use. In the satisfaction factor, the participants rated both Left Touch and Double Touch methods highly satisfactory.

TABLE II. SURVEY RESULTS ON A LIKERT SCALE (1= strongly disagree, 5= strongly agree).

	Left Touch	**Double Touch**	**One Finger Method**	**Voice Over**
Ease of use	4.25	3.00	4.25	3.75
Willingness to use	4.00	4.00	3.50	5.00
Satisfaction	4.00	4.00	3.25	3.75

VI. DISCUSSION

In this section, we discuss results of experiments

A. Speed

Among the four text-entry methods compared, it was observed that VoiceOver was the fastest one. For the accurate analysis, we used the speed from only the 3rd and 4th session, since three text-entry methods except VoiceOver showed the learnability effect. VoiceOver was still the fastest among the four different text-entry methods with 1.29 SPL. It was then followed by Left Touch (2.60 SPL), One Finger Method (3.68 SPL), and Double Touch (3.94 SPL). Left Touch was twice slower than the VoiceOver but 39% faster than the One Finger Method.

To compare this with results from previous research that used word per minute (WPM), we converted the speed unit from SPL to WPM [2][12]. The converted speed for our participants was 9.30 WPM that was faster than the speed of the methods proposed in [2], 0.66 WPM and [12], which was 2.11 WPM [12]. We speculate that the reason for large differences between our participants and the others is likely due to the following reasons; 1) all participants were experts of VoiceOver who had used the system for more than two years. 2) All participants were university students who were relatively heavy users of smart phones. This is also one of the reasons that magnify the speed difference between VoiceOver and others.

In contrast to the extensive experience of using VoiceOver, participants used other three text-entry methods for 100 minutes only. This difference was also a significant factor that affected the speed of other text-entry methods.

In case of other three text-entry methods, the speed increased with the number of sessions (Fig. 6). It indicates that there were the effects on learnability for three text-entry methods. Hence, it is possible to improve speed if users have more time to use. Two participants described that they felt experienced in using Left Touch, and that the speed would increase as time went by. Both of them mentioned that they liked to use the Braille system.

Quote 1 (P2). I think this (Left Touch) will be convenient, because I am familiar with the Braille system. It will be faster if I get used to it, since it only needs six times of touching.

Quote 2 (P3). The Braille system was made for the visually-impaired, so it is very convenient for us. I think it (using Left Touch) may become faster.

Quote 3 (P3). At first, I tried to think what to touch. For example, to touch 't', I have to touch that button. However, as I used Left Touch over time, my finger naturally moved. It felt like my finger moved automatically without even thinking.

Quote 4 (P4). In case of Left Touch, I felt my finger moved faster than my thinking, because I could remember the pattern of Braille.

The participants have conceived the shape and pattern of Braille through years, so the process of recalling Braille character is highly natural and easy to them. Using the Braille-based system, we can support natural text-entry for visually-impaired users. Hence, we assumed that it is worthwhile to make comparison among the Braille-based method to identify which factors are important in terms of improving the Braille typing speed. We report them in the following section.

1) Double Touch vs. Left Touch

Left Touch was faster than Double Touch. Both Double Touch and Left Touch are based on the two-button interface. However, the number of buttons for touching an alphabet is different. In Double Touch, a user touches at least 6 times, and 12 times in worst case, whereas in Left Touch, a user touches 6 times in every case. In addition, the mapping rule in Left Touch is more natural as the order of pushing buttons is same as the conventional order of entering Braille characters explained earlier. Hence, we believe that Left Touch is the better method to apply the two-button interface than Double Touch.

2) Left Touch vs. One Finger Method

There are two main differences between Left Touch and One Finger Method; 1) One Finger Method is based on the six-button interface, so users have to change the position of fingers. 2) Different from Left Touch, the number of touching is not fixed in the One Finger Method. In Left Touch, although the average number of touching is more than other text-entry methods such as VoiceOver and One Finger Method, a user does not have to change position of fingers. From this comparison, we believe that limiting the range of finger movements and having the fixed number of touching are more important than reducing the average number of touching. This finding is also supported by the users' quotes during the interview:

Quote 5 (P1). If I can figure out the exact position of each button, the One Finger Method will be better. However, it is very difficult for visually-impaired people.

Quote 6 (P3). I do not like the One Finger Method because the finger movement is too much.

B. Accuracy

We measured the error rates of text-entry methods using the NPL numbers. The measured data ranged from 2% to 8%, which is much smaller than the results in the previous research in which the error rate of expert group was 14.5%, and that of the average group was 33.1% [14]. Our participants might have been more careful not to make typing errors compared to those in the previous research.

C. Satisfaction

Satisfaction is a subjective factor. After completing all the experiments, we conducted the survey and semi-structured interviews to collect participants' opinion.

Both of the proposed two-button interfaces, Left Touch and Double Touch were well-received by the participants because their dependency on auditory sense was lessened. Fig. 7 (left) and (right) show the pictures of the participants

Figure 7. Different postures for VoiceOver (left) and Left Touch (right).

using VoiceOver and Left Touch taken in a noisy place during the survey.

When visually-impaired people use VoiceOver, they cannot input without hearing auditory feedback. Therefore, the participant in the Fig. 7 placed the mobile phone close to her ear (Fig. 7 (left)). In case of Left Touch, they can recognize the patterns of each letter, thereby using auditory sense as an assistive means not as the essential one. Note that the participant in Fig. 7 (right) placed the mobile phone on the table far from her ears. The participants mentioned about this advantage of being less dependent on auditory feedback during the interview, as follows:

Quote 7 (P1). When I use VoiceOver, I cannot hear any other sound. I have to concentrate on VoiceOver's audio feedback.

Quote 8 (P2). I cannot use VoiceOver in such a noisy place. When I used a folder phone, I could input without hearing any sound. However, now I cannot do that (with VoiceOver).

From this, we believe that Left Touch is more effective in a noisy place than VoiceOver, because its dependency on auditory sense is relatively less.

D. Ease of Use

Left Touch and One Finger Method were well received in terms of the ease of use. Both of them are based on the Braille system and use relatively simple input patterns.

In contrast, Double Touch received lower scores. The reason might be that Double Touch has a variable number of touching for a letter and that the order of button is different from the original Braille system as explained earlier. From this observation, we believe that distinguishing marked and unmarked dots in a Braille character by spatial differences is likely to be more user-friendly than distinguishing them using the difference in the number of touching. Note that VoiceOver also received a lower score than Left Touch. Some participants complained that the input method of VoiceOver had been too complex although they were used to VoiceOver.

E. Willingness to Use

All Participants gave five points for VoiceOver in terms of the willingness to use. The fast speed and familiarity were the main reasons behind this result, as indicated in the following quotes:

Quote 9 (P1). Until now, there is no replacement for VoiceOver.

Quote 10 (P2). I gave 5 points for VoiceOver in the 'Willingness to Use' factor because it is the most convenient for now, anyway.

Participants gave a higher score for the Left Touch than the One Finger Method because of its usability and simplicity.

F. Additional Feedback on the Two-Button Interface

In this research, we proposed two text-entry methods that are based on the two-button interface. Between Left Touch and Double Touch, we found that Left Touch is better than Double Touch in terms of speed and ease of use.

Participants suggested some interesting ideas for the potential application where two-button interface can be used. For instance, they wanted to use it in large screen interfaces.

From this feedback, we think that large screen interfaces in public places could be another exciting application for Left Touch because users do not have to fully concentrate on audio feedback, and do not have to scan the screen for input. This kind of approach matches with the ability-based design introduced by Wobbrock et al. [15] that suggested a design interface to utilize the full range of human potential not to focus on disabilities.

Quote 11 (P3). Left Touch can be used for other applications. For example, ATM has the touchscreen interface but I cannot use it appropriately. Of course, there is audio feedback, but it takes long time to use. If there were Left Touch in ATM, it would be convenient.

Quote 12 (P4). It (two-button interface) would be good if we use it in large touchscreens such as reservation machines in a train station. If we use VoiceOver in large screen, it would be difficult to scan, but we can apply the Two-button interface easily in large screens.

VII. FUTURE WORK

There were a few limitations in this research. The followings are plans to do further work.

A. Automatic Correction System

iPhone has an automatic correction system. For convenience, Left Touch and Double Touch should have such an automatic correction system like iPhone, which could greatly reduce the number of actions for deleting and restarting, thereby increasing speed of text-entry methods.

B. Abbreviation

Many visually-impaired people are familiar to use abbreviations for frequently used English words like 'with' and 'out'. However, Left Touch and Double Touch currently do not support such abbreviations. The participants were confused when they inputted some words that have well-known abbreviations. If the system supports abbreviations, it could significantly reduce the number of touching and eventually improve the speed for text-entry.

C. Finding Suitable Applications

Some participants suggested that the two-button interface would be applicable for large screen applications. As future research work, we plan to evaluate the strength of two-button interface by conducting experiments based on large screens, such as tablet PC or large touchscreen machines in public spaces. Furthermore, by conducting experiments in noisy places, we plan to evaluate the strength of low dependency on auditory feedback in our proposed methods.

D. Needs for Longitudinal Study

This study lacks the number of participants and period of using proposed methods. To get valid and statistically significant results, future work with more participants is needed. In addition, participants' experience of VoiceOver and proposed method is disparate. Therefore, for fair comparison, we plan to conduct longitudinal study for proposed methods.

VIII. CONCLUSION

In this study, we proposed two types of touchscreen text-entry methods for visually-impaired users, called Left Touch and Double Touch. The key components of the proposed mechanisms are to use the two-button interface and the Braille system. The proposed two-button interface limits the range of finger movements on a touchscreen; hence, visually-impaired users can input English letters more comfortably. Although the experiment results showed that the proposed methods were slower than the VoiceOver, we believe that familiarity played a major role for the results as indicated by the learnability effect and survey feedback. The survey results also indicated that the Left Touch method, in particular, had various strengths such as ease of use and satisfaction. All participants agreed that Left Touch was easier and simpler to use than VoiceOver. Compared to the VoiceOver that requires visually-impaired users to rely on audio feedback, the proposed schemes do not have such limitations. Based on the overall feedback from the participants, we expect that our proposed scheme can be easily used for large screen applications or in noisy settings including movie theaters, bus terminals or restaurants.

REFERENCES

[1] "Apple. Accessibility" [Online]. Available from: https://www.apple.com/accessibility/ios/voiceover/ [accessed:2017-01-17]

[2] M. N. Bonner, J. T. Brudvik, G. D. Abowd, and W. K. Edwards, "No-look notes: accessible eye-free multi-touch text entry", In Pervasive Computing, Springer Berlin Heidberg, 2010, pp. 409-426.

[3] G. Evreinov and R. Raisamo, " Tactile pointer for touchscreen manipulations", In Proc. HANDICAP, 2002, pp. 137-142.

[4] "Google. Google Translate," [Online]. Available from: https://translate.google.com. [accessed: 2017-01-17]

[5] T. Guerreiro, P. Lagoá, H. Nicolau, D. Gonçalves, and J. A. Jorge, "From tapping to touching: Making touch screens accessible to blind users", IEEE MultiMedia, 2008.

[6] "HIMS International," [Online]. Available from: http://www.himsintl.co.kr/?r=ko&m=shop&cat=6&uid=27&frameTab=1 [accessed: 2017-01-17]

[7] S. K. Kane, J. P. Bigham, and J. O. Wobbrock, "Slide rule: making mobile touch screens accessible to blind people using multi-touch interaction techniques", In Proc. of the 10th international ACM SIGACCESS conference on Computers and accessibility, 2008, pp. 73-80.

[8] S. K. Kane, J. O. Wobbrock, and R. E. Ladner, "Usable gestures for blind people: understanding preference and performance", In Proc. Of the SIG SIGCHI Conference on Human Factors in Computing Systems, 2011, pp. 413-422.

[9] I. S. MacKenzie and R. W. Soukoreff, " Phrase sets for evaluating on Human factors in computing systems", In CHI'03 extended abstracts on Human factors in computing systems, 2003, pp. 754-755.

[10] S. Mascetti, C. Bernareggi, and M. Belotti, "TypeInBraille: a braille-based typing application for touchscreen devices", In The proceedings of the 13th international ACM SIGACCESS conference on Computers and accessibility, 2011, pp.295-296.

[11] N. Paisios, A. Rubinsteyn, and L. Subramanian, "Mobile brailler: Making touch-screen typing accessible to visually impaired users", In Workshop on Frontiers in Accessibility for Pervasive Computing, 2012.

[12] J. Oliveira, T. Guerreiro, H. Nicolau, J. Jorge, and D. Gonçalves, "BrailleType: unleashing braille over touch screen mobile phone", In Human-Computer Interaction–INTERACT, Springer Berlin Heidelberg, 2011, pp. 100-107.

[13] J. Oliveira, T. Guerreiro, H. Nicolau, J. Jorge, and D. Gonçalves, "Blind people and mobile touch-based text-entry: acknowledging the need for different flavors", In The proceedings of the 13th international ACM SIGACCESS conference on Computers and accessibility, 2011, pp. 179-186.

[14] C. Souther, J. Clawson, B. Frey, G. Abowd, and M. Romero, "An evaluation of BrailleTouch: mobile touchscreen text entry for the visually impaired", In Proceedings of the 14th international conference on Human-computer interaction with mobile devices and services, 2012, pp. 317-326.

[15] J. O. Wobbrock, S. K. Kane, K. Z. Gajos, S. Harada, and J. Froehlich, "Ability-based design: Concept, principles and examples", ACM Transactions on Accessible Computing (TACCESS), 2011, 3(3), 9.

[16] G. Yfantidis and G. Evreinov, "Adaptive blind interaction technique for touchscreens", Universal Access in the Information Society, 2006, 4(4), pp. 328-337.

[17] K. Ushida, Y. Sekine, and S. Hasegawa, "IPPITSU: A one-stroke text entry method for touch panels using Braille system", In 2014 IEEE 3rd Global Conference on Consumer Electronics, 2014, pp. 374-375.

[18] B. Niazi, S. Khusro, A. Khan, and I. Alam, "A Touch Sensitive Keypad Layout for Improved Usability of Smartphones for the Blind and Visually Impaired Persons", In Artificial Intelligence Perspectives in Intelligent Systems, 2016, pp. 427-436.

[19] S. Heni, W. Abdallah, D. Archambault, G. Uzan, and M. S. Bouhlel, "An Empirical Evaluation of MoonTouch: A Soft Keyboard for Visually Impaired People", In International Conference on Computers Helping People with Special Needs, 2016, pp. 472-478.

Towards Accessibility Guidelines of Interaction and User Interface Design for Alzheimer's Disease Patients

Fatma Ghorbel[1, 2], Elisabeth Métais[2], Nebrasse Ellouze[1], Fayçal Hamdi[2], Faiez Gargouri[1]
[1] Laboratoire MIRACL, Université de Sfax, Sfax, Tunisie
[2] Laboratoire CEDRIC, Conservatoire National des Arts et Métiers (CNAM), Paris, France
E-mail: fatmaghorbel6@gmail.com, metais@cnam.fr, nebrasse.ellouze@gmail.com, faycal.hamdi@cnam.fr, faiez.gargouri@isimsf.rnu.tn

Abstract—**The number of people suffering from Alzheimer's disease is increasing. In a world which is more and more dependent on computing and Internet, this group of users is be-coming technologically isolated, due to the ill-suited design of user interfaces. Thus, in this paper, we propose a set of accessibility guidelines for designing user interfaces for adults diagnosed with Alzheimer's disease. These guidelines are identified after a comprehensive review of the literature. We identify 147 design guidelines that are grouped under 11 categories and 9 criterions. The aim of this work is to ensure that software applications and websites become accessible and easy to use to this demographic. The result of this work is a set of design guidelines, helpful for developers, designers, content producers, researchers and usability specialists. The proposed set of accessibility guidelines were applied for designing the user interfaces of a software application that target Alzheimer's patients (CAPTAIN MEMO memory prosthesis). Then, we evaluated the accessibility of the developed user interfaces. 24 Alzheimer's disease patients entered the study. The results confirmed that the developed user interfaces are accessible.**

Keywords- Human-computer interaction; User interface; Accessibility guidelines; Design-for-all; Alzheimer's Disease

I. INTRODUCTION

The prevalence of Alzheimer's Disease (AD) is increasing rapidly [1]. The AD association reports that, in 2016, the worldwide prevalence of this disease is estimated at nearly 44 million cases. With aging of the population [1]-[4], this number will increase to more than 86.7 million cases by the year 2050 [1]. The annual incidence worldwide is estimated at 1.25 million cases, which is the equivalent of one new case every 25 seconds.

Individuals with AD present particular changes that differ from other user groups; parts of them are related to AD and the other parts are related to the expected effects of age. These changes impair individuals living with AD to use standard user interfaces. The difficulty in using user interfaces prevents individuals with AD from using software application and websites that can very well enhance their quality of life [5].

The design of user interfaces dedicated to AD patients should take into account their special needs to be accessible and easy to use [5].

A considerable amount of published works focused on designing user interfaces for older adults or people suffering from dementia. However, to the best of our knowledge, there is no work that defines a set of design guidelines for designing accessible user interfaces for AD patients.

The motivation for this paper arises from the growing number of AD patients and the number of technological advances that can enhance the lives of the AD patients [3], but are nearly unusable by them due to poor design.

In this paper, we propose a number of accessibility guidelines for designing user interfaces dedicated to people suffering from AD. The aim is to remove accessibility barriers. This work can be used as a starting point for designers, developers, content producers, researchers and usability specialists to set up application and websites projects for these particular users. Dementia is a degenerative brain condition which affects people at any age [5][6]. Its most common form is AD which, by itself, accounts for 50 to 80 percent of all dementia cases [4][6]. AD is a type of dementia that occurs most at the age of 65 years or older [6]. Thus, the set of accessibility guidelines, presented in this work, are mostly identified from relevant works on design of user interfaces for both elders and people with dementia available in the literature.

The remainder of this paper is structured as follows: Section II describes the methodology used to identify, extract and systematize the set of design guidelines presented in this paper. Section III reviews the characteristics of AD patients (AD-related changes and the age-related changes). In Section IV, a selection of the most relevant works on design guidelines of user interfaces for elders, people suffering from dementia, people with dyslexia and people with aphasia, available in the literature, are presented and summarized. Section V presents the proposed set of accessibility guidelines. In Section VI, we validate the proposed design guidelines on a software application that target AD patients (CAPTAIN MEMO memory prosthesis). At last, in Section VII, we conclude the present work and we propose some perspectives.

II. METHODOLOGY

In this section, we detail the methodology used to identify the set of accessibility guidelines presented in this work. We used a User-Centered Design (UCD) approach. The methodology is described in the following four phases:

Phase 1 -"Characteristics of AD patients": In a User-Centered Design approach, we firstly study the problems of the target user group.

Phase 2 – "Studies selection": From the literature, we select a set of the most relevant works that focus on designing of user interfaces for older adults, persons with dementia, people with dyslexia and people with aphasia.

Phase 3 – "Extraction": In this phase, we perform a triage to extract the design guidelines from the selected works identified in Phase 2. Then, we regroup the initial set of accessibility guidelines according to problems identified in Phase 1. Then, we do another arrangement process to generate unique guidelines and avoid redundancy, since many guidelines, from different authors, present similar statements. The final step in Phase 3 is to add, for each category, the missing design guidelines.

Phase 4 – "Consolidation": In this phase, we do another grouping process. We group the design guidelines, contained in each category, based on a similarity criterion.

III. Characteristics of Alzheimer's Patients

This section discusses the usual changes which accompany AD patient. Most people with AD are old. Thus, they have the expected limitations associated with the age [2]. So, compared to healthy young people, AD patients suffer from AD-related changes and age-related changes.

A. Alzheimer's Disease-Related Changes

We group the disabilities related to AD into the following five groups.

"*Memory impairments*" - The most common symptoms of AD is the memory impairments [1][4]-[6], especially the short-term memory that means forgetting the recently learned information. The semantic information is normally preserved in long-term memory [2], e.g., languages.

"*Cognitive impairments*" - The cognitive ability decline due to AD [1][4][5]. Cognition is the ability to think, to generate ideas, to focus on and to remember. AD causes a decrease in cognitive abilities, such as the ability to solve matters, level of intelligence, reasoning, judgment, capability to learn and speed of information processing.

"Attention and concentration changes" - People with AD experience changes in attention and concentration. They are more easily distractible by details and noise [23].

"*Personality changes*" - Persons with AD experience changes in mood and personality [4][6]. The national Alzheimer's association reports that over 40% of AD patients suffer from depression. AD patients may refuse to learn and they are anxious about new technology [3].

"*Declining language abilities*" - AD patients suffer from a decline in language and communication abilities [4][6]. In fact, AD patients in early stage can substitute the words that have the same meaning. Patients showing moderate sign of AD have an increased difficulty in naming things.

B. Age-Related Changes

We group the disabilities related to aging into the following six groups.

"*Visual impairments*" – The elderly suffer from a decline in their vision [2]-[4][6]-[11]. Aging is related to an impairment of near-focus including a computer screen [2][7][8], a loss in visual acuity [4][5][8][10], decline in dark adaptation [3][8][10], decrease in color sensitivity [2][3][7][8] and decrease in peripheral vision [2][7]-[10]. The Alzheimer's association estimates that up to 60% of person with AD suffer from a decline in at least one visual capacity.

"*Hearing impairments*" – Age is accompanied by decreases in the auditory acuity [2]-[4][6]-[10]. At the age of 65 years and above, over 30% of women and 50% of men suffer from hearing impairments [8]. The elderly may experience another complaint that they can hear others talking, but they can't make out the words [2]. They may have difficulty to follow the synthetic speech [3]. They find it hard to follow long sentences [9].

"*Mobility impairments*" - Adults experience a decline in their motor functions [3][4][6]-[11]. Old people with manual dexterity impairments find it hard to operate with the keyboard and the pointing device [3][7]-[9]. They may have difficulty to position the cursor if the target is too small [8][9], maintain continuous movements [3] and control fine movements [9]. Because of the reduced mobility, more errors may occur during fine movements [8][9].

"*Decent/no computers skills*" – The older generations are not proficient in using computer and related technologies [3][23].

"*Decent/no literacy skills*" – Nowadays, the illiteracy rate of adults aged more than 65 years are important [23]. In addition, many adults have basic literacy skills. They may not fully understand text-based information. Older adults may have difficulties with typing since they forget how to write correctly the words [23].

"*Declining speech abilities*" – The speech ability decrease with age due to the reduced mobility of tongue and lips [9]. The elderly have difficulty to pronounce complex words. Thus, inputs via the speech modality can be limited by voice tremors. The elderly need more time to produce words sentence [9].

Based on these changes, we are convinced by the fact that AD patients face several difficulties if we adopt standard user interfaces in software applications or websites.

IV. Studies Selection

From the literature, we select the most relevant seventeen works, published between 2005 and 2015, divided into nine works on design guidelines for older adults, four works on design guidelines for people suffering from dementia, two works on web accessibility and people with dyslexia and two works on design guidelines for adults with aphasia.

A. Review of Design Guidelines of User Interfaces for Elderly People

Works on design guidelines for older adults are divided into works for designing web pages [7][11][12], mobile user interfaces [13], multi-touch user interfaces [10], multimodal user interfaces [9], user interfaces for games [3] and user interfaces for both websites and software application [2][8].

Arch and Abou-Zhara [7] summarize the main age-related changes, addressing specifically, vision decline, hearing loss, motor impairment and cognitive effects. After, they suggest teen accessibility guideline for designing websites and web applications.

Darvishy and Good [11] present 9 areas of guidance for designing elderly friendly web pages, e.g., structure, language, navigation and search. For each of these areas, the authors define a list of checkpoints which can be used to test the accessibility of web pages.

Zaphiris et al. [12] identify of a set of 38 age-centered web design guidelines which are grouped under 11 categories such as target design, links and navigation.

Al-Razgan et al. [13] discuss a set of design guidelines for touch based mobile phones that target old people. These guidelines are grouped in three categories: look and feel, interaction and functionality.

Loureiro and Rodrigues [10] identify a number of 113 accessibility guidelines that focus on the design of multi-touch interfaces for elders. The authors regroup the identified guidelines under 10 categories such as user cognitive design, text design and audio.

Jian et al. [9] review the changes related to aging, precisely, changes in vision, speech ability, hearing, motor abilities, attention, memory and intellectual ability. Then, they present a set of design principles for designing multimodal interfaces for the elderly.

IJsselsteijn et al. [3] review the expected changes related to the aging process specifically, changes in sensory-perceptual processes, motor abilities, response speed and cognitive processes. For each age-related change, they propose a number of accessibility guidelines for designing user interfaces of games that target elderly users.

Farage et al. [2] summarize the main age-related changes. The changes fall into several 5 categories: vision, hearing, touch and temperature perception, memory and cognition and balance and mobility. For each one age-related change are suggested a number of concrete design guidelines to attenuate these limitations.

Williams et al. [8] review the barriers the elderly face when using computer. Then, they present solutions for these problems. The difficulties are categorized into: cognition, auditory, haptic, visual, and motor-based troubles.

B. *Review of Design Guidelines of User Interfaces for People Suffering from Dementia*

Friedman and Bryan [14] are the first to formally present a set of web guidelines for designing user interfaces targeting people with cognitive disabilities, including AD patients.

The Web Accessibility Initiative (WAI) proposes a set of guidelines of web guidelines for people with cognitive or neuronal disabilities and the accessibility barriers to this target user group [15].

COGA presents the results of a study conducted to identify matters and solutions concerning web accessibility for person suffering from cognitive disabilities [16].

Moutinho [4] presents a set of accessibility guidelines for designing mobile phone for demented old people.

C. *Review of Design Guidelines of User Interfaces for People with Dyslexia*

De Santana et al. [17] offer a set of 41 web accessibility for people with dyslexia, including people with cognitive disabilities and older adults.

Rello et al. [18] present a number of design guidelines that aim to present texts displayed in web pages in more accessible way targeting dyslexic users. The guidelines are based in quantitative and qualitative results collected from a set of an experimental study carried out with people suffering from dyslexia. These guidelines are categorized into the following categories: font and background, colors, font size, character, line and paragraph spacing and column width.

D. *Review of Design Guidelines of User Interfaces for People with Aphasia*

Kane and Galbraith [19] list a set of 7 accessibility guidelines for designing a voting technology for adults suffering from aphasia and other communication disabilities.

Daemen et al. [20] present the design and evaluation of a storytelling software application for people with aphasia. The design guidelines are categorized into 3 categories: simplicity, structure and layout and use of accessible and portable technology.

V. ACCESSIBILITY GUIDELINES

A set of 147 distinct design guidelines resulted from Phase 3. They were grouped under 11 distinct category headings, covering the main age-related changes and AD-related changes. They were categorised into AD-related guidelines and age-related guidelines, as illustrated in Figure 1.

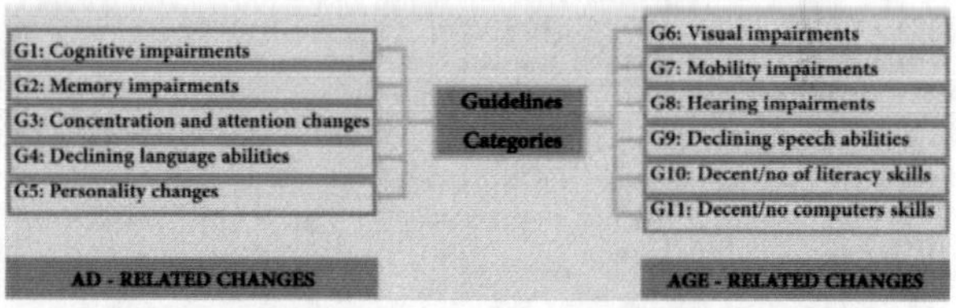

Figure 1. Guidelines categories.

In Phase 4, we did a second triage. For each category, we grouped the guidelines based on a similarity criterion. This process resulted in 9 criterions carefully labeled to represent common elements in the user interfaces. The criterions are: "*Visual elements*", "*Textual and pictorial content*", "*Navigation*", "*Customization*", "*Feedback and support*", "*Audio*", "*Inputs*", "*Multi-touch interactions*" and "*Hardware*".

The full set of accessibility guidelines ordered by category and criterion is presented in Table I.

TABLE I. THE PROPOSED DESIGN GUIDELINES

G1: Memory Impairments	
"Feedback and support"	Give feedback after every action [4][14][16]; Use short feedback messages; Give consistent feedback messages [4];

	Help users in their interaction e.g., through a speaking front end; Provide help tutorials [12]; Provide event-based reminders [2];
"Navigation"	Ensure that navigation is consistent throughout the website or application e.g., similar fonts, colors and sizes, the use of the same set of buttons menu in the same place on each screen, the use the same symbols and icons throughout the website/ application, consistent hyperlinks [10][14][16][17]; Make difference between visited and unvisited hyperlinks [12][17]; Change the color of the visited links;
"Textual and pictorial content"	Provide short paragraphs [16][17]; Provide short sentences [2][4][17];
G2: Cognitive Impairments	
"Textual and pictorial content"	Ensure that text is simple and facile to understand [2][3][4][9]-[12][14][16][17][19][20]; Avoid abbreviations and symbols [16]; Use active voice rather than passive voice [10][17]; Avoid using double negatives [17]; Don't hyphenate words at the end of phrases[14]; Provide simple examples [14]; Ensure that grammar and spelling are correct [16]; Categorise content semantically into short categories [10][11][16][19]; Express only one idea per paragraph; Provide summaries or a table of contents for lengthy content [16]; Give each page and frame a title [14]; Highlight keywords and main information [12][16]; Provide the fewest possible of choices to users [10][12]; Provide content in many multimedia mediums e.g., text, videos, pictures, audio [2][4][15]-[17][19]; Provide content through multiple modalities [3][4]; When possible, give alternative representations to numerical content e.g., charts and graphs [19]; Provide simple and facile to understand images and icons [3][10][12][16][20]; Make sure that images and icons have an alternative text (alt attribute) [12][14][15][17]; Avoid pure images and icons , place them near the significant description [9][13][15]; Provide users enough time to use or read content [12];
"Visual elements"	Highlight information via boxes [14]; Use uppercase to highlight keywords [2]; Display main information on the center of the screen [2][4][10][12]; Put a space to separate paragraphs [18]; Put a spacing line between paragraphs [17]; Underline only links [16][17]; Use different colors to categorize information visually [17]; Place the search field in the upper right or upper left side of the screen;
"Navigation"	Avoid deep hierarchies [10]; Name links in a bulleted list [12]; Provide descriptive links [11][14] e.g., do not use "click here" [17];
"Feedback and support"	Ensure that error feedback messages provide mechanisms for resolving the error [16]; Ask for confirmation before critical instructions [4]; Make actions as simple as possible [19][20];
"Multi-touch interaction"	Ensure that the screen is not off when being idle [13]; Separate keypads for numbers and letters [13];

G3: Attention and concentration changes	
"Visual elements"	Provide simple design [2][3][8][14][17][20]; Devise the layout of the screen as simple as possible [9][20]; Display only important information [2][3][10][12][16][17]; Avoid utilising too much colors [9][20]; Avoid utilising too much images; Avoid unnecessary decoration [4]; Avoid details ; Ensure that images are not only for decoration [9][12][10]; Avoid animation e.g., animated images, moving text [10][12][14][17]; Add simple and slow animation only in necessary cases; Remove from the user interfaces unnecessary elements calling attention such as ads banners [2][9][11][16]; Limit the number of the used fonts [14]; Present only one message in a single user interface [10];
"Audio"	Remove background music or sound distractions[10][16];
"Navigation"	Provide a maximum of 6 links in the menu [14];
G4: Personality changes	
"Textual and pictorial content"	Use wordings that suit the semantic field of elderly; Include pictures of old people or old thing; Add fun and humour e.g., funny emoticons;
"Feedback and support"	Ensure that error feedback messages make it clear that the user is not the cause of the problem[10]; Ensure that feedback messages are not in commando-style; Provide encouraging feedback messages to allow users experience some level of success [3];
G5: Declining language abilities	
"Inputs"	Reduce the need for keyboarding e.g., selecting choices from a dropdown list [4][14];
G6: Visual impairments	
"Visual elements"	*/*Images and icons*/* Provide large images and icons [2][7][10][16][20]; */*Text presentation*/* Provide larger font type [2][7][9][10][13][14][16][20]: from 12 pt to 14 pt for body text and 16 pt for titles [9][12][14][17][18]; Avoid decorative font type [2][7][10][12]; Utilize a sans-serif font type e.g., Arial, Helvetica, Verdana and Tahoma [2][4][10][12][14][16][17][19]; Use medium face type; Avoid justified aligned text [17]; Use left text alignment [10][12][14][16]; Avoid large blocks of italic text or bold text or underlined text [7][14][17]; Use bold only to highlight keywords or titles; Use lower cases to write the main body [10][12][14][17][22]; Avoid the use of the shadow effect; Ensure that the spacing between lines is from 1,5 to 2 [10][12][14][16][17]; Use white space [16][17]; Ensure that the text size for printing is from 12 pt to 14 pt [2][17]; Avoid lengthy lines of text (more than about 70 characters per line) [14][16][18]; Provide large distance between words [18]; Avoid narrow columns [18]; */*Colors*/*

	Use soft colors [2][10][14]; Avoid fluorescent colors [7]; Avoid combinations of green and red or yellow and blue (for users suffering from some degree of colour-blindness) [10]; Maximize the contrast between the foreground and the background colors [2][4][10][12][14]-[19]; Avoid using tones of similar lightness near to each other; Provide maximized contrast between main information and its surroundings [4][9]; Avoid patterned backgrounds [2]; Avoid background images [17]; Avoid white color background [10][12][17]; Avoid dark color background; Avoid a pure black text on a pure white background[18]; Avoid the green and blue colors[12];
"Navigation"	Avoid transparent menus [17]; Provide large menu buttons [2][7][10][20]; Use links only at the end or at the beginning of the sentence [17];
"Customization"	Allow users adjust font type, color scheme (background color, text color, and printing colors), and text size at their will [3][10][14][17]; Make it facile for users to adjust contrast without needing to utilize browser controls; Allow users zooming the screen[3];
"Audio"	Use sounds to represent information available on the visual display;
"Hardware"	Avoid utilizing small-screen devices;
G7: Hearing impairments	
"Audio"	Utilize, by default, higher volume for delivering the auditory background [2]; Increase the duration of the sound beeps [10]; Use male voices [2][10]; Use natural speech than synthetic speech [2][3][10]; Reduce the speed of the auditory background [4]; Make a pause of some seconds after each spoken sentence [2]; Do not rely only on the auditory background [4];
"Customization"	Enable users to skip the audio background [19]; Enable users to replay auditory messages [10][19]; Enable users to control the volume themselves [2][10][14][15]; Enable users to adjust the speed of the audio background [19];
"Visual elements"	Ensure that the volume control is in a facile to find emplacement [8];
G8: Mobility impairments	
"Navigation"	Use static menus, and avoid fly-out or pull-down or dropdown menus [7][12][17]; Provide an audio supported menus; Avoid using scroll [3][10][12][14][16][17]; Ascertain that the minimum possible clicks are needed to do a given instruction; Use single mouse clicks[7][12]; Avoid difficult movements e.g., dragging[9];
"Inputs"	Provide a facile way to enter characters that need pressing at the same time two keys such as '@' and '€';
"Visual elements"	Increment the size of the zone round an hyperlink; Provide a cursor to show the selected information [10];
"Hardware"	Avoid slide-out or separated keyboards [13]; Use touch screen devices [9][20];
"Multi-touch interactions"	Provide large distance between buttons [13];
G9: Decent/no computers skills	
"Navigation"	Provide a site map [12][14][17]; Show the current location all the time [10][11][12]; Make the navigation menu visible all the time [10][17]; Provide "undo" or "back" button to help users recover if lose [9][14];
G10: Decent/no literacy skills	
"Textual and pictorial content"	Use images or soundings to supplement text-based information [2]-[4][14][17]; Use video to facilitate understanding text [14]; Avoid Roman Numerals [14];
"Inputs"	Minimize the use of keyboard [9]; Use automatic inputs as possible[4]; Utilize the speech-to-text or dictation mode for typing; Use spelling checker in input and search fields [10][12][14][16][17];
"Navigation"	Present menu buttons by icons and labels [17];
G11: Declining speech abilities	
"Inputs"	Use acoustic models dedicated to seniors for the speech recognizer [9].

VI. Validation on the CAPTAIN MEMO Memory Prosthesis

In order to evaluate the effectiveness of our work in providing a better interaction for people with AD, the proposed guidelines were applied for designing the user interfaces of the CAPTAIN MEMO memory aid [21].

CAPTAIN MEMO is developed in the context of the VIVA (« Vivre à Paris avec Alzheimer en 2030 grâce aux nouvelles technologies ») project [22] to help AD patients to palliate mnesic issues. In [23], we presented the design, development and evaluation of the user interfaces of this memory prosthesis. They are user-friendly, multimodal, configurable and enjoyable. Figure 2 shows a screenshot of CAPTAIN MEMO, which shows the user interface associated to the authentication step. This interface illustrates a number of guidelines presented before, including, but not limited to, the use of images to facilitate understanding text-based information (the key metaphor associated to the connection step), the use of a black font on an orange background to maximize the contrast between the foreground and background colors, the use of droll image (old parrot).

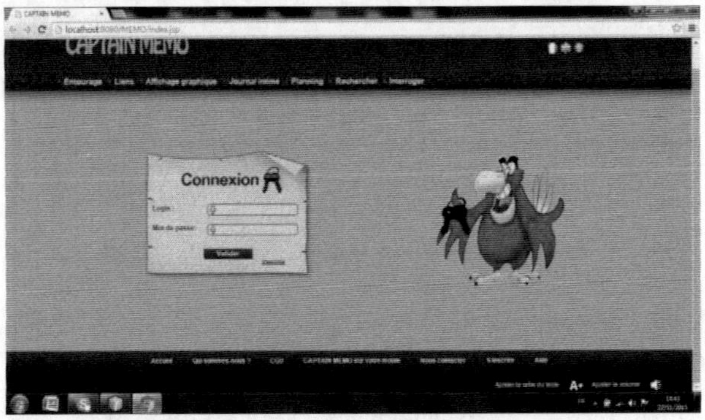

Figure 2. Screenshot of CAPTAIN MEMO which shows the user interface associated to the connection step.

The evaluation of the interfaces' accessibility and ease to use was carried out with 24 AD patients who are living in an assisted living environment in Sfax- Tunisia (Street Manzel Chaker km. 8). The participants had an average age of 64 years – the youngest is 55 years old and the oldest is 78. Most patients had AD in early/moderate stage. Their profiles were summarized in terms of age, stage of AD, difficulties in vision/hearing, computer skills and literacy skills.

This study was performed from July 2015 for about two months. Tasks were performed on tablet PC. A stylus pen is used to input commands to the touch-screen. The questionnaire covers five dimensions which include: "*Overall Reaction*", "*Visibility*", "*Speech-to-text*", "*Terminology*" and "*Auditory Background*". A five point scales are used: strongly disagree (1), disagree (2), neutral (3), agree (4) and strongly agree (5). Table II summarizes the results and the mean score for each dimension.

TABLE II. SUMMARY OF THE QUESTIONNAIRE'S RESULTS

Question	(1)	(2)	(3)	(4)	(5)	Mean
OVERALL REACTION (overall mean=4)						
Are the interfaces easy to use?		3	3	5	9	4
Is it easy to learn to use the interfaces?		7	3	10		3,15
Are the interfaces funny-to-use?			1	3	16	4,75
Are you satisfied about the interfaces?		3	3	3	11	4,1
VISIBILITY (overall mean=4.75)						
By default, can you read the main body?		4		4	12	4,2
By default, can you read headlines?				2	18	4,9
Is the ability to adjust text size useful?					20	5
Are images large enough?				2	18	4,9
SPEECH-TO-TEXT (overall mean=3.8)						
Is the speech-to-text mode helpful?	5			4	11	3,8
TERMINOLOGY (overall mean=4.72)						
Are the command names meaningful?				2	18	4,9
Icons are easy to understand?			2	3	15	4,65
Is the use of text labels improves the icon's interpretation?					20	5
Are error feedbacks helpful?		4	2	1	13	4,15
Are informative feedbacks straightforward?				2	18	4,9
AUDITORY BACKGROUND (overall mean=3.825)						
Is the voice speed reasonable?	6			10	4	3,3
Are vocal feedbacks useful?	6	2			12	3,5
Are spoken interactions helpful?	6	2			12	3,5
Is the ability to adjust volume useful?					20	5

Only 20 participants fully complete all tasks. The others just start the first test. They said that they are too old and have no motivation in learning a new technology. Those participants were the oldest with AD in moderate /late stage. They had no computer skills. We call them "patient-restricted users".

As shown in Table II, the overall mean score of the 5 dimensions is between 3.8 and 4.74. Overall, the results indicate that the users almost agreed that the developed interfaces are accessible and easy to use.

55% of all participants were strongly satisfied with the system. They said that they will use the CAPTAIN MEMO memory prosthesis frequently. Those participants suffer from AD in early stage, familiar with computers and have good literacy skills.

25% of all participants said that it is easier for them to type with a virtual keyboard since their voice volume is not enough to be captured by the device's microphone. Thus, in the next iteration, we will use acoustic models specialized for elderly persons for the speech recognizer. Illiterate participants were very satisfied with the dictation modality.

30% of all participants totally ignored the speaking front end since they did not understand words. Thereafter, in the next version, we will use slower voice speed.

VII. CONCLUSION AND FUTURE WORK

In this paper, we proposed a set of accessibility guidelines for designing user interfaces dedicated to older adults suffering from AD, refined and extracted from the most relevant works presented in the literature. This set of design guidelines is structured in a very detailed way, covering the main age-related changes and AD-related changes that might affect the usability of the interactivity in the user interfaces. Based on these design guidelines, we made the design of CAPTAIN MEMO that is developing to be used by AD patients. Afterward, a user satisfaction evaluation of the developed interfaces was carried out with individuals with AD. The results confirmed that they are user-friendly and easy to use.

We hope that the proposed set of guidelines will serve as an information base for application developers, designers, usability specialists and researchers to guiding and evaluating the design of user interfaces for AD patients.

Future work will be devoted to take into account the main characteristics of each different stages of AD. Then, we aim to set up a set of principles to adapt the user interfaces for each stages of this disease.

REFERENCES

[1] C. Riley-Doucet and D. Debnath, "Assistive technology for promoting physical and mental exercise to delay progression of cognitive degeneration in patients with dementia," The 2007 Ieee Biomedical Circuits and Systems Conference, December 2007, pp. 235-238.

[2] M. A. Farage, K. W. Miller, F. Ajayi, and D. Hutchins, "Design principles to accommodate older adults," Global journal of health science, vol. 4, March 2012, pp. 2.

[3] W. IJsselsteijn, H. H. Nap, Y. de Kort, and K. Poels, "Digital game design for elderly users," The 2007 conference on Future Play, November 2007, pp. 17-22.

[4] R. J. A. Moutinho, "A mobile phone navigator for older adults and persons with dementia," Master's thesis, Faculty of Engineering, University of Port, July 2011.

[5] C. Ancient and A. Good, "Issues with designing dementia-friendly interfaces," The International Conference on Human-Computer Interaction, July 2013, pp. 192-196.

[6] H.Niels, F. Truyen, and E. Duval, "Designing with dementia: guidelines for participatory design together with persons with dementia," The IFIP Conference on Human-Computer Interaction, September 2013, pp. 649-666.

[7] A. Arch and S. Abou-Zhara, "How web accessibility guidelines apply to design for the ageing population," The Accessible Design in a Digital World Conference, September 2008.

[8] D. Williams, M. Arif Ul Alam , S. Iqbal Ahamed, and W. Chu, "Considerations in designing human-computer interfaces for elderly people," The 13th International Conference on Quality Software, July 2013, pp. 372-377.

[9] C. Jian, N. Sasse, N. von Steinbüchel-Rheinwall, F. Schafmeister, H. Shi, C. Rachuy, and H. Schmidt, "Towards effective, efficient and elderly-friendly multimodal interaction," The 4th International Conference on PErvasive Technologies Related to Assistive Environments, May 2011, pp. 45.

[10] B. Loureiro and R. Rodrigues, "Design guidelines and design recommendations of multi-touch interfaces for elders," The Seventh International Conference on Advances in Computer-Human Interactions, March 2014, pp. 41-47.

[11] A. Darvishy and A. Good, "Inclusive websites for the elderly: user friendly guidelines for designers and managers of websites and applications," The International Conference on Human-Computer Interaction, July 2013, pp. 226-230.

[12] P. Zaphiris, M. Ghiawadwala and S.habana Mughal, "Age-centered research-based web design guidelines," The extended abstracts on Human factors in computing systems, April 2005,pp. 1897-1900.

[13] M. S. Al-Razgan, H. Al-Khalifa, and H. Alajmi, "Touch-based mobile phone interface guidelines and design recommendations for elderly people: a survey of the literature," The International Conference on Neural Information Processing, November 2012, pp. 568-574.

[14] M. G. Friedman and D. Nelson Bryen, "Web accessibility design recommendations for people with cognitive disabilities," Technology and Disability, vol. 19, pp. 205-212, 2012.

[15] S. Abou-Zahra, "How People with Disabilities Use the Web. Status: Draft Updated 1 August 2012," 2012. [Online]. Available from: http://www.w3.org/WAI/intro/people-use-Web/diversity (date of the last access: 05/11/2016).

[16] L. Seeman and M. Cooper, "Cognitive Accessibility User Research" 2015. [Online]. Available from: http://w3c.github.io/coga/user-research/ (date of the last access: 05/11/2016).

[17] V. F. de Santana, R. de Oliveira, L. D. A. Almeida, and M. C. C. Baranauskas, "Web accessibility and people with dyslexia: a survey on techniques and guidelines," The International Cross-Disciplinary Conference on Web Accessibility, April 2012.

[18] L. Rello, G. Kanvinde and R. Baeza-Yates, "Layout guidelines for web text and a web service to improve accessibility for dyslexics," The international cross-disciplinary conference on web accessibility, April 2012.

[19] S. K. Kane and C. Galbraith, "Design guidelines for creating voting technology for adults with aphasia," August 2013.

[20] E. Daemen, E. Daemen, P. Dadlani, J. Du, Y. Li, P. Erik-Paker, J. B. Martens, and B. De Ruyter, "Designing a free style, indirect, and interactive storytelling application for people with aphasia," The Human-Computer Interaction, September 2007, pp. 221-234.

[21] E. Métais, F. Ghorbel, N. Herradi, F. Hamdi, N. Lammari, D. Nakache, N. Ellouze, F. Gargouri, and A. Soukane, "Memory prosthesis," Non-pharmacological Therapies in Dementia, vol. 3, pp. 177-180, 2015.

[22] http://viva.cnam.fr/ (date of the last access: 02/11/2016)

[23] F. Ghorbel, N. Ellouze, E. Métais, F. Gargouri, F. Hamdi, and N. Herradi, "Designing and evaluating interfaces for the captain memo memory prosthesis," The Ninth International Conference on Advances in Computer-Human Interactions, April 2016, pp. 164-169.

Identifying Inexpensive Off-the-Shelf Laser Pointers for Multi-User Interaction on Large Scale Displays

Christopher S. Stuetzle
Dept. of Computer Science
Merrimack College
North Andover, Massachusetts 01845
Email: stuetzlec@merrimack.edu

Barb Cutler
Dept. of Computer Science
Rensselaer Polytechnic Institute
Troy, NY 12180
Email: cutler@cs.rpi.edu

Tyler Sammann
Dept. of Computer Science
Rensselaer Polytechnic Institute
Troy, NY 12180
Email: tylersammann@gmail.com

***Abstract*—We present a method for identifying inexpensive, off-the-shelf laser pointers in a multi-user interaction environment on large-scale displays. We identify a laser pointer's personality, a measure of its output in a particular context. Our method requires a set of inexpensive and unmodified green lasers, a large screen, a projector, and a camera with an infrared (IR) filter. The camera detects the IR spillover from the green laser beam, while ignoring color information projected onto the screen. During a calibration phase, a radial histogram of each laser's IR spillover are used to represent the laser's personality. Our system is able to identify the spots of a specific laser, allowing multiple users to simultaneously interact in the environment. In addition, we present a series of applications that take advantage of tracked and identified laser pointers to demonstrate large-scale, multi-user interactions.**

Keywords–Systems, man, and cybernetics; User interfaces; Human-computer interaction.

I. INTRODUCTION

Multi-user, large-scale interfaces, in which individual users are identified and tracked, present a challenging and worthwhile design problem. Collaborative problem solving is oftentimes easier to accomplish when sharing a large projection surface than when operating on individual screens (such as with mobile devices), and user interaction and U.I. design is simplified if all users operate on the same display. In applications in which efficient interactivity between users is important, laser pointer devices are preferable to stationary pointer devices, such as mice [1]. In most cases, the challenge of identifying individual users is tackled by physically modifying laser pointers, an effective yet often-times costly and time-consuming solution. To circumvent these drawbacks, we present the idea of describing a laser by its personality, a measure of the shape and intensity of a laser pointer's leaked infrared (IR) light, which allows us to track and identify an off-the-shelf laser pointer among a group of others for the purpose of multi-user collaborative applications.

Our contributions are:

- The *laser pointer personality*, the signature shape and intensity of a laser point's infrared light leakage, and the laser pointer personality system used to identify laser pointers by their personalities.
- Several multi-user applications that demonstrate the utility of the personality system.

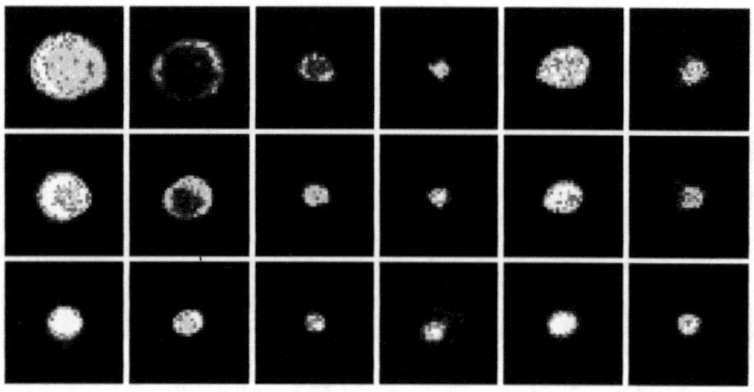

Figure 1. False color renderings of the IR spill from 6 inexpensive green laser pointers.

The rest of this paper is organized as follows. Section II describes the laser personality system. Section III discusses accuracy test results. Section IV discusses various applications that take advantage of the laser personality system. Section V closes the article.

A. Related Work

Single laser point detection is accomplished in two main ways: brightness filtering and IR filtering. Olsen and Nelson detect a laser spot on a large display screen with a two-pass system that detects red brightness with an applied convolution filter [2]. Oh and Stuerzlinger allow for multiple laser points by applying a threshold to the brightness field of the image [3]. The same technique is applied by Davis and Chen in their LumiPoint system [4]. However, depending on the brightness of the laser spot with respect to the rest of the image, this can create trouble due to its context sensitivity. Ahlborn et al. [5] present a system using multiple camera views, in which the background image is filtered out. IR filtering is employed by work by Qin et al. [6], Angelini et al. [7], and Cheng et al. [8].

In addition to laser spotting, one challenge in multi-user laser pointer systems is pointer identification. One method is to dynamically change the number of lasers present in the system at any given point in time, and to track an IDed laser spot across frames with predictive measures, such as the Kalman filter [9] [10] [8]. Another method involves the use of time division multiplexing, or the application of a laser blinking pattern, to identify a particular laser, as employed by Vogt et al. [11] [12], as well as Pavlovych and Stuerzlinger [13]. Francisco de la O Chavez et al., present a system whereby users can operate the electronic devices and appliances in their homes with a laser pointer [10]. Qinet al., present a system in which a special laser pointer is used to project several beams whose orientations indicate the angle of rotation along the beam axis of the laser [6]. Biet al. present the uPen, a laser pointer outfitted with right- and left-click buttons, designed to mimic computer mouse functionality [14]. Shizukiet al. present a series of gestures used with a laser pointer, and a series of applications using them [15]. In some applications, single laser pointer identification is all that is necessary, such as that by Miksiket el al. [16]. Each of these systems involves specialized hardware, and such additional cost. Our system requires only an I.R. filtered camera and cheap laser pointers.

II. Laser Pointer Personality System

To detect the current position of each laser pointer dot, we use a 1280 x 960 pixel monochrome, 33fps video camera. An IR pass filter in front of the camera blocks all visible light (from the projector), so we can robustly detect the bright points of IR light from the laser. We specifically use green laser pointers because the green light is produced indirectly from an infrared laser diode, and some of the infrared light remains for our detection. Most inexpensive green lasers do not include an IR filter to block this light.

We begin with a simple calibration step to determine the pixel to pixel correspondence between our camera and the 1920 x 1080 projector and projection surface, and to collect intensity data on all lasers in the system. Our system has been tested on screens as tall as 18 feet (2.44 meters). Calibration consists of hovering each laser point on several known locations on the screen for a period of time. When tracking multiple lasers simultaneously, we use the Kuhn-Munkres, a.k.a. Hungarian Algorithm [17] [18] [19] to match the lasers from frame to frame. This method produces a pairing that efficiently minimizes the sum of the distances between the positions of each laser across the two frames. We also considered using a Kalman filter [9] to track smoothly moving laser dots, but our early experiments indicated this was complicated to tune for the accelerations of the laser dots at corners or tight turns and ultimately not necessary.

In addition to the centroid of the laser spot we also extract the intensity and size of the detected IR spill to calibrate laser intensity data for identification. Inexpensive lasers exhibit unique IR spillover, as shown in Fig. 1, and this is fairly consistent for each device (once the laser has warmed up for about 15 seconds, and as long as the batteries are reasonably fresh), allowing us to track and identify the lasers over time. The pattern of spill from the laser varies most with distance of the laser to the screen. The top row of images in Fig. 1 were collected with the laser 15 feet from the screen, the middle row at 10 feet, and the bottom row at 5 feet.

We call this signature the lasers personality. During the calibration phase, we capture several frames worth of this intensity data at each of the calibration points for each laser. We examine the blob of light and calculate a radial histogram of the intensity values of the blob. In practice, 20 bins (representing a radius of 20 pixels) is sufficient to capture the uniqueness of a laser spots shape. Note that the calibration can be performed simultaneously for many lasers (with 1 person per laser), and takes less than a minute. Sample laser personality data is presented in Fig. 2.

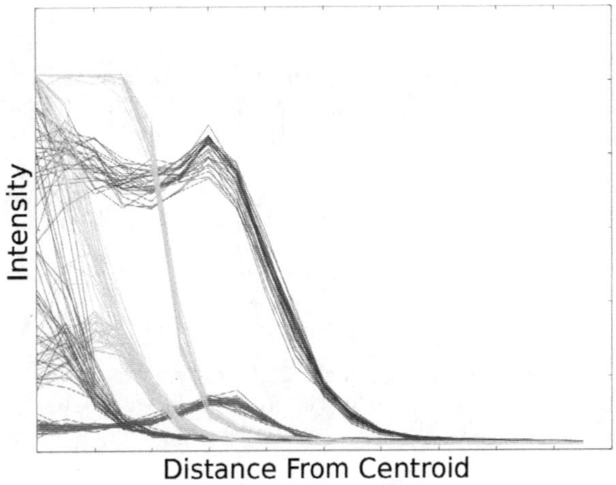

Figure 2. 30 personality measurements for each of 6 lasers from a single calibration screen location.

A. *Identifying Laser Spots: Matching Personalities*

Once calibration is complete, the system is able to match any laser spot on the projection surface with one of the calibrated lasers. When a laser spot is detected, its personality is calculated, and matched with that of one of the known lasers.

For efficiency, we utilize two passes to process the camera image. In a first coarse pass, we examine every nth pixel in the camera image and all pixels greater than a pre-set intensity threshold continue to the second pass. In the second pass, a generous window around each remaining pixel is examined. We collect all nearby pixels above the threshold and extract the largest connected component. The centroid of this component is set as the laser spot position. We then compute the histogram of pixel intensities shown in Fig. 2, matching the personalities using the sum of squared differences between the detected and known personalities.

It is important to note that the apparent laser intensity varies spatially for each laser due to a number of additional variables, including: distance from laser to screen, distance from screen to camera, and camera vignetting. We normalize for these variations by averaging all of the intensity data for all of the lasers collected at each of the calibration grid points, and normalize the input by dividing it by the spatial average. We use barycentric coordinates and interpolation to normalize laser points between calibration grid locations. Camera position normalization is especially crucial when the camera is placed at an extreme angle to the screen, and thus experiences significant perspective distortion. When multiple lasers are simultaneously detected on the screen, we leverage temporal coherence to disambiguate lasers with somewhat similar histogram personalities. We employ the Kuhn-Munkres algorithm to assign unique labels to all detected points; that is, no two lasers will be assigned the same ID, even if they both select the same ID as their first choice.

III. Accuracy Tests

The tests were performed using six lasers (given IDs 1-6) in the 19 x 23 space. The space was divided into a series of

TABLE I. RESULTS FROM ACCURACY TESTS.

Laser	a) Single Pos.		b) Arc Mov.		c) Line Mov.		d) Walking Path		e) All Lasers	
1	100.00	100.00	96.54	98.27	53.88	74.14	51.13	68.49	99.79	100.00
2	100.00	100.00	100.00	100.00	90.43	95.21	78.65	86.25	99.07	100.00
3	95.85	100.00	70.96	73.48	35.14	48.65	60.50	96.10	83.49	98.75
4	92.79	100.00	77.40	100.00	80.41	100.00	83.02	100.00	99.61	99.78
5	99.67	99.67	100.00	100.00	57.99	92.57	82.95	94.26	99.80	99.92
6	90.33	96.03	93.89	95.91	72.56	79.70	91.81	94.86	84.08	99.90
Min:	521		347		230		645		968	

testing locations at discretized 22.5 arcs with radii of 5', 10', and 15' from the center of the projection surface. The results are presented in Table **??**. Five accuracy tests were run in total, described below.

- **a) Stationary Test -** judge how well lasers could be matched to the calibrated data while stationary.
- **b) Arc Walking Test -** judge how much side-to-side movement affected the overall accuracy of the identification system.
- **c) Straight Line Walking Test -** judge how much distance from the screen affected the overall accuracy of the system.
- **d) Path Walking Test -** provide an overall averaging of the previous two tests, and to mimic movement expected by users in real-world environments.
- **e) All Lasers Simultaneous Test -** assess how accurately the laser identification system performed when several lasers were on the screen at once.

For each test and for each laser two percentages are reported: the percentage of frames in which it was correctly identified as its primary ID (left column), and the percentage of frames in which it was identified as either the primary or secondary ID (right column). The minimum number of frames collected for each test is reported along the bottom row. All units are percentages of frames.

Overall, our laser identification system is most effective when lasers remain in the general area from which their calibration data is collected while the system is in use. It is rare that a laser is mislabeled in this instance. However, when moving from place to place, the shape of the laser spot can change dramatically, and so the personality can as well. This explains the poor performance of lasers in general in tests c) and d).

These tests bring to light two noteable shortcomings of our identification system that will be tackled in the future. The first is that position is important when comparing a laser spot to a given set of laser personalities, and a lasers personality changes over the time of its use due to warming and battery drain.

IV. APPLICATIONS

We have implemented a series of five applications that effectively take advantage of multi-user interfaces for visualization, education, and problem-solving. The common thread among each of the applications is its use of input from several different users to achieve a common goal, e.g. exploration of a data visualization or solving a puzzle. Our applications are a multi-user painting program, a puzzle solving program, a terrain and hydrography data visualization tool, a graph visualization tool, and an infrastructure map visualization tool.

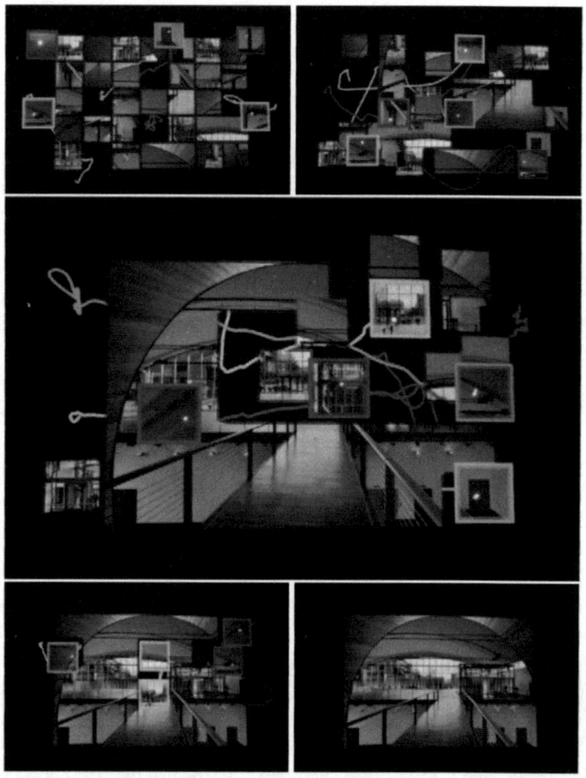

Figure 3. A visualization of the puzzle application.

The first application is a standard paint program, which allows any number of users to paint on the screen using the laser pointer as a brush, selecting color and size at will. Users hover over buttons to choose color and brush The puzzle solving program reads in an image and breaks it into n equally-sized rectangular textured tiles, randomizes them, and displays the new order on the screen, seen in Fig. 3. In the figure, five users (each represented by his own color) attempt to solve a 7x5 piece puzzle. The five images represent five points in time during the solving of the puzzle. Each border between two tiles that should not be adjacent is greyed out (top left image), but once a tile is placed next to its proper neighbor, the border fills in (middle image). Each laser point creates a trail of a unique color as it moves across the projection surface, providing feedback to individual users. The common goal of the users of this application is to reassemble the original image by clicking and dragging the tiles.

In addition, we have implemented a visualization tool for terrain hydrography. The goal of the application is to allow for the exploration of terrain hydrography data by multiple users through a laser pointer interface, utilizing the work of Metz et al. [20] and OCallaghan and Mark [21]. The application consists of a data view and a graphical user interface side-by-side, in which modes are selected in the GUI through dwell-selection. In addition to selection of modes, the laser pointers are also used to interact directly with the 3D terrain data and camera view.

We have also developed a graph visualization tool that allows users to explore data organized by nodes and edges. Our application takes as input node and connectivity information. Laser points which dwell on a node for a period of time grab the node, indicated by the laser trail turning green, and can drag the node to a new location. The graph will rearrange itself based on a mass-spring simulation, minimizing the energy in the system.

Our final application is a visualization, exploration, and editing tool for infrastructure data. The data are organized as a spatial graph of interconnected nodes and arcs in several different infrastructure systems: electric power, telecommunications, transportation, etc. The tool is used to visualize the complex network along with vulnerabilities during hurricane and flooding scenarios (e.g., where are ambulances re-routed if a local hospital is flooded). Images of all applications and videos of the system in use are available upon request.

V. Conclusion

Multi-user interaction on large-scale displays is a powerful collaborative tool with several applications. In this paper, we have presented a method for identifying off the-shelf laser pointers in an inexpensive and simple manner by calibrating each laser pointers IR spillovers intensity histogram, called the lasers personality, allowing for closest-neighbor matching of data points. The system requires only a calibration step to set up, and once it is complete multiple users can interact with interfaces in a large-scale environment. Applications tailored to multi-user collaborate problem solving efforts are presented in this paper that take advantage of our systems ability to identify laser points to explore data, manipulate data, and solve problems in a group environment. Our method is inexpensive, accurate, simple, and scalable to large screen displays.

While the system works well when users do not change how far they are from the projection surface (sufficient for many applications), there are times when this is not enough. One clear extension to this work is the introduction of continuous calibration, in which calibration data is updated as the lasers are used to account for changes in environment, including the position of the users. Additionally, the next step of adopting the system for general use is a detailed user study, which we plan to conduct in the near future. And we will extend our suite of applications for a broader audience.

References

[1] A. Pavlovych and W. Stuerzlinger, "Laser pointers as interaction devices for collaborative pervasive computing," Center for Parallel Computing, Tech. Rep., 2004.

[2] D. R. Olsen and T. S. Nielsen, "Laser pointer interaction," in *CHI*, 2001, pp. 17–22.

[3] J.-Y. Oh and W. Stuerzlinger, "Laser pointers as collaborative pointing devices," in *Graphics Interface*, 2002, pp. 141–150.

[4] J. Davis and X. Chen, "Lumipoint: Multi-user laser-based interaction on large tiled displays," *Displays*, vol. 23, p. 2002, 2000.

[5] B. A. Ahlborn, D. Thompson, O. Kreylos, B. Hamann, and O. G. Staadt, "A practical system for laser pointer interaction on large displays," in *Proceedings of the ACM symposium on Virtual reality software and technology*, ser. VRST '05. New York, NY, USA: ACM, 2005, pp. 106–109.

[6] Y. Qin, Y. Shi, H. Jiang, and C. Yu, "Structured laser pointer: enabling wrist-rolling movements as a new interactive dimension," in *Proceedings of the International Conference on Advanced Visual Interfaces*, ser. AVI '10. New York, NY, USA: ACM, 2010, pp. 163–166.

[7] L. Angelini, M. Caon, S. Carrino, O. A. Khaled, and E. Mugellini, "Multi-user pointing and gesture interaction for large screen using infrared emitters and accelerometers." in *HCI (2)'11*, 2011, pp. 185–193.

[8] K. Cheng and K. Pulo, "Direct interaction with large-scale display systems using infrared laser tracking devices," in *Proceedings of the Asia-Pacific symposium on Information visualisation - Volume 24*, ser. APVis '03. Darlinghurst, Australia, Australia: Australian Computer Society, Inc., 2003, pp. 67–74.

[9] R. Kalman, "A new approach to linear filtering and prediction problems," *Journal of Basic Engineering*, vol. 82, no. 1, pp. 35–45, 1960.

[10] F. de la O Chávez, F. Fernández de Vega, G. Olague, and J. Llano Montero, "An independent and non-intrusive laser pointer environment control device system," in *Proceedings of the 5th international conference on Pervasive services*, ser. ICPS '08. New York, NY, USA: ACM, 2008, pp. 37–46.

[11] F. Vogt, J. Wong, S. Fels, and D. Cavens, "Tracking multiple laser pointers for large screen interaction," in *Ext. Abstracts UIST*, 2003, pp. 95–96.

[12] F. Vogt, J. Wong, B. A. Po, R. Argue, S. S. Fels, and K. S. Booth, "Exploring collaboration with group pointer interaction," in *Proceedings of the Computer Graphics International*. Washington, DC, USA: IEEE Computer Society, 2004, pp. 636–639.

[13] A. Pavlovych and W. Stuerzlinger, "Effect of screen configuration and interaction devices in shared display groupware," in *Proceeding of the 3rd ACM international workshop on Human centered computing*, ser. HCC '08. New York, NY, USA: ACM, 2008, pp. 49–56.

[14] X. Bi, Y. Shi, X. Chen, and P. Xiang, "uPen: laser-based, personalized, multi-user interaction on large displays," in *MULTIMEDIA '05: Proceedings of the 13th annual ACM international conference on Multimedia*. New York, NY, USA: ACM Press, 2005, pp. 1049–1050.

[15] B. Shizuki, T. Hisamatsu, S. Takahashi, and J. Tanaka, "Laser pointer interaction techniques using peripheral areas of screens," in *Proceedings of the working conference on Advanced visual interfaces*, ser. AVI '06. New York, NY, USA: ACM, 2006, pp. 95–98.

[16] O. Miksik, V. Vineet, M. Lidegaard, R. Prasaath, M. Niessner, S. Golodetz, S. L. Hicks, P. Perez, S. Izadi, and P. H. Torr, "The semantic paintbrush: Interactive 3d mapping and recognition in large outdoor spaces," in *Proceedings of the 33rd Annual ACM Conference on Human Factors in Computing Systems*, ser. CHI '15. New York, NY, USA: ACM, 2015, pp. 3317–3326.

[17] H. W. Kuhn, "The Hungarian method for the assignment problem," *Naval Research Logistics Quarterly*, vol. 2, pp. 83–97, 1955.

[18] J. Munkres, "Algorithms for the assignment and transportation problems," *Journal of the Society for Industrial and Applied Mathematics*, vol. 5, no. 1, pp. 32–38, March 1957.

[19] J. Weaver, "Kuhn-Munkres (Hungarian) Algorithm in C++," 2010.

[20] M. Metz, H. Mitasova, and R. S. Harmon, "Efficient extraction of drainage networks from massive, radar-based elevation models with least cost path search," *Hydrology and Earth System Sciences*, vol. 15, no. 2, pp. 667–678, 2011.

[21] J. F. O'Callaghan and D. M. Mark, "The extraction of drainage networks from digital elevation data," *Computer Vision, Graphics, and Image Processing*, vol. 28, no. 3, pp. 323 – 344, 1984.

Industry 4.0 and the Futur Revolution for Human-Centered Industry

Adrien Brunet, Steffen Scholz
Institute for Applied Computer Science
Karlsruhe Institute of Technology
Karlsruhe, Germany
E-Mail: [adrien.brunet;steffen.scholz]@kit.edu

Abstract— **The development of new technologies namely in the microelectronic and the communication domains drives a new industrial revolution. As every revolution, industry 4.0 will change our way of working and bring new opportunities and challenges. This paper presents the new technologies and human-centred applications related to industry 4.0. and concludes on what it will bring to humans and societies.**

Keywords-Human-centered industrial technology; additive manufacturing; Augmented reality; industry 4.0; Robotic.

I. INTRODUCTION ON INDUSTRY 4.0

The first industrial revolution appeared in the end of the 18th century in Europe. It has seen the development of the steam engine that tremendously increased the work force of the industry. Tasks that required before many men and horses have been replaced by machine. This new invention lead to the creation of railway systems with the steam locomotive.

The second revolution came at the turn of the 20th century with the electrification of the industrial production and the adoption of the Fordism and Taylorism for the mass production

The third industrial revolution appeared in the second part of the 20th century. It concerns the development of semiconductors and programmable logic. Repetitive tasks executed my human workers have been replaced by robots and only the most complex jobs have been left to human.

Each previous industrial revolution happened simultaneously with changes in how human live and work. Today a new revolution is coming, it has different names, some call it the industrial internet of things [1] and others call it the industry 4.0. or even smart factories [2]-[4] This new revolution is emerging from the digitalisation and the connection of the industry to the internet. Figure 1 summarises the evolution of the industry since the first industrial revolution.

Considering those changes, it is important to ask the question: what will bring and change industry 4.0 for the human. The technological evolution that enable this new revolution are presented in Section II. In section III are listed the new human-centred applications. Then the hurdles on the road of lifework and societal improvement are given in Section IV and Section V is the conclusion.

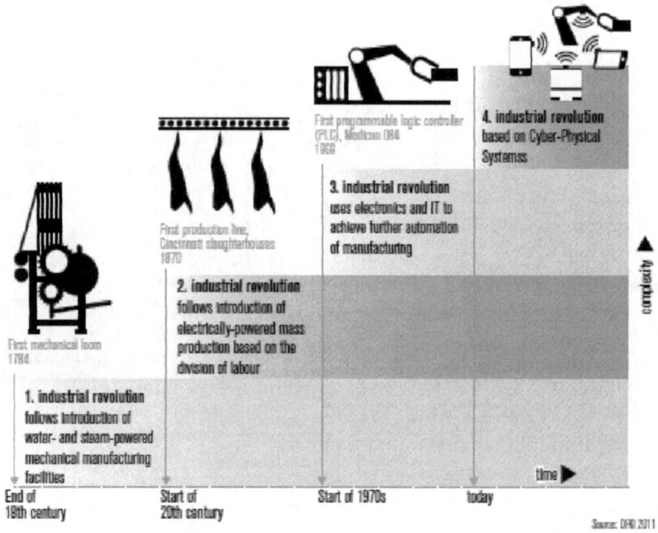

Figure 1. The four stages of the industrial revolution source DKFI 2011 [2]

II. The Origine of Industry 4.0: Technological Evolutions and Invention

Various technological evolutions and inventions (described in the following paragraphs) appeared in the last decades enabling the emergence of industry 4.0.

A. *Miniaturisation*

The first enabling technology for the industry 4.0 is actually an incremental development of the chip and semiconductor industry. Computer calculation power went in few decades from basic logic to complex meteorological model calculations. The miniaturisation and cost reduction of micro electro-mechanical systems (MEMS) filled our world of sensors, recording huge amounts of data. Dozens of sensors can be found in a smartphone such as accelerometer, gyrometer, heart rate monitor, fingerprint, light sensor, etc. In modern cars, even more sensors can be found.

B. *Communication technology*

The communication technologies made great improvement, such as in wireless communication system; nevertheless, the development of the internet was the breakthrough. It is now possible for anybody with an access to the World Wide Web to communicate with somebody else everywhere in the world. This changed radically our ways to exchange data and to conceive services. Nowadays many exchanges are dematerialized: books and music are files that can be download and read from everywhere at anytime. Object are less and less things that are made of atoms but made of bytes. This phenomenon of digitalisation is named the internet of things (IoT) [5].

C. *Cyber physical system*

Cyber physical systems (CPS) integrate computation, networking and physical process. It is this ability of machine to calculate ("to think") and to communicate that make the current evolution of the industry a revolution. Indeed, machine can harvest data, compute them locally, and adapt their reaction without human actions to be taken. For example, on a manufacturing line a temperature sensor send a voltage analysed by the machine as a value out of the safety range, then using an adapted algorithm the machine stops the process, and reduces the heat. The same machine connected to the internet and knowing more about the product history could take another decision.

D. *Cloud and big data*

The cloud and "big data" are enabling the CPS. As explained before sensors took place everywhere in our lives and this is even true in the manufacturing processes. Those sensors create data that are usually thrown away. The cloud enables company to store and compute big amount of data while they do not have locally super computer and important storage capacity. Big data analysis make it possible to answer the questions : "what is the pattern?", "what will happen next?" "what if we try this?" and "what is the best action?" This new way of analysing big amount of data is called predictive and prescriptive data analysis [1].

E. *Digitalisation and additive manufacturing*

Improvement in the previously quoted technologies as well as development in computer assisted design (CAD) technology and more recently 3D scanning of objects, accelerated the digitalisation of the industry. Nowadays libraries of 3D object exist in open source (3Dwarehouse, thingiverse, archive3D) [6]-[8] accelerating the democratisation of additive manufacturing. Additive manufacturing made possible for everyone to print a wide range of object, creating a breakthrough in spare part but also rapid prototyping and health along with other markets.

F. *General consequences of the tecnological evolutions and inventions*

It is expected that with the ability of factories to store, access and compute an increasing amount of Data, they will be able to:

- Control their energy consumption. They will be connected to a smart grid and will know when the power is available and the cheapest.
- Know the incoming and outcoming flows of raw materials, products, energy, waste, ect.
- Know when is the raw material at its best price and adapt purchasing to the manufacturing, stock and market situation.
- To be informed when a delivery will be made and if some delays are to be expected.
- Compare the actual data with previously recorded data and improve decision-making.

III. New Human-Centered Applications

Section II listed the technological evolutions that enable industry 4.0 and some of their consequences. This section focuses on the human-centred applications derived from the previous section and presents how industry 4.0 could change labour and human life in the new industrial revolution.

A. *Safe Human-Robot cooperation*

The German companies Festo [9][10] and ABB (ABB's YUMI) [11] designed robots that can work in cooperation with human. Indeed, standard robots move fast and are made of stiff material that if they interact with human they would most probably hurt them. To avoid any problem most of the robots are isolated and kept in a safe room. The idea of this new type of robot is to be able to help the worker in his tasks while preventing to hurt him. Repetitive, tiring and strength demanding task are ideal for robots while human have more dexterity and can solve more complex task.

B. Augmented reality

Augmented reality (AR) is “a technology that superimposes a computer-generated image on a user's view of the real world, thus providing a composite view”. AR and namely smart glasses such as the famous “google glass” [12] can improve work experience and productivity. AR has many different applications. Among the applications that already exist are the (1) IKEA AR catalog application that can be downloaded on tablets and allow the user to visualise virtual furniture in his/her apartment using the tablet's camera [13]; (2) Converse AR catalog application that let users to try shoes while they stay home [14]. Implemented in the industry, augmented reality could guide the worker through complex tasks, for example assembly and reduce the potential mistakes [15]. It could help localizing an object in a store house, to visualise the inside of an object for maintenance or to guide worker by superimposing useful information on real object to achieve complex processes such as in Figure 2.

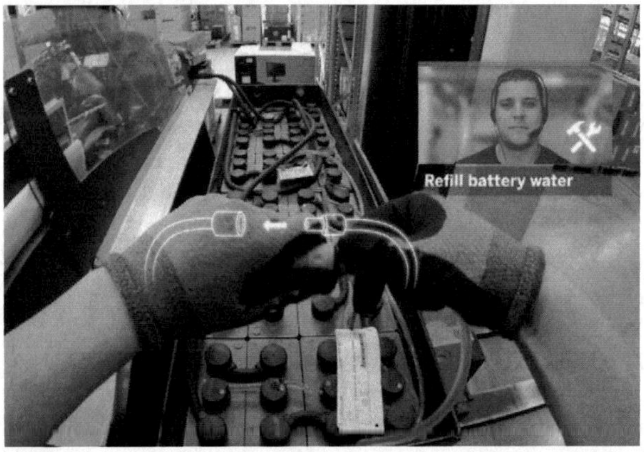

Figure 2. Augmented reality application to guide workers wearing smart glass [16]

C. Telepresence/remote maintenance

Thanks to the increasing number of sensors, many parameters of a machine can be harvested and coupled with a CAD model, thus creating a virtual twin of the machine. Instead of disassembling or coming on site for inspection, the employee can visualise and analyse the problem remotely from his office on screen. The telepresence allow the employee to remotely take action to solve the issue.

D. Agile manufacturing

Nowadays, manufacturing chains are dedicated mostly to one product and can accept changes in return for a substantial effort. With indusdustry 4.0 the production chain will be made of manufacturing modules that can be quickly reorganizised according to the demand and the available workforce while mastering the costs and the quality. This new way of conceiving production is called „Agile manufacturing“ and is part of the answer to the increasing demand of mass customization and reduced lead time.

IV. THE HURDLE ON THE ROAD OF INDUSTRY 4.0

The report of the German federal ministry of education and research (Recommendations for implementing the strategic initiative INDUSTRY 4.0) [2] published in April 2013, lists the actual challenges as follow:

- Standardisation and open standards for a reference architecture
- Managing complex systems
- Delivering a comprehensive broadband infrastructure for industry
- Safety and security as critical factors for the success of industrie 4.0
- Work organisation and work design in the digital industrial age
- Training and continuing professional development for industrie 4.0
- Regulatory framework
- Resource efficiency

V. CONCLUSION

Similarly, to the theory of creative destruction expressed by J.Schumpeter [17] robots will have to replace the work previously done by human. Nevertheless, products are becoming more and more complex and so does the production; thus, skilled workers will be more than ever required in the factories. Nevertheless, in industry 4.0 the worker will not have to follow the pace of rigid and automated production, on the contrary robots will adapt to the workers.

The productivity will be improved by the new evolutions offered by the Industry 4.0. Indeed, AR allow workers to efficiently complete more complex tasks in less time. An employee using telepresence can also improve his productivity by completing more task per day while he/she does not have to travel to carry out maintenance. This increase in productivity will reduce the costs and improve the competitiveness of every factory that will adopt industry 4.0. Because it allows machines to better control their energy consumption and reduce the travel of workers, the industrial internet of things is fundamentally environmental friendly.

To finish, it has been demonstrated that industry 4.0 will help our societies to sustain growth by increasing productivity and overcome great challenges, such as climate change, while keeping humans at the centre of the production.

REFERENCES

[1] A.Gilchrist, Industry 4.0 the industrial internet of things, 2016

[2] Forschungsunion & Acatech, Recommendations for implementing the strategic initiative INDUSTRIE 4.0, 2013

[3] K. Schwab, The fourth Industrial Revolution, 2017

[4] R Davies - European Parliamentary Research Service, Briefing, industry 4.0. Digitalisation for productivity and growth, 2015

[5] A. Rayes and S. Samer, Internet of Things From Hype to Reality: The Road to Digitization, 2016

[6] www.thingiverse.com [retrieved: february 2017]

[7] https://3dwarehouse.sketchup.com [retrieved: february 2017]

[8] archive3d.net [retrieved: february 2017]

[9] www.festo.com [retrieved: february 2017]

[10] S. Scholz, A. Brunet, T. Müller and A. Fuchsbauer, "Novel Nanoparticle Enhanced Digital Materials for 3D Printing and their Application Shown for the Robotic and Electronic Industry", proceding of the CENICS 2016 conference, pp. 27-30.

[11] ABB, A new age of industrial production. The Internet of Things, Services and People,2016.

[12] https://developers.google.com/glass/ [retrieved: february 2017]

[13] www.ikea.com [retrieved: february 2017]

[14] http://www.converse.com [retrieved: february 2017]

[15] World Economic Forum, Industrial Internet of Things Unleashing the Potential of Connected Products and Services, 2015

[16] www.itizzimo.com [retrieved: february 2017]

[17] J.Schumpeter, 1942, *Capitalism, Socialism and Democracy*

Industry 4.0 Human-Oriented Challenges using the example of Additive Manufacturing Technologies

Daniel J. B. S. Sampaio
School of Engineering – Guaratinguetá
São Paulo State University (Unesp)
Guaratinguetá, Brazil
e-mail: dsampaio@feg.unesp.br

Marc-André Weber
Division Field Corporate Excellence
Institut fuer angewandte Arbeitswissenschaft
Duesseldorf, Germany
e-mail: m.weber@ifaa-mail.de

Steffen G. Scholz
Institute for Applied Computer Science
Karlsruhe Institute of Technology
Karlsruhe, Germany
e-mail: steffen.scholz@kit.edu

Abstract—**Digitalization of the industry opens new possibilities to fulfill customer requirements such as individualized products. Additive Manufacturing is an example of a technology to do so and is part of a development towards Systems Engineering. Adapting the qualification of the workforce is a decisive factor to use successfully new technologies within the broad field of industry 4.0. This paper addresses the issue of how to integrate workforce in the changing process of digitalization based on providing examples from the Additive Manufacturing technology. It shows that work content will change and generally higher skill levels are required. Subsequently, continuous learning and the determination to do so are necessary. Implementing this is a major task for workforce and employers.**

Keywords - Industry 4.0; Digitalization; Additive Manufacturing; Workplace Change; Job Content; Qualification Needs.

I. Introduction

Industry 4.0 stands for the current revolution of the industrial production, driven by the internet technologies, and describes the technological change of today's production technology to cyber-physical production systems, so-called Smart Factories [1]. In the Smart factories environment, the manufacturing will completely be equipped with sensors, actors, and autonomous systems [2]. The term "Industry 4.0" was first presented at the 2011 Hannover Fair and describes the fourth development stage of the industrial production. The three previous stages started with the invention of the steam engine in the eighteenth century, which supported the working people in energy-intensive activities. Subsequently, the division of labor was introduced in the late nineteenth century and allowed for mass production by means of the assembly line. The use of electronic control systems, such as Numeric Control (NC) and Computer Numeric Control (CNC) machines, since the 1970s allowed faster and more precise production of goods [3]. Since the introduction of Industry 4.0, much research has been focused on it generating an extensive number of scientific, as well as practically oriented papers and contributions to this field [4].

The historical development of production techniques shows that the desire to automate production is nothing new [5], however, computational power and technical equipment was previously not as developed as it is nowadays. Decades ago, the example of "Hall 54" of the Volkswagen AG showed the practical problems of the past associated to the relation between human and machining development in the industrial production environment [6]. On top, there have been considerable problems with the operational implementation [7]. With the technological development of the last few years, a clearly improved technical infrastructure is now available, especially regarding the information technology aspect, with which many ideas of the connected industry can now be realized.

This paper focuses on additive manufacturing as an example of a part of industry 4.0. Additive manufacturing was first introduced in the 1980s and is becoming more important nowadays with the development of industry 4.0. We will exemplify human-related challenges for the use of this technology based on a qualitative description of changes. Additive manufacturing describes production of tools and products based on the computer-internal data models from formless material – such as powder – or form-neutral material – such as fiber and wires – by means of chemical or physical processes. Within additive manufacturing, different technologies are combined whose common feature consists in the fact that components are layered and material is only connected where the final product should be produced [8]. For all people using additive manufacturing, skills required will change compared to the ones necessary for "traditional" production. This covers knowledge about different types of additive manufacturing, their machine and process parameters as well as properties of the goods produced.

In Section 2, the human-oriented challenges in industry 4.0 are discussed based on the features identified in the industry 4.0 framework. In Section 3, the additive manufacturing is presented as example of industry 4.0 and changes in the way of working entailed by this technological evolution are described. In Section 4, conclusions on the major changes induced by industry 4.0 within work relations are presented.

II. Human-Oriented Challenges in Industry 4.0

The issue of what will happen to the working people is nowadays critically discussed as it had been in time of the third industrial revolution of the 1970s [9][10]. If job losses or workplace growth is predicted, is not only a question of the time horizon taken into regard and the specific type of industry in scope, but also of the political thinking and attitude of the forecasting institution. It is a question of "which type" of industry 4.0 is regarded as well, as industry 4.0 covers several topics from using a tablet computer for work up to collaboration with robots. What can be taken as given is that work itself changes by industry 4.0, and this will also lead to a change in work skill requirements on the one hand and how work will be performed in future on the other hand.

In a process inside industry 4.0, the identification of seven features as shown in Figure 1 is normally expected. It is important to note that the human is a central actor in this revolution. All other features, such as self-organized and distributed artificial intelligence, fast and automatic network integration with high flexibility, open standards, virtual real-time picture of the process, digital integrated life-cycle-management and safe and secure added-value networks have their outcomes established to achieve the requirements and needs of the central actor.

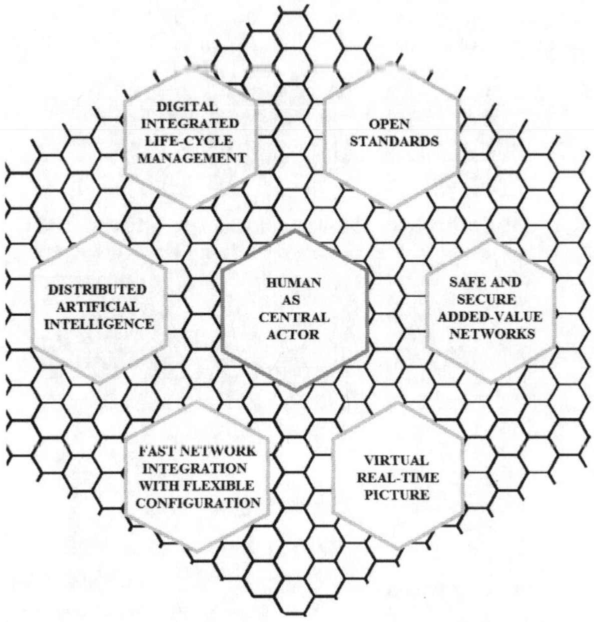

Figure 1. Industry 4.0 and its features - the human in the center.

The companies are transforming themselves by combining investments in information technology with changes in work practices, strategy, products and services. They are carrying on changes not only in their own company, but also in supplier relations and customer relationship [11]. This brings major challenges like changes in the decision rights, in the authority and responsibilities of the workers as well as in the process and workflow. The intensity of interactions with customers and suppliers will significantly increase, and so will augmented lateral communication. Among others, there might be further reductions in the management layers, and products and processes will undergo a concurrent engineering. All these factors will bring changes to the companies, and they need to find strategies of how successfully cope with those changes.

There are some general recommendations that can be given. When implementing industry 4.0, employees should be involved as early as in the planning stage, and their wishes and concerns should be taken into regard by management. It is of great use to have practical test spaces where employees can gain their own experiences with new technologies. Such pilot test environments can illustrate the benefits of digital change and may lead to a high identification with it, and finally to the recognition of its benefits. The fast development of digital technologies requires a high level of learning and change attitude as well. The management of the company plays a critical role in implementing this attitude. Only by good leadership and an appropriate fault culture, a change in thinking can be achieved [3].

Maybe it will be the case that some workers tend to retain elements of the now almost outdated work practices. Some believes, as the key for productivity is to avoid stopping the machine as long as possible and produce goods in large quantities at low rates of variety, negates the chances of flexibility offered by new production processes in industry 4.0.

III. Additive Manufacturing as Example

Additive manufacturing, as example of industry 4.0, offers the chance to produce individualized products at lot size one. Therefore, it is necessary for the workers to set their mind on each new product and machine parameters required to the specific needs for these products. Although the main process will be additive manufacturing, in detail it will make a big change if the product consists of metal or plastic, and the type of metal or plastic requires further knowledge about how to process it. The thickness of layers, therefore the number of layers, the distance of melting points next to each other and temperature are some examples that need to be taken into regard. The workers using additive manufacturing may also need knowledge for product designing, especially if the need of supporting structures for production is required. The latter shows that successful production of a product using additive manufacturing begins at the design stage when computer-aided design (CAD) models are created, therefore designers need to understand the production process and the workforce printing the products should be able to adjust data files with the designers.

To handle with the identified conditions – based on the fact that products will generally be less produced in large quantities by using additive manufacturing but at a higher level of customer individuality – the workers should be able to make decisions that were not required in their job functions before. This example shows that industry 4.0 increases the demand for skilled labor, which may in return reduce the need for low-skilled workers. It is important especially for low-skilled workers, in order to be able to work in these more complex highly skilled jobs, to undergo intense learning and a process of continuous education.

There is a consensus that industry 4.0 may not only have consequences for low-skilled workers and their operational shop floor activities, leading generally to a replacement of simple and repetitive jobs in production assembly and quality control, but also for high-skilled management representatives in administration and planning. Figure 2 shows the changes in the way of working in the industries caused by technological evolution over the last decades. In the 1960s, the industry was almost totally composed of mechanical equipment and processes with a small use of electrical systems and equipment. This reality had been changing over the years with an increasing participation of electrical systems and equipment and with the gradual introduction of software engineering and – at a later stage – of systems engineering. The trend is that by 2020 software and systems engineering will have almost as great a share as mechanical and electrical construction in the constitution of industrial production systems.

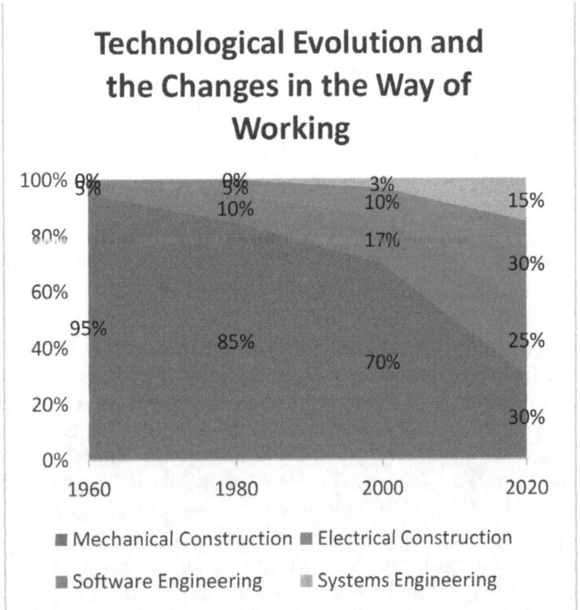

Figure 2. Technological evolution and changes in the way of working

Nevertheless, if the overall number of jobs will decline or improve is a question that cannot be answered now. However, it can be noted that – as in previous industrial revolutions – new jobs and needs for qualification are emerging and will continue to emerge. It is a task for each company on the one hand and for designing new governmental policies on the other hand, that will be required in future to help to balance the effects of industry 4.0 on the labor market.

The changes driven by industry 4.0 on the labor market are derived of the changes of the consumer markets on the one hand and of the changes of the technologies available for production on the other hand. As consumers require more individuality of products and additive manufacturing offers the possibility to do so, each industry and every company need to think of what are specific consequences they need to cope with. Digitalization affects the entire company, therefore prerequisites for a successful digitalization of the own company needs to be established both in production as in supporting indirect areas. To succeed, it is necessary to involve all people at hand and to establish standardization of processes taking into regard the principles of lean management. The change to industry 4.0 requires fundamentally questioning the existing structures and processes, and adapting them as far as necessary and possible. This includes qualification and skills as well.

A practical example is the Smart production of Microsystems based in laminated polymer films research project (SMARTLAM) research project, which was carried out under the European Union program FP7 - Factories of the Future. The main aim was to create a new concept for the manufacturing of functional micro devices based on a modular, flexible and scalable 3D integration scenario. Combining state-of-the-art 3D-compatible technologies, such as aerosol-jet printing, and laser technologies, which are capable of manufacturing three-dimensional structures and parts, with modules for handling and inspection together with a recipe-based control software, as shown in Figure 3, allowed for the successful development of a modular, scalable and easy-to-synchronise manufacturing environment for the production of complete 3D-Microsystems.

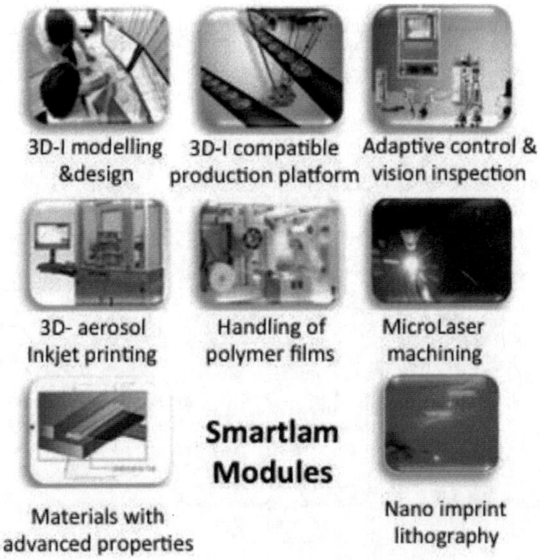

Figure 3. SMARTLAN Integrated Modules

It has shown that the 3D integration approach proposed is capable of creating the flexibility and scalability that is necessary to take the manufacturing of micro devices to another level by making it profitable outside of the area of mass production. It became clear to the project partners the need for changes in the business model and in the requirements and qualification of employees in order to face and adapt themselves to the new production paradigms from the Industry 4.0.

IV. CONCLUSION

We have shown by means of the descriptive example of additive manufacturing that industry 4.0 leads to significant changes of the industry. This is mainly driven by two developments, the wish of customers for individualized products and the upcoming of technologies that enable the companies to produce individualized products at lot size one. Additive manufacturing is an example of such a technology. Printing products according to specific customer wishes requires new skills of those creating and producing the goods, and calls for more interaction between all people on all levels involved in the production process.

The opportunities and challenges resulting from a comprehensive use of industry 4.0 appear to be far-reaching, but offer considerable potential for improvement. However, aspects, such as decisions based on insufficient process and product knowledge in respect with interdependencies of many inter-related decisions, maybe in a sense of non-cooperative use of information asymmetries, pose major challenges to the implementation of industry 4.0. The success of industry 4.0 is often a question of the system boundaries in which it is applied and operated, and one important part of it includes human aspects. Practical and scientific research is therefore confronted with major challenges that lie in the detail of how to successful use technologies such as additive manufacturing, in addition to the broad generalization of the advantages of industry 4.0 [12]. This paper addresses these issues and shows by means of examples that qualification is a major success factor and that companies need to focus on providing all possible options to appropriate skills.

REFERENCES

[1] M.-A. Weber and K. Benkel, "Industry 4.0 and Quantitative Optimization Approaches", Magazine for the entire value chain of the automotive industry, v.18, n.3, pp.12–15, 2015.

[2] H. Lasi, P. Fettke, H. G. Kemper, T. Feld, and M. Hoffmann, "Industry 4.0, " Business & Information Systems Engineering, v. 6, n. 4, pp. 239, 2014.

[3] M. Börkircher et al., "Digitization and Industry 4.0: As individual as needs - productivity gains through information," Heider Druck, Bergisch Gladbach, 2016.

[4] T. Bauernhansl, M. Hompel, and B. Vogel-Heuser, "Industry 4.0 in Production, Automation and Logistics: Applications, Technologies, Migration," Springer, Wiesbaden, 2014.

[5] W. Weller, "Automation technology in the course of time: development history of a fascinating field," [Online]. Available from:http://edoc.hu-berlin.de/oa/books/reDxmEBBdAgU/PDF/22L08GZ1anEiI.pdf. [retrieved: february, 2017]

[6] M. Heßler, "Hall 54 at Volkswagen and the limits of automation: Reflections on the man-machine ratio in the industrial production of the 1980s," Studies in Contemporary History, v.11, p.56–76, 2014.

[7] A. Zerfaß and M. Piwinger, "Handbuch Unternehmenskommunikation: Strategie, Management, Wertschöpfung, " 2nd ed. Springer Gabler, Wiesbaden, 2014.

[8] M. Schmid, "Additive Fertigung mit Selektivem Lasersintern (SLS): Prozess- und Wekstoffüberblick," Springer Vieweg, Wiesbaden, 2015.

[9] Verein Deutscher Ingenieure. VDI: *Status report: Working Environment 4.0.* [Online]. Available from: https://www.vdi.de/fileadmin/vdi_de/redakteur_dateien/gma_dateien/2016_11_GMA_Arbeitswelt_Statusreport.pdf. [retrieved: february, 2017]

[10] Spiegel, "We are facing a catastrophe," Spiegel, v.32, n.16, pp.80–100, 1978.

[11] R. Gibbons and J. Roberts, "The handbook of organizational economics, " Princeton University Press, 2013.

[12] M.-A.Weber and K. Benkel, "Importance of Optimizing Approaches and their Integration into Data Systems of Industry 4.0," In: Proff H, Fojcik TM (eds) Industry 4.0: National and international trends in mobility: technical and business aspects. Springer, Wiesbaden, pp. 435–447, 2016.

Analysis of The Cross Section of Inkjet-Printed Conductive Tracks on PET Films

A method to analyze the nano- and microstructure of inkjet-printed conductive tracks on polymer film substrates based on SEM analysis of cross sections prepared by ultramicrotomy.

Martin Ungerer[1], Waldemar Spomer[1], Lisa Veith[3], Annika Fries[1], Christian Debatin[1], Irene Wacker[2], Rasmus Schröder[2,3], Ulrich Gengenbach[1]

[1] Institute for Applied Computer Science (IAI), Karlsruhe Institute of Technology (KIT), Eggenstein-Leopoldshafen, Germany

[2] Centre for Advanced Materials (CAM), University Heidelberg, Heidelberg, Germany

[3] CellNetworks, BioQuant, University Hospital Heidelberg, Heidelberg, Germany

e-mail: ungerer@kit.edu

***Abstract*—The development of internet of things devices, smart sensor systems or wearables necessitates new fabrication technologies. The challenge is to fulfil requirements such as flexibility, low-weight and low-cost. Inkjet printing of conductive microstructures on polymer films has become increasingly important for these applications in the last decade. This additive fabrication approach is potentially more ecofriendly than conventional processes but has still not reached wider implementation in industry. One of the potential reasons is the still insufficient reliability of printed components that must sustain electrical, thermal, mechanical and chemical stress. In order to optimize the fabrication process with regard to these requirements, the nano- and microstructure of printed patterns needs to be analyzed. In the present work, a method is outlined for the nano- and microstructure analysis of inkjet-printed conductive tracks on polymer substrates by means of scanning electron microscopy of cross sections prepared by ultramicrotomy.**

Keywords-Inkjet-printing; silver nanoparticle ink; polyethylene terephthalate; sintering; ultramicrotomy; imaging by scanning electron microscopy; cross section; microstructure; nanoparticle density.

I. Introduction

In the last decade, printing technologies have become more and more important in research and development for flexible electronics [1]. The objective is to replace conventional subtractive fabrication processes of printed circuit board (PCB) manufacturing by additive processes. Printing processes can be used to fabricate conductive structures, as well as more complex electronic components on flexible polymer films.

A. Advantages of printing technologies

Various printing technologies were transferred from the realm of graphic printing to electronics manufacturing in the last decade. As manufacturing processes can be divided into those, which are well suited for mass production and those that are more suited for single part or small series production, printing processes may be also classified with regard to process productivity. Conventional printing processes based on printing forms are well suited for large-scale production whereas non-impact principles are more suited to individual part up to small series manufacturing and research applications [2] [3].

Unlike the conventional fabrication of PCB's that needs some complex electroplating, lithography and etching steps, printing processes usually need one single additive fabrication step followed by an additional curing process in order to create conductive tracks on a substrate [4] [5]. Thus material usage is optimized and the toxic waste accumulated in subtractive processing is eliminated [6]. Printing allows faster, cleaner, cheaper and more environmentally friendly fabrication of PCB's than conventional processes [5]. Additionally, printing enables large area processing of flexible polymer substrates at low temperatures and ambient conditions [7].

The implementation of printing processes for a desired electronic function in microstructure resolution demands prudent selection of the three main process components - ink, substrate and printing system. These components have to be precisely tuned to get optimum conditions for realizing features with high reproducibility [2].

B. Conductive ink

A fundamental element in printed electronics are conductive tracks [4]. They have to provide high conductivities in order to minimize the power loss. Regarding this requirement, currently two main ink types are available. One type are metal organic decomposition (MOD) inks, with oxidized metal ions as main component [8]. The most prevalent type are nanoparticle inks, where the particles are dispersed in solvents and stabilized by an organic capping agent against agglomeration [9].

Due to their high conductivity, silver-based inks are most widely used in this context [6]. For printed silver nanoparticle tracks a conductivity of about 10 % of bulk silver is acceptable for many applications [10].

The nanoparticle size severely influences the curing process. The smaller the particles, the lower the melting point compared to the bulk material [11] [12].

C. Substrate

For printed flexible electronic applications with optical functions, often low cost polyethylene terephthalate (PET) substrates are used which have a glass-transition temperature (T_g) of 78 °C and a melting point of 255 °C [13] [14]. Commercially available PET films, e.g., Melinex® ST from DuPont Teijin Films are often used in printed electronic applications. Such PET substrates are thermoplastic semi-crystalline polymer films whose maximum working temperature for printing and sintering processes (T_{max}) from about 150 °C is largely independent of their T_g due to a heat-stabilization [13] [14] [15]. Semi-crystalline polymer films have better resistances against solvents than amorphous polymers [15].

D. Inkjet-printing

Drop-on-demand (DoD) piezo inkjet printing is the most common non-impact printing principle in the field of printed electronics [7]. It allows direct, mask-less and vectorial printing of layouts on flexible polymer films [2]. The layouts are created by computer-aided design (CAD). With regard to printability, ink property parameters such as viscosity, surface energy, density, particle size and particle stability are of crucial importance [4] [5]. For example, a particle size of less than 100 nm is recommended in order to prevent print head nozzle clogging [16].

Compared to conventional electronics fabrication processes, inkjet-printed structures often suffer from non-uniformity, low line edge quality and non-reproducible morphology [17] [18]. In order to obtain an optimum line quality, the important parameters that need to be controlled are the distance between two adjacent droplets (d_d), the frequency of droplet generation (f_d), the droplet velocity (v_d), the substrate temperature (T_s) and substrate surface properties [19] [20].

E. Curing

After the printing process, the resulting structures must be cured in order to get the desired electrical conductivity [10]. First, the ink solvent has to be evaporated; then, the organic stabilizing shell has to be removed. During the sintering, a percolation-based network of conductive paths is established due to sporadic agglomeration of particles [10]. At higher temperatures, sintering necks improve the conductivity, the coalescence of the particles leads to a higher metal density of the printed feature [21]. High conductivities have been achieved by means of an oven sintering regime with 30 minutes or more at temperatures above 250 °C [1].

Despite the lower melting point of nanoparticles compared to the bulk material, a sintering regime required for such an enhanced conductivity is not compatible with many of the preferably used low-cost polymer substrates, e.g., PET [22].

Therefore, low temperature sintering methods are taken into consideration that allow either sintering at room temperature (commonly known as chemical sintering) or selective sintering where only the printed structure that needs to be cured is heated while the substrate stays at moderate temperatures [1].

Chemical sintering comprises, among other methods, sintering triggered by additives in the ink or in the substrate [23].

Selective sintering methods are photonic flash sintering, laser sintering, plasma sintering, microwave sintering and electrical current sintering [1] [10].

F. Properties of printed structures

In view of the manifold applications of printed structures, such as conductors, passive components, etc., not only their electrical characteristics must be considered, but also their mechanical and chemical properties. Printed conductive tracks have to withstand mechanical, chemical und thermal stresses that can influence their inherent porous nanostructure and thereby impair the reliability. Particularly, adhesion strength to the substrate, bendability and fatigue resistance are important properties of printed structures for applications on flexible polymer substrates. Sintering conditions substantially influence mechanical properties, such as fatigue resistance [24].

G. Hybrid electronics

To date, many electronic functional elements besides conductive tracks such as resistors, capacitors, transistors, organic light emitting diodes (OLED), organic photovoltaics (OPV) and sensors have been realized by printing technologies. However, it is currently not possible to achieve the performance of conventionally fabricated devices. Moreover, highly integrated circuits such as microcontrollers cannot yet be realized by printing. Therefore, a hybrid approach for the fabrication of more complex electronic systems on flexible polymer substrates seems to be an interesting solution in the medium term to overcome the still low performance of printed complex elements [25] [26]. Marjanović et al. define hybrid electronic integration as the combination of printed components and surface-mount technology (SMT) devices on foils [25].

For demonstration of a hybrid intralayer-integration approach, the conductive track structure of a flip-flop circuit shown in [26] was first printed via silver nanoparticle ink on a PET film. Then SMT components were mounted with conductive adhesive. Figure 1 shows the realized flip-flop

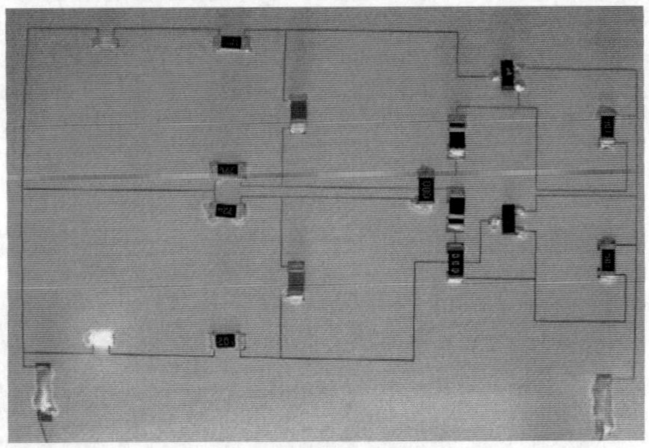

Figure 1. Flip-flop circuit with printed conductive tracks and mounted SMT-components

circuit. Tests with such circuits indicated that the system is sensitive to mechanical stress such as bending. Either the conductive adhesive that connects the SMT components fails or the conductive tracks crack or delaminate from the substrate. In order to improve the structure's resistance to mechanical stress, the microstructure of the printed tracks has to be investigated, as it directly affects the mechanical properties of the printed feature and is of high importance for reliable circuits [27].

After this introduction to hybrid electronics using additive manufacturing processes, in section II the materials and methods are described that were used for realizing test structures. In section II A., the test structure is described, in II B., the applied inkjet printer, the silver ink and the PET substrate are presented. The Section II C. illustrates the printing process and II D. the sample preparation that is needed for the analysis of the cross sections. In section III, the results of the printing process (III A.), the sample preparation (III B.) and the SEM analysis of the fabricated cross sections (III C.) are outlined. Finally, section IV gives a conclusion and an outlook.

II. Materials and Methods

A. *Test structure*

A test structure was defined for the electrical and mechanical evaluation of the properties of different ink-substrate-printer-combinations and different processing parameters. The test structure conceived for electrical and mechanical characterization consists of a 45 mm long conductive track (L) that connects two contact pads each having a length (B) of 7 mm and a width (T) of 2 mm. Figure 2 shows the geometry of the test structure (top) and some inkjet-printed samples (bottom).

B. *Material (printer, ink and substrate)*

The printer used for printing the test structures is based on our custom-built piezo-driven four-axis positioning system NAMOSE. It has a working space of 400 mm x 150 mm x 40 mm, a repeatability of less than 1 µm and a maximum speed of 200 mm/s [2]. NAMOSE is controlled by a Beckhoff-CX2040 with TwinCAT, programmable logic controller (PLC) and numerical control (NC) axis controlling. For inkjet-printing, the positioning system is equipped with a piezo-electrically driven single nozzle Microfab print head (MJ-AL-01-50-8MX) with an orifice diameter of 50 µm [2]. A NC-task synchronizes the droplet frequency (f_d) with the axis velocity (v), while the droplet distance (d_d) is maintained at its set point. Furthermore, the NAMOSE is equipped with a heated vacuum chuck and an optical observation system for controlling and adjusting droplet formation.

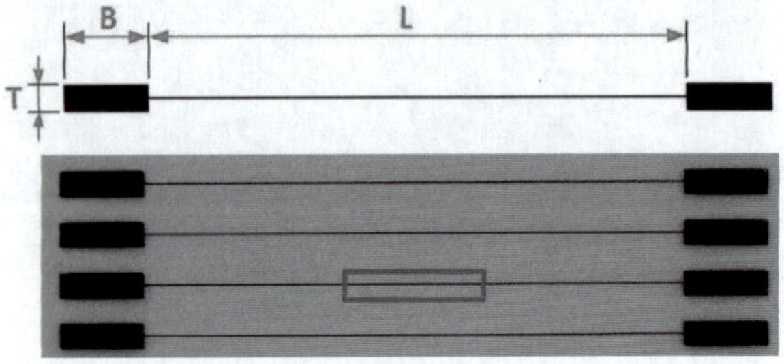

Figure 2. Inkjet test structure. Geometry (top), image of printed test structures (bottom), specimen geometry for ultramicrotomy (red box)

The silver-nanoparticle ink DGP 40LT-15C (Advanced Nano Products (ANP)) was purchased from Sigma Aldrich (736465 ALDRICH). The ink has a solid content of 30 - 35 wt %, a surface tension of 35 - 38 mN/m, a viscosity of about 10 - 17 mPa·s and is designed for application on polymer films. The manufacturer recommends a curing regime with 30 - 60 minutes at 120 - 150 °C. The main solvent of the ink is triethylene glycol monoethyl ether (TGME) [28]. The ink contains polyvinylpyrrolidone (PVP) as capping agent that leads to an electrostatic stabilization of the nanoparticles [9].

In the present work, two different PET-films were used as substrates. The 125 µm thick Melinex® ST506™ from DuPont Teijin Films is optimized for printed electronics. Both sides of this film are pre-treated for improved adhesion of inks [14]. The NB-TP-3GU100 from Mitsubishi Paper Mills is a 135 µm thick PET-film that is optimized for inkjet-printing of conductive structures based on silver nanoparticle dispersions. Due to its optimized nanoporous single side coating, it provides fast drying of water-based inks [29]. The thickness, morphology and the surface chemistry of this coating are not further specified by the supplier.

C. *Printing samples*

Test structures were printed on both substrates using the ink DGP 40LT-15C. Table I shows the printing parameters for four different samples. After printing, the samples were cured in a convection oven (Memmert UP 500) for about 60 min. at 120 °C.

After curing, the width of the central part of the test structure (see the red box in Figure 2) was measured by optical microscopy and image processing with the DIPLOM software that was developed at the KIT Institute for Applied Computer Science (IAI). The image processing yields the standard deviation of the line widths, which can be used as indicator of the line edge quality.

D. *Sample preparation for SEM-analysis*

For analyzing the cross section of central printed tracks, about 10 mm long and 1.5 mm wide rectangular specimen were cut from the printed test structures (see the red box in Figure 2).

As it is not possible at ambient conditions, to directly cut the flexible polymer with an ultramicrotome without

TABLE I. PRINTING PARAMETERS

sample	substrate	d_d [µm]	T_S [°C]	v [mm/s]
A	Melinex® ST506™	147	80	50
B	Melinex® ST506™	13	80	50
C	NB-TP-3GU100	31	RT	10
D	NB-TP-3GU100	1	RT	10

delamination of the ink, the printed samples need to be embedded into polymer blocks in order to get appropriate sections. Two different specimens were embedded parallel to each other into one embedding mould.

As embedding resin, the Embed 812 Kit from Electron Microscopy Sciences was used. The filled embedding moulds were cured over night at 60 °C in a convection oven.

After polymerization, the blocks with the embedded samples were removed from the moulds and then prepared for ultramicrotomy. For this purpose, the blocks were trimmed in a Leica Ultracut 7 ultramicrotome using a standard glass trimming knife. Then, sections of 100 nm and 200 nm thickness were cut with the same instrument but with a Diatome Ultra 35° knife at ambient conditions. The knife boat was filled with double-distilled water during the cutting process. To avoid electrostatic charging of the sample, a Diatome static line 2 ionizer was used. The cut sections are floating on the water surface of the knife boat, where they can be subsequently picked up and placed on a silicon wafer for imaging in the scanning electron microscope (SEM).

For SEM imaging, an Ultra 55 (Carl Zeiss Microscopy, Oberkochen, Germany) was used.

Particle density in the SEM images of the cross sections was measured with the software package Fiji [30]. Figure 3 illustrates the approach to determine the particle density by image segmentation. The threshold for the segmentation was manually selected for different details of a SEM-image of a cross section. The density of the particles in the sectional plane was calculated for each detail.

III. Results and Discussion

A. *Printing*

In a preliminary test, it was found that the behavior of the ink after deposition at room temperature is completely different on the two different substrates. Although the initial wetting seems to be good, printing on the Melinex® ST506™ substrate is followed by a continuous parasitic spreading combined with a resulting shape similar to a coffee-ring effect. This results in very flat, broad and fringed tracks, with poor edge qualities. The nanoporous coating of the PET-film from Mitsubishi Paper Mills avoids this ink spreading over a broad range of droplet-distances d_d. A considerable track height can be achieved, even for narrow tracks. Optimizing the droplet-distance (d_d), it is even possible to print continuous tracks with a width of less than the diameter of a single droplet. Figure 4 shows microscope images of this preliminary test. The printing parameters were the same for both substrates: the jetting frequency (f_d) was 2000 Hz, the axis speed (v) was 100 mm/s and the droplet-distance (d_d) results in 50 µm. The silver track on Melinex® ST506™ (see Figure 4 left) shows a poor edge quality, a width of about 1180 µm and a height in the range of about 100 nm, whereas the line printed on NB-TP-3GU100 (see Figure 4 right) has a good edge quality at a width of about 88 µm and a height of about 1140 nm.

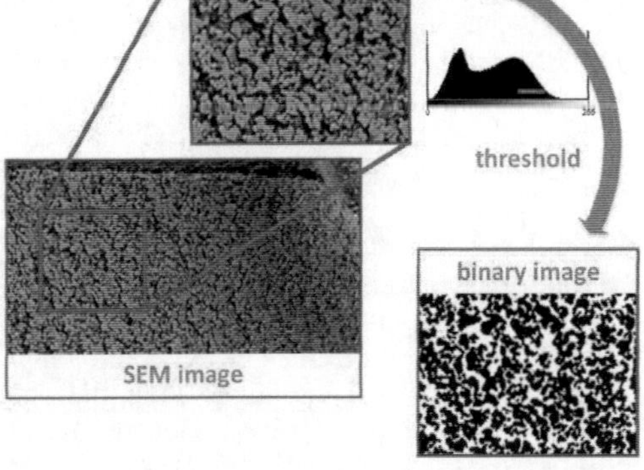

Figure 3. Determination scheme of the nanoparticle density

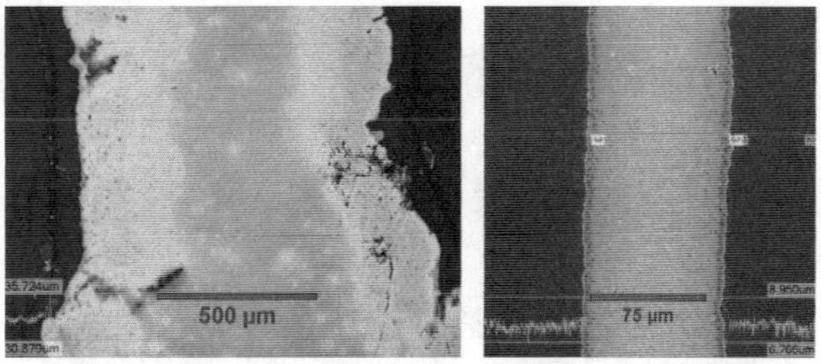

Figure 4. Microscope images of printed silver ink tracks at room temperature on Melinex® ST506™ (left) and on NB-TP-3GU100 (right)

In further tests, it was found that printing on Melinex® ST506™, with 80 °C substrate temperature results in much better track quality. This parameter was maintained for all subsequent tests with this substrate.

Concerning the sintering in a convection oven, an irreversible bulging of the NB-TP-3GU100 can be observed when heating above T_g of PET. A possible explanation for this effect could be different thermal expansion coefficients of the single side nanoporous coating and the PET bulk material. The Melinex® ST506™ foil does not show such an effect.

B. *Sample preparation via ultramicrotomy*

Figure 5 shows the block with the embedded specimens (left, a and b), the top of the block during trimming with the glass knife (center, c) and a section directly after cutting (right).

200 nm sections can be cut reproducibly but with a significant wrinkling of the embedded specimens in the sections (see Figure 5 right, d and e). Lower section

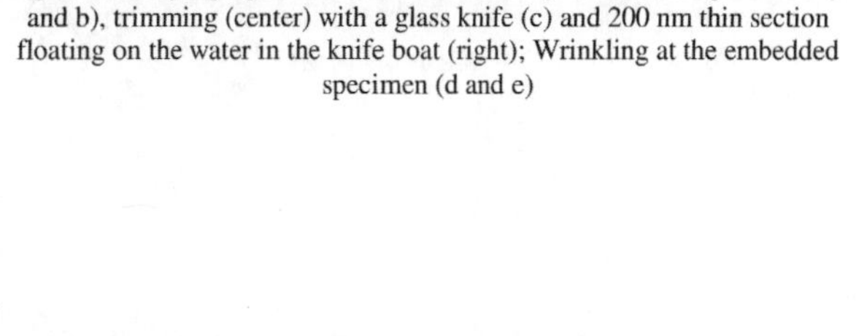

Figure 5. Sample preparation via ultramicrotomy. Embedded specimens (a and b), trimming (center) with a glass knife (c) and 200 nm thin section floating on the water in the knife boat (right); Wrinkling at the embedded specimen (d and e)

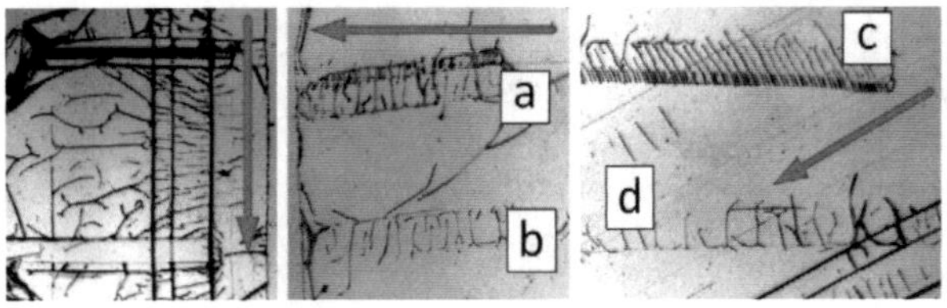

Figure 6. Influence of the cutting direction on the section morphology and the specimens (a and c: NB-TP-3GU100; b and d: Melinex® ST506™). Perpendicular (left), parallel (center) and 26° (right) to substrate plane (arrows indicate cutting direction)

thicknesses led to delamination between specimen and embedding resin.

An initial observation of the cross sections concerned the nanoporous coating of the Mitsubishi substrate: We found a 35 μm thick layer. The high thickness of this layer supports the hypothesis stated above that this might be the main reason for the warping of the substrate after thermal sintering.

Different cutting directions were tested with respect to the sample orientation in the block: perpendicular, parallel and at an angle to the embedded substrate plane. Figure 6 shows typical results indicating the effect of the cutting direction (red arrows).

When cutting is performed perpendicular to the substrate plane, the interface between the ink and the substrate is compressed and can therefore not be used for further investigation of the interface. Additionally, this section shows many wrinkles and dominant knife marks (see Figure 6 left). In contrast, sections obtained when cutting parallel to the substrate plane, show less wrinkles and knife marks (see Figure 6 center). It is assumed that this cutting direction introduces fewer mechanical stresses to the interface between ink and substrate. The sections obtained, when cutting at an angle of about 26° to the substrate plane, were also acceptable (see Figure 6 right). The embedded NB-TP-3GU100 substrate (see Figure 6 a and c) produces much more wrinkles than the Melinex® ST506™ (see Figure 6 b and d). We suppose that Melinex® film is harder than the Mitsubishi film due to its heat and surface treatment. This can

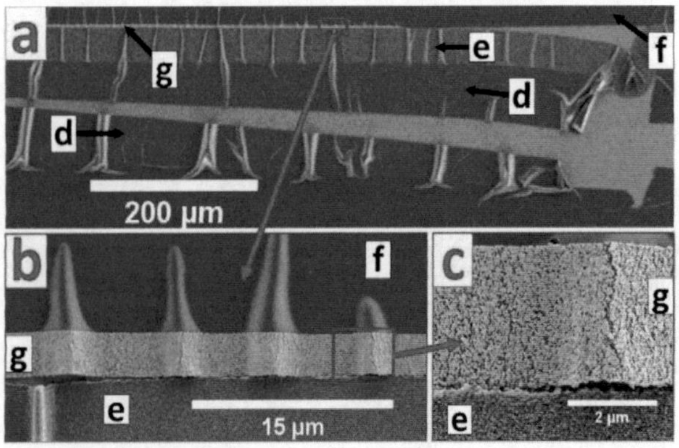

Figure 7. SEM images of a section containing a silver track (g) printed on NB-TP-3GU100 substrate (d: bulk, e: nanoporous coating, f: embedding resin); low magnification (a), high magnification (b, c); bulk substrate delamination (a); cracks and delamination of conductive cracks (b, c)

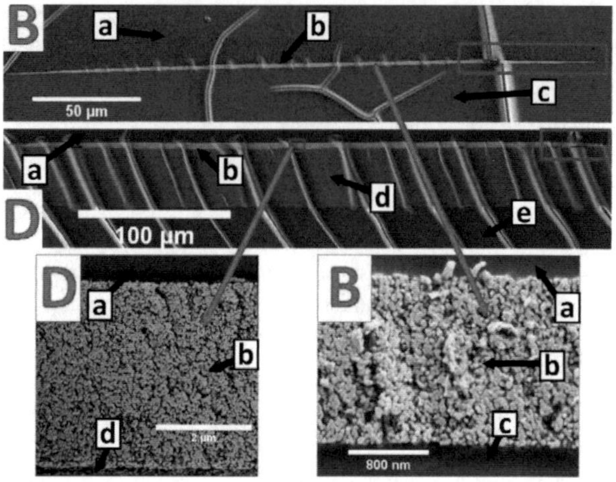

Figure 8. SEM images of sections containing the samples B (a: embedding resin, b: silver ink, c: substrate) and D (a: resin, b: silver ink, d: nanoporous coating, e: bulk substrate); low magnification (top) and high magnification images (bottom)

explain why the sections of NB-TP-3GU100 specimen show a stronger wrinkling than the Melinex® substrate.

C. SEM analysis and image segmentation

Despite varying the cutting direction, a certain degree of section wrinkling was unavoidable. This led to a degradation of the sections in terms of cracks. Sometimes delamination occurred in the section while cutting. Figure 7 shows a section from a NB-TP-3GU100 substrate cut parallel to the substrate plane (a). It can be seen that the substrate was torn during the cutting process (see Figure 7 a) and the printed ink delaminates from the coated substrate at the locations of the wrinkles (b and c).

Nevertheless, there are enough regions suitable for further analysis (compare Figure 7 b and c), since the cutting preserved the nanostructure of the cross section.

Figure 8 shows the cross section of the samples B and D. The full low magnification cross section for each sample can be seen on the top, a detail image can be found on the bottom for each sample. Using such high magnification images from SEM we determined the particle density of each sample according to the procedure described above. The particle density of the conductive tracks calculated for all four samples was between 58 % and 65 %.

Additionally, we found that the cross section of the tracks printed on Melinex® ST506™ levels off continuously in the direction of the edges (see the blue box in Figure 8 B). In contrast, the height of the silver track on NB-TP-3GU100 only decreases close to the edges (see the blue box in Figure 8 D).

IV. Conclusion and Outlook

A method was outlined for analyzing the nano- and microstructure of inkjet printed conductive tracks on different polymer substrates using ultramicrotomy. The sections produced showed wrinkling along the substrate plane partially leading to delamination. This may result from stiffness differences between the substrate material and the embedding resin, a parameter to be optimized in further investigations. Despite these delaminations, there were sufficient regions that could be used for investigation of the nanoparticle network of the printed conductive tracks. This indicates that with properly optimized embedding and cutting parameters, the described scheme is a promising method for analyzing thermal, mechanical and chemical influences on the nanostructure of printed metal nanoparticle inks and on the interface between substrate and ink.

ACKNOLEDGMENTS

The authors thank Dr. Tim Scharnweber from the KIT Institute for Biological Interfaces (IBG1) for enabling the measurements with the laser-scanning microscope.

REFERENCES

[1] J. Perelaer, and U. S. Schubert. "Novel approaches for low temperature sintering of inkjet-printed inorganic nanoparticles for roll-to-roll (R2R) applications," Journal of Materials Research, vol. 28, pp. 564–573, 2013, doi: 10.1557/jmr.2012.419.

[2] M. Ungerer, U. Gengenbach, A. Hofmann, and G. Bretthauer. "Comparative and systemic analysis of digital single nozzle printing processes for the manufacturing of functional microstructures," Proc. MikroSystemTechnik Kongress (MST 2015): MEMS, Mikroelektronik, Systeme, Oct. 2015, ISBN: 978-3-8007-4100-7.

[3] J. Lessing et al. "Inkjet Printing of Conductive Inks with High Lateral Resolution on Omniphobic "RF Paper" for Paper-Based Electronics and MEMS," Advanced Materials, vol. 26, pp. 4677–4682, 2014, doi: 10.1002/adma.201401053.

[4] H.-H. Lee, K.-S. Chou, and K.-C. Huang. "Inkjet printing of nanosized silver colloids," Nanotechnology, vol. 16, p. 2436, 2005, doi: 10.1088/0957-4484/16/10/074.

[5] Y. Kawahara, S. Hodges, N.-W. Gong, S. Olberding, and J. Steimle. "Building Functional Prototypes Using Conductive Inkjet Printing," IEEE Pervasive Comput., vol. 13, pp. 30–38, 2014, doi: 10.1109/MPRV.2014.41.

[6] T. Öhlund et al. "Assisted sintering of silver nanoparticle inkjet ink on paper with active coatings," RSC Advances, vol. 5, pp. 64841–64849, 2015, doi: 10.1039/C5RA06626C.

[7] S. H. Ko et al. "All-inkjet-printed flexible electronics fabrication on a polymer substrate by low-temperature high-resolution selective laser sintering of metal nanoparticles," Nanotechnology, vol. 18, p. 345202, 2007, doi: 10.1088/0957-4484/18/34/345202.

[8] J. Perelaer et al. "Plasma and Microwave Flash Sintering of a Tailored Silver Nanoparticle Ink, Yielding 60% Bulk Conductivity on Cost-Effective Polymer Foils," Advanced Materials, vol. 24, pp. 3993–3998, 2012, doi: 10.1002/adma.201200899.

[9] H. Andersson et al. "Inkjet Printed Silver Nanoparticle Humidity Sensor With Memory Effect on Paper," IEEE Sensors J., vol. 12, pp. 1901–1905, 2012, doi: 10.1109/JSEN.2011.2182044.

[10] J. Niittynen et al. "Alternative sintering methods compared to conventional thermal sintering for inkjet printed silver nanoparticle ink," Thin Solid Films, vol. 556, pp. 452–459, 2014, doi: 10.1016/j.tsf.2014.02.001.

[11] G. L. Allen, R. A. Bayles, W. W. Gile, and W. A. Jesser. "Small particle melting of pure metals," Thin Solid Films, vol. 144, pp. 297–308, 1986, doi: 10.1016/0040-6090(86)90422-0.

[12] P. Buffat, and J.-P. Borel. "Size effect on the melting temperature of gold particles," Phys. Rev. A, vol. 13, p. 2287, 1976, doi: 10.1103/PhysRevA.13.2287.

[13] W. A. MacDonald. "Engineered films for display technologies," J. Mater. Chem., vol. 14, p. 4, 2004, doi: 10.1039/b310846p.

[14] DuPont Teijin Films. "Product Information Melinex® ST506™," [Online]. Available from: http://www.koenig-kunststoffe.de/produkte/melinex/melinex-r-st506.pdf, [retrieved: Feb, 2017].

[15] W. A. MacDonald et al. "Latest advances in substrates for flexible electronics," Journal of the Society for Information Display, vol. 15, pp. 1075–1083, 2007, doi: 10.1889/1.2825093.

[16] U. Caglar, K. Kaija, and P. Mansikkamaki. "Analysis of mechanical performance of silver inkjet-printed structures," Proc. IEEE 2nd International Nanoelectronics Conference (INEC 2008), Mar. 2008, pp. 851–856, ISBN: 978-1-4244-1572-4, doi: 10.1109/INEC.2008.4585617.

[17] D.-H. Lee, K.-T. Lim, E.-K. Park, J.-M. Kim, and Y.-S. Kim. "Optimized ink-jet printing condition for stable and reproducible performance of organic thin film transistor," Microelectronic Engineering, vol. 111, pp. 242–246, 2013, doi: 10.1016/j.mee.2013.03.177.

[18] G. Li, R. C. Roberts, and N. C. Tien. "Interlacing method for micro-patterning silver via inkjet printing," Proc. IEEE 13th Sensors Conference, Nov. 2014, pp. 1687–1690, ISBN: 978-1-4799-0162-3, doi: 10.1109/ICSENS.2014.6985346.

[19] F. Molina-Lopez, D. Briand, and N. F. de Rooij. "All additive inkjet printed humidity sensors on plastic substrate," Sensors and Actuators B: Chemical, 166–167, pp. 212–222, 2012, doi: 10.1016/j.snb.2012.02.042.

[20] D. Soltman, and V. Subramanian. "Inkjet-printed line morphologies and temperature control of the coffee ring effect," Langmuir the ACS journal of surfaces and colloids, vol. 24, pp. 2224–2231, 2008, doi: 10.1021/la7026847.

[21] I. Reinhold et al. "Argon plasma sintering of inkjet printed silver tracks on polymer substrates," Journal of Materials Chemistry, vol. 19, pp. 3384–3388, 2009, doi: 10.1039/B823329B.

[22] J. Perelaer, M. Klokkenburg, C. E. Hendriks, and U. S. Schubert. "Microwave Flash Sintering of Inkjet-Printed Silver Tracks on Polymer Substrates," Advanced Materials, vol. 21, pp. 4830–4834, 2009, doi: 10.1002/adma.200901081.

[23] S. Magdassi, M. Grouchko, O. Berezin, and A. Kamyshny. "Triggering the sintering of silver nanoparticles at room temperature," ACS nano, vol. 4, pp. 1943–1948, 2010, doi: 10.1021/nn901868t.

[24] B.-J. Kim et al. "Improving mechanical fatigue resistance by optimizing the nanoporous structure of inkjet-printed Ag electrodes for flexible devices," Nanotechnology, vol. 25, p. 125706, 2014, doi: 10.1088/0957-4484/25/12/125706.

[25] N. Marjanović. "Hybrid electronics systems by CSEM," Proc. 8th International Exhibition and Conference for the Printed Electronics Industry (LOPEC 2016): Technical Conference, München, Apr. 2016.

[26] U. Gengenbach et al. "A toolbox for multifunctional multilayer printed systems," Proc. MikroSystemTechnik Kongress (MST 2015): MEMS, Mikroelektronik, Systeme, Oct. 2015, ISBN: 978-3-8007-4100-7.

[27] S. Merilampi, T. Laine-Ma, and P. Ruuskanen. "The characterization of electrically conductive silver ink patterns on flexible substrates," Microelectronics Reliability, vol. 49, pp. 782–790, 2009, doi: 10.1016/j.microrel.2009.04.004.

[28] Advanced Nano Products (ANP). "Nano-Silver Ink for Inkjet Printing," [Online]. Available from: http://anapro.com/eng/product/silver_inkjet_ink.html, [retrieved: Feb, 2017].

[29] Mitsubishi Paper Mills. "Technical Data Sheet: Mitsubishi Nano Benefit Series NB-TP-3GU100," [Online]. Available from: https://www.mitsubishi-paper.com/fileadmin/user_upload/PrePress/downloads/silver_nano/PET_Film_NB-TP-3GU100.pdf, [retrieved: Feb, 2017].

[30] J. Schindelin et al. "Fiji: an open-source platform for biological-image analysis," Nature Methods, vol. 9, pp. 676–682, 2012, doi: 10.1038/nmeth.2019.

Usability Analysis of Archetyped Interfaces for the Electronic Health Record: a Comparative Study

Danielle Santos Alves, Valéria Cesário Times, André Magno Costa de Araújo, Marcus Urbano da Silva
Center for Informatics (CIN) at Federal University of Pernambuco (UFPE)
Recife, Brazil
{e-mail: dsa3, vct, amca, mus}@cin.ufpe.br

Amadeu Sá Campos Filho, Magdala de Araújo Novaes
TeleHealth Center (NUTES), Clinical Hospital, Federal University of Pernambuco (UFPE)
Recife, Brazil
{e-mail: amadeu.campos, magdala.novaes}@nutes.ufpe.br

***Abstract*— Few studies about OpenEHR standards assess usability aspects. This paper aims to evaluate archetyped interfaces, built by a user interface building tool, with respect to usability requirements of health care professionals. Such an assessment is carried out by comparing two user interface building tools. We carried out experimental tests with Health professionals to evaluate the generated graphical user interfaces by a standard openEHR tool and a framework proposed by researchers to build Health applications dynamically using archetypes. Quality in Use Integrated Map (QUIM) and Questionnaire for User Interface Satisfaction (QUIS) questionnaires were used to evaluate the usability aspects. The Likert Scale was adopted to evaluate the interface concepts of the tools, such as efficiency, effectiveness and satisfaction. A T-student test was performed to compare the results, which showed that the second tool achieved better ratings in all the analyzed concepts when compared to the first tool, all being statistically significant. The usability characteristics raised by the users are listed. The conclusion is that the interface generated by the second tool brought more user satisfaction in comparison to the first tool.**

Keywords- Archetypes; Electronic Health Records; usability tests; archetyped interfaces; user interface building tool.

I. Introduction

Nowadays Electronic Health Records (EHR) are the subject of many studies, especially those related to achieving interoperability between systems for the future of international health services [1][2]. The main global initiatives focused on EHR interoperability are International Organization for Standardization (ISO), HL7 and the openEHR foundation. To standardize the content semantics, the global academic community has suggested the use of archetypes and terminology [3].

Archetypes may be conceptualized as a set of specifications that define a reference model of Health information; i.e., a language for constructing "clinical models" [3]. For this paper, we define an 'archetyped interface' as a User Interface (UI), which is generated from the specifications, restrictions and terminologies defined within archetypes. Archetyped EHR systems are those that use archetypes in their content definition.

Many authors have studied the human-computer relationship and reflected on this interaction, which relates especially to the interface component "*with emphasis on the human side, the relevance, the utility, among others*" [4].

Research on the use and reuse of archetypes to build the EHR achieved progress in the development of archetyped clinical systems, but many of these studies have not taken into consideration the usability aspects [5]. It is known that the usability aspects are very important for the successful implementation and compliance of an EHR system by the users[4].

There are several possibilities to promote the inclusion of evaluation and usability tests with potential users of EHR products during the system development. Ideally, the users are not engaged in the system design phase (formative tests), but are regularly consulted during business process validation steps and interface design prior to the approval of the final product (summative tests) [6].

Furthermore, the interface is always mentioned in studies as a relevant aspect to be improved by reducing the total number of stages of the process and the percentage of mental effort required while performing tasks, so users feel more confident when they are using the system [7][8]. This paper aims to evaluate the archetyped interfaces built by a user interface building tool with respect to usability requirements of the health care professional through a comparison between two user interface building tools.

The remainder of this paper is organized as follows: Section II describes the background and the related work. Section III presents the usability concepts adopted in the study and describes the influence factors linked to each usability concept used. In Section IV, the methodology is explained, spanning experiment design, data analysis, support instruments and the controlled experiment users. Section V shows the results and includes some discussion about the findings. Finally, Section VI presents the authors' conclusion.

II. Background And Related Work

Some recent studies have described factors that negatively and positively influenced the process of implementing a computerized system in large hospitals in the world. All these studies mentioned the importance of identifying the views of users in the context of implementation. The target population of the studies was the nursing team, which was considered the least resistant team regarding the use of computers during the computerization process [9]–[11].

A study performed at The Johns Hopkins Hospital, (Baltimore, Maryland) in 2003 and published in 2008 by the Association of periOperative Registered Nurses (AORN) Journal, shows the importance of including the nursing staff and members of the information technology staff in the pre-selection of the requirements process, as well as in the final analysis system and implementation. The researchers noticed that for the successful development and implementation of a hospital information system, a technological development is necessary (albeit not enough), alongside a scientific and methodological deepening. According to Saletnik, Niedlinger and Wilson [10], "*nurses played key roles in the planning and implementation phase of the system or of information management at Johns Hopkins*". To conclude, the authors related that "*implementation of information technology is not a purely technical project and, as such, cannot be left to the information technology (IT) department. Health is characterized by a level of complexity that defies predictability required in many IT implementations. The development team, therefore, must be prepared to learn and adapt to the problems*" [10].

In a study with 48 nursing leaders, researchers aimed to evaluate usability aspects of the management system used in the hospitals through a focus group. The researchers summarized the following results: the nurses said that there is a reduction in efficiency in the work process after the application of not fully tested computerized systems. However, they consider electronic systems essential in daily work. Nurses also reported strategic management problems and a lack of coordination during the implementation process of electronic systems [12].

Another study that aimed to analyze and evaluate the perception of the users towards EHR was based on the evaluation of 113 nurses from different shifts of a primary health care institution in Catalonia, Spain, dedicated to adult and pediatric outpatient visits. The sample evaluated nursing users (men and women) with an average age of 44.27 years. The results showed that there is no statistically significant relationship between the nurses' opinions of EHR and the ages of the subjects. However, there are significant differences in results concerning how long they have been using EHRs, as the longer the nurses work with EHRs, the greater is their degree of satisfaction. Nurses considered the contribution of EHRs positive to their nursing care. This work concluded that the usability of the EHR was satisfactory, but also emphasized that, when assessing usability, one must also take into account the training and the need for technical support during the process of implementing the EHR [9].

Many applications in the Health area failed because their interfaces were difficult to use and imposed a heavy cognitive load on its users to navigate through the system. Unfortunately, the aspect of usability is poorly analyzed by software developers, which has a negative effect on the acceptance of electronic solutions by Health professionals.

III. Usability Concepts Vs. Influencing Factors

Many authors over the years try to conceptualize the usability aspects and its metrics. International regulations also specify metrics and parameters to be considered when assessing the usability of a product [13]–[18].

In the context of information technology applied to Health, the challenge is to provide professionals (final users) with computer products that have been developed considering their applicability in contextualized practice, respecting the following usability requirements: easy to learn, use, re-using, among others. Therefore, attention is drawn to the parameters and usability metrics that are used from the moment of planning, to implementation and final evaluation, always involving users in the design (formative tests) and final analysis (summative tests) [19].

Of the 14 concepts of usability found in the literature, four were taken into consideration at this time as being the most relevant in this context that we intend to analyze. These concepts were based mainly on ISO 9241, Nilsen, and Preece, which define as important the concepts of effectiveness, efficiency, satisfaction and usage context. Besides these, the aspect "system screen or interface" was also considered for evaluation [10].

According to [10], for each concept of usability to be evaluated, some factors hereby referred to as "influencing factors" must be taken into consideration as they have a direct impact on results. For each concept, two or more influencing factors may be associated. In the present work, we selected 31 influencing factors for the main concepts. These were weighted and evaluated as part of the issues included in the usability evaluation questionnaire for archetyped clinical systems.

The influencing factors analyzed were: behavioral time; use of resources; attractiveness; pleasantness; flexibility / customization; synthesis; user orientation; consistency; generalization; familiarity; self-description; feedback; observability; compliance task; accuracy; system compatibility with the real world; migration tasks; user control and freedom; recoverability; error recovery; readability; navigability; simplicity; charging time; and help and documentation.

IV. Methodology

This project followed the ethical and legal principles of research involving human subjects, being submitted for review and approved under the number 33667214.3.0000.5208, according to the resolution number 466/12 of the National Health Council in Brazil.

To assure the validity of the tests in this section, we will describe the methods used to evaluate the usability aspects of archetyped interfaces generated by two different user interface building tools. In order to achieve this, the experiment observed some parameters: 1) Time to fill in the form: the total time spent by each user in the experiment to complete a specific task; 2) Value assigned by users to the application form: considers the scores awarded by each user to the tool regarding the usability aspects evaluated; 3) Requested usability requirements: the usability requirements listed by Health-domain users.

By carrying out this experiment, one expects to answer the following research questions: [Question 1 (Q1)]: How long each user takes to complete a task on each user interface building tool? [Question 2 (Q2)]: What is the score given for each user interface building tool and for each group? [Question 3 (Q3)]: What are the usability requirements for archetyped interfaces that will be listed by Health-domain users?

A. *Experiment Design*

For this experiment, we tried to analyze the user interface aspects that influence Health professionals. This was done by testing user interaction with two user interfaces: a) an interface dynamically generated by an archetyped interfaces tool recommended by the openEHR Foundation and b) another tool designed by the researchers.

This first experiment did not take into account aspects of database features and other aspects of security; the choice was made considering exclusively tools that carried the functionality of building interfaces, so that users involved in the experiments could analyze the main usability concepts assessed in this study, i.e.: effectiveness, efficiency, satisfaction, usage context, and system screen or interface.

The aim was to identify the strengths and weaknesses with respect to the usability concepts of the context of use, system screen (interface), effectiveness, efficiency and satisfaction. In addition, the influencing factors mentioned in Section III were also considered.

For the sake of avoiding the influence of biases, the tools were named Tool 1 (T1) and Tool 2 (T2). Tool 1 (T1) is the standard tool of the openEHR Foundation, used by researchers worldwide for archetype specification [20]. Tool 2 (T2) is a tool designed by [21] that aims to build dynamic interfaces from specified archetypes available in the database of the Clinical Knowledge Manager (CKM) [22]. Figures 1 and 2 show the interface of T1 and T2, respectively.

Both user interface building tools were evaluated by 14 users (Health professionals with expertise in information systems). From the findings of this assessment, a list of the main positive and negative aspects of the tools was produced. From the negative aspects, proposals for improvements were listed.

The subjects who agreed to participate in the experiment were placed in a computer lab where they sat randomly on machines with the same configuration, in which tools T1 and T2 were already open. In front of their machines, they had the documents indicating to which group they would be allocated (randomization). They were divided into two groups (Group 1 - G1 and Group 2 - G2). This was done to prevent researchers from knowing to which group an individual belonged, rending the experiment double-blind. All the computer screens were filmed from the beginning of the test with the tools on each machine. The collected data was stored by researchers to complement the purposes of qualitative analysis.

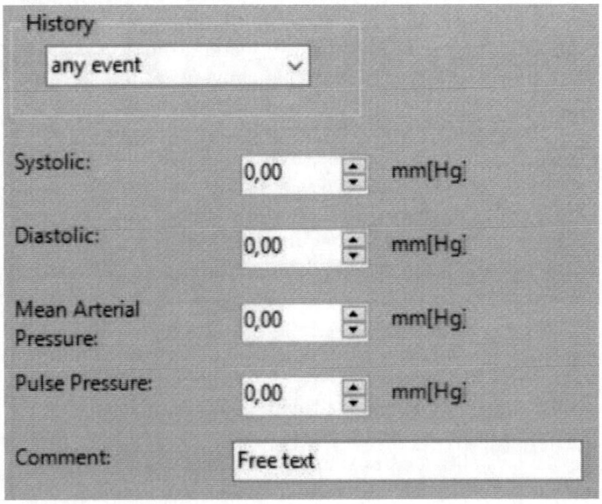

Figure 1. Example of an interface of the "Blood Pressure" archetype in Tool 1 (T1)

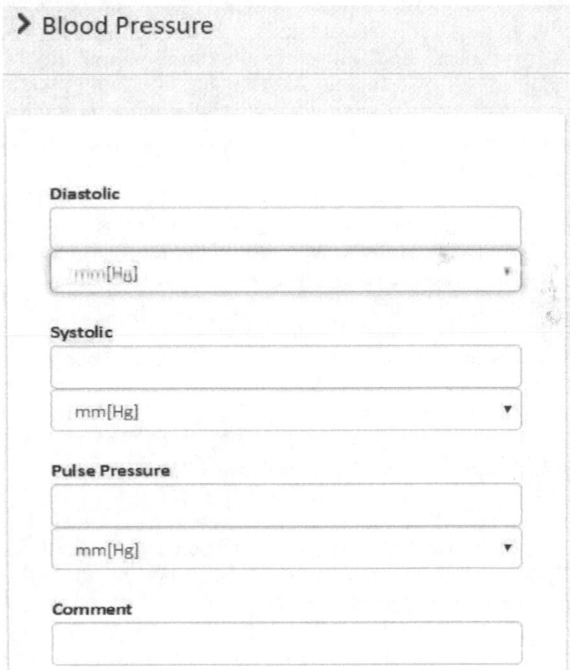

Figure 2. Example of an interface of the "Blood Pressure" archetype in Tool 2 (T2)

To eliminate the influence of previous experience with the tools and ensure that the answers are influenced only by the dependent variables detailed in the methodology of this paper, we used the technique of drawing study known as the Latin Square experiment 2x2 [21].

Latin Square is done by dividing volunteers into two groups (G1 and G2), who then evaluate T1 and T2 randomly. Participants in G1 commenced by using Tool 1 (T1), filling in the usability questionnaire for T1 and then using and evaluating Tool 2 (T2). Similarly, participants in G2 began using Tool 2 (T2) and then evaluating it. After that, they used Tool 1 (T1) and filled in the questionnaire for Tool 1.

For the experiment to represent the use of a health system faithfully, a clinical case of a fictitious patient with a maximum wealth of detail was designed and provided to the volunteers as the basis of the interface interaction exercise.

Four archetypes from the international repository CKM of the openEHR Foundation [22] were selected and used as the basic blocks for both tools. These were: patient admission; family history; problem diagnosis; and blood pressure. These four archetypes were chosen for minimally representing an admission and physical examination of the patient. They were captured and inserted as input for the interface design in both tools. It is worth noting that, during the assessment, the terminology and aspects of validation information of archetypes were not taken into account.

B. *Data analysis*

The usability questionnaire for the evaluation of archetyped interfaces was designed with the concepts (effectiveness, efficiency, satisfaction, use of context and system screen) and influencing factors of usability as explained in the section above. The questions in this survey were based on international validated questionnaires, such as Quality in Use Integrated Map (QUIM) and Questionnaire for User Interface Satisfaction (QUIS) [17][19].

For each of the concepts and influencing factors, a number of questions concerning the parameters analyzed were answered. Respondents were to analyze each question based on a Likert scale of 1 to 5, where 1 was considered the worst rating and 5 the best.

From these results, the arithmetic mean was calculated within each parameter. For this study, each concept was attributed an equal value. Tools with a final rating of 3.5 or more for each concept were considered satisfactory. In order to compare results numerically, the T-student test was applied, adopting a 95% confidence level.

C. *Support Instruments*

To perform the tests, each participant received the following support instruments: 1) Definition of archetypes and their Health application; 2) Instructions on Tool 1; 3) Instructions on Tool 2; 4) Free and clarified Consent Term; 5) map with information about the experiment; 6) Online access to usability evaluation questionnaire for each tool.

D. *Controlled Experiment Users*

According to Nielsen [15], 5 evaluators are sufficient to identify about 75% of the total usability issues at the interface and 10 are sufficient to identify 100%. For this experiment, 14 volunteers were invited - 7 for each experimental group.

Participants in the experiment were Health professionals who work in direct health care and Professors at the Federal University of Pernambuco (UFPE). These professionals were chosen on the basis of having at least a 2-year experience in health care and in-patient care in different specialties, as well as being active in various levels of complexity of health care. The full experiment took a week to complete.

V. RESULTS AND DISCUSSION

This section shows the results of the study, comparing with the literature review. The health professionals came to the lab and start responding a questionary about their sociodemographic information. Then, they test both systems. The sociodemographic profile and the user experience are shown ahead.

A. *Users Profile*

An invitation was sent to 20 Health professionals among doctors and nurses, with 14 Nursing Professionals attending the day of the experiment. All who attended were female who work in education and/or patient care. There were four Ph.D. researchers, three Ph.D. students, three experts, two Masters students and 2 undergraduates. The mean age was 34 years [25-55 years.] The training ranged from 1.5 years to 33 years with a mean of 10.5 years and the service time in the current workplace was 5.5 years [2 months - 32 years].

With regard to computer skills, all participants reported using web tools (send and receive email, do research on the Internet); 12 type and format text and prepare slides; 8 use spreadsheets; 7 use image editors; 6 use statistical software; 5 use the EHR and 3 some other Health application.

Regarding the computational skills, four users were familiar with the use of the EHR, with long experience ranging from 1 year and 2 months to 9 years. The time spent operating an EHR per week ranged from 10 to 40 hours, averaging 21.25 hours. These users were characterized based on their experience with EHR and classified as inexperienced (2 users), intermediate (1 user) and only one was considered very experienced.

B. *Quantitative results*

As it can be seen in Table I, the analysis of Tool 1 and Tool 2 was carried out and divided by study groups (G1 and G2); then, we reached a final result based on the largest quantity of positive responses for each tool. The columns show the mean value of each group for each tool.

TABLE I. RESULTS OF USABILITY TESTING OF TOOLS 1 AND 2 BY THE RESEARCH GROUP

	TOOL 1		TOOL 2	
	G1	G2	G1	G2
Fill Time	22,00	18,14	15,43	25,29
[C1] System Screen	3,02	3,66	4,38	4,14
[C2] Effectiveness	2,71	3,71	3,89	3,66
[C3] Efficiency	2,89	3,89	4,14	3,71
[C4] Satisfaction	2,71	3,67	3,93	3,66
[FI] Influencing Factors (31)	2,62	3,40	3,42	3,36
Overall average tool	3	4	4	4

G1: Group 1 assessment; G2: Group 2 assessment; T1: Tool 1; T2: Tool 2

Table I shows the time spent filling in the form, the final average of all questions for each concept of usability, the final average for the influencing factors and the overall mean rating for each Tool. The analyses were performed comparing the groups and tools.

1) Time to fill in form

As it can be seen in Figure 1, the mean value of filling time of each web form of group 1 was lower for Tool 2. For Group 2, the shortest time was for the Tool 1, i.e., when the user began the experiment by filling the form for Tool 1, they spent less time filling in Tool 2 and vice-versa. We may infer that the user was already familiar with the information (terminology) used in the archetype and with the reported case, making it easier to fill in the second form. Thus, for each group beginning of the second tool used had a lower filling time.

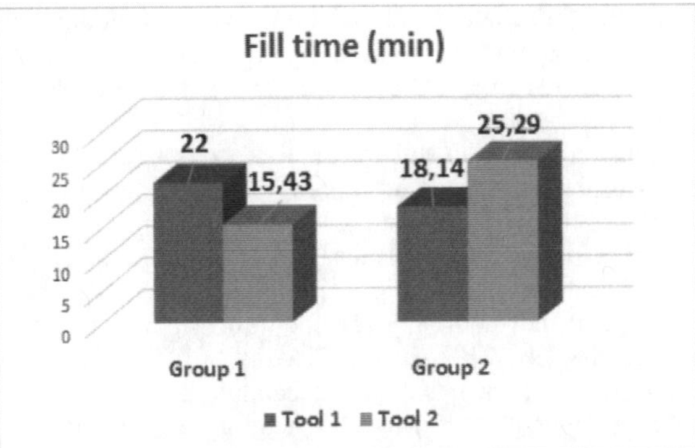

Figure 3. Average filling time for both evaluated Tools

In the statistical analysis, the filling time difference between the groups for the tool 1 and 2 was statistically significant (p = 0.005), and tool 2 had a higher average filling time.

2) System Screen

Regarding the concept 1 [C1] that evaluated the screen used, Tool 2 achieved a greater usability score for the both groups in all questions of the questionnaire. However, this result was not statistically significant (p = 0.077).

3) Effectiveness

Concerning Effectiveness [C2], Tool 2 achieved better scores than Tool 1. As compared per group, G2 preferred Tool 1, but with a minimum percentage difference with statistically significant difference (p = 0.052).

In this category, the users said that they could not complete the required tasks easily, correctly and completely. Additionally, errors that appeared were impediments to finishing the task.

4) Efficiency

Concerning Efficiency [C3], the results obtained were similar to those found in the previous concept. For Group 1, Tool 2 had a higher score than the grades assessed by the Group 2. To Group 2, Tool 1 was better regarded, with a statistically significant minimum percentage difference (p = 0.047).

The users said that while using Tool 1, they had difficulty to accomplish the tasks set; these have not been completed more quickly and completely when compared to Tool 2. In order to complete a task, users declared it was necessary to go through many steps, i.e., using a lot of graphics and mental resources.

5) Satisfaction

Satisfaction [C4] for Tool 2 achieved higher scores than Tool 1. Group 1 displayed a clear preference, whereas Group 2 attributed score average difference was only 0.01 for Tool 1 or 2. This difference was statistically significant (p = 0.055), leading to the conclusion that Tool 2 brought more satisfaction to its users.

In terms of satisfaction, Tool 1 was considered frustrating, tedious, difficult, poor in resources, and easily attached to negative feelings. Finally, Tool 1 did not promote the feeling of satisfaction, did not meet expectations, and was not attractive aesthetically.

6) Influencing factors

We evaluated 31 influencing usability factors. Group 1 considered the Tool 2 better than Tool 1. Since Group 2 found Tool 1 better, but with a little statistically significant difference (p = 0.038), the final overall average score of the tools with respect to evaluation of all concepts of usability shows that Tool 2 was preferred in comparison to Tool 1 for Group 1 and obtained the same average score (4) when compared to Group 2.

The highest average presented by Tool 2 shows that there were improvements in usability aspects presented by it, but it still had some aspects that should be improved.

A critical influencing factor was customization. Neither Tool 1 nor 2 allow for customization of the graphics and logical sequence of information in the interface.

The users said it was not possible to identify the recognizable elements of the tool interface from previous interactions with the same tool or other elements of the real world, such as a printer image on the screen identifying an impression.

Regarding the aspects of errors, the tool was not able to offer the user a clearly identified emergency exit; also, it did not allow to easily recover from unexpected situations. It was not able to help the user to recognize, diagnose and recover from errors. Finally, the software did not use simple language to present the errors and show how to circumvent them.

A positive point that was cited by the volunteers was that all the information for each Health aspect evaluated was listed in the same screen, requiring users to simply scroll down the screen to gain access to other information.

C. Final evaluation

The final results can be seen in Table II. For concept 1 [C1], which evaluated the screen, Tool 2 was preferred by both groups (G1 and G2), obtaining a mean score of 87.5, 93% and 75% approval, respectively.

Regarding Effectiveness [C2], Tool 2 was preferred by Group 1, but Tool 1 received higher marks from Group 2.

Both tools achieved the same degree of acceptance in this aspect. (80% for each specified group)

Regarding Efficiency [C3], Tool 2 was approved by 100% of the volunteers that were part of Group 1, and Tool 1 was preferred by Group 2, achieving a 75% approval rate.

On the issue of satisfaction [C4], participants in Group 1 were 100% satisfied with Tool 2 and 60% of participants in Group 2 preferred Tool 1.

TABLE II. FINAL RESULTS OF THE USABILITY TESTS FOR TOOL 1 AND 2

	FINAL RESULTS	
	G1	G2
[C1] System Screen	T2 (87,5%)	T2 (93,75%)
[C2] Effectiveness	T2 (80%)	T1 (80%)
[C3] Efficiency	T2 (100%)	T1 (75%)
[C4] Satisfaction	T2 (100%)	T1(60%)
[FI] Influencing Factors (31)	T2 (87,1%)	T1 (71%)
Overall average Tool	T2	T1=T2

G1: Group 1 assessment; G2: Group 2 assessment; T1: Tool 1; T2: Tool 2

Of the 31 influencing factors of usability, Tool 2 was approved in 87.1% of the items by Group 1, and Tool 1 was preferred in 71% of the items by Group 2.

The final overall average for each tool appointed Tool 2 as being better according to group 1, whereas Group 2 evaluated both tools similarly. This difference was statistically significant (p 0.042).

Regarding overall satisfaction, as it can be seen in Figure 4, an assessment of the degree of satisfaction has been made for each evaluated aspect.

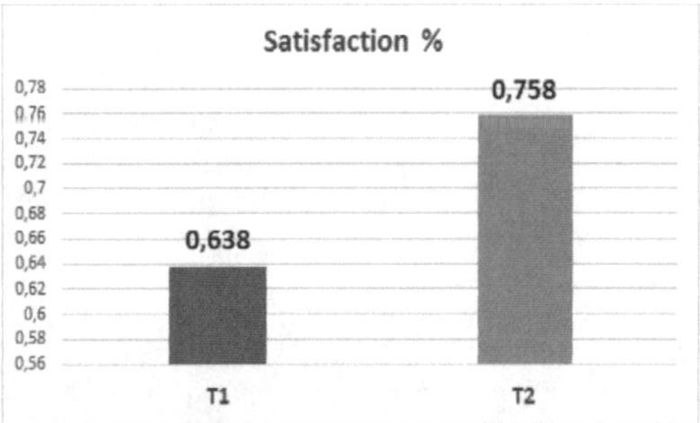

Figure 4. Satisfaction of the evaluated Tools

In general, Tool 1 achieved a degree of satisfaction of 63.8%, while Tool 2 achieved a higher level of satisfaction equal to 75.8%. This result was statistically significant (p 0.055), confirming that Tool 2 has brought greater satisfaction to its users.

VI. CONCLUSION

The contribution of this study was to make usability tests with archetyped clinical tools, which are being used worldwide as a new approach for modeling content in Health information systems, albeit having never been tested on usability aspects. From these findings, the researchers will have parameters to design future systems. The usability of interfaces archetyped had not yet been explored in the literature with much detail.

We highlight the fact that end users ought to be asked to expose their preferences early in the prototyping process of future systems. This practice has been observed in some papers on software specification. User participation since the design phase is crucial in determining the success of a computer system.

More attention should be given to the customization feature. This feature was highly requested by end users because, with customization possibilities, interface usability problems such as font size, background color, and location, can be easily addressed without dependence on computer programmers. A system with this feature is required by Health professionals, and new research on development and validation of such functionality is a possible future path.

The results reported by users will be the basis for the development of a visual library prototype of functionalities for archetyped systems. All the aspects presented will serve as input for the development of future systems, including the specificities demanded by users. The requested adjustments will be specified in a future system that is being developed by the researchers.

Another aspect observed in the study that directly impacts usability was the terminology. Although it was not the focus of this validation study, the researchers were called upon many times during testing by various professionals to answer questions about terms, even after the researchers informed that they could not provide information that would influence the test. This situation led us to believe that the terminology can increase the probability of errors while providing required information. A suggestion then would be to carryout archetype validation studies.

Even though semantics is not the focus of this study, the importance of content validation of the data found in the archetypes became apparent. In addition, coherence in the workflow sequence is of great importance for Health professionals, having a significant impact on the acceptance, use and satisfaction of the future Electronic Health Record. This validation has already been initiated in another study with some users and is part of the doctoral thesis of one of the researchers.

Knowledge of usability requirements will allow computer professionals to analyze the clinical needs expressed by customers (healthcare professionals and/or leaders) and apply this knowledge in the systems they will develop and implement.

ACKNOWLEDGMENT

This work was partially supported by the National Counsel of Technological and Scientific Development in Brazil (CNPQ)

REFERENCES

[1] T. Beale, "openEHR to ISO 13606-1, ISO 21090 mapping - Standards - openEHR Wiki," *OpenEHR*, 2014. [Online]. Available: http://www.openehr.org/wiki/display/stds/openEHR+to+ISO+13

606-1,+ISO+21090+mapping. [Accessed: 23-Nov-2014].

[2] D. Kalra, "Barriers, approaches and research priorities for semantic interoperability in support of clinical care delivery," in *SemanticHEALTH project - Semantic Interoperability Deployment and Research Roadmap*, Radboud University Nijmegen Medical Centre; Department of Medical Informatics, 2008, pp. 1–33.

[3] OpenEHR, "openEHR," *OpenEHR Foundation*, 2016. [Online]. Available: www.openehr.org. [Accessed: 30-Nov-2016].

[4] ISO/IEC, "ISO 9241-11 - Ergonomic requirements for office work with visual display terminals (VDTs) -- Part 11: Guidance on usability." p. 22, 2011.

[5] T. Beale, S. Heard, D. Kalra, and D. Lloyd, "EHR Information Model," *OpenEHR*, 2008.

[6] D. S. Alves, V. C. Times, and M. de A. Novaes, "Validation of Minimum Data of Archetyped Telehealth Clinical Report for Monitoring Prenatal Care.," *Stud. Health Technol. Inform.*, vol. 216, pp. 64–8, 2015.

[7] G. Demiris *et al.*, "Patient-centered applications: use of information technology to promote disease management and wellness. A white paper by the AMIA knowledge in motion working group.," *J. Am. Med. Inform. Assoc.*, vol. 15, no. 1, pp. 8–13, Jan. 2008.

[8] A. W. Kushniruk, K. Myers, E. M. Borycki, and J. Kannry, "Exploring the relationship between training and usability: a study of the impact of usability testing on improving training and system deployment.," *Stud. Health Technol. Inform.*, vol. 143, pp. 277–83, Jan. 2009.

[9] J. Galimany-Masclans, E. Garrido-Aguilar, M. R. Girbau-García, T. Lluch-Canut, and N. Fabrellas-Padrés, "New technologies and nursing: use and perception of primary health care nurses about electronic health record in Catalonia, Spain.," *Telemed. J. E. Health.*, vol. 17, no. 8, pp. 635–9, Oct. 2011.

[10] L. A. Saletnik, M. K. Niedlinger, and M. Wilson, "Nursing resource considerations for implementing an electronic documentation system.," *Aorn J.*, vol. 87, no. 3, pp. 585–596, 2008.

[11] P. G. Shekelle, S. C. Morton, and E. B. Keeler, "Costs and benefits of health information technology.," *Evid. rep. technol. assess*, no. 132, pp. 1–71, Apr. 2006.

[12] J. Lammintakanen, K. Saranto, and T. Kivinen, "Use of electronic information systems in nursing management.," *Int. J. Med. Inform.*, vol. 79, no. 5, pp. 324–31, May 2010.

[13] A. B. de N. T. ABNT, "Software engineering - Product quality Part 1: Quality model," 2003.

[14] L. H. Lilholt *et al.*, "Development of methods for usability evaluations of EHR systems.," *Stud. Health Technol. Inform.*, vol. 124, pp. 341–346, 2006.

[15] J. Nielsen, "Usability inspection methods," in *Conference companion on Human factors in computing systems - CHI '94*, 1994, pp. 413–414.

[16] J. Rubin and D. Chisnell, *Handbook of Usability Testing - How to Plan, Design, and Conduct Effective Tests*, 2ª. Indianápolis, Indiana: Wiley Publishing, Inc., 2008.

[17] A. Seffah, N. Kececi, and M. Donyaee, "QUIM: a framework for quantifying usability metrics in software quality models," in *Proceedings Second Asia-Pacific Conference on Quality Software*, 2001, no. 1, pp. 311–318.

[18] A. Seffah, M. Donyaee, R. B. Kline, and H. K. Padda, "Usability measurement and metrics: A consolidated model," *Softw. Qual. J.*, vol. 14, no. 2, pp. 159–178, 2006.

[19] D. S. Alves and M. de A. Novaes, "Profile of the nursing team and level of satisfaction in relation to the usability of the Electronic Patient's Record," *J. Nurs. UFPE line*, vol. 7, no. 1, pp. 143–152, 2013.

[20] OpenEHR, "openEHR - Archetype Editor," *OpenEHR*. 2015.

[21] A. M. C. de Araújo, V. C. Times, and S. C. B. Soares, "A Conceptual Data Model for Health Information Systems," *Steer. Comm. World Congr. Comput. Sci. Comput. Eng. Appl. Comput.*, pp. 236–242, 2016.

[22] OpenEHR, "Clinical Knowledge Manager," *OpenEHR Foundation*, 2016. [Online]. Available: http://www.openehr.org/ckm/. [Accessed: 04-Oct-2015].

Recognition of Human Activities in Smart Homes Using Stacked Autoencoders

Nour El Houda Mbarki, Ridha Ejbali and Mourad Zaied
RTIM: Research Team in Intelligent Machines
University of Gabes, National Engineering School of Gabes (ENIG)
nourelhouda.mbarki.tn@ieee.org, ridha_ejbali@ieee.org, mourad.zaied@ieee.org

Abstract—**There is a growing interest in the domain of smart homes. One of the most important tasks in this domain is the recognition of inhabitants' activities. To ameliorate the proposed approaches, we propose, in this paper, a Staked Autoencoder (SAE) algorithm based on a deep learning framework for recognizing activities in a smart home. Our approach is tested on the Washington State University (WSU) dataset. We will show that our proposed approach outperforms existing methods such as the Artificial Neural Networks (ANNs) in terms of recognition accuracy of activities. In particular, the SAE shows an accuracy of 87.5% in recognizing activities based on WSU smart home dataset while the ANN algorithm has shown an accuracy of 79.5% on the same dataset.**

Keywords- smart home; recognition of human activities; deep learning; stacked auto-encoders.

I. INTRODUCTION

The idea of home automation was first used in the 20th century. The main aim of home automation is to improve the comfort of living. With the progress in computer sciences and sensors' technologies, the smart home system allows users to predefine settings to manage their house remotely and gather data from the environment, to analyze it and execute necessary commands [1]. Moreover, sensors placed in homes are used to find out semantically meaningful events or activities [2]. Furthermore, a home management system utilizes machine learning, makes use of experienced systems and adopts necessary services after learning to provide appropriate services according to a user's habits [3].

A system is called a smart system when it has the ability to learn and take necessary actions or makes decisions for us. Thus, an automated home environment with the capability of learning and making decisions may be called a smart home.

Apart from reducing waste power, the objective of smart homes as sensor-based systems is to create smart, secure and comfortable environment for the aged and disabled people [4]. Therefore, sensors are needed to monitor and collect required data such as motion, temperature, analog sensors, etc [5]. In this regard, Cook et al. [6] prepared a smart apartment testbed to study human daily living activities and behaviors. Their objective was to recognize human activities throughout the collected data. The dataset was collected from 20 volunteers who performed a series of activities in the smart apartment testbed. Today, smart home technologies have rapidly developed into a large number of productions of a smart home's ready appliances. There are many different types of smart home appliances such as heating, ventilation, air conditioning, entertainment, lighting, shading, home security systems, health care applications and the control of other household appliances. These appliances were designed based on the different specific services required.

In this paper, we propose a recognition system of human activities using deep learning. The idea of using deep learning comes from its effectiveness in the pattern recognition domain. Recently, deep learning has gained its popularity as a powerful tool for learning complex and large-scale problems [7]. The model for deep learning is typically constructed by stacking multiple auto-encoders (SAEs) [8]. This deep architecture has been successfully used as a feature extractor for text, image, and sound data and as a good initial training step for deep architectures [8][9]. In this paper, we propose novel activities' recognition algorithm using the deep learning architecture as an alternative to existing shallow architectures such as Artificial Neural Networks (ANNs) [4][10]. The performance of the proposed classification method is demonstrated using the Washington State University (WSU) smart home dataset. The proposed classification method achieves an accuracy of 87.5% for classifying activities based on WSU smart home dataset (see Figure 1) while the classification based on ANN algorithm has shown an accuracy of 79.5% on the same dataset.

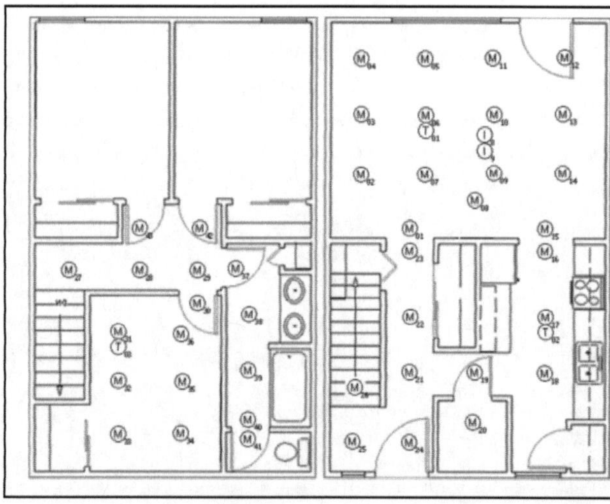

Figure 1. The installation of sensors used in the smart apartment testbed [6].

The remainder of this paper contains five sections. Section 2 includes an overview of related works. The proposed method is presented in Section 3. The experiments and the tests' results are mentioned in Section 4. As a final point, Section 5 concludes this paper.

II. RELATED WORKS

Since their creation in the early 1940s [11], Artificial Neural Networks (ANNs) have been used to solve many types of problems in robotic processing [12], pattern recognition [13], speech and handwriting recognition [14], etc.

Despite its popularity, ANNs did not escape the central problem of Machine Learning: over-learning. To move forward, new ideas were needed. After several decades of stagnation, it was G. E. Hinton [15] and his team who, in 2006, made the main breakthrough in this field. This modern machine learning technique is called deep learning [16]. The main goal of deep learning algorithms is to develop computational models that can find an optimal weighing between the input variables (also called predictors) and their corresponding class labels.

Since 2009, deep neural networks have won many official international pattern recognition competitions such as handwriting competitions at ICDAR 2009 [17] and human actions in supervision videos [18] achieving the first superhuman visual pattern recognition results in limited domains [19]. Other successful deep learning applications include object detection [20], video classification [21], and neuro-imaging studies of psychiatric and neurological disorders [22].

Regardless of the activities of recognition, the task of classification of any type of data has benefited by the advent of deep architectures [23][24]. Previously existing methods of classification mostly relied on the usage of specific features always crafted manually by human experts. Finding the best features was the subject of various researches and the performance of the classifier was strongly dependent on their quality. The advantage of the deep learning is that it can learn such features by itself reducing the need for human experts.

III. REVIEW OF METHODOLOGY

An autoencoder is a neural network that has three layers: an input layer, a hidden (encoding) layer, and a decoding layer. The network aims at reconstructing its inputs, which forces the hidden layer to try to learn good representations of the inputs [25].

In order to encourage the hidden layer to learn good input representations, certain variations on the autoencoder exist. A stacked autoencoder [7][26] is a neural network consisting of multiple hidden layers of neurons in which the outputs of each layer is wired to the inputs of the successive layer (see Figure 2).

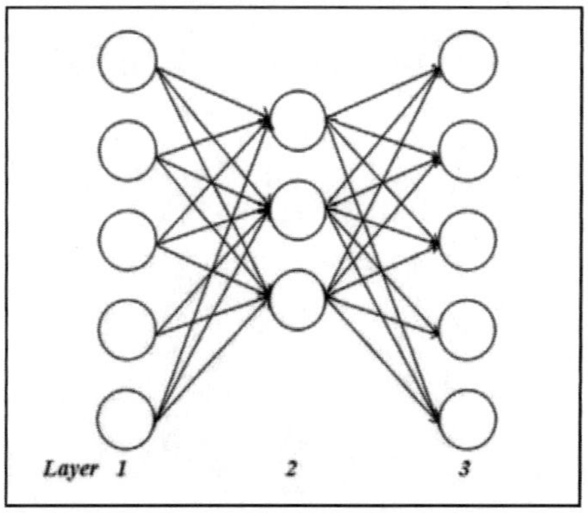

Figure 2. The structure of an autoencoder.

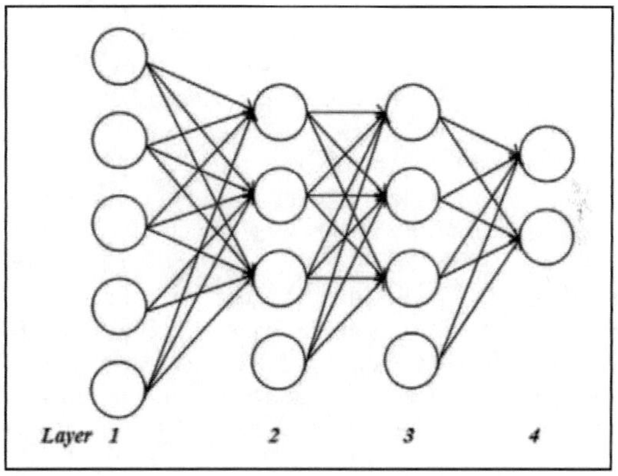

Figure 3. The structure of the stacked autoencoder used.

The SAE used in our study is constructed by two autoencoder layers and a softmax layer as shown in Figure 3. An autoencoder is the basic entity of a SAE classifier. It is composed of an encoder step (from Layer 1 to Layer 2 in Figure 2) and a decoder step (from Layer 2 to Layer 3 in Figure 2). This process can be formulated as (1) and (2), where $\boldsymbol{s}$ is a non-linearity function (the sigmoid function in our case), $\boldsymbol{W}$ and $\boldsymbol{W^T}$ are the weight matrices of this model, $\boldsymbol{b}$ and $\boldsymbol{b'}$ are two different bias vectors of this model, $\boldsymbol{y}$ is a latent variable representation of the input layer $\boldsymbol{x}$, and z represents a prediction of $\boldsymbol{x}$ when the value of $\boldsymbol{y}$ is givenand it has the same shape as $\boldsymbol{x}$.

$$y = s(Wx + b) \tag{1}$$

$$z = s(W^T x + b') \tag{2}$$

Various autoencoder layers are stacked together from an unsupervised pretraining stage (from Layer 1 to Layer 3 in Figure 3). The latent representation $\boldsymbol{y}$ obtained by an autoencoder is used as the input to its successive autoencoder layer. In these steps, the training is performed with one layer at a time and each layer is trained as an autoencoder by minimizing its reconstructing error. This reconstruction (Loss function: $\boldsymbol{L(x,z)}$) can be calculated in many ways. For our model, we use cross-entropy [27] to calculate the reconstruction error as shown in (3), where $\boldsymbol{x_k}$ and z_k denote the $\boldsymbol{k_{th}}$ element of $\boldsymbol{x}$ and z, respectively.

$$L(x,z) = -\sum_{k=1}^{d}[x_k \ln z_k + (1-x_k)\ln(1-z_k)] \quad (3)$$

The reconstruction error can be minimized using the Gradient Descent method [28]. The weights in (1) and (2) should be updated according to (4), (5) and (6), where α denotes the learning rate.

$$W = W - \alpha \frac{\partial L(x,z)}{\partial W} \quad (4)$$

$$b = b - \alpha \frac{\partial L(x,z)}{\partial b} \quad (5)$$

$$b' = b' - \alpha \frac{\partial L(x,z)}{\partial b'} \quad (6)$$

After this phase of training is complete, fine-tuning using back propagation is used to improve the results by tuning the parameters of all layers that are changed at the same time. In our model, the probability that an input vector x (in Layer 3 in Figure 3) belongs to class i can be obtained as (7), where Y is the predicted class of an input vector x, W and b are respectively the weight matrices and the bias vectors of this layer, W_i and W_j are respectively the ith and j^{th} row of matrix W, b_i and b_j are respectively the ith and j^{th} elements of vector b, and the ***softmax*** is the used function (non-linear). In equation (8), the class with the highest probability is regarded as the predicted label y_{pred} of the input vector x. The prediction error of sample data set ***DS*** (***Loss(DS)***) is calculated based on the true labels, as shown in (9), where y_i is the true label of x_i. The reconstruction error can be minimized using the Gradient Descent method as described above.

$$P(Y = i|x,W,b) = softmax(Wx+b) = \frac{e^{W_i x + b_i}}{\sum_j e^{W_j x + b_j}} \quad (7)$$

$$y_{pred} = argmax(P(Y = i|x,W,b)) \quad (7)$$

$$Loss(DS) = -\sum_{i=0}^{D} \ln(P(Y = y_i|x_i,W,b)) \quad (8)$$

IV. ACTIVITY RECOGNITION

We have used the dataset of Washington State University, obtained from the experimental study of "Assessing the quality of activities in a smart environment" [6] in the current study.

To create the dataset, 20 WSU undergraduate students recruited into the smart apartment and had them performed five activities:

- ✓ Make a phone call (5steps): in the dining room, the participant moves to the phone, looks specific number in the phone book, dials the number, and listens to the message. Then, the participant summarizes the recorded message (provides cooking directions) on a notepad.
- ✓ Wash hands (6 steps): In the kitchen, the participant moves into the sink and washes his/her hands. They use hand soap and dry their hands with a paper towel.
- ✓ Cook (7 steps): According to the directions given in the phone message, the participant cooks a pot of oatmeal. To cook it, the participant should measure water, pour the water into a pot and boil it, add oats, then put the oatmeal into a bowl with grapes and brown sugar.
- ✓ Eat (3 steps): The participant takes the oatmeal and a medicine container to the dining room and eats the food.
- ✓ Clean (5 steps): In the kitchen, the participant takes all of the dishes to the sink and cleans them with water and dish soap.

TABLE I. DISTRIBUTION OF EACH SENSOR

Sensors id	Description	Code
M01.. M26	motion sensors	01..26
I01.. I05	item sensors for oatmeal, grapes, brown sugar, bowl, measuring spoon	101..105
I06	medicine container sensor	106
I07	pot sensor	107
I08	phone book sensor	108
D01	cabinet sensor	113
AD1-A	water sensor	110
AD1-B	water sensor	111
AD1-C	burner sensor	112
asterisk	phone usage	0

The sensors were installed in a smart apartment on objects such as the phone book, the medicine container, a cooking pot, etc. to record the activation-deactivation events as the subject carrying out the five specific activities.

TABLE II. EXAMPLE OF DATA FORMAT

Activity	Date	Time	Sensor id	Activation/ deactivation
Wash hands	27/02/08	12:49:52	M14	ON
	27/02/08	12:49:53	M15	ON
	27/02/08	12:49:54	M16	ON
	⋮	⋮	⋮	⋮
	27/02/08	12:50:40	AD1-B	0.467429
	27/02/08	12:50:42	M17	OFF

This dataset included activities' names, dates and the list of the sensors activated during this activity with their type of activation and deactivation. Distribution of sensors is shown in Table I, Table II and an example of data format is shown.

A. Determining the Input and Output Layers

After preprocessing of inputs and outputs, four features of {date, day, sensor id, activation/deactivation of the sensor} for input layers were defined in a 139x4 matrix. The first autoencoder has 400 hidden units and the second autoencoder has 200.

B. Training and Testing

Activity recognitions have been varied out for 5 defined activities in a dataset. In this study, we have tried to find the best training parameters to obtain better results or higher accuracy. For this purpose, a total of 120 data, 80 data for a training set and 40 data for a test set were used. Table III presents the obtained accuracy for each activity.

The SEA algorithm showed better accuracy results compared to ANN in overall. However, the two algorithms have similar accuracy results for the tasks of phone calling and eating. The difference between SEA and ANN is mostly for the recognition of the cooking task. It may be interpreted that the longer the activity takes (cooking, with 7 steps, approximately 80 activations/deactivations), the more the SEA outperforms the ANN algorithm.

TABLE III. ACCURACY OF ACTIVITIES

Activity	**Accuracy**	
	ANN	SEA
1. Phone call	77.8%	77.8%
2. Wash hands	71.4%	85.7%
3. Cook	75.0%	100%
4. Eat	100%	100%
5. Clean	71.4%	77.8%
Total	79.5%	87.5%

Table III shows that the proposed approach of activity recognition based on stacked autoencoders has given better results than that given by artificial neural networks. These results can be explained by the ability to learn by stacked autoencoders based on deep learning as well as in artificial neural networks.

A stacked autoencoder tends to learn features that form a good representation of its input. The first layer of a stacked autoencoder tends to learn first-order features in the raw input. The second layer of a stacked autoencoder tends to learn second-order features corresponding to patterns. Higher layers of the stacked autoencoder tend to learn even higher-order features.

V. CONCLUSION

Deep Learning's Stacked Autoencoders have been used for human activity recognition according to a performance on WSU smart home dataset. The achieved results demonstrated that this algorithm has a considerable human activity recognition performance of 87.5% accuracy. It is noted that the dataset contains other parts in which activities are defined with specific errors. This part can be used to assess the consistency of activities of daily life. Furthermore, the given results are obtained for a particular environment (the smart apartment tested). In case of a different environment, it requires a new testing to create a suitable dataset.

ACKNOWLEDGMENT

The authors would like to acknowledge the financial support of this work by grants from General Direction of Scientific Research (DGRST), Tunisia, under the ARUB program.

REFERENCES

[1] T. Chu Chong and T. Chong Eng, "A Neural Network Approach towards Reinforcing Smart Home Security" Asia-Pacific Symposium on Information and Telecommunication Technologies (APSITT), pp. 1-5, 2010.

[2] T. Yoon-Sik, K. Jongik, and H. Eenjun, "Hierarchical querying scheme of human motions for smart home environment" Engineering Applications of Artificial Intelligence, vol. 25, pp. 1301-1312, 2012.

[3] S. Victor R.L., Y. Cheng-Ying, and C. Chien Hung, "A smart home management system with hierarchical behavior suggestion and recovery mechanism" Computer Standards & Interfaces, vol. 41, pp. 98-111, 2015.

[4] A. Badlani and S. Bhanot, "Smart Home System Design based on Artificial Neural Networks" World Congress on Engineering and Computer Science (WCECS), vol. 1, pp. 19-21, 2011.

[5] H. Fang, L. He, H. Si , P. Liu, and X. Xie, "Human activity recognition based on feature selection in smart home using backpropagation algorithm" ISA Transactions, vol. 53, pp. 1629-1638, 2014.

[6] D. Cook and M. Schmitter-Edgecombe, "Assessing the quality of activities in a smart environment" Methods of Information in Medicine. vol. 48, no. 5, pp. 480-485, 2009.

[7] Y. Bengio, "Learning deep architectures for AI" Foundations and Trends R in Machine Learning, vol. 2, no. 1, pp. 1-127, 2009.

[8] P. Vincent, H. Larochelle, I. Lajoie, Y. Bengio, and P. Manzagol, " Stacked Denoising Autoencoders: Learning Useful Representations in a Deep Network with a Local Denoising Criterion" Journal of Machine Learning Research 11, pp. 3371-3408, 2010.

[9] W. Li et al, "Stacked Autoencoder-based deep learning for remote-sensing image classification: a case study of African land-cover..." International Journal of Remote Sensing, vol. 37, no. 23, pp. 5632-5646, 2016.

[10] H. D. Mehr, H. Polat, and A. Cetin, "Resident Activity Recognition in Smart Homes by Using Artificial Neural Networks" International Istanbul Smart Grid Congress and Fair (ICSG), pp. 1-5, 2016.

[11] W.S. McCulloch and W. Pitts, "A logical calculus of the ideas immanent in nervous activity", the bulletin of mathematical biophysics, pp. 115-133, 1943.

[12] S.Y. King and J.N. Hwang, "Neural network architectures for robotic applications" Robotics and Automation, IEEE Transactions, pp. 641-657, 1989.

[13] T. Yoshida and S. Omatu, "Pattern recognition with neural networks", the IEEE 2000 International Geoscience and Remote Sensing Symposium. Taking the Pulse of the Planet: The Role of Remote Sensing in Managing the Environment, pp. 699-701, 2000.

[14] R. Ejbali, M. Zaied, and C. Ben Amar, "Wavelet network for recognition system of Arabic word", International Journal of Speech Technology, pp. 163-174, 2010.

[15] G. E. Hinton, S. Osindero, and Y.-W. The, "A fast learning algorithm for deep belief nets", Neural computation, pp. 1527-1554, 2006.

[16] Y. LeCun, Y. Bengio, and G. Hinton, "Deep learning", Nature, pp. 436-444, 2015.

[17] A. Graves et al., "A Novel Connectionist System for Unconstrained Handwriting Recognition", IEEE Transactions on Pattern Analysis and Machine Intelligence, pp. 855-868, 2009.

[18] V. Jain and S. Seung, "Natural image denoising with convolutional networks", Advances in Neural Information Processing Systems (NIPS), pp. 769-776, 2009.

[19] C. Szegedy, A. Toshev, and D. Erhan, "Deep neural networks for object detection", Neural Information Processing Systems (NIPS), pp. 2553-2561, 2013.

[20] D. C. Ciresan, U. Meier, J. Masci, L.M. Gambardella, and J. Schmidhuber, "Flexible, high performance convolutional neural networks for image classification", Intl. Joint Conference on Artificial Intelligence (IJCAI), pp. 1237-1242, 2011.

[21] A. Karpathy et al., "Large-scale video classification with convolutional neural networks", the IEEE Conference on Computer Vision and Pattern Recognition (CVPR), pp. 1725-1732, 2014.

[22] S. Vieira, W.H.L. Pinaya, and A. Mechelli, "Using deep learning to investigate the neuroimaging correlates of psychiatric and neurological disorders: Methods and applications", Neuroscience & Biobehavioral Reviews, pp. 58-75, 2017.

[23] S. Hassairi, R. Ejbali, and M. Zaied, "Supervised Image Classification Using Deep Convolutional Wavelets Network", the 15th International Conference on Intelligent Systems Design and Applications (ISDA), pp. 1-5, 2015.

[24] A. Eladel, R. Ejbali, and M. Zaied, "Dyadic Multi-resolution Analysis-Based Deep Learning for Arabic Handwritten Character Classification", The 27th IEEE International Conference on Tools with Artificial Intelligence (ICTAI), pp. 1082-3409 , 2015.

[25] S. Haykin, "Neural networks: A comprehensive foundation", vol. 3, no. 5, 1998.

[26] G. E. Hinton and R. R. Salakhutdinov, "Reducing the Dimensionality of Data with Neural Networks" Science, vol. 504, no. July, pp. 504-507, 2006.

[27] J. Shore and R. Johnson, "Axiomatic Derivation of the Principle of Maximum Entropy and the Principle of Minimum Cross-Entropy" IEEE Transactions on Information Theory vol. 26, no. 1, pp. 26-37, 1980.

[28] L. Bottou, "Large-Scale Machine Learning with Stochastic Gradient Descent" International Conference on Computational Statistics, pp. 177-186, 2010.

Immersed in Software Structures: A Virtual Reality Approach

Roy Oberhauser and Carsten Lecon
Computer Science Dept.
Aalen University
Aalen, Germany
email: {roy.oberhauser, carsten.lecon}@hs-aalen.de

Abstract - **Program code has been inherently challenging to visualize due to its abstract nature. With the advent of affordable virtual reality (VR) hardware products, the use of VR has become a feasible option for software tools. In this paper, we describe a VR approach for visualizing internal program code structures and evaluate its suitability for selected software development and education tasks. VR efficiency and effectiveness was equivalent to mouse and screen mechanisms, but provided an enhanced user experience for 70% of the subjects, whereas 30% experienced VR sickness.**

Keywords - Virtual reality; software visualization; program comprehension; software engineering; engineering training; computer education.

I. INTRODUCTION

With the ongoing digitalization of society, the amount of program source code produced and maintained worldwide is dramatically increasing. Google alone has at least 2bn LOC accessible by 25K developers [1], and it has been estimated that well over a trillion lines of code (LOC) exist worldwide with 33bn added annually [2]. Aristotle stated, "thought is impossible without an image", and F. P. Brooks, Jr. asserted that the invisibility of software is an essential difficulty of software construction because the reality of software is not embedded in space [3]. Common display forms used in the comprehension of source code include text and the two-dimensional Unified Modeling Language (UML). Program comprehension limitations are evident in the relatively low code review reading rates of around 200 LOC/hour [4].

Feijs and De Jong [5] present a vision of walking through a 3D visualization of software architecture with VRML. Yet the potential of VR and game engines have not been realized in software engineering (SE) tools, and their practicality with off-the-shelf VR hardware remains insufficiently explored.

In prior work, we developed a non-VR (PC display) FlyThruCode (FTC) 3D fly-through approach for navigating software structures [6]. This paper contributes VR-FlyThruCode (VR-FTC), a new VR approach for visualizing, navigating, and conveying program code information interactively in a VR environment to support exploratory, analytical, and descriptive cognitive processes [7]. A prototype demonstrates its viability, with a technical and empirical study investigating effectiveness, efficiency, and user experience (UX) factors for SE tasks and SE education.

The paper is organized as follows: the next section discusses related work; Section III then describes the solution approach. Section IV provides realization details. Section V evaluates the solution, which is followed by a conclusion.

II. RELATED WORK

Teyseyre and Campo [8] give an overview and survey of 3D software visualization tools across the various software engineering areas. Software Galaxies [9] provides a web-based visualization of dependencies among popular package managers and supports flying. Every star represents a package that is clustered by dependencies. CodeCity [10] is a 3D software visualization approach based on a city metaphor and implemented in SmallTalk on the Moose reengineering framework. Buildings represent classes, districts represent packages, and visible properties depict selected metrics, improving task correctness but slowing task completion time [11]. Rilling and Mudur [12] use a metaball metaphor (organic-like n-dimensional objects) combined with dynamic analysis of program execution. X3D-UML [13] provides 3D support with UML in planes such that classes are grouped in planes based on the package or hierarchical state machine diagrams. A case study of a 3D UML tool using Google SketchUp showed that a 3D perspective improved model comprehension and was found to be intuitive [14]. Langelier et al. [15] supports the visualization of metrics (e.g., coupling, test coverage).

As to VR, Imsovision [16] visualizes object-oriented software in VR using electromagnetic sensors attached to shutter glasses and a wand for interaction. ExplorViz [17] is a Javascript-based web application that uses WebVR to support VR exploration of 3D software cities using Oculus Rift together with Microsoft Kinect for gesture recognition.

In contrast to the above work, the VR-FTC approach leverages game engine capabilities to support an immersive VR software visualization environment multiple dynamically-switchable (customizable) metaphors; uses one VR system and controller set (not requiring gesture training) for interaction and navigation; supports tagging, searching, and filtering; and integrates information screens within the VR landscape that dynamically invoke external SE tools.

III. SOLUTION APPROACH

VR-FTC uses VR flythrough for visualizing program code structure or architecture. This inherent 3D application domain view visualization [8] arranges customizable symbols in 3D space to enable users to navigate through an alternative perspective on these often hidden structures. For example, certain information typically not readily accessible is visualized, such as the relative size of classes (not typically visible until multiple files are opened or a UML class diagram is created), the relative size of packages to one another, and the dependencies between classes and packages.

A. Principles

The principles (P:) of the VR solution approach include:

P:Multiple 3D visual metaphors: Analogous to the concept of skins, it models and supports tailoring and switching between multiple code structure visualization metaphors. While our initial implementation focused on modeling and visualizing object-oriented packages, classes, and their relationships, the approach is extensible for other programming languages. Initially, two metaphors are provided "out-of-the-box" while custom mappings to other object types are supported. In the universe metaphor, each planet represents a class with its size based on the number of methods, and solar systems represent a package. Any metric can be used to map to any visual object property (like color). Multiple packages are shown by layer solar systems over one another. In the terrestrial metaphor, buildings can represent classes, building height can represent the number of methods, and glass bubbles can group classes into packages. Relationships are modeled visually as colored pipes.

P:Group metaphor: elements (classes) are grouped and delineated in a way appropriate for that language (packages for Java) and metaphor. For instance, the terrestrial metaphor uses either a glass bubble over a city or a circle of trees at the city border, and the universe metaphor uses solar systems.

P:Connection metaphor: elements (classes) are connected in a way appropriate for that metaphor. For our two metaphors, we chose colored light beams, which often are used to portray networks on a geological background.

P:Fly-in theater screens: analogous to drive-in movie theaters common in the United States, here multiple various relatively large 2D screens are placed directly within the scene and provide menu settings and source-code and SE tool supplied information with which developers are familiar. While our original 2D FTC utilized a cockpit and heads-up display (HUD) metaphor principle simulating semi-transparent glass for providing multiple screens with context-specific information, in VR this turned out to be too close to the eyes and cumbersome for menu interaction.

The screens presented are:

- *Tags*: Setting, searching, or filtering automatic (via patterns) or manual persistent annotations/tags.
- *Source Code*: code is shown in scrollable form.
- *UML*: dynamically generated 2D diagrams.
- *Metrics*: code metrics are displayed textually due to the large number of possible metrics that may be of interest to the user; displaying a large amount of metric information visually may be disconcerting. Customization enables metrics of interest to be utilized in a metaphor (e.g., colors, object height can relate to number of class methods, font colors can indicated a threshold is exceeded).
- *Filtering*: shows elements that match selectors.
- *Project*: change metaphors, load, or import a project.

P:Flythrough navigation: 3D navigation (motion) is provided by moving the camera in space based on controller or motion sensor input. The scenery, however, remains anchored in the scene, allowing users to remember places via their geolocation relative to other elements.

B. Process

The approach process consists of:

1) Modeling: modeling generic program code structures, metrics, and artifacts as well as visual objects.

2) Mapping: mapping a model to a visual object metaphor.

3) Extraction: extracting a given project's structure (via source code import and parsing) and metrics.

4) Visualization: visualizing a given model instance within a metaphor.

5) Navigation: supporting navigation through the model instance (via camera movement based on user interaction).

IV. Implementation

The Unity engine was utilized for 3D visualization due to its multi-platform support, VR integration, and popularity, and for VR hardware both HTC Vive, a room scale VR set with a head-mounted display and two wireless handheld controllers tracked using two 'Lighthouse' base stations, and Google Cardboard with Android smartphones was used.

A. Architecture

Figure 1 shows the architecture. Assets are used by the Unity engine and consist of Animations, Fonts, Imported Assets (like a ComboBox), Materials (like colors and reflective textures), Media (like textures), 3D Models, Prefabs (prefabricated), Shaders (for shading of text in 3D), VR SDKs, and Scripts. While Google Cardboard does not use SteamVR, for the HTC Vive both are used because we needed a reticle. Scripts consist of Basic Scripts like user interface (UI) helpers, Logic Scripts that import, parse, and load project data structures, and Controllers that react to user interaction. Logic Scripts read Configuration data about Stored Projects and the Plugin System (input in XML about how to parse source code and invocation commands). Logic Scripts can then call Tools consisting of General and Language-specific Tools. General Tools currently consist of BaseX, Graphviz, PlantUML, and Graph Layout - our own version of the KK layout algorithm [18] for positioning objects. Java-specific tools are srcML, Campwood SourceMonitor, Java Transformer (invokes Groovy scripts), and Dependency Finder. Our Plugin system enables additional tools and applications to be easily integrated.

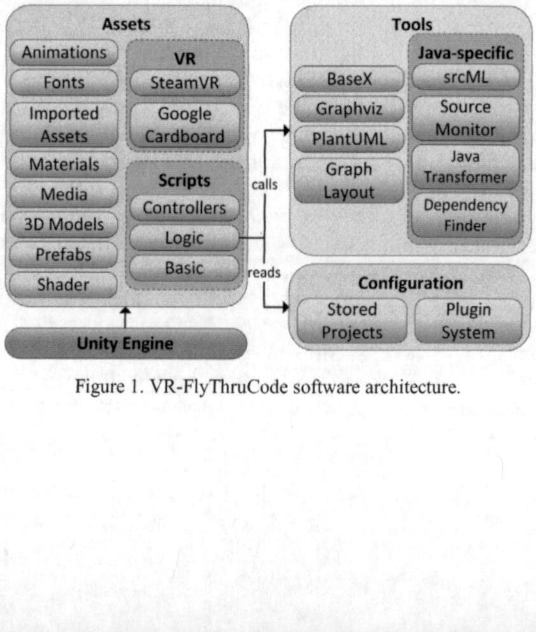

Figure 1. VR-FlyThruCode software architecture.

B. Information Extraction

For extracting existing code structure information into our model, srcML [19] is used to convert source code into XML that is then stored in the XML database BaseX, Campwood SourceMonitor and DependencyFinder are used to extract code metrics and dependency data, and plugins with Groovy scripts and a configuration are used to integrate the various tools.

C. Project structure

For an imported project the following files are created:

- *metrics_{date}.xml*: metrics obtained from SourceMonitor and DependencyFinder are grouped by project, packages, and classes.
- *source_{date}.xml*: holds all classes in XML
- *structure_{date}.xml*: contains the project structure and dependencies utilizing the DependencyFinder.
- *swexplorer-annotations.xml*: contains user-based annotations (tags) with color, flag, and text including both manual and automatic (pattern matching) tags.
- *swexplorer-metrics-config.xml*: contains thresholds for metrics.
- *swexplorer-records.xml*: contains a record of each import of the same project done at different times with a reference to the various XML files such as source and structure for that import. This permits changing the model to different timepoints as a project evolves.

D. Virtual reality

1) VR Interaction: On the HTC Vive the touchpad on the left controller controls altitude (up, down) and the one on the right hand the direction (left, right, forward, backward), which realizes *P:Flythrough navigation* by moving the camera position. The controllers are shown in the scenery when they are within the view field, as shown in the universe (Figure 2) and city metaphor (Figure 3). A virtual laser pointer was created for selecting objects, as was a virtual keyboard (Figure 4) to support text input for searching, filtering, and tagging. Menus and screens showing source code, code metrics, UML, tags, filtering, and project data were placed in the scene, in accordance with *P:Fly-in theater screens* (Figure 5 and Figure 6). To highlight a selected object, we utilized a 3D pointer in the form of a rotating upside-down pyramid (see Figure 5). This was needed because, once an object is selected, after navigating to a screen or menu one may turn around and lose track of where the object was, especially if the object was small relative to its surrounding objects.

2) Metaphor realization: To support *P:Multiple 3D visual metaphors*, a universe (Figure 6) and a city metaphor were chosen. Figure 3 shows the city metaphor where buildings represent classes with a label at the top and the number of stories represent the number of methods in that class. For the universe, *P:Group metaphor* was implemented as a solar system, whereas in the city metaphor a glass bubble. For the *P:Connection metaphor*, in both metaphors colored light beams were used to show dependencies between classes or packages (Figure 3 and Figure 7). To allow the user to remember objects, tagging is supported, which allows any label to be placed on an object (e.g., the Player Tag in Figure 7).

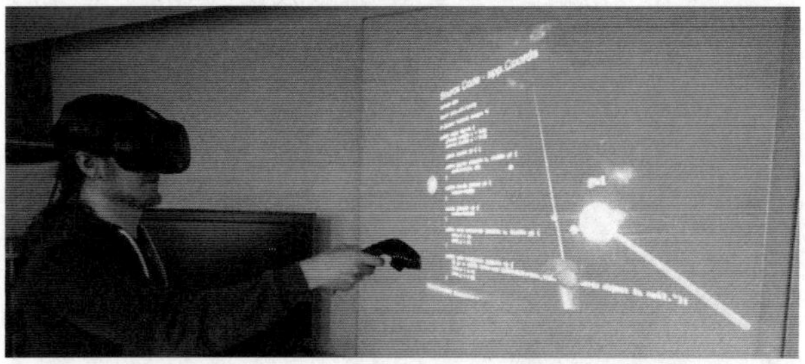

Figure 2. Subject with a Vive headset and controller (visible in a scene making a selection). Note: screen is mirroring what the subject is viewing.

Figure 3. Vive controller visible in city metaphor, buildings as classes.

Figure 4. Virtual keyboard button pressed with reticle via controller.

Figure 5. City glass bubble with pyramid pointer and program code screen.

Figure 6. Universe solar systems with pyramid pointer and menu screen.

Figure 7. Universe showing tagged class.

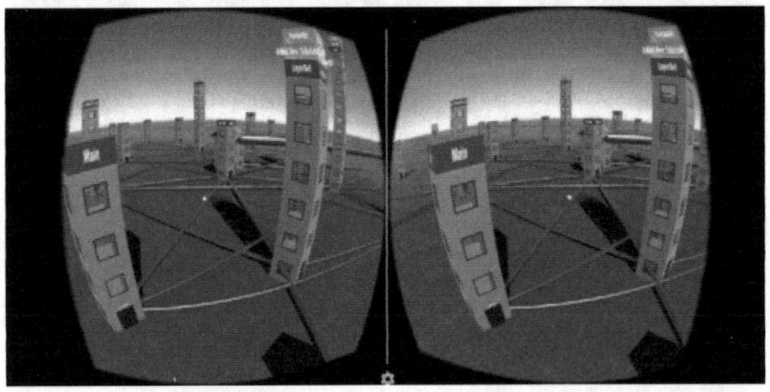

Figure 8. Cardboard stereoscopic visualization shown in the Unity Editor.

3) Google Cardboard: To support VR use with inexpensive hardware, VR-FTC was integrated with the Android SDK and Google Cardboard SDK for Unity and run with a Google Cardboard visor (see Figure 8) and utilize motion sensors within the smartphone. Using the gaze point, the reticle changes from a small closed circle to an open circle to indicate the object can be selected. The external tools were not ported.

V. Evaluation

A technical evaluation focused on assessing the application's viability on current VR hardware options. Having the same FTC application as a constant in VR-and non-VR modes, the empirical evaluation assessed differences in application usability, effectiveness, and efficiency.

The evaluation utilized an HTC Vive with a 2160×1200 447 PPI resolution, Unity 5.3.5f1 PE, SteamVR 1479163853. The desktop PC had a 4GHz i7-6700K, 32GB RAM, SSD, NVIDIA GeForce GTX980Ti with 6GB GDDR5, Win7 Pro x64 SP1. The notebook was a MSI GS60 2.5GHz i7-4710HQ, 16GB RAM, NVIDIA GeForce GTX870M with 3GB GDDR5, SSD, Win10 Home x64, which did not meet Vive's minimum requirements but allows us to determine if a notebook (popular among software developers) would suffice for our VR application.

A. Technical Evaluation

1) Resource usage: RAM was allocated for a 64-bit implementation was 220MB (with no project), 250MB (project with 27 classes), and 620MB (project with 95 classes). On the notebook, graphics card load was 80% without a project and went to 90% with a loaded project (for the PC 20%). We determined the CPU was the bottleneck, with load on the PC for a large project almost always at 100%. We believe that scripts attached to each visible class invoke their update method for each frame, and plan to optimize this in future work.

2) Google Cardboard: an inexpensive VR alternative (when one already has a smartphone), a Sony Xperia Z2 2.3GHz Quad-core 5" 1080p 423 PPI display and a Samsung Galaxy A5 1.2GHz Quad-core 5" 720p 300 PPI display were used running Android 6.0.1 with Google Cardboard. On the A5 with 720p, the pixels became discernable, and since Google Cardboard lenses magnify the screen, we believe it to be related to the lower PPI. We also observed significant drops in the frame rate. Future work will analyze this further to determine if optimizations can address this or if current smartphone performance is inadequate for this type of application.

3) Frame rate: to determine the performance impact of each metaphor and if a notebook would be sufficient, the Saxon XSLT 2.0 and XQuery processor consisting of 300K lines of code and 1635 classes was loaded and the frames per second (FPS) measured via a custom script.

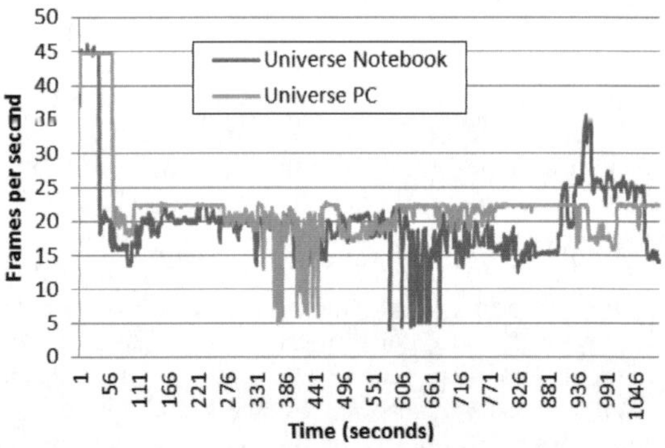

Figure 9. Universe metaphor frame rate over time on notebook and PC.

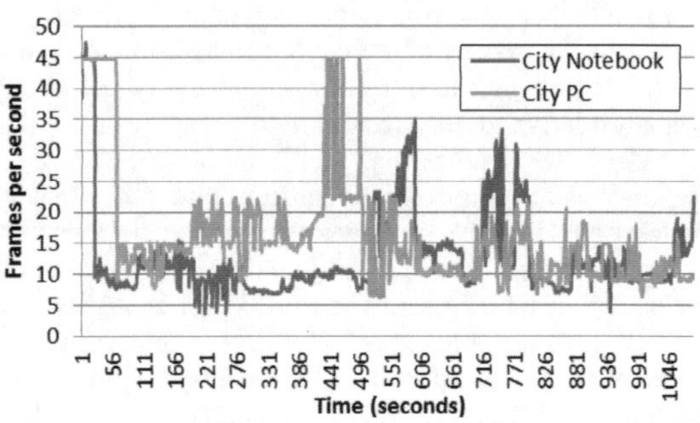

Figure 10. City metaphor frame rate over time on notebook and PC.

Figure 9 and Figure 10 show that the notebook mostly exhibited lower FPS rates than the PC, and that the city metaphor lowered the FPS rate. This is also shown by the average FPS rates for universe (notebook=20.0; PC=22.2) and city (notebook=12.7; PC=16.0). Below 15 FPS is not tolerable (early silent films had 16-20). An initial analysis found the dynamic UML generator - run in a separate process - as a main cause, and this will be addressed in future work. The universe ran better than city, since city included multiple shadows, reflections from the glass bubble, and a terrain. Higher FPS occurred when flying to an outer package such that far fewer objects were in view.

B. Empirical Evaluation

Since non-VR FTC was previously evaluated against both IDE (Eclipse) and UML (Enterprise Architect) tools [6], here we focus on comparing VR and non-VR modes keeping the FTC application a constant. For empirical evaluation of SE task suitability, because of the Google Cardboard's lack of controllers and it's the frame rate issue, only the Vive was used. Our hypotheses are (1) that VR mode is on par with non-VR in effectiveness and efficiency for SE code structure analysis tasks and education, and (2) VR mode offers an immersive and UX quality absent in non-VR.

Resource-constraints such as having only one Vive and the time-intensive 2-on-1 supervision of the experiment with a single subject at a time limited our sample size. A convenience sample of 10 computer science students of various academic semesters (1; 3-4; 6-9 grouped respectively as beginner, intermediate, and advanced) participated and self-rated their programming and UML competency (Figure 11). Object-orientation (OO) is taught in the second and UML in the fourth semester. The one first semester student had work experience in the software industry and thus knew OO and UML. Each received a short tutorial on non-VR FTC (three had prior experience). Project A consisted of 2 packages, 27 classes, and 170 methods, while Project B had 5 packages, 95 classes, and 800 methods.

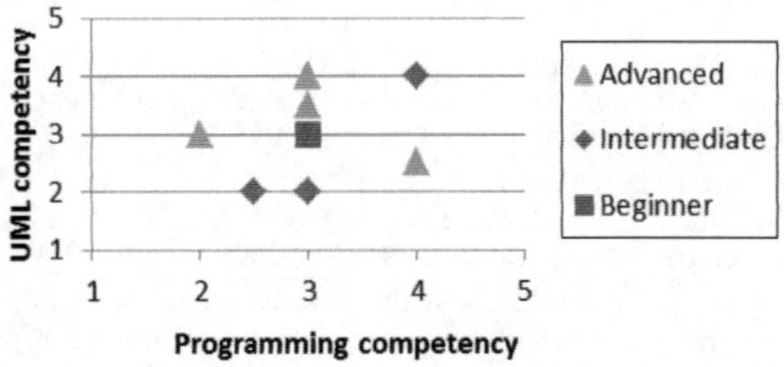

Figure 11. Participant UML/programming self-rating by semester level.

In non-VR mode, project A was loaded in the universe and thereafter the city metaphor, and likewise with B, and the same sequence repeated for VR mode. 8 questions were asked per case dealing with program code structural comprehension requiring navigation (not the same set each time), resulting in 64 questions (see Figure 12); 5 additional general questions followed giving 69 in total. So that the VR glasses need not be removed, and in order not to skew the task durations in non-VR mode, questions were asked and answered verbally and noted by a supervisor.

1) How many connections/dependencies does class X have within the package Foo?
2) How many connections/dependencies does class Y have within the package Bar?
3) Add a tag to the class X
4) Which package is the largest/smallest?
5) How many connections/dependencies does package Foo have?
6) How many connections/dependencies does package Bar have?
7) How many variables are declared in the class Y in package Foo?
8) Which classes are directly connected with the class Y?
9) Name all classes on the shortest path from A to B.
10) How many overloaded functions does the class Z have in package Bar?
11) In what package did you set your tag?

Figure 12. Sample timed task questions and requests.

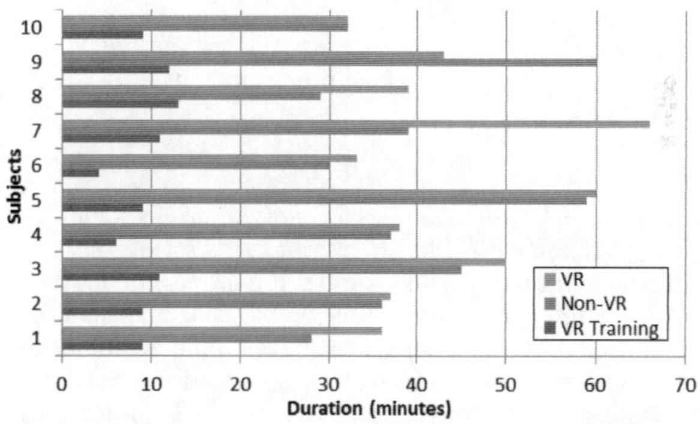

Figure 13. Sum of task durations per subject for VR and non-VR modes.

As to efficiency, on average 92.5 min were needed for the 64 questions, 43.4 in VR mode vs. 39.5 min in non-VR (10% difference), while VR training took 9.4 min. 0shows the sum of the task durations for each mode per subject, whereby subjects 8-10 had prior FTC familiarity. While VR mode was 10% slower, this was their first experience using VR. In addition, in non-VR mode the HUD is instantly available and screens can be switched, while in VR mode navigation to a screen is required. In our opinion, more VR practice would reduce this difference further.

With regard to effectiveness, given 32 questions in each mode across 10 subjects, in non-VR 300 (94%) and in VR 296 (93%) were answered correctly. Considering fatigue, we consider the effectiveness equivalent for both modes.

Subjects considered both FTC application modes suitable for these SE tasks. Comments included liking how information was visually displayed, its closeness to a reality, its clear arrangement, and that head movement could be used for exploring (which non-VR cannot provide). Subjects felt no differently after using non-VR, whereas after VR the feeling was described as impressive for seven of the ten subjects. The other three subjects reported VR sickness symptoms, a type of visually-induced motion sickness exhibiting disorientation. We plan to address the VR sickness in future work, e.g., by increasing the frame rate via optimizations and reducing the speed of camera movement. .

Our empirical hypotheses were confirmed by our results and the feedback from participants. One threat to validity is the order effect of application usage in that non-VR followed VR. Thus, non-VR times include the overhead for gaining familiarity with the application concepts, and VR mode did not have this overhead. However, 2D monitor and mouse-centric interaction was a pre-existing competency, while VR display and navigation was a new interaction paradigm for all subjects. Furthermore, subjects 8, 9, and 10 had prior familiarity with the non-VR FTC via a prior experiment, yet their task duration times did not exhibit any clear trend that prior familiarity sped up the non-VR task durations. Furthermore, the 1% difference in correctness could be attributed to fatigue since VR was done in the second hour. A further threat to validity is that the positive experience is possibly a novelty effect - VR veterans would be needed to be included to assess this factor. For better external validity, the sample size should be larger and more diverse to include professionals. However, the results can be viewed as indicative and the approach as promising if we can address the VR sickness.

VI. CONCLUSION

As virtual reality devices become more commonplace, the application of VR to SE environments for SE tasks and education will likely gain acceptance. This paper contributes a VR flythrough software structure visualization approach called VR-FTC that immerses users into multiple and customizable virtual reality metaphors for visualizing, navigating, and conveying program code information interactively to support exploratory, analytical, and descriptive cognitive processes. A game engine creates an immersive VR software visualization environment using only one VR system and set of VR controllers for VR interaction and navigation, supports tagging, searching, and filtering, integrates dynamic information screens within the VR landscape that dynamically invoke external SE tools, and supports an inexpensive VR option (Google Cardboard).

A prototype demonstrated its viability even for notebook configurations. The technical evaluation showed suitable resource usage but pointed out frame rate issues, especially for Google Cadboard. The empirical study determined that VR mode was 10% slower on average for tasks for untrained VR users with no significant difference in correctness. UX impressions were that both modes were suitable, and 70% were very impressed with the VR feeling, while 30% experienced VR sickness symptoms. That VR mode user performance was equivalent to the very common non-VR interaction in conjunction with the reported emotional effects indicates VR mode can be an appealing option for SE tools. Also, our VR training took less than 10 minutes, so training investments for VR should be minimal.

Future work includes further analysis and optimizations to address frame rate issues, visualization improvements, addressing the VR sickness symptoms, and a more comprehensive empirical study including professionals.

ACKNOWLEDGMENT

The authors would like to thank Dominik Bergen, Alexandre Matic, Lisa Philipp, and Camil Pogolski for their assistance with various aspects of the design, implementation, and evaluation.

REFERENCES

[1] C. Metz, *Google Is 2 Billion Lines of Code—And It's All in One Place.* [retrieved: Jan, 2017]. Available from: http://www.wired.com/2015/09/google-2-billion-lines-codeand-one-place/

[2] G. Booch, "The complexity of programming models," Keynote talk at AOSD 2005, Chicago, IL, Mar. 14-18, 2005.

[3] F. P. Brooks, Jr., The Mythical Man-Month. Boston, MA: Addison-Wesley Longman Publ. Co., Inc., 1995.

[4] C. F. Kemerer and M. C. Paulk, "The impact of design and code reviews on software quality: An empirical study based on PSP data," IEEE Trans. on Software Engineering, vol. 35, no. 4, 2009, pp. 534-550.

[5] L. Feijs and R. De Jong, "3D visualization of software architectures," Comm. of the ACM, 41(12), 1998, pp. 73-78.

[6] R. Oberhauser, C. Silfang, and C. Lecon. "Code structure visualization using 3D-flythrough," 11th Int'l Conf. Computer Science & Educ. (ICCSE 2016). IEEE, 2016, pp. 365-370.

[7] D. M. Butler et al., "Visualization reference models," in Proc. Visualization '93 Conf., IEEE CS Press, 1993, pp. 337–342.

[8] A. R. Teyseyre and M. R. Campo, "An overview of 3D software visualization," Visualization and Computer Graphics, IEEE Trans. on, vol. 15, no. 1, 2009, pp. 87-105.

[9] A. Kashcha. *Software Galaxies* [retrieved: Jan, 2017]. Available: http://github.com/anvaka/pm/

[10] R. Wettel and M. Lanza, "Program comprehension through software habitability," in Proc. 15th IEEE Int'l Conf. on Program Comprehension, IEEE CS, 2007, pp. 231–240.

[11] R. Wettel et al., "Software systems as cities: A controlled experiment," in Proc. of the 33rd Int'l Conf. on Software Engineering, ACM, 2011, pp. 551-560.

[12] J. Rilling and S. P. Mudur, "On the use of metaballs to visually map source code structures and analysis results onto 3d space," in Proc.. 9th Work. Conf. on Reverse Engineering, IEEE, 2002, pp. 299-308.

[13] P. M. McIntosh, "X3D-UML: user-centred design, implementation and evaluation of 3D UML using X3D," Ph.D. dissertation, RMIT University, 2009.

[14] A. Krolovitsch and L. Nilsson, "3D Visualization for Model Comprehension: A Case Study Conducted at Ericsson AB," University of Gothenburg, Sweden, 2009.

[15] G. Langelier et al., "Visualization-based analysis of quality for large-scale software systems," in Proc. 20th Int. Conf. on Automated Software Engineering, ACM, 2005, pp. 214-223.

[16] J. I. Maletic, J. Leigh, and A. Marcus, "Visualizing software in an immersive virtual reality environment," 23rd Intl. Conf. on Softw. Eng. (ICSE 2001) Vol. 1., IEEE, 2001, pp. 12-13.

[17] F. Fittkau, A. Krause, and W. Hasselbring, "Exploring software cities in virtual reality," IEEE 3rd Working Conference on Software Visualization (VISSOFT), IEEE, 2015, pp. 130-134.

[18] T. Kamada and S. Kawai, "An algorithm for drawing general undirected graphs," Information processing letters, 31(1), 1989, pp. 7-15.

[19] J. Maletic et al, "Source code files as structured documents," in Proc. 10th Int. Workshop on Program Comprehension, IEEE, 2002, pp. 289-292.

Study of Gross Muscle Fatigue During Human-Robot Interactions

Azeemsha Thacham Poyil*, Farshid Amirabdollahian† and Volker Steuber‡
School of Computer Science
University of Hertfordshire, Hatfield, United Kingdom AL10 8HJ
Email: {*a.thacham-poyil, †f.amirabdollahian2, ‡v.steuber}@herts.ac.uk

***Abstract*—This study explores the utility of Electromyogram (EMG) signals in the context of upper-limb exercises during human-robot interaction considering muscle fatigue of the participant. We hypothesise that the Electromyogram features from muscles and kinematic measurements from the robotic sensors can be used as indicators of fatigue and there is a potential to identify the muscle contribution during the activity where the Electromyogram data is correlated with the kinematic data. Electromyogram measurements were taken from four upper limb muscles of 10 healthy individuals. HapticMaster robot in active assisted mode together with a virtual environment was used to guide the participants for moving the robotic arm in a prescribed path in a horizontal plane consisting of four segments. The experiments were conducted until the participants reached a state of fatigue or until a defined maximum number of 6 trials were reached. Comparing the first and last trials indicated that the muscle fatigue had caused an increase in the average power and a decrease in the median frequency of EMG, which was more visible in Trapezius (TRP) and Anterior Deltoid (DLT) muscles in most of the analysed cases compared to Biceps Brachii (BB) and Triceps Brachii (TB) muscles. As the muscles came to a state of fatigue, the kinematic position also showed an increase in tracking error between the first and last trials. The 'near-the-body' segment movements (S1 and S4 segments) were found to have less increase of tracking error compared to the 'away-from-body' movements (S2 and S3 segments). A further analysis on this proved that the tracking error observed was mainly due to fatigue building up over the number of trials when performing 'away-from-body' movements, and not a bi-product of perception errors. We identify that Deltoid and Trapezius muscles were fatigued more. These EMG fatigue indications can be mapped to kinematic indications of fatigue mainly in the segments S2 and S3, which required away from body movements because of the role of these two muscles in lifting the arm to the shoulder height in order to perform the activity. Our extracted features have shown the potential to identify the fatigued muscles as expected. The study also showed that the Electromyogram and kinematic features have a potential to be used to highlight the extent of muscle involvement.**

Keywords*–Robotic Rehabilitation; Upper Limb Training; Fatigue Detection; Electromyogram; Kinematic Fatigue Indicators.

I. INTRODUCTION

Stroke patients during physical therapies may easily come to a state of fatigue due to their reduced muscle and cognitive capabilities. Repetitions in training exercises are thought to impact on their neuro-plasticity that aids the recovery after stroke [1], but the repetitions often result in a faster occurrence of muscle fatigue. Robots can be used to help rehabilitation exercises due to their potential to deliver large number of repetitions. But the existing physical therapies are designed without sufficiently considering the implications (pain or state of fatigue) to the patient [2][3][4]. Hence, closed loop control and adaptability to individuals becomes important criteria for the acceptance of such rehabilitation solutions. Even though adaptive robotic interactions for upper limb rehabilitation have been studied before [2][5], a commercially accepted solution for robotic interaction considering muscle fatigue could not be found yet. Electromyogram (EMG) features from the involved muscles can be used to understand the current physical state and the effort exerted by the patient [2][3] and then to alter the intensity of the training. The study may be done initially on healthy control groups in various testing conditions and for different muscle combinations before applying the solution on real patients. Such a solution can also be used in a wide-range of human-machine or human-human interactions by providing insights into the state of individual's ability to actively contribute to the interaction.

This study is focused on exploring a practical solution for better therapeutic interaction by considering the muscle fatigue indicators. The study used HapticMaster (HM) as the robotic platform, which is an admittance controlled robot developed by MOOG BV, The Netherlands. Admittance control strategy is a force-in, and displacement-out system where the user's applied force is measured and the haptic device is controlled to move proportional to that force. The robot had been utilised in a stroke rehabilitation project, GENTLE/S where 3 different interaction modes namely passive, active-assisted and active where developed [6]. The active-assisted mode is utilised in this current study, where the robot automatically compensates for the lag or lead in subject arm's position with reference to an internal trajectory model by offering support to achieve the task in time. The current research studied the fatigue development in the upper limb muscles of 10 healthy individuals using EMG and kinematic features recorded during the experiment.

The rest of the paper is organized as follows. In Section II, the past researches in this area and current gaps are briefly discussed. Section III explains the materials and methods used in the study. In Section IV, the results of the data analysis are discussed and further discussion on the results is done in Section V. Finally in Section VI, the conclusions, limitations and possible future work are presented.

II. LITERATURE REVIEW

Muscle or physical fatigue is defined as the decline in the ability of muscles to generate force or power during a physical task. Fatigue usually results in a feeling of tiredness because of the lack of strength and it develops gradually during a physical activity and is typically temporary in duration [7]. Fatigue analysis based on EMG data during upper limb exercises have been studied in the past in different contexts and it was identified that the fatigue affects the movement duration, position sense and task performance. Few researchers in the past had investigated the effect of repetitive tasks and muscle fatigue on upper limb tasks during rehabilitation training [8][9][10]. The subjects were found to get easily fatigued mentally and physically when the tasks were of long duration and of high precision [9]. The results suggested that muscle fatigue need to be considered as an important parameter during the treatment of musculoskeletal injuries as well as athletic/rehabilitation training [8][11].

EMG was used in some of the robot-assisted rehabilitation studies for detection of user's intention. For example, a robot-assisted stroke rehabilitation training system with an interactive training game was controlled through an EMG based detection of user's intention [3]. Another study detected user's intention to move based on EMG measurements, but without interactive games [4]. Even though few of them had actually tried to address the adaptability of rehabilitation training in different ways, the participant's state of fatigue is an overlooked area, which can potentially benefit the adaptation algorithms.

The HapticMaster robot was used in the past to assist (through anti-gravity compensation) in improving the difficulty in reaching away movements by chronic stroke survivors during shoulder abduction tasks [12]. An increase in the upper limb reach area was achieved through robot assisted progressive shoulder abduction loading exercises, which reduced the abnormal coupling of shoulder abduction with elbow flexion. As possible expansion of this study, robotic assistance in combination with muscle EMG studies were also proposed. A further research had experimented HapticMaster based upper limb rehabilitation training in a virtual learning environment [13]. The effects of intensive robot-assisted training were studied in multiple sclerosis (MS) patients. The hand path ratio was used as an indicator for the variation from the optimal trajectory between the start position of the hand and the target position. However, the idea of the paper was not to develop a solution that can directly read the physiological state of the patient say for example, using the muscle EMG. The user's state of fatigue and the possibility of using EMG features as fatigue indicators were not explored in either of these studies. The study had also indicated that other interfacing technologies for example, lightweight sensor-based technologies, may be a more appropriate solution [13].

HapticMaster robot and adaptive games were also used for the rehabilitation training of multiple sclerosis (MS) patients based on EMG data from shoulder muscles (Deltoid and Trapezius) [2]. The EMG data were used only for detecting whether or not the muscle fatigue develops in the patients. Only low frequency (0.8-2.5Hz) mean EMG amplitudes were used as fatigue indicators and no spectral/frequency domain features of EMG were studied. Also no kinematic study was conducted, which could help to understand the corresponding kinematic implications of muscle fatigue. The main upper limb movement involved in the training game was lifting and holding tasks. All the game movements were parallel to the frontal plane (either Left/Right or Top/Bottom) and the game did not involve any movements parallel to the sagittal plane. The HapticMaster robot in this study was used just as a haptic input/output device and no robotic assistance was used during the exercise. Hence, the EMG fatigue indicators were statistically significant in all the participants for Deltoid (DLT) and Trapezius (TRP) muscles. In presence of robotic assistance/guidance the impact of fatigue could be improved and the fatigue indicators would indicate lesser fatigue, and this was not covered in this study.

In another similiar study [5], the Root Mean Square (RMS) amplitude and median frequency of EMG signals from the Deltoid muscles (the prime mover in the task) were studied to compare the muscle fatigue in 16 MS patients and 16 healthy individuals, during a robot mediated upper limb training exercise using HapticMaster robot and a virtual game. Only vertical movements (e.g., lifting tasks) were involved and no movements parallel to sagittal plane were defined in this experiment. The study showed that the game performance was not affected by fatigue possibly due to the contribution from other compensatory muscles and there was no relation between the subjective and objective fatigue indicators for the MS patients. Even though the experiment involved movements with dynamic muscle contraction, the EMG used for fatigue study was collected during another 30 seconds isometric muscle contraction task with 90 degree shoulder anteflexion after each training bout. The maximum voluntary contraction (MVC) force was also measured at this position using HapticMaster. The changes in median frequency and RMS amplitude during fatigue were less in the MS patients than in the healthy individuals possibly due to the different weights used or the difference in muscle physiology between the two groups. However, kinematic trajectory (position) parameters were not under the scope of this study. Also the interaction was not guided by the robot and hence, the experiment rythm was not fixed. The patients should have exercised longer time to get the same amount of repetitions or use a higher weight for the exercise. As a result, the comparison of results between the MS patients and healthy participants could not give a clear picture on the usage of EMG fatigue indicators.

The HapticMaster robot was also used in another rehabilitation project, GENTLE/S for upper limb training of stroke survivors [6][14]. As an extension of these studies, [15] had tried to identify the contribution of the participants and the robot during different human-robot interaction modes and to identify who was leading (robot or the person) this interaction. The actual performance of the participant was compared with the minimum jerk model used by the robot. An adaptive algorithm was developed based on altering the movement duration and resistance parameter of the robot to change the task difficulty level. The adaptability of the system using the robot was tested against the performance of the user. But the study did not consider the muscle fatigue state of the participant during the exercise and no EMG studies were employed.

III. MATERIALS AND METHODS

This section describes the experimental setup and protocol used in the study. Additionally, the signal processing methodologies for EMG and kinematic feature extraction are briefly explained here. The muscle fatigue indicators used in the analysis are also mentioned.

A. Experiment Setup

Biometrics Ltd DataLINK hardware was used for EMG data acquisition. HapticMaster robot was configured to run in active assisted mode [15]. The Virtual Reality (VR) environment and the graphical user interface (GUI) was configured to follow a rectangular path as shown in Figure 1 and Figure 3.

B. Experiment Protocol

An experiment was designed as shown in Figure 2 and ethics approval was obtained from the University of Hertfordshire under approval reference: COM/PGT/UH/02002. Ten healthy individuals took part in this explorative study. EMG

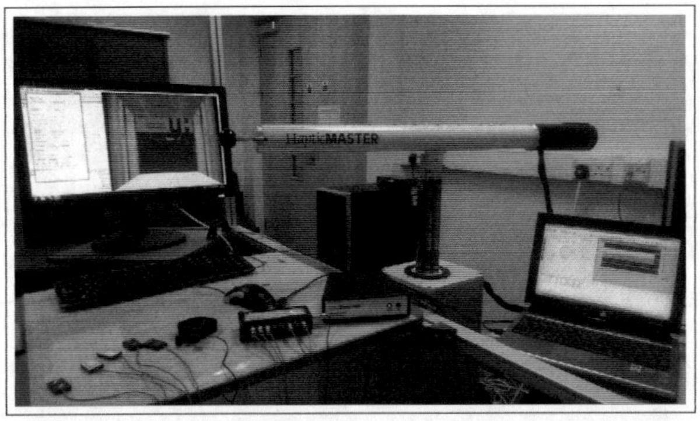

Figure 1. HapticMaster, EMG Device and Virtual Reality Environment

measurements were taken from four upper limb muscles; Trapezius (TRP), Anterior Deltoid (DLT), Biceps Brachii (BB) and Triceps Brachii (TB) muscles. The experiment involved interaction with the HapticMaster robot in active assisted mode where the robot and human participant both contributed to activities and the corresponding position of the robot end-effector was measured during interaction. In the exercise, participants moved the robotic arm in a prescribed path in a two dimensional horizontal plane consisting of four segments S1, S2, S3 and S4. The experiment consisted of 6 trials, and each trials included 10 repetitions of the rectangular motions as shown in Figure 3. The experiments would stop if a total of 6 trials were completed, or if a participant reported fatigue.

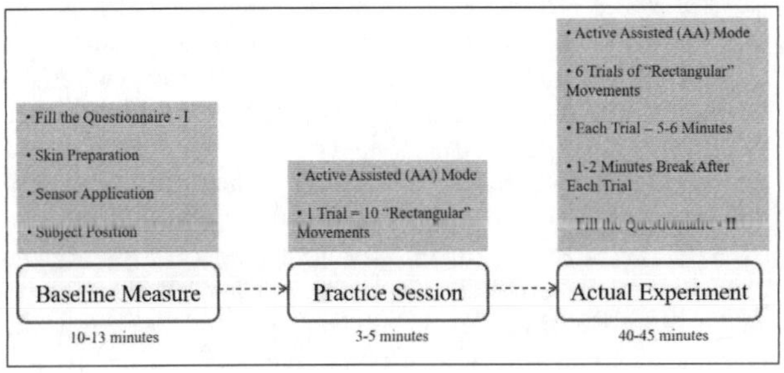

Figure 2. Experiment Protocol

The sitting position and upper limb position of participants during the experiment were as shown in Figure 3

C. Methodology

1) EMG Features: Signal processing algorithms for pre-processing and feature extraction were developed in MATLAB. The EMG signals were band pass filtered in the frequency band of 20-450 Hz using Chebyshev Type II filter [16][17][18]. A narrow notch filter was used (50Hz) to remove the power line interferences [16]. The EMG average power and median frequency were calculated for each segment and each trial.

2) Kinematic Features: The kinematic data like position and segment parameters were logged from the HapticMaster robot and the kinematic features were calculated. Minimum Jerk Trajectory (MJT) position coefficients were calculated from the actual position parameters as described by [6]. The Root Mean Square Error (RMSE) between the actual and MJT position vectors was calculated and used to assess the tracking error in position. It was believed that tracking error will increase as the muscles fatigue.

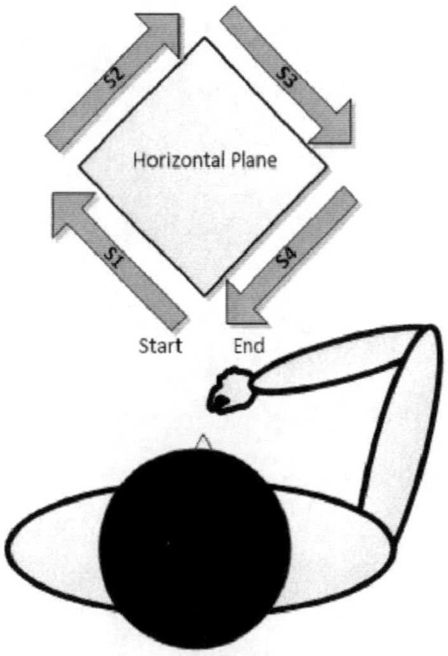

Figure 3. Sitting Position of Participants During the Experiment - Top View

3) Muscle Fatigue Detection: Kinematic (root mean square error (RMSE) in position) and EMG (Average power and median frequency) features corresponding to different trials and segments were analyzed. The change in EMG and kinematic features were studied to understand the development of fatigue in the upper limb muscles in different trials. As the muscle fatigue develops the frequency spectrum and hence, the median frequency will start shifting to lower frequency side and the EMG amplitude will start increasing [16][10][9]. Some studies had also used kinematic position parameters to indicate the performance of participants during robotic interactions [6][14][15] .

IV. Results

This section explains the different results obtained during the analysis of EMG and kinematic data. IBM SPSS version 22 was used for the statistical analysis of the results.

A. EMG Fatigue Indicators

Box plots of the features were generated for each segment to identify trends in median values of EMG features as the trials progressed. The box plots for average power and median frequency as the trials progressed for a typical subject for Trapezius muscle and 1st segment are shown in Figure 4 and Figure 5. A decrease of median frequency and an increase of average power could be noted as the trials progressed [10][5].

Summary tables were created based on the variation of different EMG features across trials as shown in Table I and Table II. Since the EMG features were normally distributed, the mean value of features in each trial for each segment was used to make decisions on the state of fatigue. The mean values between the initial and final trials were compared. The hypothesis for fatigue detection using average power parameter was that, the mean value of average power in the first trial will be smaller that the last trial [10][9]. A "1" in the corresponding cell indicates that the hypothesis is true; meaning that there is an increase in the average power as the trials progresses. A "0" indicates that there is no increase or there is a decrease in its mean value between trials. The table highlights that for the majority of cases, the average power of EMG displays an increasing trend as the trials progressed. As seen in Table I,

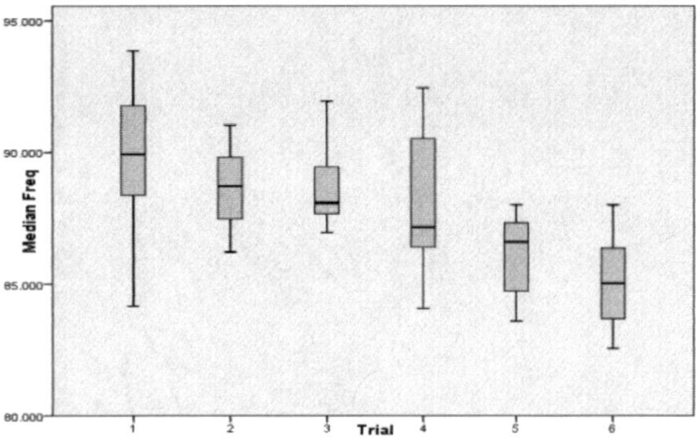

Figure 4. Box Plots for Median Frequency in Trapezius Muscle and Segment 1

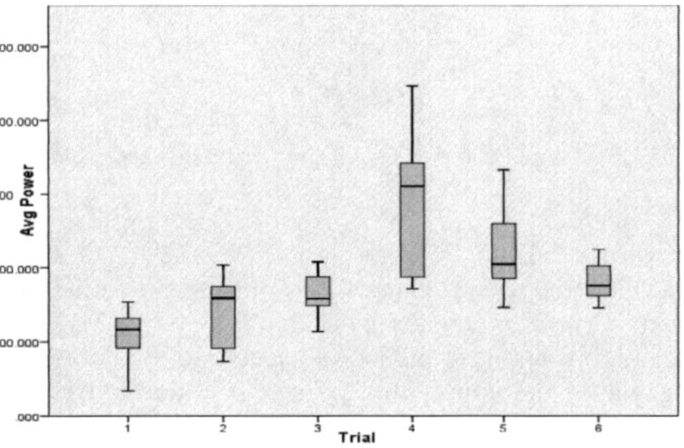

Figure 5. Box Plots for Average Power in Trapezius Muscle and Segment 1

a majority of the analysed cases in Trapezius and Deltoid muscles show an increasing trend (60% and 70% respectively) compared to Biceps and Triceps muscles (37.5% and 40% respectively).

TABLE I. SUMMARY TABLE FOR EMG AVERAGE POWER

Feature ->	EMG Average Power															
Hypothesis ->	The mean value of EMG Average Power in the first trial is smaller than that of the last trial (1 = TRUE, 0 = FALSE, NA = Not Known)															
Methodology ->	Compare the mean values of the parameter between 1st and last trials to see if there is an increase. Each trial includes 10 iterations.															
Muscles ->	TRP				DLT				BB				TB			
Segments ->	S1	S2	S3	S4	S1	S2	S3	S4	S1	S2	S3	S4	S1	S2	S3	S4
Subject 1	1	1	1	1	1	1	1	0	1	1	1	1	1	1	1	1
Subject 2	1	1	1	1	1	1	1	1	1	0	0	0	0	0	1	0
Subject 3	0	0	0	0	0	1	1	0	0	1	1	1	1	1	1	1
Subject 4	0	0	0	0	0	0	0	0	0	0	1	0	1	0	0	0
Subject 5	0	0	0	0	1	1	1	1	0	0	1	0	1	1	1	1
Subject 6	1	1	1	0	0	1	1	1	0	0	1	0	0	0	0	0
Subject 7	1	1	0	0	1	1	0	1	0	0	0	0	0	0	0	0
Subject 8	1	1	1	1	1	0	0	1	0	0	1	1	0	0	0	0
Subject 9	1	1	1	1	0	1	1	1	0	0	0	0	0	0	0	0
Subject 10	0	1	1	1	1	1	1	1	0	0	1	1	1	0	1	0
TOTAL	6	7	6	5	6	8	7	7	2	2	7	4	5	3	5	3
Fatigue Score	24				28				15				16			
Percentage %	60				70				37.5				40			

Similarly, the hypothesis for fatigue detection using median frequency parameter was that, the mean value of the feature in the first trial will be larger that of the last trial [19][20]. A "1" in the corresponding cell indicated that the hypothesis was true, which meant that there was a decrease in the median frequency as the trials progressed. A "0" meant that there was no decrease or there was an increase in its mean value. As seen in Table II, the median frequency of EMG displayed a decreasing trend as the trials progressed in Trapezius and Deltoid muscles in majority of the analyzed cases (57.5% and 62.5% respectively) compared to Biceps and Triceps muscles (37.5% and 27.7% respectively). This might be probably due to the increased fatigue state of TRP and DLT muscles compared to BB and TB muscles.

TABLE II. SUMMARY TABLE FOR EMG MEDIAN FREQUENCY

Feature ->	EMG Median Frequency															
Hypothesis ->	The mean value of EMG Median Frequency in the first trial is higher than that of the last trial (1 = TRUE, 0 = FALSE, NA = Not Known)															
Methodology ->	Compare the mean values of the parameter between 1st and last trials to see if there is a decrease. Each trial includes 10 iterations.															
Muscles ->	TRP				DLT				BB				TB			
Segments ->	S1	S2	S3	S4	S1	S2	S3	S4	S1	S2	S3	S4	S1	S2	S3	S4
Subject 1	1	1	1	1	1	1	1	1	0	1	1	1	0	0	0	1
Subject 2	1	1	1	1	0	1	0	0	0	0	0	1	0	0	0	1
Subject 3	1	1	0	0	1	1	0	0	0	0	0	1	1	0	0	0
Subject 4	1	1	0	0	1	1	1	1	1	0	1	0	1	0	1	0
Subject 5	0	0	1	1	0	1	1	1	0	1	1	0	0	0	0	1
Subject 6	1	0	0	1	1	1	1	1	1	0	1	0	0	1	1	1
Subject 7	1	1	0	1	0	0	0	1	0	0	0	1	0	0	0	0
Subject 8	1	1	1	1	1	1	1	0	0	1	1	0	0	0	1	1
Subject 9	0	0	0	0	0	0	1	1	0	0	1	0	0	0	0	0
Subject 10	0	0	0	0	0	0	1	0	0	0	0	0	0	0	0	0
TOTAL	7	6	4	6	5	7	7	6	2	3	6	4	2	1	3	5
Fatigue Score	23				25				15				11			
Percentage %	57.5				62.5				37.5				27.5			

B. *Kinematic Fatigue Indicators*

The RMSE feature was studied using SPSS box plots and MATLAB plots and summary tables were generated by comparing the median values of first and last trials. An increase of RMSE error was noted between the first and last trials. In the summary table (Table III), a value of 1 means that there was an increase in the error between first and last trials. A value of 0 means there was no increase or there was a decrease in the error. The hypothesis was that there will be an increase of RMSE error between first and last trials when the muscles come to a state of fatigue. 70% and 60% of the subjects displayed an increase of RMSE for the S2 and S3 segments respectively, whereas S1 and S4 segments had the least percentage(40% for both). The RMSE fatigue indication was hence, more during S2 and S3 segments than during the S1 and S4 segments. This might be possibly due to the fatigue developed during the trials in association with the 'away-from-body' movements involved in S2 and S3 segments.

V. DISCUSSION

This section presents further discussion on the results, the possible inference from the results and their linkage to similar studies in the past.

A. *Discussion on EMG Analysis*

It was noticed that most of the participants were challenged especially on the DLT and TRP muscles due to the horizontal position of the upper limb. It was observed that none of the participants were able to hold their upper limb in the horizontal position continuously (as it was supposed to be). This was due to the intentionally complex movement requirements [12]. Subjects could only complete the trials by lowering their upper limb below the shoulder level (hence, by not following the preferred position in the experiment design).

TABLE III. SUMMARY TABLE FOR RMSE ERROR IN POSITION CONSIDERING FIRST AND LAST TRIALS

Feature ->	Root Mean Square Error (RMSE) between Actual Position Vector on MJT Position Vector			
Hypothesis ->	The median value of RMSE parameter in the FIRST trial is smaller than that of the LAST trial (1 = TRUE, 0 = FALSE, NA = Not Known)			
Methodology ->	Compare the median values of the parameter between 1st and last trials to see if there is an increase of error. Each trial includes 10 iterations.			
Segments ->	S1	S2	S3	S4
Subject 1	0	0	0	0
Subject 2	0	0	0	0
Subject 3	0	1	1	1
Subject 4	0	1	1	0
Subject 5	1	1	1	1
Subject 6	0	1	0	0
Subject 7	1	1	1	1
Subject 8	1	1	1	1
Subject 9	1	1	1	0
Subject 10	0	0	0	0
TOTAL	4	7	6	4
Percentage	40%	70%	60%	40%

TABLE IV. SUMMARY TABLE FOR RMSE ERROR IN POSITION CONSIDERING 1ST AND 2ND TRIALS

Feature ->	Root Mean Square Error (RMSE) between Actual Position Vector on MJT Position Vector			
Hypothesis ->	The median value of RMSE parameter in the FIRST trial is smaller than that of the SECOND trial (1 = TRUE, 0 = FALSE, NA = Not Known)			
Methodology ->	Compare the median values of the parameter between 1st and 2nd trials to see if there is an increase of error. Each trial includes 10 iterations.			
Segments ->	S1	S2	S3	S4
Subject 1	0	0	0	0
Subject 2	0	0	0	0
Subject 3	0	0	1	1
Subject 4	0	0	0	0
Subject 5	1	1	1	1
Subject 6	0	1	0	0
Subject 7	1	1	1	1
Subject 8	1	0	1	1
Subject 9	0	1	1	0
Subject 10	0	0	0	0
TOTAL	3	4	5	4
Percentage	30%	40%	50%	40%

During the analysis of EMG signals, the expectation was that there will be an increasing trend for the average power and a decreasing trend in median frequency as the trials progressed. The results had indicated that both the parameters displayed such a trend as explained by the summary tables Table I and Table II. However, the average power seems to be a better indicator of fatigue compared to median frequency due to the higher percentage scores achieved. In the current experiment, the fatigue was mainly caused by the horizontal position of upper limb hence, the fatigue had affected mainly the DLT and TRP muscles. Comparison of mean values of EMG features across trials displayed higher percentage fatigue scores for Trapezius and Deltoid muscles in majority of the analyzed cases (60% and 70% respectively) compared to Biceps Brachii and Triceps Brachii muscles (37.5% and 40% respectively).

B. Discussion on Kinematic Data Analysis

The study of the kinematic features showed that there was an increase of RMSE error more visible in S2 and S3 segments than in S1 and S4 segments. This could be because S2 and S3 were the most difficult segments, which were away from the body and hence, tracking error was more visible in them. To ascertain if the increase of RMSE error between first and last trial is due to fatigue or perception error, we compared the error between the first and second trial. Another summary table was formed by comparing the median values of RMSE error between the first and second trials as in Table IV. The fatigue percentage for S2 and S3 segments were found to be 40% and 50% respectively in this case compared to the case considering the first and last trials (70% for S2 and 60% for S3). This indicated that the RMSE error due to fatigue was not as visible in the second trial as was the case in the last trial in majority of the analysed cases. This study implied that the increased fatigue score during S2 and S3 segments was not attributed to the perception error in locating the 3 dimensional reach points but was due to the development of fatigue as the trials progressed.

The S2 and S3 segments for majority of the subjects involved too much variations at the reaching point of the segment possibly due to the difficulty in accurately judging the end position of the segments. It seems that this inaccuracy increased when the subjects got fatigued as the trials progressed. This might have resulted in an increased RMSE in the final trials of S2 and S3 segments compared to the initial trials as implied by the higher percentage scores. On the other hand, the smaller percentage for the S1 and S4 segments (40%) might be because, they involved movements in space where the upper limb was closer to the body. This might make the movements easier than the other segments. This might mean that the subjects were in a more comfortable upper limb position during S1 and S4 movements or it was more easy to follow the robot in these segments. These results can be related to the findings of [15], which stated that the 'reaching away' movements were longer than the 'returning towards' movements. However, there could be a further explanation for the error in movements away from the body. The perception errors when trying to reach virtual objects away from the body could cause larger tracking errors due to overestimation of the distance to peripheral targets, which might lead to overshooting reaching movements [21][22].

The results of EMG fatigue analysis had indicated that the DLT and TRP muscles were fatigued more. Similarly, the results from the analysis of RMSE error had indicated that S2 and S3 segments displayed more error and variation in position compared to S1 and S4 segments. Hence, it can be inferred that the indication of fatigue by EMG signals (mainly from TRP and DLT muscles) were kinematically correlated with the errors and variations in position mainly in the segments, which were difficult to execute (S2 and S3) as shown by the summary tables of kinematic and EMG features.

VI. CONCLUSION AND FUTURE WORK

The research studied quantitatively which muscles where involved and fatigued in a robot assisted exercise in a 3 dimensional space in presence of a virtual environment. The EMG analysis indicated that Trapezius (TRP) and Anterior Deltoid (DLT) muscles were more in a state of fatigue compared to Biceps Brachii (BB) and Triceps Brachii (TB) muscles. The study also looked into how the kinematic features from the robot represented the muscular fatigue. The variation in tracking error during the robot assisted upper limb interactions were found to indicate physical fatigue in the muscles involved. Similar to the study by [12], we identify that DLT and TRP muscles were fatigued more. This is because of the role of the two muscles in lifting the arm to the shoulder height in order to perform the activity. The higher fatigue indication in Trapezius and Deltoid muscles can be mapped to kinematic indications of fatigue mainly in the segments S2 and S3 which were away from body, because these muscles were actively contributing to keep the horizontal position of the upper limb.

Our extracted features have shown the potential to identify the fatigued muscles as expected. The study also showed that the EMG and kinematic features have a potential to be used to highlight the extent of muscle involvement, as the positioning of the segments and the required articulations for performing those segments relate to the EMG observations. For example, the increase of RMSE error was the least in S1 and S4 segments, which were comfortable 'near-the-body' movements and considering musculoskeletal physiology, Biceps Brachii and Triceps Brachii muscles play the major roles in these segments. The summary tables for tracking error also implied that the increased fatigue score during S2 and S3 segments was not attributed to the perception error in locating the 3 dimensional reach points but due to the development of fatigue by the end of the experiment.

In the experiment, the HapticMaster robot was configured in the Active Assisted mode and all the participants in the experiment were healthy individuals. The robot was providing some assistance/guidance to the participant when there was less effort from the participant to move the end-effector along the different segments. A limitation of this study was that, the robotic assistance resulted in a reduced the muscle fatigue to the participant. However, it was also noticed that the indications of fatigue were observed even with this robotic assistance. Additionally, the experiment protocol had also defined 1-2 minutes of break period between each trial. This period was introduced in order not to harm the participant's muscles due to over challenging. However, this break period could result in a recovery from the state of muscle fatigue developed during the trial (short term fatigue) before they started the next trial. Hence, the continuity of any trend in the features used as fatigue indicators were partly lost. Hence, the experiments could have been be made a bit more difficult and the break period could be avoided so that the muscles are sufficiently tired to produce better indications of fatigue. Probably due to this reason, at the end of the experiments all the participants stated (through a questionnaire) that they were only slightly fatigued. A further study is hence planned to address these aspects.

REFERENCES

[1] B. E. Fisher and K. J. Sullivan, "Activity-Dependent Factors Affecting Poststroke Functional Outcomes," Topics in Stroke Rehabilitation, vol. 8, no. 3, oct 2001, pp. 31–44.

[2] J. R. Octavia, P. Feys, and K. Coninx, "Development of Activity-Related Muscle Fatigue during Robot-Mediated Upper Limb Rehabilitation Training in Persons with Multiple Sclerosis: A Pilot Trial." Multiple sclerosis international, vol. 2015, 2015, p. 650431.

[3] R. K. Y. Tong, W. W. F. Leung, X. L. Hu, and R. Song, "Interactive robot-assisted training system using continuous EMG signals for stroke rehabilitation," Proceedings of the 3rd International Convention on Rehabilitation Engineering & Assistive Technology - ICREATE '09, 2009, p. 20.

[4] L. Dipietro, M. Ferraro, J. Palazzolo, H. Krebs, B. Volpe, and N. Hogan, "Customized Interactive Robotic Treatment for Stroke: EMG-Triggered Therapy," IEEE Transactions on Neural Systems and Rehabilitation Engineering, vol. 13, no. 3, sep 2005, pp. 325–334.

[5] D. Severijns, J. R. Octavia, L. Kerkhofs, K. Coninx, I. Lamers, and P. Feys, "Investigation of Fatigability during Repetitive Robot-Mediated Arm Training in People with Multiple Sclerosis," PloS one, vol. 10, no. 7, jan 2015, p. e0133729.

[6] F. Amirabdollahian, R. Loureiro, and W. Harwin, "Minimum jerk trajectory control for rehabilitation and haptic applications," in Proceedings 2002 IEEE International Conference on Robotics and Automation (Cat. No.02CH37292), vol. 4. IEEE, 2002, pp. 3380–3385.

[7] Christian Nordqvist, "Fatigue: Why Am I So Tired?" 2015. [Online]. Available: http://www.medicalnewstoday.com/articles/248002.php, [Accessed on 2017-01-15].

[8] A. K. Vafadar, J. N. Côté, and P. S. Archambault, "The effect of muscle fatigue on position sense in an upper limb multi-joint task." Motor control, vol. 16, no. 2, 2012, pp. 265–83.

[9] H. R. Zadry, S. Z. M. Dawal, and Z. Taha, "The relation between upper limb muscle and brain activity in two precision levels of repetitive light tasks," International Journal of Occupational Safety and Ergonomics, vol. 17, no. 4, 2011, pp. 373–384.

[10] I. Hostens, J. Seghers, A. Spaepen, and H. Ramon, "Validation of the wavelet spectral estimation technique in Biceps Brachii and Brachioradialis fatigue assessment during prolonged low-level static and dynamic contractions," Journal of Electromyography and Kinesiology, vol. 14, no. 2, 2004, pp. 205–215.

[11] S. Minning, C. a. Eliot, T. L. Uhl, and T. R. Malone, "EMG analysis of shoulder muscle fatigue during resisted isometric shoulder elevation," Journal of Electromyography and Kinesiology, vol. 17, no. 2, 2007, pp. 153–159.

[12] M. D. Ellis, T. M. Sukal-Moulton, and J. P. A. Dewald, "Impairment-Based 3-D Robotic Intervention Improves Upper Extremity Work Area in Chronic Stroke: Targeting Abnormal Joint Torque Coupling With Progressive Shoulder Abduction Loading." IEEE transactions on robotics : a publication of the IEEE Robotics and Automation Society, vol. 25, no. 3, jun 2009, pp. 549–555.

[13] P. Feys, K. Coninx, L. Kerkhofs, T. De Weyer, V. Truyens, A. Maris, and I. Lamers, "Robot-supported upper limb training in a virtual learning environment : a pilot randomized controlled trial in persons with MS." Journal of neuroengineering and rehabilitation, vol. 12, no. 1, jan 2015, p. 60.

[14] R. Loureiro, F. Amirabdollahian, M. Topping, B. Driessen, and W. Harwin, "Upper limb robot mediated stroke therapy - GENTLE/s approach," Autonomous Robots, vol. 15, no. 1, 2003, pp. 35–51.

[15] R. Chemuturi, F. Amirabdollahian, and K. Dautenhahn, "Adaptive training algorithm for robot-assisted upper-arm rehabilitation, applicable to individualised and therapeutic human-robot interaction." Journal of neuroengineering and rehabilitation, vol. 10, no. 1, 2013, p. 102.

[16] D. G. E. Robertson, "Electromyography: Processing," 2015. [Online]. Available: www.health.uottawa.ca/biomech/courses/apa4311/emg-p2.pps, [Accessed on 2017-01-15].

[17] L. C. Miller and J. P. a. Dewald, "Involuntary paretic wrist/finger flexion forces and EMG increase with shoulder abduction load in individuals with chronic stroke," Clinical Neurophysiology, vol. 123, no. 6, 2012, pp. 1216–1225.

[18] S. Arjunan and D. Kumar, "Decoding subtle forearm flexions using fractal features of surface electromyogram from single and multiple sensors," Journal of NeuroEngineering and Rehabilitation, vol. 7, no. 1, oct 2010, p. 53.

[19] L. Grover, A. Arcelus, R. Wang, R. Huq, K. Zabjek, and D. Hebert, "Investigation Of EMG Fatigue Patterns While Using An Upper Limb Rehabilitation Robotic Device," Proceedings of the RESNA 2013 Annual Conference, no. 1, 2013, pp. 1–4.

[20] N. A. Dimitrova and G. V. Dimitrov, "Interpretation of EMG changes with fatigue: Facts, pitfalls, and fallacies," Journal of Electromyography and Kinesiology, vol. 13, no. 1, 2003, pp. 13–36.

[21] A. I. Ross, T. Schenk, C. Hesse, and S. Ullman, "The Effect of Gaze Position on Reaching Movements in an Obstacle Avoidance Task," PLOS ONE, vol. 10, no. 12, dec 2015, p. e0144193.

[22] S. M. Beurze, S. Van Pelt, and W. P. Medendorp, "Behavioral Reference Frames for Planning Human Reaching Movements," Journal of Neurophysiology, vol. 96, no. 1, mar 2006, pp. 352–362.

Wasting "Waste" is a Waste: Gleaning Deleted Text Fragments for Use in Future Knowledge Creation

Hiroaki Ikuta
School of Knowledge Science
Japan Advanced Institute of Science and Technology
Ishikawa, Japan
email: ikuta@jaist.ac.jp

Kazushi Nishimoto
Graduate School of Advanced Science and Technology
Japan Advanced Institute of Science and Technology
Ishikawa, Japan
email: knishi@jaist.ac.jp

Abstract— **While creating a document, an author externalizes his/her thought or idea to text fragments and then organizes and revises them iteratively to polish up the document. In this process, the author may partially delete the contents (i.e., text fragments) from the document because he/she determines that the fragments are not proper as parts of the document. However, these deleted text fragments may be valuable in other future attempts at knowledge creation. This paper proposes Text ComposTer, which is a document-writing support system equipped with a function of collecting the deleted text fragments. We first conduct a pilot study to assess what kind of deleted text fragments are reusable and implement Text ComposTer based on the assessment results. We conduct user studies and confirm that Text ComposTer can efficiently collect reusable deleted text fragments.**

Keywords-intangible waste; knowledge utilization; writing support system; deleted text fragments.

I. Introduction

Is it true that objects determined as waste have no value? In conventional waste management, tangible waste is found to have value to utilize for other purposes. However, intangible waste such as ignored ideas, facts, and knowledge has never been (re)utilized so far. We believe that this intangible waste is also worth utilizing for other purposes. Behind this belief, there are our experiences: a text fragment written in a draft of a document but eventually deleted from the document is sometimes worth utilizing for other purposes. For instance, the second author of this paper found that piano players often press the keys too forcefully when there is insignificant delay between key pressing and sound emission. He described this finding in a draft version of [1]. However, he determined that this finding was inconsistent with the entire context of [1]. As a result, he deleted descriptions about this finding and completed the paper as [1]. In later years, he read the draft version of [1] again when he carried out research about supporting drumstick control, and he found a way to apply the finding to this research. Finally, he completed the research and published [2]. Thus, the second author found value in utilizing the unused finding described in the deleted text fragment for other purposes. There may be a lot of other possibilities like the above example.

There are several models of the document-writing process [3][4][5]. Each proposed model suggests that writing involves a number of distinct activities that interact in complex, interconnected ways [5]. All of these models also contain an activity corresponding to editing of the contents of a document. In addition, an author of documents usually cannot write the completed version perfectly from the beginning; he/she gradually progresses to the completed version. In this process, a lot of knowledge (i.e., text fragments, parts of the document) is merely discarded as intangible waste in the writing process although it might be valuable.

Thus, intangible waste in the writing process is worth saving. Nevertheless, there are few studies on utilizing it. To the best of our knowledge, there have been no attempts to collect deleted text fragments (DTFs) to utilize them for other document writing tasks. Some existing document writing applications are equipped with functions to keep DTFs, such as "Track Changes" function in Microsoft Word and "Snapshot" function in Scrivener. However, these applications keep DTFs to reuse them in the same document for version management; not for utilizing them in the different document composition. Microsoft Word is also equipped with a function to collect text fragments as "building blocks" to reuse them in the different document composition. However, this function requires the users to intentionally save the text fragments to reuse them afterward; they are not DTFs. Therefore, there are no applications that collect DTFs to use them in future knowledge creation.

In this paper, we propose a novel document-writing support system named Text ComposTer. Text ComposTer provides functions to compose a document (i.e., Text ComposTer is a "composer") and, in addition, functions to collect DTFs to utilize them for other purposes afterward (i.e., Text ComposTer is a "composter" of text fragments as intangible waste).

The rest of this paper is organized as follows. Section II presents an overview of several related works. Section III describes a pilot study for assessing what kinds of DTFs are worth utilizing for other purposes. Section IV illustrates Text ComposTer. We show two different user studies in Section V and discuss the usefulness of Text ComposTer based on user studies in Section VI. Section VII concludes this paper.

II. Related Works

Utilizing knowledge via technologies has been the focus of attention for a long time. One of the main attempts at utilizing knowledge is an expert system in the artificial intelligence area. An expert system stores expert knowledge in a knowledge base, and users call upon the system for specific advice as needed. Liao [6] showed various kinds of expert systems. Many kinds of knowledge utilization patterns have been proposed. In addition, Mizoguchi et al. [7] pointed out problems of the knowledge base for knowledge utilization (sharing and reuse in this context), and they proposed a methodology using ontology for enhancing knowledge utilization. These studies attempted to properly formalize useful knowledge in order to utilize it.

Some interactive systems have been proposed to utilize knowledge [8][9][10]. Shibata and Hori [8] proposed a system to support long-term creative thinking in daily life. They developed a system that stored personal awareness or interests in daily life and utilized them for idea generation. Sharmin et al. [9] proposed a system to support reusing presentation slides for making slightly different materials such as a more detailed version of a base material by changing audiences. Simbelis et al. [10] proposed a system named Delete by Haiku to utilize existing text messages in a mobile phone. Delete by Haiku transforms a set of text messages that the user has selected into a *haiku*, a traditional form of Japanese poetry featuring a simple constructive form with a limited number of syllables [10].

These studies [6][7][8][9] aimed to utilize knowledge that has been determined to have potential for (re)utilizing. Simbelis et al. [10] aimed to utilize knowledge whose usefulness has not yet been determined. In contrast, we aim to utilize knowledge that has once been determined to be unuseful.

Therefore, our main research contribution in this paper is to explore a new paradigm of knowledge utilization by finding value in deleted creations in the creative process. Particularly, we start to investigate ways to utilize DTFs generated in the document-writing process.

III. ASSESMENT OF DELETED TEXT FRAGMENTS

We conducted a pilot study to assess what kinds of DTFs are worth utilizing for other purposes.

A. Experimental System

We developed a special text editor for the pilot study that is equipped with a function to collect DTFs as well as functions of a usual text editor, such as copy, cut and paste, and find and replace. This editor automatically collects and stores DTFs when it detects the following three types of user manipulations:

- Hitting elimination keys (e.g., "Delete key" and "Backspace key"),
- Inputting some characters while a string is selected, and
- Executing the replace function.

When the user hits the elimination keys, the text editor collects the eliminated string as a deleted text fragment. Similarly, when the user inputs characters while a string is selected, the text editor collects the selected string as a deleted text fragment. Also, the text editor collects the replaced string as a deleted text fragment when the user executes the replace function.

TABLE I. RESULTS OF THE PILOT STUDY

	Subject 1	Subject 2	Subject 3	Subject 4
# of characters	4726	2468	535	418
# of sentences	72	43	12	10
# of DTFs	551	124	16	99

B. Experimental Setting

We asked four Japanese people (including the first author) to perform a document-writing task using the special text editor. Each subject wrote a part of a conference paper in Japanese as the writing task.

C. Results

The results of the writing task are shown in Table I. We analyzed the results and found the following three possible factors of storing DTFs in accordance with user actions.

- Factor 1: Correcting mistypes.
- Factor 2: Revising expression.
- Factor 3: Eliminating sentences that are inconsistent with the context.

Factor 1 and Factor 2 relate to mere editorial matters. In contrast, Factor 3 relates to the content of the document. Therefore, only the DTFs obtained by Factor 3 would be useful for other purposes.

We found two issues in collecting DTFs using this editor. One of them is that collected DTFs are very messy. The reason for this is that the editor did not distinguish the deleted DTFs based on the three factors. The other issue is that the number of DTFs generated by Factor 3 was quite small. One reason for this issue is that the text fragments that are inconsistent with the context but that are suitable to utilize for other purposes are not created very often. Another reason is that the editor was not suitable for the upstream process of document composition where trial-and-error frequently occurs. Traditional text editors (including our special editor) are suitable for making clean copy rather than for the upstream process. In other words, traditional text editors cannot save the author's thoughts that are yielded in the middle of the document-writing process but that are not finally adopted in the completed version of the document.

IV. TEXT COMPOSTER

A. Approach to resolving the issues

To resolve the above two issues, we developed a novel text composition support system named "Text ComposTer," which supports all activities in document writing from the upstream process to the downstream one (e.g., generating, organizing, composing and revising [5]). Inspired by the Art #001 system [11], which supports the entire document writing process, we designed a user interface for Text ComposTer to make it possible to separately collect two kinds of DTFs (namely, factors 1 and 2 related fragments and factor 3 related fragments) in accordance with its usage.

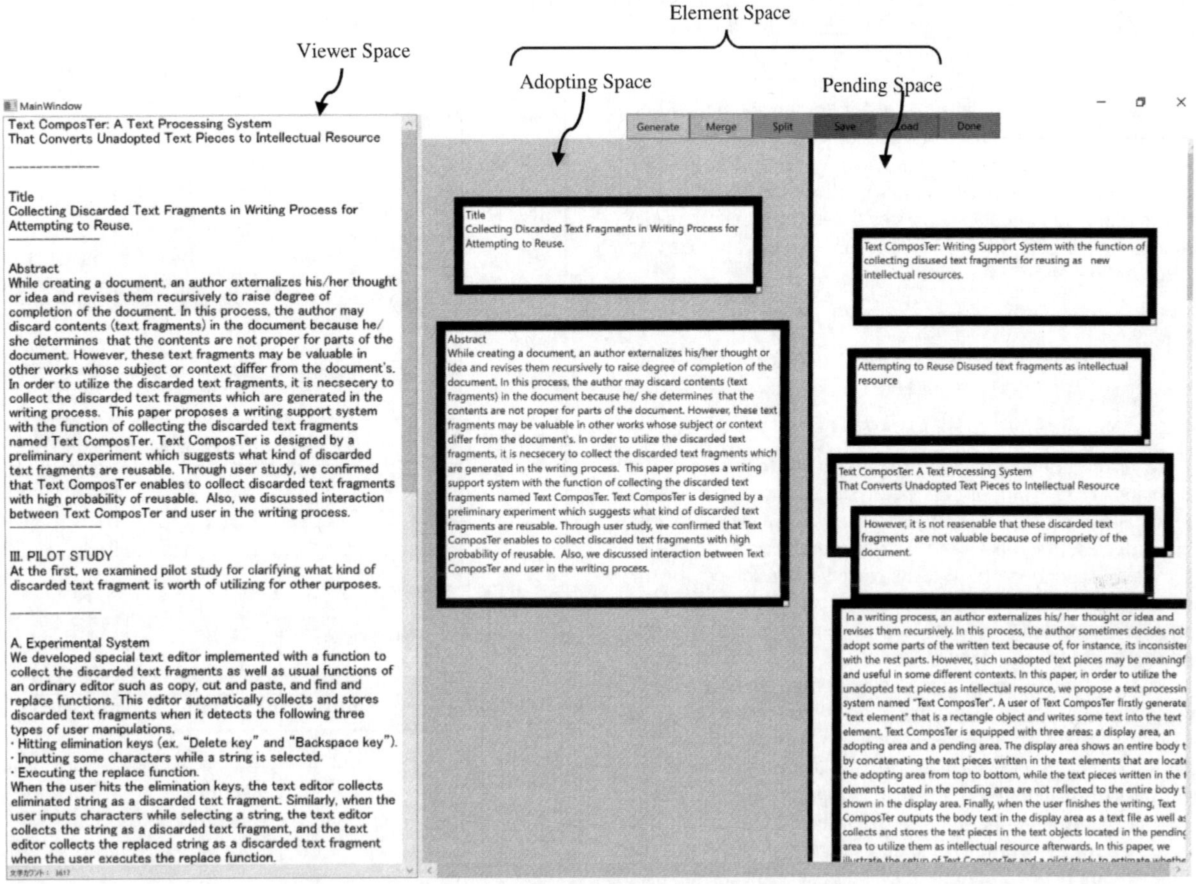

Figure 1. User interface of Text ComposTer.

B. System Overview

Text ComposTer is a native application on Windows OS™ and implemented in C# programming language. Figure 1 shows the user interface of Text ComposTer. It is roughly divided into two spaces: the viewer space and the element space. The element space is also divided into two spaces: one is the adopting space and the other is the pending space. Using Text ComposTer, a user composes a document in any language by writing sentences in a rectangle object named "element" in the element space and sequentially arranging the elements along with the flow of the narrative of the document. The viewer space shows the entire document by concatenating the sentences written in the elements that are located in the adopting space from top to bottom, while the sentences written in the elements located in the pending space are not reflected in the entire document shown in the viewer space. The user interface is equipped with six buttons (i.e., Generate, Merge, Split, Save, Load, and Done buttons) on the upper side of the element space. Each button is a trigger of following functions.

- Generate Function: The user can generate a new element in the element space by pushing the generate button.
- Merge Function: The user can merge multiple elements located in the adopting space. Text fragments written in the selected elements are merged from top to bottom and stored in an element.
- Split Function: The user can split an existing element into two elements by pushing the split button. The sentences in the original element are divided into the two new elements.
- Save Function: The user can save the current work environment of Text ComposTer as an XML-format file by pushing the save button.
- Load Function: The user can load the work environment saved previously by pushing the load button, and then select one of the saved XML files.
- Done Function: The user can output the entire document shown in the viewer space in a text-format file, as well as save the entire document by pushing the done button.

C. Collecting DTFs

Text ComposTer collects DTFs in two different grain sizes: rough-grain DTFs (R-DTFs) and fine-grain DTFs (F-DTFs). When the user pushes the done button, the text fragment in each element located in the pending space is regarded as an R-DTF, and each R-DTF is saved in XML format. An F-DTF is a text fragment deleted by one series of delete operations in an element. Namely, the F-DTF is the same as the deleted text fragment collected in Section III.

A user of Text ComposTer generates an element, then writes text in it and moves it in the element space iteratively. Finally, when the user finishes writing, Text ComposTer outputs a series of text fragments in the viewer space as a text file and also collects and stores the text fragments in the elements located in the pending space to utilize them as intellectual resources afterwards.

V. USER STUDIES

We conducted two types of user studies to investigate characteristics of Text ComposTer.

A. *User Study 1: Comparing R-DTF and F-DTF*

We asked four Japanese subjects to perform a writing task using Text ComposTer. Each subject was a master's student and wrote a research proposal in Japanese. In this user study, each subject used Text ComposTer to complete the first or second draft. We instructed each subject in the functions of Text ComposTer. We especially emphasized that, once generated, elements cannot be removed; to delete a text fragment in an element from the final document, it should be moved to the pending space. After the writing task, we asked each subject to evaluate the collected R-DTFs and F-DTFs. Particularly, we asked them to evaluate whether each R-DTF or F-DTF was "useful" or "useless" or "neither" regardless of the context of the research proposal.

Table II presents the number of collected DTFs, average character numbers of the DTFs, and standard deviation of the character numbers for grain sizes and for subjects. In user study 1, it was found that all of the R-DTFs generated by each subject were fewer, longer and had larger deviation of character numbers than correspondent values of F-DTFs.

Table III presents statistics (comprising number and ratio) of evaluation of usefulness for grain sizes and for subjects. The ratio of evaluation as "Useful" to all evaluations in R-DTFs is much greater than the corresponding ratio in F-DTFs. In addition, any R-DTFs and F-DTFs evaluated as "Useful" tend to be long strings and include technical terms.

B. *User Study 2: Comparing Text ComposTer and the Special Editor in Section III*

We asked eight Japanese master's students to perform two writing tasks using Text ComposTer and the special editor presented in Section III: Text ComposTer for one of the tasks and the special editor for the other task. The topics of the writing tasks are as follows.

T_1: Please predict form and function of mobile phones 10 years in the future.

T_2: Please devise a way to make JAIST (Japan Advanced Institute of Science and Technology, to which the subjects belong) widely known to the public. At a minimum, describe a specific way and assess the merits and demerits of its execution.

TABLE II. STATISTICS OF DTFS IN USER STUDY 1

		Number	Avg. length	SD
R-DTF	Sub. 1	5	240.6667	233.2600
	Sub. 2	8	86.6250	51.8361
	Sub. 3	0	–	–
	Sub. 4	6	97.6667	69.8538
	Total	19	106.4737	84.7984
F-DTF	Sub. 1	196	5.3163	14.4821
	Sub. 2	309	3.9029	5.7124
	Sub. 3	38	10.1842	14.4495
	Sub. 4	84	6.5176	28.7859
	Total	627	4.6571	10.0065

TABLE III. RESULTS OF EVALUATION OF DTFS IN USER STUDY 1

		Useful	Useless	Neither
R-DTF	Sub. 1	3 (50%)	3 (50%)	0 (0%)
	Sub. 2	5 (62.5%)	3 (37.5%)	0 (0%)
	Sub. 3	0 (-%)	0 (-%)	0 (-%)
	Sub. 4	3 (50%)	0 (0%)	3 (50%)
	Total	11 (55%)	6 (30%)	3 (15%)
F-DTF	Sub. 1	1 (0.5%)	195 (99.5%)	0 (0%)
	Sub. 2	5 (1.6%)	303 (98.1%)	1 (0.3%)
	Sub. 3	5 (13.2%)	12 (31.6%)	21 (55.3%)
	Sub. 4	0 (0%)	84 (100%)	0 (0%)
	Total	11 (1.8%)	594 (94.7%)	22 (3.5%)

Each writing task was limited to 30 minutes, and the number of characters of each document was restricted in the range of 100 to 400. We allowed each subject to take a break for about five minutes in each writing task. For counterbalancing, each subject was allocated to different combinations of systems used (Text ComposTer or the special editor), topics (T_1 or T_2) and order (first writing task, second task). After the writing tasks, we carried out semi-structured interviews in which we mainly asked about usability of each system and how to use each system in performing the writing task.

Table IV presents the average number of collected DTFs, average number of characters of the collected DTFs, and standard deviation of the character number for systems used and for topics. As shown in Table IV, the average number of characters of DTF collected by the special editor and F-DTF are almost the same, but their standard deviations are different.

We found that usage of Text ComposTer and the special editor differed depending on the subjects' writing styles.

TABLE IV. STATISTICS OF DTFS IN USER STUDY 2

		T_1			T_2		
		Avg. number	Avg. length	SD	Avg. number	Avg. length	SD
Text ComposTer	R-DTF	5.75	40.2727	50.1789	2.25	63.3333	47.8774
	F-DTF	74.75	4.7715	9.2677	42.25	4.5444	6.8937
Special Editor in Sec. III		41.5	6.0663	19.1707	97	6.4897	13.2141

Subject 1 started to write a document after he had finished composing the narrative of the document in his mind. In other words, he only used both systems to make a clean copy; thus the number of DTFs from subject 1 using both Text ComposTer and the special editor was quite small.

The writing styles of Subjects 2, 3, 4, 5, and 8 were as follows. First, they enumerated keywords and ideas for a document, then selected some of these keywords and ideas, and wrote the document based on the selected ones. When using Text ComposTer, they generated an element and described a keyword set or an idea in the element. Then, they arranged the elements in the adopting space and the pending space and completed the document. Finally, some elements remaining in the pending space were collected as R-DTFs. When using the special editor, on the other hand, they first wrote down a list of ideas and keywords in the special editor; then they wrote the body of the document while referring to the list. They finally deleted the list and completed the document.

Furthermore, the process of the writing task with Text ComposTer differed between subjects 2, 3, 8 and subjects 4, 5. Subjects 2, 3, 8 first generated the elements in which ideas and keyword sets are described, and then moved all these elements to the pending space. They subsequently generated an element for a clean copy of the document, and described the body of the document in the element referring to the elements located in the pending space. Subjects 4 and 5, on the other hand, first generated the elements of keyword sets and ideas in the same manner as subjects 2, 3, 8. Then, they selected some elements, put them in the adopting space, added text in these elements, and merged them into one element by using the merge function to complete the document.

In contrast, the writing styles of subjects 6 and 7 changed depending on the system. They used Text ComposTer in the same manner as subjects 2~5 and 8, while they used the special editor in the same manner as subject 1.

From these observation results, we can assume that most people who have peculiar writing styles (like subjects 1~5 and 8) tend to adhere to their own writing styles regardless of the text-writing system.

We got replies in the interview about comparison between Text ComposTer and the special editor. As an affirmative response about Text ComposTer, subjects 3, 4, 6, 7 reported that they could create many more ideas with Text ComposTer than with the special editor. They could also write the document systematically because they could organize their thoughts better using Text ComposTer. Contrarily, as a negative response about using Text ComposTer, subjects 3, 8 reported that they felt uncomfortable writing down the body of the document in the element.

VI. DISCUSSION

This section discusses the usefulness of Text ComposTer based on the results of the user studies. At first, we discuss usability of Text ComposTer, and then we discuss whether Text ComposTer can efficiently collect R-DTFs, mainly focusing on the two issues shown in Section III.

A. *Usability of Text ComposTer as a document-writing support system*

There are two significant differences between Text ComposTer and usual text editors, including the special editor: 1) similar to the Art#001 system [11], the user writes a part of the document (text fragments) in an element and composes the entire document by sorting the elements based on the storyline; and 2) if the user judges that certain text fragments in an element are not necessary, he/she moves (not deletes) the element to the pending space for elimination from the final document. These differences may cause incorrect usability as a document-writing support system.

Evaluation on the usability varied depending on the writing styles of the subjects and on whether the subjects could change their styles or not. Most of the existing text editors are based on the WYSIWYG concept: the users are always viewing the final image of the document while writing it. They are familiar with this style and they often unintentionally attempt to make the final document from the beginning. However, Text ComposTer requires users to use a totally different writing style from such ordinary text editors: it requires them to make parts at first, then to assemble them to compose the final document. Therefore, the users are required to change their document-writing style when using Text ComposTer.

The subjects who responded affirmatively in the interview would be able to change their styles, or their writing style was originally similar to that of Text ComposTer. Subjects 6 and 7 actually changed their styles depending on the tool. Subjects 3 and 4 first enumerated keywords and ideas even when they used the special editor. This style is potentially similar to that of the Text

ComposTer. Therefore, they could quickly change the style when using Text ComposTer. Although subjects 2, 5, and 8 did not respond affirmatively, they also enumerated keywords and ideas first. This means that their writing style is similar to that of subjects 3 and 4, although they did not recognize this as an advantage of Text ComposTer. In contrast, subject 1 used both tools in the WYSIWYG editor manner. For such users, it should be necessary to give them some instructions about the writing styles beforehand.

Consequently, as for the users who are potentially familiar with the writing style of Text ComposTer, its usability is acceptable. However, as for users who adhere to the WYSIWYG writing style, its usability is not good and some instructions to change their style are necessary.

B. *Can Text ComposTer efficiently collect R-DTFs?*

In this subsection, we discuss whether Text ComposTer can efficiently collect meaningful R-DTFs. Furthermore, we would like to inspect whether the following two issues revealed in the pilot study were solved: 1) collected DTFs are very messy using the special editor and 2) the number of DTFs is quite small.

In Text ComposTer, only text fragments written in the elements that are finally located in the pending space are collected as R-DTFs; DTFs generated by correcting mistypes (Factor 1) and revising expressions (Factor 2) that often cause the messiness are excluded from R-DTFs. Therefore, it became able to automatically and selectively obtain meaningful R-DTFs that are text fragments generated only by Factor 3. In addition, from the results of user study 1 (see Table II), users of Text ComposTer said that R-DTFs are more useful than F-DTFs. Consequently, we can conclude that Text ComposTer can efficiently collect meaningful R-DTFs separated from F-DTFs and can also solve the first issue.

Although Text ComposTer also has the potential to solve the second issue, whether meaningful R-DTFs can be obtained depends on the usage of Text ComposTer. We designed Text ComposTer to support the entire text-writing process from the upstream to the downstream. Namely, in the beginning of the text-writing process, the author is required to create a lot of diverse ideas regardless of the context and then composes the document in a convergent manner while gradually establishing the context. In this process, each idea is evaluated and selected if it is necessary in the context. As a result, unused ideas are usually wasted, but Text ComposTer gleans them as seeds for future knowledge creations. Therefore, we expected that the users of Text ComposTer described each keyword set or idea in an element one-by-one in the beginning, then arranged the elements to compose the documents. Finally, several unused elements were moved to the pending space.

Thus, supporting and enhancing the initial divergent process of idea creation is important for increasing the number of R-DTFs and solving the second issue. Text ComposTer is equipped with this function. However, as shown in Table IV, the numbers of R-DTFs is still small and useful ones are similar to those obtained by the special editor (see Table III). Moreover, as with the usage of subjects in user study 2, Text ComposTer can be used in different ways of text-writing. To effectively increase the number of R-DTFs, some functions and/or restrictions should be added to let the users use Text ComposTer based on our expected way of text-writing.

Such additional functions and/or restrictions are necessary from the viewpoints of improving usability and of accurately gleaning R-DTFs. We need to consider improvement of the interface of elements because the negative responses from the interviews related to the elements; subjects 2, 3, 8 in user study 2 generated elements for making a clean copy of the document, which is an unexpected usage. One reason for this problem is that the element allows different usages. It allows the user to take memos of ideas and keywords, to write a part of the body of the document, and eventually to write a clean copy of the document. This feature causes the unexpected usage where the user writes the body of the document into the elements in the adopting space by referring to the ideas or keyword sets in the elements in the pending space. This causes the problem that useful knowledge and intangible waste are mixed and cannot be distinguished.

Furthermore, we need to consider eliminating the merge function from editing functions of Text ComposTer. In user study 2, subjects 4 and 5 completed the document by merging elements into one element. Text ComposTer enables users to support the text-writing process by sorting and arranging elements in the element space. However, if the elements are merged into one element once, users of Text ComposTer become unable to easily revise the document by sorting the elements. Besides, when users want to delete a part of a document (i.e., text fragment) in the merged element, Text ComposTer collects it as an F-DTF, not an R-DTF. To collect it as an R-DTF, the user needs to split the text fragment from the original element and move the split element to the pending space. Such a manipulation introduces a high cognitive load for collecting R-DTFs. Therefore, we conclude that the merge function should be eliminated from the viewpoints of both usability and of efficiently collecting R-DTFs.

One limitation of the user studies is that the number of subjects was too small to obtain statistically significant results. Additional experiments are necessary. However, the characteristics of R-DTFs and F-DTFs collected by Text ComposTer and DTFs collected by the special editor were evidently different. Therefore, by conducting the additional experiments, we would obtain statistically significant results that are almost similar to the results of the user studies shown in this paper.

VII. Conclusion and Future Work

This paper described a novel writing support system called Text ComposTer that is equipped with functions to efficiently collect DTFs as a resource for supporting future knowledge creation. Text ComposTer was designed based on the findings of a pilot study that investigated what kinds of DTFs are proper to utilize. Text ComposTer has an advantage of collecting (re)utilizable DTFs because it can collect R-DTFs and F-DTFs separately. This advantage was confirmed in user studies. Consequently, Text ComposTer is an effective system for collecting intangible waste that has the potential to be utilized.

Our contribution of this paper is to propose a document writing application that is equipped with an effective collection function of DTFs, in particular R-DTFs. Such applications have not ever existed because of lacking a perspective of utilizing intangible waste so far. On the other hand, this paper has not yet investigated whether the collected DTFs are actually useful or not. To totally claim the usefulness of Text ComposTer, we need to carry out investigation of utilization of collected DTFs.

In near future, we would like to improve the design of the elements to more clearly separate out useful knowledge. We would also like to create an environment for utilizing DTFs (mainly R-DTFs) for future knowledge creation, and to conduct user studies to confirm the usefulness of collected DTFs. Through these studies, we would like to create a future where people know that wasting "waste" is a waste.

ACKNOWLEDGMENT

The authors sincerely thank all of the research participants who willingly cooperated in our experiments. This work was supported by JSPS KAKENHI Grant Number JP15K12093.

REFERENCES

[1] C. Oshima, K. Nishimoto, and N. Hagita, "A Piano Duo Support System for Parents to Lead Children to Practice Musical Performances," ACM Transactions on Multimedia Computing, Communications and Applications (ACM TOMCCAP), vol. 2 issue 2, Article 9, pp. 1-21, 2007.

[2] A. Ikenoue, K. Nishimoto, and M. Unoki "iDAF-drum: Supporting Practice of Drumstick Control by Exploiting Insignificantly Delayed Auditory Feedback," Knowledge Information and Creativity Support Systems, AISC 416, Springer, pp. 483-498, 2016.

[3] C. Neuwirth, D. Kaufer, R. Chimera. and T. Gillespie, "The Notes program: A hypertext application for writing from source texts," Hypertext '87 Papers. Chapel Hill, NC. pp. 121-142, 1987.

[4] J. B. Smith, S. F. Weiss, and G. J. Ferguson, "A hypertext writing environment and its cognitive basis," Hypertext '87 Papers. Chapel Hill, NC. pp. 195-214, 1987.

[5] W. J. Hunter and J. Begoray, "A Framework for the Activities Involved in the Writing Process," The Writing Notebook, vol. 7, No. 3, pp. 40-42, 1990.

[6] S. Liao, "Expert system methodologies and applications—a decade review from 1995 to 2004," Expert Systems with Applications, vol 28, Issue 1, pp. 93–103, 2005.

[7] R. Mizoguchi, J. Vanwelkenhuysen, M. Ikeda, "Task ontology for reuse of problem solving knowledge," Towards Very Large Knowledge Bases: Knowledge Building & Knowledge Sharing, IOS, pp. 46-59, 1995.

[8] H. Shibata and K. Hori, "A system to support long-term creative thinking in daily life and its evaluation," In Proceedings of the 4th conference on Creativity & Cognition (C&C '02). ACM, New York, USA, pp. 142-149, 2002.

[9] M. Sharmin, L. Bergman, J. Lu, and R. Konuru, "On slide-based contextual cues for presentation reuse," In Proceedings of the 2012 ACM international conference on Intelligent User Interfaces (IUI '12), ACM, New York, USA, pp. 129-138, 2012.

[10] V. 'V. Simbelis, P. Ferreira, E. Vaara, J. Laaksolahti, and K. Höök, "Repurposing Bits and Pieces of the Digital," In Proceedings of the 2016 CHI Conference on Human Factors in Computing Systems (CHI '16), ACM, New York, USA, pp. 840-851, 2016.

[11] K. Nakakoji, Y. Yamamoto, B. N. Reeves, and S. Takada, "Two-Dimensional Positioning as a Means for Reflection in Design," Proceedings of Design of Interactive Systems (DIS'2000), ACM , New York, USA, pp.145-154, 2000.

PassGame: A Shoulder-Surfing Resistant Mobile Authentication Scheme

Jonathan Gurary*, Ye Zhu*, Nahed Alnahash†, and Huirong Fu†
*Department of Electrical and Computer Engineering, Cleveland State University, Cleveland, Ohio
Emails: j.gurary@vikes.csuohio.edu, y.zhu61@csuohio.edu
†Department of Computer Science, Oakland University, Oakland, Michigan
Emails: nalnahas@oakland.edu, fu@oakland.edu

***Abstract*—Ubiquitous computing enabled by mobile devices, such as smartphones and tablets, causes more exposure of device users to shoulder-surfing attacks in crowded places, such as a subway train. In this paper, we propose *PassGame*, a shoulder-surfing resistant mobile authentication scheme based on board games. The design of PassGame is based on the popular game of chess. PassGame challenges a user with a random formation of chess pieces on a game board. A successful authentication requires a user to respond to the challenge so that a set of predefined rules are satisfied after adjustments made by the user. PassGame can be finished by a user without any chess knowledge. We implement PassGame on the Android operating system. Our user studies with the Android implementation show that PassGame passwords with more password strength than current mobile authentication schemes can achieve 100% recall rates when recalled one week after password setup.**

Keywords–Shoulder Surfing; Challenge Response; Gamification; Mobile Authentication; Graphical Passwords

I. Introduction

Mobile devices, such as smartphones and tablets, are becoming increasingly popular because of their nearly ubiquitous Internet access through various communication capabilities such as WIFI, 3G, or 4G networks and their numerous applications and games. While users are enjoying the benefits of ubiquitous computing enabled by mobile devices, they are also becoming more vulnerable to shoulder-surfing attacks. Consider a user on a crowded subway train. The user may want to check emails as there are a few stops before a destination. But, to check emails through a smartphone, the user has to unlock the screen with possibly several pairs of eyes watching the whole authentication process from behind. Since current authentication schemes on mobile devices are not designed to resist shoulder-surfing attacks [1], users of mobile devices are in danger of password theft and its consequences such as data breach from their mobile devices. Research suggests that mobile phone users unlock their devices an average of 48 times per day (about 3 unlocks per hour), and users perceive shoulder-surfing to be possible in 17% of these instances [2].

Designing an authentication scheme for mobile devices is a challenging task because the scheme should be both *secure* and *usable*. For mobile devices, a secure authentication scheme should be shoulder-surfing resistant for ubiquitous computing and the scheme should have a large password space, i.e., a large number of possible passwords. Usability of an authentication scheme is of the same importance for mobile devices: (1) The scheme should be easy to use. (2) Passwords generated by the scheme should be easy to remember.

In this paper, we propose *PassGame*, a shoulder-surfing resistant mobile authentication scheme based on board games. PassGame is essentially a challenge-response authentication scheme. In our current design, PassGame is based on the popular game of chess. An authentication starts with a random chess board, i.e., a chess board with randomly selected game pieces on randomly selected tiles of a game board. The random chess board serves as a challenge to the user. To finish the authentication successfully, the user responds to a challenge by making adjustments to the random game board so that a set of predefined rules are satisfied. The adjustments can be moving game pieces, adding new game pieces, and removing existing game pieces. PassGame supports both rules without any requirements on chess knowledge and rules requiring only basic chess knowledge.

In general, shoulder-surfing resistant schemes incur relatively higher usability costs such as longer password entry time. PassGame is not designed to replace existing mobile authentication schemes, such as Google's pattern unlock and the four-digit PIN widely used on smartphones. Instead PassGame can be a supplemental scheme for use in crowded places or places with camera surveillance. PassGame can also be a choice for high security authentications on smartphone operating systems supporting different security levels in authentication such as Android.

The rest of the paper is organized as follows: We review related work on graphical passwords and shoulder-surfing resistant authentication schemes in Section II. Then, we present the design details of PassGame in Section III. We present our user studies on the usability and memorability of PassGame in Section IV. We conclude the paper in Section V.

II. Related Work

A number of research efforts have been aimed to add shoulder-surfing resistance into existing schemes. Roth *et al.* [3] proposed to add the resistance to the classic 4-digit PIN by splitting the PIN entry pad into two sets (black and white buttons) and asking users to choose which set their digit is in. The process is repeated several times to confirm the choice of a digit and repeats again until all the digits are chosen. Since then many schemes to add shoulder-surfing resistance to the 4-digit PIN have been proposed, including SwiPIN [4], ColorPIN [5], and The Phone Lock [6]. While these schemes can improve shoulder-surfing resistance of PIN-based schemes, these schemes still suffer from inherently weak security strength in PINs and these schemes can be easily compromised by brute force attacks.

Zakaria *et al.* [7] proposed to improve the shoulder-surfing resistance of Draw a Secret [8] by erasing strokes as they are drawn. Their user study shows the improvement can reduce the rate of medium-strength passwords captured by an attacker after a single observation from 80% to roughly 40%. Lin *et al.* [9] proposed to add a grid to Draw A Secret. In addition to matching the Draw a Secret gesture, users in this scheme must also match the direction (e.g., up, down) in which some strokes of their gesture pass through the added grid lines.

Convex Hull Click (CHC) [10] is a graphical password scheme designed to counter shoulder-surfing attacks. CHC asks users to choose icons to represent their passwords. Rather than clicking the icons, users are required to click somewhere inside the triangular area bounded by their chosen icons. CHC suffers from long authentication times because multiple click sessions are required and it takes time for the user to find their icons. The CDS scheme [11], a combination of Draw a Secret [8] and Story [12], arranges a series of images randomly into a grid and asks users to draw a line through the images they choose to represent their passwords.

A number of shoulder-surfing resistant schemes require extra hardware [6], [13], [14], [15]. These schemes may not be suitable for mobile authentication because of hardware and software requirements and smaller screens on mobile devices.

PassGame can be considered a multi-dimensional password, as proposed in [16]. PassGame uses many dimensions such as rule, color, piece type, and number of attacking pieces.

III. The PassGame Design

In this section, we present an overview of PassGame and describe the design details of PassGame.

A. Overview

The current design of PassGame is based on the popular game chess. PassGame is essentially a challenge-response authentication scheme. In PassGame, a mobile device challenges a user with a randomly generated chess board, i.e., a chess board with randomly selected game pieces placed on randomly selected tiles. The user responds to the challenge by making adjustments on the chess game board including adding new games pieces, removing existing game pieces, and moving existing game pieces. A correct response will be an adjusted game board satisfying some predefined rules. For example, one rule of PassGame is to move game pieces by n_{tile} tiles in total. Any move of a game piece including illegal moves in the chess game is allowed. Moving a game piece to the right or the left by one tile adds or decreases one tile from the total respectively. Similarly, moving a game piece up or down by one row adds or decreases eight tiles from the total, respectively, as one row in the chess board has 8 tiles. A user can also add or decrease the number of tiles moved by adding a new game piece to the board or removing a game piece from the board respectively. As long as the sum of total tiles moved is equal to n_{tile}, the predefined number of tiles in total, the rule is satisfied and the user will be authenticated if no other rules are in use. Otherwise, the authentication is unsuccessful.

PassGame supports both rules without any requirements on chess knowledge and rules requiring basic chess knowledge. The design is to make sure every user, including those who have no knowledge of the chess game, can use the authentication scheme. The other rules require only basic chess knowledge of how game pieces attack. We include these rules requiring basic knowledge of chess to take advantage of the popularity of chess because we hypothesize that chess knowledge or previous experiences in chess games may improve memorability of PassGame passwords.

A PassGame password can be formed with multiple rules. In general, using more rules to form a PassGame password can make the PassGame password more complex, and in turn more resistant to brute force attacks and shoulder-surfing attacks.

As long as the rules of a password are satisfied, PassGame allows users to make unrelated adjustments to the board. In other words, a user can add, remove, and move game pieces that are not involved in any rules used to form a password. These unrelated adjustments to a game board allow a user to further mitigate shoulder-surfing attacks as a shoulder-surfer can not tell which game pieces are involved in the rules used to form the PassGame password.

To make PassGame more usable, the design does not enforce laws of chess. Any piece of either color can be positioned on any tile of the chess board, and multiple pieces of the same type are permitted (e.g., three kings).

In the rest of this section, we describe the generation of a random game board and then the details of each rule possibly used in a PassGame password.

B. Random Board Generation

Since PassGame authentication starts with a challenge of a random board, the generation of the random board is important for both the security and usability of PassGame. On each tile, there are 13 possibilities: the tile is empty, or it is occupied by a king, queen, bishop, knight, rook, or pawn in either of the two colors.

PassGame randomly selects one from the 13 possibilities for each tile. Pieces appear with the same frequency as they typically appear in chess middlegame, though it is also possible to get boards which are almost completely empty or full. The design is to ensure most boards have enough pieces so that there are many ways to satisfy the rules of a password.

We allow a user to request a new random board and get authenticated with the new random board. A user may request a random board for several possible reasons: (1) The user's password cannot be completed on the given random board (e.g., remove 3 black pieces from the board on a board with less than 3 pieces), (2) The user wants a board where the password can be input more easily, (3) The user wants to find a game board where shoulder-surfing is less likely, or (4) The user has modified the random board unsuccessfully and does not remember what it initially looked like. A random board often partially or completely satisfies some of a user's rules without any modifications. Thus, a shoulder-surfer may not necessarily see the user inputting all the rules that comprise their password, forcing them to guess remaining rules from the contents of the random board.

C. *PassGame Rules*

In our current design, a PassGame password can be formed with 12 rules. We present the details of the rules below.

The first 6 rules do not require any chess knowledge. So, any user should be able to use these rules.

Rule R1: Number of Tiles Moved in Total: The parameter of this rule is the number of tiles moved. To satisfy this rule, a user must make adjustments to a game board so that the number of tiles moved in total should be equal to a predefined number n_{tile}. The board can be considered as a numbered grid from 1 to 64, where the bottom left corner is 1, and the top right is 64. Moving a game piece to the right or to the left by one tile adds or decreases the number of tiles moved in total by one respectively. Similarly, moving a game piece up or down by one row adds or decreases the number of tiles moved in total by 8 respectively. Adding a game piece to a tile adds to the number of tiles moved in total by the number associated with that tile. On the contrary, removing a game piece from a tile decreases the number of tiles moved in total by the number associated with that tile.

For example, if a user sets $n_{tile} = 8$ in the password setup phase, the user can satisfy this rule by adding a piece to tile 8 if the tile is not occupied, or by moving a piece on tile 12 to tile 20 if the destination tile is not occupied. To mitigate shoulder-surfing attacks, a user can also combine multiple adjustments together to achieve the number of tiles in total. For example, if $n_{tile} = 8$, a user can move one piece forward by 20 tiles, move another piece backwards by 10 tiles, add a piece to tile 28, and remove a piece from tile 30 to make the number of total tiles moved be 8. In theory, the range of n_{tile} is $[-2080, 2080]$ as $\sum_{i=1}^{64} i = 2080$.

Rule R2: Number of Pieces in a Row: The parameters of this rule are color, row index, and number of pieces of the selected color that must exist in the selected row. To satisfy this rule, a user must adjust a game board so that the selected row has the chosen number of pieces in it of the chosen color. This can be done adding pieces or removing pieces from the row, as a randomly generated row may have more pieces than are needed. The number of possible combinations of the parameters is $3 \times 8 \times 8 = 192$ as (1) color can be black, white, or both, and (2) a chess board has 8 rows and columns.

Rule R3: Number of Pieces in a Column: This rule is similar to Rule R2 and the only difference is that R3 is defined on a column. So the number of possible combinations of the parameters is also 192.

Rule R4: Number of Pieces on a Board: This rule is similar as Rule R2 and the only difference is that R4 is defined on a game board. The parameters of this rule are color and number of pieces on the board, so the number of possible combinations of the parameters is $3 \times 64 = 192$ as (1) color can be black, white, or both and (2) a board can hold up to 64 game pieces.

Rule R5: More or Less Pieces: The parameters of this rule are color and the number of pieces added or removed from a board. To satisfy this rule, a user must add or remove the specified number of pieces in the chosen color. To further mitigate shoulder-surfing attacks, a user may want to add and remove pieces several times. As long as the final number of pieces added or removed from a board totals the specified number, the rule is satisfied. The number of possible combinations of the parameters is $3 \times 64 \times 2 = 384$ because (1) color can be black, white, or both, (2) at most 64 pieces can be added or removed from the board.

Rule R6: Specific Tile: The parameters of this rule are piece type, color, row index, and column index. The rule is satisfied when the specified piece of the chosen color is at the chosen row and column location. The number of possible combinations of the parameters is $6 \times 3 \times 8 \times 8 = 1152$ as (1) the piece type can be king, queen, bishop, knight, rook, or pawn, (2) the color can be black, white, or both colors, and (3) the board has 8 rows and 8 columns.

The next 6 rules require only basic knowledge of attacks in chess. To add more attacks, a user can add game pieces under attack, attack existing pieces, or both. Attacks can also be added by removing pieces blocking attack paths of other game pieces. Similarly, attacks can be reduced by adding blocking pieces, removing attacking pieces, or removing the pieces under attack.

Rule R7: Number of Attacks on a Piece: The parameters of this rule are piece type, piece color, and number of attacks. This rule is satisfied when a game piece of the type and color selected is attacked by the chosen number of attackers. One example is that a bishop of either color is under attack by five pieces. If there is no such piece on a random board, a user can add it to the board. If there are multiple such pieces a board, then only one of them is required to be under attack by the specified number of pieces. The number of possible combinations of the parameters is approximately $6 \times 3 \times 16 = 288$ as (1) the piece type can be king, queen, bishop, knight, rook, or pawn, (2) the color can be black, white, or both colors, and (3) the maximum number of attacks to one tile is 16 (4 diagonal attacks, 2 horizontal attacks, 2 vertical attacks, and 8 attacks by knights). Note that not every tile can have 16 attackers (e.g corner tiles can have a maximum of 5 attackers), so it may be necessary to move a piece or place a new one in order to satisfy larger numbers of attacks.

Rule R8: Number of Attacks by Pieces: The parameters of this rule are piece type, piece color, and number of attacks. The rule is satisfied when a game piece of the selected type and color is attacking the chosen number of game pieces. For a king, a queen, or a knight, there are $3 \times 8 = 24$ combinations because (1) color can be black, white, or both and (2) a king, a queen, or a knight can attack a maximum of 8 pieces. For a bishop or a rook, there are $3 \times 4 = 12$ combinations because a bishop or a rook can attack 4 pieces at most. For a pawn, there are only $3 \times 2 = 6$ combinations because a pawn can only attack two pieces at most. So the total number of possible combinations is $3 \times 24 + 2 \times 12 + 6 = 102$.

Rule R9: Number of Pieces under Attack: The parameters of this are piece color and number of pieces under attack. The rule is satisfied when the selected number of game pieces of the chosen color are under attack. Since (1) the maximum

Figure 1. A screenshot of the PassGame application.

number of attacks is 64 when a board is filled and every game piece is under attack, and (2) color can be black, white, or both, the number of possible combinations is $3 \times 64 = 192$.

Rule R10: More or Less Attacks on A Piece: The parameters of this rule are piece type, piece color, and number of attacks to add or remove. The rule is satisfied when the selected number of attacks are added or removed from a game piece of the chosen type and color. If there is no such piece on the board, a user can add it. As described in Rule R7, the maximum number of attacks on one tile is 16. Since (1) color can be black, white, or both and (2) the piece type can be king, queen, bishop, knight, rook, or pawn, the number of possible combinations is $3 \times 6 \times 32 = 576$.

Rule R11: More or Less Attacks by A Piece: The parameters of this rule are piece type, piece color, and number of attacks to add. The rule is satisfied when the selected number of attacks are added or removed from a piece of the chosen color and type. A king, queen, or knight can attack 8 pieces at most. In other words, a user can select any of the 16 possible values between -8 and 8. The number of possible combinations for a king, queen, or knight is $3 \times 16 = 48$ since color can be black, white, or both. A bishop or rook can attack a maximum of 4 pieces, so the number of possible combinations for a bishop or a rook is $3 \times 8 = 24$. A pawn can attack up to 2 pieces, so the number of possible combinations for a pawn is $3 \times 4 = 12$. The total number of combinations is 204.

Rule R12: More or Less Pieces under Attack: The rule parameters are piece color and number of attacks to add or remove. This rule is satisfied when a user adds or removes the selected number of attacks to game pieces in the chosen color. A user can add or remove up to 64 attacks. The number of possible combinations of the parameters is $3 \times 128 = 384$ since color can be black, white, or both.

IV. USER STUDY

We implemented PassGame on the Android operating system. A screenshot of the implementation is shown in Figure 1. To evaluate PassGame, we conducted user studies with participants recruited from two university communities. We used a Samsumg Galaxy Tab 3 with a 7 inch 1024×600 display and the Samsung S4 with a 5 inch 1920×1080 display.

Procedure: On the first day, participants come to our laboratory to fill out demographic information, learn the ChessPass scheme, and set a password. Before they leave the laboratory, participants must successfully authenticate themselves twice on two different random boards.

Similar to previous studies [17], we asked participants to use PassGame during the one-week-long user study to simulate regular use of the authentication scheme. We sent an email to participants 3-4 days after the first session then again 5-6 days after the first session. The email contains a link to an emulated version of the PassGame application hosted on sites.google.com/. The emulated version uses the same code and behaves in the same way as the version that participants used during the first session. We use an emulated version rather than asking participants to return to the laboratory to use the device because it is more convenient for participants and this portion of the experiment is designed solely to simulate regular use of the scheme. Use of the emulator is encouraged but not mandatory because (1) email responses are not reliable because of various reasons such as junk mail filtering, (2) we want to investigate the effect of regular use on the memorability of PassGame. Each participant had at most two successful authentications on the emulator and the attempts on the emulator happened within 36 hours from the sending time of the reminder emails.

One week after the first session, participants are invited back to the controlled laboratory environment for the second session. Participants are given the mobile device that they used during the first session and are asked to recall their passwords. At the end of the second session, participants are asked to fill out a survey rating the usability of PassGame and their favorite mobile authentication scheme.

Conditions: To evaluate the usability of PassGame with different security strength, participants were randomly grouped into one of three categories: (1) 1R: Participants in this condition were asked to make a password using a single rule. (2) 2R: Participants in this condition were asked to make a password with two rules. (3) 4R: Participants in this condition were asked to make a password with four rules. Participants are not allowed to form a password with Rule R6 only as the resulting password may not be shoulder-surfing resistant if no unrelated adjustments are included into the password. So, participants in 1R category are not allowed to use Rule R6.

Participants: We recruited participants for the user studies by distributing fliers and leaflet style advertisements. A \$10 cash incentive was offered for completing both sessions of the user study. Thirty seven participants were recruited for the user studies and 36 successfully finished both sessions. Of those who finished, 23 participants were male and 13 were female. Participants were asked "Are you skilled at using smartphones or mobile devices." On a scale from "Strongly Disagree" (1) to "Strongly Agree" (5), participants rated their skill an average of 4.28, with 32 rating their skill at 4 or higher.

Statistical Testing: We use a significance level of .05 for our hypothesis testing in this paper. For omnibus comparisons on categorical and quantitative data, we use Chi-squared and Kruskal-Wallis respectively. If the omnibus test is significant, we perform pairwise tests with Chi-squared for categorical data and Mann-Whitney for quantitative data.

TABLE I. PASSGAME RECALL RATES BY CONDITION

Conditions	Participants	Recall	Recall Rate
$1R$	12	12	100%
$2R$	14	14	100%
$4R$	10	7	70%

A. Memorability Results

As a PassGame password formed with more rules requires more rule selections and rule parameters to be memorized, we hypothesize that the recall rate of PassGame passwords decreases when the number of rules used to form PassGame passwords increases.

The recall results of the user study are shown in Table I. The results show that none of our participants had any trouble in remembering 1R or 2R passwords. The recall rate of 4R passwords is 30% lower than the rates of 1R and 2R passwords, but most participants were still able to remember their 4R passwords as well. We perform an omnibus chi-squared test on the three conditions and find a significant difference between the memorability of the conditions ($\chi^2 = 8.51$, $p = .014$). The hypothesis is supported by the data of PassGame passwords formed by 4 or less rules. We believe that the statistical difference will become more significant when the number of rules used to form a PassGame password is larger. We restrict our user study on PassGame passwords formed with no more than 4 rules because (1) a two-rule password already has more password strength than passwords of existing mobile authentication schemes, such as 4-digit PIN, and (2) PassGame passwords formed with more than 4 rules are less usable.

We examine the effect of the reminder emails on memorability. We hypothesize that using the emulator during the week will make participants more likely to remember their passwords at the end of the week. Five participants used the emulator only after receiving the first reminder email, 2 used the emulator only after receiving the second reminder email, 24 used the emulator both times, and 5 did not use the emulator at all. The omnibus chi-squared test reveals no significance ($\chi^2 = 1.64$, $p = .651$). All three participants who forget their passwords used the emulator both times, and were unable to finish authentication successfully either time. The results suggest that PassGame passwords are memorable after one week even with no reminders.

We hypothesize that chess knowledge has an impact on memorability. Thirty-one participants indicated that they knew how to play chess, while 5 indicated they did not know how to play chess. Among the 3 participants that forgot their passwords, 2 knew how to play chess and 1 did not. Our omnibus chi-squared test reveals that there is no significant difference ($\chi^2 = 1.04$, $p = .309$). The results are not compliant with our expectation. But, the results also indicate that the scheme is memorable even by persons who have no knowledge of chess.

B. Password Entry Time

Our implementation records the time users spend attempting to enter their passwords. In this section, we analyze the timing data from the final session of the user study.

On average, users in the 1R, 2R, and 4R conditions required 33, 110, and 143 seconds respectively to authenticate themselves from the moment they started the application. A Kruskal Wallis test between the three conditions finds no significant difference (H=4.996, p=.082). However, these timings values include time spent thinking, requesting new boards, and making incorrect attempts. On average, users required 1.6, 1.9, and 2.1 new randomly generated boards for the 1R, 2R, and 4R conditions respectively before successfully entering their passwords. Additionally, users required an average of 1.22, 2.07, and 2.63 authentication attempts before a success for 1R, 2R, and 4R respectively. The first correct attempt in the 1R, 2R, and 4R conditions required on average 23, 44, and 49 seconds respectively. The best 4 users in 1R required less than 7s to authenticate. We perform a Kruskal Wallis test on the timings for the first correct attempt and find that there is not a significant difference in the timings (H=3.741, p=.154).

TABLE II. USABILITY SURVEY RATINGS

Scheme	Ratings	Conve.	Speed
PassGame-1R	4	4.5	4.25
PassGame-2R	7	4.29	3.29
PassGame-4R	7	3.75	2.57
PassGame-all	7	4.06	3.22
4-digit PIN	10	5	5

We believe that these statistics will improve as users gain experience with the scheme, in particular we believe users will require fewer attempts as they get used to the scheme. Password entry times for a single correct attempt are already very similar between the conditions. The entry times for correct attempts is in line with other schemes such as Deja Vu (32s) [18], Delayed Oracle Choice PIN entry (25s) [3], or CDS (20s) [11] and superior to other shoulder-surfing resistant schemes like Convex Hull Click (72s) [10].

SwiPin [4], ColorPIN [5], The Phone Lock [6], and other schemes that improve on PIN or pattern unlock offer short login times, but at the cost of weak password strength and limited shoulder-surfing resistance. PassGame can be used as a supplementary high-security scheme in environments where the user is afraid of shoulder-surfing. The user may be willing to trade off entry time in exchange for security in these situations.

C. User Perception

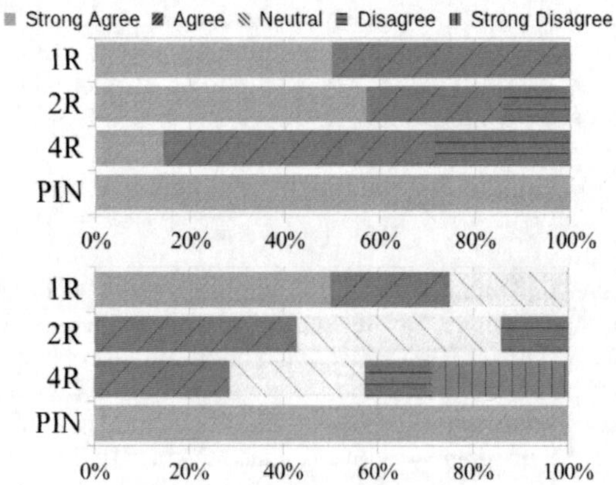

Figure 2. Usability Survey for Convenience (top), Speed (bottom).

At the end of the user study we asked participants to fill out a survey regarding the usability of PassGame and their current favorite authentication scheme. Participants were asked to rate the following statements (once for PassGame, and once for their favorite scheme) on a scale from "Strongly Disagree" (1) to "Strongly Agree" (5): (a) It is convenient to enter a password using this scheme. (b) The speed of entering a password with this scheme is fast. Additionally, we provide participants with the following definitions as a guideline: (a) Convenience: The scheme does not restrict you or take too much attention, (b) Speed: You can finish the scheme quickly. It usually does not need too many tries. For their favorite scheme, 10 participants chose 4-digit PIN, 2 participants chose Google's pattern unlock scheme, 3 chose fingerprint scanner. We sorted the usability results for PassGame based on which condition users were assigned to. The results of the usability survey are shown in Figure 2. The average usability rating is shown in Table II. For statistical analysis, we sort the usability ratings into the categories agree (4 or higher) or do not agree (3 or lower). We hypothesize that most users will think that PassGame is roughly as convenient as the 4-digit PIN or Google's pattern unlock scheme. We also hypothesize that the speed rating will decline as more rules are used. A chi-squared omnibus test on the three conditions of PassGame plus 4-digit PIN shows no significant difference in convenience ($\chi^2 = 4.11$, $p = .25$), however there is a significant different in speed ($\chi^2 = 11.04$, $p = .01$). Pairwise testing reveals the results are significant between 2R and 4-digit PIN ($\chi^2 = 7.47$, $p < .01$) and between 4R and 4-digit PIN ($\chi^2 = 10.12$, $p < .01$). At 2 rules and up, users perceive PassGame to be a slower scheme than the 4-digit PIN. We believe the difference is mainly caused by the shoulder-surfing resistance. A user usually repeats a 4-digit PIN without any thinking. But a user of shoulder-surfing resistant schemes needs to think out a valid response to a random challenge. Another possible reason is the difference in the familiarity to the scheme as the participants may be using the 4-digit PIN scheme everyday on their mobile devices and they only used PassGame for a few times.

Due to the space limit, we leave the analysis on shoulder-surfing resistance of PassGame with information theory, password space analysis, and extension of the authentication scheme in the technical report [19].

V. Conclusion

We designed PassGame to mitigate shoulder-surfing attacks on mobile authentication. We implemented PassGame on the Android operating system and conducted a user study. Our user study shows that PassGame passwords, which greatly exceed the password strength of current mobile authentication schemes, can still achieve 100% recall rates when recalled one week after password setup. In our future work, we plan to test PassGame against more sophisticated shoulder-surfing attacks, for example a machine-assisted brute force based on camera recorded password entries, and to test the viability of other games such as Checkers or Backgammon.

Acknowledgment

This work was supported in part by the National Science Foundation under Grants CNS-1460897, CNS-1338105, CNS-1343141, and DGE-1623713. Any opinions, findings, and conclusions or recommendations expressed in this material are those of the authors and do not necessarily reflect the views of the funding agencies.

References

[1] X. Suo, Y. Zhu, and G. Owen, "Graphical passwords: a survey," in *Computer Security Applications Conference, 21st Annual*, Dec 2005, pp. pp.462–472.

[2] M. Harbach, E. von Zezschwitz, A. Fichtner, A. D. Luca, and M. Smith, "It's a hard lock life: A field study of smartphone (un)locking behavior and risk perception," in *Symp. On Usable Privacy and Security*. Menlo Park, CA: USENIX Association, 2014, pp. 213–230.

[3] V. Roth, K. Richter, and R. Freidinger, "A pin-entry method resilient against shoulder surfing," in *Proceedings of the 11th ACM Conference on Computer and Communications Security*, 2004, pp. 236–245.

[4] E. von Zezschwitz, A. De Luca, B. Brunkow, and H. Hussmann, "Swipin: Fast and secure pin-entry on smartphones," in *Proceedings of the Conference on Human Factors in Computing Systems (CHI)*, vol. 15, 2015, pp. 1403–1406.

[5] A. De Luca, K. Hertzschuch, and H. Hussmann, "Colorpin: securing pin entry through indirect input," in *Proceedings of the SIGCHI Conference on Human Factors in Computing Systems*. ACM, 2010, pp. 1103–1106.

[6] A. Bianchi, I. Oakley, V. Kostakos, and D. S. Kwon, "The phone lock: audio and haptic shoulder-surfing resistant pin entry methods for mobile devices," in *Proc. of the Fifth International Conf. on Tangible, Embedded, and Embodied Interaction*. ACM, 2011, pp. 197–200.

[7] N. H. Zakaria, D. Griffiths, S. Brostoff, and J. Yan, "Shoulder surfing defence for recall-based graphical passwords," in *Proceedings of the 7th Symposium on Usable Privacy and Security (SOUPS)*, 2011, pp. 1–12.

[8] I. Jermyn, A. Mayer, F. Monrose, M. K. Reiter, and A. D. Rubin, "The design and analysis of graphical passwords," in *Proc. of the 8th Conf. on USENIX Security Symp.*, Berkeley, CA, USA, 1999, pp. 1–14.

[9] D. Lin, P. Dunphy, P. Olivier, and J. Yan, "Graphical passwords & qualitative spatial relations," in *Proceedings of the 3rd Symposium on Usable Privacy and Security (SOUPS)*, 2007, pp. 161–162.

[10] S. Wiedenbeck, J. Waters, L. Sobrado, and J.-C. Birget, "Design and evaluation of a shoulder-surfing resistant graphical password scheme," in *Proceedings of the Working Conference on Advanced Visual Interfaces (AVI)*, 2006, pp. 177–184.

[11] H. Gao, Z. Ren, X. Chang, X. Liu, and U. Aickelin, "A new graphical password scheme resistant to shoulder-surfing," in *International Conference on Cyberworlds (CW)*. IEEE, 2010, pp. 194–199.

[12] D. Davis, F. Monrose, and M. K. Reiter, "On user choice in graphical password schemes," in *Proceedings of the 13th Conference on USENIX Security Symposium*, Berkeley, CA, USA, 2004, pp. 1–11.

[13] D. Luca *et al.*, "Back-of-device authentication on smartphones," in *Proceedings of the SIGCHI Conference on Human Factors in Computing Systems (CHI)*, 2013, pp. 2389–2398.

[14] C. Winkler *et al.*, "Glass unlock: Enhancing security of smartphone unlocking through leveraging a private near-eye display," in *Proceedings of the 33rd Annual ACM Conference on Human Factors in Computing Systems, CHI*, vol. 15, 2015, pp. 1407–1410.

[15] A. De Luca, E. Von Zezschwitz, and H. Hußmann, "Vibrapass: secure authentication based on shared lies," in *Proc. of the SIGCHI conf. on human factors in computing systems*. ACM, 2009, pp. 913–916.

[16] J. Gurary, Y. Zhu, G. Corser, J. Oluoch, N. Alnahash, and H. Fu, "Maps: A multi-dimensional password scheme for mobile authentication," in *Proceedings of the 2015 International Conference on Interactive Tabletops & Surfaces*. ACM, 2015, pp. 409–412.

[17] N. Wright, A. S. Patrick, and R. Biddle, "Do you see your password?: Applying recognition to textual passwords," in *Proceedings of the 8th Symposium on Usable Privacy and Security (SOUPS)*, 2012, pp. 1–14.

[18] R. Dhamija and A. Perrig, "Deja vu: A user study using images for authentication," in *Proceedings of the 9th Conference on USENIX Security Symposium*, Berkeley, CA, USA, 2000, pp. 1–4.

[19] J. Gurary, Y. Zhu, N. Alnahash, and H. Fu, "Passgame: A shoulder-surfing resistant mobile authentication scheme, technical report 20161101a," Oct 2016, retrieved: Jan 2017. [Online]. Available: http://academic.csuohio.edu/zhu_y/techreport/20161101a.pdf

A Hybrid System Based on Wrinkles Shapes and Biometric Distances for Emotion Recognition

Rim Afdhal, Ridha Ejbali and Mourad Zaied

REsearch Groups on Intelligent Machines, University of Sfax
Sfax,Tunisia
Emails: {eng.afdhal.rim, ridha_ejbali, mourad.zaied}@ieee.org

Abstract— **Communication has an important role in human interaction. It can be vocal, bodily, textual or emotional in order to help everyone to understand others and be understood. Generally, all these types of communication aim at expressing a thought or an idea via a set of selected words, gestures, sounds or emotions. Emotions are so important to express ourselves and understand the others even without words or sounds. This paper presents a hybrid emotion recognition system based on wavelet network using 1D fast wavelet transform. The proposed application is based on two approaches. The first one is based on the shapes of the wrinkles; the second is based on the biometric distances. We combine these two approaches in order to ameliorate the classification rates. The rates given by experimental results show the effectiveness of our proposed system.**

Keywords- hybrid emotion recognition system; wavelet network; fast wavelet transform; shapes of the wrinkles; classification.

I. INTRODUCTION

Emotions play an important role in our existence [1]. It is an important field, which plays a relevant role in several studies. Let us take the example of Human Computer Interaction (HCI), which has confined its researchers to the development of techniques founded on the use of screen-keyboard-mouse triplet.

Today, the user must make a progress without obstacles in its natural environment; the finger, the hand, the face or the familiar objects are regarded as an input / output device; the border between the electronic and physical worlds tends to be blurred. These new forms of interaction usually require the capture of the observable behavior of the user and his environment. They rely on artificial perception techniques, including computer vision.

Future generations of man-machine environment are going to be multimodal by integrating new information, from taking account of dynamic behavior, from speech and facial expressions, in order to make the use of the most intuitive and natural machinery. Through human-machine interaction we try to get an idea of the emotional state of the user for ergonomic interface conception and have a better feedback. Measuring the gaze direction of the user could be an effective way to perform certain tasks in graphical interface (such as selection of a window or a text box). Expressions (defined as muscle movements) along with the spoken language, joined both in terms of physical movement required to speech (movements of lips), and in terms of emotional indicator accompanying the spoken language. They express a non-negligible part of meaning in oral communication.

This work presents a hybrid emotion recognition system based on the analysis of the shapes of the wrinkles as well as the biometric distances. To start with, we choose to analyze the facial expressions because the face is the most expressive and communicative part of a human being. In order to boost the classification rates gotten through the approach of the wrinkles, we combined the wrinkles approach with the approach of biometric distances inspired from an automatic emotion recognition approach [1] based on the facial expression.

The method based on the shapes of the wrinkles can be summarized in four steps. The first step consists of detecting the elements of the face using Viola and Jones method. The second step is used to locate the region of the wrinkles. The third step of our system consists of extracting information. The last one is the classification which is based on wavelet network using Fast Wavelet Transform (FWT) [1][2][3].

The approach of biometric distances, which is well explained in [5] can be summarized also in four main steps: detection of the elements of the face, localization of the characteristic points, tracking of features points and classification .

This paper is divided into three parts. The first part presents our proposed emotion recognition system. The second part focuses on the approach based on the shapes of the wrinkles and its different phases. In the third part, experiments are made to demonstrate the efficiency of the proposed approach by using the Chon-Kanade dataset. We finish the paper with the conclusion and the future work.

II. STATE OF THE ART

This section presents the different existing approaches in the literature corresponding to this area of research. There are several emotions recognition methods among which we cite emotion recognition by body gesture analysis [10] [11] [12].

The approach presented in [10] aims at analyzing the actions of a person in order to determine his emotional state. The analysis was based on the position and the movements of the upper part of the body (hands and head). It is restricted to the trajectory and velocity of points. These characteristic points make a triangle whose perimeter provides information about the qualitative aspects of their movement based on the approach proposed by Camuri [13]. The analysis of a movement will provide a set of qualitative aspects. In other words, the transformation of the physical measures (the position, velocity and acceleration of superior body parts) in a high level model such as righteousness, impulsiveness and fluency provides these qualitative aspects that allow their turn to recognize a particular emotion.

We can also mention the emotion recognition methods based on analyzing words [14] [15] [16]. Thanks to automatic speech emotion recognition systems, the machine becomes able to transform a signal into a sequence of words. But we must go further and learn the meaning of the word sequences and be aware of the context of the sentence pronunciation. It is at this level that the emotional dimension is involved. So we must take into consideration the intonation of the sentence in order to make the difference between a statement and a question. In addition to these approaches, many approaches were based on facial expression analysis [17][18][19][20].

This paper presents an emotion recognition system based on the analysis of the shapes of the wrinkles. We adopt this approach because the face is the most expressive and communicative part of a human being. Facial expression is a kind of visible manifestation of a spirit state, of cognitive activities, of physiological activities (tiredness, pain), of the character and the psychopathology of someone. Psychology researches have shown that facial expression plays an important role in the coordination of human conversation, and have a great influence on the listener than the textual content of the message expressed.

III. THE PROPOSED EMOTION RECOGNITION SYSTEM

This section presents our emotion recognition system. The system is the combination of two approaches the first one is the wrinkles approach [6][7], the second is an approach, which is based on the biometric distances [5].

We proposed this system in order to boost the classification rates of the emotion recognition system based on the shapes of the wrinkles, so, we decided to add the approach of the biometric distance to enhance the classification rates. Fig. 1 describes the proposed system.

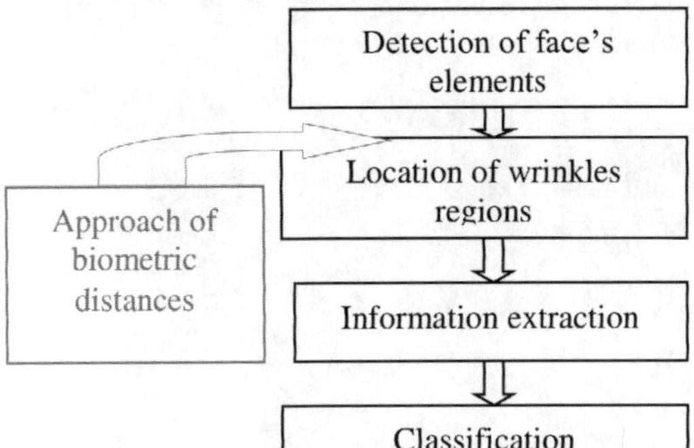

Figure1. Proposed emotion recognition system

A. *The wrinkles approach*

This approach has four stages: the detection of face's elements, the location of wrinkles regions, the information extraction and the classification.

The first phase aims at detecting the face as well as its different elements (eyes and mouth) using the viola and Jones detector. Figure 3 shows the detection of the face and its elements of the images of the Chon-Kanade databasis.

The second phase consists in locating 7 rectangles in the most important wrinkles in the face: a rectangle on the forehead, another on the chin, 2 rectangles on the corners of the eyes, 2 rectangles on the corners of the mouth and a rectangle on the upper of the nose.

The location of these regions will be at neutral state and will be relocated during the emotion. To achieve this step, we have developed an automatic method using the coordinates of the rectangles located by the Viola and Jones detector.

The third step of this approach is information extraction. The information will be extracted from the wrinkles regions by calculating the edge pixels number of each facial region expression and the neutral state. The difference between the two states will be calculated in order to prepare the training distances.

The last stage is the classification. We will use the wavelet networks [5] in order to recognize the basic emotions. This stage contains 4 steps. The first step is supposed to prepare the wavelet as well as the scaling functions. In the second step, we compute the weights by FWT [27] [28] then we compute the contributions from each library function. The last step's target is to choose the best features that best approximate the vector at the output of the network by setting a stopping criterion. At the end, we get the weight vector corresponding to the best contributions of every learning vector.

B. *Wavelet network theory*

"Wavelet networks" is a new theory which was introduced by Zhang and Benveniste in 1992 [14]. They used a combination of artificial neural networks based on radial basis, function and wavelet decomposition. Moreover, these researchers have explained how a wavelet network can be generated. It is defined by pondering a set of wavelets dilated and translated from one mother wavelet with weight values to approximate a given signal f. Eq. (1.1) represents the output of the network using a finite number of wavelets.

$$\hat{f}=\sum_{i=1}^{n} \omega_i \psi_i \qquad 1.1$$

Fig. 2 shows an example of 1D neuron from the wavelet network. In order to extend the following architecture we can add dilated and translated scaling function's versions of the corresponding used wavelet in the hidden layer of the network.

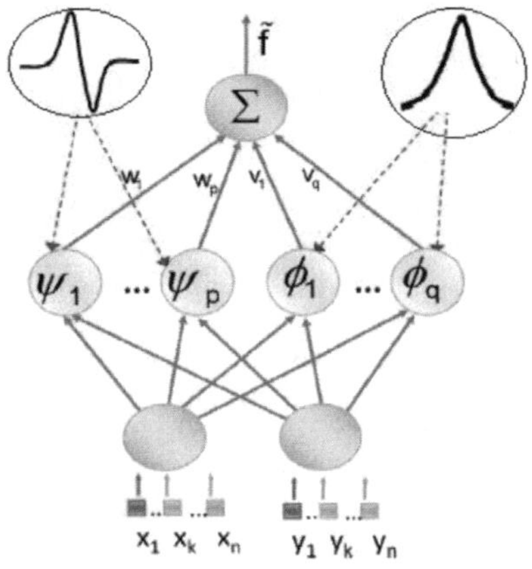

Figure 2. Wavelet network using scaling function

Many researchers [25][26] have used the projection technique of the signal f on the dual basis of the wavelets and the hidden layer's scaling functions in order to calculate the output weight connections of the wavelet network. This type of technique offers precise weights' values, but it has a main defect when it comes to determinating the hidden layer's weights to the output layer, because it leads to calculating the matrix's inversion Φ which requires an intensive calculation as the matrix is so large. Our technique is based on the FWT. The wavelet networks are not only simple but also rapid and strong. The FWT uses a simple and a fast technique in order to facilitate the calculation of the approximation and the details. The classification phase aims at creating a wavelet modeling every vector of pixels of learning.

In order to create the network of every vector, we have, first, to prepare the wavelet and the scaling functions. Then, we calculate the weights by FWT [4][21][22][23][24] and the contributions from the library function. After that, we choose the best features by setting a stopping criterion. Then, we will get the vector of weights of every learning vector. After the training, the test step determines the appropriate class of the test vector. Consequently, every test vector will be projected on the network of all the training vectors in order to get its weight. Moreover, we calculate the distance between the vector of weight of the training and the test. In addition, the distances will be sorted.

At the end, the algorithm recognizes the suitable class of the vector of the test which has the smallest distance.

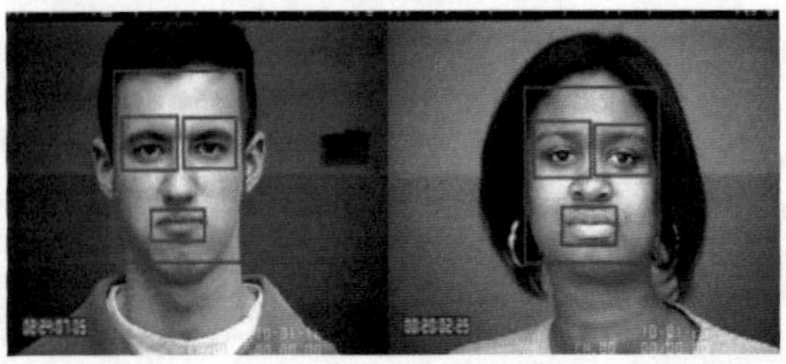

Figure 3. Detection of the face and its elements

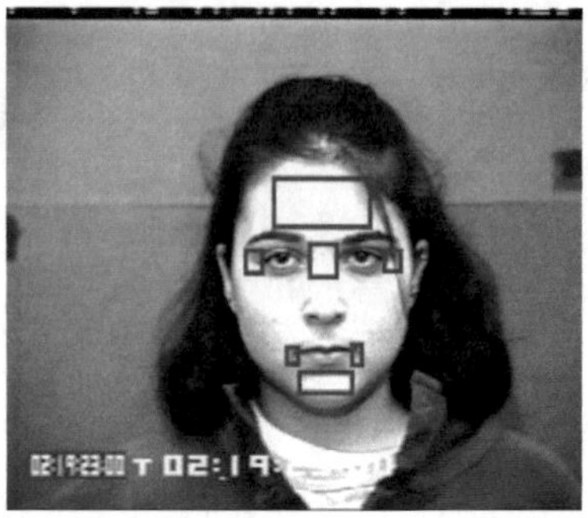

Figure 4. Location of the wrinkles regions at the neutral state

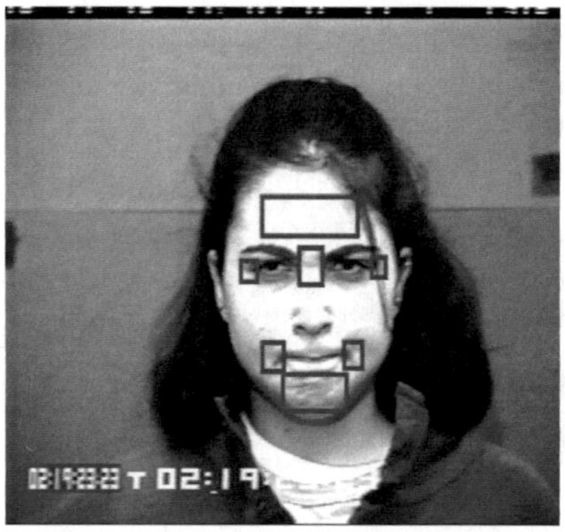

Figure 5. Location of the wrinkles regions during the emotion

IV. RESULTS

This section presents the different classification rates of our proposed emotion recognition system.

The Chon-Kanade database [9] contains a set of facial expressions images in grayscale of men and women of different ethnicities. The size of each image is 640 by 490 pixels. The orientation of the camera is front and the small movements of the head are present. This data set is very useful for facial expression recognition. Fig. 6 presents some examples of images of this data set.

Figure 6. Examples of images from Chon-Kanade dataset

TABLE I. PRESENTATION OF DIFFERENT PARAMETERS FOR EVALUATING OUR EMOTION RECOGNITION SYSTEM

	Chon-Kanade
Number of facial expressions	7
Total number of images	1070
Number of learning images	714
Number of test images	356

The classification rates of the wrinkles approach are presented in Table 1. It shows that the FWT has correctly classified the neutral emotion with a rate equal to 100%. The wrinkles regions of this emotion are not modified so the vector of difference of pixels is null. So, there are no doubts concerning this emotion.

The system classifies the emotion of joy with a classification rate equal to 72.73% and classifies the disgust with a classification rate equal to 63.44%. Finally, it classifies the fear emotion with a classification rate equal to 36.36%. It ranks sadness, anger and surprise with a classification rate equal to 54.55%. The reason for the low rates is due to the difficulty of detecting the wrinkles regions as shown in Fig. 7. Our dataset contains image of persons who did not express these emotions with the same manner. Let us take the emotion of sadness as shown in Fig. 8. There are persons who express the same emotion when their eyebrows are curved and their mouth are tight. However, there are other persons who express this emotion with released eyebrows and tight mouths. That is why we propose a hybrid system which will better improve these rates.

The hybrid system presents an enhancement of the classification rates. It classifies the emotion of joy with a classification rate equal to 90%. However, the system of the approach of the wrinkles classifies it with a classification rate equal to 72.73%. It classifies the anger with a classification rate equal to 100% but the wrinkles approach with a classification rate equal to 63.44%. Finally, it classifies the fear emotion with a classification rate equal to 80%. However, the first approach classifies it with a classification rate equal to 36.36%. We have become aware that our system made an improvement in the emotions of joy, anger, fear and neutral. We have also noticed that it is more robust than the first approach.

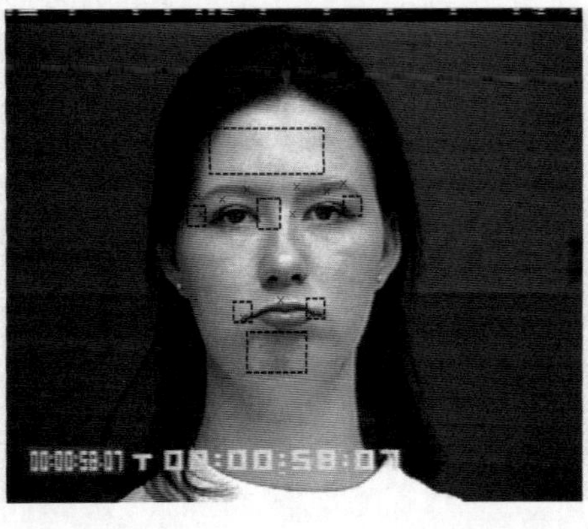

Figure 7. False wrinkles regions detection

Figure 8. Different expressions in the emotion of sadness

TABLE II. CLASSIFICATION OF THE CHON-KANADE DATA BASIS WITH FWT BY THE WRINKLES APPROACH AND THE HYBRID SYSTEM

Wrinkles Approach		Hybrid System
joy	72.73 %	90 %
anger	54.55 %	100 %
disgust	63.44 %	63.44 %
sadness	54.55 %	54.55 %
fear	36.36 %	80 %
surprise	54.55 %	54.55 %
neutral	100 %	100

TABLE III. CLASSIFICATION RATES WITH THE APPROACH DESCRIBED IN [6]

joy	37.5%
anger	62 %
disgust	62.5 %
sadness	75 %
fear	50 %
surprise	25 %

Table 3 presents the classification rates of the system described in [6]. It has classified the class joy with a rate equal to 37.5% and the class anger with a rate equal to 62%. Besides, it has classified the class disgust with a rate equal to 62.5%, the class sadness with a rate equal to 75%, the class fear with a rate equal to 50% and the class surprise with a rate equal to 25%. However, our system has classified the first class with a rate equal to 90%, the second class with a rate equal to 100%, the third one with a rate equal to 63.44%, the fourth with a rate equal to 54.55% and the fear with a rate equal to 80%.

V. CONCLUSION

The two approaches used in this work to recognize emotions are based on the wavelets networks. An algorithm of training of these networks based on the 1D Fast Wavelet Transform has been proposed and has been implemented.
Our method of emotion recognition is the combination of two approaches. The first one contains four main stages: the detection of face's elements, the location of wrinkles regions in the face, the information extraction finally the classification. The second one contains also four main stages: detection of the elements of the face, localization of the characteristic points, tracking of features points and classification. Experiments on the dataset (Chon-Kanade) are made to evaluate the efficiency of our proposed approach. The performances of the Fast wavelets networks used for emotion recognition are clear and the results obtained are encouraging. The robustness and the rapidity of the proposed training algorithm that are based on 1D Fast Wavelet Transform theory increases these performances.

Our contributions are at the level of the second stage by locating automatically the wrinkles regions on the face and at the level of classification that we used the Fast Wavelet Transform as a classifier. We are looking actually to extend this work by recognizing the secondary emotions.

ACKNOWLEDGMENT

The authors would like to acknowledge the financial support of this work by grants from General Direction of Scientific Research (DGRST), Tunisia, under the ARUB program.

REFERENCES

[1] C. Ben Amar, M. Zaied, and A. M. Alimi, "Beta wavelets. Synthesis and application to lossy image compression," Advances in Engineering SoftWare, Elseiver, special issue, Advanced Algorithms and Architectures for Signal Processing, vol. 36, no. 7, pp. 459-474, 2005.

[2] R. Afdhal, A. Bahar, R. Ejbali, and M. Zaied, "Face detection using beta wavelet filter and cascade classifier entrained with Adaboost". 8th International Conferenceon Machine Vesion (ICMV'8) November19-21, 2015 | Barcelona, Spain.

[3] R. Ejbali, Y. Benayed, M. Zaied, and A. M. Alimi, "Wavelet networks for phonemes Recognition", International conference on systems and information processing 2009.

[4] A. El Adel, M. Zaied, and C. Ben Amar, "Learning wavelet networks based on Multiresolution analysis: Application to images copy detection Communications", Computing and Control Applications (CCCA), 2011.

[5] M. Zaied, R. Mohamed, and C. Ben Amar, "A power tool for Content-based image retrieval using multiresolution wavelet network modeling and Dynamic histograms". International REview on Computers and Software (IRECOS)2012.

[6] K. Ghanem and A. Caplier, "Towards a full emotional system, Behaviour & Information Technology" 2013, 32:8, 783-799.

[7] R. Afdhal, R. Ejbali , M. Zaied, and C. Ben Amar. December 14-16. Emotion recognition using features distances classified by wavelets network and trained by fast wavelets transform., 14h International Conference on Hybrid Intelligent Systems(HIS'14) proceedings, , Golf University for Science and Technologie , Kuwait., pp.238,241.

[8] M. Frank, P. Perona, and Y. Yacoob, "Automatic extraction of facial action codes" ,2001.

[9] R. Lanjewar, S. Mathurkar, and N. Patel, 2015, "Impelementation and comparaision of speech emotion recognition system using Guassian Mixture Model (GMM) and K-nearest Neighbor (K-NN) techniques".

[10] D. Glowinski and A. Camurri,2008. "Technique for automatic emotion recognition by body gesture analysis".

[11] G. Castellano, S. D Villalba and A. Camurri, (2007). "Recognising Human Emotions from Body Movement and Gesture Dynamics". In A. Paiva, R. Prada & R.W. Picard (Eds.), Lecture Notes in Computer Science: vol. 4738. Affective Computing and Intelligent Interaction, Second International Conference, ACII 2007, Lisbon.

[12] A. Camurri, I. Lagerlöf and G. Volpe,. (2003). "Recognizing emotion from dance movement: Comparison of spectator recognition and automated techniques". International Journal of Human-Computer Studies, 59(1-2), 213-225.

[13] M. Zaied, C. Ben Amar, and M. A. Alimi.14(1–2)(2005), "Beta wavelet networks for face recognition",J. Decision Syst., Lavoisier 2005 Edition, 109–122.

[14] R. Lanjewar, S. Mathurkar, and N. Patel, "Impelementation and comparaision of speech emotion recognition system using Guassian Mixture Model (GMM) and K-nearest Neighbor (K-NN) techniques", 2015.

[15] S. Mariooryad and C. Busso, 2015, "Facial Expression Recognition in the Presence of Speech using Blind Lexical Compensation".

[16] X. Xu, Y. Li, X. Xu, Z. Wen, H. Che , S. Liu , and J. Tao,2014. "Survey on discriminative feature selection for speech emotion recognition".

[17] C. Wu, W. Wei, J. Lin, and W. Lee. "Speaking Effect Removal on Emotion Recognition From Facial Expressions Based on Eigenface Conversion", 2013.

[18] A. Halder1, R. Mandal1, A. Konar1, A. Chakraborty, and R. Janarthanan,2011. "Emotion Recognition from Facial Expression using General Type-2 Fuzzy Set".

[19] J. Hakura, R. Domon, and H. Fujita, 2013. "Emotion Recognition Method Using Facial Expressions and Situation".

[20] C. Chang, J. Tsai, C. Wang, and P. Chung,2009. "Emotion Recognition with Consideration of Facial Expression and Physiological Signals".

[21] S. Hassairi, R. Ejbali, and M. Zaied, "Sparse Wavelet Auto-Encoders for Image Classification", International Conference on Conférence Digital Image Computing: Techniques and Applications (DICTA), 2016.

[22] M. Zaied, C. Ben Amar, and M A Alimi, "Award a new wavelet based beta function", International conference on signal, system and design, SSD031,185-191, 2003.

[23] R. Ejbali,Y. Benayed, M. Zaied, and A. M. Alimi,"Wavelet networks for phonemes recognition", International conference on systems and information processing, 2009.

[24] B. Guedri, M. Zaied, and C. Ben Amar, "Indexing and images retrieval bycontentHigh Performance Computing and Simulation", (HPCS), 2011.

[25] A. El. Adel, M. Zaied, and C. Ben Amar, "Learning wavelet networks based on Multiresolution analysis: Application to images copy detection Communications", Computing and Control Applications (CCCA), 2011.

[26] W. Bellil, C. Ben Amar, M. Zaied, and M. A. Alimi, " La fonction Beta et ses dérivées: vers une nouvelle famille d'ondelettes", First International Conference on Signal, System and Design, SCS'04, 201-207,2004.

[27] O. Jemai, R. Ejbali, M. Zaied, and C. Ben Amar, "A speech recognition system based on hybrid wavelet network including a fuzzy decision supportsystem", Seventh International Conference on Machine Vision, 2014.

[28] M. Zaied, R. Mohamed, and C. Ben Amar, "A power tool for Content-based image retrieval using multiresolution wavelet network modeling and Dynamic histograms", International REviewon Computers and Software (IRECOS), 2012.

[29] R. Ejbali, M. Zaied, and C. Ben Amar, "Multi-input Multi-output Beta Wavelet Network: Modeling of Acoustic Units for Speech Recognition", International Journal of Advanced Computer Science and Applications, 2012.

[30] R. Ejbali, M. Zaied, and C. Ben Amar, "Intelligent approach to train wavelet networks for Recognition System of Arabic Words", International Conference on Knowledge Discovery and Information Retrieval, 2010.

Nano Inks for Additive Manufacturing – A Safe-by-Design-Approach

Katja Nau[1], Tobias Müller[1], Daniel J.B.S. Sampaio[2], Steffen G. Scholz[1]

[1]Institute for Applied Computer Science
Karlsruhe Institute of Technology
Karlsruhe, Germany
e-mail: nau@kit.edu

[2]School of Engineering – Guaratinguetá
São Paulo State University (Unesp)
Guaratinguetá, Brazil
e-mail: dsampaio@feg.unesp.br

Abstract—**Additive manufacturing (AM) enables a new manufacturing paradigm, such as the rapid, distributive manufacture of complex 3D objects. Nanoparticles are in particular suitable for ink formulation of novel PolyJet inks to obtain functionalities embedded in the AM process. However, the impact and interaction of nanomaterials on environment and human health is widely discussed today. This paper deals with a safe-by-design-approach that is developed in this context.**

Keywords-additive manufacturing; nano safety; safe-by-design; human-centred industrial technologie.

I. Introduction

Additive manufacturing (AM) is a technique for creating 3D objects by building up material, layer by layer, with the control of a digital design. The term 3D printing is often used to refer to AM but it is important to keep in mind that 3D printing is actually one of the several AM processes. 3D printing was developed by a Massachusetts Institute of Technology team led by Emanuel Sachs in the late 1980s [1]. AM processes have some important advantages over traditional manufacturing techniques. The design of products is more flexible because of its additive approach, permitting a range of geometries beyond the capabilities of other methods. The development of new products is also faster because of the ease of moving from design to prototyping and then to production since it takes place directly on the basis of digital 3D data. It is possible to create functional parts without the requisite for assemblage [2].

Nanotechnology is science, engineering, and technology conducted at the nanoscale, which is about one to 100 nanometers, and involves the ability to see and to control individual atoms and molecules [3]. When shrinking the size scale from macro to nano, materials can change their fundamental properties, exhibiting unique optical, thermal or electrochemical properties that differ from the properties of the bulk material. These properties strongly depend on the size and the shape of nanostructures [4][5]. The integration of nanotechnology with AM can complement existing techniques and create entirely new nanocomposites having unique properties that can lead to expansion of AM application areas and reduce some of the AM limitations. Investigations have shown that the introduction of inorganic nanostructures such as carbon nanotubes, metal nanoparticles, and ceramics can meaningfully affect sintering features and final mechanical properties of the produced parts [6].

The addition of metal nanoparticles generally decreases sintering temperatures, improves part density, and decreases shrinkage and distortion of printed parts in comparison to micro-scale fillers [7]. Metal nanoparticles embedded into polymer materials can also provide improved electrical conductivity in fabricated objects [8]. Incorporation of carbon nanotubes in printing media offers a potential route to improving mechanical properties of the final parts and to increasing electrical and thermal conductivities [9]. The addition of carbon nanotubes in bio-scaffolds can yield excellent enhancement of cell proliferation. Adding semiconductor and ceramic nanoparticles to printing media can lead to improvements in mechanical and wear properties of the final parts. In addition, ceramic nanoparticles can be effectively used for bone tissue engineering. Even with the mentioned design, material and environmental advantages, the adoption of AM as a means for fabricating end-use components has been limited by the narrow choice of materials that can be used with this technology and challenges in the fabrication like nozzle clogging/wear, aggregation within printing media and rough surface finish of printed parts. Additionally, differences in built process parameters and/or in some AM processes parameters, like ambient conditions, can result in variations in properties and dimensions between parts built on different machines of the same kind. Overcoming these issues will require advances in both process control methods and material diversity [10].

One of the initiatives that intends to lead to advances in AM technologies is a EU-funded project called DIMAP (novel nanoparticle enhanced **DI**gital **MA**terials for 3D **P**rinting) [11] that, based in an idea born among various industrial and research centres across Europe, aims to develop applications not only limited to rapid prototyping but that address production processes, enhancing digital materials with novel nanoparticles for 3D printing in order to increase design possibilities and handling with needs for adapting and updating actual printing technology components.

Another important point is that DIMAP is also taking in account the risks of today's nanoscale technologies [12]. These nano related risks cannot be treated the same as the risks of longer-term molecular manufacturing, it would be wrong to put them together and make the same policy considerations since they offer different problems and therefore require special solutions. Nanotechnology manufacturing can bring unfamiliar risks and new classes of problems, consequently the impact and interaction of nanomaterials on environment and human health is widely discussed today [13].

This paper presents work of the EU project DIMAP as shown in Section II. Section III shows the safe-by-design approach, based on the prior knowledge of the used chemicals and nanomaterials that is going to be validated using two concrete demonstrators, an additive manufactured robotic arm and additive manufactured luminaires. Current work on nano safety aspects is presented in Section IV.

II. OVERALL APPROACH OF DIMAP

The overall objective of the DIMAP project is to enhance digital materials with novel nanoparticles for 3D printing in order to increase design possibilities. In order to develop these two specific innovative demonstrators, four novel digital materials, novel multi-material 3D printer and a safe-by-design approach should be investigated in parallel and developed as shown in Figure 1.

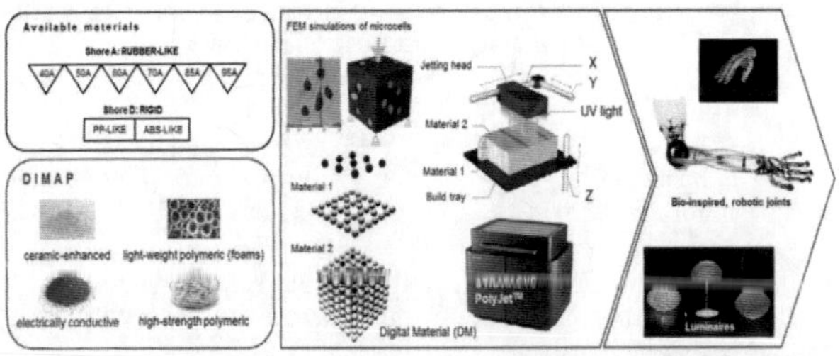

Figure 1. Concept for novel nanoparticle enhanced Digital Materials for 3D Printing

The challenges created by the selected applications require the development of novel ink systems with incorporated nanoparticles, with four different inks being in the scope of the project: electrically conductive inks, ceramic inks, high strength polymeric inks and lightweight polymeric inks as shown in Figure 2. In order to cope with these new material classes, the existing PolyJet technology should be further developed and therefore improved.

Material	Type	Particle properties
Ceramic enhanced	Al_2O_3 ZrO_2 AlN BN	15 - 100 nm
Electrically conductive	Ag	~70 - 80 nm
Low-weight structures	Polyolefines, Blowing agents	non particulate
High strength polymeric	Polyimides	non particulate

Figure 2. Selected materials to enhancement inside DIMAP

A safe-by-design and work place safety approach is carried out in parallel with the purpose of minimizing the risk due to the use of nanoparticles. This is shown in more details in the next section.

III. SAFE-BY-DESIGN APPROACH

The growing of nanotechnology-based products is increasing together with the conscience that some nanomaterials can bring unsafe effects and in order to try to control the risks, safe-by-design approaches are gaining attention and importance as tools to develop safer products and production processes [14]. It is important to first define what is included in the design process and then think about the safety aspects. There is no agreement in the literature about a clear boundary of the design process [15].

In this work, a proposed safe by design methodology for 3D printed nano-based products is presented centred in a systematic design analysis that can detect exposure scenarios and present the solutions to control the possible risks, endorsing possible barriers to reduce or even block them. The Figure 3 shows an overview of the proposed approach indicating all the elements that are encompassed and also the possible exposures for each element, emphasizing the importance of a safe-by-design approach.

The approach starts with the knowledge of all necessary chemicals and nanomaterials used during all process steps because their properties are used as basis to understand the toxicity of each production stage and final nanotechnology-based product. Each used material is evaluated and for each a very detailed Safety Data Sheet (SDS) has to be filled. This first step is very important since the SDS is the basis for the analysis made inside the methodology.

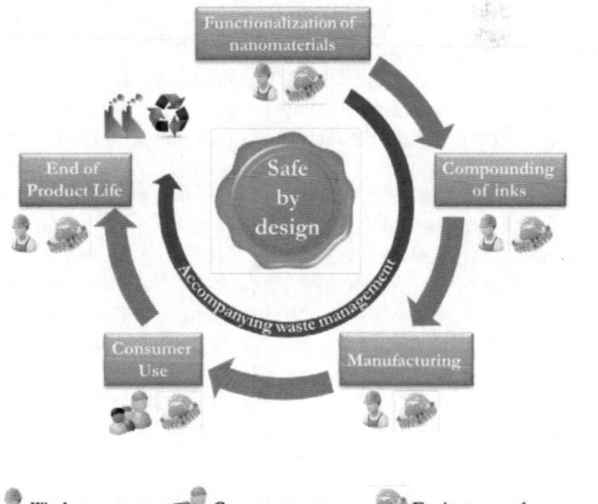

Figure 3. Safe by Design approach based in a systematic design analysis

The next step is the potential risk investigation where personal monitoring devices should be used to measure and analyse exposure to nanoparticles during the material preparation and printing steps. A life cycle assessment should be also carried out to determine the impact of the printed product throughout the whole production, usage and disposal. Assessment of the exposure rates during manufacturing, usage and end of life are then carried out. The waste produced starting from the synthesis of each used material until the end of life of the final product is also analysed and considered in this assessment. As last step, solutions are given for the detected exposure scenarios that should be applied to reduce or even eliminate the found risks and re-evaluated after application.

IV. CURRENT WORK

Within the DIMAP project various nanomaterials are used in inks for 3-D printing. The safe-by-design approach started with the determination of the composition of the inks on the one hand and the potential exposure hotspots within the DIMAP work packages on the other hand. Material safety datasheets were analysed or generated for each new or modified material. Another aspect of the safe-by-design approach is, as mentioned above, the exposure of humans to nanoparticles during the whole process of AM. At present, little is known about the release of nanomaterials from 3D printers. But the potential exposure to airborne nanomaterials from these printers needs to be measured in the personal breathing zone using nano-specific personal samplers or monitors.

Within DIMAP, such a small and easy to use sampler is currently applied to determine the particle release at, in and around the printer. Measurements are carried out in ambient conditions, as well as with the printer running, being able to compare different materials, different printing techniques, printer models and, to a limited extent, the dependence of exposure on different manufacturing parameters.

V. CONCLUSION AND FUTURE WORK

The main aim of the DIMAP project is to develop novel multi-material systems for PolyJet inks. Therefore, DIMAP will improve and advance the current technology by widening the range of available materials. However, the impact and interaction of nanomaterials on environment and human health is widely discussed today. Work is currently at an early stage concerning the measurement of (nano)particles in the process chain of AM. Different work place scenarios will to be analysed. The release of (nano)materials during work process, exposure to workers, potential hazard and a potential risk have to be assessed.

As an outcome of the project a safety guideline will be established in order to support the industry in applying AM in an even wider spectrum.

ACKNOWLEDGMENT

The DIMAP project is funded by the European Union's Horizon 2020 Program for research and innovation under Grant Agreement No. 685937.

REFERENCES

[1] E.M. Sachs, J.S. Haggerty, M.J. Cima, and P.A. Williams, "Three-dimensional printing techniques", U.S. Patent No. 5,204,055. Washington, D.C.: U.S. Patent and Trademark Office, 1993

[2] A.M. Dollar and R. Howe "Joint coupling design of underactuated hands for unstructured environments" 30 (9) pp. 1157-1169 2013. DOI: 10.1177/0278364911401441

[3] M.C. Roco, R.S. Williams, and P. Alivisatos, Nanotechnology Research Directions: Iwgn Workshop Report. Vision For Nanotechnology R&D In The Next Decade. National Science And Technology Councilarlington Va, 1999

[4] Y.W. Jun, S.M. Lee, N.J. Kang, and J. Cheon, "Controlled synthesis of multi-armed CdS nanorod architectures using monosurfactant system", Journal of the American Chemical Society, 123(21), pp. 5150-5151, 2001.

[5] C. Burda, X. Chen, R. Narayanan, and M.A. El-Sayed, "Chemistry and properties of nanocrystals of different shapes", Chemical reviews, 105(4), pp. 1025-1102, 2005.

[6] S. Chaturvedi and P.N. Dave, "Design process for nanomaterials", Journal of Materials Science, 48(10), pp. 3605-3622, 2013.

[7] W. J. Sames, F. A. List, S. Pannala, R. R. Dehoff, and S. S. Babu, "The metallurgy and processing science of metal additive manufacturing", International Materials Reviews, 61:5, pp. 315-360, 2016, doi: 10.1080/09506608.2015.1116649

[8] S. Schlabach, R. Ochs and T. Hanemann, and D.V. Szabo, "Nanoparticles in polymer-matrix composites", Microsystem Technologies, 2011, 17, pp. 183-193, doi: 10.1007/s00542-010-1176-8.

[9] M.F. De Volder, S.H. Tawfick, R.H. Baughman, and A.J. Hart, "Carbon nanotubes: present and future commercial applications", science, 339(6119), pp. 535-539, 2013.

[10] O. Ivanova, C. Williams, and T. Campbell, "Additive manufacturing (AM) and nanotechnology: promises and challenges", Rapid Prototyping Journal, v. 19, n. 5, pp. 353-364, 2013.

[11] http://www.dimap-project.eu [retrieved Feb 2017]

[12] S. Scholz, A. Brunet., T. Müller, and A. Fuchsbauer, "Novel Nanoparticle Enhanced Digital Materials for 3D Printing and their Application Shown for the Robotic and Electronic Industry", proceeding of the CENICS 2016 conference.

[13] P.C. Ray, H. Yu, and P.P. Fu, "Toxicity and Environmental Risks of Nanomaterials: Challenges and Future Needs", Journal of environmental science and health Part C, Environmental carcinogenesis & ecotoxicology reviews. 2009; 27(1): pp. 1-35. doi:10.1080/10590500802708267.

[14] F. Silva, P.M. Arezes, and P. Swuste, "Systematic design analysis and risk management on engineered nanoparticles occupational exposure", Sho2015: International Symposium on Occupational Safety and Hygiene, pp. 350-352, 2015

[15] A. Hale, B. Kirwan, and U. Kjellén, "Safe by design: where are we now? Safety science, v. 45, n. 1, pp. 305-327, 2007

Bonding of Flexible Mulitlayer Printed Systems based on PET-Substrates – An Investigation of Challenges and Promising Approaches

Liane Koker[1], Anu Paul[1], Didem Kinay[1], Jan-Hendric Rakebrandt[2], Heino Besser[3], Daniel Moser[1], Martin Ungerer[1], Ulrich Gengenbach[1]

[1]Institute for Applied Computer Science
[2]Institute for Applied Materials
Karlsruhe Institute of Technology
Karlsruhe, Germany
e-mail: liane.koker@kit.edu

[3]Karlsruhe Nano Micro Facility
Eggenstein-Leopoldshafen, Germany
e-mail: heino.besser@kit.edu

Abstract — **Flexible, thin and smart multilayer printed systems have a wide range of applications, reaching from human-centred alarm systems to industrial applications like condition monitoring within the scope of Industry 4.0. During the production process for flexible mulitlayer printed systems, the bonding of the individual substrate layers is an important step. Thereby, the functionality of the components and lines printed onto the different layers must not be affected. In this paper, the challenges of the bonding process of flexible printed systems based on Polyethylene Terephthalate (PET) substrates are demonstrated and possible approaches for bonding are introduced and compared to each other.**

Keywords – multilayer printed systems; bonding of PET; transmission laserwelding; direct thermal bonding; adhesive bonding; surface activation.

I. Introduciton to Printed Systems

A. Potentials of flexible multilayer printed systems

The term of printed systems is used in the context of this paper for systems based upon thin polymer foils, called substrates, comprising printed components and conductive lines, in the following aggregated with the term "printed elements". The ongoing development of functionalized inks opens the possibility to print a large variety of different materials onto varying substrates. Thereby, printing techniques are applied, that are being well established for the printing of color on paper, reaching from screen printing to inkjet printing [1].

One motivation for producing printed electronic systems is cost optimization. Using roll-to-roll techniques, the production of large quantities of printed materials is possible. Alternatively, existing products can be replaced by cheaper and therefore disposable printed systems [2]. Thereby, mainly single-layer systems are used.

Here, another approach is taken [3]. Printing technologies offer the potential of producing multifunctional, highly integrated smart systems. The potential can be realized by printing task-specific elements onto one side of each substrate using different printing techniques. These single layers can contain electrical circuits, sensor elements, optical or fluidic components. One approach is to separate functions between layers (see Figure 1). In order to combine the layers and to enable interaction between the different domains, the single layers are bonded, resulting in a multilayer system. The use of flexible substrates allows for the production of flexible systems.

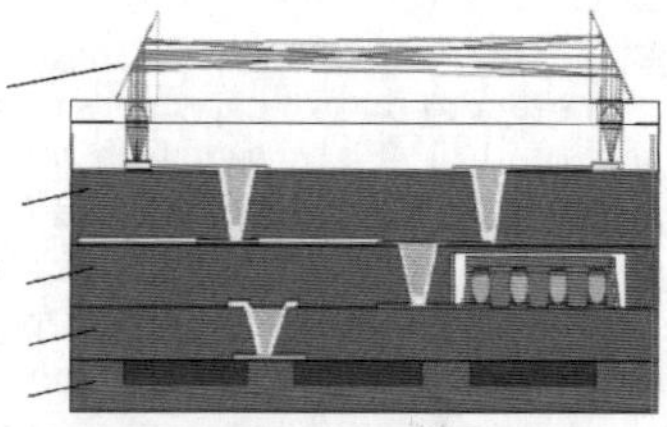

Figure 1. Visualization of the setup of a multilayer printed system by the example of an electro-optical sensor (cp. [3]).

Potential applications are diverse. When implementing sensors and wireless communication they reach from human-centered to industrial applications. Examples for human-centered alarm systems are illustrated in Figure 2. They include thin and nearly invisible smoke detectors, humidity monitoring on walls for mildew prevention or within smart plasters to prevent dehydration, e.g., of elderly people. Industrial applications of smart multilayer printed systems are conceivable for industry 4.0 and decentralized production, where condition monitoring of workpieces, machines and goods during manufacturing, transport and application is necessary [4]. Here, printing technologies can be used for generative production technology with tailor-made customized monitoring systems, allowing for small production quantities down to a single piece.

B. Setup and manufacturing of multilayer printed systems

For the setup of the printed systems described here, transparent flexible polyethylene terephthalate (PET)

Figure 2. Visualization of examples for human-centered alarm systems: dehydration sensors or other smart plasters, smoke detectors, humidity sensors for mildew prevention.

substrates are used. In order to demonstrate the manufacturing feasibility, sheets of 150mm x 150mm are being processed, whereby the transfer to mass production techniques is considered. Conductive lines are printed on top of these substrates by using inks filled with metal particles, e.g., silver nano particles [5]. To print resistors, highly resistive inks containing, e.g., carbon particles are applied. Subsequently, the printed elements have to be sintered in order to evaporate the solvent of the ink. The particles get in contact to each other, going from a percolation-based conduction to forming of sinter necks and grain growth, ultimately leading to porous, metallic structure. Thermal sintering of silver nanoparticles occurs at temperatures of 120°C to 150°C [6][7]. Investigated alternatives are flash light sintering or current sintering.

In order to realize capacitors and field effect transistors, a stack of different materials has to be printed. Therefore, special inks have to be developed to realize the dielectric and the electrolyte [7][8]. For the time being, the printed components require large areas compared to conventionally manufactured surface mounted devices (SMD). But they are very thin and flat and thereby flexible. In order to setup fully printed electronic circuits, the integration and interconnection of these printed components on one layer is necessary. This class of integration technique is called intralayer-integration [3]. It also includes the embedding of conventional components like silicon bare dies (see Figure 1).

The second class is called interlayer-integration. It comprises the mechanical bonding of the layers as well as establishing electrical, optical and fluidic interconnections between the layers.

Two approaches of the design for electrical vias are illustrated in Figure 3. The first approach is to print a full metal pad on the lower layer and a metal frame pad placed around a hole on the top layer. By filling the hole with conductive adhesive, the two metal pads are connected electrically. Disadvantageous are thereby the change of production techniques and the protruding of conductive adhesive over the level of the top layer. Bridging steep-walled holes with conductive ink is not possible due to the evaporation of the solvent during sintering, that results in a strong reduction of ink volume. In order to enable a continuous printing process and to avoid the use of conductive adhesive, it is necessary create conical holes. The metal area on the lower layer can now be electrically connected by printing a continuous conductive line on the top layer (see Figure 3 right). The realization of conical holes, however, is more elaborate than the one of steep-walled holes.

For the production of multilayer printed systems, two general processes are being investigated:

1. Printing and assembly of all elements on the substrates and subsequent bonding of the printed substrates
2. Succession of printing and assembly of elements on one layer, bonding of the subsequent layer and printing of elements on the top layer of the bonded stack

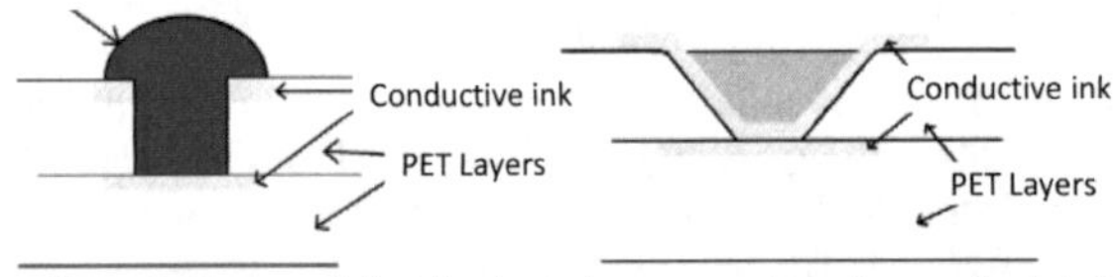

Figure 3. Design of electric vias to interconnect two layers of printed systems by filling a hole with conductive ink (left) or overprinting a conical hole (right).

Both processes are illustrated in Figure 4. The advantage of the first approach is the separation of production processes. Process parameters of printing techniques for different domains, like high sintering temperatures, do not affect the other layers. Theoretically, even the bonding of all layers in one step would be conceivable. The integration of vias, however, will require a layer-by-layer bonding process. Furthermore, the bonding of layers with assembled protruding components is hard to realize, since the bonding processes require a compression of the individual layers. This can be easier realized when using the second approach. The latter does also allow for both, printed and conductive adhesive vias, to be applied.

In Section I, multilayer printed systems and the general processes for their production were introduced. In Section II,

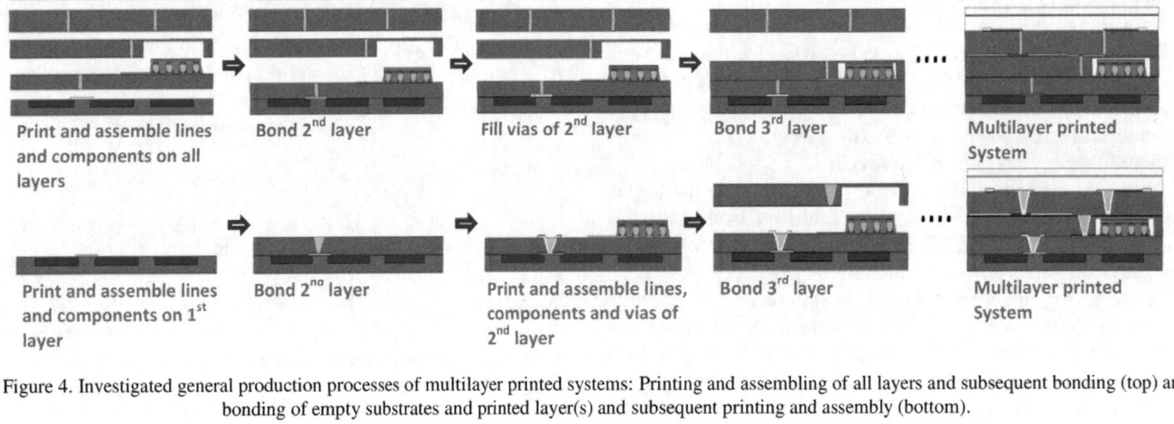

Figure 4. Investigated general production processes of multilayer printed systems: Printing and assembling of all layers and subsequent bonding (top) and bonding of empty substrates and printed layer(s) and subsequent printing and assembly (bottom).

the requirements for the bonding process to join individual printed system layers are defined, a general approach for bonding is explained and the three favored bonding methods are presented. These are transmission laserwelding, adhesive bonding and direct thermal bonding. After the comparison of the bonding methods in Section III, the conclusion of this paper is drawn in Section IV.

II. Bonding Methods

A. *Requirements for the bonding process*

The objective of the bonding is the provision of a strong bond between the layers that allows for flexing of the final system without delamination. Thereby, the functionality of the printed system must not be affected by the bonding process. The flexibility of the bonded layers should be comparable to the flexibility of bulk material of equivalent thickness. In order to enable the second bonding process, the printability of the surface must be preserved. Appealing bond quality, including smooth surfaces, is also aspired for the final systems. The preservation of transparency is desirable but not necessary, since optical elements will presumably be omitted during bonding. The bonding time is also considered, including all process steps that are necessary to bond the substrates, e.g., application of adjuvant bonding materials. The importance of the bonding time strongly depends on the batch size of the respective system. Further aspects are bonding costs and process complexity.

For the investigation, PET Melinex ST 506 substrates of 125 µm or 175 µm thickness are being used to ensure sufficient stiffness for substrate handling [9]. In future work, it is envisaged to reduce substrate thickness to enhance the flexibility of the layer stack. The substrates have a glass transition temperature of 78°C [10] and a melting point of 265°C [9]. Due to the roll–to-roll manufacturing process, the thermal shrinkage of the substrate is anisotropic.

In experiments with the different bonding techniques, first the parameters have to be determined that enable a sufficiently strong bond between the layers. The bond strength will be analyzed using T-peel tests in accordance to DIN EN ISO 11339. Afterwards, the possible damage of the bonding process on the printed elements is investigated for the given parameters. In order to determine the influence on conductive lines, for example, special standardized test structures were designed (see Figure 5). Their conductivity is measured before and after bonding.

B. *General approach*

The investigated bonding techniques can be classified as direct bonding and indirect bonding [11]. Adhesive bonding, using either liquid adhesives or lamination films, is a well established indirect bonding technique. For direct bonding, on the other hand, no additional material is added at the interface. One approach is to transfer thermal energy into the bond area – either localized or simultaneously over at the entire surface. Another possibility is to influence the polymer surface. Hereby, either solvent bonding techniques or different kinds of surface treatment and modification can be used.

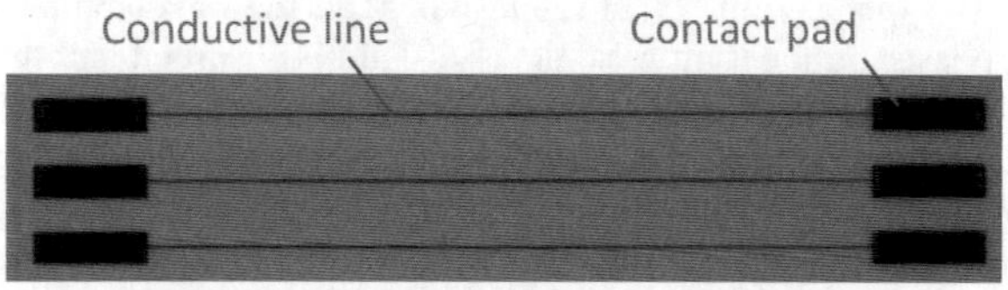

Figure 5. Test structures of printed conductive lines.

Due to the material and geometry of the given application, the three approaches that are further investigated and compared to each other are laserwelding, direct thermal bonding, if necessary in combination with surface activation, processes and adhesive bonding.

In order to reduce bonding complexity and bonding costs, the aspired objective is to find a layout-independent bonding process, that can be equally applied to any printed system. If a negative impact of the bonding process on the printed structures cannot be avoided, however, a potential compromise solution is to omit the printed structures during the bonding process. The resulting setup is illustrated in Figure 6. The most important areas to be bonded are the outer substrate frame and the area around vias to increase via stability. Additional bonding areas must be defined in order to achieve the aspired bonding strength. The individual areas are staggered to avoid negative effects of stacking, like local stiffening or interferences of the bonding process with already bonded interconnections. It is obvious, that this approach will not only result in a loss of available element area, but also in extensive effort. Special bonding keep-out areas have to be included into the circuit design rules of the printed systems, and individual programming of bonding equipment is required for every layout. The flexibility, on the other hand, might be increased if only small areas of the substrates are bonded. The effects of the application of layout-dependent as well as layout-independent bonding will be analyzed for every investigated bonding technique.

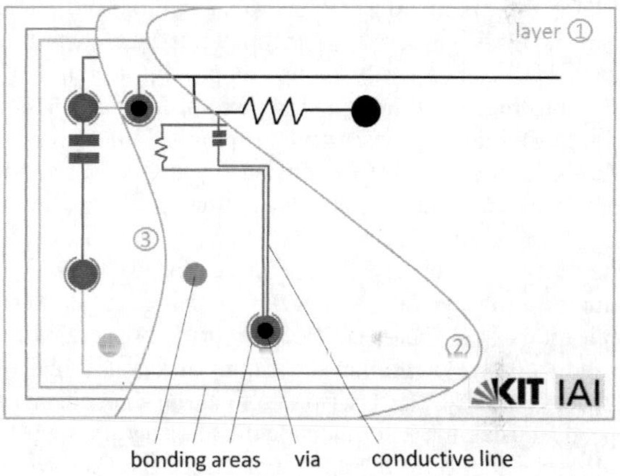

Figure 6. Illustration of layout-dependent bonding procedure.

C. *Transmission laserwelding*

Transmission laserwelding of two polymer parts is based upon heat generation in the joint area of the parts that are tightly clamped together [12][13]. Therefore, the laser light passes the upper part that is transparent for the wavelength of the laser. In the joint area, the laser light is absorbed and the absorbed energy results in heat generation. This leads to melting of the polymer surfaces and thus to bonding of the clamped parts.

One approach to realize absorption of laser light in the joint area is to use lower bond parts that are absorbent for the laser light [13]. In order to weld two transparent polymer parts, special coatings like a thin sputtered carbon layer or Clearweld™ are applied at the bond interface [14][15]. Clearweld™ is a liquid that, once applied on a foil, quickly dries to a thin layer absorbing in the wavelength range of 900 nm to 1100 nm. The use of fiber lasers with higher wavelength than infrared even allows laserwelding without additional coatings for a variety of thermoplastics [16]. Since the bond is formed between the molten surfaces of the thermoplastic polymers, the achievable bond strength is very high, up to the cohesive strength of the bulk material. The local transfer of heat leads to thermal stress and can result in deformation of the polymer parts.

For the bonding of transparent PET foils that shall be used for the production of transparent multilayer systems, Clearweld™ is chosen as absorbing interface layer. The Clearweld™ can be easily applied by printing techniques or doctor blading, resulting in a thin uniform layer on the PET surface. During the laserwelding process, the greenish-yellow Clearweld™ layer is consumed and the final bond is again transparent [12]. Both, the Clearweld™ application and the subsequent laserwelding process, can be applied either localized for layout-dependent design or over the entire area of the layers. For layout-dependent localized application of the Clearweld™, either masks, structured rolls or individually programmed printing processes can be applied. Similarly, the laserwelding can be applied layout-dependent using masks or individual laser programming.

In order to protect the printed elements, the Clearweld™ is applied to the lower, blank side of the top layer. Using the first general production process described in section I.A, the Clearweld™ is either applied before or after printing and assembly of all elements on one layer. If applied before printing, the Clearweld™ is exposed to heat and mechanical forces caused by sintering and handling processes that might damage the coating. During a Clearweld™ application after printing and assembly, on the other hand, the printed elements are exposed to handling forces. Protruding elements would impede a conformal coating. Thus, the implementation of the second process is probably more advantageous. The coating is applied to an empty substrate, laserwelded to a lower printed layer and subsequently printed on and assembled. The main challenge is to preserve a printable surface by preventing deformation due to localized thermal stress intrusion.

In first experiments depicted in Figure 7, the applicability of laserwelding on transparent PET substrates coated by Clearweld was demonstrated using a laserwelding machine built within the framework of the SMARTLAM project [17]. The aim of the current investigations is the definition of laserwelding parameters that enable suitable bond strength and do not affect the printed elements.

D. Adhesive bonding

For adhesive bonding, an intermediate layer of adhesive is applied to the surface of at least one bonding part. The bonding parts are then pressed together and the adhesive is cured. The associated reaction of linking the single monomers of the adhesive to form large molecules is called polymerization. Adhesives can be classified in accordance with the polymerization mechanism: polyaddition or chain reaction polymerisation and polycondensation or step reaction polymerization [18]. Curing is enabled or supported by processing conditions like elevated temperature, pressure or UV-irradiation [19]. Another approach is the use of two different components that start curing after being mixed together. Adhesive bonding can be used to bond similar or dissimilar bonding parts. If choosing a suitable adhesive matching with the bonding parts, very high bond strengths can be realized [18][19]. Though adhesive bonding is a well-established bonding method, the application of uniform layers of adhesive on large areas is challenging. The introduction of an additional material into a system might reduce the system stability, e.g., to temperatures and can be critical for medical applications. For optical applications, special gradient-index matched adhesives can be applied. One advantage of adhesive bonding is that the influence of uneven surfaces, e.g., due to protruding elements, can be compensated at a certain extent.

There is a variety of adhesives designed for PET bonding (e.g. [20][21]). Using adhesive bonding for the large area substrates, the adhesive can be applied in form of a liquid film directly before the bonding process. Alternatively, the use of precoated PET foils containing a dry film of adhesive is possible. Methods of adhesive application are dispensing, doctor blading, dipping, spray-coating etc. or the use of adhesive films. Surface treatment can be applied in order to increase the wettability of the PET surface and thus the molecular forces between adhesive and substrate, leading to improved bond strength [18][22][23].

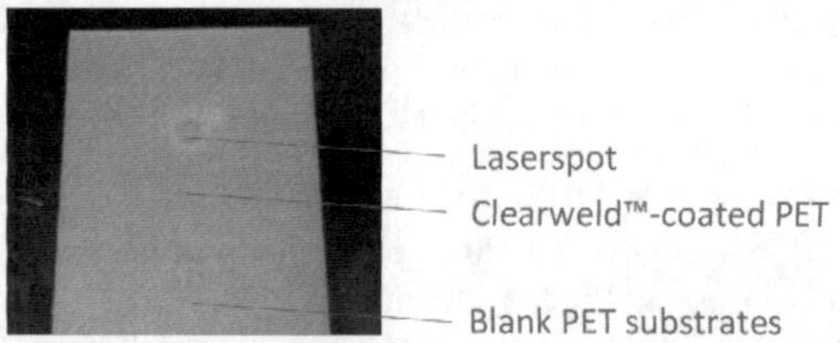

Figure 7. Laserwelding of Clearweld™-coated PET substrates.

A possible impairment of the printed elements can be caused either by chemical reactions between printed elements and adhesive or supporting conditions like UV-irradiation, or by mechanical stress during adhesive application. The latter can be omitted by the application of the adhesive only onto the lower, blank side of the top substrate or by using sensitive methods of application. The occurrence of chemical reactions has to be investigated for all types of ink being used for the production of a printed system, or has to be avoided by applying layout-dependent adhesive bonding techniques. Another aspect to be considered is that vias punched into the top substrate must not be filled by liquid adhesive. For layout-independent application, this can only be avoided by using pre-coated PET substrates allowing for punching via holes into substrate and coating. The lowest substrate is thereby not coated. When using pre-coated substrates for the first production process, special care must be taken during handling and preceding production steps in order not to damage the adhesive layer or to prematurely activate curing.

E. Direct thermal bonding

During direct thermal bonding, the two bond parts are heated and simultaneously pressed together. Usually, heated rolls are used to enable a high surface pressure of the bond area (see Figure 8). The combination of pressure and temperatures near or above the glass transition temperature leads to polymer softening in the bond area, enabling interdiffusion of polymer chains [11]. The achieved bond strength is very high, ideally reaching up to the cohesive strength of the bulk material. The required high temperatures, however, may cause deformation.

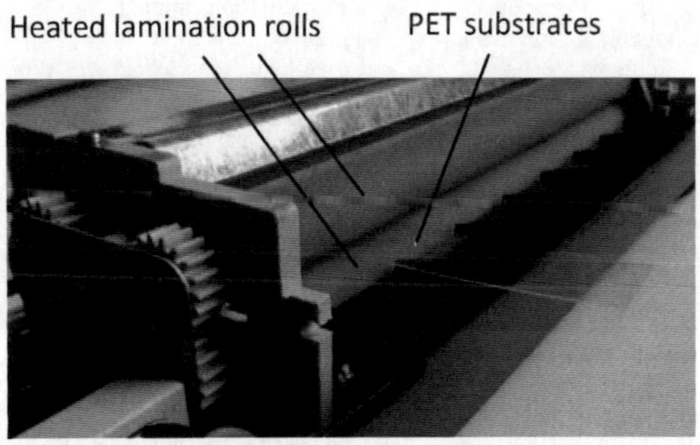

Figure 8 Direct thermal bonding of PET substrates

When using the relatively simple process of thermal bonding in order to bond thin PET substrates, all elements are heated. A layout-dependent protection of individual areas during the bonding process is not possible. One approach to reduce the process temperature significantly is to activate the substrate surface before bonding. Surface activation methods include, amongst others, the use of coupling agents [24], ultraviolet, ozone and plasma surface treatment [25][26]. Depending on the activation procedure, a layout-dependent masking of the printed structures is conceivable during this process step.

For both general bonding processes, all printed elements and mounted discrete components must withstand the bonding temperature and pressure, excluding the topmost layer, when using the second approach. Anisotropic thermal shrinkage and subsequent bending of the substrate must be prevented. The approach of first printing and assembling the individual layers, additionally leads to mechanical stress of the elements applied directly by the lamination roll. A roll-based thermal bonding of layers containing protruding components is not possible.

Due to the simplicity of the process, the thermal bonding will be further investigated, presumably in combination with surface activation methods. For first experiments, a thermal lamination machine (Dahle 70453) is used.

III. Comparison and Discussion

In Table 1, an overview of the three different bonding techniques that were described in the above sections is presented. Based upon the literature review and first experiments, estimates about the fulfillment of the main requirements of the bonding techniques are made. Thereby, some of the assumptions have to be further investigated in practical tests.

With transmission laserwelding, very high bond strength can be achieved. This is reduced if only parts of the area are welded, using the layout-dependent approach. The bond quality has to be investigated, especially regarding the printability on the top surface. Due to the serial process of local heating, visible lines or patterns resulting from the scanning of the Laser beam have to be expected and local deformation might occur, leading to uneven surfaces or bending of the entire substrate. The Clearweld™ coating process step and the serial welding result in rather slow bonding time. The process complexity is low to medium. Layout-dependent programming of the welding machine or even localized coating increase complexity. The costs of Clearweld™ coating and laser machines are medium, extra programming time and/or the production of masks increase

TABLE I. Comparison of different bonding techniques to be applied for bonding flexible transparent PET substrates containing printed elements to setup multilayer printed systems. Assesments of the determining factor, reaching from ++ as very good to – for very bad performance.

Bonding technique		**Bond strength**	**Bonding quality**	**Bonding time**	**Process complexity**	**Bonding costs**	**Flexibility of the system**	**Trans-mission**
Laser welding	Layout-independent	++	0 to +	-	0 to +	0	0	-- to -
	Layout-dependent	0 to +	- to +	-	- to 0	- to 0	0 to +	- to 0
Adhesive bonding	Layout-independent	+ to ++	+	-	0 to +	- to +	--	-- to 0
	Layout-dependent	0 to +	-- to 0	-	- to 0	- to 0	-	- to 0
Direct thermal bonding	Without surface activation	0 to +	- to +	++	++	++	0	- to 0
	With surface activation	+ to ++	+ to ++	+	+	0 to +	0	- to 0

the costs. The flexibility of the system is not affected by the laserwelding process, the reduction of the transmission caused by visible lines or unused Clearweld™ coating has to be further investigated. Due to the high laser power that has to be introduced in order to melt the PET surfaces, an impairment of the printed elements must be expected in the bonded areas.

Choosing the appropriate adhesive, very high bond strength can be realized by adhesive bonding. The reduction of bonded area in the layout-dependent approach reduces the overall strength. Applying the adhesive onto the entire area, good results can be achieved for the bond quality. Depending on the adhesion layer thickness, existing unevenness of the substrate surfaces might even be compensated. For layout-dependent adhesive bonding, on the other hand, uneven surfaces have to be expected due to the local intrusion of an extra layer. The overall bond time, including the application of adhesive, possibly with preceding surface activation, bonding and curing is rather high. The complexity and thus the bonding costs strongly depend on the need of surface activation, choice of adhesive and method of adhesive application and curing. They are increased for layout-dependent bonding due to programming or the use of masks. The flexibility is reduced due to the additional layer. The impairment of transmission depends on the choice of the adhesive. Possible damage of the printed elements due to chemical reactions of the ink with the adhesive have to be further investigated.

Using direct thermal bonding, ideally very high bond strengths can be realized. Presumably, a preceding surface activation is necessary to achieve the desired bond strength and/or to reduce the process temperature. If thermal stresses can be avoided, the bond quality is expected to be good. The fast bonding process and the low process complexity result in relatively low bonding costs. Time, complexity and costs are significantly increased if the implementation of the additional processing step for surface activation is necessary. The flexibility of the system will not be affected by the bonding method. Minor or no interference of the transmission is expected. At temperatures of 120°C or more, substantial influences of the bonding process on the substrate and the printed elements have to be expected.

IV. Conclusion

In this paper, three selected bonding techniques were described that can be applied for bonding of transparent flexible PET foil substrates containing printed elements to produce multilayer printed systems. The techniques are transmission laserwelding of Clearweld™-coated substrates, adhesive bonding and direct thermal bonding, presumably in combination with a surface activation process. It was shown that for all investigated bonding processes the approach of bonding a blank PET substrate on top of a printed layer or a stack of layers and subsequently printing the next layer on the blank substrate is preferable in comparison to printing all layers and subsequently bonding them. This conclusion leads to the requirement of preserving the printability of the surface of the bonded empty substrate during the bonding process. A comparison of the different bonding techniques shows, that all of them have the potential to be used for the present application if the appropriate bonding parameters can be found, enabling a strong bond and simultaneously keeping the functionality of the printed elements and the printability of the top surface. The current state of the investigation indicates that direct thermal bonding is the most promising approach due to its low complexity and relatively fast bonding time. The final decision, however, requires a comprehensive experimental investigation of the application of the different bonding techniques.

Acknowledgement

The authors would like to thank the Helmholtz Association of German Research Centres (HGF) for supporting this work by program-oriented funding and the Ministry for Science and Art Baden-Württemberg for its funding within the scope of the Brigitte-Schlieben-Lange program (BSLP). Further thanks go to the Karlsruhe Micro Nano Facility (KNMF) for assistance with the laser welding tests and the colleagues from Thin Film Technology (TFT) at KIT for the Clearweld™ application.

References

[1] H. Kipphan, Handbuch der Printmedien [translation from German: Handbook of print media]. Springer, 2000.

[2] V. Subramanian et al., "Printed electronics for low-cost electronic systems: Technology status and application development" 38th European Solid-State Device Research Conference (ESSDERC 2008), 2008, pp. 17-24.

[3] U. Gengenbach et al.; „Ein Baukastensystem für multifunktionale, mehrlagige, gedruckte Systeme [translation from German: A modular system for multilayer printed systems]" Mikrosystemtechnikkongress in Karlsruhe (MST 2015), 2015.

[4] A. Gilchrist, Industry 4.0 – The Industrial Internet of Things. Apress, 2016.

[5] J. G. Korvink, P. J. Smith and D.-Y. Shin, Inkjet-Based Micro-manufacturing, Wiley–VCH, 2012.

[6] M. Ungerer et al., "Analysis of the cross section of inkjet-printed conductive tracks on PET" The Tenth International Conference on Advances in Computer-Human Interactions (ACHI 2017) Special, in this issue, 2017.

[7] M. Mikolajek et al., "Direct Inkjet Printing of Dielectric Ceramic/Polymer Composite Thick Films", Advanced Engineering Materials, vol. 17, no. 9, pp. 1294-1301, 2015.

[8] T. T. Baby et al., "A General Route toward Complete Room Temperature Processing of Printed and High Performance Oxide Electronics", *ACS Nano* vol. 9, no. 3, pp. 3075-3083, 2015.

[9] Dupont Teijin Films. *Datasheet Melinex ST 506,* 2006. [Online] Available from: www.dupontteijinfilms.com/FilmEnterprise/Datasheet.asp?Result=Print&ID=269&Version=US 2017.02.28

[10] Dupont Teijin Films. *Latest Developments In PolyesterFilm for Flexible electronics.* 2004. [Online] Available from: http://people.ccmr.cornell.edu/~cober/MSE5420/page2/files/DTF%20PEN.pdf 2017.02.28

[11] C.-W. Tsao and D. L. DeVoe, "Bonding of thermoplastic polymer microfluidics", Microfluid Nanofluid, vol. 6, pp. 1-16, 2009.

[12] R. Klein, *Schweißen von Lasertransparenten Kunststoffen mit Laser [translation from German: Welding of laser transparent polymers with laser],* 2008. [Online] Available from: http://www.wolf-produktions

systeme.de/de/veroeffentlicht/technologieseminar/technologieseminar2008/vortrag3.pdf 2017.02.28

[13] A. Roesner, A. Boglea and A. Olowinsky, "Laserdurchstrahlschweißen von Thermoplasten [translation from German: Transmission laserwelding of thermoplastics]"', Laser Technik Journal, vol. 5, no. 4, pp. 28-32, 2008.

[14] R. Klein, Laser Welding of Plastics: Materials, Processes and Industrial Applications. Wiley–VCH, 2011.

[15] W. H. Cawley, *Use of Infrared Absorbers to Laser Weld Plastics*, 2007 [Online] Available from: http://www.clearweld.com/edufiles/Use%20of%20Infrared%20Absorbers%20to%20Laser%20Weld%20Plastics%20_2_.pdf 2017.02.28

[16] J. Brown, *Transparent Laser Plastic Welding - Clear Polymer Bonding for Medical Devices*, 2012 [Online] Available from: www.lpkfusa.com/articles/lq/Transparent_Lase_Plastic_Welding.pdf 2017.02.28

[17] S. Scholz et al., "A modular flexible scalable and reconfigurable system for manufacturing of Microsystems based on additive manufacturing and e-printing" Robotics and Computer-Integrated Manufacturing, vol. 40, pp. 14-23, 2016.

[18] A. Baldan, "Adhesively-bonded joints and repairs in metallic alloys, polymers and composite materials: Adhesives, adhesion theories and surface pretreatment" J. of Materials Science, vol. 39, no. 1, pp. 1-49, 2004.

[19] S. Ebnesajjad, Adhesives Technology Handbook. William Andrew, 2008.

[20] DuPont Packaging & Industrial Polymers, *Bonding 'Unjoin-able' Polymers*, White Paper, 2011 [Online] Available from: www2.dupont.com/Packaging_Resins/en_US/assets/downloads/white_papers/Bonding_Unjoinable_Polymers_Lee_92011.pdf 2017.02.28

[21] Dymax, *Ultra Light-Weld 3043 RPET & PET Rapid Bonder*, Datasheet, 2013 [Online] Available from: www.dymax.com/images/pdf/pds/3072.pdf 2017.02.28

[22] E. Gonzalez et al., "Remote Atmospheric-Pressure Plasma Activation of the Surfaces of Polyethylene Terephthalate and Polyethylene Naphthalate" Langmuir, vol. 24, pp. 12636-12643, 2008.

[23] R. Wolf and A. C. Sparavigna, "Role of Plasma Surface Treatments on Wetting and Adhesion" Engineering, vol. 2, no. 6, pp. 397-402, 2010.

[24] C. Goh, S. Tan, E. Ngoh and J. Wei, "Surface Treatment of Polyethylene Terephthalate (PET) Film for Lamination of Flexible Photovoltaic Devices" Energy Procedia, vol. 15, pp. 428 – 435, 2012.

[25] T. Homola, L. Y. L. Wu and M. Cernakrnak, "Atmospheric Plasma Surface Activation of Poly(Ethylene Terephthalate) Film for Roll-To-Roll Application of Transparent Conductive Coating" The Journal of Adhesion, vol. 90, no. 4, pp. 296-309, 2014.

[26] T. Tamai, M. Watanabe and K. Mitamura, "Modification of PEN and PET film surfaces by plasma treatment and layer-by-layer assembly of polyelectrolyte multilayer thin films" Colloid and Polymer Science, vol. 293, no. 5, pp. 1349-1356, 2015.

Concept of an Active Optical Subsystem for Use in an Ophthalmic Implant

Ingo Sieber, Thomas Martin, Georg Bretthauer, Ulrich Gengenbach
Institute for Applied Computer Science
Karlsruhe Institute of Technology
76344 Eggenstein-Leopoldshafen, Germany
e-mail: ingo.sieber@kit.edu

Abstract—**This paper describes the concept of an active optical subsystem for use in a demonstration model of an ophthalmic implant in the context of human centered systems. The active optical subsystem consists of the three principal components optics, actuator, and amplification linkage. The main focus of the work presented is on the robust concept and mode of operation of the active optical subsystem.**

Keywords-robust design; tolerance analysis; freeform optics; optical modeling and simulation; design optimization; ophthalmic implant

I. Introduction

In ophthalmology, restoration of the accommodation ability of the human eye is still an unsolved problem. The process of accommodation means the adjustment of the refraction power of the human eye with respect to the object distance. The loss of the ability to accommodate is due to an aging process of the human eye leading to a stiffening of the lens. Different approaches for restoration of the accommodation ability are currently under discussion [1]-[4], but none of them solves the problem in its entirety [5].

The concept of the Artificial Accommodation System (AAS) follows a mechatronic approach and will be implantable into the capsular bag of the human eye [6]. The following components represent the functional units of the AAS:

- An active optical subsystem,
- an information acquisition system,
- an information processing system,
- a communication unit,
- housing, and
- an energy supply system.

Figure 1 shows a schematic representation of the AAS [7]. There are depicted the main components and the position of the implanted system within the capsular bag of the human eye. A demonstration model of such an implant solution was designed and realized at a scale of 2:1 [8].

The active optical subsystem is of vital importance to the implant since the optical performance of the AAS depends on its reliable function.

The article is organized as follows: Section 2 presents the active optical subsystem of the AAS with all its components. Section 3 covers the set-up of the demonstration model and shows exemplarily its mode of action. The paper is completed by the conclusions drawn in Section 4.

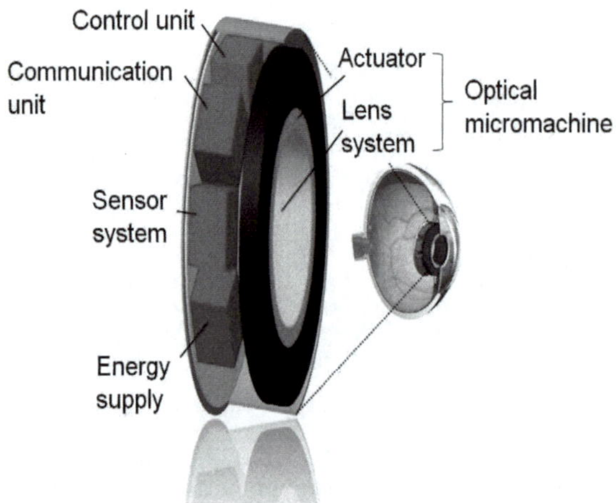

Figure 1. Schematic representation of the AAS and its position within the capsular bag of the human eye [7].

II. The Active Optical Subsystem

The three principal components of the active optical subsystem are presented and discussed in the following subsections.

A. Optics

Figure 2 shows a sketch of the optical components used in the demonstration model of the ophthalmic implant. The ray path is from left to right. The AAS features a modular concept, where the housing as well as optical surfaces integrated in the housing will be used for different optical principles. Originally, the housing was designed for an optical subsystem using an axially moveable lens to adjust refraction power [9]. Hence, the optics integrated in the housing are negative aspheric lenses. The first lens integrated in the housing is for beam expansion, the second lens integrated in the housing has the task to focus the rays on the retina (or camera chip in case of the demonstration model). Both optics are described by aspheric surfaces [7].

Manufacturing of the housing with its integrated optics was realized using a precision glass molding process. The influences of the manufacturing tolerances were analyzed by measuring the molded surfaces and a subsequent integration of the measured data into the optical simulation model [10].

The task of the varifocal optics inside the housing (between the optics integrated in the housing) is to adjust the refraction power due to the visual requirements. One optical

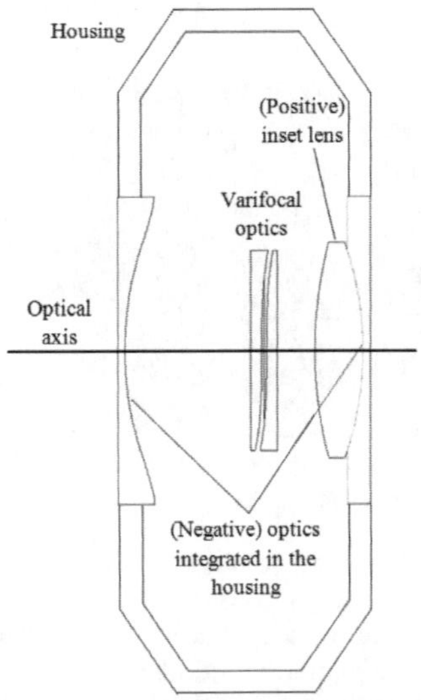

Figure 2. Optics of the demonstration model.

concept, which can be used as varifocal optics is the principle invented by Alvarez and Humphrey in 1970 [11]. According to this principle, the refraction power is varied by a mutual shift of two cubic-type lens parts perpendicular to the optical axis as shown in Figure 3. To combine the above described housing design with this varifocal concept, an aspherical inset lens has to be designed to add a positive refraction power to the negative lens of the rear side (see Figure 2) [7].

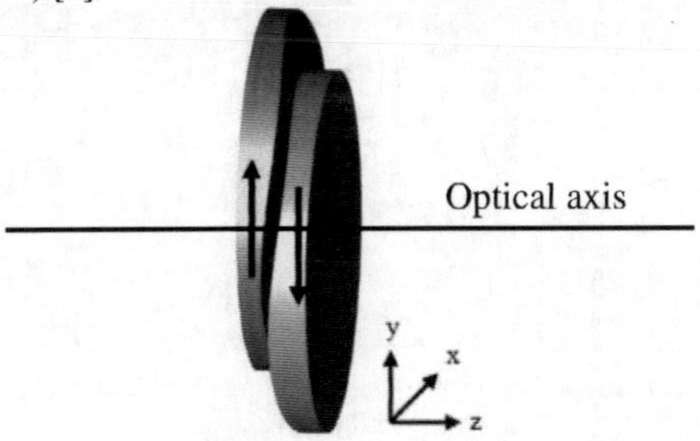

Figure 3. Alvarez-Humphrey optics.

Alvarez-Humphrey optics were studied extensively [12–14] and proposed for different technical [15]–[17] as well as ophthalmic applications [18], [19]. The opposing surfaces are conjugated and of cubic shape. Design parameters of the Alvarez-Humphrey (AH) lenses are the lateral movement v of the lens parts and the "form" parameter A determining the shape of the lens surface. The polynomial description of the surface sag is given by (1):

$$z(x,y) = A((y - v)x^2 + 1/3(y - v)^3). \qquad (1)$$

The relation between the lateral movement v and the change of refraction power ΔD is given by (2) [20]:

$$\Delta D \sim A\, v. \qquad (2)$$

Adjustment of the refraction power by means of a lateral shift of lens parts is advantageous in all applications where the space available along the optical axis is limited, as is true for the demonstration model at hand. Requirements of the optics and its design are presented in [21]. To compensate for aberration effects as well as for manufacturing tolerances a comprehensive design approach was used [22] resulting in a robust freeform surface of the AH optics, which is represented by a polynomial of seventh order using 35 parameters [7]. Also the robust design of the AH optics results in two different descriptions of the opposing freeform surfaces violating the conjugation of the original AH concept. The AH optics was manufactured by two competing processes: ultraprecision diamond machining and microinjection molding. While diamond machining is suitable only for small series fabrication microinjection molding is a replication process with the potential of mass fabrication [23, 24]. For both processes the effect of manufacturing tolerances on the performance of the optical subsystem was analysed and compared against each other by simulations based on a measurement data enhanced model [25].

B. Actuator

As described above, design parameters of the AH optics are the lateral mutual shift of the lens parts, v, as well as the form parameter A. To preserve a constant ΔD a reduction of v, which is requested to minimize the actuation stroke, leads evidently to a higher value of A (see (2)), which in turn significantly increases aberration effects and hence limits imaging quality. As a trade-off a maximum mutual shift of the lens parts of 180 µm with an actuator rest position at 40 µm displacement allows for a change of 4.6 dpt in optical power and was found to be a reasonable compromise for the demonstration model [26].

The requirements of the actuator with respect to cycle lifetime, power consumption, fail-safe behavior, response time, and space can be found in [26]. As the final actuator for the demonstration model a piezoelectric stack actuator (Noliac A/S, NAC2001-H06, Noliac, Kvistgaard, Denmark) was chosen. This actuator offers a nominal stroke of 4.9 µm of which a maximum of 2.9 µm is used during operation [27].

C. Amplification linkage

To provide a maximum lateral shift of a lens part of 140 µm (resulting in a displacement of the lens part of 180 µm on basis of the actuator rest position of 40 µm) an amplification ratio of around 48 of the maximum actuator stroke of 2.9 µm is required. For reasons of miniaturization and reduction of assembly processes, a monolithic design with flexure hinges was selected. The planarity of the linkage enables a Deep Reactive Ion Etching (DRIE) process for fabrication of the linkage in single-crystal silicon [26]. Figure 4 shows the linkage manufactured by DRIE fulfilling the transmission requirements [26]. The opening in the upper part of the linkage is the host structure for the piezoelectric stack actuator. The lens parts are to be assembled into the round mounts in the middle of the linkage. Minimum structure widths of about 24 µm were realized by means of the DRIE-process. The linkage is enclosed by a solid frame serving both as interface to the subsystem mount and as handling frame during system assembly.

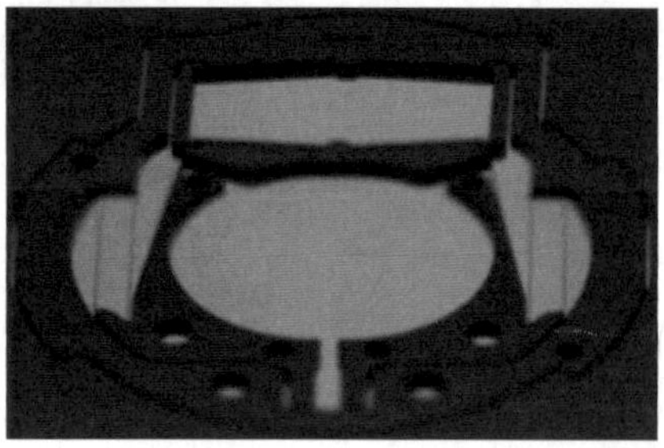

Figure 4. Silicon linkage manufactured by DRIE [7].

III. SET-UP OF THE ACTIVE OPTICAL SUBSYSTEM

Assembly of the AH optics, the actuator, and the silicon linkage yields the varifocal optics. Figure 5 depicts two photographs of the varifocal optics in two different actuation states. On the left hand side, the piezo stack actuator is expanded. The expansion leads to a mutual outward shift of both lens parts and therefore to a relative decrease in refraction power of the optics. On the right of Figure 5 the contraction of the actuator is shown leading to an inward movement of the lens parts and an increase of the optics' refraction power. This effect is visible comparing the grid size in the image: while reducing the refraction power the grid size of the image scales down (Figure 5, left) compared to an increase of refraction power as shown in Figure 5 on the right hand side.

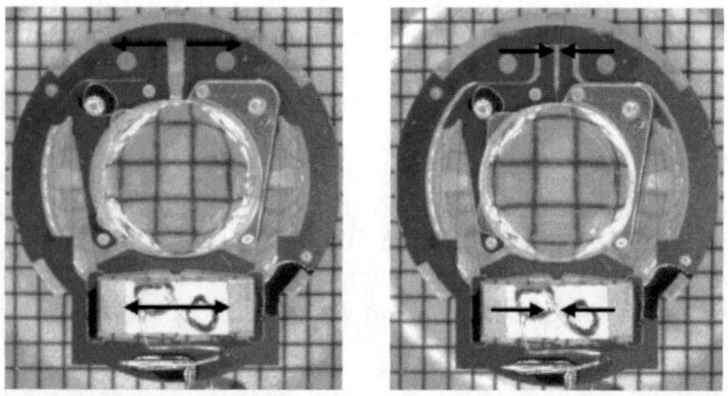

Figure 5. Varifocal optics. **Left**: expanded actuator and decreased refraction power, **right**: contracted actuator and incresed refraction power.

As described in Section 2, the optical subsystem consists of the varifocal optics assembled in a housing where both the entrance and exit windows provide optical power by means of curved optical surfaces integrated in the housing. Since the AAS features a modular concept where varifocal optics of different kind can be exchanged the optics integrated in the housing have to be adapted to the optics used. Combining the negative rear-side optics with an AH optics, an aspherical inset lens has to be designed to add a positive refraction power to the negative lens of the rear side. The exact description of the optics integrated in the housing and the aspheric inset lens can be found in [7]. Figure 6 shows the varifocal optics assembled on its mount in the rear half shell of the glass housing.

Figure 6. Varifocal optics assembled to the rear half shell of the glass housing.

The active optical subsystem combined with a sensor cross and electronics for control, information acquisition & processing, and communication is depicted in Figure 7. The sensor cross of the demonstration model consists of photodiodes and is segmented:

- The central segment is for measurement of the environmental luminance.
- Two outer segments are for measurement of the pupil diameter.

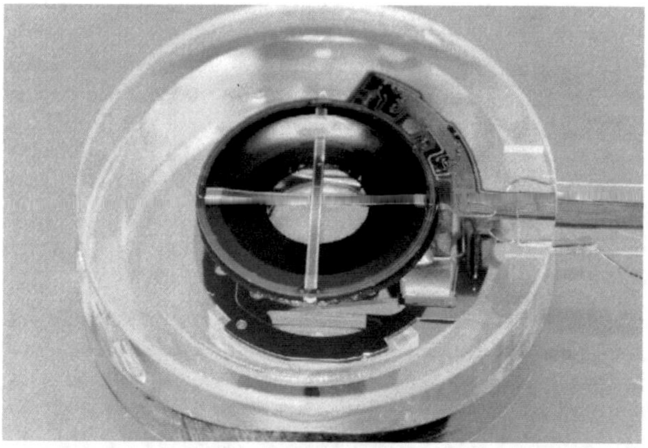

Figure 7. Active optical subsystem consiting of the varifocal optics assembled to the housing.

On the basis of these two measurands the accommodation demand and hence the adjustment of the refraction power can be derived [5].

Mode of action of the active optical subsystem is shown in Figure 8 for two different adjustments of the system's refraction power. On top of Figure 8 a concentric pattern at a distance of approximately 3 m is imaged sharply on a camera chip while the pen in the foreground is out of focus and is imaged only blurred. Readjusting the varifocal optics for the near sight images the pen at a distance of approximately 0.3 m sharply while the image of the concentric pattern appears blurred.

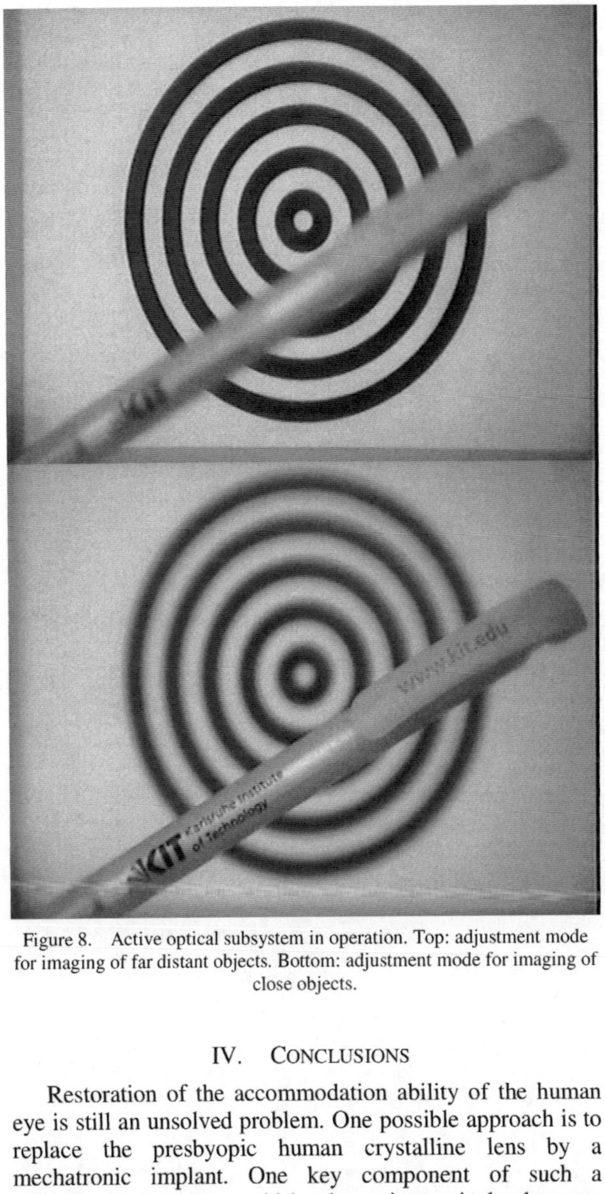

Figure 8. Active optical subsystem in operation. Top: adjustment mode for imaging of far distant objects. Bottom: adjustment mode for imaging of close objects.

IV. CONCLUSIONS

Restoration of the accommodation ability of the human eye is still an unsolved problem. One possible approach is to replace the presbyopic human crystalline lens by a mechatronic implant. One key component of such a mechatronic implant would be the active optical subsystem consisting of varifocal optics and a tailored actuation principle. As varifocal optics an Alvarez-Humphrey optics is presented, which is able to adjust the refraction power by a mutual shift of two freeform lens components perpendicular to the optical axis. For designing freeform optics, the robust design approach is essential [28] consisting of monolithic integration principles to minimize assembly efforts as well as an optimization of the functional components with respect to robustness against remaining assembly and manufacturing tolerances.

Actuation is conducted by a piezoelectric stack actuator while a silicon linkage provides the necessary displacement amplification. The result leads to a robust design of the active optical subsystem, which is integrated in a demonstration model at a scale of 2:1. A first impression of the mode of action of the demonstration model is shown for imaging objects in two different distances.

ACKNOWLEDGMENT

The authors would like to acknowledge Olaf Rübenach from Ingeneric GmbH for manufacturing of the optics integrated in the housing, Eric Beckert, FhG IOF, for ultraprecision diamond machining of the AH-optics, and Allen Yi, Ohio State University, for microinjection molding of the AH-optics. Parts of this work were funded by Bundesministerium für Bildung und Forschung (BMBF) (16SV5472K).

REFERENCES

[1] G. Bretthauer, U. Gengenbach, O. Stachs, and R. F. Guthoff, "A new mechatronic system to restore the accommodation ability of the human eye," Klin Monatsbl Augenheilkd 227, pp. 935-939, 2010.

[2] R. R. Krueger, X. K. Sun, J. Stroh, and R. Myers, "Experimental increase in accommodative potential after neodymium-yttrium-aluminum-garnet laser photo disruption of paired cadaver lenses," Ophthalmology 108 (11), pp. 2122-2129, 2001.

[3] K. R. Johannsdottir and L. B. Stelmach, "Monovision – a review of scientific literature," Optometry and Vision Science 78 (9), pp. 646-651, 2001.

[4] M. Lavin, " Multifocal intraocular lenses - part1," Optometry today 5/2001, pp. 34-37, 2001.

[5] U. Gengenbach, et al., "Concept and realisation of an optical microsystem to restore accommodation", at-Automatisierungstechnik 64 (10), pp. 839-849, 2016.

[6] M. Bergemann, U. Gengenbach, G. Bretthauer, and R. F. Guthoff, "Artificial Accommodation System - a new approach to restore the accommodative ability of the human eye," World Congress on Med. Phys. and Biomed. Engin., pp. 267-270, 2006.

[7] I. Sieber, T. Martin, and U. Gengenbach, "Robust Design of an Optical Micromachine for an Ophthalmic Application," *Micromachines* 7(5):85, 2016.

[8] U. Gengenbach, et al., "Systemintegration on hard- and software level on the example of a 2:1 scale functional model of an Artificial Accommodation System," In Proceedings of the MikroSystemTechnik Kongress 2015, pp. 234–238, 26–28 October 2015.

[9] M. Bergemann, I. Sieber, G. Bretthauer, and R. F. Guthoff, „Triple-Optic-Ansatz für das künstliche Akkommodationssystem," Der Ophthalmologe 104, pp.311-16, 2007.

[10] I. Sieber and O. Rübenach, "Integration of measurement data in the comprehensive modelling approach," Proc. SPIE 8884, pp. 88841F-1, 2013.

[11] L. W. Alvarez and W. E. Humphrey, "Variable-power Lens and System," U.S. patent 3,507,5651, 1970.

[12] A. W. Lohmann, "A new class of varifocal lenses," Appl. Opt. 9, pp. 1669–1671, 1970.

[13] L. W. Alvarez, "Development of variable-focus lenses and new refractor," J. Am. Optom. Assoc., 49, pp. 24–29, 1978.

[14] S. Barbero, "The Alvarez and Lohmann refractive lenses revisited," Opt. Express 17, pp. 9376–9390, 2009.

[15] S. Barbero and J. Rubinstein, "Adjustable-focus lenses based on the Alvarez principle," J. Opt. 13, 125705, 2011.

[16] S. S. Rege and T. S. Tkaczyk, M. R. Descour, "Application of the Alvarez-Humphrey concept to the design of a

miniaturized scanning microscope," Opt. Express 12, pp. 2574–2588, 2004.

[17] I. A. Palusinski, J. M. Sasian, and J. E. Greivenkamp, "Lateral-shift variable aberration generators," Appl. Opt. 38, pp. 86–90 1999.

[18] S. Barbero and J. Rubinstein, "Power-adjustable sphero-cylindrical refractor comprising two lenses," Opt. Eng. 52, 063002, 2013.

[19] A. N. Simonov, G. Vdovin, and M. C. Rombach, "Cubic optical elements for an accommodative intraocular lens," Opt. Express 14, pp. 7757–7775, 2006.

[20] I. Sieber, et al., "Design of freeform optics for an ophthalmological application," Proc. SPIE 9131, pp. 913108-1-11 2014.

[21] I. Sieber, T. Martin, A. Yi, L. Li, and O. Ruebenach, "Optical Design and Tolerancing of an Ophthalmological System," Proc. SPIE 9195, pp. 919504-1-10 2014.

[22] I. Sieber, "Comprehensive modeling and simulation of micro-optical subsystems," Proc. SPIE 8550, pp. 855002-1-11, 2012.

[23] L. Li, et al. "Design and fabrication of microinjection molded miniature freeform alvarez lenses", Proceedings - ASPE/ASPEN Summer Topical Meeting: Manufacture and Metrology of Freeform and Off-Axis Aspheric Surfaces, pp. 13-16, 2014.

[24] L. Li, et al., "Fabrication of Microinjection Molded Miniature Freeform Alvarez Lenses, " Applied Optics 53(19), pp. 4248–4255, 2014.

[25] I. Sieber, et al., "Optical performance simulation of freeform optics based on a measurement data enhanced model," Appl. Opt. **55**(24) pp. 6671-6679, 2016.

[26] T. Martin, P. Schrank, U. Gengenbach, and G. Bretthauer, "Design of an actuator for the lateral-shift optics of an intraocular implant," Proc. Actuator, pp. 152-155, 2012.

[27] T. Martin, U. Gengenbach, P. Ruther, O. Paul, and G. Bretthauer, "Realization of Actuator Systems for an Implantable Artificial Accommodation System," in Proceedings of the 14th International Conference on New Actuators, Bremen, Germany, 23–25 June 2014, pp. 169–172, 2014.

[28] I. Sieber and M. Dickerhof, "Robust Design Approach in Micro Optics". Proc. SPIE, 7717, 77170H, 2010.

"Was it easy"? "Yes". "Will you use it"? "No". Elderly Trying Out a Kinect Interface

Guri Verne
Department of Informatics
University of Oslo
Norway
e-mail: guribv@ifi.uio.no

Abstract—**This paper describes a qualitative study that seeks to give a rich description of the experiences and viewpoints of elderly about their use of digital technologies in general and videoconferencing in particular. Interviews and workshops were methods for data collection. The workshops included a discussion group session in addition to a session of trying out gesturing as a response to a videoconference call. A prototype of a gestures-based interface for interacting with a videoconference system intended for use in their homes was tried out. The participants had clear views of technologies they used and liked, and they wanted to maintain physical fitness as long as possible. Although they found the gestures easy to perform, they did not want to use this technology in their homes. This apparent self-contradictory response is discussed.**

Keywords-elderly; videoconference; gestures; Kinect; design.

I. INTRODUCTION

Welfare technology for the elderly is intended to improve their health and quality of life while preserving their autonomy and well-being. The aim is for public health services to be able to take care of an increasing population of elderly. As more people live longer and need care from public services, the elderly that are accepted into care homes are less able to take care of themselves than previously. Elderly who cannot take completely care of themselves live longer in their own homes supported by public care services and welfare technology is expected to play a role in this support.

The term "welfare technology" denotes a rather wide class of technologies. There are several approaches to the development of welfare technology. Some focus on assisted living and remote surveillance [1][2][3], others focus on exercising [4][5][6], while others again focus on communication and socializing [7][8][9].

Social connections are considered important for a healthy life in old age. Loneliness is found to correlate with functional decline and even death [10]. Videoconference technology is one means of supporting connections with and between elderly in their homes. This paper reports from a project where videoconference technology is developed to support communication between elderly in their homes, municipal care personnel, and with friends and family. The elderly do not need to use a PC as the TV set that is already present and familiar to the elderly will be used for the videoconference. To enable also elderly who do not use a PC to use the videoconferencing technology, an interface based on gestures instead of a mouse or a remote controller will be tried out. The ambition is to base the gestures on previous habits and bodily knowledge which are experienced as easy for the elderly users [11]. A Kinect camera was used to capture and interpret the gestures. The gestures that are chosen build on naturally occurring gestures for greeting someone or answering the phone and will be presented below.

This paper presents the experiences from two workshops with elderly participants. The workshops served a dual purpose of eliciting the elderly participants' experiences with digital technologies and trying out gesturing as an interface to a videoconference prototype. The workshops were part of a user-centered development process and were aimed at giving input to the design process.

This study is a qualitative case study as the elderly participants' own views are the focus of the study [12]. A result of the study is that many elderly use more digital technology than they say they do. Even though the elderly participants found the gestures easy to perform, they did not want to use gestures-based videoconferencing in their homes.

The rest of the paper is structured as follows. In the next Section, related works about welfare technology, videoconferencing and gestures-based communication are presented. The method is described in Section III, while Sections IV-V presents findings from the study. In Section VI, the results are discussed, while Section VII concludes the paper.

II. ELDERLY AND THEIR USE OF TECHNOLOGIES

Early work on elderly and technology showed that practical experience from using computers earlier in life reinforced their positive attitudes towards computer use as they grew older [13]. The emotional dimension of staying engaged with life and society, and adapt to changes in technology is important with elderly users of ICT. They are concerned that they can continue living autonomously and continue activities that they value [14][15]. If the technology fits with their lives and values, elderly people can learn new technological skills and use them for their own purposes. In addition to practical purposes, using any device is coupled with affective and emotional experiences, for example expectations, satisfaction, values, joy, or frustration. Also, the age group between 71-92 years can be active producers of online content and interact with strangers sharing the same interest [14].

However, technology often becomes too difficult to use in practice [9][16]. Assistive technologies installed into the homes do often not meet the elderly person's needs. Some devices become abandoned and some deliberately disabled [1].

A. Videoconferencing

An experiment with using videoconferencing with elderly functioned well in semi-controlled environments in a lab [17]. When the videoconferencing equipment was moved into the homes of the elderly and put into use there, it did not function so well [9]. Various difficulties arose. Elderly who managed to use the remote controller and the TV set and respond to videoconference calls in the controlled test, did not respond with the same high level of fidelity when they were in their own homes where contextual and contingent events got their attention and priority. Also, light conditions in the homes turned out to be different and less favourable for the video camera than in the lab, and this caused the view to be of less quality for the nurse in the other end. In one case, a woman was in her bed and did not answer the call within time.

The different responses between lab conditions and the home will be of importance if this technology is considered for use in a real life work setting. The nurse may need to contact the person in a traditional way, for example visit the home in question or telephone the elderly, if there is no response. The no-response could indicate that a serious situation has occurred, and the nurse will need to find out. The video call will in this situation mainly provide her with extra work as she will have to resort to the traditional means for contacting the elderly person at home if the call is not answered.

B. Experiences with Kinect camera

The Kinect camera is developed as a motion-sensing input device for gaming computers. The camera comes with software specifically tailored to recognize certain gestures and movements, and is used in a variety of contexts and applications. The Kinect with its software can interpret specific gestures, making completely hands-free control of electronic devices possible. It uses an infrared projector and camera and a special microchip to track the movement of objects and individuals in three dimensions. There are expectations that gesture interaction will be experienced as natural and easy as it builds on bodily communication and movements [18][19]. However, gestures-based interaction needs to be learned for sufficient precision [20]. A mutual adaption takes place: users have to adapt to the technology by learning to move in particular ways, and the algorithms adapt to the users' movements [21].

To be read by the camera so that the user's "skeleton" can be detected and movements identified with sufficient precision, the Kinect requires exaggerated gestures. Controlling oneself to perform the exaggerated movements may be difficult. To be able to move in a way that is recognized by the algorithms, the user benefitted from being able to "technomorphise"; that is, adapt to how the user believes that the machine will interpret his or her movements [19]. Although the gestures need to be learned, hands free control open for a larger space for possible human computer interactions.

The Kinect is used in many applications related to elderly and health care, in particular to encourage older adults to exercise [4][22][6]. A literature review from 2014 of Kinect applications in elderly care classify its use into fall detection, fall risk reduction, evaluation of Kinect's spatial accuracy, rehabilitation methods and exercise games [23]. The camera's accuracy is discussed by [22] who finds that the camera lacks precision in some situations, for example when a user is in wheelchairs, or when body parts are occluded. There is a perceptual asymmetry between the Kinect user and the computer, in terms of the resources available for both parties to interpret the interaction. The user perceives the whole space where the Kinect is situated, while the computer only "senses" the users' movements through a motion recognition camera. Only gestures that function as input is "seen" and identified by the algorithms [24].

III. METHODOLOGY AND METHOD

This study is a qualitative interpretive case study [25][26][27]. In two workshops, 22 elderly participants discussed their experiences with and views on digital technology. They were also invited to try gesturing to the Kinect camera in a simulated response to an incoming videoconference call. Interpretive research aims to understand what gives meaning for other people and takes as the starting point that our knowledge about other people's thoughts and experiences comes from social interactions. The methods for data gathering were interviews and participant observation in the two workshops.

Interviews: As a preparation for the workshops, two women in their seventies were interviewed about their experiences and use of digital technologies. The in-depth interviews lasted about one hour and a half, and took place in their homes in the fall of 2015. The women were recruited through a women's NGO for health and society. The interviews were recorded and transcribed. Topics from the analysis of the interviews were used in the guidelines for the discussion groups in the workshops. The two interviewees did not participate in the workshops.

The workshops consisted of a discussion group session where each participant was invited to try out the selected gestures to a Kinect camera. The workshops took place in the spring of 2016. They served a double purpose: discussing the participants' experiences with and thoughts of using digital technologies in their homes as well as trying out the prototype for gesture interaction with an incoming video conference call. The project wanted to test whether the selected gestures were easy to perform.

In the discussion group, the participants were engaged in talking about their views of using videoconferencing from the living room TV set in their homes. The videoconference prototype functioned in the discussion group as a "thing to think with" [28] in the way that it triggered the participants to express concrete viewpoints on videoconferencing technology. The author and other members of the project acted as facilitators in the discussion group, and two project members run the gesturing test. The author had planned and arranged the workshop, and took notes during the discussion. The participants did not want the discussion recorded.

The gesturing test was set up as a wizard-of-oz test simulating an incoming videoconference call. The sound of a telephone ringing could be heard, and the TV screen showed a large icon of a green vibrating telephone receiver. When the participant performed the selected gesture, the ringing stopped and a simulated videoconference session was set up. The participant was after some time encouraged to perform the same gesture to close the call.

The TV screen connected with the PC and Kinect camera was located in the same room at some distance from the discussion group. After trying the gestures in front of the Kinect camera, the participants were asked a few questions about which gestures they preferred. The Kinect session was video recorded and transcribed. The notes were transcribed afterwards. After both workshops, the facilitators discussed their notes. The analysis consisted of looking for recurrent issues in the transcription of the interviews, the notes from the discussion groups and the video recordings.

The first workshop took place in a municipality in the south east of the country, called South Mun in this paper. The six participants were recruited from a women's NGO for health and society in South Mun. They were all active in their community and of good health. They did not receive any municipal care services in their homes. We did not ask for their exact age; however, they volunteered information about being in their seventies.

The second workshop took place in a day care centre for elderly located in the north of Norway, here called North Mun. The sixteen participants lived in their own homes and received varying degrees of municipal care services. They were recruited through the day care centre. This group was on the average older than the first group, many were in their eighties and the oldest was 95 years old. All participants had some physical or cognitive issues. Some was very cognitively alert but had some physical challenges, while others suffered from some degree of dementia. This day our workshop was scheduled by the personnel as the (entertainment) event for the day.

All six participants in the first workshop tried the gestures, while nine out of sixteen in the second. The personnel at the care centre took an active role in facilitating the second workshop and encouraging the participants to try the gesturing. Since they knew their clients, they could talk in a loud voice to someone with reduced hearing or comment on their knowledge of the participants' life situation or technology experience, or in other ways act as interpreters between their clients and us, the outside guests.

IV. TRYING OUT GESTURES

The Kinect was programmed to recognize three specific arm movements for accepting an incoming videoconference call: a) hand waving like you say "hello", b) grabbing with the arm like picking up the telephone receiver, and c) merely moving the arm to an upwards and sideways position at one's right side. In the women's group at South Mun, all six participants tried the gestures, and nine out of fifteen participants in North Mun volunteered to try out the movements to be recognized by the Kinect.

Figure 1. The three gestures for answering a call:
a) hand up, b) grab "the receiver", c) waving hello.

All participants that tried out the gestures for interacting with the prototype received oral instruction before and during the test. The participants in North Mun needed more follow up instructions. In some cases, there were some technical problems, for example the Kinect camera did not recognize the body or hand of the participant in front and the participant had to wait a little while the test leader tinkered with the technology. When the Kinect did not recognize the test user's "skeleton" or she did not immediately succeed, she became insecure as to how the gesture should be performed. The test leader provided instructions and guided the movements in detail if necessary for the user to succeed. With detailed guidance, most participants succeeded in performing all three gestures with adequate response from the Kinect. In some occasions, they had to try more than once before the Kinect recognised the gesture. One woman did very well with the arm gestures, and it turned out that she had played Kinect games with her grandchild.

The participants preferred different gestures. In South Mun, they were asked to rank their preferences, and four out of six preferred the hand up gesture, see Figure 1 a). None preferred the "grab the receiver" gesture (Figure 1 b), while two preferred the hand waving (Figure 1 c). Table I shows their preferences in detail. P1-P6 represents the preferences of each participant, where Roman numeral i is considered the easiest gesture. Hand up was considered the easiest overall and received the lowest overall score.

TABLE I. PRIORITIES OF PARTICIPANTS TRYING THE GESTURES

	P1	P2	P3	P4	P5	P6	Score
Hand up	ii	i	ii	i	i	i	8
Grab	iii	ii	iii	ii	ii	ii	14
Wave	i	iii	i	iii	iii	iii	14

The Kinect recognition algorithm was only programmed for right-handed movements, and left handed gestures were not recognized. Of the nine elderly at the day care centre that tested the gestures, two preferred to use the left hand. One of them had a painful right handed shoulder, and he needed to be reminded of using his right hand several times during the test. He seemed to have some pain or discomfort from using the right hand.

One man reacted to the hand up gesture. He said that it resembled a "Heil Hitler" movement of the arm. The movement is not similar but the man obviously associated this gesture with the nazi greeting. He made this comment several times when he responded with the hand up gesture during the test.

The workshop at the day care centre was scheduled as the main program for the day we visited there. Participants that had finished their gestures testing, hang around the TV set and watched the others perform. As the day progressed, more of the participants gathered around in the TV set, and created an atmosphere with funny comments, laughter and sometimes bantering to the one trying out the gestures.

In some occasions, the user performed the movement successfully; however, a slight delay between the ringing sound and the gesture that can be seen on the videotape indicate that the participant does not move the arm as a response to the ringing sound, but according to the instructions by the test leader.

In both workshops, the participants observed the test leader tinkering with the technology. They observed him while setting up the PC, TV and Kinect before the test session. In some occasions, some tests could not be performed because the camera did not pick up their skeleton even after several attempts.

Most participants stated that that the gestures were easy. They preferred different movements, seemingly independently of the ease with which they succeeded in answering the simulated incoming conference call. To the question about what she found easiest, one woman responded "I think it is simple as it is, that we answer the phone the usual way".

V. EXPERIENCES AND VIEWPOINTS

One of the elderly women who was interviewed as a preparation for the workshops, accepted the interview request with the comment that she was "not so experienced with technology". However, during the interview, she described a lot of digital technologies that she used. She said that she used her tablet a lot, and talked about using e-mail, Facebook, online banking, and reporting the reading of the electricity meter online. She started using Facebook when her childhood friends who lived on another part of the country asked her to join so that they could keep in touch. She did not use Skype because she did not like the interface, but she used Facetime with her granddaughter who lived in another part of the country.

She had downloaded and installed an app for buying public transport tickets and found it very practical while moving about. She preferred one app for cloud storage of her family pictures instead of another, and explained that she preferred the one with less clicks to show the pictures. She upgrades the operating system and the apps herself, and when in doubt about what to do, she asked her children or grandchildren. She demonstrated that she was very familiar with the TV set and the remote controller, and she switched between sources to let me hear online radio stations through the TV set. However, she didn't like if her grandchildren rearranged the cable connections between the devices during a visit without putting it back together before they left. She felt unsure about how to put it back together.

All the women who participated in the discussion group in South Mun were retired and in their seventies. Some volunteered information about their earlier professional life: two had worked as a school teacher, one as a kindergarten teacher, and one had worked in a bank. They describe days with lots of activities. During the summer season, they often go to their summer houses or are active in other ways so they are not available for meetings between May and August. They stay in touch or take care of their grandchildren. They are active with organizational work in their NGO, where documents and minutes from meetings are emailed as pdf-files to the mostly retired female members. Most of them are physically active, although to different degrees. Except for the participant working in the bank, they had little or no practical experience from using computers in their previous working life.

As with the interviewee mentioned above, the participants use more technology than they explicitly say when first asked. They all use ICT in some ways, although it does not look like ICT to them. Most of them had smart phones. One described herself as "not clever" with technology. She "has cut out the PC", and uses her iPad and the iPhone. She uses online banking apps on both these devices, depending on whether she is at home or in the cabin, and reads online newspapers. She has used Facetime on her iPhone for contact with her grandchildren, but she did not use it so often. She finds that it does not give her so much even though she can see snippets of her grandchildren at the summer house or on fishing trips. On later consideration, she remembers a recent occasion where her son had lost his phone at a shopping mall, but could borrow an iPad and get in touch with her through facetime to her iPad when she did not answer her own telephone. On this occasion, she found Facetime very useful.

After returning to the discussion group after trying out gesturing, the participants gave some immediate feedback from their experience with the videoconference and the Kinect camera. Many express concerns that videoconferencing will come instead of and not in addition to the care personnel's physical contact with their clients. However, one woman commented that she could have benefitted from videoconferencing to stay in touch when she a few years ago broke one arm and leg at the same time and had to stay indoors for three months while recovering.

One expresses doubt as to how simple the technology will be in practical use. She compared it with the introduction of online banking, where many problems occurred and nobody was there to help. One woman had experience from playing gestures-based computer games (from a different technology) with her grandchildren, and she was slightly familiar with gesturing commands.

One woman responded to whether she will use the videoconference technology with the Kinect that she would not have used it. She "would go and pick up the phone. I need to move about, and not rot while sitting". Another said that this technology "is for those who are well versed and would like to keep in touch". One added that her late mother who suffered from dementia could not have used it, as "one will need a good head" to use it. Another said it was suitable for those who have "a good head and a lousy body", indicating that the interaction requires some understanding of the technology and that it is most useful for those who cannot move about easily. This they all agreed to.

Activities that are learned at an earlier stage in life can be kept up into old age and also into some degree of dementia [16]. On this basis, the participants were asked whether they would consider taking videoconferencing into use before they strictly needed it, so that its use could become an established habit before they get too old to learn. They all responded "no". Many of the participants who said that they would not want this technology at home, suggested that others might find it useful, for example if you are young and computer savvy but bedridden for some reason.

The participants at the day care centre in North Mun were in average older and less healthy and active. Some was cognitively challenged with various degrees of dementia, while others were cognitively clear but had various physical health issues that required care. They all received a minimum of municipal services, at a minimum they were accepted into regular meetings at this centre based on their application. The centre had a waiting list and accepts clients based on their needs. Some received care services in their homes as well.

Some of the participants there had previous experience from using computers in their working life, although they did not use digital technologies now. One woman said that she had had a mobile phone but that she did not use it anymore. She used a land line telephone at home. One woman had talked with her son in the US via Skype when visiting her daughter. Her daughter had set up the call.

After he had tried the gesturing, one man found the videoconferencing could be useful in his life situation. He asked if he could be called from a country abroad, because he has a grandchild there. Another man though it could be good for his son, who was "very intelligent" but bedridden.

In North Mun the winter weather can be quite cold and windy with lots of snow. When asked if they would consider videoconferencing as a means to keep in touch during periods with challenging weather in the winter months, one said with pride "We are northerners! We are used to ice and snow! As long as I can move about, I would prefer going down to [the café at the shopping centre] and meet the others there."

VI. Discussion

The dual objective of the workshops functioned well to stimulate the participants to tell us about their experiences with using digital technologies and their viewpoints on gesturing for videoconferencing which they tried out. The workshops were neither intended as a user study aimed at providing quantitative data about e.g. the time to respond to an incoming call nor a usability test where the user is asked to do several tasks with the equipment to be tested [29]. The prototype was too unfinished to appear as a product to be tested in a controlled environment.

This paper seeks to give a rich description of the elderly participants' experiences and viewpoints. However, as this study did not try out videoconferencing via other kinds of interfaces, we cannot differentiate between their viewpoints about this prototype for a gesturing interface and videoconferencing with more traditional interfaces.

The title of this paper is a quote from several brief interviews done immediately after the participants had tried the gesturing. Even though they found the gestures easy to perform with success, they did not want to use such technology at home. In addition to the TV screen, which is familiar to them and in regular use, the technology includes one unpopular device, the PC, and one mostly unfamiliar device, the Kinect camera. This result is in line with several studies about use of technology in the home.

As technology makes some old tasks obsolete, new tasks emerge – and the new tasks belong to a different domain than the old, familiar task. New tasks may increase the level of complexity around the user [30]. Setting up and maintaining home networks is a challenge for families [31]. The participants in both workshops could observe that the technology to be tried out needed some tinkering to function properly – if at all. They can anticipate problems with actual installation and maintenance of the Kinect camera and the accompanying PC in their homes, where many already have some unused technology [32][33][1].

Technology that is entered into the homes of people without their interest in that particular technology will often stay unused. Nansen et al. found that even though the older participants in their study both mastered the Kinect and found it fun to do, they preferred their usual activities to the Kinect: an old woman would rather watch tennis on TV, and her husband would rather stay outdoors working with the plants in his garden in daytime and doing his jigsaw puzzles when inside. There was no room for new activities with the Kinect in their habitual daily life [21].

Elderly people in the study of Culén did not consider technology to be a solution to their needs for social contact [8]. Loe argues that old women use or reject old and new technologies in their daily life according to how nicely it fits into their lives; whether the technology functions for continuity and control in their lives or the opposite [15]. Their considerations go "beyond usability" [14]: Without a personal objective for taking some technology into use, the experience will not necessarily be meaningful or useful. Elderly's understandings of usefulness "point to the relevance of perceptions and feelings of safety and self-efficacy" [14]. ICT introduced for personal growth is perceived differently than ICT for compensating for reduced capabilities. Loss of independence is feared by the elderly [14]. This finding is in line with the views of the participants who said they would prefer to maintain physical fitness by walking to the café or moving about to pick up the phone.

The Kinect experience when gaming is about having fun. The exaggerated movements that is required for the Kinect camera to recognise the gestures are easily laughed about, and laughing together is what makes it fun [19]. We saw that the participants in North Mun were laughing and bantering when they watched some of the others. Gestures, such as turning lights on or off in a smart house with exaggerated movements are not fun, and Harper and Mentis argue that the Kinect is not fit for controlling the lights or doors in for example a smart house (ibid.). A question is whether gesturing to a Kinect camera that will need to be always on will be a good way to interact with a videoconferencing service for elderly people who want to stay healthy. In line with [15], perhaps this technology will fit better into the lives of technology interested people with health issues that immobilises them and confine them to the home. The Kinect is a more familiar technology with younger people.

Design that builds on elderly's habits and competences will be in a better position to fit smoothly into their lives. Habits enable elderly people to continue life as they cherish it. Their habits will be a resource for continuing life as they know it into their really old days. Habits can be a resource for design [16]. To get in touch with elderly people's habits and activities, participatory design will be well suited with its focus on user participation and situated practices [34]. Early engagement of elderly participants in the design process helped to support their engagement in the design process [35]. Voicing their values is an important prerequisite for elderly people's participation in design [36]. The elderly participants' response after trying the gesturing created a challenge for the design team, who decided that the next design step would be to try out various button-based interfaces to the videoconferencing. Further research will show how the future elderly users will respond to such an interface.

VII. CONCLUSION

The elderly women in their seventies used more digital technologies than they explicitly state at first. They use smartphones and tablets, but avoid using a PC. They have some experience with Facetime, which they prefer over Skype. They do have some experience with Skype, which they mostly use when it is administered by children or grandchildren to keep in touch with family members.

All participants in the two groups expressed concern that they would prefer to meet people physically. They want to maintain physical fitness by moving about as long as possible, for example by walking to the café for meeting friends or moving outdoors even in wintery weather. Some found that if they were physically restrained from moving about, videoconferencing with a Kinect interface could be useful.

Most participants succeeded in performing the gestures, although with guidance to fine tune their movements. Even though they said the gestures were easy to perform in front of the Kinect and the TV screen, almost all the participants said that they are not interested in taking videoconference technology with Kinect interface in use in their homes. They found the gestures easy to do, but did not want the equipment at home. They considered the gestures for video-conferencing with Kinect as requiring "intelligence" or "a good head".

The elderly workshop participants' responses show that they take more than usability into account when they consider technology for use in their homes. The results of this study indicate that they consider their own competence to use and maintain the technology as well as how the technology will fit into their lives and support activities they cherish – to support their need for well-being and autonomy as they continuously adapt to growing older.

ACKNOWLEDGMENT

A big thank you goes to the participants of the interviews and workshops who willingly gave us their time and attention! I will also thank the colleagues in the BRIS project for developing the technology that were used in the workshops. The project is funded by the Regional Research Funds in Norway.

REFERENCES

[1] T. Greenhalgh et al., "What matters to older people with assisted living needs? A phenomenological analysis of the use and non-use of telehealth and telecare," *Soc Sci Med,* vol. 93, pp. 86-94, Sep 2013.

[2] R. Procter et al., "The Day-to-Day Co-Production of Ageing in Place," *Computer Supported Cooperative Work (CSCW),* vol. 23, pp. 245-267, 2014/06/01 2014.

[3] A. Danielsen, H. Olofsen, and B. A. Bremdal, "Increasing fall risk awareness using wearables: A fall risk awareness protocol," *Journal of Biomedical Informatics,* vol. 63, pp. 184-194, 10// 2016.

[4] S. Ganesan and L. Anthony, "Using the kinect to encourage older adults to exercise: a prototype," presented at the CHI '12 Extended Abstracts on Human Factors in Computing Systems, Austin, Texas, USA, 2012.

[5] A. Nawaz et al., "An Exergame Concept for Improving Balance in Elderly People," in *ICTs for Improving Patients Rehabilitation Research Techniques: Second International Workshop, REHAB 2014, Oldenburg, Germany, May 20-23, 2014, Revised Selected Papers,* H. M. Fardoun, V. M. R. Penichet, and D. M. Alghazzawi, Eds., ed Berlin, Heidelberg: Springer Berlin Heidelberg, 2015, pp. 55-67.

[6] F. Ofli et al., "Design and Evaluation of an Interactive Exercise Coaching System for Older Adults: Lessons Learned," *IEEE J Biomed Health Inform,* vol. 20, pp. 201-12, Jan 2016.

[7] L. Savolainen, E. Hanson, L. Magnusson, and T. Gustavsson, "An Internet-based videoconferencing system for supporting frail elderly people and their carers," *Journal of Telemedicine and Telecare,* vol. 14, pp. 79-82, 2008.

[8] A. L. Culén, "Later Life: Living Alone, Social Connectedness and ICT," in *Digital Human Modeling. Applications in Health, Safety, Ergonomics and Risk Management: Ergonomics and Health, 6th International Conference, DHM 2015,* Los Angeles, 2015, Springer International Publishing, pp. 401-412.

[9] S. G. Joshi and A. Woll, "A Collaborative Change Experiment: Post-experiment Evaluation of Home Telecare for Elderly Home Dwellers," *Procedia Manufacturing,* vol. 3, pp. 82-89, 2015/01/01 2015.

[10] C. M. Perissinotto, I. S. Cenzer, and K. E. Covinsky, "Loneliness in Older Persons: A predictor of functional decline and death," *Archives of internal medicine,* vol. 172, pp. 1078-1083, 2012.

[11] T. Bratteteig and G. Verne, "Old Habits as a Resource for Design: On Learning and Un-learning Bodily Knowledge," *International Journal On Advances in Intelligent Systems,* vol. 9, 2016.

[12] M. D. Myers. (Living version). *Qualitative Research in Information Systems.* Available: http://www.qual.auckland.ac.nz/

[13] A. White and J. Weatherall, "A Grounded Theory Analysis Of Older Adults And Information Technology," *Educational Gerontology,* vol. 26, pp. 371-386, 2000/06/01 2000.
[14] E. Hernández-Encuentra, M. Pousada, and B. Gómez-Zúñiga, "ICT and Older People: Beyond Usability," *Educational Gerontology,* vol. 35, pp. 226-245, 2009/02/04 2009.
[15] M. Loe, "Doing it my way: old women, technology and wellbeing," *Sociol Health Illn,* vol. 32, pp. 319-34, Feb 1 2010.
[16] T. Bratteteig and G. Verne, "From Difficult Artifacts to Easy to Use Designs," presented at the Ninth International Conference on Advances in Computer-Human Interactions (ACHI), Venice, Italy,, 2016.
[17] S. G. Joshi and A. Woll, "A Collaborative Change Experiment: Diagnostic Evaluation of Telecare for Elderly Home Dwellers," in *Digital Human Modeling. Applications in Health, Safety, Ergonomics and Risk Management: Ergonomics and Health: 6th International Conference, DHM 2015, Held as Part of HCI International 2015*, Los Angeles, 2015, Springer International Publishing, pp. 423-434.
[18] J. R. Parker, "Buttons, Simplicity, and Natural Interfaces," *Loading...* vol. 2, 2008.
[19] R. Harper and H. Mentis, "The mocking gaze: the social organization of kinect use," in *Proceedings of the 2013 conference on Computer supported cooperative work*, San Antonio, Texas, USA, 2013, ACM, pp. 167-180.
[20] D. A. Norman, "Natural user interfaces are not natural," *interactions,* vol. 17, pp. 6-10, 2010.
[21] B. Nansen et al., "Reciprocal Habituation: A Study of Older People and the Kinect," *ACM Trans. Comput.-Hum. Interact.,* vol. 21, pp. 1-20, 2014.
[22] S. Obdrzalek et al., "Accuracy and robustness of Kinect pose estimation in the context of coaching of elderly population," in *Engineering in Medicine and Biology Society (EMBC), 2012 Annual International Conference of the IEEE*, 2012, pp. 1188-1193.
[23] D. Webster and O. Celik, "Systematic review of Kinect applications in elderly care and stroke rehabilitation," *Journal of NeuroEngineering and Rehabilitation,* vol. 11, p. 108, 2014.
[24] L. Loke, A. T. Larssen, T. Robertson, and J. Edwards, "Understanding movement for interaction design: frameworks and approaches," *Personal and Ubiquitous Computing,* vol. 11, pp. 691-701, 2007.
[25] H. K. Klein and M. D. Myers, "A set of principles for conducting and evaluating interpretive field studies in information systems," *MIS Quarterly,* vol. 23, pp. 67-93, 1999.
[26] R. E. Stake, "Qualitative Case Studies," in *The Sage Handbook of Qualitative Research*. vol. 17, N. L. Denzin, Y., Ed., ed: Sage Publications, 2005, pp. s. 443-466.
[27] G. Walsham, "Doing interpretive research," *European Journal of Information Systems,* vol. 15, pp. 320–330, 2006.
[28] E. Brandt, "How Tangible Mock-Ups Support Design Collaboration," *Knowledge, Technology & Policy,* vol. 20, pp. 179-192, 2007.
[29] S. MacKenzie, "User studies and usability evaluations: from research to products," in *41st Graphics Interface Conference*, Halifax, Nova Scotia, Canada, 2015, Canadian Information Processing Society, pp. 1-8.
[30] G. Verne and T. Bratteteig, "Do-it-yourself services and work-like chores: on civic duties and digital public services," *Personal and Ubiquitous Computing,* vol. 20, pp. 517-532, 2016.
[31] R. Grinter, W. K. Edwards, M. W. Newman, and N. Ducheneaut, "The Work to Make a Home Network Work," in *ECSCW 2005: Proceedings of the Ninth European Conference on Computer-Supported Cooperative Work*, Paris, France, 2005, Springer.
[32] J. Halloran, E. Hornecker, M. Stringer, E. Harris, and G. Fitzpatrick, "The value of values: Resourcing co-design of ubiquitous computing," *CoDesign,* vol. 5, pp. 245-273, 2009/12/01 2009.
[33] E. Christiansen and P. K. Andersen, "Digital Living at Home - User Voices about Home Automation and a Home-Keeping Design Discourse," presented at the Nordic Contributions in IS Research, 2013.
[34] J. Simonsen and T. Robertson, Eds., *Routledge International Handbook of Participatory Design* (Routledge International Handbooks. Routledge, 2012.
[35] S. Lindsay, D. Jackson, G. Schofield, and P. Olivier, "Engaging older people using participatory design," in *Proceedings of the SIGCHI Conference on Human Factors in Computing Systems*, Austin, Texas, USA, 2012, ACM, pp. 1199-1208.
[36] T. W. Leong and T. Robertson, "Voicing values: laying foundations for ageing people to participate in design," in *Proceedings from the 14th Participatory Design Conference:*, Aarhus, Denmark, 2016, ACM, pp. 31-40.

The Hand Gesture Recognition System Using Depth Camera

Ahn,Yang-Keun
VR/AR Research Center
Korea Electronics Technology Institute
Seoul, Republic of Korea
e-mail: ykahn@keti.re.kr

Park,Young-Choong
VR/AR Research Center
Korea Electronics Technology Institute
Seoul, Republic of Korea
e-mail: ycpark@keti.re.kr

Abstract— **This study suggests a method for hand gesture recognition using a depth camera in a smart device environment. The hand gesture recognition can be made through the detection of fingers or the recognition of a hand. For the detection of fingers, the hand skeleton is detected through Distance Transform, and the finger detection is made by applying the Convex Hull algorithm. The hand recognition is done by comparing a newly recognized hand gesture with already learned data using the Support Vector Machine (SVM). For this, the hand's center, finger length, hand axis, axis of fingers, arm center, etc.. are reviewed. After recognition of a hand gesture, the corresponding letter is displayed. For the evaluation of the proposed method, an actual smart device system was implemented for experiments.**

Keywords-Hand Gesture; Gesture Recognition; Text Input System; Sign Language; Sign Language Recognition.

I. INTRODUCTION

Nowadays, with the growth of the mobile and smart TV industries and the development of smart devices, smart equipment and devices can commonly be found in diverse places. The growth potential of these markets has motivated some leading companies to compete for the acquisition of competitive smart device technologies, further expanding their use and availability. For example, Google has acquired Flutter, and Intel has purchased Omake Interactive, while Microsoft has developed Kinect jointly with Primesense.

Recently, a new product called Leap Motion has been developed, which addresses the growing demand for an efficient input method for smart devices. With the increasing use of smart devices, the amount of information displayed on a screen has steadily grown. Generally, current technologies use a remote controller or mobile devices for input. However, these methods are not convenient, in that users have to carry such devices all the time. To resolve such inconvenience, new input methods based on the use of hand gestures, like the one developed by Leap Motion, have begun drawing significant attention.

The hand recognition methods that have been proposed to input text on a screen include: recognition based on the learning of hand gestures using a neural network [1]; recognition by extracting a finger candidate group after removing the palm area [2]; teaching by extracting the characteristics of a hand using Support Vector Machines (SVM) [3]; recognition of the fingers by opening a hand [4]; depth-based hand gesture recognition [5][6][7][8]. In the case of the neural network, recognition is possible on the condition that a hand moves from a fixed position, a limitation which causes many constraints in consumer use. Furthermore, this method only allows a limited number of inputs, and therefore is not suitable for text input. The method of removing the palm area allows free movement, but it is difficult to distinguish separate fingers when they are put together. The method of recognizing the fingers after opening a hand is a good algorithm for hand recognition, but the number of hand gesture patterns is limited. Finally, the method of teaching the characteristics of a hand using SVM is considered an efficient approach, but it also has a shortcoming in terms of the number of hand gesture patterns that can be recognized.

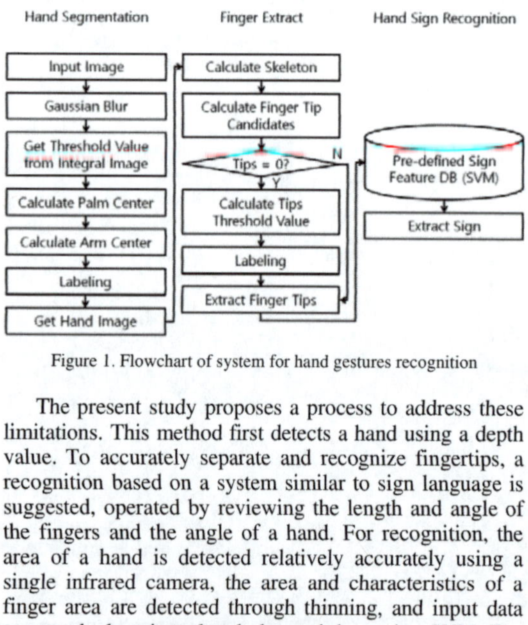

Figure 1. Flowchart of system for hand gestures recognition

The present study proposes a process to address these limitations. This method first detects a hand using a depth value. To accurately separate and recognize fingertips, a recognition based on a system similar to sign language is suggested, operated by reviewing the length and angle of the fingers and the angle of a hand. For recognition, the area of a hand is detected relatively accurately using a single infrared camera, the area and characteristics of a finger area are detected through thinning, and input data are matched against already learned data using SVM. The number of hand gesture patterns used in this study is about 30.

This study suggests a system which consists of the following three parts: of Hand Segmentation, Finger

Extract and Sign Recognition. Figure 1 shows the flowchart of the process adopted for the system.

II. Hand Detection

When a depth image is input, a smoothing operation is performed to remove noise. The Gaussian kernel is known as an effective smoothing method for noise elimination. Then, objects are separated using the binarization technique. Infrared lighting is applied while using an infrared camera, and the distance between objects is expressed in different brightnesses, making binarization possible. Subsequently, an integral image is produced to calculate a threshold value (T). As shown in (1), using the integral image, the average depth value is calculated, which amounts to a window of size w. Here, the value of w is 20.

$$S(x,y)=\frac{\begin{array}{c}G(x+w,y+w)-G(x+w,y-w)-\\G(x-w,y+w)+G(x-w,y-w)\end{array}}{(2w+1)^2}\quad (1)$$

In (1), $G(x,y)$ means an integral image, and $S(x,y)$ signifies an average of depth values located within the w area on the basis of an (x,y) coordinate. T is a value obtained by adding 50 to the minimum value of $S(x,y)$.

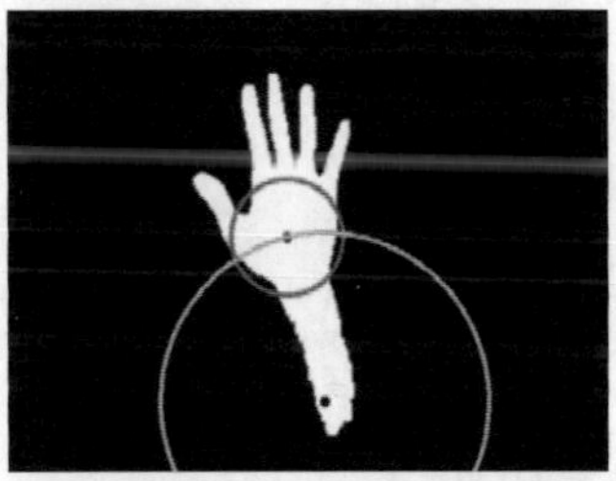

Figure 2. Hand center, arm center, and distances

Figure 3. Detection of hand area

After extracting a candidate group for the hand, the arm part is eliminated to display the hand part more accurately. For the removal of the arm part, the palm center ($P(x,y)$) and palm area (L) are calculated using Distance Transform ($D(x,y)$). The arm center ($A(x,y)$) is calculated to be an average of the areas with a depth image value between T and T+50. Based on the above, the Euclidean distance ($Eu(P(x,y),A(x,y))$) of $A(x,y)$ and $P(x,y)$ is calculated. On the basis of $A(x,y)$, the depth values within Eu are calculated as the arm part. The palm part is what is within L on the basis of $P(x,y)$. Figure 2 shows the arm center and removed area as well as the palm center and palm area. Figure 3 shows the resulting hand detection image.

III. Finger Detection and Hand Gesture Recognition

The system proposed by this study uses two different methods for finger detection: thinning and application of a minimum depth value.

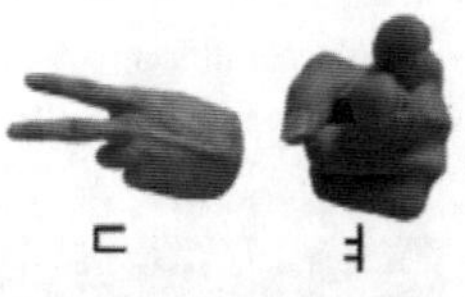

Figure 4. Two cases of finger detection(Left: ㄷ, Right: ㅕ)

These two methods are used together because, as shown in Figure 4, it is not possible to detect all of the fingers of hand gestures of the sign language using only one method. For example, referring to [ㄷ] in Figure 4, finger detection can be done through thinning only. In contrast, in the case of [ㅕ], finger detection can be made by using a minimum depth value, but not through thinning.

A. Finger Detection Using Thinning

To detect fingers, the hand skeleton needs to be identified first. Compared with the hand contour method applied previously, the method of detecting the hand skeleton offers some advantages. For example, the fingertips can be identified more accurately, and the fingers can also be detected more easily. To calculate the hand skeleton, as shown in Figure 5, an image of the hand part is gained using Distance Transform.

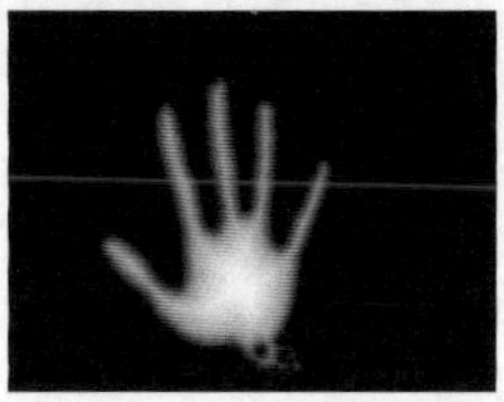

Figure 5. Result of Distance Transform using Histogram Equalization

After applying Distance Transform, the hand skeleton ($Sk(x,y)$) is detected. (2) shows the algorithm for skeleton detection.

$$Sk_1(x,y) = \begin{cases} if, D(x,y) \geq L/10 & 1 \\ else, & 0 \end{cases}$$
$$c = 0, if\{D(x,y) < D(x+dx, y+dy)\}, c = c+1$$
$$Sk_2(x,y) = \begin{cases} if, c \leq 2 & 1 \\ else, & 0 \end{cases} \quad . \quad (2)$$
$$Sk(x,y) = \begin{cases} if, Sk_1(x,y) = 1 \,\&\, Sk_2(x,y) = 1 & 1 \\ else, & 0 \end{cases}$$

In (2), dx and dy signify a 3 x 3 mask and have values between –1 and 1. c is a variable for counting cases where an adjacent pixel value ($D(x+dx, y+dy)$) is larger than a current pixel value ($D(x, y)$). If the value of c is 3 or greater, that case is ignored since it does not form a line. $Sk(x, y)$ is recognized as a pixel (i.e., skeleton) when both conditions of Sk_1 and Sk_2 are satisfied. Figure 6 shows the result of hand skeleton detection and the palm part.

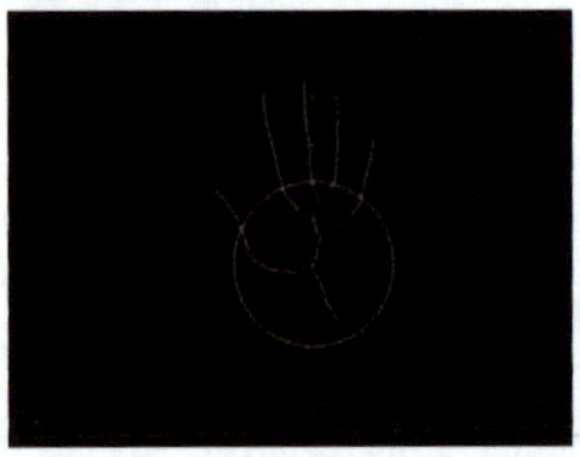

Figure 6. Display of hand skeleton and palm area

When the hand skeleton is detected, the fingertips are identified for the detection of fingers. For this, the Convex Hull(C) algorithm is applied, which is shown in (3).

$$C \equiv \{\sum_{j=1}^{N} \lambda_j p_j : \lambda_j \geq 0 \text{ for } all\ j \,\&\, \sum_{j=1}^{N} \lambda_j = 1\} \ . \quad (3)$$

In (3), $p_1, \ldots, p_N$ means the locations of $Sk(x, y)$, and N is the number of the pixels of $Sk(x, y)$. Figure 7 shows a candidate group of fingertips when the Convex Hull(C) algorithm is applied.

When the Convex Hull(C) algorithm is applied, some areas which are not the fingertips are recognized as if they are fingertips. To resolve this, such areas are removed if they are found to belong to the palm part identified before. Figure 8 shows the fingertip parts after eliminating the irrelevant areas.

When the fingertips have been detected, to detect the fingers reverse tracking is started from the fingertips to the palm. The reverse tracking is done using a recursive function from the detected fingertips to the palm until no skeleton is found.

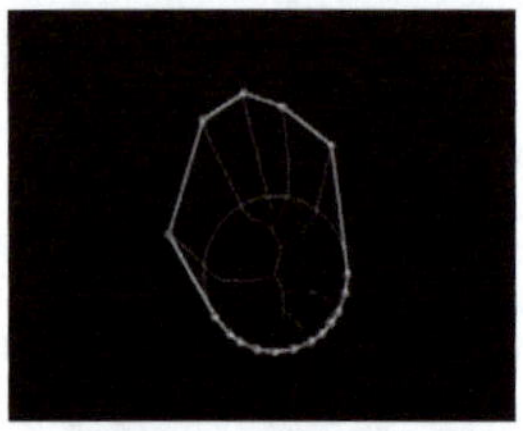

Figure 7. Application of Convex Hull

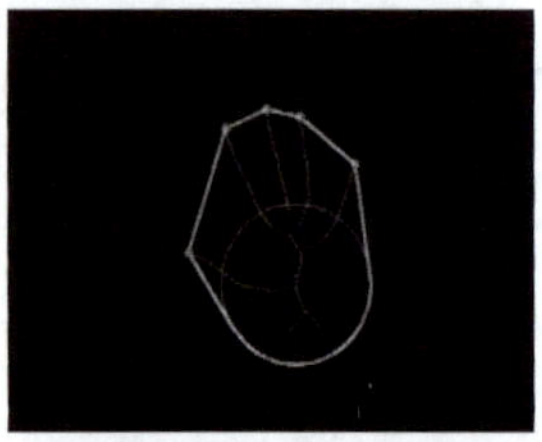

Figure 8. Detection of fingertips

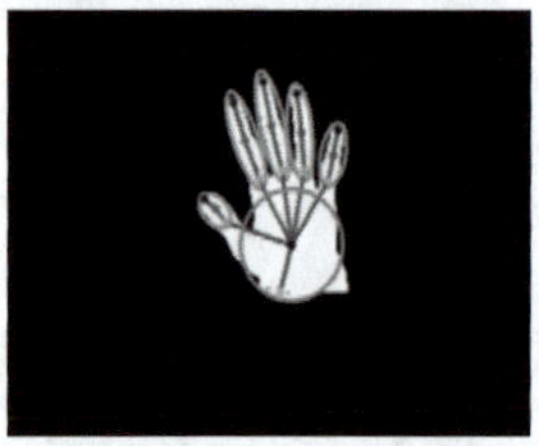

Figure 9. Detection of hand characteristics

The point which is closest to the skeleton around the middle part of a finger is recognized as the middle phalanx of a finger. Figure 9 shows the result of finger detection and the characteristics of a hand.

B. *Finger Detection using Minimum Value*

It is assumed that the thinning-based finger detection fails if there is no recognized hand shape using the thinning technique. If the finger detection through thinning fails, an attempt is made to detect fingers based on the minimum value (i.e., the closest distance to the camera) of a depth image.

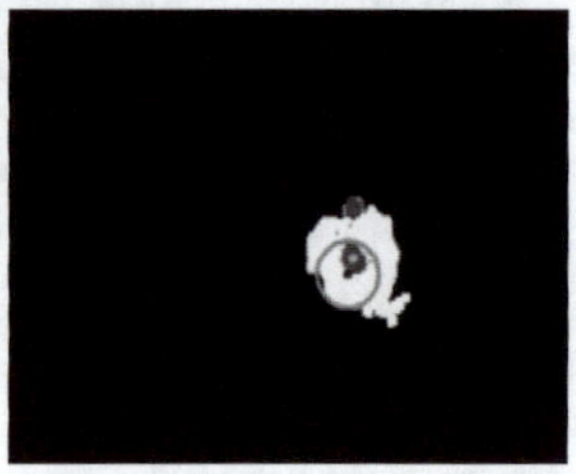

Figure 10. Finger detection using minimum value(ㅓ)

For this, first, a minimum depth value (Dm) should be gained. The threshold value (Tm) for finger detection is obtained by adding 55 to the Dm value. The reason for adding 55 is based on experimental experiences. Now, the binarization is complete, and a candidate area of fingertips is detected through labeling. If this area has a size of 1/2 or more of the palm part, that area is ignored. Figure 10 shows the result of this process.

C. Hand Gesture Recognition

Basically, the recognition of hand gestures is done using the SVM. Based on data already learned, a newly input hand gesture can be recognized. For recognition, the necessary input data are entered according to the detection method. For finger detection through thinning, the hand center, palm size, axes of arm and palm, finger length, and axis of fingers should be offered. In the case of finger detection using a minimum value, the number of fingertips, area size and ratio of width to height of the area needs to be given. For fast learning, the linear SVM was adopted. However, as some errors were found, some factor values were changed, creating a more efficient SVM detector.

IV. System Configuration

To evaluate the text input performance of the system proposed by this study, which is based on the recognition of hand gestures, an actual text input system SignKII was implemented.

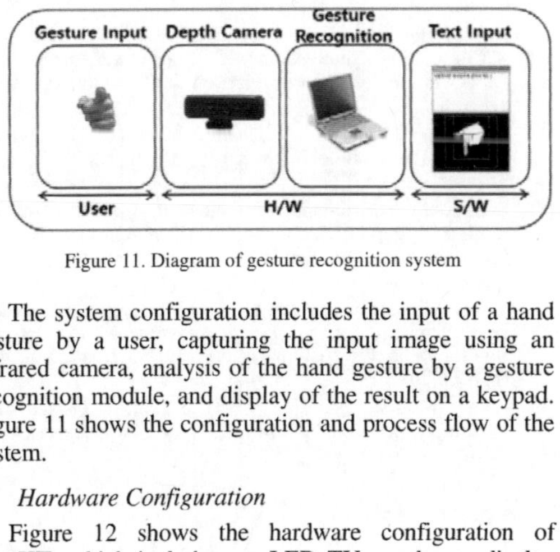

Figure 11. Diagram of gesture recognition system

The system configuration includes the input of a hand gesture by a user, capturing the input image using an infrared camera, analysis of the hand gesture by a gesture recognition module, and display of the result on a keypad. Figure 11 shows the configuration and process flow of the system.

A. Hardware Configuration

Figure 12 shows the hardware configuration of SignKII, which includes: an LED TV, used as a display device, positioned at eye level; an infrared camera for image input, located under the LED TV; and a desktop PC, used as a gesture analysis module, connected to the camera through a USB interface as well as to the LED TV through the output module and HDMI.

B. Software Configuration

Figure 13 shows the software configuration of the SignKII system, which includes: a main screen for the display of the input image (upper middle); binarization screen for the display of binarization results and a detection screen for the display of finger detection and characteristics (right upper); keyboard input results (left); and input examples (lower middle, right lower). The system performance has been improved by presuming empirical parameters using SignKII software. A threshold value of 10% of the value obtained when the user took the gesture of the designated character is designated as the parameter threshold value.

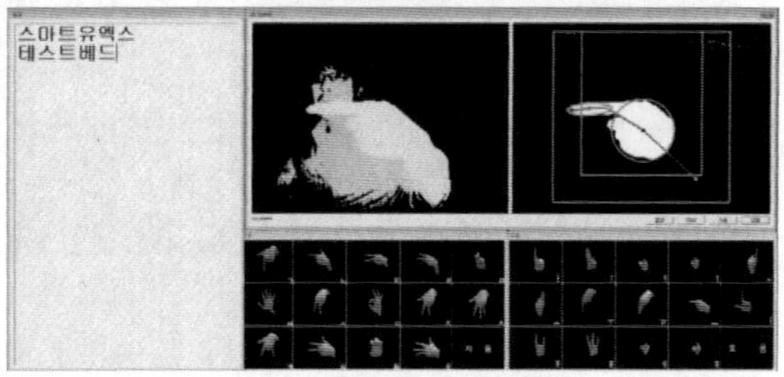

Figure 12. Gesture recognition system GUI

C. Input Configuration

Figure 14 shows the hand gestures for the input of consonants.

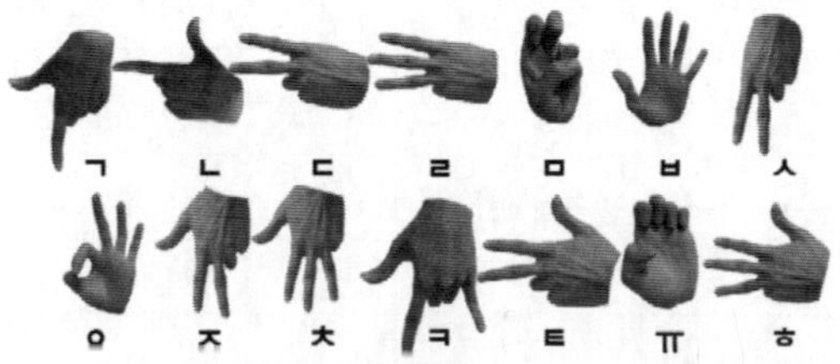

Figure 13. Examples of SignKII consonant input

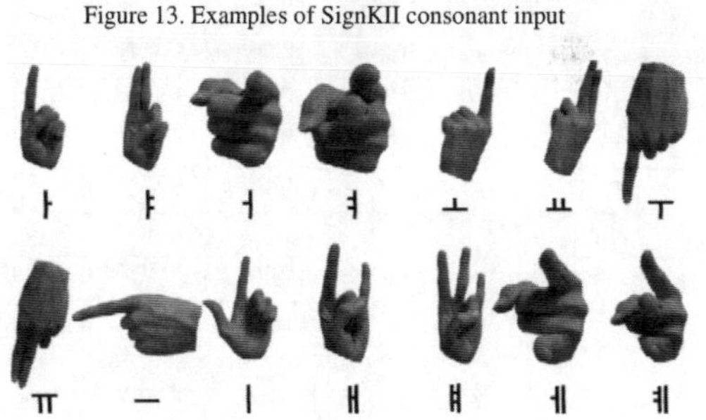

Figure 14. Examples of SignKII vowel input

Figure 15 shows the hand gestures for the input of vowels as applied in the SignKII system.

V. Experiment Results

In this paper, we experimented hand gesture recognition rates independently, because there were no korean input system that we could compare our system before. The development environment is as follows: Window7 OS, Visual Studio 2010, and MFC. The hardware configuration includes: DS325 infrared lighting camera of SoftKinetic, HDMI interface display, desktop PC Intel i7-2600k CPU and 3.48GB. As for the S/W performance, the distance range from a camera is from 11cm to 30cm, and the optimal distance for gesture recognition is 20cm±5cm. Figure 16 shows the signKII system.

Figure 15. SignKII system

TABLE I. CHANGE OF RECOGNITION RATES ACCORDING TO HAND GESTURE AND ANGLE

Gesture	-10	-5	0	5°	10
ㄱ	100%	100%	100%	0%	0%
ㄴ	100%	100%	100%	0%	0%
ㄷ	0%	100%	100%	100%	0%
ㄹ	0%	100%	100%	0%	0%
ㅁ	100%	100%	100%	0%	0%
ㅂ	100%	100%	100%	100%	100%
ㅅ	0%	100%	100%	100%	0%
ㅇ	50%	100%	100%	50%	0%
ㅈ	100%	100%	100%	100%	100%
ㅊ	100%	100%	100%	100%	0%
ㅋ	100%	100%	100%	100%	100%
ㅌ	0%	100%	100%	100%	100%
ㅍ	100%	100%	100%	100%	100%
ㅎ	0%	100%	100%	100%	100%
ㅏ	100%	100%	100%	0%	0%
ㅑ	100%	100%	100%	0%	0%
ㅓ	100%	100%	100%	100%	100%
ㅕ	100%	100%	100%	100%	100%
ㅗ	0%	0%	100%	100%	100%
ㅛ	0%	0%	100%	100%	100%
ㅜ	0%	0%	100%	100%	100%
ㅠ	0%	0%	100%	100%	100%
ㅡ	0%	100%	100%	100%	100%
ㅣ	100%	100%	100%	100%	100%
ㅐ	100%	100%	100%	100%	100%
ㅒ	0%	100%	100%	100%	100%
ㅔ	100%	100%	100%	100%	100%
ㅖ	100%	100%	100%	100%	100%

Experiments were conducted in such a way that one user performed each gesture 100 times. Considering that hand gesture recognition is sensitive to the rotation of a hand (with the rotation of a hand, a totally different recognition result can be shown), experiments were performed mainly in connection with rotation. For example, the difference between 'ㄱ'and 'ㄴ'can be recognized due to hand rotation despite the same hand gesture. Table 1 shows the recognition results.

VI. CONCLUSION

This study proposed an algorithm for improved hand gesture recognition based on previous studies. Based on experiments, the SignKII system was implemented. The results of the experiments demonstrated that recognition rates were very high even though the performance was affected at some hand angles. Future research will focus on more efficient and easier recognition based on hand motions as well as hand gestures.

REFERENCES

[1] C. Nolker and H. Ritter, "Visual Recognition of Continuous Hand Postures," IEEE Transactions on Neural Networks Neural Networks, vol. 13, pp. 983-994, Jul. 2002.

[2] Y. Fang, K. Wang, J. Chen, and H. Lu, "A Real-time Hand Gesture Recognition Method," Multimedia and Expo, 2007 IEEE International Conference on, Jul. 2007.

[3] P. Suryanarayan, A. Subramanian, and D. Mandalapu, "Dynamic Hand Pose Recognition using Depth Data," Pattern Recognition (ICPR), 2010 20th International Conference on, Aug. 2010.

[4] Z. Ren, J. Yuan, and Z. Zhang, "Robust Hand Gesture Recognition Based on Finger-Earth Mover's Distance with a Commodity Depth Camera," Proceedings of the 19th ACM international conference on Multimedia, pp. 1093-1096, Nov. 2011.

[5] C. Wang, Z. Liu, S. C. Chan, "Superpixel-Based Hand Gesture Recognition With Kinect Depth Camera," IEEE Transactions on Multimedia, vol. 17, pp.23-39, 2015.

[6] S. Jadooki, D. Mohamad, T. Saba, et al., "Fused features mining for depth-based hand gesture recognition to classify blind human communication," Neural Computing and Applications, 2016.

[7] W. L. Chen, C. H. Wu, C. H. Lin, "Depth-based hand gesture recognition using hand movements and defects," International Symposium on Next-Generation Electronics (ISNE), 2015.

[8] C. H. Wu, W. L. Chen, C. H. Li, "Depth-based hand gesture recognition," Multimedia Tools and Applications, 2016.

FPGA-based Power Efficient Interactive Augmented Reality Learning Applications for Children

Abdul-Rahman Algharbi, Farida Hamid
School of Communication and Electronics
October University for Modern Sciences and Arts
Giza, Egypt
e-mail: aralgharbi@gmail.com
e-mail: faridaaddala@gmail.com

Noha Younis
National Center for Radiation Research and Technology, Atomic Energy Authority
Cairo, Egypt
e-mail: nyounis@msa.eun.eg

Abstract— **Most human-computer interaction systems, specifically, Augmented Reality, are designed based on general purpose processors. Consequently, their power consumption is considerably high, as systems work at Gigahertz rates. In this paper, power efficient interactive augmented reality learning applications for children are designed and implemented. Interaction is performed by hand gestures and markers. The power consumption of the proposed system is reduced by developing and implementing the recognition and tracking processes on a Field Programmable Gate Array platform to exploit its parallelism feature. This enables the system to work, portably, at lower operating frequencies, without violating the required real-time performance. The most suitable five hand gestures for 3 to 10-year-olds were determined, then the implemented system was tested by 100 children. Implementation results revealed that only 25 MHz are sufficient for the applications to run in real-time at 30 fps, with a recognition rate of 93.2% on average. This significantly reduces the overall power consumption of the proposed system, comparing with other systems.**

Keywords; Augmented Reality (AR); hand gestures; AR markers; FPGA; Human Computer Interaction (HCI)

I. INTRODUCTION

Augmented Reality (AR) is a direct or indirect combination between real and virtual worlds in real-time, by using computer generated graphics, sounds, or videos. AR is used for various applications, such as medicine, entertainment, and marketing as a kind of Human Computer Interaction (HCI). Augmented reality is also used in educational fields, as it can improve the pedagogical methodology by enhancing children's concentration [1]- [5]. However, such systems do not offer a direct virtual interaction between the students' body and the virtual object, which is necessary to keep them attracted and to enrich their imagination. Most interactive AR systems use markers that are represented by either barcode [6], or certain objects, attached to data gloves [7]. Interaction can, also, be achieved by means of bare hand gestures [8][9], or by hand gestures together with markers [10] [11]. The main challenge in such interactive AR systems is detecting, recognizing and tracking markers and/or gestures in real-time, with high accuracy. Object detection is developed, in some systems, using hardware devices such as gloves, supported with sensors, to digitize the detected hand-gesture/marker [7] [12] [13]. Though such systems are robust and provide high recognition rates, their power consumption is high. Also, gloves are not user friendly as they limit the user's movement. This is in addition to the inflexible size of gloves that cannot fit all human hands' sizes, specifically, children's. Other systems use depth cameras, such as Kinect, which provides HCI systems with the hand skeleton and depth such that the remaining detecting steps become easier [14] [15]. However, it is expensive and power consuming, and is only compatible with Windows operating systems. Moreover, there is another part of the power, consumed by the software program that is developed to execute the remaining recognition and tracking operations. Such power consumption is considerably high as the program is executed at gigahertz rates to achieve a real-time performance. In [10], a mobile AR system was proposed for teaching and learning, using a low power low processing device, to control simple hand gestures that in turn control presentation slides. Another effective method to reduce the power consumption is implementing the high computationally complicated functions on a Field Programable Gate Array (FPGA) platform, where a wearable backpacked computer and tracking gloves are used [16]. However, the system does not provide a high recognition rate, since it is built in Handel-C that was later converted to a Hardware Descriptive Language. Also, the user should wear gloves and a heavy computer while using it, which isn't suitable for children. Another FPGA-based hand gesture HCI is proposed in [17], where an Artificial Neural Network (ANN) was implemented on FPGA to recognize hand gestures. Again, a data glove was used to detect the proposed gestures.

To reduce the power consumption, an FPGA-based interactive AR system is proposed, where the high computationally complicated hand-gesture/marker detection, recognition, and tracking processes are designed and implemented on an FPGA. The power consumption is, then, reduced by operating the implemented system at lower frequencies. This is achieved by gaining the benefit of the parallelism feature from the FPGA to execute more than one function in parallel, in a way that the required real-time performance is not affected. As a result, the proposed low power consuming design can be used portably anywhere that suits children, especially in Kindergarten and primary levels.

The implemented applications have been applied on normal and autistic children to find how far it improves their concentration.

The remainder of the paper is organized as follows: Section II demonstrates an overview of the proposed hand-gesture/marker AR system. The software and hardware architectures are explained in Sections III, and IV, respectively. In Section V, the Hardware-Software interface is described, whereas the practical implementation results are discussed in Section VI. Finally, the conclusion and future work are presented in Section VII.

II. SYSTEM OVERVIEW

The proposed system supports four different learning applications for children, as shown in Figure 1. The first and second applications use hand gestures to control and interact with virtual objects, displayed on the Personal Computer (PC) monitor. The third and fourth applications use markers, instead. In the first application -called "Animal Homeland"- the child grabs a virtual animal using his/her hand and places it on its home land. In the second application -called "Planting"- the child learns about the planting phases by planting virtually, using hand gestures. In the third application -called "Machinery"- the child uses different mono-color markers to assemble machinery objects, such as an airplane. The fourth application, "Atom System", helps children to realize the main particles of the atom (i.e., protons, neutrons and electrons). In this application, children move multi-colored markers that represent the atom particles, to virtually display their rotations around the atom.

To minimize the computational complexity, caused by recognizing and classifying different objects of various applications, the system was designed such that the user selects an application, first. This is done by means of the Graphical User Interface (GUI), depicted in Figure 1, which has been developed using Unity, the game engine [18]. Then, the application number is sent from the PC to the FPGA, where classification and tracking are done for only the gestures/markers of the selected application. Figure 2 illustrates the system setup, where the system input is the successive frames, captured by a CMOS webcam, which is connected to the PC. The scene includes a white background, on top of which, a hand gesture/marker moves. 'A' and 'B' represent the areas of the detected object at zero and maximum heights, respectively, which are used to get the object depth, as explained later. The output of the FPGA, which represents the recognized gesture/marker and its 3D position, is sent to the PC. Then, the monitor displays the gesture/marker, after mixing it with a virtual object that is determined, based on the received data from the FPGA. Figure 3 shows the block diagram of the proposed system that consists of Software (SW) and FPGA – based architectures. Both architectures are discussed in the following sections.

I. SOFTWARE-BASED ARCHITECTURE

Captured frames are automatically stored in the PC RAM, since the camera is, directly, connected to the PC to display the user's hand on its monitor, while interacting with virtual objects. Consequently, to minimize the size of the FPGA utilized RAMs, it is more efficient to carry out the first step of detection, which is color segmentation, in the PC. For hand-gesture-based applications, a skin color filter is applied, that range is selected using MATLAB. For Marker-based applications, a color filter is applied instead, based on the colors of the markers. Afterwards, a binary conversion of the segmented frame is executed. Both color segmentation and binary conversion are developed using Unity. Figures 4 and 5 show the skin color segmentation of the applied five hand gestures and the markers, respectively. The five gestures were selected after visiting several schools; the children were given small figures, to hold by hand, then they were asked to perform several gestures. Accordingly, the most feasible five

Figure 1. GUI of the proposed multi-application interactive AR system.

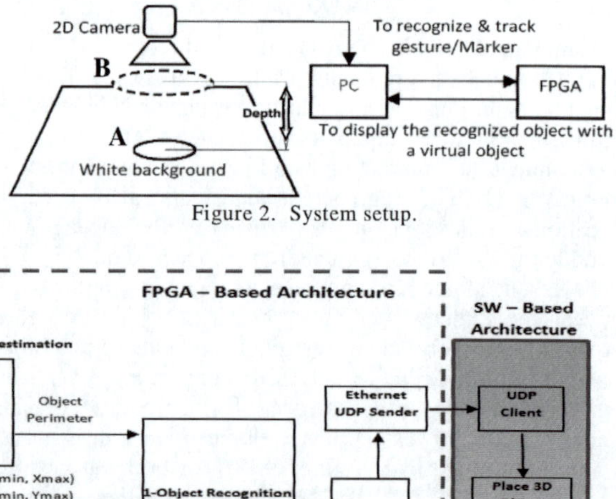

Figure 2. System setup.

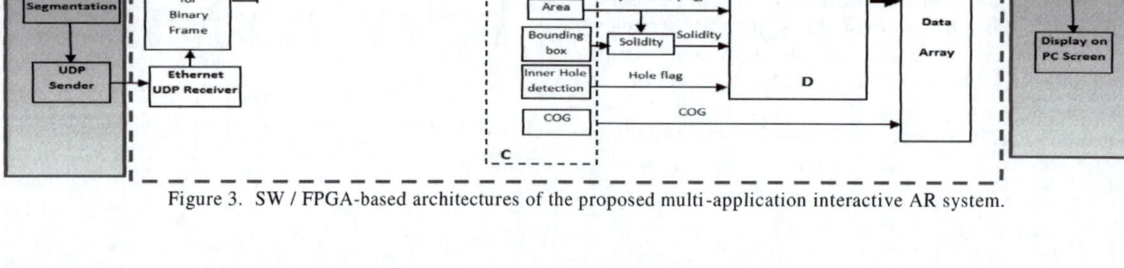

Figure 3. SW / FPGA-based architectures of the proposed multi-application interactive AR system.

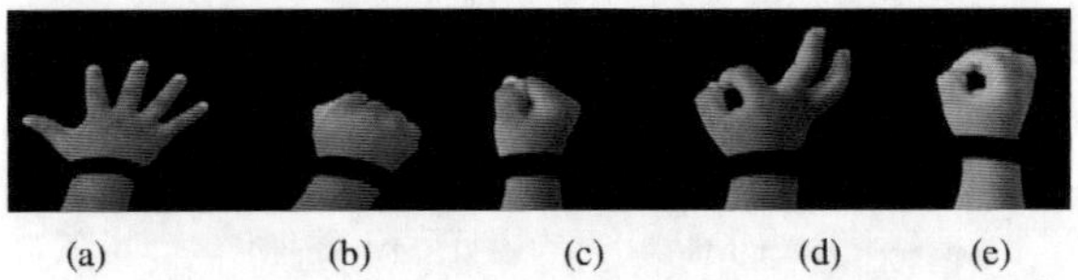

(a) (b) (c) (d) (e)

Figure 4. Skin color segmentation of gestures, used in the 1st and 2nd applications: a) Open hand, b) Horizontal fist, c) Vertical fist, d) Three fingers, e) With hole.

(a) (b)

Figure 5. Color segmentation of the AR Markers, used in (a) 3rd application, and (b) 4th application.

gestures -shown in Figure 4- for 3-to-10-year-olds were determined. The gestures, shown in Figure 4 are performed without any rotation or twisting during interaction. To isolate the detected hand from the rest of the arm, a green ribbon is worn on the child's wrist, if he/she is not wearing long sleeves. The binary frame is, then, sent to the FPGA for recognizing and tracking. N×M represents the camera resolution. For marker-based applications, the colors of the markers are also sent to the FPGA to ease classification, as children may use markers of other applications that have appropriate features as those used in the selected application.

II. FPGA-BASED ARCHITECTURE

Since the application is first selected, a limited number of hand gestures or markers should be recognized. Hence, shape-based features are selected for classification, to reduce the computational complexity. The extracted features are the object perimeter, area, bounding box, solidity, Center of Gravity (CoG), and the object depth.

A. Object perimeter extraction

The received binary frame is stored in an N×M RAM, implemented in the FPGA. The perimeters of all segments in the frame are, first, extracted by dilating each shape in the original binary frame with the structuring element, shown in Block A of Figure 3. The dilated frame is then XORed with the original binary frame, to give a new N×M array that includes only perimeters [19]. Then, the structuring element, shown in block B of Figure 3, is used to go through all shapes in the frame, and the number of binary-one-pixels for each connected segment is accumulated, to get the perimeter length. The largest estimated perimeter represents the marker/gesture perimeter. Other segments are considered noise, and therefore deleted, except the ones enclosed inside the object perimeter, as they are used to detect the inner hole of the gesture, if any, as explained later. Also, the minimum and maximum X and Y coordinates of the object perimeter -(X_{min}, X_{max}) (Y_{min}, Y_{max})- are saved to extract other features.

B. Parellel extraction of featurs

To gain the benefit of the parallelism feature from the FPGA, the calculation of the area, bounding box, CoG, as well as the inner hole detection of the gestures, shown in Figure 4 (d) and (e), are processed in parallel. This reduces the power consumption and processing time, considerably.

To increase the recognition rate of the gestures of Figure 4 (d) and (e), their inner hole is detected after extracting the object perimeter. This is done by comparing the perimeter of shapes that are bordered by (X_{min}, X_{max}) and (Y_{min}, Y_{max}). The segment represents an inner hole of the gesture if the ratio between the perimeters of the candidate hole and the object is greater than 0.01%. Otherwise, it is considered noise. Figure 6 shows the inner hole, enclosed inside the hand gesture of Figure 4 (d).

The Object area is calculated by (1), where max x_y and min x_y represent the maximum and minimum X coordinates, respectively, which exist on the object edge at a specific y.

In parallel, the coordinates of the CoG, (X_C, Y_C), are calculated by (2) [20]. Also, the width, *W*, and length, *L*, of the bounding box are calculated using (3) and (4), respectively.

Another feature, to be extracted, is the solidity. It is used since it is not affected by the distance between the object and the camera, as it represents the ratio between the object area and the convex area. In the implemented system, the *bounding box* is used instead of the convex area to reduce the computational complexity. The solidity, S, is then estimated by (5).

$$A_d = \sum_{y=Y\min}^{Y\max} (\max x_y - \min x_y) \quad (1)$$

$$X_C = \frac{X_{max}-X_{min}}{2}, Y_C = \frac{Y_{max}-Y_{min}}{2} \quad (2)$$

$$W = X_{max} - X_{min} \quad (3)$$

$$L = Y_{max} - Y_{min} \quad (4)$$

$$S = \frac{A_d}{(WxL)} \quad (5)$$

C. Object recognition and 3D pose localizations

The perimeter, area, and solidity of the five gestures were pre-calculated for 140 different hands to define the upper and lower limits of their thresholds. In Figure 7, the five gestures from "Open" to "With hole" represent the five gestures of Figure 4, from Figure 4(a) to Figure 4(e). Figure 7 shows that the (open) and (3 Fingers), gestures can be recognized based on any of the three features, whereas the (Vertical) gesture can be recognized based on the area and the perimeter features. Though the (With hole) and (Horizontal) gestures are overlapped in all features, the inner hole detection is used to distinguish them. Similarly, for marker recognition, the colors and the normalized values of the area and solidity of all utilized markers were calculated, and listed in Table I.

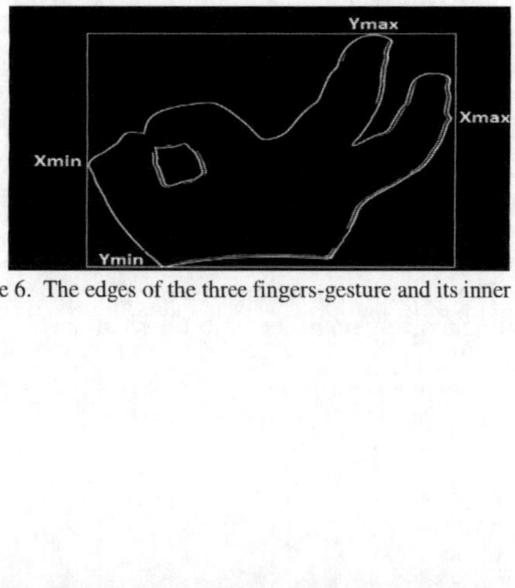

Figure 6. The edges of the three fingers-gesture and its inner hole.

For 3D pose localization, more than a single 2D cameras, or depth sensors are usually used [14] [15]. This is mandatory if the utilized gestures/markers rotate or twist during interaction. In the proposed system, neither rotation nor twist is required. Thus, the object depth can be calculated using only one 2D camera, based on the change of the object area at different heights, with respect to the camera, as shown in Figure 2. For any different user, both A and B areas shown in Figure 2, are calibrated once, for all gestures, such that after object recognition they are used to estimate its depth, Z, by applying (6). A is the biggest possible hand area in pixels, whereas B is the smallest possible hand area in pixels. H, represents the height at which the camera is fixed, with respect to the background, and 'Δ' is the difference between the areas A and B that is independent of A_d. However, 'Δ' varies if the distance between the camera and the background is changed.

$$Z = (A_d - A) * H/\Delta \tag{6}$$

III. HARDWARE - SOFTWARE INTERFACE

To interface the FPGA with the PC, Ethernet and User Datagram Protocol (UDP) are used. UDP is selected because the it transfers data directly without dividing them into chunks, and it does not depend on a certain Operating System (OS). The N×M binary frame is sent to the FPGA via Ethernet, followed by an m-bit data that represent the application number, and the marker color. For the proposed system, 4 bits are adequate to represent m. On the other side, a data vector is sent from the FPGA to the PC, via Ethernet, after executing the recognition and tracking processes. This vector carries the required information of the recognized object and its 3D position. The first Q bits of the data vector represent the recognized gesture/marker, where Q is determined according to the maximum number of different objects used in one application. In the proposed system, the maximum number of objects in one application is five; hence, Q is equal to three bits. The remaining parts of the data vector are 24 bits that represent the 3D position of the detected object, (X_C, Y_C, Z), where each coordinate is represented with eight bits. Wireshark analyzer monitored the packets sent via Ethernet to the FPGA. Also, it monitors the packets received from the FPGA, and provides error check methods, which in turn, diagnose and correct errors that can result from the VHDL code. A C# program was developed using Unity to capture the received data and check if they passed by all network layers and the OS accepted it. After that, the user's hand is combined with the 3D virtual model that is selected and located on the screen according to the received data vector.

Figure 8 illustrates the functions, designed and developed by Unity, where the data base of the application, selected by the GUI, is passed to the UDP receiver that also receives the data vector from the FPGA. The received data packet is then stored temporarily in the PC's RAM, such that each new packet deletes the old one. Afterwards, the data are analyzed according to the selected application and the received 3D coordinates, where the center of the detected object is combined with that of the virtual 3D object in the Integration Unit. The continuous response of the virtual object is controlled by the Controller Unit, based on the data vector.

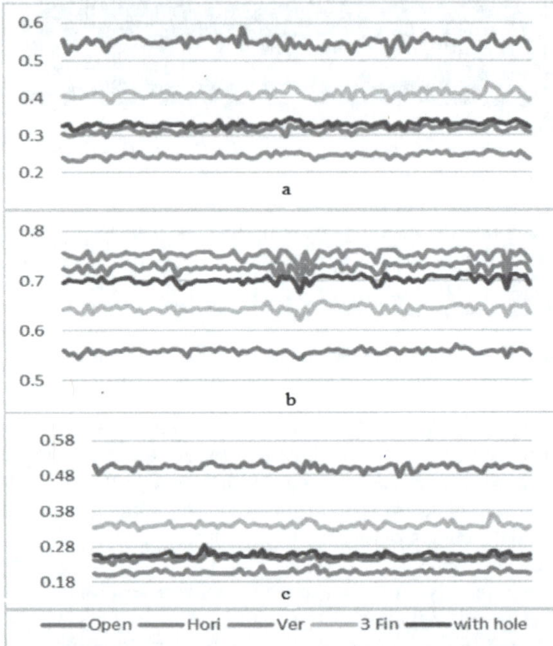

Figure 7. Normalized values of (a) Area, (b) Solidity, and (c) Perimeter of 140 different hands for the applied five hand gestures, in the system.

TABLE I. NORMALIZED VALUES OF THE MARKERS FEATURES

Marker	Color	Area	Solidity
Motor	Green	0.30421875	0.65847
Tale	Green	0.225143229	0.84043
Wheel	Green	0.317083333	0.5021
Wing	Green	0.331158854	0.91021
Proton	Blue	0.323385417	0.66774
Electron	Red	0.36265625	0.74883
Neutron	Yellow	0.300859375	0.62123

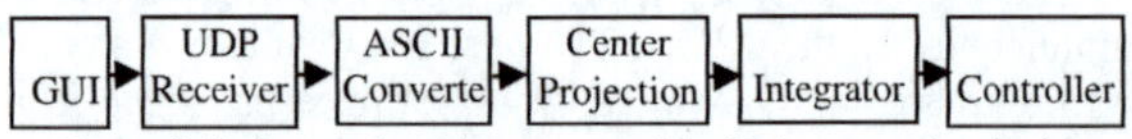

Figure 8. Software algorithm, executed by Unity game developing

IV. IMPLEMENTATION RESULTS AND DISCUSSION

Several visits were paid to nurseries and schools to evaluate the practical accuracy of the implemented system, and to see how well kids interact with it. The practical testing setup consisted of a webcam with a 640×480 resolution. The camera is fixed at height of 70 cm above a 50 cm × 25 cm white background. The software–based architecture runs on a 2.2 GHz processor.

Table II lists the recognition rate of each hand gesture after testing it on 100 children, and that the average recognition rate is 93.2%. Also, it can be noticed that the lowest recognition rate was of the "3 Fingers" gesture. This is because the gesture was slightly difficult for kids who are less than 5 years old to steadily perform, especially the first time they practice the applications. On the other side, the accuracy of the utilized markers approaches 100% because their shapes, features, and colors are constant, unlike gestures.

TABLE II. RECOGNITION RATE OF THE UTILIZED HAND GESTURES

Gesture	Open	Hori	Ver	3Fin	With Hole
Recognition (%)	96	93	92	90	95

Table III lists the FPGA utilized resources of the proposed system that was estimated by Xilinx Integrated Software Environment (ISE) tool, after implementing it on the low power Spartan3, S1600e-4fg320 device. The FPGA chip is mounted on a MicroBlaze development Kit-Spartan3E-1600E that features an Ethernet interface to the PC. Table III indicates that the implemented system uses less than 5% of the FPGA resources, which allows further modifications to improve the recognition rate and increase the number of gestures and markers. In addition, the implementation reports revealed that the maximum operating frequency at which the FPGA-implemented system can work is 102.817 MHz. However, the implemented system successfully works in real-time at only 25 MHz, when the camera works at 30 fps.

The power consumption of the implemented system was estimated, using XPower analyzer, provided by Xilinx. It is found that the FPGA–based implemented part consumes 5.65 mW at 25 MHz. Using higher frame rates is not demanded, since hand speed varies from medium to slow rates. Hence, it is more efficient to use lower frame rates, such as 15 fps, to reduce the operating frequency required for a real-time performance. This, in turn, optimizes power consumption much better.

In addition, practical testing showed that normal children were very excited while practicing the applications without finding any difficulty performing the selected hand gestures. On the other side, autistic children were more interested in marker based applications, but they were hardly obeying their teachers when told to do the selected hand gestures. However, after an adequate effort from the teachers, autistic children could, so far, interact with the applications by gestures.

Figure 9 (a) shows kids interacting with animals by dragging them to their homeland, using different hand gestures. Figure 9 (b) illustrates the planting steps starting with holding the planting pot by the "With hole" gesture, putting a seed inside the pot using the "three figures" gesture, dropping water by the "vertical fist" gesture, and finally growing the plant by the "open hand" gesture. In Figure 10 (a) the child holds and drags different shaped green markers to assemble an airplane that flies at the end. In Figure 10 (b) the child uses three different colored markers that represent the main particles of the protons, neutrons and electrons. The child moves the colored markers and locates them on the circles in the middle, that represent the atom structure. Afterword, the electrons -red balls- start rotating around the atom in the fourth step.

To determine whether the learning outcomes of the applications have been successfully received by the students and how far such interactive applications enhance their concentration, some matching quizzes were given to 25 normal children ranging from 4 to 8-year-olds. The quizzes results differed according to the child's age and the application, however, the results were 75% on average, after the first time of practicing the applications.

TABLE III. FPGA UTILIZED RESOURCES OF THE IMPLEMENTED SYSTEM

Logic Utilization	Used	Available	Utilization
Number of Slice Flip Flops	412	29,504	1.3 %
Number of 4 input LUTs	927	29,504	3.1 %
Number of occupied Slices	553	14,752	3.7 %
Number of RAMB16s	1	36	2.77 %
Number of BUFGMUXs	1	24	4.1 %

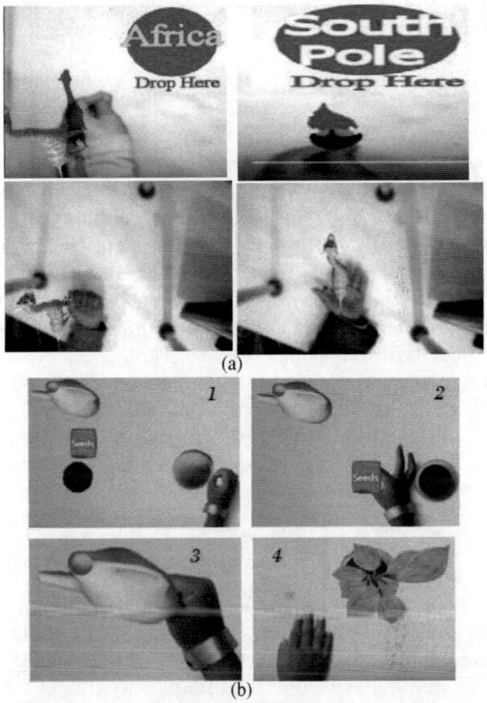

Figure 9. Kids practice (a) the first and (b) the second applications.

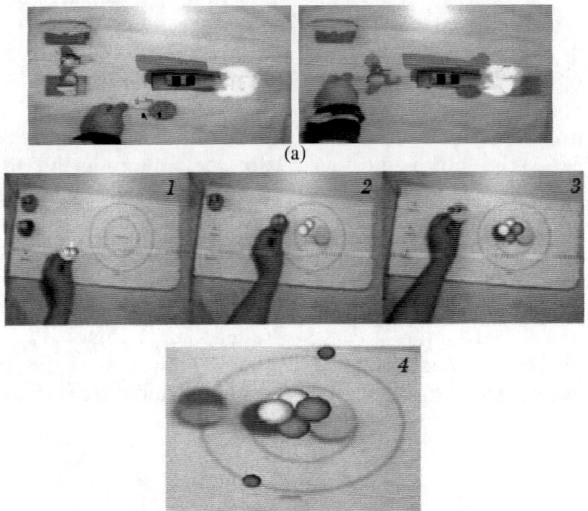

Figure 10. Kids practice (a) the third and (b) the fourth applications.

TABLE IV. COMPARISON BETWEEN THE PROPOSED SYSTEM AND OTHER INTERACTIVE AR AND HCI SYSTEMS

System	G	M	R (%)	FR	F_{OP} (MHz)	P_{HW} (mw)	Technology Used
[9]	2	None	90	U	1600	> 12000 (for Kinect [21])	Intel Core i5 processor & Kinect camera.
[10]	4	3 colored ribbons	93.3	U	U	U	Low Processor (U).
[15]	1	9	U	25	2800	> 12000 (for Kinect and Video Camera)	Intel Core i5 processor, Kinect & Video cameras.
[16]	None	2 color balls	U	25	U	6000	Celoxica RC200 reconfigurable computer, Virtex II, Head worn PAL resolution camera, and Tracked glove.
Proposed system	5	7	93.2	30	25 at 30 fps	(5.65: for FPGA-based design)	General purpose processor & FPGA (UR < 5 %).

Table IV summarizes a comparison between the proposed system and some other hand gesture and marker based HCI systems, where G and M are the number of used gestures and markers, respectively, R is the recognition rate, FR is the frame rate, F_{OP} is the applied operating frequency for real-time recognition and tracking, P_{HW} is the amount of power, consumed by the hardware equipment, UR is the FPGA Utilized Resources, and U stands for undefined. From Table IV it is noticed that for real-time performance, the operating frequency and power consumption of the proposed system are lower than those of the other systems. Another important point is that, the markers, used in the proposed system, are handmade, unlike the complicated barcode markers, used in [7], [12] and [16]. Using such simple and cheap markers makes children feel included as they participate in creating the 3D objects, and it makes the system more reliable, as its reusable resources are affordable.

V. CONCLUSION AND FUTURE WORK

A low power interactive AR learning system for children was proposed. The high computationally complicated recognition and tracking functions were implemented on an FPGA to minimize the operating frequency without violating real-time performance. This helps using the proposed applications anywhere that fits children. Implementation and testing results show that the recognition rate of the implemented system is 93.2% on average. Comparing the proposed implemented system to some other systems, it is found that the proposed system is more efficient in terms of power consumption, and reliability. For future work, a general form is currently being finalized by the authors, to get the optimal FPGA operating frequency, at which the system can work in real-time, as a function of the frame rate. This will enable working at rates even lower than 25 Mhz. Also, more hand gestures and markers can be recognized by adding additional features as only 5% of the FPGA resources are utilized. In addition, a custom Printed Circuit Board (PCB) will be manufactured that contains only the necessary components for the implemented system to minimize size and cost.

ACKNOWLEDGMENT

Authors thank Prof. Khayri Abdel Hamid for his sincere support, and for breaking many barriers the authors faced, during working in this manuscript.

REFERENCES

[1] M. Mafner, M. Schoning, M. Antczak, A. Demenko, and K. Hameyer, "Methods for computation and visualization of Magnetic Flux Lines in 3D," *IEEE Trans. Magn.*, vol. 46, no. 8, pp. 3349 – 3352, Aug. 2010.A.

[2] S. Matsutomo, T. Miyauchi, S. Noguchi, and H. Yamashita, "Real-Time visualization system of magnetic field utilization Augmented Reality Technology for education," *IEEE Trans. Magn.*, vol. 48, no. 2, pp. 531-534, Feb. 2012.

[3] M. Sugimoto, "A mobile mixed-reality environment for children's storytelling using a handheld projector and a robot," *IEEE Trans. Learn. Technol.*, vol. 4, no. 3, pp. 249 – 260, Sep. 2011.

[4] D. B. Chin, I. M. Dohmen, and D. L. Schwartz, "Young children can learn Scientific Reasoning with teachable agents," *IEEE Trans. Learn. Technol.*, vol. 6, no. 3, pp. 248 – 257, Sep. 2013.

[5] L. Escobedo, M. Tentori, E. Quintana, J. Favela, and D. Garcia-Rosas, "Using Augmented Reality to help children with Autism stay focused," *IEEE Pervasive Computing*, vol.13, no.1, pp. 38-46, Mar. 2014.

[6] B. Zhen, A. F. Blackwell, and G. Coulouris, "Using Augmented Reality to elicit pretend play for children with Autism," *IEEE Trans. Vis. Comput. Graph.*, vol. 21, no. 5, pp. 598-610, May 2015.

[7] S. Prasad, P. Kumar, and K. P. Sinha, "A wireless dynamic gesture user interface for HCI using hand data glove," *in International Conference on Contemporary Computing (IC3)*, Noida, India, pp. 62-67, Aug 2014.

[8] L. Figueiredo, V. Teichrieb, and R. Anios, "Bare hand natural interaction with augmented objects, " *In IEEE International symposium on Mixed and Augmented Reality (ISMAR)*, Adelaide, Australia, pp. 1-6, Oct. 2013.

[9] J. M. Teixeira, B. Reis, S. Macedo, and J. Kelner, "Open/Closed hand classification using Kinect data," *in 14th Symposium on Virtual and Augmented Reality (SVR)*, Adelaide, Australia, pp. 18-25, May 2012.

[10] S. Prasad, S. K. Peddoju, and D. Ghosh, "Mobile Augmented Reality based interactive teaching & learning system with low computation approach," *in IEEE Symposium on Computational Intelligence in Control and Automation (CICA)*, Singapore, pp. 97-103, Apr. 2013.

[11] S. Jinwook, K. Minje, Y. Yoonsik, S. Jonghoon, and H. Tack-Don, "Interactive features based Augmented Reality authoring tool," *in IEEE International Conference on Consumer Electronics (ICCE)*, Las Vegas, USA, pp. 47-50, Jan. 2014.

[12] L. Dipietro, A. M. Sabatini, and P. Dario, "A survey of Glove-Based Systems and their applications, " *in IEEE Trans. on Systems, Man, and Cybernetics*, vol. 38, no. 4, pp. 461-482, Jul. 2008.

[13] Z. Huang, W. Li, C. Peylo, and P. Hui, "CloudRidAR: A cloud-based architecture for mobile Augmented Reality," *in Telekom Innovation Laboratories*, Berlin, Germany, 2012.

[14] R. Lo, et al., "Augmented Reality system based on 3D camera self-gesture sensing," *in IEEE International Symposium on Technology and Society (ISTAS)*, Toronto, Canada, pp. 20-31, Jun. 2013.

[15] C. Stritzke and R. Radkowski, "Interactive hand gesture-based assembly for Augmented Reality applications," *in Advances in*

Computer-Human Interactions, Paderborn, Germany, PP. 303-308, 2012.

[16] W. Piekarski, R. Smith, G. Wigley, B. Thomas, and D. Kearney, "Mobile hand tracking using FPGAs for low powered augmented reality," *in 8th International Symposium on Wearable Computers (ISWC'04)*, Mawson Lakes, Australia, pp. 190-191, Oct.2004.

[17] S. Oniga, A. Tisan, D. Mic, A. Buchman, and A. Vida-Ratiu, "Hand postures recognition system using Artificial Neural Networks implemented in FPGA," *in 30th International Spring Seminar on Electronics Technology*, Cluj-Napoca, Romania pp. 507-512, May 2007.

[18] Unity, <https://unity3d.com/ > 2016.11.16

[19] R. E. Woods and R. C. Gonzalez, *Digital Image Processing*, 3rd ed., Miami, Pearson International Edition, 2007.

[20] M. Kolsch, M. Turk, "Fast 2D hand tracking with Flocks of Features and Multi-Cue integration," *in Conference on Computer Vision and Pattern Recognition Workshop (CVPRW '04.),* Washington, USA, pp. 158-158, Jun. 2004.

[21] <http://www.datasheet-pdf.com/datasheet-html/K/i/n/Kinectsensor_MicrosoftCorporation.pdf.html> > 2016.11.

Designing Icons on User Interfaces for 4-6 year Old Children

Shan Yan
Digital Worlds Institute
University of Florida
Gainesville, United States
email: shanyan923@ufl.edu

***Abstract*—A new generation of children, called "digital natives", live in a world where technology is forever being used in their daily lives. Digital media, such as games and applications, are increasingly being designed with kids in mind. However, interface and icon design for kids are not just a matter of simplification or scaling-up buttons. Children should not be dumbed down during the design process. Given that children's cognitive abilities vary at different ages, it's imperative to avoid assumption of an icon or image will be targeting all ages. Designing for a 4-year-old may not be age appropriate for a 7-year-old. This paper discusses how to design icons for children from 4 to 6, on user interfaces, by investigating cognitive development theory and applying the concept of user-centered design into children-centered design. Along with that, it will compare different user interfaces on different media platforms like applications, games, and websites for kids. With the children's unique characteristics at different ages in mind, designers can address age-appropriate design to those characteristics.**

Keywords-icon design; children; cognitive development.

I. INTRODUCTION

Many media research studies have shown that children have become a large user group for digital products such as websites, applications, and video games. A report from Common Sense Media in 2013 pointed out that 72% of children under 8 years old in the United States own a mobile device for a different purpose [1]. Under such circumstance, younger users need more appropriate interface design. However, as some studies have pointed out, it is not hard to find general guidelines for interface design, but only a few have responded to the development world of today's children [2][3][4][5]. We cannot design for children just based on intuition or memories from adult's childhood [6]. The new generation of children thinks and processes information fundamentally different from their predecessors [7]. A study from Andrew Large and Jamshid Beheshti suggested that specific interface design guidelines are required for kids rather than just relying on general design guidelines [4].

When working with children, they do not always follow the strict requirements of experimental procedures, so the completion rates and data collection of this subject pool are usually not ideal [8]. This problem makes interface design for these "digital natives [7]" more challenging for designers. To crack this hard nut, designers should better understand their intended small-age users' characteristics [10]. Piaget's theory about the four stages of cognitive development may help us know why children behave differently at different age.

The purpose of this paper is to employ findings from literature review to investigate some specific guidelines for icon and interface design for 4 to 6 year old by adopting children's cognitive development theory and user-centered design concept. The main reason to choose this age group is that they have been missing from most literature [8]. Lots of relevant studies focus on children older than 7 year old.

There are mainly three parts in this paper. Section II discusses the importance of icon and interface design for children; design for children is different from design for adults. According to Piaget's development stage theory, Section III explains why design icon and interface for children should take different age segments into account. Section IV lists some problems in current icon design for children and attempts to incorporate user-centered design concept in the procedure of design for children users. Other than that, it provides some specific guidelines for icon and interface design for children.

II. ICON AND INTERFACE DESIGN IS IMPORTANT FOR CHILDREN AND SHOULD BE DIFFERENT FROM DESIGN FOR ADULTS

When we own a new electronic device such as PC, iPad or smartphone, the way we interact with an unknown system is through activating the icons or other visual indicators on the graphic user interface (GUI). The term icon originates from a Greek word *eikon*, which refers to likeness, image or portrait. In the field of computer science, an icon is a small picture of symbol that represents a program, command, file, directory or device [9]. Usually, users can activate an icon on the graphic user interface (GUI) through a mouse, pointer, finger or voice commands. Icon interface has been extensively used on various smart devices because it has compact universal pictographic representations of functionality [11] and confronts fewer language obstacles [12]. Many studies have pointed out that children and young adults tend to rely on visual indication or visual cues rather than textual information [3][13][14][15]. Some researchers from Taiwan measured 104 children's information search efficiency of finding icons (databases) in the virtual environment. The final statistical analyses demonstrated that children's searching efficiency improves through using the graphical interface, compared to using text-focused interface [3]. Children at 4-6 year old still have poor reading ability, so appropriate icon and interface design are important for them to easily retrieval information from digital products such as website, game, and application [16].

When kids open a website or an application, they think in the different ways as adults [3][17][18]. Adults use websites and applications to find information, do shopping, and communicate with friends, etc. Meanwhile, most of the kids consider digital media as a way to entertain themselves [19]. Jakob Nielsen found that lots of usability aspects apply for both kids and adults. Meanwhile, he also discovered that there are some different aspects. Table I [20] in his study summarizes the main similarities and differences in user behavior between children and adults when they use websites. It illustrates how children and adults think and behave differently as they use digital products. For instance, look at the seventh column in the first row, when users confront multiple or redundant navigations on user interface, children feel more confused. Then in the row that says Back button in the first column, it shows young kids barely use that icon, yet older kids and adults are relying on it. Those comparisons just indicate that younger children have a different interpretation to the same design than older children and adults. In addition to that, designers should also consider children's immature cognitive development, and void experience of association to produce high recognizable and age-appropriate icon design for them.

A. *Immature Executive Function*

Neuroscience scholars discovered that the executive functions controlled by the frontal lobes allow adults to concentrate on relevant information on user interface and filter irrelevant information [21]. Children aged from 3 to 8 have relatively immature executive functions and short-term memory [22], which hinder their ability to have a good command of interpreting the icon and visual cues on graphic interface as adults do. Hence, children may not be able to recognize some icons that we adults take for granted.

B. *Void Experience of Associating Icon Metaphor*

A study from National Taichung University of Education found that the users' prior experiences could contribute to storing images and build up conceptual neural networks in our brain [22]. When an icon delivers a message, adult users can retrieve their previous long-term memory to interpret it. However, due to the void experience, children user would have difficulty associating the icon metaphors with the real objects. For example, we adults are quite familiar with the save icon (Figure 1), which we still frequently used in the Microsoft Word software (Figure 2). Most of adults can recognize this icon because it is widely used on websites and applications. However, the image of this save icon is a 3.5-inch floppy disk (Figure 3), the primary means of backing up files or transferring them between computers in the 1990s. We are no longer using this storage device. Apparently, children today cannot recognize this icon without training because floppy disk does not exist in their world. Therefore, it is important for adults and designers to avoid assuming that children's world experiences and adult experiences are comparable, with regard to icon metaphor association. Children will feel quite confused if this assumption is

TABLE I. MAIN SIMILARITIES AND DIFFERENCES IN USER BEHAVIOR BETWEEN CHILDREN AND ADULTS [20]

	Children	Adults
Goal in visiting websites	Entertainment	Getting things done Communication/community
First reactions	Quick to judge site (and to leave if no good)	Quick to judge site (and to leave if no good)
Willingness to wait	Want instant gratification	Limited patience
Following UI conventions	Preferred	Preferred
User control	Preferred	Preferred
Exploratory behavior	Like to try many options Mine-sweeping the screen	Stick to main path
Multiple/redundant navigation	Very confusing	Slightly confusing
Back button	Not used (young kids) Relied on (older kids)	Relied on
Reading	Not at all (youngest kids) Tentative (young kids) Scanning (older kids)	Scanning
Readability level	Each user's grade level	8th to 10th grade text for broad consumer audiences
Real-life metaphors e.g., spatial navigation	Very helpful for pre-readers	Often distracting or too clunky for online UI
Font size	14 point (young kids) 12 point (older kids)	10 point (up to 14 point for seniors)
Physical limitations	Slow typists Poor mouse control	None (unless disabled)
Scrolling	Avoid (young kids) Some (older kids)	Some
Animation and sound	Liked	Usually disliked
Advertising and promotions	Can't distinguish from real content	Ads avoided (banner blindness); promos viewed skeptically
Disclosing private info	Usually aware of issues: hesitant to enter info	Often recklessly willing to give out personal info
Age-targeted design	Crucial, with very fine-grained distinctions between age groups	Unimportant for most sites (except to accommodate seniors)
Search	Bigger reliance on bookmarks than search, but older kids do search	Main entry point to the Web

Figure 1. Save icon.

Figure 2. Save icon on Microsoft Word interface.

Figure 3. Floppy disk.

applied in the design for them. The icon metaphors used in interface should be familiar to children and connect to the physical world [20][23].

III. Why Icon and Interface Design for Children Should Consider Different Age Ranges

Children undergo dramatic physiological and cognitive changes as they grow up [3][24]. Children at different age segments have different user characteristics. Adult's mental and physical situation usually remain pretty stable in the long term. Shneiderman argued that any design should be built upon an understanding of its target users. He also stated that age group and gender should be considered as important user characteristics alongside education, ethic, personality, training and so forth [3][25]. In addition, Sultan Idris Education University did a study on children's ability to design icons based on the given tasks, the finding shows younger and older children have a different understanding of the same icon representation and their meaning. Children under 8 year old have difficulty in recognizing even some simple icons like undo icon and move-to-first-page icon [26]. Figure 4 in this study report shows children interpret a given word differently according to their age [26]. It reveals that age plays an important role in icon recognition and visual information perception ability.

According to Piaget's theory [27][28][29], children have four stages of cognitive development: the sensorimotor stage (0-2 years), preoperational stage (2-7 years), concrete operational stage (7-11 years), and formal operational stage (adolescence through adulthood). Most children under 2 and half years old have few experiences with standard input devices like mouse trackball and keyboard to interact with technology. And children older than 14 years old have entered into puberty and are likely to behave as adults [30]. However, children aged 4-6 year old are in the development process of the preoperational stage, and they begin to develop various cognitive skills, such as language, memory, imagination and so forth. But they are unable to understand concrete logic yet, so they tend to know this world only through making connections between events and phenomena. Their ability to process information mentally is still very limited [8]. Statement from Piaget and Inhelder and Piaget [28][31] also identified that the children aged 2 to 4 like to

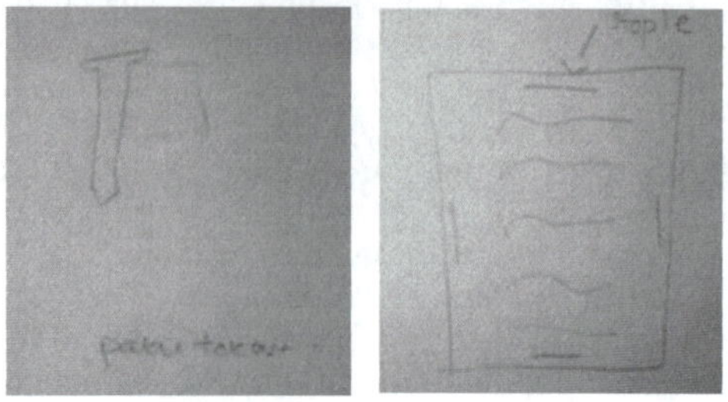

Figure 4. A girl aged 5 years old (left) and a girl aged 11 years old (right) interpretate of a giving word "paste" [26].

engage in symbolic play, such as pretend play. It means they start to use symbolic representations. Later, children at preoperational stage achieve an important cognitive milestone when they behave better at language expression, draw and play [8]. Making use of symbol such as icons on user interface for children at this age group will help them get the hang of smart devices and understand things faster and efficient.

IV. How to Design Icon for 4 to 6 Year Old

Though there exist many studies and guidelines of user interface design, most of them still focus on adult users, only a small amount of them have taken children youthfulness as user characteristic [3][32]. This situation is typical in touch-screen interface designed for children. A study from Romania noticed that only a few works had addressed children's interaction behavior with touch-screen devices. Most existing touch interactions are designed for a generic user population. Those designers just assumed that all users could be able to target small graphical items precisely, and drag and drop them smoothly and effortlessly on the screen interface [8]. Nevertheless, as the study pointed out, children's touch interaction patterns are different from adults. Children have smaller finger size, and their motor and cognitive ability are limited in accordance with their age and developmental stage [8][32][33][34]. In fact, small children are more complicated than they appear initially [24]. Designers should avoid dumbing down their young users by simply enlarging the icon size and brightening the color in UI design. Therefore, specific interface design guidelines are required for small-age children, rather than just relying on general design guidelines [3]. If needed, designers can also actively include the young user themselves in the design process.

Icon and interface design for children can incorporate the concept of "User-centered design". Most designers are familiar with the term "User-centered design"(UCD). Donald Norman's research laboratory at the University of California, San Diego, originated the term 'user-centered design' (UCD) in the 1980s. The role of the designer in the user-centered design is to facilitate task for users, to make sure that users can use the product as intended, and with a minimum effort to learn how to use it [35]. Table II lists the four phases of the UCD process. A rule for user-centered design practices is that no design suits all users. Designers should design based on the knowledge of the target users [4]. However, as Shneiderman argued [10], it is less common to find in practice that small-age users are being considered in the interface design guidelines. Sabina Idler, who is the founder of UXkids, mentioned the notion of child-centered design (CCD). She recommends designers to take what we have learned from UCD and to apply it to design for kids [36]. Based on the concept of UCD, and Sabina's explanation of CCD, Figure 5 demonstrates the five phases of icon design for children. The first step is to have an idea; then designers should conduct some field research to understand their children user characteristics. Next, it is time for designers to produce design solution for a particular product. After that, usability testing is required to make the design evaluation and designers can modify their design based on the feedback from children users.

A. Field and User Research

Having a good understanding of target user's needs is an evitable part of the design process. If users are preschoolers who have limited language expression and cognitive ability, designers should do more research on characteristics of children users. In this case, understanding the cognitive psychology at various age stages could help designers put themselves into children's shoes.

1) Children from Age 4 to 6 are in the Preoperational Stage: According to Piaget's theory of cognitive development, children aged 4 to 6 are in the preoperational stage (2-6 years). Piaget developed term "Preoperational" for children who don't understand concrete logic yet and can only see objects and people from their perspective [24]. They are starting to have the ability to communicate via simple language and use symbols such as words, numbers, and images to represent real objects [6]. But kids at this stage are in the process of learning how to think abstractly, so they still are having trouble articulating thoughts and behaviors clearly. Hence, even if some icons and symbols are universally understood for adults, they make no sense in children's minds. So, designers ought to think twice before using any icons and symbols that adults take for granted.

2) Children Privacy and Parental Consent: Before conducting the on-site research or test for children, one thing should be kept in mind is that many countries have strict regulations about collecting personal data from kids younger than 13. Designers and researchers are required to obtain parental or guardian consent before conducting any testing. In the United States, detailed explanations of the rules could be found in the U.S. Children's Online Privacy Protection Act (COPPA) laws [24]. Apart from getting permission, it is highly recommended to let the parents understand your research objectives [37].

B. Produce Design Solution

When designing icon graphics for 4 to 6 year old, the following aspects should be taken into account. The design concept can be applied to the user interface on different platforms.

TABLE II. FOUR PHASES OF USER-CENTERED DESIGN

User-centered Design Phases	
Specify the context of use	Identify target user, what they will use it for, under what conditions
Specify requirements	Identify user goals or business requirements
Create Design Solutions	Realize rough concepts to complete design
Evaluate Design	Conduct usability testing with actual users

1) Icon Graphics Should Match User's Mental Models: Icon metaphor should depend on user familiar mental models, for the purpose of reducing cognitive effort [3]. In other words, icon design should remind the user of real objects that they are already known [12] [38]. Many studies [39][40][41][42] shows that concrete icon sets tend to be more visually complex than abstract icons since the detailed interpretation of real world objects would allow users to access their existing knowledge and life experience related to these items to infer meaning. However, icon design should avoid being too complex, as it will increase the extra processing time for user to recognize [43]. Jeeves [3] example found that metaphors are related to age and culture. Chinese Academy of Science did a research about how the development of visual attention aged from children to adult affects interface design [44], the finding use series of data to point out that children participants need significant longer reaction time on user interface than adolescence and adult participants.

In addition, for children who usually don't have much life experience and haven't received icon recognition training, learning a new set of visualized symbols is much difficult than recognizing images they observe in daily life. According to the study from Nation Taipei University of Technology [45], a design guideline is using icons based upon simplified images that relevant to children's real life experience, as they can easily perceive the actual meaning on the user interface database. Figure 6, the screen shot of TV icons from website Sprout and CBeebies for preschoolers, is an example in practice. The biggest difference in these two icon graphics is that the right one has

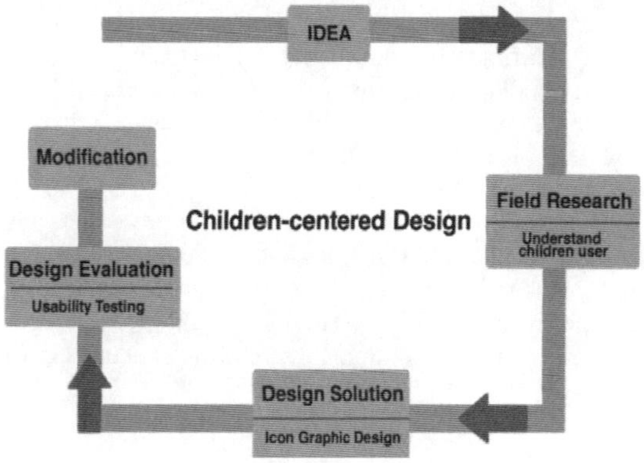

Figure 5. Children-centered design phases.

two television antennas. Those antennas are not matched with nowadays children's mental model because the truth is we no longer use TV with antennas and have not for quite a long time. Most of the kids nowadays are watching the TV in Figure 8 at home or school rather than the counterpart with antennas. Though the antenna makes the TV icon "childish" and more kid-friendly, it is at odds with children user's sense of rightness, and result in a low recognizability.

2) Semantic Distance: Semantic distance in interface design means the closeness between the icon and the function it represents [39]. When designing interface for children, icon graphic should match its function to avoid misunderstanding. Some researchers agreed that semantic distance plays an important role in determining interpretability [38][39][46]. Townsend [2] also recommended in his research that icon designed for children user should "clearly depict, indicate and distinguish a program's commands and operations" and "should suggest and indicate a command intention rather than just duplicate or represent a particular pictorial form." Currently, some icons designed for children users tend to be looking good but not accurately matching the meaning of function [3]. For instance, the two icons represent the game section in Figure 8, the graphic in the right one is a wheel with an arrow on it, and the left one is a game console. Apparently, most kids today know what a game console looks like, this graphic let them easily remind of video gameplay experience in real life. However, the wheel graphic does not accurately match the video game concept. Children may play wheel spin game in real life, but this cannot represent various kinds of video games in their mind. As a result, icon graphics need to be carefully selected, accurately matched with the label text to avoid any misinterpretations [3] for children users.

3) Maintain Visual Hierarchy on User Interface: Color combination and color contrast on user interface would significantly influence the visual search performance of user [43]. Studies [47][48][49] show that proper use of color could enhance the graphical display effectiveness, which can lead to fewer search times for user. Children at the preoperational stage prefer bold and primary colors and high contrast in graphic layouts [50], because bright colors immediately catch their attention [3] and trigger their interest to explore. But some studies also stated that incorporate too much color into a user interface could be counterproductive, as it may generate a "fruit salad" look [49] feeling to the user. At the same time, it could also slow down children user's visual search time on the interface. In the example shown in Figure 9, Webkinz Jr. is a website design for kids aged 3 to 6, to play learning games online. You can tell from the picture that designers intend to use lots of bright colors to attract children's attention of exploring. Also, the four icons at the bottom are quite colorful. However, the visual hierarchy on the interface is not evident, which makes children under 6 years old have trouble navigating it. Screenshot in Figure 10 is a good iconic interface design. It is an early math application for preschoolers, named *Eggy Substract to 20*. The color on the interface is bright enough, and the graphic design is kid-friendly. The icons on *Eggy Substract to 20* maintain have high color contrast with the background. For children user, it is easier for them to complete visual search and further navigate to the contents they want. Hence, user interface design for children should incorporate an appropriate amount of color and high contrast to increase visual search efficiency [43].

Figure 6. TV icon on children website Sprout (left) and CBeebies (right).

Figure 7. Children watching TV.

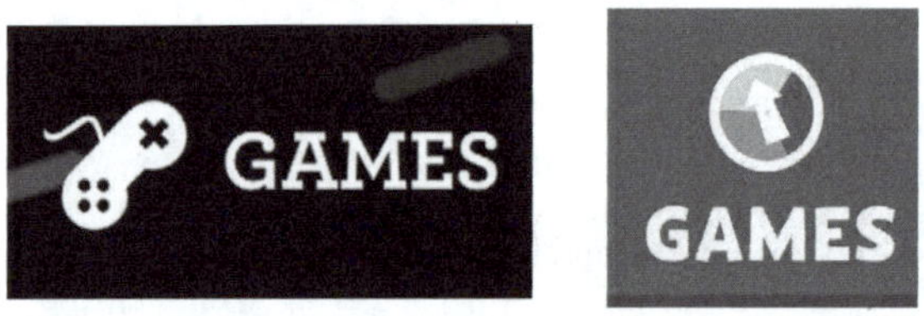

Figure 8. Game icon on children website Sprout (left) and PBSkids (right).

4) Indication of Icon Clickability: Children love feedback, such as animation and sound when they interact with the game or application. A study result from University of Calgary [2] argued that animated icons are easier to decipher the meaning than static images for children. Children show an obvious preference for the moving icons. So incorporating animated icons in a user interface for children could have a merit. The click animation in Figure 11 is a good illustration of this point. When the mouse cursor moves to the icon, the animation appears to give children users feedback and attract their attention. It uses a children-friendly way to indicate that icon is clickable.

C. Design Evaluation-Usability Testing with Children

Figure 9. User interface of website Webkinz. Jr.

Figure 10. Screen shot of early math application- Eggy Substract to 20.

Figure 11. CBeebies Icon Animation.

For designers, it is highly recommended to get feedback from children about your design and make some proper modifications. In Human-Computer Interaction (HCI) field, we usually use usability testing to do evaluation. This notion initially focused on adults [51][52], later children's different requirement became noticeable, and it leads to more children-centered methods in usability testing. In a study from Malaysia [51], some researchers attempted to find out issues that have been overlooked in performing testing with children. They point out that some testers, especially younger ones, seemed to have trouble communicating with children. As we know, usually children are taught to not to trust strangers easily. When you first meet a kid, it is suggested to establish relationships by engaging him or her into some small talk to find out more about each other. Topics like birthday, favorite computer games, or favorite subjects at school [30] could trigger children's interest. Other than that, some children are quite introversive, and not willing to talk too much. In this case, a good way is to use "friendship pairs" [37] during the communication with children. Friendship pairs in conducting research refers to obtaining information from participants, by speaking to their outgoing peers who know about their experience of using any websites or apps. However, even the children users are willing to talk to the tester; another challenge is that they can be very unpredictable regarding actions and behaviors [51]. And most of the children aged from 4 to 6 year old are still not ready to sit at task and follow directions from an adult. Besides, children at this age stage usually have difficulty expressing their likes and dislikes in words [30]. Under this circumstance, we could apply observation in the evaluation process. When children users are sighing, smiling or sliding under the table, it can indicate they like or dislike your design to a certain degree.

As for some other aspects, such as preparation, lab environment and so on need to be taken care during the usability testing with children, we can use Figure 12 and Figure 13 from previous studies [46][51] about usability testing with children to summarize the specific guidelines for testers.

V. CONCLUSION

This paper attempts to investigate some guidelines for icon and interface design for 4 to 6 year olds by analyzing children user characteristics, incorporating Piaget's development stages theory and user-centered design concept. The design procedures could be summarized as having an idea, conducting field research, producing design solution, doing design evaluation by usability testing, and making some modifications. In general, based on findings from different studies, design icon on interface for children should strike a balance between a plain, unimaginative but functional design and a colorful and animated design.

REFERENCES

[1] Common Sense Media, "Zero to Eight: Childrens Media Use in America 2013," *The Education Digest*, Vol. 79, pp. 59-63, Feb. 2014, Avaliable from: http://www.commonsensemedia.org/research/zero-to-eight-childrens- media-use-in-america-2013

[2] T. Jones, "Recognition of animated icons by elementary-aged children," Research in Learning Technology, Vol.1, Iss. 1, pp. 40-46, May. 1993.

[3] J. A. Large and J. Beheshti, "Interface Design, Web Portals, and Children," Library Trends, Vol. 54, pp. 318-342, Mar. 2006, doi: 10.1353/lib.2006.0017.

[4] T. Jamaliah, A. Wan, and B. Noor, "Investigating Children Preferences of a User Interface Design," Proc. The 13th International Conference on Human Computer Interaction

(ICHCI 2009), Aug. 2009, pp. 510-513, ISBN: 978-3-642-02573-0, doi: 10.1007/978-3-642-02574-7_57.

[5] H.B. Hutchinson and B.B. Bederson, "Children's interface design for searching and browsing," Doctoral Dissertation, University of Maryland at College Park, 2005, ISBN: 0-542-47108-6.

[6] H. Gelderblom and P. Kotzé, "Designing Technology for Young Children: What we can Learn from Theories of Cognitive Development" The SAICSIT 2008 Annual Research Conference of the South African Institute of Computer Scientists and Information Technologists (CSIT '08), ACM Press, South Africa, Oct. 2008, pp. 66-74, doi: 10.1145/1456659.1456668.

[7] M. Prensky, "Digital Natives, Digital Immigrants Part 1," On the Horizon, Vol.9 Iss:5, pp.1-6, 2001, doi: 10.1108/10748120110424816.

[8] R. Vatavu, G. Cramariuc, and D. M. Schipor, "Touch interaction for children aged 3 to 6 years- Experimental findings and relationship to motor skills," International Journal of Human-Computer Studies, Vol. 74, pp. 54-76, Feb. 2015, doi: 10.1016/j.ijhcs.2014.10.007.

[9] LINFO, "Icon Definition." [Online]. Avaliable from: http://www.linfo.org/icon.html

[10] B. Shneiderman, Designing the user interface: Strategies for effective human-computer-interaction, 3rd ed., Reading, Mass: Addison Wesley Longman, 1998.

[11] L. Uden and A. Dix, "Iconic Interfaces For Kids On The Internet" IFIP World Computer Congress, Beijing, pp. 279-286, Oct. 2000.

[12] S. Huang, K. Shieh, and C. Chi, "Factors affecting the design of computer icons," International Journal of Industrial Ergonomics, Vol. 29, Iss. 4, pp. 211-218, Apr. 2002, doi: 10.1016/S0169-8141(01)00064-6.

[13] R. Fidel, R. Davies, M. Douglass, J. Holder, C. Hopkins, B. Kushner, and et al., "A visit to the information mall: Web searching behavior of high school students," *Journal of the* American Society for Information Science, Vol. 50, Iss. 1, pp. 24-37, Jan. 1999.

[14] S. G. Hirsh, "Children's relevance criteria and information seeking on electronic resources," Journal of the American Society for Information Science, Vol.50, Iss. 14, pp. 1265–1283, Dec. 1999.

[15] A. Large and J. Beheshti, "The Web as a classroom resource: Reactions from the users," *Journal of the American Society for Information Science, Vol. 51, Iss.* 12, pp. 1069–1080, Oct. 2000.

[16] M. Wiebe, D. Geiskovitvch, A. Bunt, J. Young and M. Glenwright, "Icons for kids: Can young kids understand graphical representations of App store categories," In Proceedings of Graphics Interface 2016: Victoria, British Columbia, Canada, Jun. 2016, pp. 163-166, doi: 10.20380/GI2016.20.

[17] D. F. Bjorklund, Children's thinking: Developmental function and individual differences, 3rd ed., Belmont, CA: Wadsworth, 2000.

[18] R. S. Siegler, Emerging minds: The process of change in children's thinking. New York: Oxford University Press, 1996.

[19] S. Idler, "Comparing Usability for Kids and Adults (Part 1)." [Online]. Avaliable from: http://uxkids.com/blog/comparing-usability-for-kids-and-adults-part-1

[20] R. Budiu and J. Nielsen, "Usability of Websites for Children: Design Guidelines for Targeting Users Aged 3–12 Years, 2nd edition, " Nielsen Norman Group Report, 2010.

[21] Treeincement, "What are Executive Functions." Video. [Online]. Avaliable from: https://www.youtube.com/watch?v=8cCNhKqQXOM

[22] S. Chiu, C. Koong, and S. Fan, "Icon Design Principles for Preschoolers: Implications Derived From Child Development," Procedia - Social and Behavioral Sciences, Vol. 64, pp. 228 – 237, Nov. 2012 [12 th International Educational Technology Conference- IETC 2012], doi: 10.1016/j.sbspro.2012.11.027.

[23] T. Gossen, M. Nitsche, and A. Nürnberger, "Search User Interface Design for Children: Challenges and Solution" The 2nd European Workshop on Human Interaction and Information Retrieval (EuroHCIR 2012), Aug. 2012, pp. 59-62, ISSN: 1613-0073K, doi: 10.1.1.416.5911.

[24] D. Gelman, Design for Kids: Digital Products for Playing and Learning. Rosenfeld Media Press, Brooklyn, New York, 2014.

[25] W. Horton, The icon book: Visual symbols for computer systems and documentation. New York: Wiley, 1994.

[26] M. H. M Yatim, A. S. Shariff, N. S. Fathil, N. A. A. Zaki, and et al., "Managing Icon Presentation in Children Software-Interpretation from Children Perspectives" The 7th International Conference on IT in Asia (CITA 2011), IEEE Press, Jul. 2011, doi: 10.1109/CITA.2011.5998953.

[27] J. Byrnes, "Piaget's Theory," In Encyclopedia of Infant and Early Childhood Development, 1st ed., Vol. 2, New York, NY, USA: Elsevier, pp. 543–552, 2008.

[28] J. Piaget, The Psychology of Intelligence, 2nd ed., Routledge, London, 2001.

[29] A. de Ribaupierre, Piaget's Theory of Child Development. International Encyclopedia of the Social and Behavioral Sciences, pp. 11434–11437, 2001, doi: 10.1016/B0-08-043076-7/01576-X.

[30] L. Hanna, K. Risden, and K. Alexander, "Guidelines for Usability Testing with Children," Interactions Vol. 4, Iss. 5, pp. 9–14, Sep. 1997, doi: 10.1145/264044.264045.

[31] J. Piaget and B. Inhelder, The Psychology of the Child. Basic Books, New York, 1969.

[32] L. Anthony, R. D. Vatavu, and J. O. Wobbrock, "Understanding the consistency of users' pen and finger stroke gesture articulation" In Proceedings of the 2013 Graphics Interface Conference, Canadian Information Processing Society, Toronto, ON, Canada, Canada, May. 2013, pp. 87–94.

[33] L. McKnight and B. Cassidy, "Children's interaction with mobile touch-screen devices: experiences and guidelines for design," International Journal of Mobile Human Computer Interaction (IJMHCI), Vol. 2, Iss. 2, pp. 1-18, 2010, doi: 10.4018/jmhci.2010040101.

[34] J. Rick, A. Harris, P. Marshall, R. Fleck, N. Yuill, and Y. Rogers, "Children designing together on a multi-touch tabletop: an analysis of spatial orientation and user interactions" The 8th International Conference on Interaction Design and Children (IDC 09) ACM, New York, NY, USA, Jun. 2009, pp. 106–114. doi: 10.1145/1551788.1551807.

[35] C. Abras, D. Maloney-Krichmar, and J. Preece, User-Centered Design. Bainbridge, W. Encyclopedia of Human-Computer Interaction, 2004.

[36] S. Idler, "Children-Centered Design is User-Centered Design, But then Different." [Online]. Avaliable from: http://uxkids.com/blog/child-centered-design-is-user-centered-design-but-then-different

[37] G. Gallavin, "UX for Kids' Products: Designing for the Youngest of Users." [Online]. Avaliable from: https://www.usertesting.com/blog/2015/04/29/ux-for-kids

[38] R. S Goonetilleke, H. M. Shin, H. K. On and J. Fritsch, "Effects of training and representational characteristics in icon design," International Journal of Human-Computer Studies, Vol. 55, Iss. 5, pp. 741-760, Nov. 2001, doi: 10.1006/ijhc.2001.0501.

[39] S. Isherwood, S. J. McDougall, and M. B. Curry, "Icon Identification in Context- The Changing Role of Icon Characteristics With User Experience," The Journal of the Human Factors and Ergonomics Society, Vol. 49, Iss. 3, pp. 465-476, Jun. 2007, doi: 10.1518/001872007X200102.

[40] U. Arend, K. P. Muthig, and J. Wandmacher, "Evidence for global feature superiority in menu selection by icons," Behavior and Information Technology, Vol. 6, pp. 411–426, 1987.

[41] M. Garcia, A. N. Badre, and T. Stasko, "Development and vali- dation of icons varying in their abstractness," Interacting with Computers, Vol. 6, Iss. 2, pp.191–211, Jun. 1994.

[42] A. J. K. Green and P. J. Barnard, "Iconic interfacing: The role of icon distinctiveness and fixed or variable screen locations," In D. Diaper, D. Gilmore, G. Cockton, and B. Shackel. Eds. *INTERACT '90, The IFIP TC* 13 Third International Conference on Human-Computer Interaction. Oxford, U.K.: North Holland/Elevier Science & Technology, pp. 457–462, 1990.

[43] K. Huang, "Effects of computer icons and figure/background area ratios and color combinations on visual search performance on an LCD monitor," Displays, Vol. 29, Iss. 3, pp. 237-242, Jul. 2008, doi: 10.1016/j.displa.2007.08.005.

[44] X. Zhang, J. Shi, T. Liu, and C. Jing, "The Development of Visual Attention Controlling Aged From Children to Adult and Its Effect on Interface Design," Computing, Control and Industrial Engineering, International Conference on, Vol. 2, pp. 292-295, 2010, doi: 10.1109/CCIE.2010.190.

[45] K. Wu, Y. Tang, and C. Tsai, "Graphical interface design for children seeking information in a digital library," Visualization in Engineering, Vol. 2, Iss.1, pp. 1-14, Dec. 2014.

[46] S. J. P. McDougall, M. B. Curry, and O. de Bruijn, "The effects of visual information on users' mental models: An evaluation of pathfinder analysis as a measure of icon usability," International Journal of Cognitive Ergonomics, Vol. 5, Iss. 1, pp. 59–84, 2001.

[47] R.E. Christ, "Review and analysis of color coding research for visual displays, " Human Factors, Vol. 17, Iss. 6, pp. 542 – 570, Dec. 1975.

[48] G. Murch, "Colour graphics—blessing or ballyhoo?" Computer Graphics Forum, Vol. 4, pp. 127-135, Jun. 1985, doi: 10.1111/j.1467-8659.1985.tb00202.x.

[49] J. Ling and P. Schaik, "The effect of text and background colour on visual search of Web pages ," Displays, Vol. 23, Iss. 5, pp. 223-230, Nov. 2002, doi: 10.1016/S0141-9382(02)00041-0.

[50] C.Naranjo-Bock, "Effective Use of Color and Graphic in applications for Children Part I: Toddlers and Preschoolers." [Online]. Avaliable from : http://www.uxmatters.com/mt/archives/2011/10/effective-use-of-color-and-graphics-in-applications-for-children-part-i-toddlers-and-preschoolers.php

[51] H. Hafit, F. H. A. Razak, and H. Haron, "Usability Testing with Children- What We Have Overlooked," In: Stephanidis C. (eds) HCI International 2011 – Posters' Extended Abstracts. HCI 2011. Communications in Computer and Information Science, Vol. 173, Springer, Berlin, Heidelberg, , pp. 147-150, doi: 10.1007/978-3-642-22098-2_30.

[52] A. Druin, "The Role of Children in the Design of New Technology," Behaviour and Information Technology, Vol. 21, Iss. 1, pp.1–25, Feb. 2002, doi: 10.1080/01449290110108659.

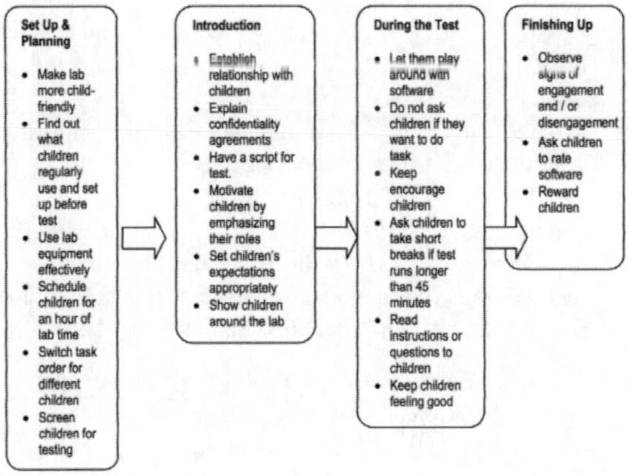

Figure 12. Guidelines from Hanna, Risden and Alexander [30][51].

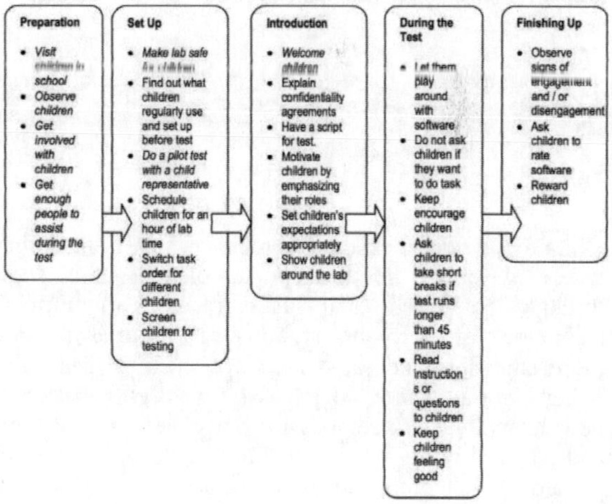

Figure 13. Additional steps in usability testing with children [51].

User Experience with Intelligent Proactive Technology in Automotive: A Longitudinal Study in Context

Mathilde Duczman, Aurélie Thévenin
Dept. Research & Innovation, UX Design
Renault
Guyancourt, France
e-mail: mathilde.duczman@gmail.com,
aurelie.thevenin@renault.com

Eric Brangier
Université de Lorraine, PErSEUs EA 7312, User-Lab
Faculté des sciences humaines et sociales
Metz, France
e-mail: eric.brangier@univ-lorraine.fr

Abstract— In the next few years, cars will tend to be smarter and provide more intelligent services, better connected and better adapted to user's habits than ever. Information system will be able to learn about behavior and then display personalized content in a proactive way. In order to develop user oriented car systems, the goal of our research is to study user experience related to the use of a learning and proactive application in automotive sector. We collected quantitative and qualitative data by observing evolution of driving style and by interviewing 13 end-users. Our results show that the learning and proactive application (a) negatively impacted driving safety; (b) did not really help users to anticipate dangerous events; (c) did not really help users to plan a new route; but (d) was considered as interesting to personalize their driving experience, with parameters related to real-time, privacy, transparency, unobtrusiveness and personalization. Based on our findings, we discuss essential aspects to consider learning and proactive informational systems as a gamified user experience.

Keywords-User Experience; intelligent car; proactive information system; gamification.

I. Introduction

In the last decades, the automotive sector has emerged as a key player in the development of innovating services through connected and autonomous car. Embedded technology is improving day after day, in order to provide more enjoyable and satisfying experience to their user by being more attractive, adaptive and intelligent. All of these new technologies present a same objective: improving safety and global driving experience. Most of the existing vehicles are already integrating smart and connected services, such as advanced driving assistance systems that help drivers to detect dangerous events, anticipate situations and help in overall decision making process. Some of them present more intelligent behavior by even taking decision and directly acting for the drivers. In one word, technology tends to be more proactive. Proactivity is defined [1][2] as the ability of device to act on its own initiative, on behalf of user needs and intentions, in order to help him/her to realize his/her tasks. The particularity of proactive technologies is working in an autonomous way, and proposing personalized information at the appropriate moment, regarding to user's activity [3][4]. In the next few years, these smart technologies will be able to send more and more relevant information and personalized suggestion to the driver by integrating learning abilities.

But what would be the effects on the driver and on his/her experience of driving? In a context where the industrial operates to offer better service by deploying technology, user needs and requirements need to be intently studied and took into account in a design process. In this research, we then specifically study user experience with a learning and proactive application. User experience refers to users' perception of one product qualities and to his responses towards this product such as emotional or physical reactions [5]. The aim of this article is then to study effects of a learning and proactive application on users' perceptions and reactions by focusing on their real driving activities and lived experience.

In this study, research questions are:

- What are the effects of a learning and proactive information system on driving activity and user experience?
- What features of a learning and proactive information system could influence the user experience?
- What recommendations of interaction design can be addressed?

In Section 2, we will describe the context and methodology of our study. Section 3 will present our main findings that we will then discuss in section 4.

II. Ergonomic Evaluation of Proactive Technology: Methodological Implications

This section describes context and methodology. We first present the assessed application and then describe method that we have set to answer our research questions.

A. Context

Renault research teams have recently developed a first version of a learning and proactive driving information application, named as "Driving coach" (Fig. 1 and 2). It aims at assisting drivers in their daily trips by helping them to plan their route and to anticipate dangerous events on their usual routes. In a contextually and autonomous way, the application is proactive: it displays personalized content to the user without any request of him. The application presents two main proactive functionalities for the driver:

- Predictions of Destination: It aims at helping the user to plan his route before a trip by displaying address of usual destination. This functionality allows the user to be directly guided to that destination with optimized routes, with few physical operations.
- Predictions of Dangerous Spots (PDS): PDS are defined by specific places where the user needs to make (1) hard braking, (2) hard acceleration or (3) hard cornering in bends on his usual routes. More the driver is making trips, more the application is able to recognize places that might be dangerous for him. The aim of the functionality is to predict PDS and then warn the user 500 meters before PDS, in order to help him to anticipate these spots and to control them by not making hard breakings, hard accelerations or hard bends.

Two modes are also proposed to the user for interacting with Driving Coach application: Challenge Mode and Companion Mode. Both present the same functionalities, except that Challenge Mode is offering more gamified means and procedures such as rewards to collect and challenges to take up. These game design elements aims at providing more enjoyable interactions and inducing user's behaviors [6].

Considering both these gamified aspects and abilities to display personalized content in a proactive manner, we can then wonder what are the overall effects of such an intelligent and personalized application on the user experience?

Figure 1. Screenshot of the proactive functionality "Predictions of Destination" in Driving Coach application

Figure 2. Screenshots of the proactive functionality of "Predictions of Dangerous Spots" in Driving Coach application

B. General orientation

This research follows a first work that had inspected the ergonomics of the system with ergonomic criteria based on accessibility, usability, emotionality and persuasiveness [7]. But this heuristic inspection does not assess the effects of proactivity over a long period of use. To do that, a longitudinal study is needed. Indeed, according to the literature, more the system is able to learn about user's habits and preferences, more it will be able to send personalized and relevant content to the user. Nevertheless, before being able to send relevant content can also depend of time and frequency of using the system. For these reasons, users may wait for several days before receiving information, which can affect user experience. To answer our research questions, we have conducted a study over a period of 6 weeks to assess how user interact with a proactive information system.

C. Recruiting

15 persons employed in Renault society have been recruited to participate to this study (12 males and 3 females). Participants were recruited according to the following conditions:

- Being familiar to the R-Link environment (Renault multimedia device embedded in cars),
- Having connectivity in car for being able to install and use the application "Driving coach",
- Not sharing the car with another driver,
- Realizing every journey with the same car on which Driving coach" would be installed.

Users were also asked to inform the examiners of their driving habits in order to constitute heterogeneous sample of participants having different types of journey, short, medium and long distance.

In order to collect heterogeneous and complementary data about how the persons were using the Driving Coach application and how they were feeling during this using period, observations had been conducted within two different manners. Indeed, our sample was divided in two groups:

- Group 1 was constituted of 6 participants. They were asked to use the application and to make a daily report on both troubling and pleasant aspects they observed and how they felt in these situations. They were interviewed every two weeks in order to collect their verbalization towards the main functionalities over time. At the end of the six weeks period, they were interviewed about their global satisfaction while using the application.
- Group 2 was constituted of 9 participants. They were asked to freely use the application, with no obligation to make a daily report or even to use the application. They were only interviewed at the end of the test to collect their feedback and reactions about the application.

D. Material and Equipement

Experiment material is composed of:

- "Driving Coach" application, installed in every car for each user of Group 1 & Group 2;
- Smartphone with a "recording" application for each user of Group 1. They were asked to make vocal comments for each troubling or pleasant situation they encountered during the six weeks test;
- Smartphone car charger with lighter socket for users of Group 1.

E. *Longitudinal using test*

As seen, it might take a long time for the user to get personalized information and suggestions, according to his habits and journeys frequency. For this reason of time delay, using tests had been conducted over a period of 6 weeks (Fig. 3). We considered this period as sufficient for the user to both familiarize with the learning and proactive driving information application, and to get personalized content throughout the proactive functionalities.

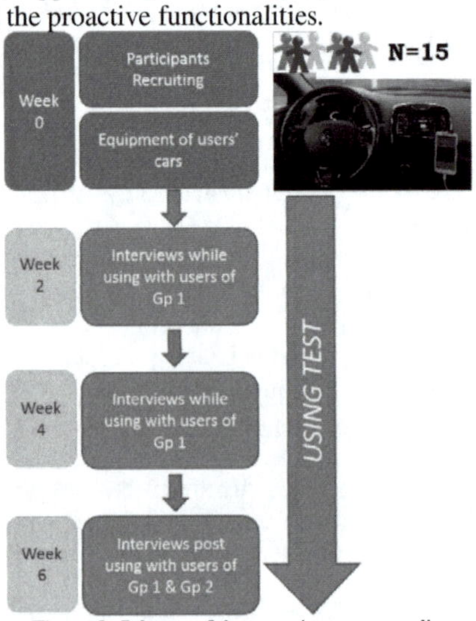

Figure 3. Scheme of the experiment proceeding

F. *Quantitative data collection*

Monitoring of driving activity was about observing what would be the impact of the application on the way of driving of the users. As we said previously, the objective of the application was to help users to adapt their driving style to proactive functionalities aiming at help them to anticipate dangerous events and to plan their journey: In other words, studying the impact of the application on driving activity correspond to study efficacy. Efficacy can be defined as the capacity of a system to reach a specific objective [8]. Efficacy refers to the expected effect and deals with the performance of a user to successfully reach a goal thanks to a system's features. In our case, measuring efficacy of the application "Driving Coach" aims at assessing pragmatic aspects of the application. That is to say, does the application really help users to plan their route and to anticipate dangers? We then focused on three data:

- Data to describe overall driving style evolution, by observing vehicle data of the participants to assess if the Driving Coach application would be useful and helpful to improve user driving style.
- Data to describe the success of PDS predictions; by observing if the users were adapting their driving style when they received personal suggestions to be careful on dangerous spots. To measure success of PDS predictions,
- Data to identify the success of destination prediction; by observing selection rate of the predicted destination.

G. *Qualitative data collection*

Lived experience with the Driving Coach application was studied by conducting explicitation interviews with users during and after the longitudinal test. This method aims at helping the users to remember specific situation, be aware of their actions and describe their lived experience [9][10][11]. Through specific techniques such as non-directive questioning and revivals, the interviewers establish a state of evocation for making the participant describe actions through verbalizations [12]. Explicitation interviews helped us to get the participants remember the most precisely the situation in which they were while using the application and how they were feeling at these moments. The 13 users that participated to the full period of test were asked to express their feelings and interest towards the application and if the application helped them to change their driving style. The aim was to identify, through user verbalizations, critical aspects in the application that can impact overall experience with such intelligent product. To analyze our results about the lived experience, we classified positive and negative comments in a smartsheet according to the overall application and its proactive functionalities. With this classification, we could then identified comments related to perceived utility, satisfaction/dissatisfaction and sources of satisfaction that we consider as crucial aspects of the learning and proactive application impacting the lived experience. In our study, we define satisfaction as the level of comfort that the user is feeling when he uses a product [8]. Satisfaction results from a subjective evaluation of the user, considering further aspects than just efficacy, such as aesthetics, need of the product or pleasure towards the product.

III. ANALYSIS OF RESULTS

During the first week, 2 users had stopped the test because of robustness and compatibility problems with their driving habits. We then focused on the results collected about the 13 other users.

A. *Record analysis during driving activity*

The main objective of the application was to help drivers to realize their daily trips by first helping them to anticipate dangerous driving events on their usual routes, and also help them to choose a route for going to their daily destinations. To assess the efficacy, we first decided to focus on the evolution of user's driving style along the 6 weeks period of test. We then observe how the users succeeded to master dangerous spots which were predicted on their usual routes and to finish how they could be helped to choose a route to go to their daily destination.

1) Impact on driving style evolution

For measuring driving style evolution of the participants, we have first calculated an index for each participant based on dangerous events that could happen during their test (sharp braking, sharp acceleration, sharp cornering) and based on the distance they travelled. This index is named as "Unsafety index", which is a ratio calculated as following:

$$\frac{\text{Sum of dangerous events per one user} \\ \text{(sharp braking, sharp accelerating, sharp cornering)}}{\text{Distance travelled}}$$

The higher the Unsafety Index is, the riskier the driving style of one user is. Unsafety index was calculated for each of the 13 users, at 3 steps during the 6 weeks period: after 1 week, 3 weeks and 6 weeks of using.

In our data analysis of the overall driving style evolution, we first observe an overall constant worsening during the using test period Indeed, results are showing an average deterioration of the Driving style along the test period (Table 1 and Fig. 4). According to these data, as long as the participants are using the application, they are realizing more dangerous events such as braking, acceleration, bends while they are supposed to realize less dangerous actions.

TABLE I. DANGEROUS INDEX FOR EACH USER AFTER 1 WEEK, 3 WEEKS AND 6 WEEKS OF TEST

User	After 1 week of test	After 3 weeks of test	After 6 weeks of test
1	0.21	0.52	0.58
2	0,55	1,51	1,59
3	0,81	0,7	0,94
4	0,32	0,56	0,60
5	0,57	0,69	0,67
6	0,55	0,61	0,58
7	0,91	1,24	1,46
8	0,44	0,95	0,76
9	1,40	1,37	1,79
10	1,13	1,69	1,80
11	0,63	0,49	0,68
12	0,87	0,74	0,76
13	1,88	1,84	1,99
Average	**0,79**	**0,99**	**1,09**

However, analysis of results for each participant also show 4 main types of variations in their driving style evolution along the test period (Fig. 4):

- Five users got a constant worsening during the 6 weeks period.
- Five users got improved in the middle of the test before getting worse at the end of the test than in the beginning.
- Three users got worse in the middle of the test.
- Only one user got improved at the end of the test period, compared to the beginning.

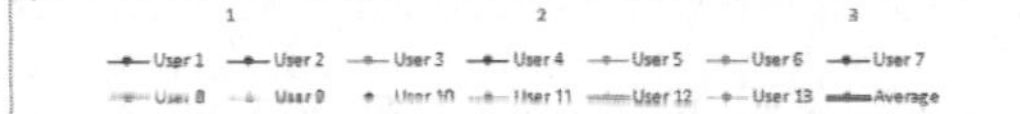

Figure 4. Graphic of driving style evolution for each participant according to their Unsafety index at the three periods of using

Ten users had deterioration in their driving style while using the application. This can be explained by the fact they were tempted to test the limits of the application and observe how it behaved by adjusting their driving style in an intentional way. What we finally observe in results analysis is that that no one of the participants got a constant improvement during the test period while the application was supposed to help the drivers to adopt a better way of driving.

2) *Impact on ability to master predictions of Dangerous Spots*

The first functionality of the Driving Coach application was about predictions of personal dangerous spots on usual routes of the users. Among the displayed information, only 61 percent of the predicted dangerous spots were passed by users. This means that in 39 percent of cases in which users were alerted of a personal dangerous spot on their route, the functionality was not efficient because users were not adapting their driving style and though did not succeed to master the predicted dangerous spots (Table 2).

TABLE II. OVERALL NUMBER AND PERCENTAGE OF PASSED PDS BY USERS FOR EACH PDS PREDICTION RECEIVED

Number of PDS predictions for all users	Number of passed PDS for all users	Overall Percentage rate of passed PDS
988	725	61,84 %

According to us, two assumptions can explain these results:

- Users could not pay attention to the information they received because it appeared too late on the screen, after they received information. According to a previous study that we have conducted with inspection methods [7], we indeed observed problems of robustness which negatively impacted real-time information display.
- Users did not even tried to master the predicted dangerous spots because they did not care about information they received and did not perceived any utility of these information in the context they were driving.

Impact on ability to plan routes with destination prediction

Among the 13 users, 10 have received at least one prediction of destination at the beginning of trips they made during the test period. In 41 percent of the cases in which the users received these predictions, we observe they did not accept to display the predicted route for going to their destination. We consider this percentage too low to say that the application was efficient and able to assist the user in their route planning.

B. Analysis of the interviews focused on lived experience

Results about overall lived experience with the learning and proactive application "Driving Coach" were analyzed by classifying positive and negative comments obtained during explicitation interviews with the 13 users in a smartsheet.

From verbalizations, we first identify comments related to perceived utility, satisfaction/dissatisfaction and then highlighted main sources of satisfaction/dissatisfaction.

1) *Perceived utility*

During explicitation interviews, each participant was wondered to express about their feeling of improvement on their driving style. Among the 13 participants, 11 consider they did not improve their driving style: *"I don't think that I changed my way of driving"; "I already had a soft driving"; "To be honest, I did not radically change my driving habits".*

The application is even perceived as useless: "it doesn't present a lot of interest"; "I don't need it, it doesn't provide me anything"; "on a regular trip, it is less relevant because we know it" ; « I've made a trip into Paris last week-end, it didn't tell me anything whereas I don't know Paris. I would have appreciated to get information for helping me to anticipate things ».

2) Satisfaction/Dissatisfaction comments

- In spite of the lack of perceived utility, all participants agreed about 2 main positive aspects of the proactive behavior of the "Driving Coach" application: The application is seen as a way of being aware of the way of driving, provided that the information is displayed in a real-time manner: *« I've been sensitized to my way of driving but it did not make me change »; "it is more an application which helps you to stay watchful, than teaching you to drive differently and helping you to anticipate"; "it confirms for me that I have a manner to drive too sharply and too fast, that's it".*
- The proactive functionality of destination prediction has been appreciated because of minimization of offered tactile commands: *« it avoids to handle the app »; "it is simple because we don't need to look for the information into the device"; "I found that it was clever to recognize my trips, it is something convenient. It is reassuring".*

All participants are nevertheless expressing negative feelings about the learning and proactive behavior of the intelligent informational system. We then distinguish many feelings of frustration and discomfort related to the application: *"it didn't get any interest" ; "I didn't feel secure at all" ; "it made me nervous" ; "some messages for being cautious are unfair, you just want to slap it!" ; "Once, the app told me to prepare to brake in 500 meters whereas I was stopping. We feel embarrassed because the app is telling something wrong".*

3) Sources of Satisfaction/Dissatisfaction comments

Among the negative comments that we collected through the explicitation interviews, we could identify 5 main sources of dissatisfaction of the application that need to be improved:

- Robustness of the application: *"When you go out of an alert zone, it says there is less than 50 meters after 3 km, this is painful"; "it can be interesting but it has to start immediately, it needs to be quick, instant"; "the problem is that it is very long to be launched but when we start the car, we usually want to launch the navigation immediately, and in that situation, this can be already too late for some users".*
- Temporal compatibility with the driving task, which means delivering proactive messages at the good time : *"If I receive information about being careful to the next bends whereas I'm already into it, I won't pay attention anymore to the messages because things already happened"; "if the information is given into the 10 seconds before the area, this might be interesting". ; "there is some places where we cannot brake like we would like to do it".*
- Level of comprehensibility of the messages, which means that the user needs to know and understand why he gets a proactive message in a situation. This might be with explanations if the information is not displayed in a logical way during his activity : *"Why in the morning it considers I'm going to work?"; "I got the messages twice and then I've never seen it anymore, I've never understood why?" ; "I got the message only once, I didn't understand why it didn't warn me each time" ; "sometimes, with exactly the same way of driving, the application didn't tell me anything and sometimes it got woke up and kept saying be careful; I didn't understand why?".*
- Mental workload, legibility and unobtrusiveness regarding to the driving activity : *"When you get a suggestion, you might pay less attention to your driving situation, it can be risky" ; "It is good because he directly proposes to go at my place with only two steps"; "it is an easy way to display GPS, it avoids to look for a destination"; "I saw at a certain point that he suggested me to go at that place and it helped me , it is good, it spares me to handle the device and look for the information".*
- Privacy, which means respecting data which can be estimated as confidential according to the user: *"It's ok because I'm alone in my car. If something else is with me, and I don't want him to know where I'm used to go, this might be embarrassing"; "it was surprising about that and was wondering how it knows that?*
- Personalization, which means offering means to the user to personalize the way he can receives proactive information: *"Maybe it can display something that you can personalize, it would be more user-friendly"*

IV. DISCUSSION - CONCLUSION

This research is about a longitudinal evaluation of users experiences with a learning and proactive information system in car. The information system that we assessed aims at display personalized information in a proactive way, without any request of the user.

Our objective was twofold: to assess the impact of a learning and proactive system on driving style; and to study the lived experience by conducting explicitation interviews with the drivers sample.

The main functionalities were to help users to anticipate personal dangerous driving events and also to help them planning their routes to their usual destinations. Longitudinal tests have been conducted with 15 participants during 6 weeks in order to study the effects of a driving proactive information system on the user's behavior and feelings. In our methodology, qualitative data obtained by explicitation interviews helped us to understand how the users behave with the application and to explain what aspects negatively impacted driving activity and overall lived experience with the application.

The results of this study emphasize the fact that the learning and proactive information system assessed leads to low efficiency, reduced satisfaction and sometimes frustration and misunderstanding.

- Success percentages that we obtained were considered too low to talk about efficacy of the application to help users to anticipate dangerous driving events and to plan their route for going to their usual destinations.

- Plus, results have showed that using the application during 6 weeks negatively impacted the driving activity over the test period. We observed an overall deterioration of the driving style, while the application was supposed to help the driver to anticipate dangerous events and to plan their route.
- According to explication interviews results, we could identified six crucial aspects of the learning and proactive behavior of the application that could explained its negative impact on the overall activity and experience. In the verbalizations of the users, we had identified problems of robustness, temporal compatibility (relevance regarding to the driving task and real-time feedback), comprehensibility of information (lack of explanation and transparency), mental workload (lack of legibility and obtrusiveness), privacy (lack of respect with confidential and personal data), and personalization (means offered by the application to personalize the way that information are displayed). Some of these aspects, such as relevance, transparency, obtrusiveness were also mentioned in previous research work as key factors in human-interface interaction in the way it can impact acceptance of proactive information system [3]. For the future steps of the ergonomic design process of information proactive system, we must conduct further research work to formulate appropriate guidelines that take into account these human factors considerations.

In spite of the overall lack of interest and perceived utility according to our sample of users, proactive behavior of an automotive information system can be interesting added value to the user in the way it provides personalized content without requesting, handling or searching anything in the multimedia device. In our study, results show that users were mostly disturbed by robustness aspects of the application which also negatively impacted relevance of the information, due to technical incompatibility that is currently being improved. The six crucial aspects that have been mentioned as critical points in user interface interactions need to be confirmed by conducting further experiment on bigger samples, with experimented and also novice users. Plus, these results have been obtained with R-Link environment. Additional experiment on another kind of automotive environment would also be useful to confirm our results. Finally, further studies need to be conducted, such as participatory design to involve users in the design process and decide how to improve the current interfaces and interactions. Brainstorming, design studio, personas or focus group could help to answer these central questions in a design process of a learning and proactive information system: When, why and what information should be presented during activity to enhance and enlarge the foreseen part of driving experience?

With this point of view, evaluation is not enough! Collect future expectations and future requirements of users are needed. Indeed, the anticipation of human needs and activities is based on the analysis of numerous factors and data, and on scenario planning as it is done in prospective. Prospective ergonomics [13][14][15] emphasizes the investigation of the use of artifacts to discover their strengths and flaws, and sources of satisfaction and dissatisfaction that could lead to the design of innovative artifacts. Prospective ergonomics, and not only corrective or preventive, will be the next step of this research.

ACKNOWLEDGMENT

The authors would like to thank all participants and project partners for their contribution to the experiment. This work was supported by Renault innovation and research team, Cloudmade society and University of Lorraine.

REFERENCES

[1] D. Tennenhouse, "Proactive computing," Communications of the ACM, vol. 43, pp. 43-50, 2000.

[2] A. Salovaara and A. Oulasvirta, "Six modes of proactive resource management," Proceedings of the third Nordic conference on Human-computer interaction (NordiCHI 2004), 2004.

[3] R. Bader, "Proactive Recommender Systems in Automotive Scenarios", DR, Technische universität München, 2013.

[4] K. Myers and N. York-Smith, "Proactive behavior of a Personal Assistive Agent. Metareasoning in Agent-Based Systems," Proc. AAMAS Workshop on Metareasoning in Agent-Based Systems, 2007, pp.31-45.

[5] M. Thüring and S. Mahlke, "Usability, aesthetics and emotions in human-technology interaction," in International Journal of Psychology, vol. 42,pp.253-264, 2007.

[6] C. Marache-Francisco and E. Brangier, "Gamification and human machine interaction : a synthesis," Le travail humain, vol. 78, n°1, pp. 165-190, 2015.

[7] M. Duczman, E. Brangier and A. Thévenin, "Criteria based approach to assess the user experience of driving information proactive system: integration of guidelines, heuristic mapping and case study," in *Human Factors in Transportation.*, 2016.

[8] E. Brangier, J. Barcenilla, "Designing a product easy to use: adapting technologies to human" ("Concevoir un produit facile à utiliser: Adapter les technologies à l'homme"). Paris, France : Éditions d'Organisation, 2003.

[9] P. Vermersch,"The explicitation interview" ("L'entretien d'explicitation"). Paris, France : ESF, 1994.

[10] B. Cahour, "Affects in cooperative interaction situation: methodological proposition" ("Les affects en situation d'interaction coopérative : proposition méthodologique"). Le travail humain, vol. 69, pp. 379-400, 2006.

[11] C. Petitmengin, A. Remillieux, B, Cahour and S. Carter-Thomas, "A gap in Nisbett and Wilson's findings? A firstperson access to our cognitive processes," Consciousness and Cognition, vol. 22, pp. 654–669, 2013.

[12] A. Light, "Adding method to meaning. A technique for exploring people's experience with technology," Behaviour and Information Technology, vol. 25, pp. 175-187, 2006.

[13] E. Brangier, J-M. Robert, "Prospective ergonomics : basis and issues" ("L'ergonomie prospective : fondements et enjeux "), Le Travail Humain, vol. 77, pp. 1-20, 2014.

[14] J-M. Robert, E. Brangier, "What is prospective ergonomics? A reflection and position on the future of ergonomic," Ergonomics and Health Aspects (HCI 2009) LNCS, 2009, pp. 162–169.

[15] J-M. Robert, E. Brangier, Prospective ergonomics : origin, goal, and prospects. Work, vol. 41, pp. 5235-5242, 2012.

Serious Games Evaluation Using Eye-tracking and Affective Computing Techniques Case Study of OSH Training Course

Iwona Grabska-Gradzińska[1] and Jan K. Argasiński[2]
Department of Games Technology
Jagiellonian University
Kraków, Poland
Email: iwona.grabska@uj.edu.pl[1], jan.argasinski@uj.edu.pl[2]

***Abstract*—The aim of this paper is to provide theoretical and empirical assumptions of framework for evaluation of serious games. When it comes to games, whose main purpose is to train and educate, the category of "fun" is often overlooked, while the category of "education" is interpretated as "teaching how to win the game" instead of "teaching the right decision-making practice". However, in our opinion "fun" is crucial for the success of the whole educational process. "Fun", being a kind of user experience is a sum of player's affects and engagement, and only the properly constructed gameplay can ensure didactic success. In our considerations, we propose pattern and DPE – based (Design, Play, Experience) model for describing and designing games enhanced by eye-tracking methods for analysis of the player's decision-making process and affective computing techniques of evaluating player's engagement. A preliminary case study of simple Occupational Safety and Health (OSH) training game is presented. The ultimate goal is to construct additional – affective – patterns that will ensure designer's way to fully satisfy player's experience in a serious play that will lead him to acquire the essential skills, from the training point of view.**

Keywords–Serious games design, Education process, Decision-making, OSH training, Evaluation methods, Eye-tracking system, Affective computing.

I. Introduction

The aim of this study is to provide insight into serious games evaluation methods using eye-tracking and affective computing techniques.

A. Motivation

The contributed model was used to test Polish academic web browser based on OSH game entitled "Janek w opałach" ("Johnny in Distress"). We believe that it is possible to examine reception of any videogame (particularly serious) by using proper framework and tools, which provide helpful, physiological metrics of player's concentration, perception and commitment (immersion) in the presented game world. The project is now in the course of implementation at Jagiellonian University's Department of Games Technology. The first obtained results encourage further research.

In Section I, the problem is presented and key concepts are described. Section II is devoted to presentation of state of the art in the discipline of affective computing. Section III is dedicated to considerate methodology of performed investigation. The last Section shows preliminary results of the conducted study.

B. Serious Games

In the book "Serious Games", the authors D. Michael and S. Chen state: "A serious game is a game in which education (in its various form) is the primary goal rather than entertainment" [10]. The most important fact about the serious games is that pursuing "serious" purposes (most often – as in the quoted definition – educational, but also therapeutic and others) they remain all the time games – so belong to the field of pleasurable activities. Numerous studies point to the fact, that the entertainment factor – fun – has a very positive impact on the participants' attitude to exercise, but also on the 'breaking' cognitive barriers to educational or therapeutic processes [2][3][4][5]. In this way, serious games are not only edutainment (the knowledge given in an attractive form), but represent something qualitatively different, an alternative form of interaction, which use brings important benefits to the user. Regardless their unique properties, serious games remain games. That means general rules governing their design and creation remain similar as in the case of "normal" games, designed for entertainment purposes only.

C. Games and Game Systems

In fact there is no good definition of game or game system. For every possible characterization, there could be a counterexample provided. In the context of affective serious games the important thing is that they are systems that have mechanics. They can be defined after M. Sicart as "methods invoked by agents to interact with game states" [9] or mention Bjork's and Holopainen's component framework for game systems that contains components such as "boundary" (Rules, Modes, Goals), "holistic" (Game Instance, Game Session, Play Session, Extra-Game Activities), "temporal" (Actions, Events, Closures, End Conditions, Evaluation Functions), and "structural" (Interface, Game Elements, Players, Game Facilitator, Game Time). The elements of this system provide the player with opportunity to interact with the game, overcome given obstacles and achieve goals are mechanics. Mechanics regulate gameplay and therefore are crucial elements of the whole system. Operating mechanics is also the main, distinctive source of players "fun".

D. Patterns in Game Design

Patterns are recurring themes that occur through the game's mechanics. Authors of the book "Patterns in Game Design" [1] perceive them as "a language for talking about gameplay" where "each pattern describes a part of the interaction possible in games, and together with other patterns they describe the possible gameplay in the game". In this framework, the provided patterns are presented through their consequences, relations and references to the gameplay. Combining different mechanics is expected to lead to the formation of emergent entireness

E. Serious Games Design

A popular way to represent the educational objectives is Bloom's Taxonomy. It locates the results of teaching in three areas: cognitive, psychomotoric and affective. A common way to analyze games is an MDA (Mechanics, Dynamics, Aesthetics) framework that takes into account Mechanics, Design and Aesthetic features of the entertainment systems. We would like to use its expansion – DPE (Design, Play, Experience) point of view (see [11] for more information). The basic element in the process of designing serious game is already discussed in "fun" category, as a factor characteristic of the games, yet critical to the educational or therapeutic processes. In paper, we would like to present an approach to design and evaluate affective video games that allow the player to capture (create metrics) the "fun" category for the design improvement iterations purposes.

F. Affective Patterns

The ultimate goal of work is to propose the inclusion of the concept of patterns to DPE framework and a tool for describing mechanics responsible for the "fun" factor in the games. Affective patterns would be "building blocks" from which emotional interactions with the user can be built in order to increase his/her involvement and ultimately control motivation and achieve educational and therapeutic effects.

II. State of the Art

Evaluation of games using data obtained from various sensors and trackers is very fast growing area of computer science.

A. Affective Computing

In her paradigm-establishing book, Rosalind Picard states that "affective computing is the study and development of systems and devices that can recognize, interpret, process and simulate human affects" [7]. The author of the mentioned book believes that including emotional factors in information processing systems can significantly enrich their capabilities. This can occur wherever important factors are correlated with human-computer interaction or decision making.

Within presentation the main focus are systems that recognize emotions and – to some extent – are able to react to them for the needs of creation of serious games and simulations. Intriguing and extensive subject of systems built to emulate "possession" of emotion is not the subject of our interest.

In order to build affective systems, the first thing to do would be to define affective states. This is not an easy task, but only the proper model of emotions will give possibility to set difference between emotional states, which is a crucial operation. Classification scheme needs to be developed that uses specific features form input signals to recognize user emotions.

The research involves use of biosensors (wearables) and specially treated data obtained from standard controllers (like high-resolution mouse, gamepad or motion cameras). The possibilities also include using features such as facial/gesture/pose recognition, speech/voice processing and many others. The need for theory becomes obvious after collecting any preliminary data. In common literature there is a multitude of proposals (i.e. theories by James-Lange, Canon-Bard, Schachter-Singer, etc.). Among numerous available options the James-Lange based appraisal theory by Jesse Prinz [7] was chosen. This bottom-up concept stating that basic bodily reaction is (rather) result of non- cognitive processes allows for sensible amount of intentionality in somatic feedback theory.

B. Eye-tracking

Eye-tracking is more and more often used in games, especially as a controlling device, but also as a researcher's tool for game analysis. Eye-tracker as an evaluation tool was also used in discussed inquiries to investigate the visual search patterns and heat maps describing the main area of interest on the screen [12][13]. Examinations were conducted with use of eye-tracking device to analyze search tasks [14] and measure information acquisition in educational game [18]. Due to their close relation to attentional mechanisms, eye-tracking examination can be used while analyzing the cognitive processes such as language comprehension, memory, mental imagery and decision making [16], especially for decisions based on the choice among a countable set of alternatives

III. Methodology

The main element that must be taken into consideration while designing a (serious) game is mechanics.

A. Pattern framework and DPE

In the study, they have already been considered (after Sicart, see: [9]) as elements that player can interact with in order to change state of the system, as such mechanics are main game-shaping elements. First thing to do when analyzing "Janek w opałach" would be to extract main design patterns that govern the play. It can be done through application of Bjork's and Holopainen's aforementioned framework (see: [1]). The most obvious selection includes patterns such as: Awatars,

Buttons, Clues, Collecting, Controllers, Delayed Effects, Early Elimination, Exploration, Direct Information, Indirect Information, Extra-Game Information, Game State, Overview, Guard, Helpers, Irreversible Actions, Rescue and Survive. Conducted inquiry also showed presence of some misused patterns, such as: Tension, Identification, Illusion of Influence, Emotional Immersion, Consistent Reality Logic. The detailed description of patterns and their relations and consequences is presented in [1].

Reconstructed gameplay overview can be interpreted in relation to DPE (Design, Play, Experience) model. It focuses on user experience seen as individual player's game story, with accompanying affects and resulting engagement. These phenomena are associated with designer's practice (prepared story, mechanics, user interface) and particular course of play (resulting in storytelling, dynamics – "mechanics in motion" and interactivity). When the components are duly assembled, the result can be overall experience of "fun" (see Figure 1).

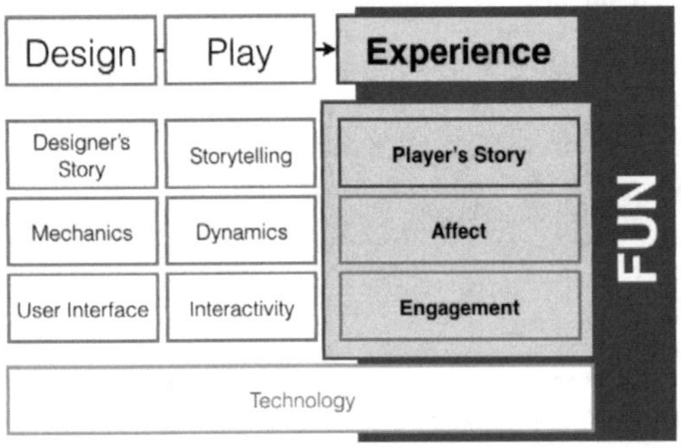

Figure 1: Design, Play, Experience model.

B. Biosensors

In the conducted preliminary experiments, various biosensor platforms such as: Empatica E4 (Developed in the Affective Computing Lab at MIT), e-Health Sensor Platform (Arduino/Raspberry-Pi shield developed by Cooking Hacks) and Microsoft Band 2 (popular fitness tracker) armed with custom made software, were used. In the paper, the results obtained with MSB2 are presented. As it is unspecialized equipment for everyday use and the long-term goal of research is to create a solution that allows obtaining feedback loop by the end users with their own equipment. Collected information were about GSR (Galvanic Skin Response) and HR (Heart Rate).

C. Eye-tracking

The approach presented in this paper is based on the dependence between the gaze direction immediately before making decision and player's strategy. Researchers agree [17], that users have a tendency to shift their attention more towards alternatives they subjectively perceive as being attractive and thus consider to choose. In the case of serious game, the choice is not as obvious as in the multiple-choice tasks, but every time the decision is connected with the hint visible on the screen.

Efficiency of the training can be measured using category of decision made on the base of elements of the game connected to the two game patterns featured in [1] (p. 141): "direct information pattern" (DIP) and "indirect information pattern" (IIP - see Figure 2). The first pattern is connected with gathering information about the game state from the elements connected to the game interface and game control elements. The second means collecting knowledge while interacting with others in the game and speculate using deductive or inductive reasoning. Decisions made in the game on the basis of DIP are useless in the real word situation, because of the lack of game interface indicators in the real emergency situation. Decision made on the basis of IIP shows player skills and knowledge translatable to the real

The goal of the paper is to show the repeatable eye movement schemas and correlate them with the cognitive process of making choices and making decisions to investigate efficiency of the training.

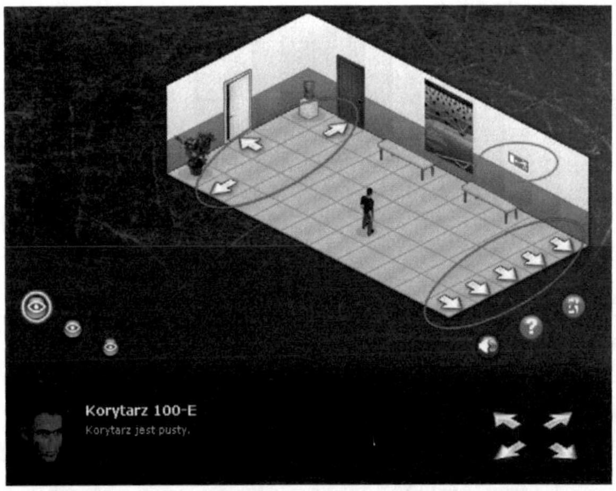

Figure 2: Game scene with indicated DIP (red line) and IIP (blue line).

Figure 3: Emergency exit sign used in the game.

From the long list of decision-making situations the one was chosen by researchers and presented below: problem of perception of emergency signs (presented in Figure 3) in decision-making process. The reasons making this example representative to the general problem of serious games are:

- The game situation is relevant to the real world problem: way choosing to escape the building,

- the problem is crucial from the OSH point of view and represents the core of the training,
- there are two types of hints visible in the screen during the decision making process: one connected with pattern "direct information" and the second connected with "indirect information",
- the scene of the game during the process of decision making is immovable, so both gaze plot and heat maps are available.

IV. Preliminary Results

The research was based on the serious game, based on Occupational Safety and Health (OSH).

A. Case study

In this case aim of the player is to find the way out of the burning campus building. The game has been used at Jagiellonian University, as a part of the OSH training course for students and staff since 2008. The game view is in isometric perspective. The game is rather an ordinary representation of the "adventure game" genre with no time pressure or arcade skills required. The main task of the player is to navigate the areas and safety regulations related to decision-making.

Data was collected from 30 voluntary participants (students of the Jagiellonian University) during the sessions of gameplay. The used equipment was: The Eye Tribe (specification in [15]) – for eye tracking and Microsoft Band 2 for bio-signals (GSR, HR). After finishing the game (usually after 10-15 minutes), the participants were asked to fill custom made questionnaires with two one-dimensional axis (Was experience "unpleasant – neutral – pleasant" and "boring – neutral – fascinating"). The questionnaire also included the "cloud" text with emotional keywords, where participants could mark expressions describing their feelings about the game (i.e. sadness, joy, rage, fear...).

B. Results

Both the eye tracking and affective preliminary data seem to suggest the grouping pattern which can be a base to make the general picture of "Janek w opałach" as a serious game. Although the presentation of the full result will need to be confirmed in additional studies.

In the category of "decision-making" there was one problem taken into consideration: choice of the direction to get out of the building. There were two types of hints, each connected with one game pattern. For OSH training, the essential part is the decision made on the basis of "indirect information pattern".

The results were unexpected and worrying. This educational game does not teach users to pay attention to emergency signs during the evacuation from fire, as there are very attention-grabbing yellow arrows showing possible movement on the stage (elements of Heads Up Display, not the scenery) and they were the only noticeable tips. In 90 percent cases, the players chose the one of the top-left yellow arrow. No one gave a single look to emergency signs.

In the category of "fun", the general attitude to the game was taken into consideration. The second problem was that game was generally considered very dull. In participants' reports, most of them marked "neutral" on "pleasant-unpleasant" axis and "neutral" to "boring" on "arousal" axis. Greater part of respondents did not choose any keywords from the "affective cloud" or chose "irritation". It can be observed on averaged graphs showing trends in changes in GSR and HR (see Figure 4 and Figure 5).Note: there are no markers of concrete values or precise timeline on graphs on purpose – the core interest were changes in tendencies, attaching to specific numbers obtained with device of such low precision, as MSB2 can be delusive and lead to false conclusions.

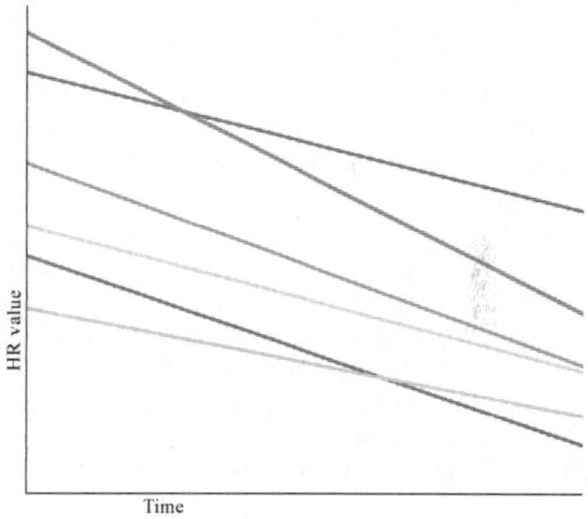

Figure 4: Averaged tendencies in changes in HR.

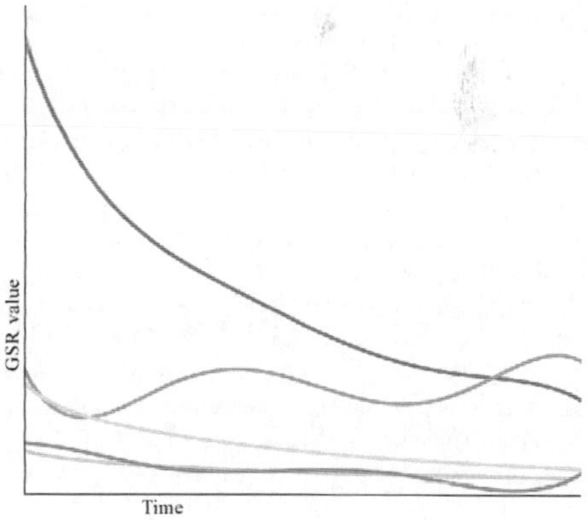

Figure 5: Averaged tendencies in changes in GSR.

V. Conclusion and Future Work

We belive that above results should be taken into consideration while preparing "Janek w opałach 2.0".

The authors would like to emphasize that presented tests are work in progress but we are confident that the combination of affective computing techniques and eye-tracking is a promising direction of research on the evaluation of serious games. Another step is to prepare and conduct further study with more accurate custom-made sensors and dedicated application that will allow to examine gameplay variants.

REFERENCES

[1] S. Bjork and J. Holopainen, *Patterns in Game Design*, Charles Rivers Media, Boston, USA, 2004.

[2] J. Cannon-Bowers and C. Bowers, *Serious Game Design and Development: Technologies for Training and Learning, Information Science Reference*, New York, USA, 2010.

[3] E. Hudlicka, "Affective Computing for Game Design" in *Proceedings of the 4th Intl. North American Conference on Intelligent Games and Simulation (GAMEONNA)*, McGill University, Montreal, Canada, 2008

[4] E. Hudlicka, "To feel or not to feel: The role of affect in human computer interaction" in *International Journal of Human-Computer Studies* 59, 2003, pp. 1-32.

[5] D. Michael and S. Chen, *Serious Games: Games that Educate, Train and Inform*, Thomson Course Technology, Boston, USA, 2006.

[6] C. Pelachaud (ed.), *Emotion-Oriented Systems, John Wiley and Sons Inc.*, Haboken, USA, 2012.

[7] R. Picard, *Affective Computing*, MIT Press, Cambridge, USA, 1997.

[8] J. Prinz, *Gut Reactions. A Perceptual Theory of Emotion*, Oxford University Press, Oxford, UK, 2003.

[9] M. Sicart, "Defining Game Mechanics" in *Game Studies* 8, 2008. [http://gamestudies.org/0802/articles/sicart]

[10] G. Yannakakis and A. Paiva, "Emotions in games" in R. Calvo, S. D'Mello, J. Gratch, and A. Kappas, (eds.), *The Oxford Handbook of Affective Computing*, Oxford University Press, Oxford, UK, 2014, pp. 459–471.

[11] E. Ferdig, *Handbook of Research on Electronic Gaming in Education*, Information Science Reference, New York, USA, 2009.

[12] S. Almeida, *Augmenting Video Game Development with Eye Movement Analysis*, Universidade de Aveiro 2009.

[13] K. Kiili, A. Koivisto, E. Finn, and H. Ketamo,"Measuring user experience in tablet based educational game" in P. Felicia (ed.), *Proceedings of the 6th European Conference on Games-Based Learning*, ECGBL 2012, Cork, Ireland, 4-5 October 2012, pp. 242-249.

[14] A. T. Duchowski, "A breadth-first survey of eye-tracking applications" in *Behav Res Methods Instrum Comput* 34(4), 2002, pp. 455-470.

[15] D. Knoepfle, J. Wang and C. F. Camerer, "Studying Learning in Games Using Eye-Tracking" in *Journal of the European Economic Association* 7, JEEA, 2009, pp. 388–398.

[16] D. C. Richardson and M. J. Spivey, *Eye-Tracking: Characteristics and Methods*, CRC Press, Boca Raton, 2008.

[17] M. A. Lindner et al., "Tracking the decision making process in multiple-choice assessment: Evidence from eye movements" in *Applied Cognitive Psychology* 28(5), 2014, pp. 738–752.

[18] https://theeyetribe.com/ [retrived: 01.2017]

The Usability State of Nine Public Self-Service Applications in Denmark

Jane Billestrup, Jan Stage, Anders Bruun
Institute of Computer Science
Aalborg University
Aalborg, Denmark
{jane,jans,bruun}@cs.aau.dk

***Abstract*—Empirical usability research have documented usability problems in public websites and self-service applications. This paper uses data from usability evaluations of nine Danish public self-service applications from six self-service areas by five different self-service providers, to examine similarities in the usability problems found across self-service applications. The study found that the types of usability problems are present across self-service applications, self-service areas, and self-service providers. However, it is also found that the total number of problems have decreased significantly in the self-service applications that were usability evaluated in 2016. In this paper, we have shown that though the amount of found usability problems is significantly lower, three types of usability problems were present in both old and new self-service applications. These general types were button placement, attaching of files, and meaning of concepts.**

Keywords-Digitalisation; Usability; Usability Evaluation; Self-Service Applications; User-Centred Design

I. Introduction

European countries are currently developing digital self-service applications for their citizens. These efforts are being launched to improve citizens' services and to reduce costs [7]. The Digital Economy and Society Index (DESI) measures the level of digitalisation in EU countries. According to DESI, Denmark is one of the leading countries in regards to digitalisation [7]. In 2012, a digitalisation process was launched in Denmark, with the goal that by the end of 2015, 80% of all communication between citizens and the municipalities should be conducted digitally; this also included digital public self-service applications [17]. In this paper, applications and self-service applications refer to digital forms used for applying for e.g., a new passport, this activity was until recent times conducted on paper, but has been digitalized in recent years.

Having public self-service applications does not mean that citizens are necessarily willing to use these applications. The usage depends on whether citizens find these applications easy to use [5] as poor design can prevent citizens from using these websites [15].

In Denmark self-service applications are developed by different companies, and several companies are developing similar self-service applications and competing about selling their applications to the municipalities 98 municipalities. The citizens do not experience that the applications are developed by different self-service providers as all applications follow the same design style guide, though the content and layout vary between the different companies.

To support the Danish initiative, the joint IT organisation of the municipalities in Denmark (KOMBIT) developed two sets of user-centred guidance materials in 2012 and early 2013, to support self-service providers in developing user-friendly self-service applications [2]. Similar initiatives have been taken in countries, such as the United States, the United Kingdom, and South Africa [18] [22].

In this paper, we analyse the usability problems found across self-service applications and self-service providers to find commonalities in the usability problems. The purpose was to ascertain if the usability of self-service applications has been improved and if there are general usability problems across self-service applications. The categories of usability problems identified here have previously been published. The purpose and the content of this paper differs from [21].

In the following section, we present the method of collecting and analysing the data for this study, Section III describes the findings. Section IV discusses these findings, and Section V presents the conclusion.

II. Method

For this study, we use lists of usability problems gathered from usability evaluations of nine Danish self-service applications developed by five self-service providers for six different self-service areas. These evaluations were conducted between 2010 and 2016 [1] [3] [11].

A. Case Companies

This study includes three of the largest and most experienced companies in regards to developing public self-service applications in Denmark, one medium sized experienced company, and one small company with little experience in developing public self-service applications. Table 1 shows the year the usability evaluations were conducted and the relation between companies and self-service applications.

Usability evaluations were conducted of nine different public self-service applications from five different self-service providers, in six different self-service areas. The table also shows that the applications were evaluated in four usability evaluations.

TABLE I. SHOWS THE RELATION BETWEEN COMPANIES AND SELF-SERVICE APPLICATIONS AND NUMBER OF USABILITY PROBLEMS FOUND

Year of Evaluation	Tested Self-Service Solutions	Number of Test Persons	Company and Usability Problems	Total number of usability problems
2010	Building permits	10	Company E 7/26/38 +4	75
2014	Assistive technologies	8	Company A 2/17/17 Company B 5/18/14 Company C 0/11/6 Company D 1/15/13	36 37 17 29
2014	Marriage certificates	4	Company B 1/3/2	6
2016	Address change Rent subsidy Medical practitioner	6	Company E 2/3/0 Company D 1/3/3 Company C 2/4/0	5 7 6

B. *Self-Service Applications*

This section provides a description of each self-service area included in this study.

1) Building Permits (2010)

The self-service application for building permits is used when citizens apply for conducting construction work where a building permit is needed, such as building a garage. The evaluated building application was a digitalised paper application developed by company E. The application was developed before the approach of user-centred design was introduced in the development of public self-service applications.

2) Assistive Technologies (2014)

The self-service application for procurement of assistive technologies is used if a citizen needs to apply for assistive technologies, such as a hearing aid. These applications were developed just after the introduction of user-centred design in public self-service applications by companies A, B, C and D.

3) Marriage Certificates (2014)

The self-service application for marriage certificates is filled out by citizen's wanting to get married either in a church or by having a registry-office wedding. This application was developed just after the introduction of user-centred design in public self-service applications by company B.

4) Address Change (2016)

The self-service application for an address change is used when citizens are moving to a new address. This application was developed more than two years after the introduction of user-centred design in public self-service applications. This self-service application was developed by company E.

5) Rent Subsidy (2016)

The self-service application for rent subsidy is used if citizens have a low income and live in rented accommodation. This application was developed more than two years after the introduction of user-centred design in public self-service applications by company D.

6) Medical Practitioner (2016)

The self-service application for changing medical practitioner is used if a citizen wants to change to another medical practitioner. This application was developed more than two years after the introduction of user-centred design in public self-service applications by company C.

C. *Usability Evaluations*

All usability evaluations were conducted as think-aloud evaluations on a PC in a Chrome browser. The building application, assistive technology applications, and marriage certificate application were conducted in a usability laboratory. The applications of address change, rent subsidy and medical practitioner were conducted at a student café.

1) Test Persons

In regards to the number of test persons for each evaluation, we are aware that the correct number of test persons has been discussed extensively in the research community e.g., [6] [10] [13] [16] [20]. All usability evaluations in this study were conducted with between four and ten test persons. All test persons in each test received the same instructions and the same tasks. The tasks were scenario based and were tasks a user would typically complete in these systems.

For the building application, the evaluation was conducted in 2010 with ten test persons. All test persons were experienced in conducting "do-it-yourself" (DIY) work. Their DIY experiences varied; two had only painted their homes, and eight had either restored parts or all of their homes. Experience with filling out online forms for the municipality varied from none to a few times for eight of the participants. The two remaining participants were more experienced and had filled out forms for the municipality more than ten times.

For the procurement of assistive technologies, the evaluation was conducted in 2014 with eight test persons. The four different self-service applications in this self-service area were usability evaluated during the same usability evaluation, where the four applications were given to the users in a different order to even out bias. Seven participants had experience with filling out public applications, of these, three had experience with public self-service applications; of these three, two had experience with the public self-service application for assistive technologies.

For ordering of a marriage certificate, the evaluation was conducted in 2014 with four test persons. Three test persons had experience with public self-service applications, though neither with this particular application.

The three self-service applications for address change, rent subsidy, and changing medical practitioner were usability evaluated in one evaluation with the same test-persons in 2016 with six test persons. All users had filled out a self-service application for an address change in the past; four participants had used the self-service application for a rent subsidy and changing medical practitioner before this usability evaluation.

2) Data Analysis from Usability Evaluations

All data were analysed using the instant data analysis (IDA) method [12] by researchers. All usability problems were categorised as either critical, serious or cosmetic, in regards to levels of confusion and frustration of the participants, and whether they were able to fill out the forms correctly [14].

3) Results of Usability Evaluations

All results were documented in a list describing and categorising each usability problem. At least two people took part in the characterisation of the problems. The lists of usability problems across all nine self-service applications consisted of a total of 218 usability problems (21 critical, 100 serious, 93 cosmetic, and four uncategorised problems); no usability problems were removed prior to the analysis. The distribution of the usability problems across self-service applications, self-service providers and severity can be found in Table 1. The +4 by company E in the building application means that there were two problems where the severity was uncategorised as this categorisation required a deeper knowledge of the domain than the researchers had acquired; it was left to the case workers to conduct the classifications of these four usability problems.

D. Data Analysis

The usability problems were analysed using a descriptive coding as described by Saldana [19]. All 218 problems found across the lists of usability problems were coded in regards to the character of the problem. The descriptive coding provided us with a list of three categories after removing all specific problems only found in one self-service application. Subsequently, all the problems in each category were discussed between two researchers to validate the categories and ascertain if the problems in each category were comparable across self-service applications and self-service providers. All problems not directly comparable were removed, leaving only the problems appearing across self-service applications. The three categories were named: button placement, attachment of files, and meaning of concepts.

III. FINDINGS

In this section, we present the findings from the categories button placement, attachment of files, and meaning of concepts, respectively. We also compare the results of the usability evaluations between applications from each self-service provider.

A. Button Placement

Usability problems in relations to button placement were found in four of the six self-service areas. It was mainly the placement of the "next-button" that confused the test persons.

In the building application, the buttons were placed at the top of the application, which made the test persons overlook the buttons, as this placement made these buttons difficult for them to find. Similar problems were found in two assistive technology self-service applications. The "next" button was hidden until the test person scrolled down to the bottom of the page, in the self-service applications for address change, and changing medical practitioner. It was later discovered that the buttons were only hidden in some Internet browsers. Subsequently, four different browsers have been checked: Chrome, Firefox, Safari and Internet Explorer. In Chrome the "next" button was hidden, in Firefox the button was partly visible and in Internet Explorer and Safari, the button was fully visible. The only indication of hidden buttons was the scrollbar located on the left side, which some test persons missed.

B. Attachment of Files

In the applications for building permits, rent subsidy, and changing medical practitioner, some test persons did not understand how to attach a file. When the test persons had chosen a file to attach, they did not understand that they then had to press the "attach" button to get the file attached. Instead, some test persons clicked the "next" button, which meant that the document did not get attached.

When trying to attach files, the test persons in both the building application and two of the assistive technologies applications had difficulties seeing that a file had been attached. When a test person experienced problems understanding how to attach a file they tried to follow the guidelines; however, these were constructed to be browser specific and did not match the actual flow in the Chrome browser used for the usability evaluations.

C. Meaning of Concepts

Meaning of concepts is used as a broad categorisation of problems in regards to what the users read in the applications. This category covers wording, and term users do not understand, consequences of a conducting a specific action, like clicking yes or no, and unclear use of language, meaning that users do not understand what is expected of them.

The test persons experienced problems understanding the wording and terms used in the applications for building permits and all four applications for assistive technologies. The test persons had insecurities about clicking yes or no, as the consequences of choosing one or the other were not clearly stated, e.g., the test persons had to decide whether the municipality was allowed access to their medical file, but neither an explanation as to why or the consequences of choosing no was stated if they chose not to allow access.

In one of the applications for assistive technologies, the test persons had to click either yes or no in a radio button to the question "Do you consent to this?" The wording confused the test persons as they became insecure about what "this" meant. In the marriage application, one section had to be filled out by both parties which confused the test persons as the wording made them believe both parties had to be present in the same room to do that, which was not the case. In the application for address change, several test persons did not understand when to use a power of attorney, or what to use it for.

IV. DISCUSSION

In this section, we discuss our findings. Each of the three categories of usability problems described in the results section is compared to Nielsen's ten usability heuristics.

A. *Comparison of Applications From One Self-service Provider*

We have only evaluated one self-service application from company A, and both evaluations of the self-service applications from company B was conducted in 2014, which means that neither of these would be interesting to compare. Self-service applications from company C and D were evaluated in 2014 and 2016, and self-service applications from company E were evaluated in 2010 and 2016. In this section, we will compare the number of usability problems compared to the type of applications and describe the tendencies in regards to the design of self-service applications.

1) Company C

In 2014 the application for procurement of assistive technologies was usability evaluated. This evaluation provided 17 usability problems in total, of which none were categorised as critical, 11 were categorised as serious, and six were categorised as cosmetic problems. This application was developed as a digitalized paper application and was part of a larger healthcare system.

The application looked identical to a paper application citizens used to fill out by hand, both in terms of format and design. The application was developed to provide the basic information the caseworkers needed to handle the application and did not intend to ease the workload of the caseworkers or to make the application process easier for the citizens [1].

In 2016 their application for changing medical practitioner was evaluated. This usability evaluation showed six problems in total, of which two were critical, and four were serious, and none were cosmetic. The application from 2016 was developed as a wizard and not as a digitalized paper application.

A segment of the application from 2014 is shown in Figure 1 on the top, and the application from 2016 is shown at the bottom.

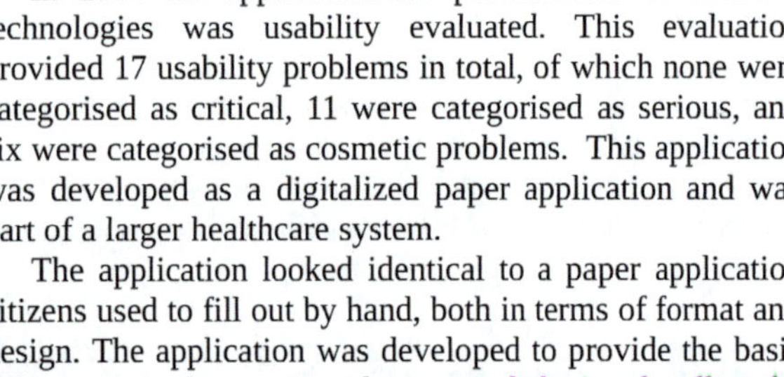

Figure 1. Shows parts of both applications from company C

2) Company D

In 2014 the application for procurement of assistive technologies was usability evaluated. That evaluation provided 29 usability problems in total, of which one were categorised as critical, 15 were categorised as serious, and 13 were categorised as cosmetic problems. This application was developed as a digitalized paper application and was part of a larger healthcare system. In 2016 the application for rent subsidy was evaluated; this evaluation identified seven problems. Of these, one usability problems was categorised as critical, three as serious, and three was classified as cosmetic usability problems.

The application from 2016 was developed as a wizard and not as a digitalized paper application. Segments of both applications are shown in Figure 2. The application from 2014 is shown at the top and the application from 2016 is shown at the bottom of Figure 2.

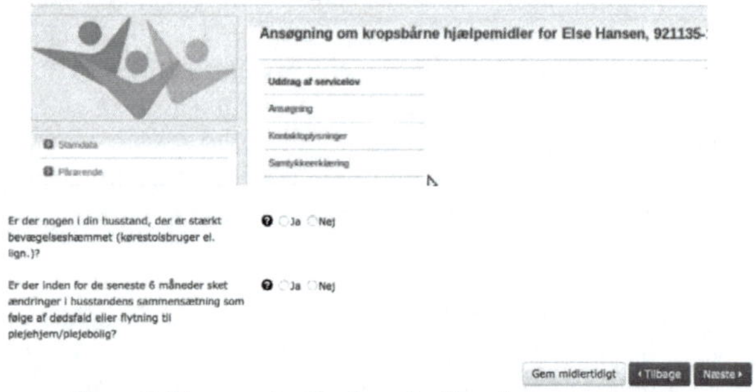

Figure 2. Shows parts of both applications from company D

The application from 2014 is shown to the left, and the application from 2016 is shown to the right.

3) Company E

In 2010 the application for applying for a building permit was usability evaluated. That evaluation provided 75 usability problems in total, of which seven were categorised as critical, 26 were categorised as serious, and 28 were categorised as cosmetic problems. This application was developed as a digitalized paper application.

In 2016 the application for changing address was evaluated; this evaluation identified five problems. Of these two were critical, three were serious, and none were classified as cosmetic usability problems.

The application from 2016 was developed as a wizard and not as a digitalized paper application. Segments of both applications are shown in Figure 3.

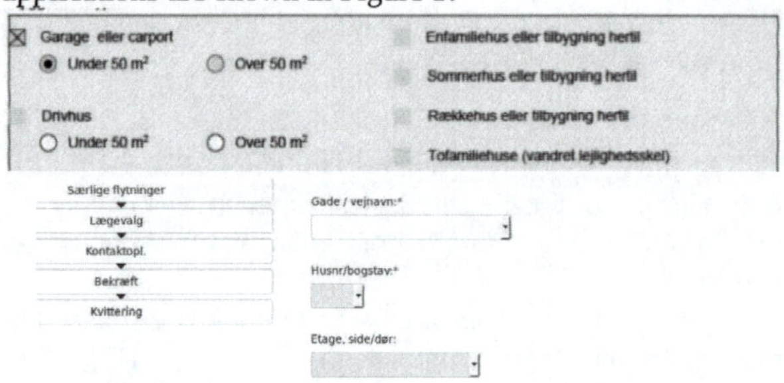

Figure 3. Shows parts of both applications from company E

The application from 2010 is shown on the top, and the application from 2016 is shown on the buttom of Figure 3.

B. Button Placement

In the building application, the "next" button was placed counter-intuitive to the test persons. However, most problems in regards to button placement were present because the self-service applications were not optimised to different browser types.

Geminus Ranking logs Internet activity in Denmark to give access to statistical data about technology and Internet usage. According to Geminus, Chrome is the most used Internet browser on computers in Denmark [8]. This indicates that a large amount of Danish citizens would experience hidden "next" buttons, which could lead to confused and annoyed citizens who might not be interested in using self-service applications[5] [15].

C. Attachment of Files

Our results showed two types of problems in regards to file attachments. One type of problem was test persons not understanding how to attach a file; they pressed the "next" button instead of the "attach" button. Some tried to follow the guidelines in the self-service application. However, the guidelines were optimised for another browser, meaning that the steps did not fit.

A citizen experiencing these types of problems will likely lead to their inability to correctly attach a file. This means that they will either need to ask for help or send an application that might be incomplete. If they press the wrong button, they may not even be aware that their application is incomplete.

The other problem type is users not seeing when a file has been attached, which shows that the relevant information was either too small, or too much information was on the screen meaning that there was too little focus on the essentials, leading to users not noticing when a file had been attached.

D. Meaning of Concepts

Test persons experiencing problems with understanding meaning of concepts were found in all the evaluated self-service applications. The wording used was mainly directed at professionals or people with some amount of domain knowledge, and was not necessarily understandable for citizens. Or, the language was simply unclear. This problem made some test persons confused and afraid to make mistakes; as a result, some test persons stopped for a longer period, trying to figure out the consequences of choosing one option over the other. Several test persons stated that they would have given up and contacted the municipality by phone if this was not a test and they experienced this kind of doubt when filling out a public self-service application.

E. Usability Problems Across Self-Service Providers and Year of Evaluations

Table 2 shows a decrease of the numbers of found usability problems between 2014 and 2016 for company C and D, and between 2010 and 2016 for company E.

TABLE II. SHOWS THE NUMBER OF FOUND USABILITY PROBLEMS FROM EACH SELF-SERVICE PROVIDER AND USABILITY EVALUATION

Company	Year	Critical	Serious	Cosmetic	Uncategorised	Total number of usability problems
C	2014	0	11	6		17
	2016	2	4			6
D	2014	1	15	13		29
	2016	1	3	3		7
E	2010	7	26	38	4	75
	2016	2	3	0		5

Billestrup et. al. found that the Danish self-service applications for procurement of assistive technologies, which were usability evaluated in 2014, were not developed with a user-centred approach, though this approach had officially been implemented as guidelines by the joint IT organisation of the municipalities during this period [1].

As the number of found usability problems have dropped significantly between the evaluations conducted in 2010 and 2014 to the ones conducted in 2016, this indicates that some improvements have been made; this could indicate that a more user-centred approach has been enforced by companies during this period or simply that the evaluated applications from 2016 have been developed as wizards, designed to help the users. Also. In 2014 it was decided that all new public self-service applications should be usability evaluated which itself also could have had an impact [4] as usability evaluations might have caught some issues before the citizens had to use these applications. A decreasing number of usability problems could also indicate that citizens have increased their understanding of using public self-service applications over the past few years.

V. CONCLUSION

In this paper, we analysed the usability problems across self-service applications and self-service providers. The purpose of this study was to gain a greater understanding of the broader usability issues in public self-service applications. Our results show three types of usability problems found across self-service applications and self-service providers.

We have shown that public self-service applications need to be optimised for different browsers as this otherwise can lead to usability problems for the users. This should also include optimisation for different technologies such as tablets and smartphones, as Geminous rankings show that 56% of Internet usage in Denmark is not conducted from a computer but other devices, e.g., smartphones and tablets [9].

The first evaluation was conducted in 2010, two years before the user-centred design approach was implemented in the development of public self-service applications in Denmark. In 2012 the user-centred design approach was implemented, meaning that the systems usability evaluated in 2014 and 2016 were evaluated after the introduction of a user-centred focus. Though Billestrup et al. found that this was not the case in with self-service applications developed in 2014 [1].

This study showed that the number of problems has decreased since the introduction of the user-centred design approach, and we have shown an indication of more usable self-service applications, as the number of usability problems was significantly lower in 2016. However, we have also shown that though the amount of found usability problems was significantly lower, three types of usability problems were present in both old and new self-service applications.

This means that the approach taken by focusing on a user-centred approach, using wizards, and conducting usability evaluations has not been sufficient in eliminating some general and reoccurring usability problems found across self-service applications, self-service providers and self-service areas.

A. *Limitations and Future Work*

This study is limited to a single country by its focus on the Danish self-service applications and problems found across these self-service applications. As for future work, it would be interesting to compare our findings to similar studies from other countries.

Another limitation is that the lists of usability problems we have analysed for this study did not state how many test persons experienced each of the listed problems.

We are aware that many unknown factors could implicate the changes in the self-service applications besides the companies using a more user-centred development approach these unknown factors should be investigated further.

References

[1] J. Billestrup, M. Larusdottir, and J. Stage, "A Case Study of Four IT Companies Developing Usable Public Digital Self-Service Solutions". *In proceedings the Ninth International Conference on Advances in Computer-Human Interactions, ACHI, 2016.*

[2] J. Billestrup, a. Bruun, and J. Stage, "UX Requirements to Public Systems for All: Formalisation or Innovation". *Proceedings of INTERACT 15th IFIP TC. 13 International Conference on Human-Computer Interaction, Vol. 22, p. 2015407, 2015.*

[3] A. Bruun, J. J. Jensen, M. Skov, and J. Stage, "Usability Evaluation of an electronic building application". White paper, 2010.

[4] User Evaluation of public self-service evaluations, 2016. *http://www.kl.dk/Administration-og-digitalisering/ Brugertest-bidrager-til-oget-brugervenlighed-id211070/ [retrieved: January, 2017].*

[5] T. Clemmensen and D. Katre, "Adapting e-gov usability evaluation to cultural contexts". *In proceedings of Usability of e-government systems*, 2012.

[6] D. A. Caulton, "Relaxing the homogeneity assumption in usability testing". *Behaviour & Information Technology*, vol. 20 no. 1, pp. 1-7, 2001.

[7] DESI Index, 2016. https://ec.europa.eu/digitalagenda /en/scoreboard/ [retrieved: January, 2017].

[8] Geminus Rankings, browsers, 2016. http:// rankings.dk/en/rankings/web-browsersgroups .html [retrieved: January, 2017].

[9] Geminous Rankings, devices, 2016. http://rankings.dk/en/ rankings/pc-vs-nonpc.html [retrieved: January, 2017].

[10] W. Hwang and G. Salvendy, "Number of people required for usability evaluation: The 10±2 rule". *Commun. ACM, vol.* 53, no. 5, pp. 130–133, 2010.

[11] K.B. Jørgensen and M. L. Stentoft, Usability Analysis of Public Self-Service Applications. Student report, 2016.

[12] J. Kjeldskov, M. B. Skov, and J. Stage, "Instant Data Analysis: Conducting Usability Evaluations in a Day". *Proceedings of the third Nordic conference on Human-computer interaction, NordiCHI*, ACM, pp. 233-240, 2004.

[13] E. L-C. Law, and E. Hvannberg, "Analysis of combinatorial user effect in international usability test". *Proceedings of CHI, pp. 9-16*, 2004.

[14] R. Molich, "User-Friendly Web Design" (in Danish). Ingeniøren Books, Copenhagen, 2nd edition, 2003.

[15] S. Wangpipatwong, W. Chutimaskul, and B. Papastratorn, "Understanding citizen's continuance intention to use e-government website: A composite view of technology acceptance model and computer self-efficiency". *The Electronic Journal of e-Government*, vol. 6, no. 1, 2008.

[16] J. Nielsen, "10 Usability Heuristics for User Interface Design". *Fremont: Nielsen Norman Group*, 1995.

[17] Digital applications. Organisation of the Municipalities in Denmark, 2012. http://www.kl.dk/Administration-og-digitalisering /Lov-om-obligatorisk-digital-selvbetjening-og-di gital-post-er-vedtaget-id105354/ [retrieved: January, 2017]

[18] M. C. Pretorius and A. P. Calitz, "The South African user experience maturity status for website design in provincial governments". *Proceedings of the 12th European Conference on eGovernment*, ESADE, pP. 589-599, 2012.

[19] J. Saldaña, *"The coding manual for qualitative researchers"*. Sage, 2015.

[20] M. Schmettow, "Sample Size in Usability Studies". *Commun. ACM* vol. 55, no. 4, pp. 64–70, 2012.

[21] J. Billestrup, N. Bornø, A. Bruun, and J. Stage, "Usability problems found across public self-service applications and self-service providers". In: *Proceedings of OzCHI*. ACM, pp. 623-625, 2016

[22] B. Soufi, and M. Maguire, "Achieving usability within e-government websites illustrated by a case study evaluation". *In Symposium on Human Interface and the Management of Information*, Springer-Verlag, pp. 777-784, 2007.

Methods for Analyzing Millennials' Characteristics and Contexts of Media Usage in Multi-Device Environments

Mingyu Lee[1], Jiyoung Kwahk[1], Sung H. Han[1],
Kyudong Park[2], Ju Hwan Kim[2], Dawoon Jeong[1]
[1]Department of Industrial Management & Engineering
[2]Department of Creative IT Engineering
POSTECH, Pohang, Republic of Korea
e-mail: {mk3215s2, kjy, shan, kdpark, juankim, jdw0303}@postech.ac.kr

Seokmin Oh, Gunho Chae
User Experience Center
Samsung Electronics Co., Ltd.
Seoul, Republic of Korea
e-mail: {seokmin0717.oh, gunho.chae}@samsung.com

***Abstract*—It is an era of multi-device. Today's users produce and consume media by using various devices in various environments. Especially millennials have been in contact with digital devices likes PC, tablet, and smartphone since childhood, so their behaviors to produce and consume media by using the digital devices can be displayed diversely compared with other generations. Their needs on the media products can also be diverse. In developing process of media products, it is important to grasp users' media usage patterns and divide them into several groups that show similar characteristics to appropriately respond to their needs. By doing this, it is possible to understand the user more precisely, and developers or marketers can develop appropriate functions or strategies for each group to improve the users' satisfaction. For that reason, this study is a research related to investigation of millennials' behavior to produce and consume media by using multiple devices. It suggests a method to group millennials by their context of media use based on a survey of their media and related devices usage. The result of the study can be used to develop a user model or user scenario for product development and marketing.**

Keywords—Millennials; Multi-device experience; Media; User modeling; Use case.

I. INTRODUCTION

It is an era of multi-device. With the development of information and communication technology, various types of devices have been developed. Users can utilize a number of devices to achieve their own needs, including desktop computers, laptops, smartphones, tablet PC, cameras, media players, and TVs. Nowadays, users perform activities that span devices, rather than using different devices for different activities [1]. Even if users do the same activities, they use the appropriate devices according to occasion and location. Cisco estimates that there will be around seven internet-connected devices per person by 2020 [2]. Due to the multi-device environment, designers and marketers have become more anxious. Even if you create a service or function, they need to consider many devices associated with it (Figure 1). If internet of things (IoT), where all things are connected to the Internet, become more widely commercialized, there would be much more devices to consider.

Designers and marketers need to take a deeper look at the device as well as the user. As users are able to use many devices, their usage patterns have become more diverse. As a result, users shouldn't be viewed as a group, and it is necessary to divide them into several segments according to the patterns and purposes of use.

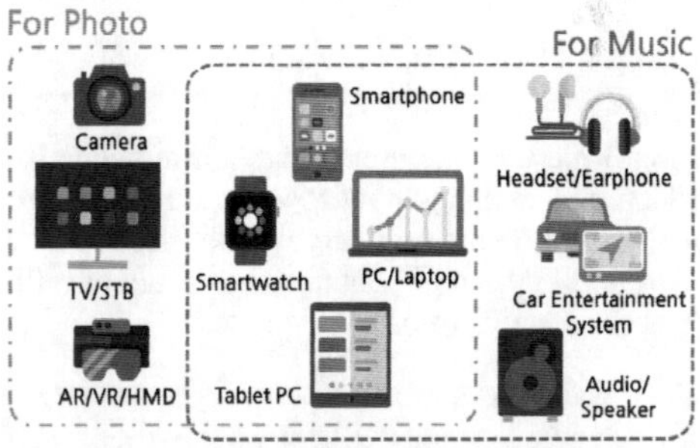

Figure 1. Many devices associated with media (Photos and music)

In particular, millennials are experts in multi-devices [3]. Millennials, also known as Generation Y or Net Generation (or Generation N), are a cohort that directly follows Generation X [4]. Generally, researchers define millennials as births from the early 1980s to the early 2000s [4]. According to a survey of Americans' generation and gadgets, millennials have more devices than previous generations, such as Generation X and Baby Boomer Generation (Table 1) [5]. In addition, since they have been in contact with devices since childhood, they have better understands how to connect and use digital devices. Thus, it is expected that millennials show much diverse usage patterns and needs in a multi-device environment than other generations. Even the purpose of utilizing multi-devices can be different.

It means that we require a deeper understanding of millennial Generation. Especially when using media, it is necessary to understand how millennials consume the media, for what purpose they use the media devices, and in which environment they are consuming the media. This can help developers to develop appropriate functions or services for millennial Generation.

This study is a basic research on media usage behavior of millennial Generation in the multi-device environment. In particular, this study proposes a way to classify millennials into several types based on the survey on them and to derive where and when they use media with multiple devices. This study suggests an objective and quantitative analysis method that utilizes statistical techniques.

TABLE I. % OF AMERICANS IN EACH GENERATION THAT OWN EACH DEVICE [5]

	Cell phone	Desktop	Laptop	MP3 player	Tablet PC
Millennials	95%	57%	70%	74%	5%
Generation X	92%	69%	61%	56%	5%
Younger Baby Boomers	86%	65%	49%	42%	4%
Older Baby Boomer	84%	64%	43%	26%	3%
Silent Generation	68%	48%	30%	16%	1%
G.I. Generation	48%	28%	10%	3%	1%

Section 3 presents the user survey on millennials' media usage. Section 4 explains how to derive the user groups of millennials based on the user survey data. Section 5 accounts for how to derive the representative use cases of millennials for two types of media (music and photos).

II. EXISTING STUDIES ON CHARACTERISTICS OF MILLENNIALS

There were many studies that had characterized millennials. These studies yielded common characteristics of millennials compared to other generations, such as Baby Boomer or Generation X. According to a survey of millennial generations conducted at the Pew Research Center in 2010 and 2014, millennials had the characteristics of being individual, confident, self-expressive, liberal, and not afraid of change [6]. In addition, they valued the family and were less likely to identify with a particular political party [6]. They were identified as "digital natives", who tried to do many things using digital devices [7]. Millennials in adulthood were detached from institutions and networked with friends [7].

Much research has been conducted on the analysis of the media use characteristics of millennials. These studies have analyzed the way they consume music or TV/video contents. According to these studies, millennials had the following characteristics:

- This generation streams music through technological devices, via the use of social media among other platforms [8].
- To this generation, it is important habits not only to download music online but also to share music [9][10]. They express emotions, share with friends, and reinforce each other's relationships through music [9].
- This generation downloads digital music. However, this generation purchases CDs to express the tribute to the artists [11].
- This generation wants to listen to music instantly whenever and wherever [8].
- This generation is a user of the online platform to access and share music files [11][12].
- This generation consumes video contents with the second screen devices rather than on the TV [13].
- This generation is good for multitasking, and they consume the video contents in multitasking environment [13].

However, previous studies had analyzed the millennials as only one group of user and derived unique characteristics for whole millennials by comparing them with the other generations. Millennial Generation is a generation with a population size of about 20 years. Generally, about 25% of the world's population is millennials. It is difficult to interpret their characteristics, seeing millennials as a group. For a more sophisticated understanding of Millennial Generation, it is necessary to analyze the millennials more finely.

III. USER SURVEY

In this study, we conducted a user survey to identify the media usage of millennials. The purpose of this survey was to collect basic data for user analysis.

TABLE II. SUBJECTS OF THE SURVEY

Millennials who are actively using media	- Millennial Generation (the early 20s to mid 30s)
	- Actively use music, photos, and videos
	- Connect various electronic devices to utilize media

The survey was conducted on millennials (Table 2). In this study, we defined births from the mid-80s to early 2000s as Millennial Generation. However, the survey was conducted only for those aged 20 years or older, because it was judged that adolescents have limits to use media due to academic reasons. We expected that millennials are familiar dealing with digital devices and they have the highest desire to achieve their needs by utilizing various types of devices. In addition, millennials are the primary consumers of various media devices, so they must be considered to develop media devices or create marketing strategies.

This study focused on the media usage. In particular, we focused on creating and consuming photos and videos and listening to music. Therefore, respondents who did not produce or consume media were preferentially excluded.

The following items were surveyed (Table 3). First, demographic information of respondents was collected. Age, sex, occupation, and family members of the respondents. Next, the respondents' degree of interest in the media was collected. We collected that the number of times they used music, pictures, and videos for a day. Respondents were also asked to answer the question about the degree of interest in media devices.

TABLE III. SURVEY ITEMS

Survey items	Descriptions
Demographic information	Basic demographic information such as age, sex, and occupation of the respondents
Degree of interest in the media	How much are the respondents interested in media and media-related products
Products in use (Devices & Apps)	The types, names, manufacturers, model names of the products or apps that the respondents are using
Context of using the products	The purpose of each product, where to use it, and when to use it
Cognitive Style	Psychological test for the classification of the respondents' psychological types (short MBTI)

In addition, information about the media devices and apps in use were collected, such as the types (smartphone, tablet PC, TV, laptop, camera, audio, etc.), the manufacturers (Apple, Samsung, LG, Canon, Bose, etc.), and model names of the devices and apps. We also asked when, where, and for what purpose each device was used. Finally, we added a questionnaire item (short version of Myers-Briggs Personality Test) to identify the relationship between respondents' personality and their media usage.

360 millennials participated in the survey, and it was conducted for a week. A web-based questionnaire was constructed for the convenience of the survey. Respondents were able to access the questionnaire via the web URL. For those who participated in the survey, were provided with certain rewards.

IV. USER CLASSIFICATION

In this study, we tried to classify media usage of millennials into several types. People have their own needs of using media. It is most ideal if you are able to provide customized strategies for all of them. However, this is technically and costly difficult. Instead, if we can group users with similar tendencies and derive their common characteristics, we can achieve a better strategic effect than treating all millennial users equally.

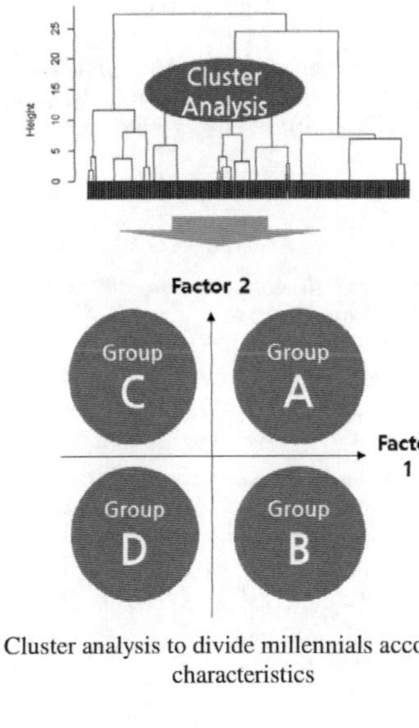

Figure 2. Cluster analysis to divide millennials according to common characteristics

The data collected from user survey was used to divide user groups. The data were divided into two sets. First one was the data for classifying the user groups, such as the number of products and apps currently in use (Figure 2). The remaining data was used as data to determine the characteristics of the group.

After 4 groups were derived, an additional data analysis was performed to derive the characteristics of the groups. We checked for differences between groups for the other variables, including age, gender, occupation, interest in new products, frequency of purchasing new products, and results of personality test (Figure 3). For the data analysis, analysis of variance (ANOVA) and cross-tabulations were used. ANOVA was performed for continuous variables such as age. If there were significant differences, post-hoc analysis was performed to determine which groups differed from each other. Cross-tabulations was performed for nominal or ordinal variables such as gender and occupation. Likewise, when there were significant differences, post-hoc analysis identified the groups that differed.

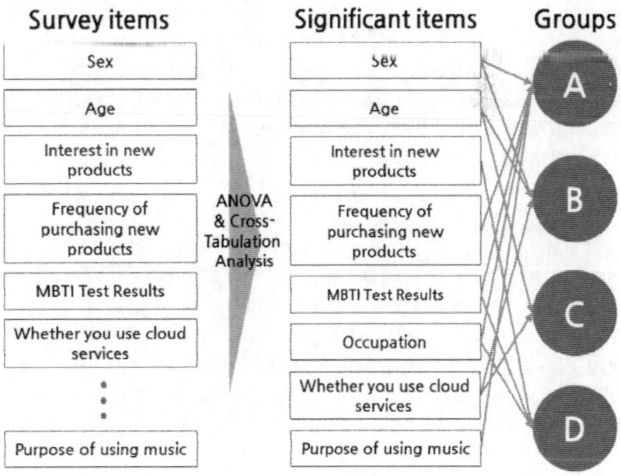

Figure 3. Statistical analysis to define characteristics of each group

Each group was defined based on the characteristics. A name and an image that can represent each group was constructed. The proportion of each group was derived. The characteristics of the group were classified into demographic characteristics, the products in use, and the context of media usage (Figure 4).

TABLE IV. EAMPLE OF THE TATA ON LOCATION, TIME, AND PURPOSE OF USING MEDIA (PHOTOS AND MUSIC)

Sub No.	Media types	Location			Time			Purpose		
		Living room	...	Office	Time to relax	...	Time to study	To listen	...	To share
Sub01	Music	O	...	X	O	...	X	O	...	O
Sub02	Music	X	...	O	O	...	O	O	...	X
Sub03	Music	X	...	O	O	...	O	O	...	X
Sub04	Music	O	...	O	O	...	O	O	...	O
Sub05	Music	O	...	O	X	...	X	O	...	X
...	...	...	...	...	...	...	...	...	...	...

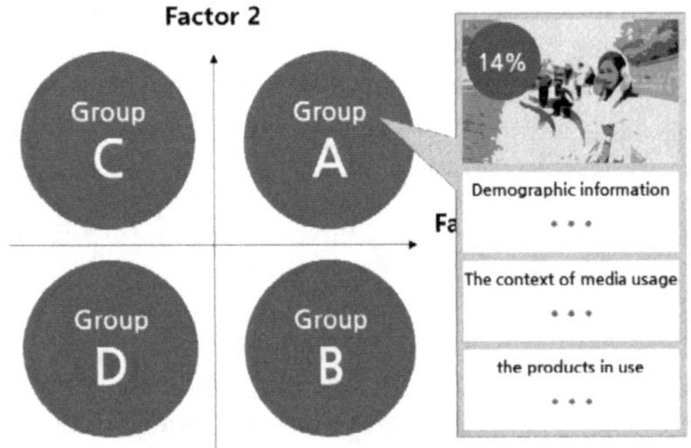

Figure 4. Example of classification results

V. USE CASE

In a multi-device environment, the types of devices can be vary depending on the place, time, and purpose of using the media. As a result, the behaviors and needs of the user also can be differed. In order to accurately understand the behaviors and needs of the user, it is necessary to know precisely where, when and why the user uses the media. In this study, we tried to derive millennials' typical use cases of music and photos, based on the data that was responded to when, where, and for what purpose the millennials used the media.

First of all, the data on location, time, and purpose of using media (photos and music) were collected from users (Table 4). "O" meant that users normally use music or photos at the place, at that time, and for that purpose. We used this data to analyze the correlation between Location, Time, and Purpose. If the correlation between 'living room' and 'time to relax' was high, we could derive that the respondents usually used music to relax in the living room. Also, if the correlation between 'living room' and 'to listen' was high, we could find out that they usually listened to music for their relaxation in the living room.

In this way, we were able to derive the millennials' typical use cases of music and photos. In addition, we added frequency for each use case, and we were able to identify how representative each use case was.

VI. CONCLUSION

This study was a basic research to investigate and classify millennials behaviors to create or consume media and use of media related devices. This study suggested a method to develop user groups of millennials and their context in use of media based on a survey of millennial users. Especially, the method was based on an objective and quantitative analysis that utilizes statistical techniques.

ACKNOWLEDGMENT

This research was supported by User Experience Center in Samsung Electronics Co., Ltd.

REFERENCES

[1] D. Dearman and J. S. Pierce, "It's on my other computer!: computing with multiple devices," In Proceedings of the SIGCHI Conference on Human factors in Computing Systems, ACM, pp. 767-776, April, 2008.

[2] D. Evans, "The internet of things: How the next evolution of the internet is changing everything," CISCO white paper, vol. 1, 1-11, 2011.

[3] D. Lee and K. Engelman, "The Impact of Mobile on CPG CRM Strategy: a Kraft Canada Case Study," International Journal of Mobile Marketing, vol. 7, 5-22, 2012.

[4] N. Howe and W. Strauss, Millennials Rising: the Next Great Generation. Vintage, 2009.

[5] K. Zickuhr, "Generations and their Gadgets," Washington, DC: Pew Internet & American Life Project, 2011.

[6] Pew Research Center (2010). *Millennials: Confident, Connected, Open to Change*. [Online]. Available from: http://www.pewsocialtrends.org/ 2016.02.01

[7] Pew Research Center (2014). *Millennials in Adulthood: Detached from Institutions, Networked with Friends*. [Online]. Available from: http://www.pewsocialtrends.org/ 2016.02.01

[8] P. H. Saldana, "Boomers, Millennials, and The Music Experience," University Honors theses. Paper 238, 1-19, 2016.

[9] J. Beekhuyzen, and L. von Hellens, "How does technology influence online music access and Use? A taxonomy of empirical studies," ACIS 2008 Proceedings, 70, 86-96, 2008.

[10] A. R. Brown, "Popular music cultures, media and youth consumption: Towards an integration of structure, culture and agency," Sociology Compass, vol. 2, 388-408, 2008.

[11] D. Bahanovich and D. Collopy, "Music experience and behaviour in young people," University of Hertfordshire, 2009.

[12] S. J. Tepper and E. Hargittai, "Pathways to music exploration in a digital age," Poetics, vol. 37, 227-249, 2009.

[13] A. M. Gould, "Millennial Media Consumption and the Birth of the Anytime, Anywhere Television Viewing Experience," Doctoral dissertation, Drexel University, 1-55, 2014.

User Experience Design of Smart Headwear for Bike User

Jae-hyun Choi, Sung-soo Bae, Juhee Kim, Sangyoung Yoon, Soon-won Chung
U2 System, Inc.,
Seoul, Republic of Korea
e-mail: choi2000@u2system.co.kr, ssbae@u2system.co.kr, kjh@u2system.co.kr, syyoon@u2system.co.kr, soonwonchung@u2system.co.kr

***Abstract*—With the recent development of technology for wearable devices, user experience design is considered as the important design strategy. The purpose of this study is to conduct practical user experience design for smart headwear for bike user. To find smart headwear contents, the user needs and pain points were extracted from the user research. In developing the user experience (UX) design elements, persona and user journey map were created to provide differentiated experience contents for bicycle user. In this study, smart headwear through UX design process could provide the guidance for route during the cycling, coping with accidents, and bicycle trip. The smart headwear development with UX design process could suggest the UX content direction and the business success model. This study could be helpful to establish the UX strategy for smart devices for bicycle users.**

Keywords-user experience; smart headwear; wearable device; bicycle user; user interface.

I. Introduction

The technologies of wearable devices and digital life have been developed last decade. Smart glasses gained interests since the Google Glass was launched in 2013 and other manufacturers put various models on the market. However, it is difficult to find examples of effective usage on everyday life or profitable cases.

Recently, the services and contents for cycle users were developed with the smartphone and wearable device. Volvo and Strava introduced new alert system to reduce chances of collisions between cars and cyclists using global positioning system (GPS) information data [1]. Moreover, increase of the cycle users and success on cycle tourist could boost the wearable device industry. Jung reported the usage of cycle increased sharply in nine cities in North America and the transportation rate of cycle increased to 5.8% in 2009 from 1.1% in 1990 [2]. Successful cycle tour business could be found in France. In 2007, 7.3 million people, 3.5% of tourists who visited France, used bicycle tour and 0.8 million people, 3.0% of tourists who visited Paris, used bicycle tour [3].

The aim of this study is to introduce practical user experience design process from exploiting user experiences to applying the user experience (UX) concepts to wearable device. Focus group discussion and in-depth interview to exploit users' needs and pain points were described in Section 2. Development of personas and journey map and workshop in order to provide a differentiated service were described in Section 3. In Section 4, all findings were applied to wearable device for bicycle users.

II. User Experience Research

A. Methods

Focus group discussion and in-depth interview are good methods to collect broad and clear user experiences. Nine bicycle users separately recruited from three groups, such as daily leisure bicycle users, expert road bike users, and wearable device users. Daily and expert users participated in focus group discussion and wearable device users participated in in-depth interview.

Awareness and behavioral characteristics of bicycling, bicycle usage experience and objects of bicycle usage were collected from daily and expert user groups. And behavioral characteristics related with smart devices and smartphone during bike-touring were collected through an interview with the wearable device users (Figure 1).

B. Results

Needs and pain points were categorized into three riding tour phases. First, few information on difficulties on the riding course, and issues related with safety likes maintenance and protection of robbery were raised during preparation phase of riding tour. Second, problems on safety and accident were main concerns including communication with riding members during phase of riding tour. Lastly, after riding, major interests were riding photos and data related with riding likes riding distance and average velocity.

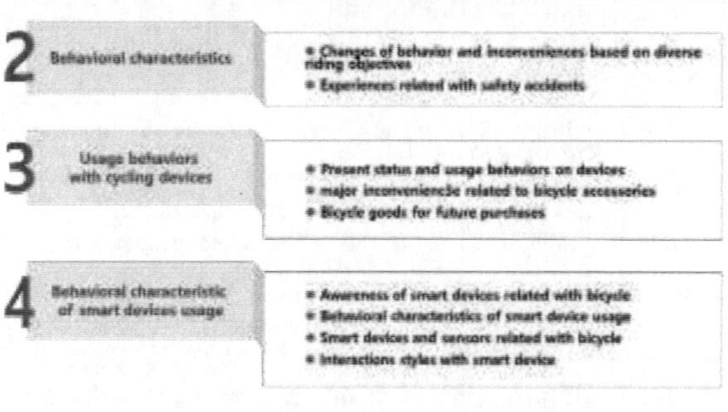

Figure 1. Major interview contents for bicycle users

Cycle users hoped the wearable device for cycling could provide the precise information on riding and exercise, information on riding course and surroundings and cautions on risky conditions. However, the short battery time of device and interference of calling and listening music caused by a wind were major concerns.

Consequently, the concepts of wearable device for cycling could be summarized into "safety motivation", "social activities with self-motivation", "tour assistant" and "health monitoring".

III. BUILDING UX CONCEPT

A. *Persona and User Journey*

Collected user opinions and comments were refined and used for creation of personas and journey map that were suggested by Alan Cooper [4], software designer and programmer. These methods could be effective and give easier way for understanding users. For creating personas, democratic variables, objectives of bicycle riding, inherent tendency of bicycle usage were considered and classified into similar personal characteristics.

There were two common negative emotions on four personas. The bike user concerns about safety and accidents took great portion during cycling. The expert bike rider who is more than six road bikes a week, and the persona needs for riding courses, objective riding data, and navigation functions. When riding for travel, there were requirements for movement such as navigation and route information. In the case of commuting bike rider had the needs for contemplating about accidents and requirements on crossway in urban area. For a riding bicycles for health care, the main focus has been on the need for information on living conditions, exercise and personal training functions, and achievement of goals, mainly on track records and on compensation and motivation.

The user journey map was developed based upon characteristics shown in Table 1. Journey map was composed after each persona's bicycle usage phase was settled and was defined behavioral criteria for each phase, such as emotional variance, needs, and user requirements.

TABLE I. GOAL FOR PERSONA

Persona	Goal
Expert bike rider	To renewal own record for preparing competition
Traveling bike rider	To find a bicycle course for traveling
commuting bike rider	To commute and use bike as a form of transportation
Bike rider for healthcare	To care about health from cycling

Four personas were consequently created, such as expert bike rider, Traveling bike rider, commuting bike rider, Bike rider for healthcare. Figure 2 present the hallmarks, pain-points and needs of each persona and the output example.

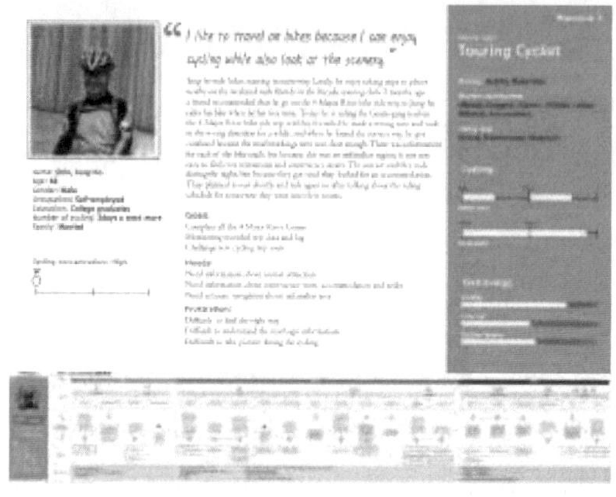

Figure 2. Persona & User Journey map

B. *User Experience Concept*

The workshop was carried out for extracting the UX concept, shown in Figure 3. Collected data were classified into safe riding, bicycle information, navigation, sharing route and information, bike accessory, record and feedback. Idea generating process was discussed in order to solve the pain points and needs of each persona. UX concept and strategy were drawn during idea workshop.

Finally, values and experiences that a wearable device could provide to bicycle users were summarized into four key UX contents: safety, tour, social, and health. Figure 4 displays key UX contents.

Figure 3. Idea workshop and affinity diagram

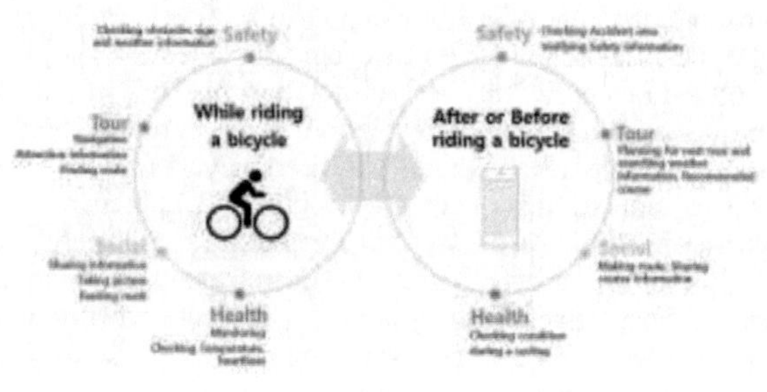

Figure 4. Key UX contents

This study drew concrete ideas to enhance the user experience through the headwear with four main contents drawn. First of all, the safety function is that prevents dangerous accident and helps cope with it after an accident, which helps the users ride safely by providing alarms for speeding bumps and places where accidents occur frequently so that the users can let others know that through emergency call and quickly cope with it.

Secondly, the social feature makes the user experience of riding the bicycle more pleasant by the function of saving and sharing own driving records and routes and the function of motivating for riding through competitions and games.

Thirdly, the features for tours are to provide the information and navigation about the area where the user is cycling. Users can easily get the information about the area and can find the correct tour route even if the user is not familiar with the area.

Last, the health care function provides exercise state information while driving such as exercise status monitoring, exercise goal-setting and achievement rate display, so that the user can effectively control user pace, monitor the physical condition through body temperature and heart rate measurement, and prevent Glycogen depletion by informing the user of time for food and water intake.

IV. APPLICATION TO SMART DEVICE

A. *User Interface Design*

With the derived key contents, an application for mobile and headwear was designed. Each function was defined, and a screen considering the user's gaze was designed. Experiment was conducted for inspecting the relationships between eye dominance and the user's cognitive performance before user interface design. A total of 36 bicycle riders who have been cycling consistently were recruited and participated in the experiment. Recognition time, error rate and user preference scores were measured during riding a bicycle on a stationary stand for safety reasons. As a results, quantitative experiment with eye tracker showed that recognition time had 20% delay and error ratio increased almost 10% when the device was located on non-dominant eye. The interaction effect of ocular dominance and age group was significant with respect to recognition time and error ratio. The recognition time of the users in their 40s was significantly longer than the other age groups when the display was placed on the non-dominant eye, while no difference was observed on the dominant eye. Error ratio also showed the same pattern. Although no difference was observed for the main effect of ocular dominance and bike usage, the interaction effect between the two variables was significant with respect to preference score.

Headwear display screen connected to a mobile device is divided broadly into Event Area and Information Area as Figure 5. The part of the screen which is most noticeable visually was assigned to the Event Area and it was designed so that information checked continuously such as current speed and mileage would be positioned in the Information Area.

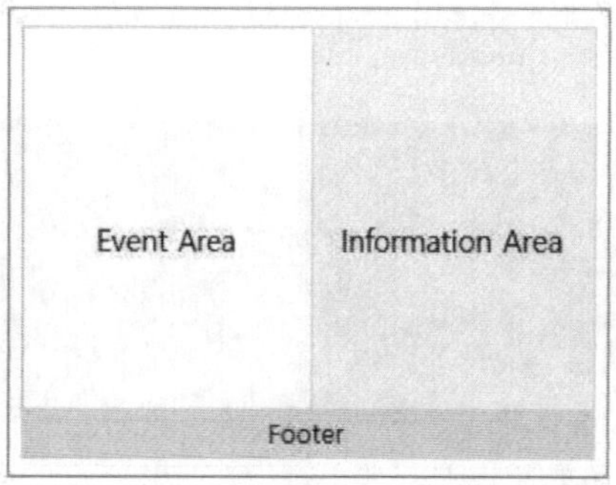

Figure 5. Smart Headwear display layout

In order to seek interaction to provide the users with an emotional new experience while they are riding the bicycle, four visual concepts were proposed and this study went through a user verification process. Like shown in Figure 6, designs were provided as follows: the design that forms honeycomb-shape in which multiple contents are connected based on the hexagon shape, the design in which each content has a bubble-shaped module and each information appears like soap bubble spreads, and the past information disappears as the bubble bursts, the design of sunflower concept in which contents appear round and turn like petals, which provides interaction centered around directions contents; and design of Bi-Circle, which embodies circle shape in bicycle mode, and provide visual information simply using two big circles.

In the detailed visual design, it was embodied by choosing Bi-circle as the most highly preference from the survey about four concepts corresponding to the headwear display.

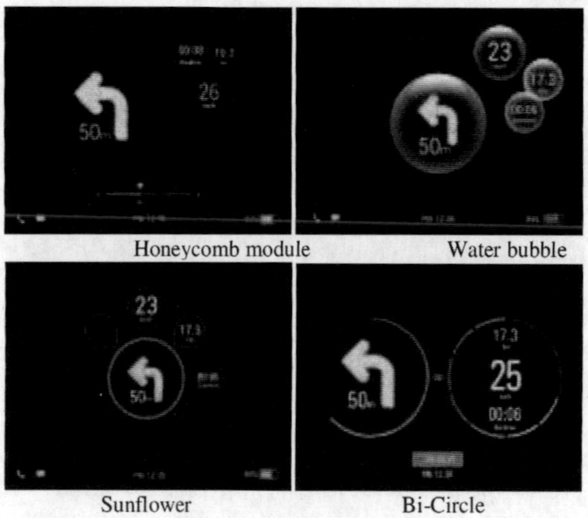

Figure 6. Visual design concept

B. *Visual Design*

When the headwear device is turned on, the first screen is displayed in the wearable device. Figure 7 shows the connection attempt screen.

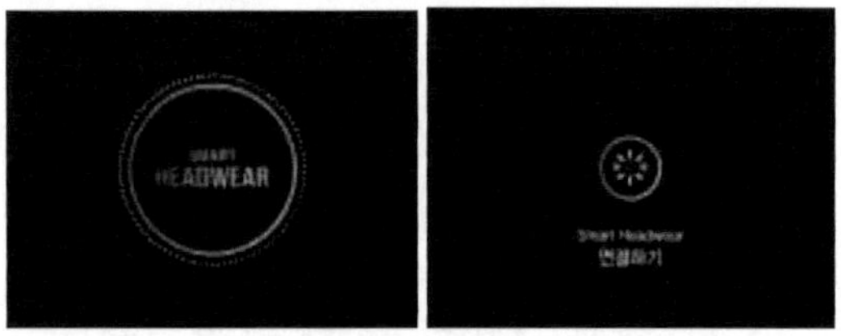

Figure 7. Connecting screen on Headwear display

The main feature is that the contents are not arranged on the left part during ordinary bicycling so that the sight could be less disturb. When navigation shows in the screen that the direction is indicated on the left side, the state of battery is displayed with rounded shape and the POI (point of interest) information is displayed on the center (Figure 8).

Figure 8. Riding Screen on Headwear display

This application provides the state on the display and rings a warning sound if the user's body temperature gets out of the normal range, through the body temperature sensor on the headwear while on the bicycle (Figure 9). In addition, it alerts a dangerous situation by blinking the translucent red background and automatically sends an SOS message to a preset acquaintance, if such a situation lasts for over 3 seconds.

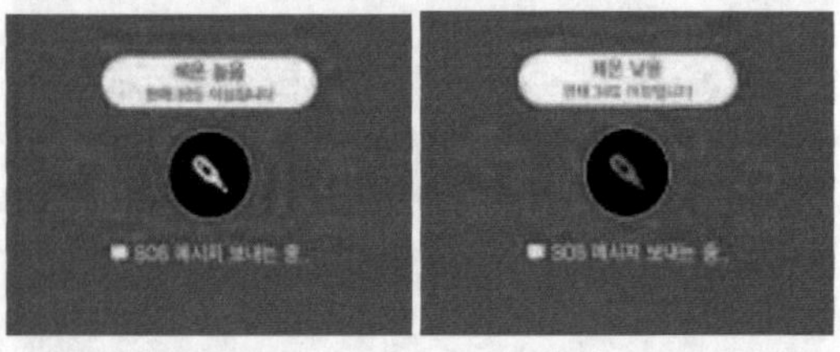

Figure 9. Warming Screen on Headwear display

C. *Prototype Creation*

Prototype was made as a video type for verifying design of Headwear in detailed visual design. The background animation provided real situation for cycling as the Figure 10.

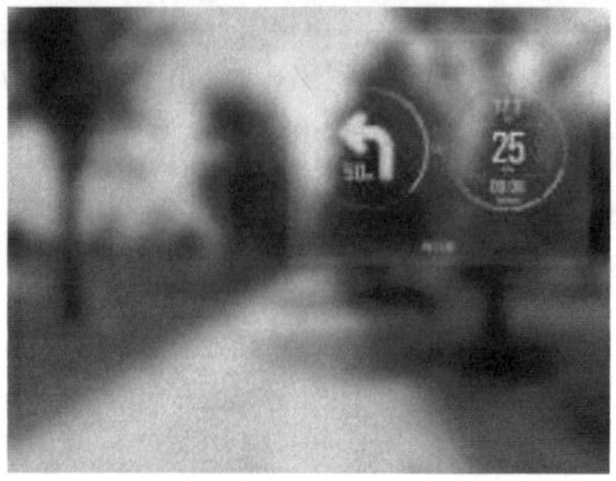

Figure 10. Video prototype screen

V. DISCUSSION

This study introduced the practical UX process with single-lens wearable device for cycle users.

Overall, the expectation was met from the output for the new headwear application. Despite the project interest in the UX design process, it was not easy to analysis the large amount of collected data from user because it was needed to be concerned about the related interaction between the App and device. It was not easy to analyze the data of cycle users during FGD and to extract the most needed contents for wearable device. First, numerous concept meeting was placed to resolve the needs and pain points during cycling. Smart headwear could give limited functions technically, so there were a lot of troubles how to enhance the user experience during cycling. Especially, safe cycling to prevent accidents and information on route and local area were discussed intensively. In addition, there were many suggestions how to give natural interaction between headwear and smartphone and how to offer emotional experience. In order to clearly define target user, major grouped needs and pain points were classified, and personas were created.

This study considered the effect of ocular dominance when the user gazed the display of wearable device. Most popular single-lens smart device, Google glass, were recommended to locate on user's dominant eye. Moreover, this study empirically identified that cognitive performance could be decreased when the device was placed on non-dominant eye, cognitive performance could be decreased. Results showed that the recognition time and error ratio increased significantly. This study developed the smart device for the right-eye dominant only, however, experiment results proposed the necessity of device for left-dominant eye users for safe cycling.

Besides ocular dominance, small display size was also a problem to address. Optimized contents and layout of information were determined not to disturb user's front view.

Another problem was that the user wearing the device could not see the information on the display of device in sunny day condition. This problem should be settled down, considering the cycling condition.

This study is progressing. The central concern has been for personal device associated with information on safe cycling and navigation for more emotional experience. There are some aspects tour and social network service that it can be concerned about future works.

VI. Conclusion

This study tried to apply UX approach to develop the headwear that could enhance the bicycle user experience. In order to achieve the goal, massive data were collected from many cycle users, then persona and journey map were created for more understanding users. Working prototype was developed and was tested in laboratory experiment.

For further research, specific feature should be implemented on Smart Headwear to build a new business model. It is significant that this study can provide insight as a UX design approach about new wearable services for cycling user. It is necessary to embody the function development implementation and related services provided from the extension of this study which is ongoing. Results of the study could provide the UX approach and apply to wearable device.

Acknowledgment

This research project was supported by the Sports Fund of Seoul Olympic Sports Promotion Foundation from Ministry of Culture, Sports and Tourism.

References

[1] Cycling Weekly, *Could Volvo's new alert system help prevent collision with cyclists?* [Online]. Available from: http://www.cyclingweekly.co.uk/ [retrieved: 2017.2.22]

[2] I. Jung, "Study on Ordinary life bicycle in Metrocity", Technical Report of Ministry of the Interior, pp. 22-24, 2013.

[3] S. Hong, "Policy for the bike tourist in Seoul", SDI Policy Report, 2011.

[4] A. Cooper, The Inmates are Running the Asylum: Why High Tech Products Drive Us Crazy and How to Restore the Sanity, Indianapolis: Sams Publishing, 1999.

Designing a Feeding Support System for Infants using IoT

Kyudong Park[1], Jiyoung Kwahk[2], Sung H. Han[2]
Department of Creative IT Engineering[1]
Department of Industrial and Management Engineering[2]
POSTECH
Pohang, South Korea
Email: {kdpark, kjy, shan }@postech.ac.kr

***Abstract*— The main goal of this on-going research is to design a feeding support system based on technologies with Internet of Things (IoT). For that reason, we conducted user observation and in-depth interview with three parents for developing the system based on better understanding of users. We found two pain points, which are the measurement of temperature and quantity of feeding milk, in current feeding behavior. Thus, designed prototype can measure the temperature and record the quantity of feeding automatically with sensors. The prototype consists of sensor client, representation client, and server. Sensor client obtains feeding amount and time information and sends them to the server via the internet. The server statistically analyzes the dataset and gives useful information about the baby. Representation client visualizes the stored data effectively and gets an alarm setting for feeding time. The next step of the research is to perform a user study to evaluate user experience and establish a strategy for analyzing data with machine learning approaches.**

Keywords-UX design; Feeding system for infants; Internet of Things

I. INTRODUCTION

Recently, technologies based on Internet of Things (IoT) have got a roaring attention of academic as well as the industrial field. Kevin Ashton proposed the first concept of IoT in forms of Radio Frequency Identification (RFID) in 1999 [1]. The ultimate objective of IoT is to construct more comfortable and convenient environment through exchanging the information seamlessly between objects [2]. Nowadays, IoT technologies are composed of 1) device for detecting and sensing an object, 2) network for connecting to the internet, and 3) platform for knowledge management considering semantics. These were mainly developed as separate technologies, but now, interdisciplinary approaches, such as human-computer interaction (HCI), ergonomics, cognitive science, and data science are vibrantly discussed and studied.

This paper is organized as follows. Section 2 presents the design process. Section 3 demonstrates the needs of users. Section 4 contains a detailed explanation of the proposed prototype. Section 5 draws conclusions and future work.

II. DESIGN PROCESS

In this project, we adopted human-centered design (HCD) process for developing a product based on better understanding of users. There are five main activities in HCD process according to the ISO 13407 standard as shown in Figure 1 [3]. We focused "understand and specify the context of use" and "specify the user requirements" activities to find users' needs. Based on the needs, the prototype was designed, but it is still under development. After producing design solutions, an evaluation will be performed with users.

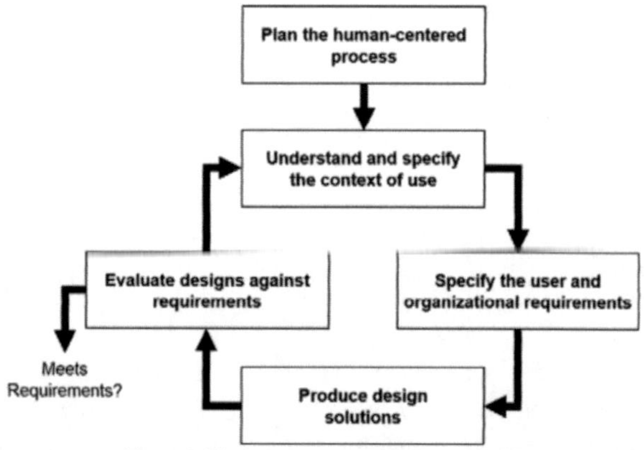

Figure 1. The human-centered design cycle [3]

III. NEEDS FINDING

A. *Understand and specify the context of use*

The topic with formula milk feeding has been steadily studied worldwide and regarded as important because it is directly related to the infant health [4][5]. In this study, we conducted user observation and in-depth interview with three parents to find needs.

Most feedings with formula milk use a baby bottle. Thus, parents and babysitter have to pay particular attention to air penetration into the bottle (causing diarrhea), and internal washing and disinfection of the bottle. Furthermore, when parents make a formula milk, they first boil tap water and pour the exact amount of water into the bottle. In this process, more than 70 degree Celsius water is necessary because of the sterilization of Cronobacter Sakazakii, which can cause bacteremia and meningitis with the use of powdered infant formula [6]. Then, add the right number of scoops to the bottle, give the bottle a good shake until all the powder has dissolved, and leave it to cool naturally. They have to test the temperature by tipping a little milk to the inside of their wrist. It should feel just warm, not hot. After feeding, they have to check the quantity of feeding and write it down in a notebook or mobile application by hand.

B. *Specify the user requirements*

We found two pain points in current feeding behavior. First is the measurement of temperature. Appropriate feeding temperature is 37 degree Celsius, but skin sensation using wrist is limited to measure the suitable temperature:

"If I give my son a slightly hotter milk powder than normal, he will have loose bowels"

Second is the measurement and record of the quantity of feeding milk. This is an essential process because weight, height, and quantity of feeding are important factors to check the infant's health. However, it could be a very tiresome to measure the quantity by the gradation on the bottle, and write the value in the note or mobile application:

"I have to remember the amount of milk powder in the bottle when I start feeding. After finishing, I subtract the remaining amount. Then, I write it down in my note."

Thus, we propose a product that can measure the temperature and record the quantity of feeding automatically.

IV. Proposed Prototype

The proposed system consists of sensor client, representation client, and server (Figure 2). Sensor client will obtain data including feeding amount and time, and send it to the server using a network. Data will be collected to the server and processed. The server will statistically analyze the dataset, and give useful information about the baby. Representation client, such as mobile application, will visualize the stored data, and get an alarm setting for feeding time and private data including baby's weight and height.

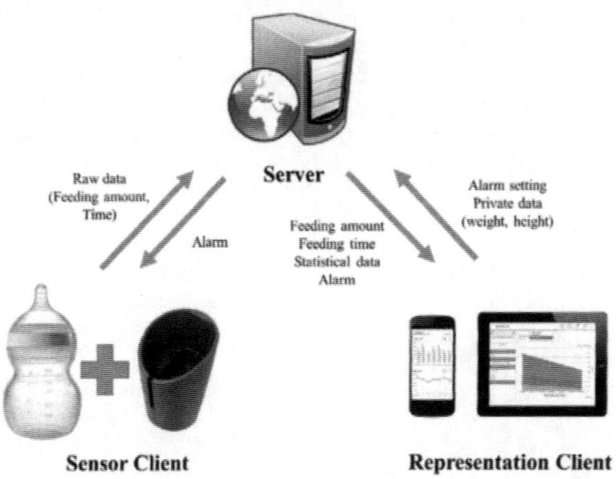

Figure 2. The overall structure of the proposed system

A. *Sensor client*

Sensor client has a form of the cup holder that user can put the feeding bottle on. There are sensors for measuring the weight and temperature located at the bottom of the holder. For measuring the weight of the bottle with powder milk, we use an amplifier (HX711) and load cell, which creates an electrical signal from measured force. Contactless temperature sensor using infrared light (MLX90614) is installed in the client. The main advantages of contactless approach are 1) measurement time is short, and 2) the sensor has a long life because it is not contaminated from the object.

We also adopt Arduino UNO board for receiving data from the sensor and transmitting the data to the server. Arduino UNO is a microcontroller board based on the ATmega328. And it has a small size and easy-to-use hardware and programming language based on Java so that it is efficient in satisfying users' changeable requirements. Internet connection will be supported by Wi-Fi shield (ESP-8266).

B. *Representation client*

Representation client performs visualization function that gives an effective way to communicate with processed data from the server through visual imagery in forms of mobile application. As shown in Figure 3, users can check feeding amount, time, and patterns of feeding behavior. Also, users can enter the weight and height of their baby for more detailed analysis and can set the timer for periodic alarm.

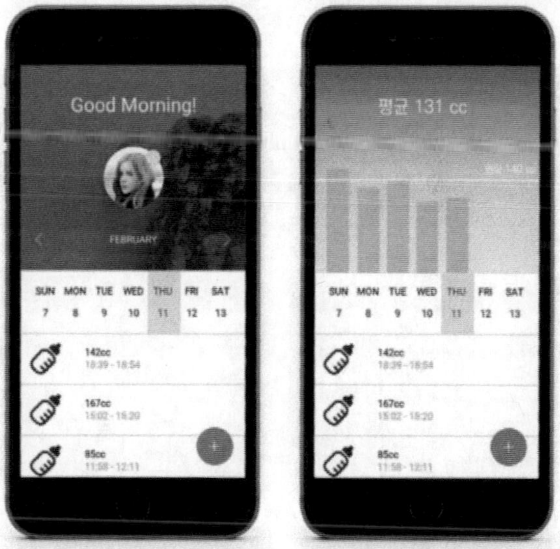

Figure 3. The prototype of representation client

C. *Server*

The server connects with sensor client and representation client by storing and transmitting feeding data. Basically, time (feeding start event and feeding finish event) and quantity of milk (at feeding start and at feeding finish) will be stored on the server. After collecting dataset from users, the server will be able to infer meaningful information about infants, such as feeding pattern, desired feeding time, the age-appropriate amount of formula milk, etc., by machine learning techniques.

V. Conclusion and Future works

In this study, feeding support system for infants is proposed with IoT concept. Through the observation and the interview, we found two pain points; measurement of proper temperature and record of the amount of feeding milk. Considering them, the prototype is designed using IoT.

Further studies need to be carried out in order to evaluate its usability and user experience by a user study. More than 20 users including parents having a baby, as well as staffs in a postnatal care center will be recruited for testing our product and service. Participants will be asked to use our product to feeding with formula milk in terms of longitudinal study at least 2 weeks. Also, diary study would be adopted to capture user experience (UX) in daily context.

Further research should be undertaken to analyze the data collected from the server. Recently, novel services combining IT and healthcare, such as MI band by Xiaomi have been released. Mi band can detect and track how many steps users have walked and how much users have slept. It means Xiaomi now collects walk and sleep data of millions of users, and the data is key to create added value. In the same vein, collected dataset from our proposed service is also very important in perspective of business and research. In the academia, deriving meaningful insights from the healthcare-related data has been studied [7]-[9]. Marlin et al. [7] developed a probabilistic clustering model for finding patterns from physiologic time series data contained in e-health care records. Keogh et al. [8] detected abnormal signal from the time-series data in medical datasets. We could apply these approaches to develop an algorithm detecting meaning events from the feeding dataset.

References

[1] K. Ashton, "That 'internet of things' thing," RFiD Journal, vol. 22, no. 7, pp. 97-114, 2009.

[2] L. Atzori, A. Iera, and G. Morabito, "The internet of things: A survey," Computer networks, vol. 54, no. 15, pp. 2787-2805, 2010.

[3] M. Maguire, "Methods to support human-centred design," International journal of human-computer studies, vol. 55, no. 4, pp. 587-634, 2001.

[4] P. Ziegler, R. Briefel, N. Clusen, and B. Devaney, "Feeding Infants and Toddlers Study (FITS): development of the FITS survey in comparison to other dietary survey methods," Journal of the American Dietetic Association, vol. 106, no. 1, pp. 12.e1-12.e50, 2006.

[5] R. J. Schanler, R. J. Shulman, and C. Lau, "Feeding strategies for premature infants: beneficial outcomes of feeding fortified human milk versus preterm formula," Pediatrics, vol. 103, no. 6, pp. 1150-1157, 1999.

[6] K. K. Lai, "Enterobacter sakazakii infections among neonates, infants, children, and adults: case reports and a review of the literature," Medicine, vol. 80, no. 2, pp. 113-122, 2001.

[7] B. M. Marlin, D. C. Kale, R. G. Khemani, and R. C. Wetzel, "Unsupervised pattern discovery in electronic health care data using probabilistic clustering models," In Proceedings of the 2nd ACM SIGHIT International Health Informatics Symposium, ACM, pp. 389-398, 2012.

[8] E. Keogh, J. Lin, A. W. Fu, and H. VanHerle, "Finding unusual medical time-series subsequences: Algorithms and applications," IEEE Transactions on Information Technology in Biomedicine, vol. 10, no. 3, pp. 429-439, 2006.

[9] S. J. Roberts, "Extreme value statistics for novelty detection in biomedical data processing," IEE Proceedings-Science, Measurement and Technology, vol. 147, no. 6, pp. 363-367, 2000.

Suggesting Design Method for Performance Evaluation System Based on IoT Data: Considering UX

Its Application to Lane Keeping Assistance System

Hyeji Jang[1], Jiyoung Kwahk[1], Sung H. Han[1], Minseok Song[1], Dong Gu Choi[1], Kyudong Park[2], Dohyeon Kim[1]
Department of Industrial Management and Engineering[1]
Department of Creative IT Engineering[2]
POSTECH
Pohang, South Korea
Email: {wdfokj, kjy, shan, mssong, dgchoi, kdpark, kdohyeon}@postech.ac.kr

Young Deok Won[3], In Sub Jeong[3]
ADAS Performance Development Team[3]
Hyundai Motor Company[3]
Namyang, South Korea
Email: {nicewyd, jis}@hyundai.com

***Abstract*— The rapid development of Internet of Things (IoT) technology makes it possible to connect various objects among each other and to collect sensor data from the objects. Connected car, achieved by advanced driver assistance system (ADAS), is one of the representative example of IoT technology. Since massive amount of IoT data could be effectively analyzed with appropriate methods, it is helpful to introduce supportive systems for the analysis. This study proposes a method to design supportive system for the analysis of IoT data considering user experience (UX). The suggested method is applied to design the supportive system for lane keeping assistance system (LKAS), which is one of the ADAS.**

Keywords-Internet of Things; connected car; user experience; system design; advanced driver assistance system; lane keeping assistance system

I. INTRODUCTION

A. *IoT and Connected Car*

The rapid development of Internet of Things (IoT) technology makes it possible for connecting various smart objects together through the internet and providing more data of interoperability methods for application purpose [1]. According to European commission [10], IoT means a worldwide network of interconnected objects that is uniquely addressable, based on standard communication protocols. IoT is rapidly applied to various area, connecting many parts of our life. It brings us a new level of convenience by connecting physical and virtual objects [2].

The connected car is a representative example of IoT. It means that vehicles are not part of the connected world, rather continuously Internet-connected, generating and transmitting data, which can be helpfully integrated into applications [4]. For example, dashboard application is linked to social media services and sensors attached in cars help drivers in variety of ways for car maintenance. With the growing attention to IoT, scale of the connected car market already exceeds 25.2 billion dollars in 2014 [2].

The vehicle-to-vehicle (V2V) network is essential to realize the connected car. Advanced driver assistance system (ADAS) supports the V2V network with technologies, such as vision/camera systems and sensor technology [3]. For this reason, research of ADAS has actively been proceeded.

B. *Data Colleced from IoT*

Enormous amount of data is easily and quickly collected from various sensors, which are attached on a number of IoT objects. For example, there are quantified-self sensors (sensors that measure the personal biometrics of individuals like heart rate) and automotive sensors (sensors that measure quantitative automotive performance metrics like speed and braking activity) [4] attached in vehicles. These kinds of sensors collect data related with operations and status of car in real time.

The result of analyzing IoT data may be useful in various ways. The effort to analyze the IoT data is easily found in the healthcare field. In fact, a growing number of researches have been conducted using the IoT data in this field [11]. However, because the IoT data is collected in real time, its amount is significantly large. Supportive tools can be helpful to go through this process. Designers should provide decent user experience and enhance usefulness by considering UX when they design this kind of tools. Therefore, this study suggests design method for ADAS performance evaluation system based on the IoT data collected from connected car. In addition, this study aims to apply the suggested method on LKAS performance evaluation system.

In Section 2, theoretical points of whole process and techniques used to design the system from UX point of view are introduced. Section 2 also includes detailed implementation method and advantages of using each technique. Suggested system design method was applied to make performance evaluation system for lane keeping assistance system (LKAS). Section 3 shows application process and practical result.

II. METHOD

This study suggests six main steps for system designs from writing out user persona to creating key screen designs. This process needs to be iterated several times to derive more systematic and accurate system designs. Enough iterations of the process reduce any potential risks of the system and allow the actual software development more smoothly.

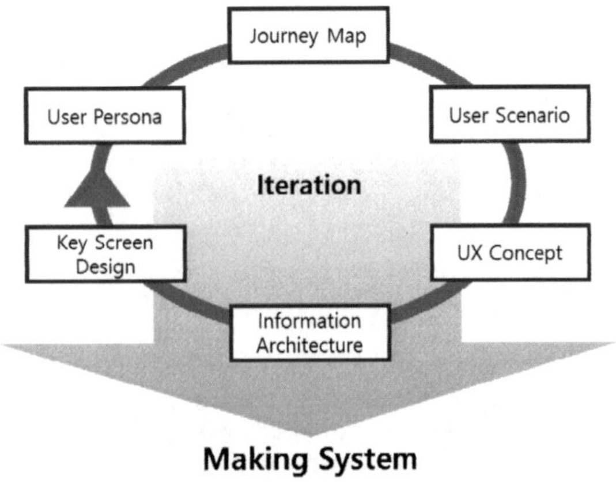

Figure 1. Whole process of making system

The main objective of the system designer is to derive proper key screens. To design persuasive key screens, systematic analysis on system users has to be preceded. This study deals from creating user persona, which is to reflect user analysis on the system, to developing information architecture (Figure 1). This section provides detailed explanations on the five steps for system designs.

A. *User Persona*

User centered design is significantly important for efficient system design. It considers the requirements of users to develop the system instead of simply considering technical requirements. For this purpose, designers need to identify and analyze the main users of the system. The actual observation data of how users behave provides valuable information to the designers [5]. User persona is a method for this purpose. According to Cooper and Reimann [6], user persona is a collection of realistic and representative information on users. That information is collected for the purpose of to catch the significant aspects of user behavior for designers.

The target for the user persona is not just limited to current users of the products and services. It includes all the users who has potentials to change any of the tasks of the products and services. The user persona can be developed by asking questions like "what the users do", "what frustrates them", "what makes them satisfied" and more [7]. Those questions mainly consider the role and main tasks of users related with the system, the characteristics of the tasks, and needs and pain points of current tasks. Preparing user persona allows to determine interaction characteristics like navigation scheme and the visual designs [7].

Stakeholder relationship, the relationship between users analyzed by user persona, can be created in this step. It shows the products, services, and the tasks of users. It allows how the products and services influence the relationship among users. In addition, it is able to find additional opportunities of utilize the system, which have not been thought of in the early stages of system design. These processes of user persona can derive the final outputs that can be provided to users.

B. *User Journey Map*

User journey map shows the behavior of the system users [8]. All the user tasks, considering the user persona which has been developed in the previous stage, can be illustrated as a diagram. User journey map has two different types, current process and expected process with the system. First, the current process shows the flow of user tasks before introducing the new system. It allows how users interact currently on the flow of tasks. Therefore, it easily figures out any problems in the current flow of the tasks. For example, overwhelming workload applied on a certain user can be found and no cooperation or communication occurred between users with the current process can be recognized. Second, the expected process with the system shows the flow of user tasks after introducing the new system. Comparing the two user journey maps helps to understand the flow of user tasks as well as what has been improved.

C. *User Scenario*

User scenario is a flow of user tasks on how the system can be effectively and valuably utilized. With user scenario, users can predict when the system can be helpfully utilized. Among different scenarios, it is able to set the priority of the scenario and select the most frequently usable scenario. Several methods can be applied when listing the scenario. For example, designers can conduct interviews asking about user tasks on potential type of references on features of similar systems. Those methods can help designers to determine the deepness of the user scenario that is covered by the system. The user scenario states functions that can actually be implemented, as well as functions that will be implemented in future. The system becomes more powerful by preparing the case of the system's expansion, considering the potential functions to be implemented. The usage frequency or checking the importance of each scenario can be used as a reference to set up the concept of system.

D. *Define Key UX Concept*

The type of UX concepts that would be mainly considered needs to be concerned when developing the system. It is important to define the key UX concepts since the characteristics of the system can be changed on which UX concept is used. Clarity, digestibility, familiarity are the examples of UX principles [9]. This step builds the base for the entire structure of the system by exploring proper UX concepts that well represent the characteristics and objective of the system.

E. *Information Architecture (IA)*

Information Architecture (IA) is a flow of information reflected upon the user scenario and system UX concept. UX and IA are closely connected. By forming IA, the necessary information for establishing the system can be identified. The proper IA takes the task flow in consideration and makes the flow smoother. In addition, the information can be classified with clear classifiers. In short, a good IA helps users to understand their surroundings and find what they are looking for [12]. The actual system is built based on IA. The IA needs to consider all the steps mentioned in the previous stage.

III. APPLY TO LKAS PERFORMANCE EVALUATION SYSTEM

This study applies the introduced method for system designing on LKAS performance evaluation system. LKAS is one of the key features of ADAS in connected-car. LKAS supports car to keep the lane by recognizing the lane with camera and applying torques on steering. Data collected from several sensors attached on the connected-car can be utilized to evaluate the performance of LKAS. The system suggested by this study can help as a reference in evaluating the ADAS for connected-cars.

A. *System Characteristic*

The system introduced in this study differs from the general performance evaluating system. The general IoT data analysis system has two separate stages, data collection stage and data analysis stage. However, the system in this study performs the two stages simultaneously. Therefore, there are strong requirements for short evaluation time of the system and no additional analysis for users. The collected data are vehicle driving information including vehicle velocity, steering angle, torque applied, etc. Since large amount of data are collected in very short period of time pre-processing is necessary. The pre-processing includes selecting significant factors and filtering out unnecessary data.

B. *User Persona*

It is expected that there are four types of system users in LKAS evaluating system. First, performance evaluator is the

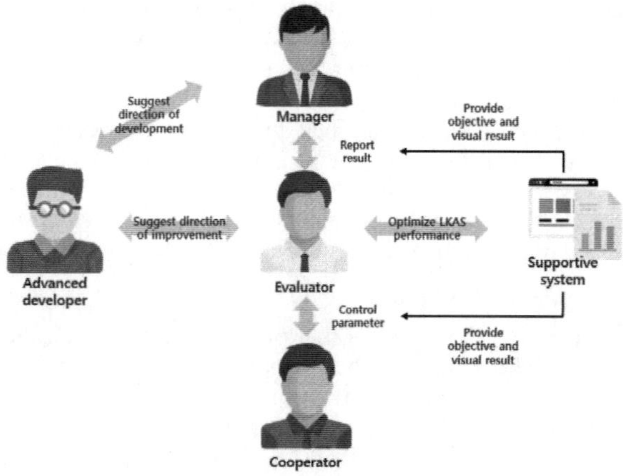

Figure 2. Stakeholder relationship

user who actually evaluates the performance of LKAS and makes decisions about LKAS tuning. The mission of this evaluator is to optimize the performance of LKAS through driving tests. They have enough understanding of LKAS operating principles and of collected data. The most important paint point is evaluating the driving test results subjectively. In other words, all the decisions are made based upon evaluator's personal thoughts. It causes many problems when reporting the result to others. In addition, because of the absence of the objective evaluation criteria, the evaluation process depends on subjective feeling rather than systematic and quantitative approach. As a result, the reliability of the reporting will decrease.

The second user is cooperator, who is in charge of controlling LKAS parameters. They control the parameter related to LKAS based on the evaluation results of the evaluator. Cooperator also have great knowledge of LKAS operating principles and of collected data as well as the behavior of vehicles according to the change in LKAS parameters. The main pain point for the cooperator is that they have to control the parameters with only subjective evaluation results.

The third and fourth system users are manager and advanced developer, respectively. Manager provides a big

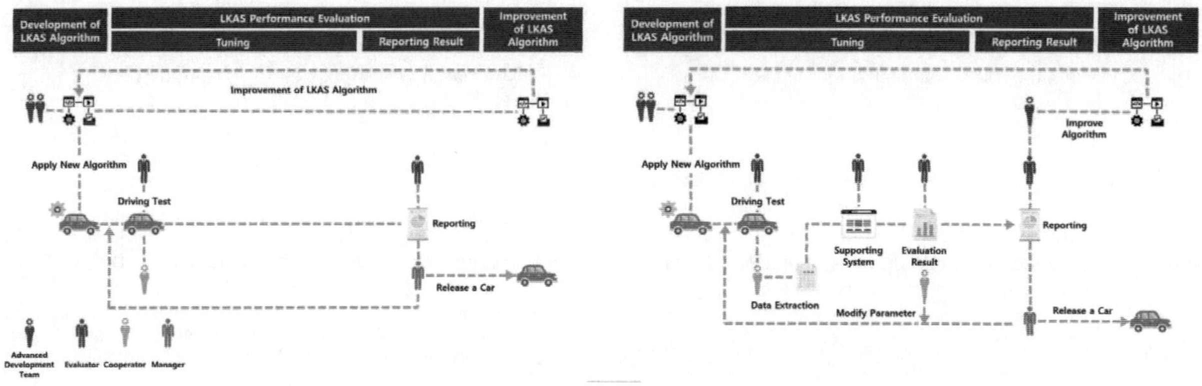

Figure 3. Current user journey map (left) and expected user journey map (right)

outline of LKAS to other users. The advanced developer deals with developing high-performance LKAS algorithms. They have similar pain points like the cooperator that they are not able to identify objective results of LKAS performance. It makes difficult for advanced developers to clearly set the direction that they have to pursue.

The stakeholder relationship can be drawn from the above user persona (Figure 2). It shows the work relationship among users and how the system helps the current workflow.

C. User Journey Map

Figure 3 shows the task flow of LKAS optimization process. The picture on the left side is current process and right side is expected process with the system. These journey maps are derived from the user persona. We can easily see the difference between task flows. In current journey map, because there is no objective results of the evaluation, algorithm development and adjustment of LKAS are in separate procedures. With the expected process with the system, these separated processes can be integrated as a single process. It also improves communication among the users. By comparing the two journey maps, it can be easily identified that the problems are solved with the introduced system.

D. User Scenario

Considering characteristics of each scenario, three phases are suggested in this study (Figure 4). Phase 1 is composed of scenarios that is essential to the system. Phase 2 covers the scenarios achieved in advanced version. Scenarios with highly advanced function are contained in phase 3. Each scenario is assigned by considering the possibilities to be implemented, user requirement, etc.

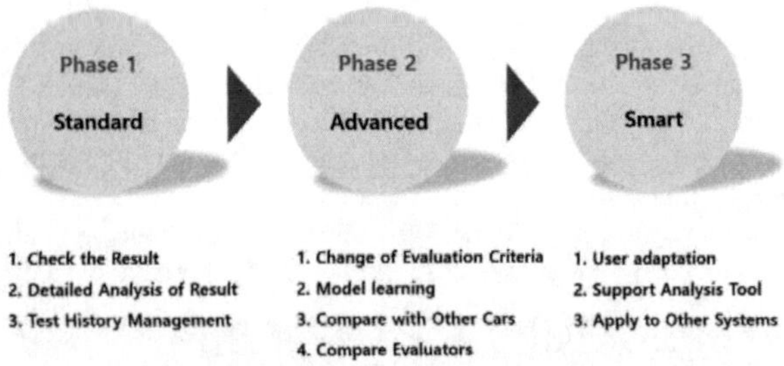

Figure 4. User scenario with three phases

E. Define Key UX Concept

The term 'simplicity' and 'glanceable' are chosen as key UX concepts for the system, considering characteristics of the system and user scenarios. 'Simplicity' means the design of the system should be simple and easy for users. It can be achieved with the simple screen construction and navigation. In addition, the system has to provide proper shortcuts by figuring out the tasks that takes long period of time. Similarly, 'glanceable' means that the design which is shown on the screen should be quickly understood by users without particular attentions.

F. Information Architecture (IA)

IA for the system is developed by reflecting the steps shown in Figure 5. We distinguish the background information and future functions. Background information is the information that has to be considered on the back-side of

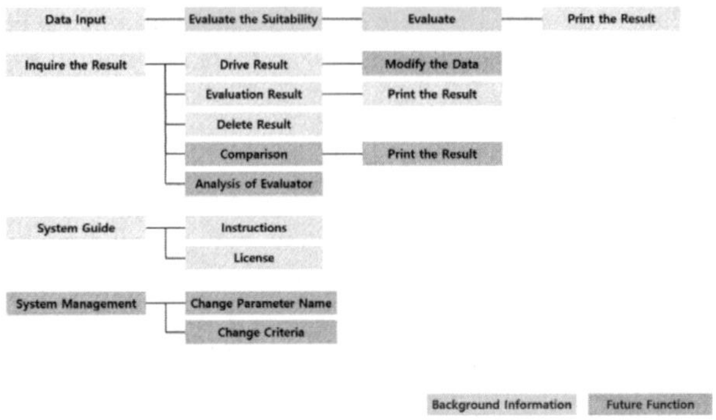

Figure 5. Information architecture

the system. Future function is the information that is achieved in the advanced version. System developers can refer this IA when they actually implement the system.

IV. CONCLUSION

This study suggests the method to consider UX when we design the performance evaluation system based on the data collected from IoT. The introduced method is applied to LKAS, one of the ADAS. With the suggested method, designers can systemically reflect the requirement of the user from user's aspect. In addition, it helps the advancement of the system in the future by considering advanced version. It will be applied to various systems for analyzing enormous data collected from connected products and services.

Although only researcher's analysis is considered in this study, in actual situation, designers are able to use various methods to reflect user's needs. By considering user's behaviors, characteristics, pain points and requirements, it is expected that designers can provide better UX.

ACKNOWLEDGEMENT

This research was supported by Hyundai-NGV.

REFERENCES

[1] B. Xu et al., "Ubiquitous data accessing method in IoT-based information system for emergency medical services," IEEE Transactions on Industrial Informatics, vol. 10, no. 2, pp. 1578-1586, 2014.

[2] J. Gubbi, R. Buyya, S. Marusic, and M. Palaniswami, "Internet of Things (IoT): A vision, architectural elements, and future directions," Future generation computer systems, vol. 29, no. 7, pp. 1645-1660, 2013.

[3] Microsemi, Introduction to ADAS and Secure Connected Car, WP0199 White Paper, 2015

[4] M. Swan, "Connected car: quantified self becomes quantified car," Journal of Sensor and Actuator Networks, vol. 4, no. 1, pp. 2-29, 2015

[5] P. T. A. Junior, and L. V. L. Filgueiras, "User modeling with personas," In Proceedings of the 2005 Latin American conference on Human-computer interaction October, 2005, pp. 277-282, ACM.

[6] A. Cooper, and R. M. Reimann, About Face 2.0 The Essentials of Interaction Design. John Wiley & Sons. 2nd edition, 2003.

[7] K. Goodwin, Perfecting Your Personas. Cooper Interaction Design. Cooper, San Francisco, CA, 2004, available from Internet, 2005.

[8] A. Richardson, "Using customer journey maps to improve customer experience," Harvard Business Review, vol. 15, no. 1, 2010.

[9] UX think. Using Scenarios. [Online]. Available from: https://uxthink.wordpress.com/2010/11/30/using_scenarios/ 2017.01.29

[10] European Commission, "Internet of things in 2020 road map for the future," Working Group RFID of the ETP EPOSS, Tech. Rep., Available from: http://ec.europa.eu/information society 2017.01.28

[11] C. Perera, A. Zaslavsky, P. Christen, and D. Georgakopoulos, "Context aware computing for the internet of things: A survey", IEEE Communications Surveys & Tutorials, vol. 16, no. 1, pp. 414-454, 2014.

[12] The information architecture institute. [Online]. Available from: http://www.iainstitute.org/what-is-ia 2017.01.29

The Idea Generation Process for Support Tools Enhancing Pedestrian Experience of the Mobility Handicapped in Smart City

Dong Yeong Jeong[1], Jiyoung Kwahk[1], Sung H. Han[1], Joohwan Park[1], Mingyu Lee[1], Kyudong Park[2], Ju Hwan Kim[2], Hyeji Jang[1], Dawoon Jeong[1]
Department of Industrial Management of Engineering[1], Department of Creative IT Engineering[2]
Pohang University of Science and Technology
Pohang, Republic of Korea
e-mail: {comnet924, kjy, shan, pkjhwan, mingyu.lee, kdpark, juankim, wdfokj, jdw0303}@postech.ac.kr

Abstract— **The objective of this paper is to develop ideas for support tools of the mobility handicapped. As the smart city is under the spotlight based on the information and communication technologies, development of support tools for the mobility handicapped has a chance to go forward in advanced using the technologies of the smart city. There were several researches to develop support tools for the mobility handicapped, but most of them focused mainly on the walkability. This paper suggests the process to develop ideas of the support tools to enhance holistic Pedestrian eXperience (PX). The process was helpful in developing ideas for support tools especially for the mobility handicapped in this study. The process consists of seven steps, and description and outcomes of each step will be presented.**

Keywords-Pedestrian Experience; Support tools; Idea generation; PX principles; The mobility handicapped

I. INTRODUCTION

Ramp and handrail on the sidewalk are the typical tools for people who have a problem on mobility. The people who need help on mobility are called the mobility handicapped [1]. The mobility handicapped can be classified by their duration of handicap; the temporary mobility handicapped and non-temporary mobility handicapped. The non-temporary mobility handicapped includes the disabled, the aged, and a child [2]. The temporary mobility handicapped includes a pregnant woman, an injured person, and a person with luggage [2]. If we consider this broad definition of mobility challenges, it is obvious that anyone can confront mobility challenges at least temporarily. Therefore, mobility challenges should be considered as one of the most important parts of social welfare service now.

So far, a variety of support tools have been developed based on information and communications technology (ICT) to help vulnerable pedestrians [3]. With the emergence of smart city, which means that public infrastructures are connected and communicate with each other based on the ICT, expectations on its positive benefits are escalating [4][5]. Everything can be digitalized through the sensors built in the formerly analog infrastructures. Various organizations can provide services to the citizen using the public data. Because of the rapid advance in scientific technology, the smart city can become an important part of our life. Smart city has been studied in various fields; "Natural resources and energy," "buildings," "government," "economy and people," "Transport and mobility," and "livings" [4]. The last two fields are related to the mobility handicapped. It can be a great chance to develop effective and efficient support tools for the mobility handicapped using the public data.

Despite the potential of smart city to provide a variety of support tools for the mobility handicapped, few studies were found that considered the problems and needs of the mobility handicapped systematically. Due to the lack of empathetic understandings of user needs, most of them focused mainly on walkability such as the ease and safety of walking, ignoring such factors as affective or social aspects of pedestrian experience.

This study suggested the systematic process to develop idea on effective and efficient support tools for the mobility handicapped based on their own needs and problems. We borrowed the UX concept to find out the factors outside of ease and safety.

UX is an experience that consists of all aspects of users' interactions with a certain product or service [6]. The paradigm of UX is shifted to the pedestrian environment from the electronic devices. This paper defines the concept of Pedestrian eXperience (PX) as "pedestrian cognition, affect, behavior occurred from the interaction with a pedestrian passage and its' related environment in a specific context." Fig. 1 presents conceptual framework of PX.

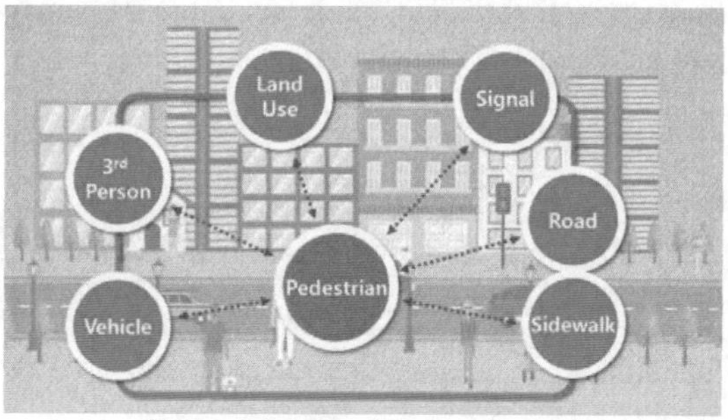

Figure 1. Conceptual Framework of PX

This paper focused on the non-temporary handicapped; the disabled, the aged, a child. The non-temporary mobility handicapped might have more problems and needs than temporary one. The problems and needs in the walking situations were considered in this paper. According to the Korean Ministry of Land, when the mobility handicapped travel, they mostly use sidewalk than the other transport systems [7]. Therefore, the infrastructure that is the most urgent to be improved is sidewalk [8].

In Section 2, existing studies about pedestrian experience and support tools are introduced with their limitation. Section 3 describes the overall process of the idea generation. The results of the complete process are also presented. In Section 4, the significance of the suggested process is explained.

II. LITERATURE REVIEW

The existing studies related to PX and support tools for the mobility handicapped are introduced in this section. The necessity of this research is understandable from the limitations of the existing studies.

A. *Literatures related to Pedestrian eXperience (PX)*

Most literatures related to PX deal with pragmatic factors such as walkability and safety significantly rather than hedonic factors such as affect and sociability. Park considered five factors of walkability; "sense of safety," "sense of security," "comfort," "convenience," "visual interest". He only considered visual interest as a hedonic factor of the pedestrian environment that is vague [9]. Lo suggested Portland pedestrian planning parameters [10] with 7 factors, but he did not consider hedonic factors at all. Ewing suggested 9 principles, but he also focused on pragmatic factors with only one hedonic factor, tidiness [11].

Kari suggested 5 factors including social related factor [12]. He suggested pragmatic factors; "safety," "comfort and convenience," "functional characteristics," and hedonic factors; "aesthetics," "social characteristics". Although he suggested well-balanced factors between pragmatic and hedonic, he did not answer what the aesthetic factor means sufficiently. He only considered attractiveness and visual condition of the environment as detailed factors of aesthetics that are vague. The experts of the User eXperience (UX) can suggest specific hedonic factors that affect PX borrowing the UX concept.

B. *Literatures related to support tools for the mobility handicapped*

The literatures related to support tools for the mobility handicapped usually focus only on the walkability and safety using robotic system. For example, Ni et al. developed robotic system that guides and enables the visually impaired to avoid obstacle on the road [13]. Fontanelli et al. suggested guidance mechanism for a walking robotic assistant [14]. Jiang et al. also developed motion algorithms of walking-assistant robot [15]. There were other researches that utilized mobile and smart devices to assist the mobility handicapped. Scheggi et al. developed a vibrotactile bracelet that gives directional cues to the aged [16]. Miller developed walking assistant application of smartphone that recognizes an object on the road and let the pedestrian know the object and its' direction [17].

However, the mobility handicapped also have the problems in the outside of the walkability and safety. The hearing impaired, who does not seem to be a disabled, can be embarrassed when a stranger asks a passerby for directions. It can lead low sociability of the mobility handicapped. It is essential to find out what the mobility handicapped have problems regarding PX. Also, the researches usually have been focused on the visually or physically impaired or aged. It was relatively hard to find the researches for improving PX of the hearing impaired or a child.

III. SUGGESTION OF THE IDEA GENERATION PROCESS

This study suggests the process of generating support tool ideas that improve PX of the mobility handicapped. The key point of the process is to consider experience of the pedestrian. We do not only focus on the walkability, but considering whole experiences on the road. The process we suggest includes 7 steps (Figure 2). Detailed explanations of each step are described below.

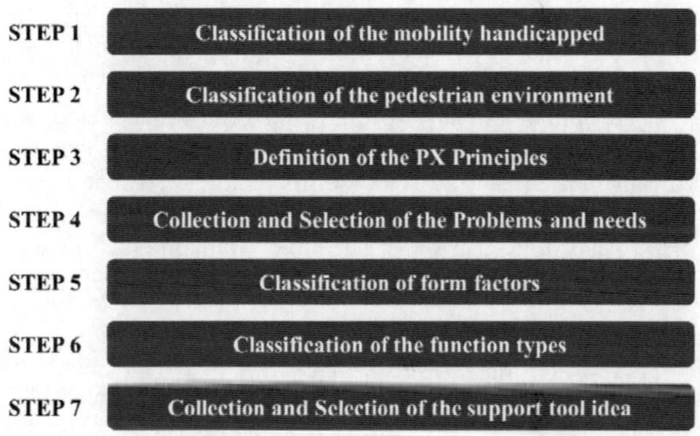

Figure 2. Seven steps of the idea generation process

A. *Step 1: Classification of the mobility handicapped based on their walking characteristics*

The walking characteristics of the mobility handicapped are figured out based on the physical/cognitive/behavioral characteristics of them. We can classify the types of the mobility handicapped based on their walking characteristics, not the demographic factors. The results can be utilized when defining "who" has problems and needs in step 4.

The literature survey was conducted to find out the walking characteristics of the mobility handicapped; the visual/hearing impaired, physically challenged person, mentally handicapped, the aged and child. The literature about physical/cognitive/behavioral characteristics of the mobility handicapped were also collected, and walking characteristics were inferred from them. Also, interview was conducted. 9 participants who works for the mobility handicapped were recruited, and they told us the walking characteristics of the mobility handicapped.

We could define the types of the mobility handicapped based on the walking characteristics, not the demographic factors. The results would let us focus on the unusual walking characteristics that can leads problems and needs, not being restricted to a specific type of the mobility handicapped. The 34 pedestrian characteristics of the mobility handicapped were deduced from the physical, cognitive, and behavioral characteristics of the mobility handicapped (Table 1). The 34 pedestrian characteristics were classified into 15 categories.

Walking characteristics could be helpful to understand the mobility handicapped, which make us generate contexts of the problems and needs easily in the step 4. Combining with the PX principles and pedestrian environment, the contexts of the problems and needs will be better specified.

B. *Step 2: Classification of the pedestrian environment*

The spaces of the pedestrian environment were classified, and the related objects were arranged. Furthermore, time related factors were also considered to generate more various ideas. The results can be utilized when defining "where and when" the problems and needs happened in step 4.

The literature survey was conducted to collect the elements of the pedestrian environment. The collected elements were classified through the open card sorting. The field observation was also conducted to supplement the lists of the elements of the pedestrian environment. 87 Pedestrian environment's elements were arranged as 8 spaces (Table 2).

The human/animal, weather, and time related elements were also considered through the brainstorming to generate various ideas in step 4. The mobility handicapped can have a variety of problems and needs depends on the weather and time. Also, they can have a trouble when interacting with other people and animals.

TABLE I. THE PEDESTRIAN CHARACTERISTICS OF THE MOBILITY HANDICAPPED

The pedestrian characteristics of the mobility handicapped
The eye height is lower than the non-mobility handicapped
Walking speed is slower than the non-mobility handicapped
Easy to trip and fall to the ground
Difficult to communicate with others
Using means of assistance for walk
Difficult to acquire the information about surrounding envirnment
Relying on the non-visual sensation when walking
Having unsafe walking & crossing habit
Difficult to use devices while walking
Difficult to avoid approaching objects and obstacles
Necessary to get a great deal of rest while walking
Difficult to walk outside on rainy and snowy days
Difficult to walk on the low accessibility environment
Physical/Cognitive disabilities appear to the third person
Physical/Cognitive disabilities do not appear to the third person

TABLE II. CATEGORIES OF THE PEDESTRIAN ENVIRONMENT

Categories	Sub-categories
Space	Exclusive pedestrian road
	Community road
	Exclusive vehicle road
	Crosswalk
	Pedestrian overpass/underpass
	(Bus/Taxi) Stop
	Subway station
	Park
Human/Animal	Fellow traveler
	Third party
	Crowd
	Animal
Weather	Spring
	Summer
	Autumn
	Winter
Time	Day-time
	Night-time

C. *Step 3:Definition of the PX Principles*

The PX principles means the recommended design rules of every system that enhance the pedestrian experience. This can be the classification standard of the pedestrian's problems and needs. The PX principles do not only consider walkability. Affects, safety, and sociability are also considered to improve the satisfaction of pedestrian experience. The results can be utilized when defining "why" the problems and needs happened in step 4.

The literature survey was conducted in the UX and PX fields. PX includes walkability concept. The most of the PX literature were related to walkability. 24 UX literatures and 7 PX were collected, and three results of the previous project of the researcher's organization were also utilized. Open card sorting was conducted to categorize principles, and brainstorming of UX experts was conducted to supplement the PX principle.

There were 6 principles categorized as "walkability", 6 as "affect", 4 as "safety," and 4 as "sociability". PX principles can be utilized to find out overall problems and needs on walking experience that are not only bounded on walkability. The defined principles were checked if the problems and needs of the mobility handicapped are matched with each principle (Table 3).

TABLE III. PX PRINCIPLES

Category	Explanation
Walkability	The pedestrian environment should be designed to let pedestrian use elements of pedestrian environment easily and comfortably
Affect	The pedestrian environment should be designed to let pedestrian satisfy affective desire
Safety	The pedestrian environment should be designed to make pedestrian safety from the hazard
Sociability	The pedestrian environment should be designed to make pedestrian being sociable

Problems and needs were collected through the interview with 9 workers related to the mobility handicapped. From the interview, "friendliness" was added in the affect principle.

D. *Step 4: Collection and Selection of the Problems and needs of the mobility handicapped*

The problems and needs of the mobility handicapped are figured out in this step. The results of the steps 1-3 are utilized in this step to find out specific contexts of the problems and needs.

Two major methods can be utilized in this step. First method is focus group interview (FGI) with the mobility handicapped. From step 1 to 3, we have acquired the characteristics of the mobility handicapped through literature surveys and interviews with workers related to the mobility handicapped such as social worker and kindergarten teacher. It is essential to meet the mobility handicapped directly to understand them deeply.

Second method is 'Morphological Analysis (MA)' that let us to consider almost every possible context of problems and needs. The results of the step 1-3 is utilized in MA (Figure 3). Based on the two methods, problems and needs of the mobility handicapped on walking are figured out.

Figure 3. Process flow diagram of Step 1-4

E. *Step 5: Classification of form factors*

The form factors of a support tool are considered in this step. Possible candidates are investigated, and classified. The list of the form factors is utilized when considering "what" solves a problem in step 7.

There are several types of products that are called "form factors". Form factors can be utilized to implement functions such as receiving information and giving services to the pedestrian using ICT.

The products in the pedestrian environments can be considered as form factors such as traffic lights/signs, street lamps. The products possessed by pedestrian also can be utilized to develop support tools such as smart phone, watch, glasses. The lists of the form factors can be collected by literature survey and experts' in-depth interview.

F. *Step 6: Classification of the function types*

The function types are considered in this step. The list of the function types is utilized when considering "how" to solve a problem in the ideation step like form factors.

As there are several types of products, there are several function types. The lists of the function types can be constructed by the literature survey and brainstorming. Alarm is representative function type of the support tool. It is usually used when people need to be noticed. Diagnosis is another function type that is usually used when people want to know the overall condition of a system. A game can also be another function type, which can be used to educate people with fun.

G. *Step 7: Collection and Selection of the support tool idea for the mobility handicapped*

The specific support tool ideas are developed in this step. The results of steps from 4 to 6 are utilized for the ideation process (Figure 4). The ideas can be constructed by the context of problems and needs, form factor, and function type.

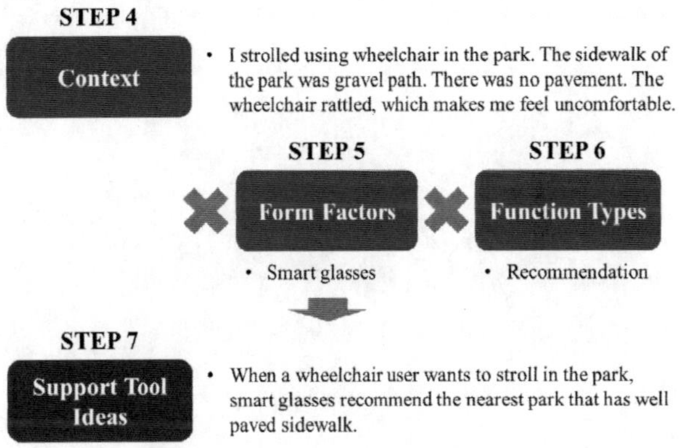

Figure 4. Process flow diagram of Step 4-7

The results of the steps 4-6 can be utilized in this step using 'MA'. MA can be a powerful tool to develop various ideas. Combination between contexts, form factors, and function types would lead us to consider every major problems and needs.

Another ideation tools can be used in this step such as brainstorming and TRIZ to supplement the idea sets from MA. After ideation, high quality ideas should be selected using specific standards such as feasibility, creativity, effectivity using analytic hierarchy process (AHP).

Ideas that have high relation with each other can be grouped to be developed in the one product. For example, there can be integrated recommendation service that would guide one to the nearest well paved park.

IV. DISCUSSION

The suggested systematic idea generation process includes MA, which can allow us to consider as many contexts as possible. Although user research is conducted, the problems and needs that the users do not recognize by themselves cannot be considered. MA is effective methodology to generate users' potential problems and needs.

This process emphasizes PX that includes not only pragmatic perspectives but also hedonic perspectives such as affect and sociability of the pedestrian. The existing studies in Section 2 only focused on the pragmatic perspectives, which is considered as more critical issues than hedonic ones.

However, after UX concept had emerged in the electronic device field in the 21st century, affect and sociability also became an important part of the products and services. In contrast, affect and sociability of the mobility handicapped are rarely considered in the pedestrian environments. Regarding PX principle as a factor of MA, idea designer can think outside the box and generate creative support tool ideas.

Design thinking refers to "a methodology used by designers to solve complex problems, and find desirable solutions for clients" [18]. The process of the design thinking consists of divergent and convergent thinking. The suggested systematic idea generation process can be a kind of design thinking process, which highlights divergent thinking. Adopting MA and emphasizing PX, Divergent thinking can be conducted more actively (Figure 4). Quantitative and qualitative improvement of the idea generation is expected simultaneously.

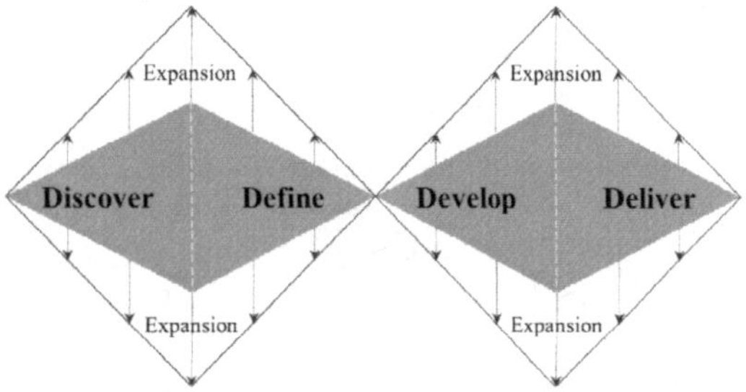

Figure 5. Double diagram of design thinking process

The idea generation process has not been completed yet. The steps 1-3 have been finished, and the step 4 is now in progress. The steps 5-7 are going to conducted. After conducting the all steps, the lists of the all problems and needs can be utilized as the data base, each can be a topic of the basic research of the mobility handicapped. Likewise, each support tool idea can also be utilized as a topic of the development research.

V. CONCLUSION

This paper suggested the process for generating ideas of support tools to enhance pedestrian experience of the mobility handicapped. Defining the principles that covers various aspects of pedestrian experience helped us explore support tool ideas beyond walkability. We hope the results of this study can contribute in making the world one step closer to an equitable society. It is also expected that the suggested process can give insights to other researchers who try to develop ideas of support tools in the other domains as well.

ACKNOWLEDGMENT

This research was supported by the National Research Foundation of Korea (NRF) grant funded by the Korea government (MSIP) (No. NRF-2016R1A2B2011158)

REFERENCES

[1] Ministry of Governmt Legislation. *The mobility enhancement for the mobility impaired act.* [Online]. Available from: http://www.moleg.go.kr/english/korLawEng;jsessionid=BLwxHY0ZxbDgktEncVSH3cw9F5T4TNFtdzaWD3QSiaffZ9iaQtbfALTmURGjG4Gf.moleg_a2_servlet_engine2?pstSeq=52706&brdSeq=33&pageIndex=41 (accessed February 24, 2017)

[2] W. Kim, S. H. Lee, and S. H. Kim, "A Study on Travel Behavior of the Mobility Handicapped and Custom-made Transit Information System," Seoul Metropolitan Research, 9(2), pp. 105-119, 2008.

[3] J. A. Jang, "ICT Based Assistance Technologies for Vulnerable Road User's Walkability," The Magazine of Korean Society of Civil Engineers, 62(1), pp. 21-29, 2014.

[4] P. Neirotti, A. De Marco, A. C. Cagliano, G. Mangano, and F. Scorrano, "Current Trends in Smart City Initiatives: Some stylised facts," Cities, 38, pp. 25-36, 2014.

[5] T. Nam and T. A. Pardo, "Smart City as Urban Innovation: Focusing on management," policy, and context. Proc. of the 5th international conference on theory and practice of electronic governance, ACM press, Sept. 2011, pp. 185-194.

[6] J. Park, and S. H. Han, "Defining user value: A case study of a smartphone," International Journal of Industrial Ergonomics, 43(4), pp. 274-282. 2013.

[7] Ministry of Land, Infrastructure and Transport, "A Study on the Convenience Facilities of Travel, 2015," 2016.

[8] Ministry of Land, Infrastructure and Transport, "A Study on the Convenience Facilities of Travel, 2014," 2015.

[9] S. Park, "Defining, Measuring, and Evaluating Path Walkability, and Testing Its Impacts on Transit Users' Mode Choice and Walking Distance to the Station," *Doctorial thesis*, University of California, Berkeley, 2008.

[10] R. H. Lo, "Walkability: what is it?," Journal of Urbanism, 2(2), pp. 145-166. 2009.

[11] R. Ewing, S. Handy, R. C. Brownson, O. Clemente, and E. Winston, "Identifying and measuring urban design qualities related to walkability," Journal of Physical Activity and Health, 3(s1), pp. 223-240, 2006.

[12] S. Kari, "Pedestrian experience: Affordances and habits in utility walking–Case Otaniemi campus," Master's Thesis, Aalto University, 2016.

[13] D. Ni, A. Song, L. Tian, X. Xu, and D. Chen, "A walking assistant robotic system for the visually impaired based on computer vision and tactile perception. International Journal of Social Robotics, 7(5), pp. 617-628, 2015.

[14] D. Fontanelli, A. Giannitrapani, L. Palopoli, and D. Prattichizzo, "A passive guidance system for a robotic walking assistant using brakes," IEEE 54th Annual Conference on Decision and Control, IEEE Press, Dec. 2015, pp. 829-834.

[15] S. Y. Jiang, C. Y. Lin, K. T. Huang, and K. T. Song, "Shared Control Design of a Walking-Assistant Robot," IEEE Transactions on Control Systems Technology, pp. 1-8, 2017.

[16] S. Scheggi, M. Aggravi, and D. Prattichizzo, "A vibrotactile bracelet to improve the navigation of older adults in large and crowded environments," Proc. 20th IMEKO TC4 Int. Symp. and 18th Int. Workshop on ADC Modelling and Testing Research on Electric and Electronic Measurement for the Economic Upturn, pp. 798-801, 2014.

[17] A. Miller, "Walking Assistant-A Mobile Aid for the Visually-Impaired," Doctoral dissertation, California Polytechnic State University San Luis Obispo, 2014.

[18] Creativity at Work. *Design Thinking as a Strategy for Innovation.* [Online]. Available from: http://www.creativityatwork.com/design-thinking-strategy-for-innovation/ (accessed February 28, 2017)

Development of the Support Tool Preventing Violations in Nuclear Power Plants

Dawoon Jeong, Sung H. Han, Dong Yeong Jeong, Bora Kang
Department of Industrial & Management Engineering
POSTECH
Pohang, Republic of Korea
email: {jdw0303, shan, comnet924, purple31}@postech.ac.kr

***Abstract*— The aim of this study is to develop guidelines and the support tool for preventing violations in nuclear power plants and to evaluate the effects of developed support tool. Nuclear industry needs ways to prevent violations, which is one of human errors. Human error is the major reason of nuclear accidents which result in a global impact. For fundamental and effective prevention of human errors, approach by types of human errors is needed. For idea generation, morphological analysis and brainstorming were conducted. Guidelines were used as one factor of morphological analysis for support tool idea generation. Six high scored ideas of support tool functions in feasibility were developed into smart safety helmet. Effects of developed smart safety helmet were evaluated through interview and survey. Participants responded positively in usability and effectiveness. The result of this study can be used for preventing violations in nuclear power plants. Also it is applicable to various industry where workers wear a safety helmet.**

Keywords-violations; nuclear power plant; prevention; support tool; guidelines; safety helmet;

I. INTRODUCTION

The accident at a nuclear power plant is very rare [1]; however, it can lead severe damage [2]. The results of the nuclear accident are not only death of workers and neighborhood residents, but also contamination of soil and water. Neighboring countries can also suffer from the radiation leakage issues [3]. Typological approach of accident causes is needed to find effective ways preventing nuclear accidents.

Human error is one of the reasons of nuclear accident. It is usually classified under 'slips and lapses', 'mistakes', and 'violation' [4]. This study focuses on 'violation' because research about 'slips and lapses' and 'mistakes' is relatively popular [5][6][7]. For example, Itoh et al [8] considered only slips and mistakes for understanding of internal mechanisms on a man-machine interface used by nuclear power plant operators. Also, Yun and Lee [9] evaluated only safety of smart mobile from slips or mistakes of workers in nuclear power plants.

Although research about violations is not popular, basic research about violation was carried out through defining violation based on failure analyses [10] and classifying types of violations [11]. However, the practical approach is necessary for preventing violations because present violation prevention methods such as campaign and posters are limited to activate workers. One of the practical approach is the support tool based on Internet Of Things(IoT). IoT can collect workers' information through sensors and give feedback on their work behavior. Also, IoT can lead hands-free communication among workers so it could catch their violation and make them stop to do violation. Moreover, IoT support tools enable workers to communicate each other and check progress of task frequently. Thus, data from IoT devices can be used for current violation analysis and personalized task suggestion. Accordingly, IoT can make smart workplace of the nuclear power plant.

Therefore, this study developed guidelines and the support tool preventing violations in nuclear power plants and evaluated the effects of the support tool. This research focused on routine violations. Routine violation can be happened more frequently than other types of violation in nuclear power plants. To generate ideas of guidelines and support tool, morphological analysis(MA) and brainstorming were used. Support tool is mainly for operators and test/repair workers who are work at the coalface.

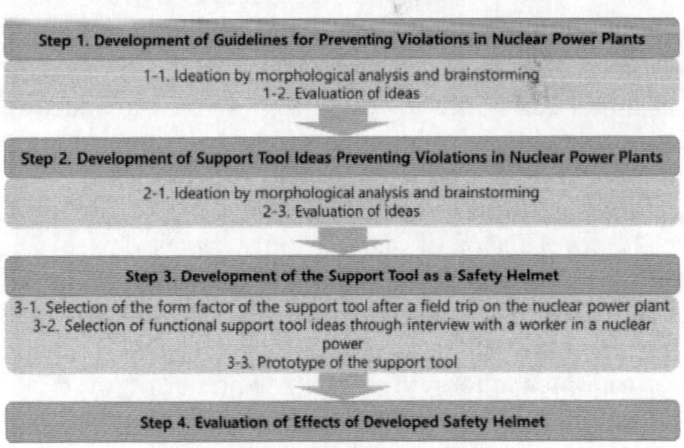

Figure 1. Research process

The research process is shown as Figure 1. This paper explains the study step-by-step.

II. DEVELOPMENT OF GUIDELINES FOR PREVENTING VIOLATIONS IN NUCLEAR POWER PLANTS

First, three user experience(UX) engineering experts developed the guideline ideas for preventing routine violations in nuclear power plants. They used MA and brainstorming for idea generation.

A. *Ideation by morphological analysis and brainstorming*

MA is one of idea generation tools by combining factors which stimulate ideas. This method is effective when generating ideas for solving problems because as many as possible number of cases can be considered [12][13]. The factors used for achieving guideline ideas are three; organization-related violation characteristics, occurring mechanisms of routine violation, and job types. Kang et al. [10], which is a prior study founded organization-related characteristics(OC) and occurring mechanisms of routine violation.

In this study, OC which is composed of 11 factors about operation of organization/safety and 3 factors in education/training and 3 occurring mechanisms of routine violation were combined. After that, possible combinations and three job types in the nuclear power plant were combined to generate ideas.

Additionally, experts conducted brainstorming based on the causes and definition of routine violation. Consequently, total 58 ideas were derived.

B. *Evaluation of ideas*

Three UX experts evaluated ideas using 3-point Likert scale based on the viability and suitability. Poor ideas were ruled out and then 30 ideas were derived.

These ideas were developed as guidelines. One example of guidelines is "design interface in workspace through worker-centric ergonomic design to conduct tasks according to manual easily".

III. Development of Support Tool Ideas Preventing Violations in Nuclear Power Plants

A. *Ideation by morphological analysis and brainstorming*

Three UX engineering experts chose the three factors for MA; form factor of support tools, types of support functions, and guidelines in section 2. Support tool ideas were derived by combining these three factors.

The form factor of support tools means device or tool such as smartphone/tablet, safety helmet, and big display to realize functional ideas. Also, the types of support function refers to functional role of the idea such as provision of information, monitoring/feedback, and reporting system. The 20 form factors of support tools and 6 types of support function were collected from the literature about preventing human error in various fields such as information and communication and safety engineering and industrial fields such as construction, shipbuilding, and chemistry.

Guidelines for preventing violations are the result of section 2. Similar guidelines in 30 guidelines were merged into 8 guidelines. Then, this eight guidelines were used in MA.

For efficient process of support tool idea generation, the form factor of support tools was combined with support function. Then, 67 possible combinations between them were combined with guidelines. 74 ideas were deducted from MA.

Brainstorming was additionally conducted to supplement ideas. Violation occurrence situations were derived and classified as cue in brainstorming session. 13 situations were drawn from analysis of 27 representative cases of nuclear accidents in Republic of Korea by human error since 2005. Furthermore, seven situations were extracted from industrial accidents by human error in recent five years. Based on these 20 situations, researchers brainstormed 16 ideas.

B. *Evaluation of ideas*

Researchers evaluated ideas by feasibility. Feasibility means how easy the idea be realized technically. This is because ideas which can be conducted a spot inspection should be prototyped. Three UX experts assessed ideas using 5-point Likert scale. Ideas over 3.5 average points in feasibility were selected.

IV. Development of the Support Tool as a Safety Helmet

A. *Selection of the form factor of the support tool after a field trip on the nuclear power plant*

The ideas which were generated using one specific form factor can be matched with other form factors. For example, the idea; "The support tool gives warning to the cofactors when they becomes far away from each other" was derived based on a wearable band. However, this idea can be applied to other form factors such as safety helmet, smartphone/tablet, and emergency beeper. For that reason, the ideas were matched with all possible form factors thorough discussion.

To select the form factor of the support tool, researchers visited the nuclear power plant. After the field trip, safety helmet was selected as the form factor of the support tool. This is because safety helmet is existing protect equipment. Accordingly, workers would feel less burdensome than other form factors such as wearable band and emergency beeper. Also, workers should wear the safety helmet in workplace in nuclear power plants. Therefore, applicable place is more various than other form factors such as large displays and smartphone/tablet.

B. *Selection of functional support tool ideas through the interview with a worker in a nuclear power plant*

Interview with a worker in the nuclear power plant was conducted to consider viability of functional ideas of the safety helmet.

Based on the interview, researchers exclude functions which already existent and are unnecessary. In case of ideas related to wireless communications, interviewee said that they were hard to be applied because of technological problem such as interference. However, technological problem could be solved after the technological developments naturally. Therefore, we included ideas which cannot be applied because of technology. Selected functional ideas are shown in Table 1.

TABLE I. SELECTED FUNCTIONAL SUPPORT TOOL IDEAS

Types of Functional Ideas	Functional Ideas
Management of wearing a safety helmet	• Turn on/off of the safety helmet when a worker contacts the safety helmet to a terminal on entrance/exits • Warning 10 seconds after when a worker takes off the safety helmet • Providing voice message about safety when a worker wears/takes off the safety helmet • Sensing health information of a worker through sensors in the safety helmet and providing the information for health care
Communication aid	• Communication with workers within certain distance • Communication with workers in certain workplace • One to one communication • Communication between a supervisor and a worker periodically for checking attention to work
Assistance in Maintaining of distance among workers	• Warning if workers are too far apart for maintaining distance among them during cooperation work

C. *Prototype of the support tool*

Selected of functional support tool ideas realized in form of the safety helmet(Figure 2, Figure 3). It has sensors on the forehead part and headset. Display which shows health information was made.

Figure 2. Prototype of the support tool(Safety helmet)

Figure 3. Prototype of the support tool(Terminal)

TABLE II. FUNCTIONS OF THE SUPPORT TOOL

Types of Functions	Functions
Management of wearing a safety helmet	• Warning and providing messages about safety when a worker does not wear the safety helmet during 10 seconds • Warning and providing messages about safety when a chin strap comes untied
Wireless communication	• Communication with a cooperator • Communication between a director and a worker
Assistance in Maintaining of distance among workers	• Warning if the distance among workers over 10 meters
Health care	• Providing health information such as heart rate and oxygen saturation when a worker contact the safety helmet to the terminal on entrance/exit

Functions were refined as Table 2 because of time and cost.

V. EVALUATION OF EFFECTS OF DEVELOPED SAFETY HELMET

The experiment including interview and survey was conducted to evaluate effects of the prototype of the support tool. Eight workers participated and they wear a safety helmet during working in the nuclear power plant. Their work experience is over one year. The average of work experience is 5.69 years and standard deviation(s.d.) is 4.28 years. They are all male and their average age is 37.38 and s.d. of age is 7.67.

The experiment was progressed as Fig. 4. Subjects listened to explanation about the support tool and then operated it himself for understanding. In the interview, they said pros and cons of functions of the support tool freely based on experience in the previous stage. Also they should try all functions again. Therefore, they could consider usability and effectiveness of preventing violations. After the interview, the survey was conducted. The survey was composed of questions about usability and effectiveness of violation preventive functions. Participants answered in 5-point Likert scale. Detail questions in the survey are shown in Table 3.

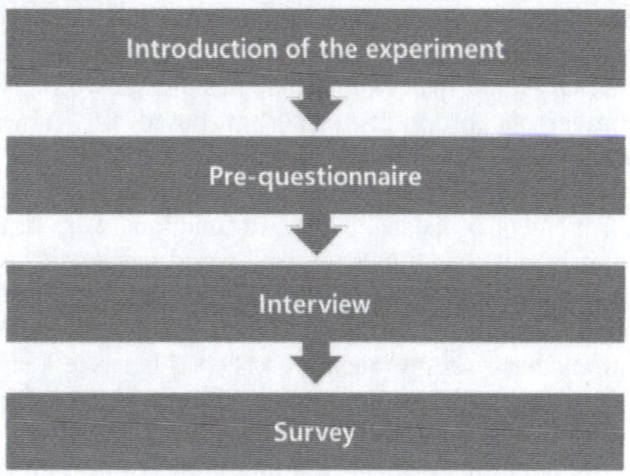

Figure 4. Process of the experiment

TABLE III. CONTENTS OF SURVEY

Question No.	*Description*
1	The sound of warning messages to wear a safety helmet is clearly heard.
2	Warning messages to wear a safety helmet will reduce cases that a worker does not wear a safety helmet.
3	The way to check health information of the worker such as heart rate and oxygen saturation is easy to learn and memorize.
4	A worker can check his/her health information such as heart rate and oxygen saturation clearly on the display.
5	A worker can check his/her health information such as heart rate and oxygen saturation easily and quickly on the display.
6	Health care function can induce workers to wear a safety helmet.
7	The sound of warning messages to maintain distance among workers is clearly heard.
8	Warning messages to maintain distance among workers will reduce cases that a worker works individually during cooperative work.
9	The way to use voice communication function is easy to learn and memorize.
10	Information about status of voice communication function is clearly provided.
11	A worker can use voice communication function easily and quickly.
12	Voice communication function can reduce cases of not checking working status between a work director and a field worker.
13	The sound of voice messages before/after the work is clearly heard.
14	Voice messages before/after the work can raise safety consciousness.
15	This safety helmet will reduce violations which happen routinely such as not wearing a safety helmet, unchecking work status, and working individually during cooperative work.

The results of the survey are shown in Figure 5 and Figure 6. Almost every participant agreed that the developed safety helmet prevents violations. Also everyone said that health care function can lead workers to wear the safety helmet except one participant who answered "disagree". Therefore, this support tool is expected to reduce violations.

Participants responded positively to usability questionnaires. There is no negative answer in whole questions about usability. Thus, it means that people can use the prototype of the support tool without great difficulty.

Considerations to improve the support tool were extracted from the results of the interview. There were total 22 considerations. Among them, considerations which are mentioned by more than two participants are shown in Table 4. Improvement proposals came up based on subjects' opinions in the interview and discussion between two UX engineers.

Improvement proposals related to functions were drawn. In case of health care function, providing more detail health information in real time would be better. In case of assistance function to maintain a certain distance among workers, distance set up function is needed because keeping distance among workers would be different depending on task types. Also, workers should be able to turn off the function maintaining distance if a task does not need to keep a certain distance. Communication among all collaborative

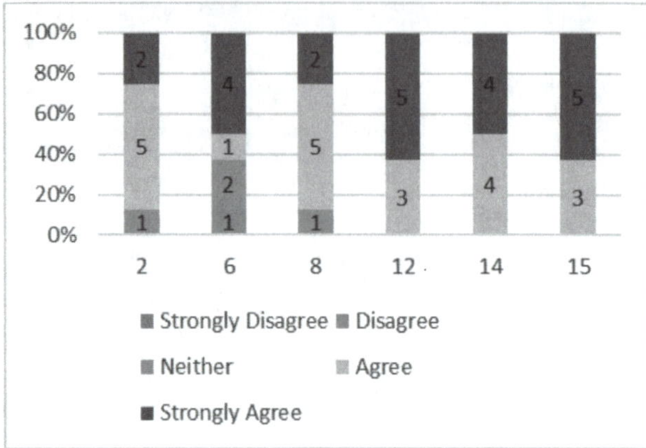

Figure 5. The freqeuncy of response by evaluation questions – Possibility of preventing violations

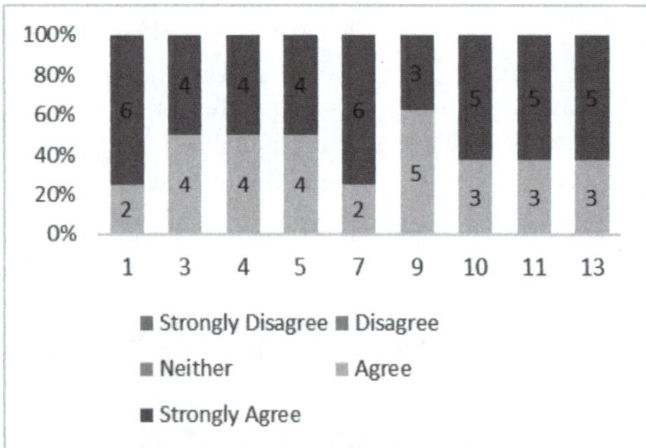

Figure 6. The freqeuncy of response by evaluation questions – Usability

TABLE IV. THE FREQUENCY OF CONSIDERATIONS FOR IMPROVEMENT

Considerations for Improvement	*Related Function/Design Factor*	*Frequency*
A lot sweat	Headset	5
Short distance for maintaining	Assistance in Maintaining of distance among workers	4
Difficulty in binding a chin strap	Chin strap	2
Impossibility of providing health information in real time	Health care	2
No turn off button of assistance in maintaining of distance among workers	Assistance in Maintaining of distance among workers	2
Undue pressure	Headset	2
Heaviness	Safety helmet	2

workers would be better than one-to-one communication. Moreover, process of changing communications target should be easier.

Improvement proposals related to design elements were generated. Location of the switch should be changed to the site where a worker does not press the switch by mistake. Otherwise, it would be better to make the power of the support tool be turned on or off automatically when a worker goes in or out the workplace. A form of earphone is also recommended. This is because earphone arrest noise enough and more convenient for workers in the workplace which does not product noise a lot. Wearing recognition should be moved to optimal position where it can sense well. Optimal position could achieve through the ergonomic experiments.

In other researches about development of a safety helmet to prevent safety accident, there are some possible improvement proposals. Jang et al. [14] made check system for wearing a safety helmet with wireless sensor network. This system logs whether a worker wears a safety helmet or not through sensor module at chin strap in real time. Therefore, it aids a work director to check wearing condition easily and quickly. Providing information and warning about safety helmet wearing condition to both a worker and a work director would be better. Also, data from logging safety helmet wearing condition can be used to analyze violations.

Hong et al. [15] developed the safety helmet with alarm bell to prevent safety accident. They said that the alarm bell rings when stress and heart rate from electrocardiogram(ECG) and brain wave sensors go over certain range. This safety helmet has similar function compared to health care function. However, this tracks health information and alarm in real time and uses different sensors. To provide various and helpful health information, ECG and brain wave sensors can be added.

In this study, support tool ideas were generated mainly based on guidelines about prior checking and task guidelines. Therefore, tracking data and collecting data were out of our research scope. However, tracking and storing health information and warning immediately such as safety helmets in Jang et al. [14] and Hong et al. [15] can be good health care function.

VI. CONCLUSION

In this study, guidelines and support tool ideas for preventing routine violations were generated using MA and brainstorming. Through visiting real nuclear power plant and interview, ideas were selected and developed to the functions of the support tool, safety helmet. After the development, the effects of this safety helmet were evaluated by workers who wear safety helmets during working in the nuclear power plant. As a result, the safety helmet is not difficult to use and good for preventing violations such as not wearing helmet and rare communication.

The developed safety helmet will prevent not wearing safety helmet and performing alone during cooperative work. Moreover, communication support function induces workers to converse actively and smoothly so every task can go according to plan. Also this support tool could be applied to other industries where workers wear safety helmets. Additionally, guidelines and developed support tool help workers in nuclear power plants cultivate safety consciousness. If the safety helmet will be designed with consideration for comfort, more workers will try to wear the safety helmet. Also, violations because of not wearing a safety helmet will decrease a lot.

People in nuclear industry tend to avoid talk about violations because violation receives negative attention in the society. Accordingly, it was hard to recruit workers as participants and collect their ideas and experience. This is because various opinions of workers were not reflected in idea generation and development of the support tool.

Currently, the wireless communication technology is difficult to be applied in nuclear power plants because of interference. After solving that problem and developing various support tool based on IoT, a nuclear power plant can be a smart workplace.

Therefore, more ideas for preventing violations could be generated by collaboration with workers in nuclear power plants later. Additionally, various form of support tool could be developed besides the safety helmet. Thus, this methodical approach could be applied to study other violations.

ACKNOWLEDGMENT

This work was funded by grants from Korean Federation of Science and Technology Societies (Grant-# NRF-2015M2A8A4025069).

REFERENCES

[1] Y. Lee, "A Comparison of the Recent Human Errors In Nuclear Power Plants," Jornal of the Ergonomics Society of Korea. vol. 31, pp. 288-292, 2012.

[2] C. Shim and J. Hong, "The Impact of Radioactive Disasters on Human and Ecosystems," KEI Working Paper, pp. 1-59, 2011

[3] L.R. Anspaygh, R. J. Catlin, and M. Goldman, "The global impact of the Chernobyl reactor accident," Sience. vol. 242, pp. 1513-1519, 1988.

[4] J. K. Park and Y. Lee, "A Human Error Classification according to the Task Information Requirements in Nuclear Power Plants," Proceedings of the Ergonomics Society of Korea, p. 91-95, 2008.

[5] D.A. Norma, "Design Rules based on Analyses of Human Error," Communicationsof the ACM. vol. 26, pp. 254-258, 1983.

[6] J. Julius, E. Jorgenson, G. W. Parry, and A. M. Mosleh, "A Procedure for the Analysis of Errors of Commission in a Probabilistic Safety Assessment of a Nuclear Power Plant at Full Power," Reliability Engineering & System Safety. vol. 50, pp. 189-201, 1995.

[7] D.Y. Jeong, S. H. Han, H. Moon, B. Kang, and Y. Lee, "Characteristics of Human Violations in a Nuclear Power Plant," Proceedings of the Ergonomics Society of Korea, pp. 27-32, 2015.

[8] J.I. Itoh, S. Yoshimura, T. Ohtsuka, and F. Masuda, "Cognitive Task Analysis of Nuclear Power Plat Operators for Man-Machine Interface Design," Proceedings of the

topical meeting on advances in human facotrs research on man/computer interactions, pp. 96-102, 1990.

[9] J.H. Yun and Y. Lee, "Development of a Human Error Evaluation Method for Introducing Smart Mobile to Nuclear Power Plants," Proceedings of the Ergonomics Society of Korea, pp. 190-195, 2011.

[10] B. Kang, S. H. Han, H. Moon, and Y. H. Lee, "A New Definition of Violation Based on Accident/Failure Analyses in Nuclear Power Plants in a Nuclear Power Plant," Proceedings of the Ergonomics Society of Kroea, pp. 22-26, 2015.

[11] B. Kang, S. H. Han, D. Y. Jeong, and Y. Lee, "Conceptual Models of Violation Error in Nulcear Power Plant," Journal of the Korean Society of Safety. vol. 31, pp. 126-131, 2016.

[12] M. Lee, S. H. Han, J. Park, and H. Jang, "A framework for developing smart device design guidelines with consideration of UX of the disabled," Proceedings of the Ergonomics Society of Korea, pp. 170-175, 2016.

[13] G. Q. Huang and K. L. Mak, "Web-based morphological charts for concept design in collaborative product development," Journal of Intelligent Manufactiruing. vol. 10, pp. 267-278, 1999.

[14] M. Jang, M. Yeom, I. Song, O. Kwon, E. Kee, and S. Choi, "Check system for wearing hard hat with wireless sensor network," Proceedings of Conference on Information and Control Systems, pp. 209-210, 2007.

[15] C. Hong, M. Shin, J. Yoon, and H. Kim, "Safety helmet with alarm bell to prevent safety accident," Proceedings of the Ergonomics Society of Korea, pp. 65, 2016.

Development of Web based UX Diagnosis System for Small and Medium Sized Home Appliance Manufacturers in the IoT Era

Joohwan Park, Jiyoung Kwahk, Sung H. Han,
Bora Kang, Mingyu Lee, Dong Yeong Jeong,
Hyeji Jang, Dawoon Jeong
Dept. of Industrial & Management Engineering
POSTECH
Pohang, Korea
e-mail: {pkjhwan, kjy, shan, purple31, mk3215s2, comnet924, wdfokj, jdw0303}@postech.ac.kr

Jungchul Park
Dept. of Safety Engineering
Korea National University of Transportation
Chungju, Korea
e-mail: jcpark@ut.ac.kr

Jaehyun Park
Dept. of Industrial & Management Engineering
Incheon National University
Incheon, Korea
e-mail: jaehpark@inu.ac.kr

Abstract — **The purpose of the study is to develop a web based User eXperience (UX) diagnosis system that helps the small and medium sized home appliance manufacturers prepare for the opportunities of Internet of Things (IoT) era. To provide a UX diagnostic system that is compatible with various product types of the home appliance manufacturers, a total 109 questionnaire items for UX evaluation were developed based on the UX design principles and design elements. The functional requirements of the proposed diagnosis system were constructed based on the needs and requirements that collected from the designers of the small and medium sized manufacturers though in-depth interviews. A UX diagnostic system was developed as a web based platform that supporting overall UX diagnosis process, from the questionnaire generation, survey distribution, user survey data collection, and visualization of the analyzed UX diagnosis result. The proposed system is designed to uncover various possible UX design flaws related to specific design elements and UX design principle. The proposed system provides both quantitative and qualitative diagnosis results, such as UX design scores and users' comments and opinions about the products. The usability, validity, and usefulness of the developed system were evaluated by the experts through case study. The developed system is expected to be useful for home appliance designers of the home appliance manufacturers by providing systems to evaluate the current state of their products and uncover the UX design issues through a web based survey. The following study will be focused to provide design elements, UX design principles, and questionnaire items for evaluation of the home appliances' IoT features.**

Keywords- User experience; IoT; Home appliance; UX diagnosis system; Survey system

I. Introduction

UX (User eXperience) became very popular and important concept to be considered by product designers to achieve competitive advantage in the market. The User Experience can be defined as a person's overarching experience that consists of all aspects of users' interaction with a product, system or service [1]-[3]. The detailed aspects that influence the UX satisfaction of the users may can be varied by the application domains and academic fields, however, usability [3]-[5], affect [3], and user value [3], [6]-[12] of the products are considered to be the most important criteria for UX evaluation by many researchers.

Nowadays, designers of the home appliance manufacturers also started to consider the UX of their product to enhance the user satisfaction. Home appliance is a set of electronic devices that assisting household jobs. Home appliance manufacturers who have enough resources are trying to enhance the UX of their products by investing their resources to introduce state-of-art UX design techniques. However, the Small and Medium sized Enterprise (SME) manufacturers that taking a large portion of the Korean home appliance market usually does not have enough resources and tools for product UX enhancements. As the Internet of Things (IoT) technologies are leading trend of the home appliance market, gradually SME manufacturers are forced to develop new home appliances that have various new IoT features. As a result, it is needed to propose a UX diagnosis system that can reduce the risk of the failures that caused by design by supporting the development process of the SME manufacturers. The diagnosis system has to be afforded to SME manufactures and compatible to their various home appliance product spectrum. The purpose of this research is to develop a UX diagnosis system for designers of the SME home appliance manufacturers based on the requirements and needs that reported by the designers. This study is research that covers the UX diagnosis of traditional home appliance types before the extended research on the UX evaluation of the IoT features of home appliance.

In Section 2, research target home appliance products were defined and the requirement of the designers were explored and analyzed. In Section 3, the proposed diagnosis system was designed and developed. In Section 4, the architecture and interfaces of developed system were described. In Section 5, the case study was proceeded to validate the system's usability. In Section 6 and 7, the discussion and conclusion were followed.

II. Requirement Analysis on Home Appliance Products Designers

Currently, a lot of types of the home appliances are distributed on the market. The types of the home appliance product are varied as the number of the household jobs. This research covers the 6 categories and 27 sub-categories of the home appliance types (See, table 1).

TABLE I. TARGET HOME APPLIANCES OF THE RESEARCH

Category	Home Appliance
Cleaner	Vacuum cleaner, Robot vacuum, Handheld vacuum
Kitchen	Rice cooker, Electric kettles, Blender, Water filter/purifier, Electric range, Microwave oven, Electronic oven, Toaster, Dishwasher
Laundry	Iron, Washing machine
Beauty	Hair dryer, Hair straighteners, Electric shaver
Heater/Air Conditioner	Fan, Dehumidifier, Humidifier, Air purifier, Heater, Fan heater
Health Care	Hearing aid, Massager, Handheld massager

The requirements of the UX diagnosis system were needed to be defined based on the demands of the designers. In-depth interview sessions were placed to collect the opinions and demands of the designers on the UX evaluation and diagnostic tools they have experienced. A total nine SME designers who take the role of operating designers, engineers, and Chief Executive Officers (CEO) of six SME home appliance manufacturers were participated in the interview. Designers shared their needs, pain-points, and episodes that they experienced during UX diagnosis or product design enhancement process. They also provided valuable opinions about the ideal concept and the role of the UX diagnosis system based on their experiences (See, table 2). These opinions were translated into the system design requirements to reflect the designers' demands of researchers

III. UX Diagnosis System Design

The system was designed through following three steps. At first, the UX design principles and design elements were defined. And questionnaire items for UX evaluation were generated by combining the principles and design elements. At last, the web based diagnosis system was developed.

A. *UX design Principles and Design Elements*

To define major criteria for evaluating UX satisfaction of the home appliance products, the UX related principles and evaluation criteria were collected through home appliance designer interview and literature review. The collected UX design principles were merged into 14 UX design principles and categorized into three UX aspects such as usability, affect, and user value (See, table 3).

TABLE II. SME DESIGNERS DEMANDS ON UX DIAGNOSIS SYSTEM

Category	Demands
Accessibility	▪ The system has to be easily accessible by external participants ▪ Survey session needs to be around 15 minutes to reduce cognitive workload ▪ Survey process and questionnaires have to be easy and simple
Usability	▪ Easy for participants to rate products ▪ Easy for designers to use the system ▪ Easy/clear terminologies need to be used
User Characteristics	▪ Demographic information of the user has to be analyzed ▪ The answering tendency of the participants' demographic characteristics towards each UX element is very important information for market segmentation and strategy
Customizability	▪ Designers may need to select, add, modify, remove questionnaire items ▪ System need to provide customizability for designers
Comments Analysis	▪ User comments are also a very important source of the ideas, issues, opinions ▪ It is needed to provide functions to collect and analyze user's comments
Comparison	▪ Comparison between products are very important to provide understanding about current market's UX levels and criteria for judgement
Price Decision	▪ The system may can provide the criteria for the pricing decision
Pros/Cons Analysis	▪ System need to provide information about current weak point and the strength of the product

TABLE III. UX DESIGN PRINCIPLES FOR HOME APPLIANCES

UX Aspect	UX Design Principle
Usability	▪ Informativeness ▪ Learnability ▪ Efficiency ▪ Physical suitability
Affect	▪ Attractiveness ▪ Delicacy ▪ Luxuriousness ▪ Stability ▪ Harmoniousness
User Value	▪ Safety ▪ Hygiene ▪ Durability ▪ Performance ▪ Functionality

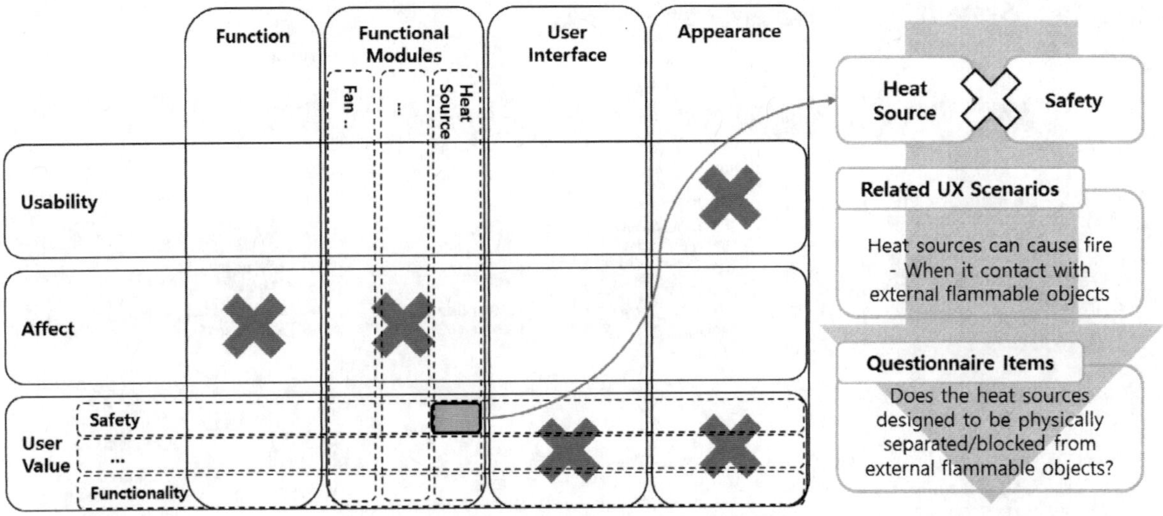

Figure 1. Development Process of Questionnaire Items

It is also important to investigate the source of the poor UX for design enhancement. Design elements of the home appliance were defined as the logical and physical components of products that can be designed by designers and influence the UX satisfaction of the users such as function, interface, and appearance of the product. The design elements of various home appliances that could affect to the UX satisfaction were collected from literatures, user reviews, and expert interviews.

TABLE IV. DESIGN ELEMENTS OF HOME APPLIANCES

Category	Design Element
Function	▪ Function
Functional Module	▪ Ventilation Opening ▪ Filter/Dust Bag ▪ Fan/Motor ▪ Heat Source ▪ Sensor ▪ Handle/Grip ▪ Wheel ▪ Feet ▪ Cover/Lid ▪ Replaceable Module ▪ Power Supply Cable ▪ Battery ▪ Bottle/Vessel
User Interface	▪ Visual Information/Display ▪ Sound/Speaker ▪ Haptic Stimulus ▪ Control
Appearance	▪ Color/Painting ▪ Texture ▪ Shape

A total number of 21 design elements were defined and classified into four categories, such as the function, functional module, appearance, and user interface elements (See, table 4).

B. Development of UX Evaluation Questionnaire Items

It is important to develop detailed questionnaire items that could be related to various home appliance design flaws. The proposed system uses UX design principles as evaluation criteria and design elements as the targets to be evaluated. The questionnaire items were developed based on the combinations of these two factors. As fourteen UX design principles and twenty-one design elements were defined, a total of 294 combinations were available.

To develop the questionnaire items based on the possible use scenarios related to design flaws, scenarios that could be happened during context of use were constructed and reviewed for each combination. Questionnaire items were developed based on the scenarios to ask users if the target product is appropriately designed to prevent the related UX problems. For example, combining a heat source with the safety principle, safety related problematic scenarios could be deduced and following questionnaire items were developed based on these scenarios (See, Figure 1).

As a result, a total 109 questionnaire items were defined based the UX related principles and design elements of the home appliance types. Each questionnaire item was designed to be related to the specific UX design principle and the specific design element.

C. UX Diagnosis System Development

The UX diagnosis system was developed as a web-based responsive survey system that running on Apache Tomcat. The system was designed to be web-based survey system. The system design followed the requirements that collected from the designers of SME designers by providing related functions to evaluate the home appliance and inspect possible design flaws.

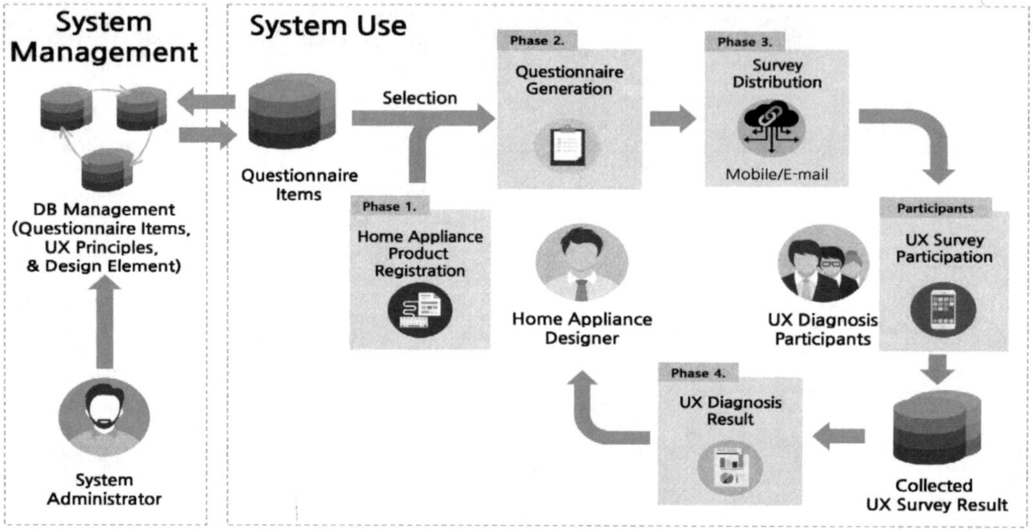

Figure 2. UX Diagnosis System Architecture

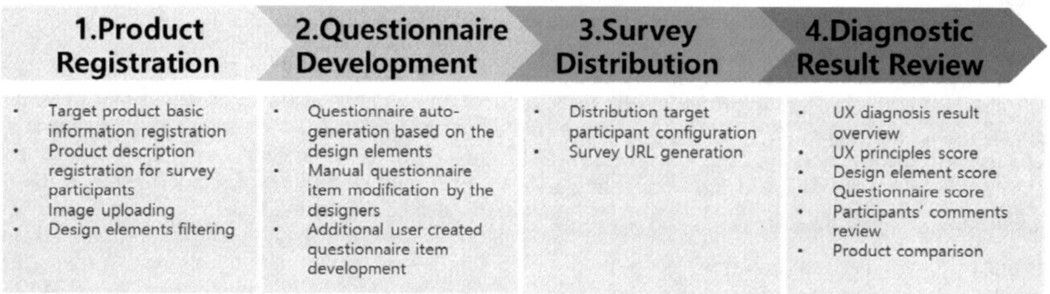

Figure 3. UX Diagnosis Process and Designers Tasks

IV. RESULT: UX DIAGNOSIS SYSTEM

On the proposed UX diagnosis system, home appliance designers can follow four steps to generate, distribute, and read the result of the UX diagnosis survey (See, Fig. 2). The developed system provides questionnaire items and related functions to support home appliance designers through the UX diagnosis process (See, Fig. 3).

The first stage is the product registration phase. SME designers can register the information about the product to be evaluated. The information about the product such as major functions and images were designed be presented to survey participants as supplemental information to provide better understanding about questionnaire item.

The second stage is questionnaire development phase. The system generates questionnaire automatically based on the design elements consisting the target product. The designers can modify any questionnaire items to specify the terminologies to fit on the product components, and also remove any questionnaire items if they were considered not to be important (See, Figure 4). The designers can also add any questionnaire items to collect additional user opinions.

The third stage is survey distribution. The UX diagnosis system generates a Uniform Resource Locator (URL) of the survey that can be distributed through email or message. The survey participants can access to the survey on any devices through internet connection by clicking the survey URL.

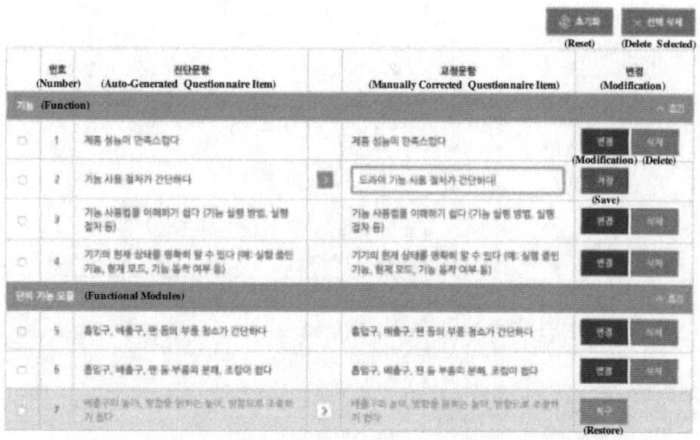

Figure 4. Questionnaire Item Modification Interface

During the survey, each questionnaire item was presented to participants with supplementary information such as images and related design element description. The participants were instructed to rate with 0 to 100 scale for each questionnaire item (See, Figure 5). The participants can provide any comment or opinion to describe why they rate so through the survey process.

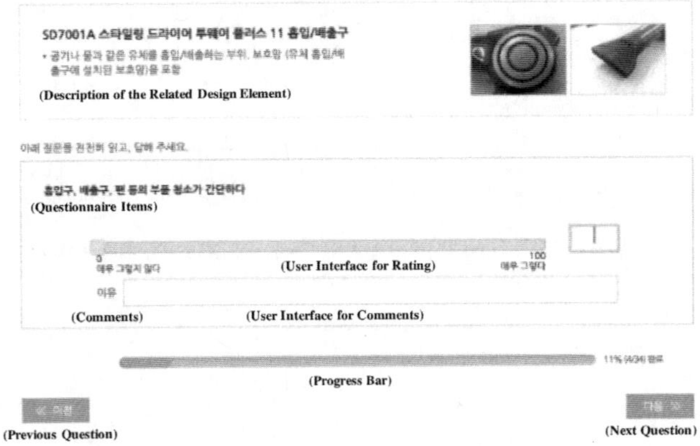

Figure 5. Survey Questionnaire Interface for Participants (Translated)

The last stage is the diagnostic result review. The web diagnosis system generates the diagnostic report for SME designers based on the survey participants' responses. Designers can review which UX design principle or design element were evaluated high or low by participants with the proposed system. The diagnostic result contains visualized information about the response of each demographic group. The designers also can review the critical design issues and related opinions on the diagnostic report to get a hint for the further design enhancements.

The system provides several distinct interfaces to visualize the products' scores and participants' responses. For examples, the product comparison function generates reports to visualize the UX diagnosis results of products through side-by-side view (See, Figure 6). This interface uses a bar - chart to visualize the scores of each product to be easily compared by the designers.

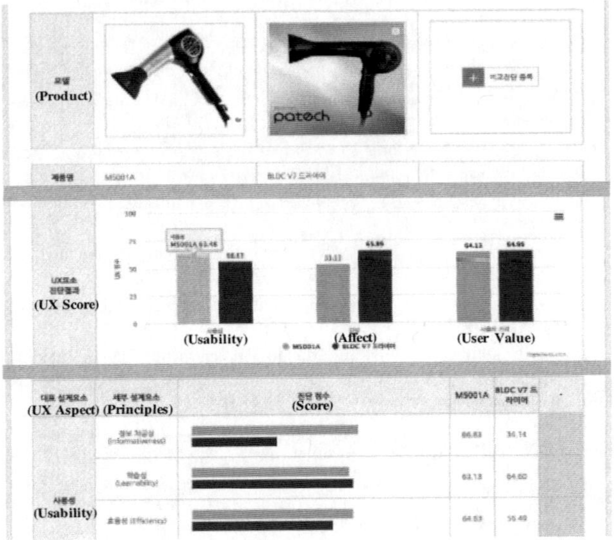

Figure 6. Result: Product Comparison

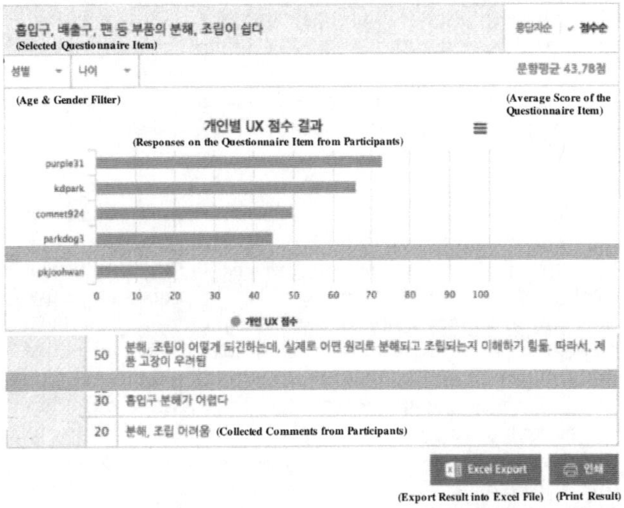

Figure 7. Result: Participants' Responses on Specific Questionnaire Item

The system also provides the interface to show the participants' responses to each questionnaire item, such as rating score, gender, age, and comments (See, Figure 7).

V. CASE STUDY: SYSTEM USABILITY EVALUATION

To validate the usability of the proposed system for the realistic home appliance UX diagnosis purpose, the usability of the proposed system was evaluated by expert group consists of UX experts and SME designers. The UX expert group consisted of six UX experts who have a Doctor of Philosophy (Ph.D.) degree of UX related domains and nine industrial designers of the SME manufacturers.

TABLE V. AVERAGE USABILITY EVALUATION RESULT

SUS Questionnaire Item	UX Expert	SME Designer
I think that I would like to use this system frequently.	91.3	77.2
I found the system unnecessarily complex.	88.9	80.0
I thought the system was easy to use.	85.1	83.9
I think that I would need the support of a technical person to be able to use this system.	81.9	73.9
I found the various functions in this system were well integrated.	88.1	76.7
I thought there was too much inconsistency in this system.	82.8	82.2
I would imagine that most people would learn to use this system very quickly.	84.7	85.6
I found the system very cumbersome to use.	82.3	81.7
I felt very confident using the system.	87.2	87.8
I needed to learn a lot of things before I could get going with this system.	81.7	82.8
Mean score	**85.4**	**81.2**

System Usability Scale (SUS) is usually used as a system usability evaluation questionnaire [13]. SUS is one of the most qualified and simple usability evaluation tools that uses ten questionnaire items for software usability evaluation. To verify the usability of the proposed system, experts reviewed the proposed system and evaluated the usability of the system. UX diagnosis results of nine home appliance products were collected from ten users and presented to experts as examples. The overall average SUS score was over 80 points on the both groups (See, table 5).

VI. DISCUSSION

Several survey participants reported that it is hard to perform objective evaluations on specific product design because of the lack of the expertise. As the psychophysical scale methods are used to quantify the users' subjective judgement to measurable index, when users do not have enough experience it can be hard to quantify the subjective judgement on the product [14]-[16].

There was a concern that reported by SME designers about the bias caused by participant variability. Reliability of the rating score may differ because the relative indicators may change depending on the user's evaluation criteria. Some researcher pointed out the possible bias that based on the inter- and intra- subject variabilities [17]-[20]. The number of participants must be compensated at least ten and more participants are required to overcome the inter- and intra-subject variability when using the magnitude estimation technique [20].

As the home appliance industry is currently following the trend of the IoT, the proposed diagnosis system needs to be enhanced to compatible with the IoT home appliance products. The deduced UX design principles and design elements are developed based on the popular and representative products on the market, not based on state-of-art IoT products. It means they are currently not sufficiently comprehensive to cover the various IoT based functions and IoT related functional modules that consisting IoT home appliance products. The future research is currently planning to expand provided system to support IoT home appliance products.

The purpose of this research is to develop a UX diagnosis system for designers of the SME home appliance manufacturers based on the requirements and needs that reported by the designers. This study covers the UX diagnosis of basic home appliance types, and the extended research on the UX evaluation of the IoT features of home appliance will be followed.

VII. CONCLUSION

The developed system is designed based on the demands of the designers of the SME home appliance manufacturers. The developed system provides the systematic UX diagnosis system that is compatible and flexible to various home appliance types. The inspection and diagnosis result of the proposed system could be helpful for SME manufacturers to find design flaws of their product and hints for further design improvement.

ACKNOWLEDGMENT

This research was supported by Technology Innovation Industrial Program funded by the Ministry of Trade, industry & Energy (MI, Korea) [10054722, User experience evaluation system for consumer electronic products to enhance competitiveness of small and medium enterprises]

REFERENCES

[1] International Standardization Organization (ISO), "ISO 9241-210: 2010, Ergonomics of human system interaction-Part 210: Human-centred design for interactive systems," International Standardization Organization (ISO), Switzerland, 2009.

[2] A. P. Vermeeren et al., "User experience evaluation methods: current state and development needs," Proceedings of the 6th Nordic Conference on Human-Computer Interaction: Extending Boundaries. ACM, 2010, pp. 521-530.

[3] J. Park, S. H. Han, H. K. Kim, Y. Cho, and W. Park, "Developing elements of user experience for mobile phones and services: survey, interview, and observation approaches," Human Factors and Ergonomics in Manufacturing & Service Industries, vol. 23(4), pp. 279-293, 2013.

[4] International Standardization Organization (ISO), "ISO 9241-11:1998," International Standardization Organization (ISO), Switzerland, 2012.

[5] D. Hix, and H. R. Hartson, Developing user interfaces: ensuring usability through product & process. John Wiley & Sons Inc., 1993.

[6] M. Hassenzahl, and N. Tractinsky, "User experience-a research agenda," Behaviour & information technology, vol. 25(2), pp. 91-97, 2006.

[7] F. D. Davis, "Perceived usefulness, perceived ease of use, and user acceptance of information technology". MIS quarterly, vol. 13(3), pp. 319-340, 1989.

[8] M. Igbaria, S. J. Schiffman, and T. J. Wieckowski, "The respective roles of perceived usefulness and perceived fun in the acceptance of microcomputer technology," Behaviour & Information Technology, vol. 13(6), pp. 349-361, 1994.

[9] V. Venkatesh, "Determinants of perceived ease of use: Integrating control, intrinsic motivation, and emotion into the technology acceptance model," Information systems research, vol. 11(4), pp. 342-365, 2000.

[10] H. Van der Heijden, "Factors influencing the usage of websites: the case of a generic portal in The Netherlands," Information & management, vol. 40(6), pp. 541-549, 2003.

[11] S. J. Hong, and K. Y. Tam, "Understanding the adoption of multipurpose information appliances: The case of mobile data services," Information systems research, vol. 17(2), pp. 162-179, 2006.

[12] A. Marcus, "Cross-cultural user-experience design". In International Conference on Theory and Application of Diagrams, 2006, pp. 16-24.

[13] J. Brooke, "SUS-A quick and dirty usability scale," Usability evaluation in industry, vol. 189(194), pp. 4-7, 1996.

[14] D. Meister, Behavioral analysis and measurement methods. Wiley-Interscience, 1985.

[15] G. A. Gescheider, Psychophysics: the fundamentals. Psychology Press, 1997.

[16] J. S. Dumas, and B. A. Loring, Moderating usability tests: Principles and practices for interacting. Morgan Kaufmann, 2008.

[17] G. A. Gescheider, "Psychophysical scaling," Annual review of psychology, vol. 39(1), pp. 169-200, 1988.

[18] R. P. Hellman, "Stability of individual loudness functions obtained by magnitude estimation and production," Attention, Perception, & Psychophysics, vol. 29(1), pp. 63-70, 1981.

[19] A. W. Logue, "Individual differences in magnitude estimation of loudness," Attention, Perception, & Psychophysics, vol. 19(3), pp. 279-280, 1976.

[20] S. H. Han, M. Song, and J. Kwahk, "A systematic method for analyzing magnitude estimation data," International Journal of Industrial Ergonomics, vol. 23(5), pp. 513-524, 1999.

Design and Evaluation of Mobile Interfaces for an Aging Population

Ljilja Ruzic, Christina N. Harrington, and Jon A. Sanford
The Center for Assistive Technology and Environmental Access (CATEA)
Georgia Institute of Technology
Atlanta, GA, USA
e-mail: ljilja@gatech.edu, cnh@gatech.edu, jon.sanford@design.gatech.edu

Abstract—**The design and evaluation of mobile interfaces for older adults are becoming more important as the population ages and their use of technology increases. Current design strategies, which are used to guide the design of mobile interfaces, are either not primarily developed for mobile platforms or are not focused on the aging population with diverse limitations. Adaptation and integration of the existing strategies were necessary to create an inclusive and comprehensive set of guidelines for interactive mobile interfaces for older adults. The paper presents an overview of the Universal Design Mobile Interface Guidelines (UDMIG) and the related evaluation checklist. UDMIG v.2.1 and the evaluation checklist were developed to ensure usability of future mobile technologies by older adults through a universal design strategy that accommodates all users to the greatest extent possible. This paper contributes to human-computer interaction research by including this population of users and advancing the technology uses for the mobile touchscreen interfaces for aging population.**

Keywords-aging; design; evaluation; mobile interfaces.

I. INTRODUCTION

Older adults encounter many barriers associated with aging while interacting with mobile applications [1]-[4]. Lack of physical space (e.g., small touch and physical buttons), confusion with their location within the context, use of menus that require precise movements, use of small fonts, content placement, and use of large contents that require memory recall, are some of the barriers that lead to longer and less successful task completion [5][6].

The design and evaluation of mobile interfaces for older adults is becoming more important as the population ages and their use of technology increases. Current design strategies that guide the design of user interfaces are either not primarily developed for mobile platforms or are not focused on the aging population with diverse limitations. Moreover, there is a lack of evaluation tools for mobile applications designed for older adults. Four established design strategies for desktop and mobile user interfaces for the general and aging population were analyzed: Universal Design (UD), Design for Aging (DfA), Universal Usability (UU), and Guidelines for Handheld Mobile Device Interface Design (MID). Adaptation and integration of the existing strategies were necessary to create an inclusive and comprehensive set of guidelines for interactive mobile interfaces for older adults. In addition, the evaluation checklist was created to support the user testing of mobile applications designed for an aging population.

The research paper presents an overview of the Universal Design Mobile Interface Guidelines, UDMIG v.2.1, and the related evaluation checklist. UDMIG v.2.1 and the evaluation checklist were developed to ensure usability of future mobile technologies by older adults through a universal design strategy that accommodates all users to the greatest extent possible.

This paper is organized into five sections. Section II describes the related work that covers four sets of design guidelines used to develop the resulting UDMIG. Section III describes the final version of the design guidelines. Section IV addresses the related evaluation checklist. Section V summarizes the paper and proposes future work.

II. RELATED WORK

The purpose of UD is to design for everyone and by doing so, to overcome the barriers to usability that come with aging [7][8]. It consists of seven principles of universal design and twenty-nine guidelines. In contrast to UD, DfA [9] focuses on specific limitations of older adults. DfA is a strategy that explores the factors that constrain the use of products and user interfaces by older adults, as well as aspects of human-computer interface design that accommodate older users with age-associated disabilities and limitations [10]. It has fifty-two design guidelines grouped into six categories that cover design of visual, auditory, and haptic presentation of information, input and output devices, and effective interface design.

Based on UD, which initially covered the design of physical environments (e.g., buildings, spaces, products, graphics), UU was developed to support usability, inclusivity, and utility of information and communication technology [11]. It contains eight guidelines, called the Eight Golden Rules of Interface Design. Guidelines for Handheld Mobile Device Interface Design [12] were based on UU, modifying its eight design guidelines and adding the guidelines applicable to mobile and touchscreen platforms.

While UD, DfA, UU, and MID represent design strategies that are currently used to guide the design of mobile interfaces, none are sufficiently comprehensive to ensure that mobile user interfaces will be usable by older adults. UU, DfA, and UD guidelines were not originally developed for mobile interfaces, although UD has recently included this platform to a certain extent. MID fails to acknowledge diversity and the ranges of limitations that the aging population faces.

Moreover, there is a lack of relevant and comprehensive evaluation tools that support usability and equitability assessment of mobile touchscreen interfaces for an aging population. The existing assessment tools are either designed for other environments (e.g., products, services, spaces, buildings) or developed to support the design of mobile interfaces for general population, thus failing to acknowledge the diversity of limitations of older adults.

UD checklist [13][14] is an evaluation tool, which assesses the design based on both UD principles and ranges of users' abilities (i.e., vision, hearing, speech, cognition, dexterity, communication, balance, stature, upper and lower body strength and mobility, life span) to indicate the degree to which the outcome met the criteria for each design principle and each type of ability, respectively. This tool only considers the architectural spaces, does not assess the specific design features and evaluates the proposed and not the actual designs. The Universal Design Performance Measures for Products [8] uses twenty-nine UD guidelines as performance measures, and the five-point rating scale from strongly disagree to strongly agree, with a choice of not applicable to identify strengths and weaknesses of a product. This assessment tool is intended to be used by experts on aging and disability to evaluate the usability of the products throughout the life cycle, develop usability testing and focus groups, and identify and promote UD features of products. It is limiting in the application to complex and integrated products. The second version of this tool called the Product Evaluation Countdown [15], was developed for use by end-users with their ranges and levels of abilities to test the actual demands of products. Universal Design Assessment Protocol (UDAP) [8][16] assesses UD principles by ability as well as across the range of abilities, evaluating design at the level of each UD guideline, thus providing a more precise analysis. However, the tool proved to be very complex and impractical to actually quantify UD with its six hundred and twelve-cell matrix. The Global Universal Design Commission, Inc. (GUDC) created GUDC Rating System that covers design process, site and building elements, customer service, and facilities management, which is building-type specific [8]. WCAG 2.0 checklist [17] was developed to design accessible web pages to users with disabilities. It is also used to primarily evaluate the accessibility of HTML content. However, neither one of these evaluation tools was developed for the usability evaluation of the mobile user interfaces.

Heuristic evaluation [18] is widely used for web and mobile interface usability assessment. This usability engineering method was made to be an easy, fast, and cheap way of evaluating user interface design during the project lifecycle. An evaluation framework for mobile interfaces [19] is developed to allow designers and users to quickly test the prototypes on the actual devices. A number of other evaluation checklists and frameworks for testing the usability of mobile applications for the general population have been proposed [20]-[22]. However, these usability assessment tools do not recognize a variety and ranges of limitations an aging population faces.

III. Universal Design Mobile Interface Guidelines, UDMIG

The first version of the guidelines, UDMIG v.1.0, which has been previously reported [23][24], was created by applying DfA, UU, and MIG to seven UD principles and related guidelines. This version relied too much on principles and guidelines of universal design, failed to incorporate person-environment interaction approach that was a unique contribution of DfA, contained inconsistent language and level of specificity, and needed further refinement. As a result, UDMIG v.2.0 [25] was developed within a framework based on the two organizing principles: the Person-Environment (P-E) Fit Model [26], and Guideline Approach (i.e., prescriptive- vs. performance-based).

The P-E Model [26] assessed the match or fit between a person's ability and the demands of the environment to promote healthy aging. Usability of mobile applications is achieved when there is a match between a person's ability and the design of the interface. In UDMIG v.2.0, the person component is a part of all the guidelines as it describes how to accommodate people with different abilities. The fit component includes those guidelines that describe the design of the touchscreen mobile interface as a whole (i.e., interface context), as well as those that guide the design of the specific design elements of the mobile interface with which users interact. The environment component recognizes the requirements of the overall space and context of use (e.g., lighting and glare). Only the fit component is addressed in this paper.

Guidelines were also categorized into prescriptive- vs. performance-based. Prescriptive guidelines focus on means and methods of achieving usability by dictating what must be done to achieve a usable outcome. This is largely achieved without specifying the design of the outcome. In contrast, performance guidelines focus on the product or results of the design process. Performance-based guidelines suggest what the usable outcome should be without regard to how that outcome is achieved. As a result, performance guidelines provide greater flexibility in design outcomes by providing opportunities for designers to rely on their own interpretation and creativity to achieve a usable outcome.

A. UDMIG v.2.1

UDMIG v.2.0 was refined and regrouped to better fit its organization into the interface context and design elements guidelines (See Table 1). Features guidelines were renamed into the design elements guidelines so that the resulting UDMIG v.2.1 precisely distinguish between the design characteristics and elements of the mobile interfaces. Design characteristics are specified based on the design elements guidelines and indicate clearly what exactly needs to be developed and designed for a usable outcome.

Interface context guidelines guide the design of the mobile touchscreen interface as a whole. For example, the mobile user interface needs to be designed in a way that the complexity is eliminated, and information arranged consistent with its importance to allow for natural use.

TABLE I. UDMIG V.2.1

Design Elements Guidelines	Interface Context Guidelines
1. Choice in methods of use	1. Same means of use
2. Accuracy and precision	2. Design appealing to all
3. Minimization of hazards and unintended actions	3. Simple and natural use
4. Informative feedback	4. Consistency with expectations
5. Different modes of use	5. Internal locus of control
6. Simple error handling	6. Maximized "legibility" of essential information
7. Easy reversal of actions	7. Clear and understandable navigation structure
	8. Dialogs that yield closure
	9. Range of literacy and language skills
	10. Right-, left- or no-handed use
	11. Adaptation to users' pace
	12. Multiple and dynamic contexts
	13. Low physical effort
	14. Variations in hand and grip size
	15. Natural body position

Source: L. Ruzic Kascak, Designing Mobile Health and Wellness Self-Management Applications for Individuals Aging with Multiple Sclerosis, unpublished

Design elements guidelines cover the design of the specific elements within the mobile touchscreen interface that users interact with. For instance, a user interface is designed to provide the user with the option to change the color contrast (e.g., white on black vs. black on white).

IV. UDMIG V.2.1 EVALUATION

Prescriptive design guidelines and standards are easy to interpret and to objectively test in the wild. Assessment of performance guidelines is multidimensional since it incorporates both activity and participation [8]. All performance-based guidelines are subject to interpretation by experts as well as end-users to a certain extent, which makes objective measurement slightly difficult. UDMIG v.2.1 Checklist rates all the design guidelines using the 5-point Likert scale. It is intended to be used by users as well as by the experts in the field to objectively assess usability and equitability of the mobile interfaces.

A. UDMIG v.2.1 Checklist

The checklist rates agreement with each of the UDMIG v.2.1 guidelines. This evaluation sheet can help you think about your needs and those of other potential users when interacting with mobile applications.

1) Design Element Guidelines

1. This application provides alternate means of interaction such as speech input, hands-free, or eyes-free interaction.
   □1 Strongly Disagree □2 Disagree □3 Neither □4 Agree □5 Strongly Agree

2. I am able to find the information I am looking for easily.
   □1 Strongly Disagree □2 Disagree □3 Neither □4 Agree □5 Strongly Agree

3. The design of this application minimizes the occurrence of unintended actions (e.g., prompt messages, button placement, etc.).
   □1 Strongly Disagree □2 Disagree □3 Neither □4 Agree □5 Strongly Agree

4. A. This application provides informative feedback (e.g., a beep when pressing a key, an error message, etc.) that I am using it in the right way.
   □1 Strongly Disagree □2 Disagree □3 Neither □4 Agree □5 Strongly Agree

   B. I am able to tell that I have successfully completed an action in this app.
   □1 Strongly Disagree □2 Disagree □3 Neither □4 Agree □5 Strongly Agree

5. This application provides different modes of feedback such as audio, tactile, or visual feedback.
   □1 Strongly Disagree □2 Disagree □3 Neither □4 Agree □5 Strongly Agree

6. The most important design elements in this application are readily available, and the app provides warnings of errors.
   □1 Strongly Disagree □2 Disagree □3 Neither □4 Agree □5 Strongly Agree

7. I can easily reverse my actions if I make a mistake in using this application.
   □1 Strongly Disagree □2 Disagree □3 Neither □4 Agree □5 Strongly Agree

B. Interface Context Guidelines

1. I find this application useful and accessible.
   □1 Strongly Disagree □2 Disagree □3 Neither □4 Agree □5 Strongly Agree

2. The design of this app appeals to me.
   □1 Strongly Disagree □2 Disagree □3 Neither □4 Agree □5 Strongly Agree

3. The interface of this application is easy to understand and not complex.
   □1 Strongly Disagree □2 Disagree □3 Neither □4 Agree □5 Strongly Agree

4. Interaction in this app is consistent with my expectations and intuition.
   □1 Strongly Disagree □2 Disagree □3 Neither □4 Agree □5 Strongly Agree

5. I am able to control the output of my actions when using this app.
   □1 Strongly Disagree □2 Disagree □3 Neither □4 Agree □5 Strongly Agree

6. A. This application provides adequate contrast between background colors against the images and text.
   □1 Strongly Disagree □2 Disagree □3 Neither □4 Agree □5 Strongly Agree

   B. Fonts and graphics are legible in this app.
   □1 Strongly Disagree □2 Disagree □3 Neither □4 Agree □5 Strongly Agree

7. Navigation throughout this app is understandable, and I can easily find my way from one screen to the next.
   □1 Strongly Disagree □2 Disagree □3 Neither □4 Agree □5 Strongly Agree

8. I am able to tell my status throughout the use of this app.
   □1 Strongly Disagree □2 Disagree □3 Neither □4 Agree □5 Strongly Agree

9. I can easily understand the terms and language used throughout this app.
   □1 Strongly Disagree □2 Disagree □3 Neither □4 Agree □5 Strongly Agree

10. The app provides right- or left-handed and single- or no-handed access and use.
    □1 Strongly Disagree □2 Disagree □3 Neither □4 Agree □5 Strongly Agree

11. This application features an appropriate pace of interaction for me.
    □1 Strongly Disagree □2 Disagree □3 Neither □4 Agree □5 Strongly Agree

12. I can configure output to my needs and preferences (e.g., text size, brightness).
    □1 Strongly Disagree □2 Disagree □3 Neither □4 Agree □5 Strongly Agree

13. The amount of force required to perform actions in this app was adequate.
    □1 Strongly Disagree □2 Disagree □3 Neither □4 Agree □5 Strongly Agree

14. Buttons, keys, and icons are large enough for me to select without error.
    □1 Strongly Disagree □2 Disagree □3 Neither □4 Agree □5 Strongly Agree

15. I feel comfortable using this app regardless of my previous experience with mobile applications.
    □1 Strongly Disagree □2 Disagree □3 Neither □4 Agree □5 Strongly Agree

UDMIG v.2.1 checklist is developed to be used by both experts in the field (e.g., designers, researchers, disability and gerontology experts) and older adults. The checklist is a usability and equitability evaluation instrument that can be used to identify usability problems during the design process as well as to test the final product.

V. CONCLUSION AND FUTURE WORK

UDMIG v.2.1 and related evaluation checklist were developed to ensure usability of future mobile applications by older adults. A universal design approach was used to accommodate all users to the greatest extent possible. Based on each UDMIG v.2.1 guideline, a representative statement with the 5-point Likert scale was created. The purpose of the checklist is to rate the agreement with each of the guideline. It was developed for end-users and usability experts to evaluate the usability and equitability of the mobile interfaces for an aging population.

The future work will require validation of the guidelines and the checklist through the application of UDMIG v.2.1 and evaluation of both the guidelines and the checklist with older adults and other users who represent variety and ranges of abilities. The planned work includes development and testing of an eHealth mobile application for individuals aging with Multiple Sclerosis (MS). People with MS represent an ideal user group for application and evaluation of UDMIG v.2.1 and the checklist. They are a diverse user group with symptoms that vary widely from individual to individual and within an individual over time. UDMIG v.2.1 checklist will be evaluated with both experts in the field and individuals with MS.

ACKNOWLEDGMENT

This research was supported by a grant from the National Institute on Disability, Independent Living, and Rehabilitation Research (NIDILRR grant number 90RE5016-01-00) under the auspices of The Rehabilitation Engineering Research Center on Technologies to Support Successful Aging with Disability (RERC TechSAge). NIDILRR is a Center within the Administration for Community Living (ACL), Department of Health and Human Services (HHS).

REFERENCES

[1] A. Holzinger, G. Searle, and A. Nischelwitzer, "On some aspects of improving mobile applications for the elderly," International Conference on Universal Access in Human-Computer Interaction (HCII2007), Springer, Jul. 2007, pp. 923-932.

[2] M. Ziefle, "The influence of user expertise and phone complexity on performance, ease of use and learnability of different mobile phones," Behaviour & Information Technology, vol. 21, pp. 303-311, Jan. 2002.

[3] M. Ziefle and S. Bay, "How older adults meet complexity: aging effects on the usability of different mobile phones," Behaviour & Information Technology, vol. 24, pp. 375-389, Sep. 2005.

[4] M. Ziefle, S. Bay, and A. Schwade, "On keys' meanings and modes: The impact of different key solutions on children's efficiency using a mobile phone," Behaviour & Information Technology, vol. 25, pp. 413-431, Sep. 2006.

[5] A. Chadwick-Dias, M. McNulty, and T. Tullis, "Web usability and age: how design changes can improve performance," Conference on Universal Usability (CUU 2003), Nov. 2003, pp. 30-37.

[6] S. A. Becker, "A study of web usability for older adults seeking online health resources," ACM Transactions on Computer-Human Interaction (TOCHI 2004), Dec. 2004, vol. 11, pp. 387-406.

[7] C. M. Law, J. S. Yi, Y. S. Choi, and J. A. Jacko, "A systematic examination of universal design resources: part 1, heuristic evaluation," Universal Access in the Information Society, vol. 7, pp. 31-54, Apr. 2008.

[8] J. A. Sanford, Universal Design as a Rehabilitation Strategy: Design for the Ages. New York, NY: Springer Publishing Company, 2012.

[9] A. D. Fisk, W. A. Rogers, N. Charness, S. J. Czaja, and J. Sharit, Designing for older adults: Principles and creative human factors approaches. Boca Raton, FL: CRC Press, Taylor & Francic Group, 2009.

[10] M. Zajicek, "Interface design for older adults," Proc. The 2001 EC/NSF Workshop on Universal Accessibility of Ubiquitous Computing: Providing for The Elderly (WUAUC'01), ACM, May 2001, pp. 60-65.

[11] B. Shneiderman and C. Plaisant, Designing the user interface: strategies for effective human-computer interaction. Pearson Education India, 2010.

[12] J. Gong, and P. Tarasewich, "Guidelines for handheld mobile device interface design," Proc. DSI 2004 Annual Meeting, Citeseer, Nov. 2004, pp. 3751-3756.

[13] G. Finkel and Y. Gold, "Actualizing universal design," Journal of Leisurability, vol. 26, pp. 25-30, 1999.

[14] The Executive Policy Committee, "Universal Design policy, " vol.5, Dec. 2001.

[15] E. Mpofu and T. Oakland, Rehabilitation and health assessment: applying ICF guidelines. Springer, 2010.

[16] J. Sanford, E. Mpofu, and T. Oakland, "Assessing universal design in the physical environment," Rehabilitation and Health Assessment, pp. 255-278, 2010.

[17] Web Content Accessibility Guidelines 2.0 Overview. [Online]. Avalable: https://www.w3.org/WAI/intro/wcag.php [Accessed: 20-Jan-2017].

[18] J. Nielsen, "Usability inspection methods," ACM Conference Companion on Human Factors in Computing Systems (CHI '94), Apr. 1994, pp. 413-414.

[19] M. de Sá and L. Carriço, "An evaluation framework for mobile user interfaces," 12th IFIP Conference on Human-Computer Interaction, Springer, Aug. 2009, pp. 708-721.

[20] Y. G. Ji, J. H. Park, C. Lee, and M. H. Yun, "A usability checklist for the usability evaluation of mobile phone user interface," International Journal of Human-Computer Interaction, vol. 20, pp. 207-231, Jul. 2006.

[21] J. Heo, D. H. Ham, S. Park, C. Song, and W. C. Yoon, "A framework for evaluating the usability of mobile phones based on multi-level, hierarchical model of usability factors," Interacting with Computers, vol. 21, pp. 263-275, Aug. 2009.

[22] D. H. Ham, J. Heo, P. Fossick, W. Wong, S. Park, C. Song, and M. Bradley, "Conceptual framework and models for identifying and organizing usability impact factors of mobile phones," Proc. The 18th Australia Conference on Computer-Human Interaction: Design: Activities, Artefacts and Environments (OZCHI '06), ACM, Nov. 2006, pp. 261-268.

[23] L. Kascak, C. B. Rébola, and J. Sanford, "Integrating Universal Design (UD) Principles and Mobile Design Guidelines to Improve Design of Mobile Health Applications for Older Adults," Proc. IEEE International Conference on Healthcare Informatics (ICHI 2014), IEEE Press, Sep. 2014, pp. 343-348.

[24] L. R. Kascak, E. Y. Liu, and J. A. Sanford, "Universal Design (UD) Guidelines for Interactive Mobile Voting Interfaces for Older Adults," 9th International Conference on Universal Access in Human-Computer Interaction (HCII2015), Springer, Aug. 2015, pp. 215-225.

[25] L. Ruzic and J. A. Sanford, "Universal design mobile interface guidelines (UDMIG) for an aging population," in CFP Mobile EHealth, Springer, in press.

[26] M. P. Lawton and L. Nahemow, "Ecology and the aging process," The psychology of adult development and aging, pp. 619-674, 1973.

Design Thinking as a Process for Innovative Older Adult Applications

Claudia B. Rebola
Industrial Design
Rhode Island School of Design
Providence, USA
crebola@risd.edu

Elizabeth Hermann
Landscape Architecture
Rhode Island School of Design
Providence, USA
ehermann@risd.edu

Abstract—**Design Thinking is a critical methodology used by designers to work through and solve complex problems, and to develop solutions aimed at creating a preferred future. Designing for aging requires focused expertise, considerations, and principles for bringing about effective solutions for this target population. While there is vast knowledge within each of these areas of knowledge and practice, little has been discussed and presented at the intersection of the two – design thinking and aging. This paper introduces a system for design thinking addressing the needs of older adults. The system is comprised of a seven-phase "P" methodology: Position, Purpose, Prosthetics, Place, Participation, Potential and Presentation. This paper discusses a case study of the application of this methodology in a project titled "Aging and Health(care) 3.0: Place of Aging," a collaboration across Industrial Design and Architecture. The significance of this paper is to introduce approaches that better identify critical opportunities when designing for older adults. This paper discusses approaches that are contextual and personal in the realm of designing for *one* in the context of *many*, with the aim of redefining care for healthy aging.**

Keywords-Design Thinking; Critical Making; Design for Aging; Methodologies

I. INTRODUCTION

Design practices have become more complex, yet essential, for addressing challenging societal problems. While design once was considered a more linear iterative activity for problem-solving, user requirements have expanded the design process making it more inclusive and comprehensive. The incorporation of the social sciences in design has resulted in switching practices from a designer-centered design to a user-centered design approach [1][2]. User-centered design approaches have been dominating the design disciplines in order to design products that better serve users [3]. IDEO, a global design company, was one of the pioneers in harnessing the power of specific methods to develop a more critical, nuanced and responsive design process. Since then, a plethora of alternative methods have emerged in response to better understanding user needs [4]–[7]. While design methods are still suitable for better identifying user requirements, usability and adoption, they limit their impact on contemporary design practice and rhetoric. Even though participatory design aims at involving the targeted user in the design process for meeting the needs of the stakeholders [6][8], the method can challenge critical insights. The emergence of design thinking is responsible to address complex issues within complex social issues that focus on understanding user experiences in our built environment [9]. Design thinking supports the belief that designers should be more involved in the big picture of socially innovative design; that design is a collaborative effort; and that ideas have to be explored in a hands-on way with stakeholders [10].

Building on the strengths of design thinking, this paper discusses the curricular process of a class exercising empathy towards users, cooperative activities, design prototyping and contextualization. A set of design activities was envisioned as a system to address the problem area of abandonment of older adults in our society. The rationale was to customize a methodology that can go beyond participatory design by collectively setting principles for designing for impact in the population—in this case, behavioral change and well-being of older adults by reformulating health by focusing on *care*. The goal was to set forward the need for design thinking for improving the perception and integration of older adults in the community.

The paper is structured as follows. In Section II, we introduce principles for design and well-being, as well as objectives for designing solutions for the aging population. In Section III, we describe a seven-phase "P" methodology: Position, Purpose, Prosthetics, Place, Participation, Potential and Presentation. The subsections describe in detail each phase and its application. Lastly, section IV discusses concluding thoughts about the "P" methodology reflecting on its application in a project titled "Aging and Health(care) 3.0: Place of Aging," a collaboration across Industrial Design and Architecture.

II. DESIGNING FOR OLDER ADULTS

Designing for older adults requires focused expertise, considerations and principles for bringing about effective solutions for the population. There are a number of sources aimed at giving easily accessible information as a primer for designing for older adults [11]. Fisk et al offer a practical introduction to human factors and older adults by illustrating practical translations of scientific data into design applications. Similarly, Universal Design principles provide guidance for designing products and environments involving the consideration of the human factors across populations of varied abilities [12]. Universal Design holds the promise to design products and environments to be usable by all people, to the greatest extent possible, without the need for adaptation or specialized design.

A. Principles of Well-Being in Aging

The International Plan of Action on Ageing in 1991/1992 held as its main objective "to add life to the years that have been added to life" [13]. Building on this objective and considering Universal Design principles, the following guiding principles were proposed in parallel with design activities:

- AGENCY: Independence in decision-making and actions.
- DIGNITY: Ability to maintain one's image of oneself and one's values.
- IDENTITY: Recognized as an individual person by others.
- RELEVANCY: One has purpose in one's own and others' eyes.
- CONNECTIVITY: Integrated into the rest of society
- CURIOSITY: One keeps discovering and learning (progressive)
- ECCENTRICITY: Ability to behave outside of expected or normative actions.
- LOVABILITY: How others care about you and respect you regardless of your quirks.

B. Design objectives for the Aging Population

Clarifying design objectives is a central component for the success of any project. A design process cannot exist in isolation. Design objectives guide the creativity and critical thinking. Without objectives, the design process can arrive at solutions that may not meet the requirements of the end user. Design objectives are not a list of requirements from the user, neither scoping the project but advancing a comprehensive approach to delineate a guide on how to advance human beings by design. When designing for the aging population, the design objectives should reflect integration, implementation, inspiration and progression.

In delineating the objectives, integration refers to proposing products and/or systems to build intergenerational, supported and connected communities. The goal is to develop bottom-up approaches across generations that can help older adults have access to a community of care. Implementation is about proposing products and/or systems to have a successful effect and long-lasting impact within the aging population. The goal is to develop solutions that are feasible for implementation in the near future and more importantly, sustainable from the point of view of self-maintaining. Inspiration is about proposing products and/or systems that are forward thinking and enablers. The goal is to celebrate the aging populating with creative, attractive and pervasive solutions that avoid physical, visual or experiential segregation. Lastly, progression is about proposing products and/or systems that allow positive growth. The goal is to develop solutions that grow with the aging population and inspire them to do more and be more.

III. "P" PROCESS

Exercising the aforementioned design objectives and principles, the goal was to create a curriculum that would focus on understanding and questioning current conventions around aging, and portray how design - from the products, systems, platforms, programs, services, experiences, digital and non-digital perspective - can impact health and well-being in dwellings for a meaningful aging of future generations.

The design thinking approach for addressing the needs of older adults starts with people and ends with people. Through interactions among research, interventions, and implementation (see Figure 1), the system provides the basis to contextualize problem setting and problem-solving grounded in needs. The design methodology described here is comprised of a seven-phase "P" structure: Position, Purpose, Prosthetics, Place, Participation, Potential and Presentation. The following sections describe in detail these phases applied to a project "Aging and Health(care) 3.0: Place of Aging", a collaboration across Industrial Design and Architecture. The sections are structured with the curricular approach used in the course (see Table 1).

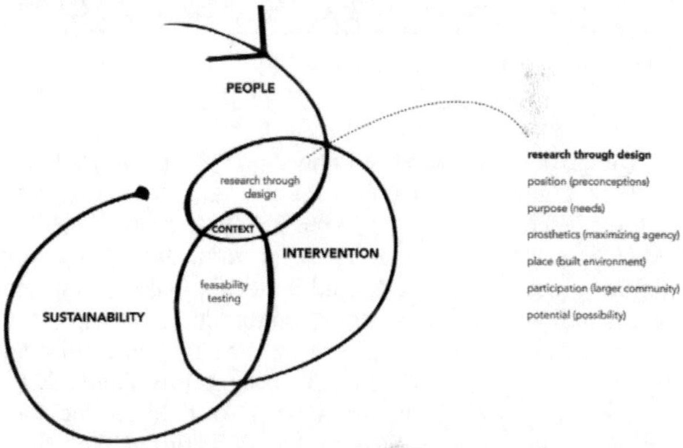

Figure 1. Design Thinking as a Processs

TABLE I. RESEARCH THROUGH DESIGN METHODOLOGY

Step	"P" Process		
	User Centered Approach	*Research*	*Design*
1	Position	Recognize	Scoping
2	Purpose	Understand	Defining
3	Prosthetics	Identify	Exploring
4	Place	Locate	Applying
5	Participation	Engage	Co-creating
6	Potential	Propose	Generating
7	Presentation	Report	Validating

a. Curricular approach for Aging and Health(Care) course

A. Position

The goal of this step is to move beyond preconceptions and build a deeper understanding of users through direct evidence. It requires an attentive observation of the population with the aim of discovering experience perceptions of older adults. While an abundance of observations exists within the literature, the aim is to learn about the population firsthand with sensitive and critical eyes, and to go "out" and record observations of encounters. The goal is to have the designer obtain an open-ended and exploratory *personal* view. This step requires exercising observational and interviewing skills that can be materialized through a video outcome summarizing the insights. One interesting aspect of the outcome is that it should be a conceptual representation of data collections excluding voice. *Voiceless* representations force reflection, and help avoid potentially erroneous a preconceptions. The end result is an evidence-based storytelling around being an older adult in America (see Figure 2).

Figure 2. Example of preconceptions observations—stillness in age.

B. Purpose

The goal of this step is to understand the personas/types of users going beyond preconceptions and building them with evidence. For this step, types should be constructed as prototypes. Prototypes serve as material typologies for applying design thinking and critical making in the understanding of users. The construction of persona prototypes involves the translation of observations, building from the previous step, to reflective insights (see Figure 3).

Questions to guide the development of this step include: How individuals physically carry themselves in public? How individuals engage with others (actively approaching others, cheerful, withdrawn)? How individuals react to change or stress? Are there family members present in their lives (and what are the age groups)? Are they experiencing physical limitations? Can they move around on their own or are they dependent on others? Do they and how do they engage in activities? Answering these questions provides insights for categorization. The aim is to develop a *situated* classification criterion. Each category should be based on multiple variables and carefully considered, while setting the range of each category (and its variables) before determining that there now is a different category. This part of the process involves identifying the critical factor/s (the 'tipping point') separating one category/type and another.

While there is a need to create personalized typological categories, it is worth knowing how, over time, psychologists have attempted to classify personality types. The most widely used classification systems that sort humans by how they understand and respond to the world around them include the Myers-Briggs Type Indicator (MBTI) based on Carl Jung's theory that we experience the world in four basic ways: sensation, intuition, feeling, and thinking [14]; the Five Factor Model (FFM) openness to experience, conscientiousness, extraversion, agreeableness, neuroticism; and the Keirsey Temperament Sorter uses Plato's temperament categories of the Artisans, Guardians, Idealists and Rationals [15]. This model is broken into two categories each, where each of these has two role variants, and then filters the 16 categories through "rings" of: abstract vs. concrete; cooperative (complying) vs. pragmatic (adapting); directive (proactive) vs. informative (reactive); expressive vs. attentive. Overall, for this step, it is worth considering typological studies in other fields. The ones below are not all about appearance. Rather, appearance is a factor of how something is structured, how it performs, when and how it was made, available materials and technologies, alterations and stresses upon it over time, the circumstances and the histories of those who created it.

Figure 3. Example of a purpose prototyped personas.

C. Prosthetics

With aging, older adults find themselves needing support where they live. Aging in place aims at keeping older adults in their "home" places for as long as they can. Yet, aging at "home" challenge *self-care* even in activities of daily living, the common, everyday tasks people do to become be *self-sufficient* such as bathing, eating and dressing. Some activities require re-learning to remain independent and healthy. With age or when becoming ill, the body and mind lose dexterity, balance, motor skills and the brain's keen awareness of the body's signals. Many of these activities have a strong and direct impact on our health. The question is, what tools, as prosthetics, people use to remain independent in one's environment?

The goal of this step is to understand activities and devices supporting the aging population; and how these activities are contextual. There is a need to consider questioning the role of place and environment: What are the living conditions? How the environment enables or constrains us? What is the landscape of aging in terms of abilities and disabilities? What type of tools do older adults use to support their daily living? Are these tools wearable prosthetics, environmental prosthetics? What are the cultural/social implications of adopting these "prosthetics" for aging?

The key is to identify the interplay between artifact and place as there are associated activities that need to be identified as issues (i.e., bathing has associated issues such as balance). This step involves working with older adults and constructing a photo storyboard representing the critical perspective (analysis) on a single need of older adults aging in place. Storyboarding is a suitable technique for documenting insights (see Figure 4). Photo storyboarding can represent taxonomies of needs helping visualize problems/opportunities: how older adults do those activities through time? What insights come from observing, photographing and annotating older adults environment and activities? In addition, this step can benefit from creating customer journeys by understanding and visualizing what older adults do on a daily basis? What problems might they have? What has become a "new normal"?

Figure 4. Example of a prosthetics visualizations.

D. Place

The goal of this step is to define what is the *place* for aging. Historically, and today in many parts of the world, one ages in the home of a family member, usually that of a grown child and their family. In this case, aging is done within an intergenerational setting where any assistance needed is readily at hand. Moreover, aging within the family means the older person is a respected member of the group, revered for their wisdom, origin stories, memories shared with the rest of the group, and their lifetime of being the protector and provider for the clan. Yet, in other parts of the world, and certainly in the United States, families are widely scattered having relocated for jobs or other opportunities. Moreover, in a large number of households, there is either only a single parent, or there are two where both have full professional working lives. In either case, there is seldom someone at home able to take care of an aging parent. In the United States, aging members of our society typically stay in their own home as long as they are able to fend for themselves, and when home is no longer an option, they move on to some type of assisted-living facility where, more often than not, their community consists of other elderly adults who can no longer care for themselves. Some of the most often heard complaints about such facilities – even the very best – are that they are "full of old people;" that the individual feels like an "inmate" (i.e., "imprisoned" with little agency); and that they are a nobody, surrounded by people and a place with which they have no history. So, what do we mean by 'place'?

We spend a life time finding our particular place in the world and as we age and days become increasingly marked by loss – one's abilities, one's memory, one's friends and family members – one's place of return, one's sanctuary, and the physical manifestation of one's agency and rootedness in this world – one's home – takes on significantly greater importance. Yet, not all adults can age in place in the sense they can stay in their own home for the duration of their life. The reasons may be economic, they may be physical, or they may have to do with decisions being made by others. Whatever the case, many of the new places aging adults are moved to do little to address the fundamental loss of 'one's place in the world' and 'home.' This step looks critically at recent housing solutions for older adults from various parts of the world. The intent is to develop an understanding of what issues are being addressed in the design of these facilities, what aspects are not, and what role might a designer play in developing places and conditions that restore the aging to their 'place in the world' (albeit a new one), a more meaningful version of 'home' and all that implies about purpose, identity, memory and agency. The outcomes of this phase should be a map (see Figure 5) summarizing the components of place. If necessary, maps of older adults showing their movement and activities in place can help visualize components of place.

This step involves having a critical perspective on *place* and summarizing insights on the 'place of aging' by visiting local housing options ranging from nursing homes, a variety of income neighborhoods, assisted living facilities and various retirement communities. There is a need to think across scales from the overall location within the town or city, to relationship to adjacent streets, houses, schools, store, to the grounds of the facility, to the building itself, to the details of the building's layout and design including corridors, common spaces, private spaces, bedrooms and bathrooms, interfaces between indoor and out – views, access, to mention a few.

E. Participation

The goal of this step is to develop methods and tools for empowering older adults to co-create solutions to their concerns and needs, and to develop solutions that involve the larger community in an essential way. This step requires partnering with someone in the aging community (presumably someone met during the previous steps) to develop an intervention responding to concerns or specific needs they have articulated. What this means is that the researcher/designer, as someone familiar with creative problem-solving processes, needs to develop methods that allow the elderly partner to think like a designer/inventor and co-create a way to address their concerns. This approach places the researcher/designer as a teacher, and to do so in a way that is sensitive to the changes and fears that older adults are confronted with. Moreover, while the older adult partner may never again be able to address their own needs alone, the researcher/designer can help them obtain the tools they need to continue to have agency going forward.

Figure 5. Example of a place development.

The Participation step involved developing methods and tools for giving a member of the aging community a process by which they can become the designer's creative partner in addressing concerns they have articulated (see Figure 6).

Figure 6. Example of participation though a meal preparation.

The goal is to develop a process, service, product or space that addresses these concerns, and include the larger community in the solution. The participation can be in the form of cultural probes such as booklet that in text and image lays out the process of the entire endeavor [16]. However, other participatory methods can be envisioned for collecting insights building on the previous steps.

F. Potential

The goal of this step is to propose possibilities—design interventions to make a change on the health and well-being of the aging population. Design interventions are defined as innovative older adult applications not limited to artifacts, but systems, platforms, programs, services, experiences, digital and non-digital (see Figure 7). The goal is to develop interventions which allow the community to take charge of generating the change.

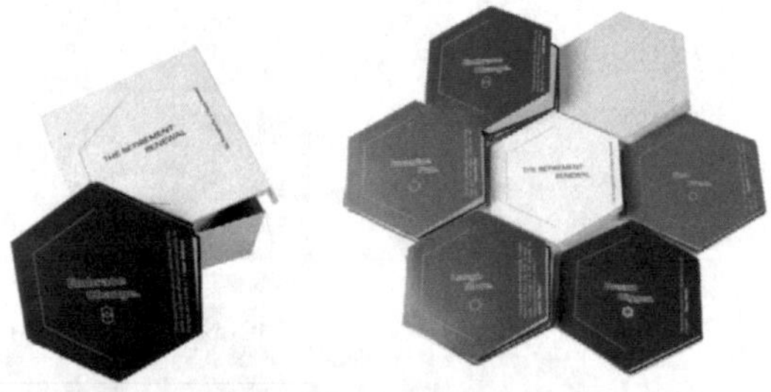

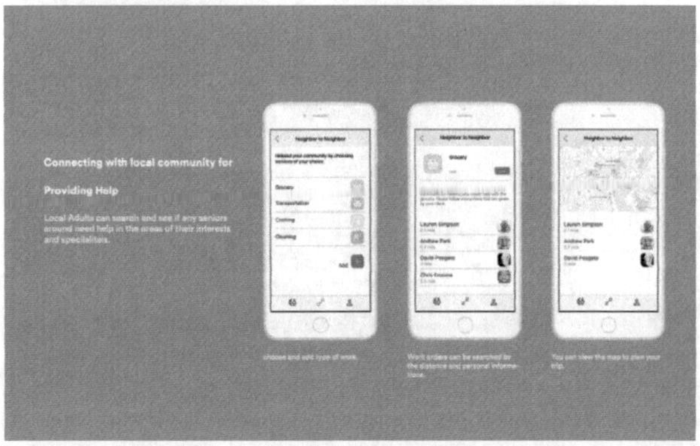

Figure 7. Examples of potential interventions.

Students were guided in the design of the interventions and encouraged to consider the following: How the interventions are designed as a creative response connected to health? How stakeholders are engaged with the designed intervention? How implementable, feasible is your designed intervention? Can the interventions be designed to be socially adopted and self-sustainable? Do designed interventions respond to the principles of the class (Independence, Progression, and Integration)?

G. Presentation

As the last step of the process, students build a presentation of their final projects. While a "potential" proposition may evolve across the length of the project, students needed to look back at every step of the process and develop a presentation supporting their design decisions. In addition to describing the overall goal and the criteria used to envision programs, the presentation should also discuss details about use and implementation. Such details should be presented with the stakeholders in the program and visualize/map the value for each of them (i.e., the gains for the older adult might be different from the gains of the community). In addition, it should discuss incentives for the stakeholders: Why should they participate in the program? What are their gains?; the feasibility of the program: Is it a realistic solution? What resources are needed?; the financial needs: Who would sponsor the program? Of what organization would finance the program?; the implementation plan: How it would unfold the first months versus the first year, growth in next years? ; and lastly and more importantly, its sustainability: How would the program would survive through time? What resources would keep it alive? How can its enrollment be guaranteed? And how does this program address the principles presented in this class.

IV. CONCLUSION

Building on the strengths of design thinking, this paper discusses the curricular process of a class exercising empathy with users, cooperative activities, design prototyping and contextualization. This paper introduces a system for design thinking for older adults. The system is comprised of a seven-phase "P" methodology: Position, Purpose, Prosthetics, Place, Participation, Potential and Presentation. These steps allow to interchangeably mix the roles of researcher, designer, and participant into one system to advance better solution for the aging population. The methodology is built on a research-through-design approach with the goal of integrating stakeholders and designers in a unified system. More importantly, it is a methodology that celebrates a systematic understanding of issues from different scales ranging from the designer to the user and place. This paper is an attempt to provide an organized methodology that the design for aging community and related disciplines can adopt for course curriculum to speculate in the future place of aging. The significance of this paper is to introduce approaches that better identify critical opportunities when designing for the older adults. It is to discuss approaches that are contextual and personal, in the realm of designing for one in the context of many aiming at redefining care for healthy aging.

ACKNOWLEDGMENT

We would like to thank the Academic Affairs at the Rhode Island School of Design and the Academic Enrichment Grant for supporting the collaboration across departments, Industrial Design and Architecture/Landscape Architecture Urban Systems, for new curricular development. Special thanks to Tracie Costantino, Dean of Faculty, for granting mechanisms that support endeavors like this project.

REFERENCES

[1] E. B. N.Sanders, "From User-Centered to Participatory Design Approaches," Design and the Social Sciences: Making Connections: CRC Press, pp. 1–8, 2002.

[2] V. J. Papanek, Design for the Real World : Human Ecology and Social Change, 2nd ed, Chicago, IL: Academy Chicago, 1985.

[3] IDEO, Human-Centered Design Toolkit: An Open-Source Toolkit To Inspire New Solutions in the Developing World, 2nd ed: IDEO, 2011.

[4] B. Hanington and B. Martin, Universal Methods of Design: 100 Ways to Research Complex Problems, Develop Innovative Ideas, and Design Effective Solutions. Beverly, MA: Rockport Publishers, 2012.

[5] L. Sanders and P. J. Stappers, Convivial Toolbox: Generative Research for the Front End of Design, Amsterdam: BIS Publishers, 2013.

[6] E. B. N. Sanders, E. Brandt, and T. Binder, "A Framework for Organizing the Tools and Techniques of Participatory Design," The 11th Biennial Participatory Design Conference, Nov-Dec, 2010, pp. 195–198.

[7] V. Kumar, 101 Design Methods: A Structured Approach for Driving Innovation in your Organization, 1st ed, Hoboken, N.J: Wiley, 2012.

[8] L. Sanders, "An Evolving Map of Design Practice and Design Research," Interactions, vol. 15, no. 6, pp. 13–17, 2008.

[9] J. Kolko, "Design Thinking Comes of Age," Harvard Business Review, September Issue, 2015.

[10] E. Bjögvinsson, P. Ehn, and P. A. Hillgren, "Design Things and Design Thinking: Contemporary Participatory Design Challenges," Design Issues, vol. 28, pp. 101–116, 2012.

[11] A. D. Fisk, W. A. Rogers, N. Charness, S. J. Czaja, and J. Sharit, Designing for Older Adults: Principles and Creative Human Factors Approaches, 2nd ed, Boca Raton, LA: CRC Press, 2009.

[12] The Center for Universal Design: About UD: https://www.ncsu.edu/ncsu/design/cud/about_ud/udprinciples.htm

[13] United Nations: Implementation of the International Plan of Action on Ageing and related activities: http://www.un.org/documents/ga/res/46/a46r091.htm

[14] The Myers & Briggs Foundation: MBTI® Basics: http://www.myersbriggs.org/my-mbti-personality-type/mbti-basics/

[15] Keirsey Temperament: Overview of the Four Temperaments: http://www.keirsey.com/4temps/overview_temperaments.asp

[16] B. Gaver, T. Dunne, and E. Pacenti, "Design: Cultural Probes," Interactions, vol. 6, no. 1, pp. 21–29, 1999.